GARDENING

Addison-Wesley Publishing Company, Inc.

Reading, Massachusetts
Menlo Park, California
Don Mills, Ontario
Wokingham, England
Amsterdam
Sydney
Singapore
Tokyo
Mexico City
Bogotá
Santiago
San Juan

GARDENING

The Complete Guide to Growing America's Favorite Fruits & Vegetables

The National Gardening Association

GARDENING

The Complete Guide to Growing America's Favorite Fruits & Vegetables

Many of the designations used by manufacturers and sellers to distinguish their products are claimed as trademarks. Where those designations appear in this book and Addison-Wesley was aware of a trademark claim, the designations have been printed in initial caps (e.g., Wall O'Water).

Library of Congress Cataloging-in-Publication Data
Main entry under title:

Gardening: the complete guide to growing America's favorite fruits & vegetables.

Includes index.
1. Vegetable gardening — United States. 2. Fruit culture — United States. I. National Gardening Association (U.S.)
SB320.6.G37 1985   635   85-30809
ISBN 0-201-10866-6
ISBN 0-201-10855-0 (pbk.)

ISBN 0-201-10866-6 (hardcover)
      0-201-10855-0 (paperback)

ABCDEFGHIJ–KR–89876

GARDENING was set in the Sabon and Univers families of typefaces by Compset, Inc., of Beverly, Massachusetts.

The color separations and camera work were supplied by Color Response, Inc., of Charlotte, North Carolina.

W. A. Krueger Company of New Berlin, Wisconsin, printed and bound the book on 65-pound Warrenflo stock from Lindenmeyr Paper Company.

Cover photograph: John Still

Back cover photographs: (*top and bottom*) Thomas E. Eltzroth; (*middle two*) Didier Delmas

Designer	*Brent Marmo,*
	The Brownstone Group, Inc.
Illustrations	*Elayne Sears*

National Gardening Association

Project Coordinators	*Laura Carlsmith*
	Lynn Ocone
Editors	*George Thabault*
	Susan Littlefield
	Andrea Chesman
	Judy Chaves
	Michael Leff
	Ruth Page
	Kit Anderson
	Ed Robinson
Editorial Research	*Bruce Butterfield*
	Cynthia Norman
	Lydia Kaye
Photo Research	*Heather Hale Hutchins*
Staff Support	*Barbara Godfrey*
	Peggy Ticehurst

Addison-Wesley Publishing Company

Editors	*Genoa Shepley*
	Anne Eldridge
Editor-in-Chief	*Doe Coover*
Production Supervisor	*Lori Snell*
Production/Operations Manager	*Barbara Wood*
Manufacturing	*Ann DeLacey*
	Lu Anne Piskadlo
Copy Editor	*Janice Byer*
Proofreader	*Cecilia Thurlow*

Contents

Acknowledgments

A book of this depth and magnitude has to draw on the knowledge and enthusiasm of a number of people. In this case no fewer than 135 dedicated gardeners and members of the National Gardening Association offered a range of skills and expertise.

First thanks go to our past president, Jack Robinson, whose vision and perseverance led to the project.

A lot of the tips and techniques that are mentioned in this book came from many more of our 250,000 members nationwide. We want to thank those individuals who took the time and interest to send us their ideas.

We would also like to thank the many photographers whose work appears here, especially Didier Delmas, who worked on site in our test garden; Elayne Sears, whose artwork illustrates the finer points of how-to; and Brenda Olcott-Reid, who compiled valuable information on fruit varieties and rootstocks.

Finally, we would like to express our appreciation to some of the many knowledgeable vegetable and fruit growers and experts throughout the country who shared their experiences, suggestions, criticisms, and love of gardening with us. Their help has been essential in creating this book.

Virgil Adams
Albin Anderson
Dr. J. R. Baggett
Mel Bartholomew
Aldo Biagiotti
Dr. P. K. Biswas
Judi Blucher
Prof. John Bouwkamp
Mrs. G. A. Bowen
Prof. Bertie Boyce
Weldon Burge
Frank Campobasso
David Cavagnaro
Dan T. Chambers
Peter Chan
James E. Chezem
Winston Cooke
Betty and Jerry Corvan
Rosalind Creasy
Greg Dinkel
Don Dobbs
Gene and Nelda Edwards
Marilyn Elliott
Edine Forsberg
Ray Fowler
Carleton S. Francis, III
Steve Frowine
Irene Fuderer
Stuart Garner
Sal Gilbertie
Arthur Goodnough
Sue Gray
Janet Gyer
Bart Hall-Beyer
Shirley Hamernik
Mark Hebert
Norman Heggemeier
James Hoeft
James R. Hoff
Teresa K. Howe
Emily Hickey
Henry Johnson
James D. Johnson
Sue Johnson
Rob Johnston
Kathy Kapusta
A. N. Kasimatis
Roger Kline
Ken Klotz

Dr. David Kollas
Bob Kurle
Lance Ladd
Frank "Ben" Lawson
Norm Lee
Rand B. Lee
Lherif Loraamm
Dr. Sauveur Mahotiere
Jim Manchester
Shirley Marriott
Dale Marshall
Ginny Marshall
Ivan Martin
Louise Matthews
John E. Mayer
Dr. Jeffrey McCormack
Dr. Elwyn Meader
Robert Mendelsohn
K. R. "Mike" Michel
Brett Miller
David Miskell
Albert Lee Moran
Jean Natter
Gary Nelson
Charles O'Dell
John Page
Bill Park
John Parker
Dr. D. R. Paterson
Clifford Pearson
Rudy Perkins
Dr. Clinton E. Peterson
Jesse Pomazal
Prof. Wayne Porter
L. A. Potter
Dr. Arthur Pratt
Prof. Robert J. Precheur
Dr. Ron Prokopy
Marshall Richards
Caroline Riggins
Josephine B. Ruud
Sue Sack
Dudley Sanders
Holly Shimuzu
Steve Solomon
Evelyn Stash
Ralph Stevenson
Elizabeth Strauch
Lee Sutton

Prof. Fred Taylor
Betty Thomas
Bob Thomson
Dr. L. E. Van Valkenburgh
Lance Walheim
John P. Watson
Bonnie and Les Whiteside
Dr. Gene Wild
Jim Williams
Robert Woolley
John F. Wood
Alice Yeager
Kelly Yeaton
D. J. Young

Preface

If there's one thing we've learned at the National Gardening Association, it's that there is no one correct way to garden.

There are as many ways to garden as there are varieties of seeds and gardeners to grow them. No one of them is best for every gardener in every location at all times. In this book, we have tried to describe, vegetable by vegetable, fruit by fruit, each plant's basic needs, the variety choices, and a number of techniques worked out by experienced gardeners. We've also included problem-solving information about bugs and diseases.

To a great extent, our knowledge comes from our own members, gardeners in the mountains and at sea level, gardeners in the Deep South and in the far North — over a quarter million home and community gardeners. They range from people who see nothing wrong with using chemical fertilizers to those who wouldn't touch the chemicals with a 10-foot rake, from gardeners who always plant intensively in raised beds to those who have plenty of space and prefer the old-fashioned, single row, flat-on-the-ground method.

The National Gardening Association is a member-supported, nonprofit organization that was founded in 1972. Our sole purpose is to help people become successful gardeners at home and in community groups, and we stress the sharing of information among our members. We are a resource for information, services, and publications related to gardening. Our monthly magazine, *National GARDENING*, gives straightforward tips and techniques that we have gleaned from gardeners, and it addresses problems in gardening with proven solutions from our members across the country.

Gardening is intended to be an enjoyable resource book, one you will want to refer to again and again as you plan your garden in the spring, prepare the soil, plant, nurture, and harvest the food produced through your own efforts. We do not impose one point of view or one method in this book. Rather, we give you the option to choose among tried and true methods because everyone likes to do things a bit differently.

The information you will find in these pages is designed to help both the beginner and the expert gardener, whether gardening in the East, Midwest, South, or West. If we address a problem that should not be answered on a national level, we direct you to other resources such as the Extension Service. If we've missed some useful gardening information that you've acquired, please let us know.

We wish you good gardening and happy reading.

Charles Scott
President
National Gardening Association

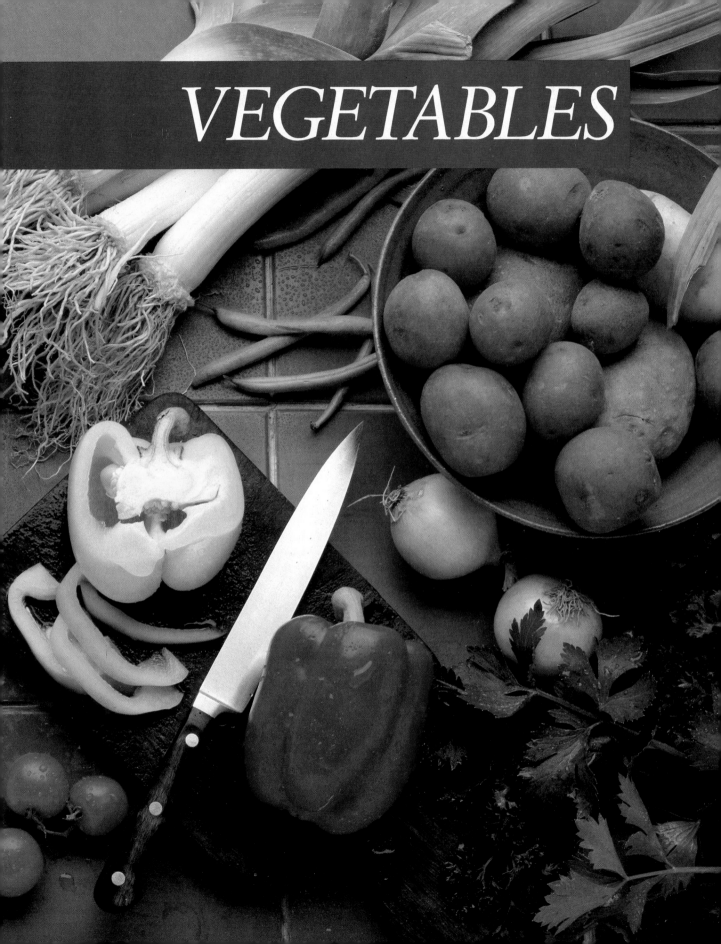

VEGETABLES

Planning

The difference between a good garden and a great garden is often in the planning. Although there are no hard and fast rules for planning a garden, a few basic principles will steer you toward success: plan your garden to fit your needs. Most important, use your imagination. Your garden should be a place where your personality and creative instincts can merge with nature's own designs.

This section covers the elements of planning: positioning your garden to its best advantage, deciding when to plant what, discriminating among the hundreds of seed variety choices available through seed catalogs and garden centers. We hope that gardeners find in these pages both insight and inspiration for creating a great garden.

Choosing a Site

The first step in planning a new garden is deciding where to put it. Don't be discouraged if you lack an ideal spot — few gardeners have one. Here are some things to think about when selecting the garden site and suggestions for ways of dealing with less-than-ideal conditions.

Sunlight

Your garden will do best if it gets full sun; 6 hours a day of direct sun is the *minimum* needed by most vegetable plants for optimum growth. However, if your only spot for a garden gets less than this, don't give up. Some crops, especially leafy ones like lettuce and spinach, produce reasonably well in a partly shaded location. Root crops such as carrots and beets need more light than leafy vegetables, but may do well in a garden that gets only morning sun. Fruiting plants such as peppers, tomatoes, and beans are sun worshipers and will yield poorly, if at all, with less than 6 hours of direct sun. The best advice for a shady site is: start small and experiment with the more shade-tolerant vegetables to see which do best.

You don't have to plant all your vegetables together in one plot. If your only sunny spot is in the front yard, you might plant a border of tomatoes and peppers along the front walk and set lettuce plants in a shadier spot out back.

If the shade in your garden comes from nearby trees and shrubs, your vegetable plants will be competing for water and nutrients as well as for light. Tree roots extend slightly beyond the "drip line," the outer foliage reach of the tree. If possible, keep your garden out of the root zone of surrounding plantings. If this isn't possible, just give everything extra water and fertilizer.

Black walnut trees pose a particular problem, as their roots give off a substance called juglone that inhibits the growth of some plants. Tomatoes are sensitive to juglone; plants growing in the root zone of a black walnut often wilt and die. Try to leave at least 50 feet between your garden and walnut trees.

Drainage

Plant roots need air as well as water. Water-logged soils are low in air, which is why soil drainage is an important consideration in choosing a garden site. Heavy clay soils are usually not as well drained as sandy ones. Puddles of water on the soil surface after a rain indicate poor drainage. One way to check your garden soil's drainage is to dig a hole about 10 inches deep and fill it with water. Let the water drain, then fill the hole again the following day and clock how long it takes for the water to drain away. If water remains in the hole more than 8 to 10 hours after the second filling, your soil drainage needs improvement.

Drip line

Root Zone

Tree roots usually extend beyond the tree's drip line. If your garden is near trees, it will probably require extra fertilizer and water for good production, as the tree will compete with the vegetables for water and nutrients.

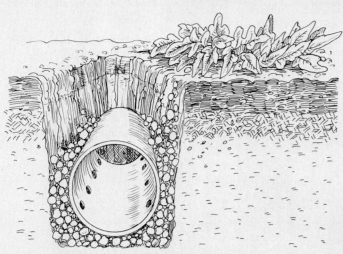

Tile drains will help you transform an overly soggy garden area into a productive parcel.

Adding lots of organic matter to the soil is a long-term way to improve soil drainage (see page 29). Or you can build raised beds on a poorly drained site (see page 40). If your soil is really soggy, due perhaps to a high water table, tile drains buried in the ground may be the only solution. Consult a landscape contractor for information on this fairly expensive option.

Soil can also be *too* well drained. Very sandy soil dries out quickly and needs frequent watering during dry spells. Adding organic matter to sandy soil will gradually increase the amount of water it can hold.

Slope

A gentle slope to the south is ideal, especially in cold climates. Soil warms up faster in the spring and the likelihood of frosts affecting plants is lessened. Cold air is like water; it runs downhill and settles in low spots. Frosty air will move past plants on a slope. In hot climates, a north slope may help keep plants cooler during the heat of midsummer.

Too great a slope can cause erosion problems, however. On any sloping site, it's a good idea to orient rows across rather than down the slope to catch runoff. On very steep slopes you may need to build terraces to hold soil in place.

Wind

In some parts of the country, high winds can wreak havoc with tall crops like corn and pole beans and can make them dry out rapidly. If wind is a problem in your area protect the garden from the prevailing winds with a windbreak (several rows of plants or a fence). You will get maximum wind protection for your crops if you plant them downwind at a distance three to five times the height of the windbreak.

Size and Convenience

While the average garden is about 600 square feet, or about 20 by 30 feet, your garden can be as large or as small as your space and time allow. Consider how much of each crop you would like to end up with and then consult the chart on pages 26–27 for the space requirements of the vegetables you want to grow. If you're a first-time gardener, 600 square feet is plenty of space to take care of. A busy person may want a smaller garden, say 10 by 20 feet.

If the soil is in good condition, a novice gardener can keep up with a 400-square-foot garden by devoting about a half-hour each day at the beginning of the season. In late spring and through the summer, a good half-hour of work every 2 or 3 days should keep the garden productive and looking good.

Try to plan your garden so that it is close to water sources and to the house. If you plan on bringing in truckloads of soil amendments or additions such as manure, put your garden in a spot that can be easily reached by a vehicle.

Lead Contamination

The possibility of lead contamination in your soil may also affect the location of your garden. Although lead is not used in most paints manufactured today, it was a common ingredient until about 1955. As lead-base paint weathers and peels from buildings, the lead accumulates in the soil around foundations. Plants growing in soil with a high lead content can take up the element, making them unsafe to eat. Soil that is high in lead can also be dangerous to children, who might inadvertently ingest it while playing outside.

If you own an older house that you suspect has been coated with paint containing lead at some point, or if you suspect that your garden site may have had a pre-1955 frame building on it in the past, consider the following precautions:

- Have a soil test done to check lead levels. Be sure to ask specifically for a lead test; it is not usually part of a standard soil test. Your Extension Service or municipal health department can give you information on testing soil for lead.
- If possible, plant the food garden away from the sides of buildings you suspect may have been painted with lead-base paint.
- Keep the soil pH above 6.5 and the level of organic matter high. This will reduce the amount of lead the plants absorb from the soil.

• Wash vegetables thoroughly before eating to remove any lead-contaminated soil. Peel root crops.
• Grow fruiting plants such as tomatoes and beans rather than leafy crops such as spinach and lettuce. More lead accumulates in leaves than fruits.

Automobile exhaust also contains lead, which settles on the aboveground parts of plants. Locate your garden at least 50 feet away from a busy road or put a fence or hedge between your food plants and the road. Wash vegetables before eating.

Lead arsenate was a commonly used orchard pesticide several decades ago. If you live on the site of an old orchard (or suspect you may), it is a good idea to have your soil tested for lead.

Designing a Garden

Fortunately, drawing a garden plan doesn't require landscaping expertise. Once you have determined the location and dimensions of your garden, sketch the area to scale on a piece of graph paper. Taking into account the space requirements of crops you want to grow (see pages 26–27), whether you want to plant in rows or beds (see pages 52–53), and how much of each fruit or vegetable you want at harvest, fill in this space with your favorite crops. There are any number of possibilities for a garden design and just a few things to keep in mind: limitations — you can't plant everything, so choose carefully; the shade factor — tall crops such as corn should be placed where they won't deprive other crops of sun; and accessibility — plan your garden with walkways so you can get at your plants easily without damaging their roots.

With a plan, you won't buy more seeds than you need. Of course, this requires strength of character as well as an accurate plan. As you review your garden plan, complete with space budgeted for walkways and expanding crops, you may realize that you can't grow as much as you want to.

Planning on paper will also help you use garden space more efficiently. It's a good way to see the possibilities for succession planting (following one crop with another) and interplanting (planting a quick-maturing crop close to a slower-maturing one and harvesting the first before the two compete for space). For example, you may see that you can follow your peas with a crop of late broccoli, and you'll be ready with transplants in July. Or you may see that there is space to tuck a few lettuce plants among your tomatoes while the vines are still small.

An important consideration in garden design is how you will sow seeds for most of your vegetables. There are three basic options: in single rows, in wide rows, or in beds. Because each garden and gardener is unique, the plans on pages 18–25 are intended as ideas for planning your own garden, not blueprints to be followed slavishly.

Choosing Varieties

Part of the fun of planning is in choosing from a number of different vegetable varieties available. One important factor to consider is length of season. With tomatoes, peppers, and sweet corn, you can select varieties maturing at different times to have a steady harvest starting 60 days after planting and continuing for 5 or 6 weeks.

Cooking characteristics come into play, too. Certain varieties of beans and peas, for example, freeze better than others. Peppers may have thin or thick walls or have flavor ranging from bland to fiery hot.

Some squash and melon varieties grow in compact areas; these crops vary quite a bit in flavor as well.

Vegetable varieties developed for commercial gardeners may mature uniformly — often during the same week — while other varieties yield the same size crop over a period of weeks.

The individual chapters on vegetables and fruits that follow have more in-depth discussions of variety traits, which will be helpful when you peruse the seed racks and plants at the garden center or study the mail-order seed and nursery catalogs.

Hybrids

As you look through seed catalogs or read seed packets, you may notice the phrase F-1 hybrid (or simply hybrid) before or after the names of some varieties. Generally, these seeds are more expensive than others.

Hybrid seeds are the result of a cross between selected groups of plants of the same kind, called inbred lines. To produce an inbred line, a variety is bred to itself for ten to twelve generations. The result is a group of plants that is almost identical genetically. Different inbred lines are then crossed to produce hybrids, or the F-1 generation. If the breeder hits upon the right combination of inbred lines, the F-1s show what is called hybrid vigor — a significant increase in qualities such as early and uniform maturity and increased disease resistance. This increased vigor can

(continued on page 26)

This plan is a 750-square-foot rectangular plot with a wide variety of plants grown in rows. Study this for ideas on succession planting, intercropping, wide-row planting, and crop placement within the garden. Your choice of succession crops will depend on the length of the season in your area and the particular varieties you choose. This plan was drawn with central and northern states in mind.

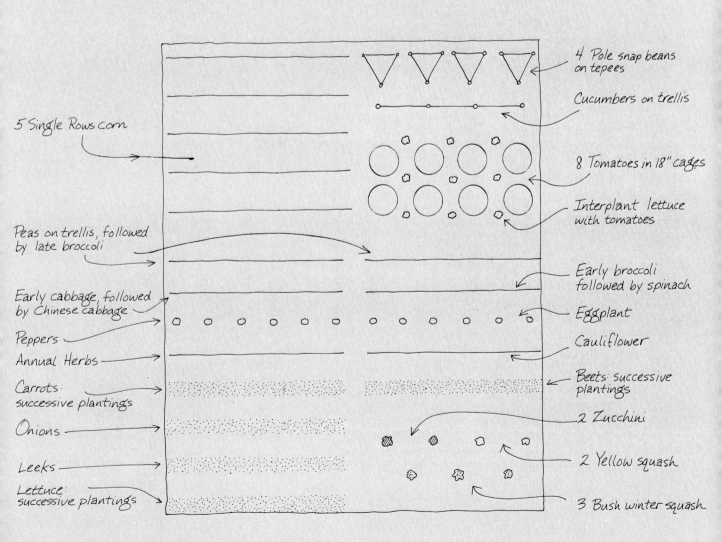

4 Pole snap beans on tepees

Cucumbers on trellis

5 Single Rows corn

8 Tomatoes in 18" cages

Interplant lettuce with tomatoes

Peas on trellis, followed by late broccoli

Early broccoli followed by spinach

Early cabbage, followed by Chinese cabbage

Eggplant

Peppers

Cauliflower

Annual Herbs

Beets: successive plantings

Carrots: successive plantings

2 Zucchini

Onions

Leeks

2 Yellow squash

Lettuce: successive plantings

3 Bush winter squash

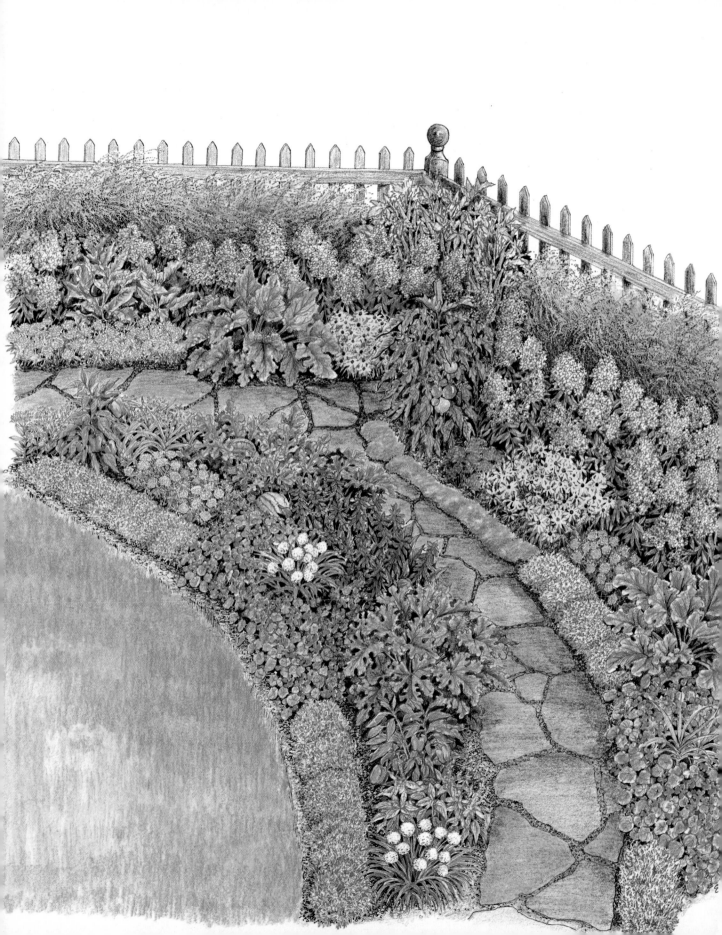

A vegetable garden is not limited to a rectangle planted in rows and set in the middle of the lawn, nor even to vegetables. This plan shows how you can incorporate ornamental plants among your vegetables to make a border that enhances the landscape while providing bounty for the table. Of course, you can also include flowers in the rows of a traditional garden, or plant only vegetables in a border along a fence.

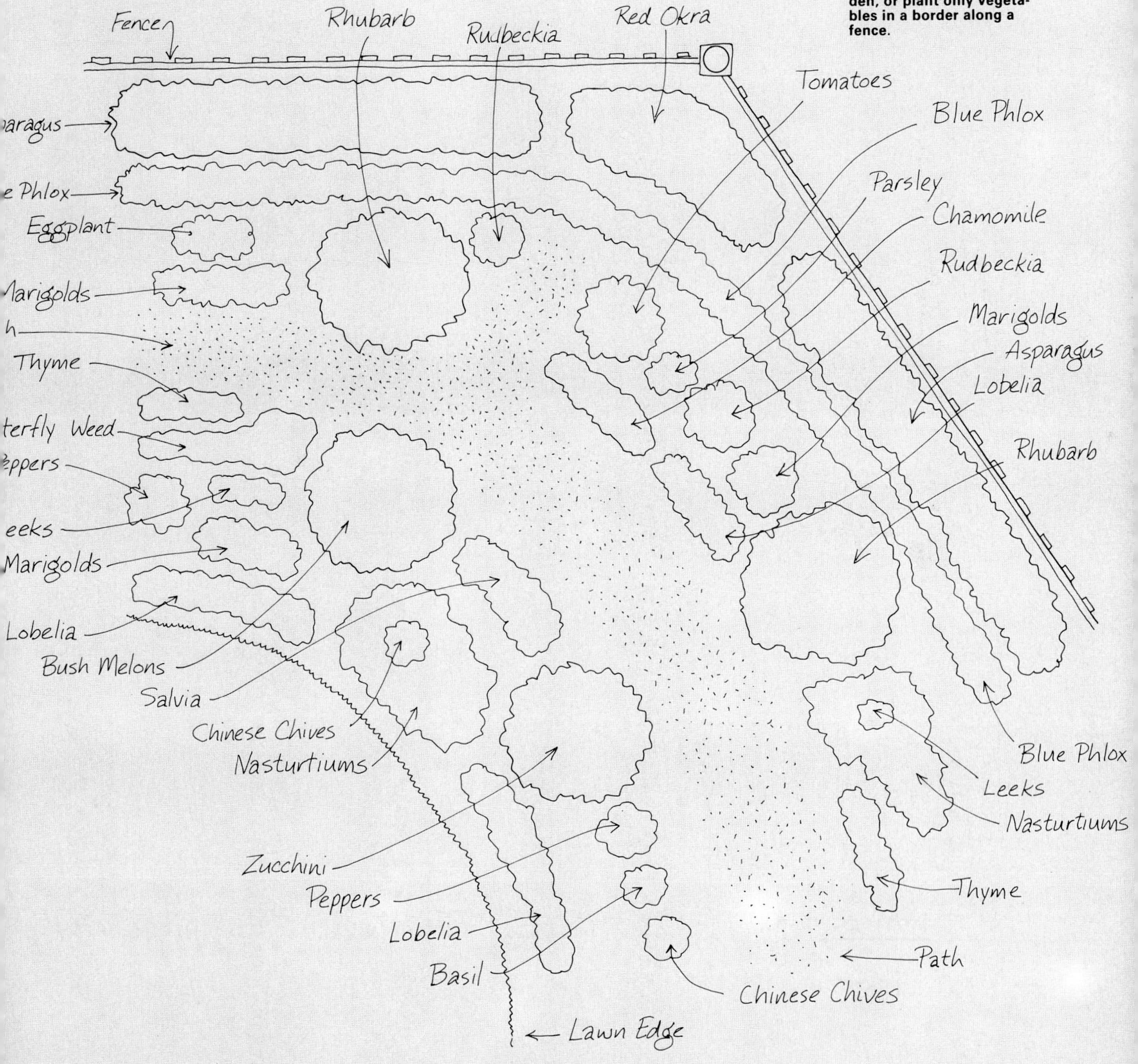

Fence

Rhubarb

Rudbeckia

Red Okra

Tomatoes

Blue Phlox

Parsley

Chamomile

Rudbeckia

Marigolds

Asparagus

Lobelia

Rhubarb

Asparagus

e Phlox

Eggplant

Marigolds

h

Thyme

terfly Weed

eppers

eeks

Marigolds

Lobelia

Bush Melons

Salvia

Chinese Chives

Nasturtiums

Blue Phlox

Leeks

Nasturtiums

Thyme

Zucchini

Peppers

Lobelia

Basil

Chinese Chives

Path

Lawn Edge

Lack of space is a problem for many gardeners, so we've included a plan showing that even a 3-foot-square plot can provide the makings for many tasty salads.

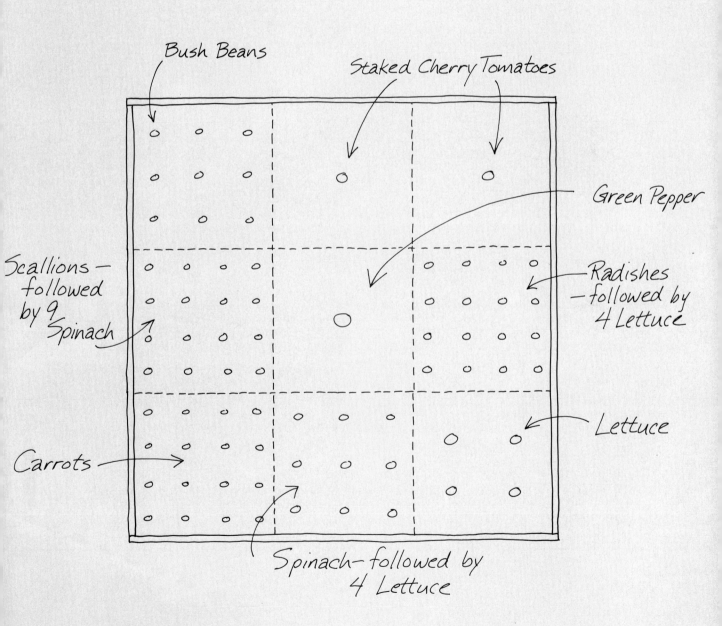

Bush Beans

Staked Cherry Tomatoes

Green Pepper

Scallions — followed by 9 Spinach

Radishes — followed by 4 Lettuce

Carrots

Lettuce

Spinach — followed by 4 Lettuce

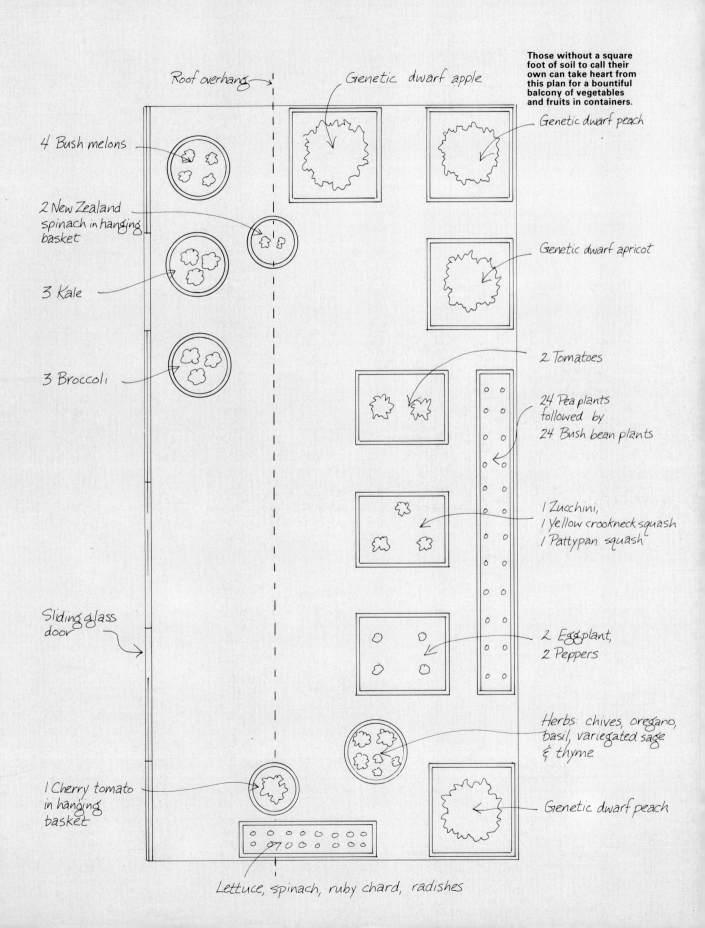

Roof overhang →

Genetic dwarf apple

Those without a square foot of soil to call their own can take heart from this plan for a bountiful balcony of vegetables and fruits in containers.

4 Bush melons

Genetic dwarf peach

2 New Zealand spinach in hanging basket

3 Kale

Genetic dwarf apricot

3 Broccoli

2 Tomatoes

24 Pea plants followed by 24 Bush bean plants

1 Zucchini, 1 Yellow crookneck squash 1 Pattypan squash

Sliding glass door

2 Eggplant, 2 Peppers

Herbs: chives, oregano, basil, variegated sage & thyme

1 Cherry tomato in hanging basket

Genetic dwarf peach

Lettuce, spinach, ruby chard, radishes

make hybrids worth the extra cost. The added expense is mainly a product of the space and labor required to maintain the inbred lines that serve as the parents of the hybrid. Also, to make the actual cross the flowers of one inbred line must often be hand-pollinated with the pollen from the other inbred line.

If you choose hybrid seeds, you'll need to buy a new batch every season, rather than save your own. When hybrid plants cross with themselves and form seeds, these seeds lose the specific combination of genetic information that gave the hybrid its good qualities. If you plant seeds saved from hybrids, you'll end up with a very mixed bag of plants.

Disease Resistance

Watch for the letters V, F, or N after some tomato variety names in catalogs or on seed packets. These letters indicate that the variety is resistant to certain diseases: V stands for resistance to verticillium wilt, N to certain nematodes, and F to fusarium wilt. If the F is followed by 1 & 2, the variety is resistant to two races of fusarium wilt.

Planning Guide

This chart will help you sketch out your garden plan. For example, if you start with an idea of how much harvest you can handle, you can determine the approximate length of row required. For example, 25 heads of lettuce will take approximately 25 feet of row. The recommended distances between rows will tell you how much space to leave between crops.

Keep in mind that the information here is useful as a general guideline. You may choose to vary the distance between rows, for example, depending on the method of cultivation. Hand-hoeing the area between rows can usually be done adequately in 18- or 24-inch-wide pathways; rototilling is faster, but pathways should be 30 or 36 inches wide. If you are gardening intensively in beds, you can space plants slightly closer than indicated in the chart.

The days to maturity and the yield figures are averages. Some of these figures will be different in your garden, depending on specific growing conditions and varieties.

Crop	Seeds/ plants per 100 ft. of row	Frost tolerance*	Planting depth (inches)	Spacing between rows (inches)	Spacing between plants (inches)	Soil temp. for germ.**	Average days to germ.	Average days to maturity	Average yield per 100 ft. of row
Asparagus	65 pl./1 oz.	very hardy (R)	½	36–48	18	50–95 (75)	7–21	2 years	30 lbs.
Beans, snap (bush)	½ lb.	tender	1–1½	24–36	3–4	60–95 (85)	6–14	45–60	120 lbs.
Beans, snap (pole)	½ lb.	tender	1–1½	36–48	4–6	60–95 (85)	6–14	60–70	150 lbs.
Beans, lima (bush)	½ lb.	very tender	1–1½	30–36	3–4	60–85 (80)	7–12	65–80	25 lbs., shelled
Beans, lima (pole)	¼ lb.	very tender	1–1½	36–48	12–18	60–85 (80)	7–12	85–90	50 lbs., shelled
Beets	1 oz.	hardy	½	15–24	2	40–95 (85)	7–10	50–60	150 lbs.
Broccoli	45 pl./¼ oz.	very hardy (P)	¼	24–36	14–24	40–95 (85)	3–10	60–80	100 lbs.
Brussels sprouts	55 pl./¼ oz.	very hardy (P)	¼	24–36	14–24	40–95 (85)	3–10	90–100	75 lbs.
Cabbage	55 pl./¼ oz.	very hardy (P)	¼	24–36	14–24	40–95 (85)	4–10	60–90	150 lbs.
Carrots	½ oz.	hardy	¼	15–24	2	40–95 (80)	10–17	70–80	100 lbs.
Cauliflower	55 pl./¼ oz.	hardy (P)	¼	24–36	14–24	40–95 (80)	4–10	70–90	100 lbs.
Celery	200 pl.	hardy	⅛	30–36	6	40–75 (70)	9–21	125	180 stalks
Chinese cabbage	65 pl./¼ oz.	hardy (P)	¼	18–30	8–12	40–105 (80)	4–10	65–70	80 heads
Corn	3–4 oz.	tender	2	24–36	12–18	50–105 (85)	6–10	70–90	10 dozen
Cucumbers	½ oz.	very tender	1	48–72	24–48	60–105 (95)	6–10	50–70	120 lbs.
Eggplant	⅛ oz.	very tender (P)	¼–½	24–36	18–24	65–95 (85)	7–14	80–90	100 lbs.
Leeks	½ oz.	very hardy	½–1	12–18	2–4	45–70 (75)	7–12	130–150	125 lbs.
Lettuce, heading	¼ oz.	very hardy	¼–½	18–24	6–10	32–75 (75)	4–10	70–75	100 heads
Lettuce, leaf	¼ oz.	very hardy	¼–½	15–18	2–3	32–75 (75)	4–10	40–50	50 lbs.
Muskmelon	50 pl./½ oz.	very tender	1	60–96	24–36	65–105 (95)	4–8	85–100	50 fruits

P—plants
R—roots
NA—not applicable
* Very hardy—plant outside 4 to 6 weeks before last spring frost date

Hardy—plant outside 2 to 3 weeks before last spring frost date
Tender—plant outside on date of last spring frost
Very tender—plant outside 1 to 2 weeks after last spring frost date
** Range of germination temperature; optimum germination in parentheses

Tomatoes, spinach, peas, and cucumbers are just a few of the vegetables that have been bred to resist certain diseases. Building in resistance to disease is one of the major efforts of plant breeding, and the list of accomplishments grows longer each year.

Fungicide-treated Seed

Gardeners are sometimes surprised to open a packet of corn seeds and find them bright pink instead of yellow. These colors indicate that the seed has been coated with a fungicide, a chemical that protects seeds from rot organisms that attack germinating seeds in cold, wet soils. Seeds of corn, beans, and peas are often sold treated as indicated on the seed packet. Some seed companies sell only untreated seeds, some sell only treated seed for certain crops, and others give the gardener a choice.

Gardeners can also treat seeds themselves with seed protectant powders containing fungicides. If you do use treated seed, remember that fungicide is a poison. Keep the seeds out of the reach of small children, and wear gloves when you handle the seeds.

Planning Guide *(continued)*

Crop	Seeds/ plants per 100 ft. of row	Frost tolerance*	Planting depth (inches)	Spacing between rows (inches)	Spacing between plants (inches)	Soil temp. for germ.**	Average days to germ.	Average days to maturity	Average yield per 100 ft. of row
Okra	2 oz.	very tender	1	36–42	12–24	65–80	7–14	55–65	100 lbs.
Onion, seed	1 oz.	very hardy	½	15–24	3–4	32–95 (80)	7–12	90–120	100 lbs.
Onion, sets	400–600 pl.	very hardy	1–3	15–24	3–4	NA	NA	80–120	100 lbs.
Parsley	¼ oz.	hardy	¼–½	15–24	6–8	50–85 (70)	14–28	70–90	40 lbs.
Parsnips	½ oz.	hardy	½	18–30	3–4	32–85 (70)	15–25	120–170	100 lbs.
Peas	1 lb.	very hardy	2	18–36	1	40–85 (75)	6–15	55–90	20 lbs.
Peppers	⅛ oz.	very tender	¼	24–36	18–24	60–95 (85)	10–20	60–90	60 lbs.
Potatoes, Irish	6–10 lbs. seed potatoes	very hardy (R)	4	30–36	10–15	NA	NA	75–100	100 lbs.
Pumpkins	½ oz.	very tender	1–2	60–96	36–48	65–105 (95)	6–10	75–100	100 lbs.
Radishes	1 oz.	hardy	½	14–24	1	40–95 (80)	3–10	25–40	100 bunches
Rhubarb	20 pl.	very hardy (R)	4	36–48	48	NA	NA	2 years	75 lbs.
Southern peas	½ lb.	very tender	½–1	24–36	4–6	60–95 (85)	7–10	60–70	40 lbs.
Spinach	1 oz.	very hardy	¾	14–24	3–4	32–75 (70)	6–14	40–60	40–50 lbs.
Squash, summer	1 oz.	tender	1	36–60	18–36	65–105 (95)	3–12	50–60	150 lbs.
Squash, winter	½ oz.	very tender	1	60–96	24–48	65–105 (95)	6–10	85–100	100 lbs.
Sweet potatoes	75–100 pl.	very tender (P)	NA	36–48	12–16	NA	NA	100–130	100 lbs.
Tomatoes	50 pl./⅛ oz.	tender	½	24–48	18–36	50–95 (80)	6–14	70–90	100 lbs.
Turnips	½ oz.	very hardy	½	14–24	2–3	50–105 (80)	3–10	30–60	50–100 lbs.
Watermelon	1 oz.	very tender	1	72–96	36–72	65–105 (95)	3–12	80–100	40 fruits

P—plants
R—roots
NA—not applicable
* *Very hardy*—plant outside 4 to 6 weeks before last spring frost date

Hardy—plant outside 2 to 3 weeks before last spring frost date
Tender—plant outside on date of last spring frost
Very tender—plant outside 1 to 2 weeks after last spring frost date
**Range of germination temperature; optimum germination in parentheses

Preparation

Soil is more than just plain dirt. It is a dynamic mixture of mineral particles, living organisms, organic matter, air, and water that is the foundation not only of your garden, but of all plant life on earth.

All soil began as rock. In a weathering process that began eons ago and continues today, rock from the earth's crust is slowly broken down into small particles through the action of frost, temperature changes, wind, water, and acids produced by decaying organic matter. Living organisms, from earthworms to microscopic bacteria, along with the remains of plants and animals in various stages of decomposition, combine with the minerals to form a complex, constantly changing system that provides plants with the water, air, and nutrients they need.

Given the origins of soil, then, it should come as no surprise that adding organic matter to your garden always improves it. This is the key to soil preparation. The following pages give you a more in-depth look at the components of soil and how the whole system works, what different fertilizers will add to your garden, and finally how to begin the real work — digging your garden.

The best way to get to know your soil is by working with it, digging through it, examining it, testing it, and improving it.

Soil

Texture and Structure

Pick up a handful of moist soil and rub it between your thumb and fingers. If it has a smooth, slippery feel, it contains a high proportion of clay; a gritty feel tells you that your soil contains a lot of sand.

Soil is divided into three main textural categories depending on the size of the particles it contains. Sand particles are the largest, clay the smallest, and silt falls between the two. Soil with a large proportion of silt particles is called loam. Most soils contain a combination of particle sizes, and soil scientists have come up with subcategories to describe them. For example, a soil with 25 percent clay, 25 percent silt, and 50 percent sand is called a sandy loam.

Soil texture is important to the gardener because it influences the amounts of water, air, and nutrients the soil can hold. Clay soils hold a lot of water, but not much air; sandy soils are well aerated, but can't hold water well. Clay soils are potentially more fertile than sandy ones.

Loam is what all gardeners long for. A compromise between sand and clay, it has good aeration and drainage, holds adequate moisture for plant growth, and retains nutrients well. If you don't have loamy soil in your garden, don't despair. There are ways to improve less-than-ideal soils.

You can't change the texture of the soil you have, but you can influence another important characteristic — its structure. Structure refers to the physical arrangement of the soil particles. Soils that have a granular structure, with the individual soil particles clumped together into larger aggregates, are best for plant growth because they have good aeration and drainage. Organic matter added to the soil helps improve soil structure. It breaks down to form humus (partly or thoroughly decomposed vegetable matter), which helps to cement soil particles together into aggregates. Adding organic matter to a poorly drained soil that is high in clay will improve aeration and drainage; if added to a sandy soil the water-holding capacity of the soil will increase.

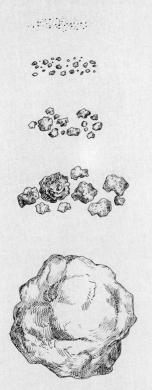

Rock particles, the basis of soil, range in size from those found in clay, hardly discernible to the naked eye, to the slightly larger particles found in silt, to the larger-still particles of sand and gravel.

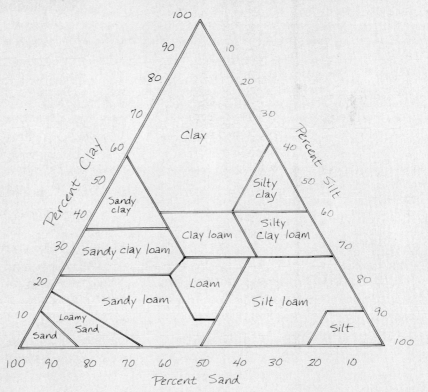

Soil scientists use this textural triangle to categorize soils based on the content mix of clay, silt, and sand. Loam, a mixture of all three sizes of particles, is the ideal soil for growing plants.

Microorganisms

When you add manure, leaves, or grass clippings to your soil, microorganisms break them down, making the nutrients they contain available to plant roots and creating humus. There are two major groups of soil microorganisms: fungi and bacteria.

Fungi go about their business even when the soil is cold and wet and at extremes of pH. They keep the decay process going under conditions that are unsuitable for the fussier bacteria. Bacteria require good aeration, a near-neutral pH, moist but not wet soil, and warm temperatures. Most are active when the soil temperature is between 70 and 100°F, so they become active about the time you set out such heat-loving plants as tomatoes and peppers.

While the primary role of fungi and some soil bacteria is to break down organic matter, other bacteria play an important role in making nitrogen available to plant roots. The end result of the first stage of breakdown by the general decomposers is ammonium nitrogen. The next step in the process is called nitrification. When moisture and temperatures are suitable, two special types of bacteria convert the ammonium nitrogen into nitrate nitrogen, the form in which most plants take up most of their nitrogen. These bacteria are somewhat active when the soil temperature is as low as 30 to 40°F, but don't reach the peak of their activity until it hits the 80 to 90°F range.

That's one of the reasons plants need warm soil to grow well. It is also why adding manure, blood meal, and other organic sources of nitrogen to cold soils in early spring may not provide plants with enough of the nitrate nitrogen they need. For early crops it's better to use a readily available chemical fertilizer that has nitrogen already in the nitrate form.

If you add a lot of undecomposed organic matter to the soil your plants may begin to show signs of a nitrogen deficiency — yellowing of the older leaves of the plant and a slowdown of growth. This is because soil microorganisms need more nitrogen than the undecomposed organic matter can supply. Instead, they take up nitrogen from the soil, making it unavailable to plants. As their food supply decreases, the microbes begin to die off. Then the nitrogen in their tissues becomes available to plants, and all is well again.

pH

The pH scale runs from 0 to 14. The midpoint, 7.0, is neutral; lower numbers are acidic, higher ones alkaline. Each value on the scale is ten times greater or less than the one before or after it. A pH of 6.0 is ten times more acid than a pH of 7.0, and one hundred times more acid than a pH of 8.0. Changing the pH slightly can cause a relatively large change in acidity.

If the pH is not within a suitable range, plants cannot take up nutrients such as phosphorus and potassium even if they are present in the soil in high amounts. On the other hand, the solubility of certain minerals such as manganese may increase to toxic levels if the soil pH is too low.

Keeping soil pH in the 6.0 to 7.5 range not only keeps nutrients available to most plants, but provides a suitable environment for bacteria and fungi. Some gardening experts may recommend trying to achieve a soil pH of 6.8; that is ideal for many vegetables, but you shouldn't worry as long as your soil is in the 6.0 to 7.5 range.

In general, if your soil is too acid you will need to add lime; if it is too alkaline, you will add sulfur. A soil test is the best way to determine your particular soil pH; the lab results usually prescribe the amounts of lime or sulfur needed to adjust the pH of different soil types.

When you test the pH of a soil sample you are measuring the concentration of hydrogen ions in the soil solution (the water between the individual soil particles). The more hydrogen ions in solution, the greater the acidity.

Think of a soil particle as having niches in which plant nutrients (alkaline ions such as calcium, magnesium, and potassium, and other ions such as hydrogen, aluminum, and sodium) can be stored. Sandy soil particles have fewer storage niches and are relatively infertile. Clay soil particles have more niches and are potentially more fertile. Storage niches can hold nutrients in reserve, releasing them as needed into the soil solution where they can be taken up by plant roots.

In areas with abundant rainfall — such as the eastern half of the country and the Pacific Northwest — rainwater percolating down through the soil picks up hydrogen ions from the acids at the soil surface. These acids are the end products of the decomposition of organic matter. The high concentration of acidic hydrogen ions in the soil solution fills any empty niches on the soil particles with hydrogens and pushes alkaline ions off. Once in solution, these alkaline ions leach down into the subsoil out of reach of plant roots. Thus, where rainfall is plentiful, soils are often acidic.

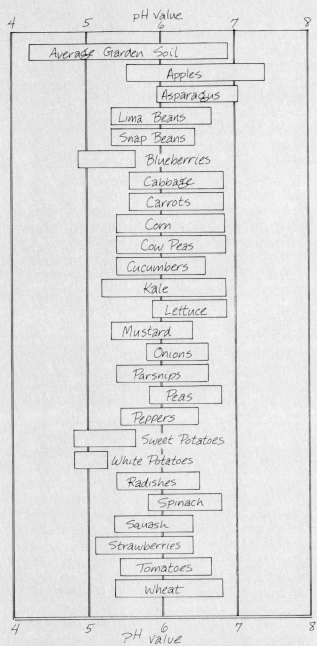

pH Value

| | 4 | 5 | 6 | 7 | 8 |

Average Garden Soil
Apples
Asparagus
Lima Beans
Snap Beans
Blueberries
Cabbage
Carrots
Corn
Cow Peas
Cucumbers
Kale
Lettuce
Mustard
Onions
Parsnips
Peas
Peppers
Sweet Potatoes
White Potatoes
Radishes
Spinach
Squash
Strawberries
Tomatoes
Wheat

pH Value

This chart shows the ideal pH ranges for growing various crops. A pH of 7.0 is neutral; the lower numbers are acidic, the higher ones alkaline. Most crops do best in the range of 6.0–7.5 (slightly acidic); only a few need special pH conditions.

To raise the pH (decrease the acidity), gardeners add lime to provide calcium ions to replace some of the hydrogen ions. (Clay soils, whose particles have more niches than sandy soils, will need a greater amount of lime to change the pH by the same amount.)

In arid regions just the opposite problem arises. With little rainfall to leach out alkaline ions produced by the weathering of soil minerals, soils become alkaline. If the soil pH is too high (generally, above 7.5 to 8.0), nutrients such as phosphorus, iron, and zinc may be tied up in the soil, unusable by plants. To correct this situation, gardeners can add sulfur, which is oxidized by soil bacteria to form sulfuric acid that provides hydrogen ions to replace some of the akaline ions attached to the soil particles.

Changing Soil pH

You will get the most accurate liming and sulfur recommendations from a professional soil-testing service. If you do your own pH testing and need to raise the pH, the rule of thumb is: for an increase of one unit (e.g., 5.5 to 6.5) add 30 pounds of ground limestone per 1,000 square feet on sandy soil, 50 pounds on sandy loam, 70 pounds on loam, and 80 pounds on heavy clay. If your soil is high in organic matter, increase these amounts somewhat. Decrease them if your soil is low in organic matter.

Most gardeners add lime in the form of ground limestone; the more finely it's ground, the faster it works. If your soil test indicates a need for magnesium, use dolomitic limestone to provide that as well as calcium. Hydrated lime acts faster in the soil than ground limestone, so use less; but it is also more caustic and can damage plant roots if applied too heavily. Quicklime can destroy soil humus, so we don't recommend using it at all.

To lower the pH one unit (e.g., 7.5 to 6.5) add 5 pounds of sulfur per 1,000 square feet on sandy soils, 20 pounds per 1,000 square feet on heavy clay, about 7 to 10 pounds on sandy loam, and 10 to 15 on loam.

"Sodic" soils, frequently found in western states, are alkaline soils in which many of the storage niches on particles have sodium ions as tenants. Large amounts of sodium break down soil structure, compacting the soil so it is poorly drained and aerated. Adding agricultural gypsum provides calcium ions to replace the sodium ions without changing the pH. If you add sulfur to sodic soils, you reduce the sodium content and the pH at the same time.

Soil Testing

You can get a soil test at a private soil-testing lab and, in most states, at soil-testing labs at state universities. The price of a routine test varies — state tests are usually quite inexpensive. A routine test generally includes tests for pH, phosphorus, potassium, and soil texture. Depending on the lab, they may also test for other nutrients, such as nitrogen and magnesium. Private soil-testing services are generally more expensive than state labs, but may offer more extensive tests. Both will make recommendations for the amount of lime or sulfur needed to amend the pH and the amount of fertilizer to add for the crops you intend to grow. Nonroutine tests (for lead or micronutrients, for example) may be offered at an extra charge. (Micronutrient testing should be a last resort to a plant growth problem. First check soil pH and adjust if necessary; test for major nutrients and fertilize according to the result, then add organic matter such as manure. If there is still a growth problem, micronutrient testing is the next step.) To find out about state soil-testing services, contact your local Extension Service office.

Many home soil-testing kits are available at garden centers. While the results may not be as accurate as those of a soil-testing lab, a home kit is handy for gardeners who like to monitor their soil frequently throughout the season.

Changes in pH and most nutrients are gradual. If you are correcting a soil imbalance, you may want to test the soil every year. For maintaining soil that is in good balance, test every 3 to 5 years. Fall is a good time to have a soil test done. Labs aren't as busy, and it's the best time to add lime and phosphorus-containing fertilizers because they work slowly in the soil.

Plant Nutrients

Sixteen elements are known to be essential for healthy plant growth. Plants need carbon, hydrogen, and oxygen in large quantities because they are the essential ingredients, along with energy from sunlight, for photosynthesis, the process by which green plants take carbon dioxide from the air and water from the soil to produce sugars to fuel their growth. Apart from watering plants, gardeners can trust nature to supply these "big three."

Plants also need nitrogen, phosphorus, and potassium in relatively large quantities. These three elements are often called macronutrients. Plants take up these three nutrients from the soil. If they are not abundant in the soil, they can be supplied by using fertilizers.

Nitrogen (N) is responsible for the healthy, green color of your plants. It is a key part of proteins and chlorophyll, the plant pigment that plays a vital role in photosynthesis. Plants with a deficiency of nitrogen show a yellowing of older leaves first, along with a

general slowdown in growth. (In plants like tomatoes, nitrogen deficiency may be indicated by a reddening of the stems and the undersides of the leaves.) There can be too much of a good thing, however; a plant with too much nitrogen will have lots of soft, dark green foliage, an underdeveloped root system, and delayed flowering and fruiting.

Nitrogen can come from inorganic sources such as chemical fertilizers, from decomposing organic matter and organic fertilizers such as blood meal (dried animal blood) and cottonseed meal (a by-product of cottonseed oil mills), and from the air, through the action of nitrogen-fixing bacteria. Nitrate nitrogen (the form in which most plants take up most of their nitrogen) moves easily through the soil and can be leached out of range of plant roots by rain and irrigation water. So besides being needed by plants in large quantities, nitrogen is one of the nutrients most likely to be lost from the root zone. You'll need to see that your plants receive a steady supply of nitrogen throughout the growing season.

Phosphorus (P) is associated with good root growth, increased disease resistance, and fruit and seed formation. Plants lacking in phosphorus are stunted, with dark green foliage, followed by reddening of the stems and leaves. As with nitrogen, the symptoms appear on the older leaves first. Sources for phosphorus include soil minerals, organic matter, inorganic fertilizers such as rock phosphate, and organic fertilizers such as bone meal (crushed bones). Soil pH plays a big role in the availability of phosphorus to plants; a pH of 6 to 7.5 will keep this important nutrient most available. Unlike nitrogen, phosphorus doesn't move quickly through the soil. Therefore, it is a good idea to mix phosphorus-containing fertilizers into the root zone before planting, rather than sprinkling them on the surface.

Potassium (K) promotes vigorous growth and disease resistance. The first sign of a deficiency is a slowdown in growth; more severe deficiency shows up as browning of the edges of leaves. Older leaves are affected first. Soil minerals provide potassium, as do organic matter and inorganic fertilizers such as potassium sulfate, rock sand, and granite dust.

Calcium, magnesium, and *sulfur* are known as secondary nutrients. They are needed in substantial quantities, but not to the same extent as nitrogen, phosphorus, and potassium. In areas where the soil is acid, liming to keep the soil pH in the range for good plant growth usually provides adequate calcium and magnesium (the latter if dolomitic limestone is used). Most alkaline soils are naturally well supplied with these elements. Few soils are deficient in sulfur. A common ingredient in many chemical fertilizers, it also falls from the sky when rain and snow wash industrial pollutants out of the atmosphere, and it is present in organic matter.

Micronutrients include *iron, manganese, copper, boron, molybdenum, chlorine,* and *zinc.* These elements are needed by plants in extremely small amounts. Too much is usually as harmful as too little. Often a micronutrient deficiency is the result of a pH imbalance. The problem can often be corrected by changing the pH rather than adding more nutrients. In some cases, it is not practical to change the pH to the degree required to increase the amount of a micronutrient; or you may need to provide a plant with a micronutrient quickly while you go about the longer-term solution of changing the soil pH. In such cases, micronutrients are applied as *chelates.* Taking their name from the Latin word for "claw," chelates are chemicals added to other chemicals, in this case micronutrients, to keep them available to plants even though soil conditions are unfavorable. Chelated micronutrients may be applied to the soil or sprayed on the foliage.

Fertilizers

When you buy a commercial fertilizer, its analysis will be listed on the label with three numbers. These three numbers are helpful to the gardener in several ways. First of all, they let you know what nutrients are in a particular fertilizer. The first number indicates the percentage of nitrogen (N) in that particular fertilizer; the second, the percentage of phosphate (P_2O_5); and the third, the percentage of potash (K_2O). A fertilizer with an analysis of 5-10-10 contains 5 percent nitrogen, 10 percent phosphate, and 10 percent potash. The remaining material in a commercial fertilizer, the percent not accounted for by the analysis numbers, is generally inert filler of some kind.

A fertilizer containing a balanced supply of the three major nutrients, such as 5-10-10 or 10-10-10, is called a complete fertilizer. Bone meal has an analysis of 3-20-0. It's a good source of phosphate, but won't provide any potash.

Most fertilizer recommendations for maintenance fertilization (rather than for correcting a specific defi-

ciency) are made on the basis of the amount of nitrogen needed by a particular crop. For example, suppose you have a recommendation for 3 pounds of 5-10-10 per 1,000 square feet, but all you have on hand is 5-10-5. You'd still apply 3 pounds of 5-10-5 — even though its percentage of potash is less than that of the 5-10-10 — in order to apply the same amount of nitrogen.

Commercial fertilizers are labeled with the percentages of the three major nutrients they contain, always in the same order. This bag contains 5 percent nitrogen, 10 percent phosphorus, and 5 percent potash. A complete fertilizer for general use contains a balanced supply of these major nutrients.

Three Different Kinds of Nitrogen

The label on the fertilizer package should give you an analysis and a list of the compounds that provide these nutrients. For example, the label may tell you that of the total percentage of nitrogen, so much is ammoniacal nitrogen, so much nitrate nitrogen, and so much water-insoluble nitrogen. Nitrogen in the nitrate form is fast acting. Depending on the specific nitrate compound, it either has no effect on soil pH or raises it somewhat. Ammoniacal nitrogen, on the other hand, is not available to most plants until the action of soil microorganisms converts it to nitrate. It does not leach from the root zone as easily as nitrate nitrogen and has an acidifying effect on the soil. Water-insoluble nitrogen has been formulated so that it is released slowly over a period of time. In general, a fertilizer with nitrogen in both the nitrate and ammoniacal forms will provide plants with both immediate and longer-term sources of nitrogen without much effect on the soil pH. Fertilizers with a lot of water-insoluble nitrogen are good for container plants that need frequent watering because they don't wash too quickly from the soil.

Approximate Ratio of Primary Nutrients in Some Common Fertilizers

Fertilizer	Nitrogen	Phosphate	Potash	Comments
Ammonium nitrate	33.5	0	0	Has no effect on soil pH
Ammonium phosphate	12	62	0	Provides both nitrogen and phosphorus
Ammonium sulfate	20	0	0	An acidifying fertilizer
Blood meal, dried	12	3	0	Expensive source of nitrogen
Bone meal	3	20	0	Excellent source of phosphorus but expensive
Calcium nitrate	15	0	0	Tends to raise pH
Cottonseed meal	7	2	2	Fairly expensive when compared to other sources of nitrogen
Cow manure, fresh	.5	.1	.4	Apply in fall if possible; otherwise apply 3–4 weeks before planting
Cow manure, dried	1.3	.9	.8	Sold packaged, usually inexpensive
Granite dust	0	0	5	By-product of building stone industry; potassium not quickly available
Greensand	0	1.5	5	The potassium dissolves rapidly into the soil solution
Horse manure, fresh	.6	.3	.5	Slow release of nutrients
Potassium chloride	0	0	60	Also called muriate of potash
Potassium nitrate	13	0	44	Has little effect on soil pH
Potassium sulfate	0	0	50	Common source of potash
Rock phosphate	0	31	0	Phosphorus more available if applied along with manure and compost rather than spread over garden
Sheep manure, dried	1.4	1.0	3.0	Often sold in 25- or 40-lb. bags at garden centers
Sodium nitrate	15	0	0	Tends to raise pH
Soybean meal	6	0	0	Good source of nitrogen; not available in all regions
Superphosphate	0	20	0	Phosphorus is quickly available
Triple superphosphate	0	44	0	More concentrated source
Urea	45	0	0	Concentrated nitrogen source that is quickly available; use carefully

Chemical and Organic Fertilizers

There is no definitive answer to the question of which type of fertilizer, chemical or organic, is better. Gardeners must weigh the pros and cons to decide which products are best suited to their particular needs.

Chemical fertilizers are synthetically manufactured. They include fertilizers such as sodium nitrate, potassium chloride, and superphosphate. Different chemical fertilizers may be combined to produce a complete fertilizer, one with a balanced supply of nitrogen, phosphate, and potash, such as 6-18-6, 5-10-5, or 10-10-10. Chemical fertilizers are widely available, relatively inexpensive in general, easy to store, and come in a wide array of formulations and forms, which lets a gardener come up with a precise fertilizer program tailored to his or her needs. Unless they have been manufactured in a slow-release form most chemical fertilizers are quite rapidly available to plants.

You can buy chemical fertilizers in liquid, granular, powder, or pellet form. A fertilizer that comes as a liquid or a dry powder to be mixed with water is completely soluble and its nutrients are most quickly available to plants. This is an advantage when plants need a quick boost, such as right after transplanting.

On the negative side, chemical fertilizers add no organic matter to the soil and contribute nothing to the improvement of soil structure. Because they are more concentrated than natural fertilizers, they can have a greater effect on soil pH, which can damage soil microorganisms. And finally, the manufacture of chemical fertilizers requires large amounts of energy, usually supplied by nonrenewable sources.

Natural fertilizers, which include animal and green manures, blood meal, cottonseed meal, granite dust, and rock phosphate, also have their pros and cons. On the positive side, many contribute organic matter to the soil, improving its structure, and they can be a good source of micronutrients. Most natural fertilizers supply a slow but steady diet for plants. Also, some natural fertilizers, such as manure, may be inexpensive.

On the other hand, some natural fertilizers are bulky and hard to store. Their slow release of nutrients, in some cases dependent on the action of soil microorganisms, may not provide plants with an adequate supply when needed. Few natural fertilizers have a balanced ratio of nutrients; rather, they must be combined in order for plants to receive a good diet. For example, cow manure is low in phosphate in relation to nitrogen and potassium. To supply the deficient phosphate a gardener would have to add another high-phosphate fertilizer such as bone meal. Complete fertilizers are available in which all the nutrients are from organic sources. As with complete chemical fertilizers, all three major nutrients are present, but usually in a lower concentration, such as 1-2-1.

Wood Ashes

Wood ashes are a source of potash and phosphate, although the exact amounts of these nutrients depend on the type of wood burned (hardwoods generally contain more nutrients than softwoods), the completeness of combustion, and whether the ashes have been stored in a dry spot to prevent leaching of nutrients. A general analysis is usually in the range 0 percent nitrogen, 1 to 2 percent phosphate, and 4 to 10 percent potash. But the major benefit of wood ashes is as a liming agent to raise the pH of the soil.

Wood ashes are considerably more soluble than ground limestone and cause a rapid change in soil pH. You should not add wood ashes to your soil indiscriminately. Add them only if you need to raise the soil pH to improve plant growth. If you spread wood ashes in the garden each spring, don't use more than 2 pounds per 100 square feet. If you spread ashes once every 3 to 4 years, you can use up to 10 pounds per 100 square feet. Check the pH of your soil regularly to make sure you are not raising the pH too much.

Another reason to be moderate with wood ashes is that they contain small amounts of heavy metals such as cadmium and copper. These metals can begin to accumulate in plants if excessive quantities of wood ashes are added to the soil.

Green Manures and Cover Crops

One easy way for gardeners to add organic matter to their soil is to grow green manure crops. These are plants grown to be chopped and tilled or spaded into the soil when they are still green (but before they blossom and produce seeds, which could create a future weed problem). The succulent plant material breaks down quickly, adding nutrients and improving soil texture. These crops are usually grown during the main gardening season in a separate portion of the garden that will be used the following year.

Cover crops are similar to green manures; often they are the same plants. The difference is that the primary purposes of a cover crop are to prevent soil erosion and choke out weeds, usually when the soil is bare of crops before and after the harvest.

The plants used as green manures and cover crops can be divided into two broad categories, legumes and nonlegumes. Legumes are plants that have developed a mutually beneficial relationship with a group of bacteria of the genus *Rhizobium*. These bacteria enter the roots of legumes where they colonize special cells around which nodules form. These nitrogen-fixing nodules have a distinct pink color. They receive carbohydrates from their hosts for food and in return take from the air nitrogen that is otherwise unavailable to plants and convert it to forms plants can use, a process called nitrogen fixation.

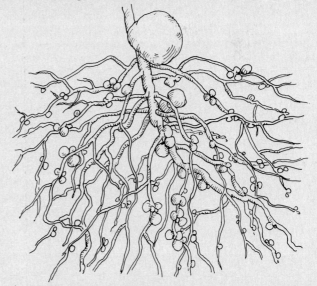

The association of bacteria and legumes, referred to as nodulation, is a mutually beneficial one. In return for providing legumes with available nitrogen, the *Rhizobia* bacteria get carbohydrates from the plant to use as an energy source. The nodules, usually a distinct pink color, are where the bacteria have colonized on the roots.

The nitrogen fixed by these bacteria not only benefits their current hosts. Nearby nonleguminous crops benefit when nitrogen passes into the soil as old nodules are sloughed off the roots. And if legumes are tilled back into the soil, succeeding crops benefit from the increased nitrogen.

There are many types of *Rhizobia* and each kind chooses a particular group of legumes with which to set up housekeeping. To make sure that the proper strains of *Rhizobia* are present in the soil, you can buy commercial inoculant powders containing live bacteria. These are mixed with the legume seed before planting.

When you buy inoculant, read the label to be sure it contains the correct type of *Rhizobia* for the crop you intend to grow. A farm supply store may carry a wider selection of inoculants than a garden store.

Remember when you handle the inoculant that you are handling living creatures; plant as soon as possible after stirring the inoculant in with your seeds. Add a bit of vegetable oil to the mixture so the bacteria will adhere to the seeds. Once a particular group of *Rhizobia* is established in the soil, it is not necessary to reinoculate each year as long as legumes of the same family are grown each season.

Green Manure Crops

Name	Pounds of seed per 1000 sq. ft.	When to Sow	Comments
Legumes			
Clover, common sweet	½	spring or fall	Early spring seeding is best in the North. Seed in fall in lower South; needs a soil pH above 6.0; biennial.
Clover, crimson	1	spring or fall	Good winter annual, but not hardy north of New Jersey.
Cowpea	2½	late spring	Withstands drought and moderate shade well; do not sow until weather is warm; annual.
Lespedeza	1	early spring	Good for acid soils with low fertility; South only; annual.
Lupine	2½	spring or fall	Good on acid soils; annual.
Soybeans	2½	spring or summer	A warm weather crop; do not sow until the ground is warm and the weather is settled; annual.
Vetch, hairy	1½	spring or fall	Grows best in cool moist weather; very winter hardy; annual.
Nonlegumes			
Buckwheat	1½	late spring	Quick growing; plant only after ground is warm; excellent green manure crop in North; thick growth, smothers weeds; annual.
Kale	¼	summer or fall	Can be eaten after serving as winter cover; in northern areas interplant with winter rye for protection; plant at least 6 weeks before first frost; annual.
Millet	1	late spring	Sow only after ground is warm, a week or 10 days after normal corn planting time; fast growing; annual.
Oats	2½	spring or fall	Winter oats (sown in fall) are suitable only in areas with mild winters; annual.
Rye grass, annual	2	spring or summer	Yields abundant organic matter; won't survive heavy freezes; protects ground for early tilling in spring; not a true annual, but usually only lives one year.
Winter Rye	2	fall	One of the most important winter cover crops; can be sown late in fall; makes a good growth in spring to till under.
Fescue grass	1	as needed	Good for areas with mild winters, humid climate; southern U.S. and Pacific coast; short-lived perennial that behaves as an annual.
Sudan grass	1	late spring	Widely adaptable across the country; sow after ground is warm; a fast grower; annual.

The soil conditions that promote optimum nitrogen fixation include good drainage and aeration, adequate moisture, a pH between 5.8 and 7.0, lots of calcium in the soil, warmth (a soil temperature of 66 to 68°F is best), and not too much nitrogen in the soil (if there is plenty of available nitrogen, the plants will simply use that and not admit the *Rhizobia* into their roots).

Although nonlegumes won't add as much nitrogen to the soil, many are very useful as green manures and cover crops for the organic matter they add to the soil. In most parts of the country a spring crop of oats or annual rye can be planted and tilled under early enough to allow a late planting of vegetables for a fall harvest. This is a good strategy for gardeners who want to build up their soil rapidly with organic matter while still getting vegetables from the plot.

Winter rye is a good choice as a cover crop in northern sections of the country because of its winter hardiness. It can be sown in the fall after crops are harvested and tilled under in the spring before planting.

Buckwheat not only adds lots of organic matter to the soil but is a good crop for crowding out weeds because it grows so densely. If weeds are a big problem, two successive plantings of buckwheat may be necessary to smother them. Till in this and other annual crops before they begin to set seed. Buckwheat is probably the easiest crop to dig in with a spade or shovel, so it is a good choice if you don't have a tiller.

Compost

Making compost is a way for gardeners to turn a wide array of readily available organic materials, such as grass clippings, household garbage, and plant residues, into a uniform, easy-to-handle source of organic matter for the garden. Although it is true that when these materials decompose into finished compost the mixture is usually low in plant nutrients, composting allows you to enrich your soil in an efficient, inexpensive way. Although you can add undecomposed organic matter to the soil with nearly the same result, most gardeners find that dark, crumbly compost is easier to handle than half-rotten household garbage.

Building a good compost pile involves much more than just tossing organic materials in a pile in the corner of the yard, though many people use this method with varied success. A well-made pile heats up quickly (a sign that decay organisms are at work), decomposition proceeds at a rapid rate, and the pile doesn't give off any bad odors. A good pile is one in which the

organisms doing all the decay work can take up carbon and nitrogen in proportion to their needs.

It is easy to come up with the correct proportions of carbon and nitrogen if you build your pile in layers. Choose a well-drained spot and start with a 4- to 6-inch layer of organic materials that are high in carbon — plant residues from your garden, grass clippings, household garbage, leaves, etc. The more finely chopped these materials are, the more surface area there will be for decay organisms to attack, and the faster they'll decompose.

Follow this with a thin layer of materials high in nitrogen, such as a 1- to 2-inch layer of manure or a light, even coating of blood meal, cottonseed meal, or a chemical fertilizer high in nitrogen. Cover the second layer with a couple of inches of garden soil. This will insure that plenty of decay organisms are present and will cover any materials in the carbon layer that might attract flies, such as household garbage. Add a dusting of ground limestone or wood ashes. Repeat these layers until the pile is no more than 5 feet high; if the pile is higher than this, too little oxygen may reach the center of the pile, in which case anaerobic decay organisms will take over and produce bad odors. Five feet is a good maximum width for the pile as well.

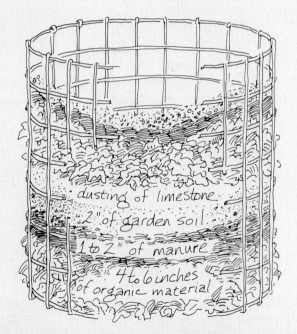

When you layer materials in a compost pile in this order, you will ensure the proportions of carbon and nitrogen that decay organisms need to work efficiently. You can repeat these layers to a total height of about 5 feet. The depression helps retain needed moisture.

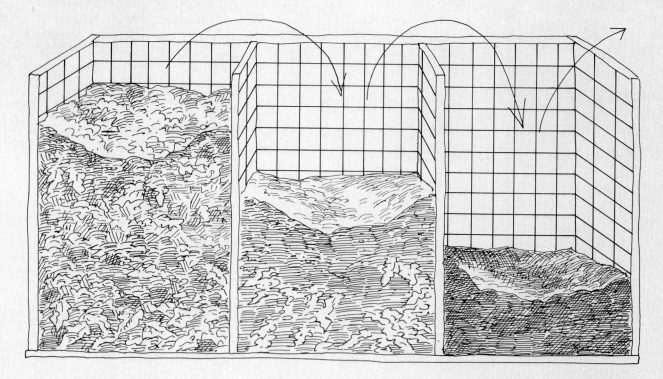

Your compost pile can be freestanding or enclosed. Wire fencing makes a good container because it lets in plenty of air. Proper moisture is important for decay organisms. Moisten each layer as you build the pile, but don't get it soggy. Make a depression in the top of the pile to catch rainwater when the pile is completed. If there is a long spell of dry weather, water the pile.

Once your pile is completed, it will begin to heat up in the center as the decay process begins. Turn the pile periodically, forking the material from the outside of the pile into the center. This will aerate the pile, prevent it from overheating, and will ensure that all the material decomposes uniformly.

How often you turn the pile and how quickly the compost is "done" depends on how quickly decay is taking place. If all the material you added is shredded, the pile may be ready for turning in a week. If there are lots of big pieces of organic material in the pile, wait several weeks or more before turning. Green, succulent organic matter like fresh grass clippings decays faster than dried plant material. On the other hand, cool fall temperatures or a spell of rainy days that turn the pile soggy will slow things down.

Compost is finished when the interior of the pile is no longer hot and all the material in the pile has broken down into a uniform, dark, crumbly substance.

A three-bin composting arrangement allows you to compost a steady supply of plant residues and organic household leftovers. Forking partially decomposed matter into successive bins both aerates each pile and makes way for fresh materials. The material collapses as it decomposes and is "done" when it has cooled and is a uniform, dark, crumbly substance.

Leaves are commonly composted before being added to garden soil. Uncomposted leaves should not be added directly to soil because they give off organic compounds as they begin to decay that can inhibit the germination of seeds and reduce yields temporarily.

There are a few things you shouldn't add to your compost pile, such as diseased or infested plant material. Although a well-made pile heats up enough to kill off many insects and disease organisms, this heating is usually not uniform enough to be relied on. For the same reason don't add weeds that have gone to seed as they may not be killed. Also, try not to get pieces of quack grass roots in the pile; even a small piece of root can produce a new plant. Avoid grass clippings from lawns treated with herbicides. Some herbicides may not break down during the composting process. Meat scraps and fats break down slowly and may attract unwanted animals to the pile. Never put dog or cat feces in your compost pile. They may carry diseases that can be transmitted to humans.

Preparing a New Garden

Your first step is to clear the area, removing existing plants, sod, brush, and large rocks. As this can be quite a task, it is usually best to start preparing the soil for a new garden at least one season in advance.

Start by removing any rocks on the surface, then clear rough ground by mowing the site as much as possible. You can rent a "brush-hog," or high-wheel mower, for tough situations. If there are woody plants growing on your proposed site, cut them down and grub out the roots with a mattock. Once the vegetation is down to a fairly manageable level, you can remove the sod. If you leave it in, the perennial grass roots will create weed problems later.

Clearing Sod

First, water the area to be cleared a couple of days before beginning to dig. The soil is easier to work if it is slightly moist.

Next, mark the edges of the plot. Use strings and stakes to define the border, then slice down through the sod with a straight spade.

Gardeners who have access to a rototiller can use it to loosen the sod. A tiller with the tines in the rear is the most effective for this job. After the sod is sufficiently broken up, remove the chunks by hand and set them aside.

If you are clearing the garden with hand tools, skim off the sod with a spade. This is not as difficult as it sounds; once you develop a rhythm, it goes fairly

quickly. Starting at the edge of the garden, slide the spade underneath the sod. Don't go deeply; you only want to remove the sod and about an inch of roots. Lever the spade up, tearing the sod along its uncut edge. Flip the loosened sod back onto itself, then continue to skim off another spade's worth. When the rolled up sod begins to get too heavy to push along, slice it off and set it aside.

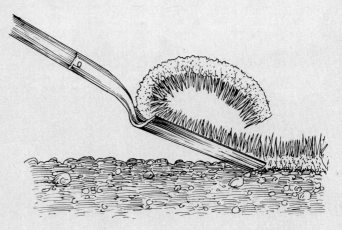

Skimming sod by hand with a sharp-edged spade is fairly easy for a smaller new garden site.

An easy way to clear the garden is to cover it completely with black plastic the summer *before* you plant. The vegetation under the plastic will die and can be tilled under in the fall or early spring.

Don't leave broken up sod on the soil surface or shallowly buried; some of it will reroot and you'll be battling perennial grasses in your garden. If you're working the garden by hand, pieces of sod can be buried upside down at least 12 inches deep. Sod can be added to your compost pile or stacked in piles to decompose.

Loosening the Soil

Once the sod is removed, loosen the soil. If the soil is dry, water well, then let it set for 2 days before digging. Don't work the soil when it is too wet. It should crumble easily in your hand with a flick of a finger.

If you use a rototiller, adjust the tines so that the initial pass over the garden is fairly shallow. As the soil is loosened, set the tines to dig deeper with successive passes until the top 8 to 12 inches of soil is loosened.

You can hire or borrow a heavy-duty rototiller to help break up sod at the site of a new garden. Remove the sod to lessen weed problems in the years ahead.

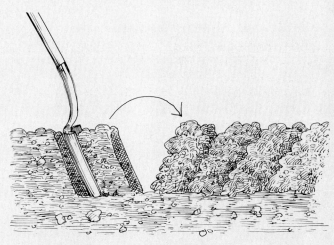

If you have good loam for soil or perhaps are starting a garden for the first time, hand digging the soil to the depth of a spade or fork is sufficient.

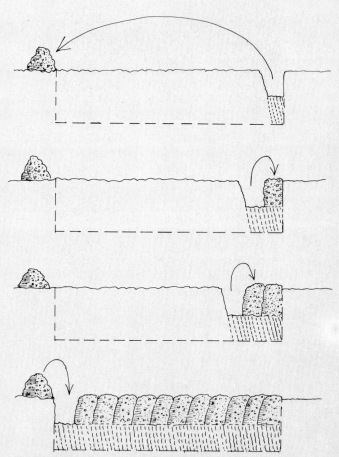

Double-digging is more work, but it loosens the soil to a greater depth, which lets plant roots penetrate deeper in search of water and nutrients, particularly helpful in clay. Dig the upper portion with a spade and loosen the subsoil with a digging fork. The resulting bed may be fluffed up higher than shown.

To loosen the soil by hand use a straight spade and a digging fork. The garden can either be dug to one spade's depth or double-dug, going down 20 to 24 inches. Double-digging is more work but it does loosen the soil to a greater depth, which lets plant roots penetrate deeper in search of water and nutrients. If you're double-digging, dig the upper portion with a straight spade and loosen the subsoil with a digging fork.

Finishing Touches

Once the soil is loosened, break up large clods of soil by sifting them through the tines of the digging fork. If you dig the area the fall before planting, it's a good time to mix in organic matter such as fresh manure or compost and lime, if necessary. (Don't add fresh manure sooner than 4 weeks before planting as it may burn the roots of young plants.) Slow-acting natural fertilizers are best added in the fall, if possible, to provide nutrients for the following growing season.

Preplanting Fertilizer

To get your garden ready just before planting it, add nitrogen to get plants off to a good start and correct phosphate or potash deficiencies that your soil test may have uncovered.

If your soil fertility is low, you may need to add more fertilizer initially than you would if soil had been built up and was high in organic matter. Although a soil test is always the most accurate way to decide on the amount of fertilizer to apply, a general rule for vegetable gardens is to apply 3 to 4 pounds of 5-10-10 fertilizer or its equivalent per 100 square feet during initial soil preparation.

Raised Beds

Raised bed gardening has been somewhat of a gardening fad in America for the past decade or so. There are definite advantages to raised bed gardening, but the method is not for all gardeners.

The advantage to an elevated planting area is that it has much greater topsoil depth and concentration of nutrients than the soil around it. If your garden spot is soggy, the raised level of the bed will improve soil drainage. It will usually keep newly planted seeds from washing away in heavy downpours that ordinarily wash soil away or create puddles in the garden.

Soil compaction around plants will be reduced with raised beds. Because you will walk in the pathways and not in the beds themselves, the soil will stay looser, allowing air and water to reach plant roots more easily. This benefit is greatest if the beds are permanent — located in the same spot each year.

In a traditional garden, all the soil is fertilized and improved with organic matter, even though some of it will be pathways each season. With raised beds, you can lavish your attention only on those areas that will be producing plants. High fertility allows you to plant intensively, spacing crops close together for greater yield from a smaller area.

One drawback to raised beds is that they may take some time and effort to build, especially if you decide to make permanent beds. You may find it difficult to cultivate them with power tools. Finally, the roots of elevated plants will dry out faster than level plants and will require more watering.

If you are unsure of how well raised beds will perform in your garden, don't make permanent beds the first season. Stake out only a few bed areas to try the technique.

You can use a rototiller to loosen the soil in the area before shaping a raised bed, but spading with good hand tools should allow you to loosen the soil more deeply than with a tiller. In fact, to give your test raised beds the best chance, prepare the area with the double-digging method to a depth of about 24 inches, if possible.

The resulting bed of loose soil will be about 4 to 6 inches above ground level. Adding organic matter such as peat moss or well-decomposed manure or compost should also help.

After a season or two of raised bed success, you may want to define and retain the beds with a wooden enclosure of some kind. Old planks, beams, landscaping timbers, or railroad ties can be used. Either cut your materials to fit your existing beds or reshape the bed dimensions to fit your framing materials. You may want to treat the wood with copper naphthenate, a preservative available from hardware stores. (Do not use creosote- or pentachlorophenol-treated timbers, as they can be harmful to plants.)

It's a good idea to sink your retaining materials a few inches into the soil for added support. Try to have the top of the enclosure an inch or two higher than the soil level to keep soil from washing away.

With permanent beds you can mulch or sow grass in the walkways for a good, clean look and to make working around the beds easier in wet weather. If you use grass, mow regularly and keep the borders edged to prevent the grass from invading the garden.

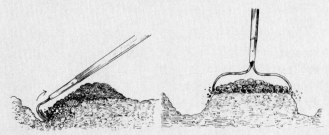

You can make raised beds (*above*) simply by drawing soil from walkway areas onto the top of already loosened soil. Raised beds can work well without any retaining wall (*right top*), but you can keep walkways mown or mulched and keep bed edges better weeded with walls of wood (*middle*), stone (*bottom*), or other materials readily available in your area.

Planting

After waiting through winter and then patiently preparing the garden soil for the upcoming season of growth, it's a landmark day when planting time finally arrives.

Even if you're getting a jump on the season by starting some of your own transplants indoors before outdoor planting is possible, the feel of vegetable seeds in your hands marks a turning point in the year.

Planting seeds can be a very quick process, but it pays to work deliberately and do it right, whether indoors or out. The following section will guide you through the planting process with information on correct seed spacing, planting depth, soil and germinating conditions, and fertilizing so you can produce smooth-growing, vigorous plants.

Starting Seeds Indoors

You might wonder why you should bother to start your own seeds indoors when nursery-grown transplants are so readily available later in the season. For one thing, you'll have a much wider choice of varieties. Your local garden store or nursery may carry only three or four varieties of started tomato plants, for example, whereas seed catalogs offer you hundreds of varieties.

As long as you provide the proper growing conditions, you can produce strong, healthy plants that are ready for the garden when you need them. You won't have to settle for leggy, root-bound plants that can't take the rigors of transplanting well. You won't risk inadvertently introducing club root fungi into the garden by planting infected seedlings, or an infestation of whiteflies that are hiding on nursery transplants.

If you garden on a large scale, growing your own transplants from seed can mean considerable savings. And there's nothing quite like the excitement of seeing those first seedlings pushing through the soil. You may have two feet of snow outside, but you can enjoy a little spring by sowing seeds indoors.

The best candidates for an early start are plants that tolerate root disturbance and that benefit from a jump on the season. There's no need for most gardeners to start root crops such as beets, carrots, and parsnips indoors because they are cold-hardy enough to go into the garden early in the season. Melons, squashes, and cucumbers don't take kindly to transplanting, but do need a long time to mature, so they are best started in individual containers, as is cauliflower, which may fail to form a head if its roots are disturbed. Crops such as corn, beans, and peas are very finicky about transplanting and are usually sown directly in the garden.

Easy transplanters, which can be grown in flats, are broccoli, Brussels sprouts, cabbage, celery, eggplant, leeks, lettuce, onions, parsley, peppers, and tomatoes. Vegetables that need to be transplanted with care, and are best started in individual containers, are cauliflower, cucumbers, muskmelon, squash, and watermelon. Eggplants, peppers, and tomatoes are sometimes started in shallow flats and transplanted to deeper individual containers before transplanting to the garden.

Containers

Just about anything that holds several inches of soil and in which drainage holes can be punched is suitable for growing seedlings. There are lots of low-cost possibilities — milk cartons, paper or Styrofoam cups,

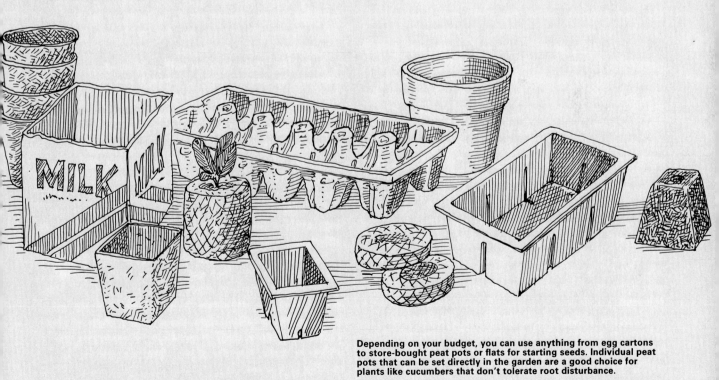

Depending on your budget, you can use anything from egg cartons to store-bought peat pots or flats for starting seeds. Individual peat pots that can be set directly in the garden are a good choice for plants like cucumbers that don't tolerate root disturbance.

cottage cheese containers, homemade wooden flats. Garden stores sell a wide variety of plastic, fiber, pressed peat, and Styrofoam flats and containers for just about every budget. Flats — shallow, wide, seed-starting trays — let you start many seedlings in a small space, which is helpful when it comes to watering and moving plants around. Individual peat pots that can be set directly in the garden are a good choice for plants like cucumbers that don't tolerate root disturbance. For the gardener who puts a premium on convenience, premade growing cubes are a good idea.

You will want to surface-sterilize plastic, wooden, clay, and Styrofoam containers before each use to kill damping-off fungi that attack young seedlings. Dip containers in a solution of 9 parts water to 1 part household bleach, then rinse in clear water.

Growing Media

The most practical seed-starting medium for many gardeners is a commercially prepared "soilless" or "peat-lite" mix, available at most garden stores. As the name implies, there is no true soil in the mix; it is usually a combination of peat moss, vermiculite and/or perlite, ground limestone to bring the pH into the proper range, and fertilizer for good plant growth. It is light-weight, holds moisture well while having good aera-tion and drainage, and is free of the disease organisms, insects, and weed seeds that may be present in soil.

You can make up your own soilless mix and perhaps save some money. For simply germinating seeds before moving them on to more spacious quarters indoors, you need only provide a medium that will support the tiny plants and supply their roots with water and air. The nutrients stored in the seed nourish the seedling at this stage of growth. A good seed germination mix is 2 parts peat moss, 1 part vermiculite, 1 part perlite, and 1 tablespoon ground limestone per gallon of mix.

To grow transplants to garden-planting size indoors, you will need a mix with more nutrients. To the above mix, add 2 tablespoons 20 percent superphosphate and 1 teaspoon 5-10-5 fertilizer per gallon of mix. Trace elements, which can be purchased at many garden cen-ters, should be added; read the package label for spe-cific amounts. This mix can also be used for germinat-ing seeds.

There are several disadvantages to starting seeds indoors in garden soil. First, it must be pasteurized to kill off disease-causing organisms, insects, and weed seeds. You can pasteurize it yourself by bringing all soil ingredients to 160°F in the oven for 30 minutes, but baking soil gives off a pretty strong odor that may not endear you to other household members, or you can buy packaged, pasteurized potting soil. Second, soil that is well drained in your garden will not be as well drained when put in a pot. You will need to mix in materials such as peat and perlite to improve aera-tion and drainage. Finally, soil is heavy, an important consideration when you are moving containers in and out of the house during the hardening-off process. However, soil is a good source of nutrients; deficien-cies are less likely when some soil is in the growing mix. One recipe for a growing mix containing soil is: 1 part *pasteurized* garden loam or commercial potting soil, 1 part peat moss, 1 part vermiculite or perlite, 1 teaspoon ground limestone per quart, and 1 teaspoon 20 percent superphosphate or bone meal per quart.

Sowing Seeds

After choosing the proper container and growing medium, follow these steps to sow your seeds:

1. Fill containers to within ½ inch of the top with moistened growing medium. Soilless mixes are dusty and hard to wet initially. Put the mix in a plastic bag, pour in water, and mix with your hand or a strong wooden spoon, closing off the opening of the bag as much as possible to keep the dust in. Gently firm down the medium with a flat board.

2. In flats, make furrows with a blunt stick or by pressing the narrow edge of a board into the medium. Seeds can be broadcast over the surface, but row plant-ing makes thinning and transplanting easier. As a gen-eral guideline, sow seeds that will be transplanted soon after they come up at about five to eight seeds per inch. Sow those crops that will be thinned and left in the same container more sparingly, three to four seeds per inch.

To plant seeds in individual containers, put two to four seeds in each. Later, thin the seedlings, leaving the strongest ones.

Sow seeds at the correct depth, cover with fine soil or vermiculite, then water gently with a mister (a stronger stream can wash seeds too deeply into the soil). Label the containers (broccoli and cabbage seed-lings look a lot alike), then cover with a sheet of clear plastic or glass to hold in moisture. If necessary, use stakes to make sure the plastic does not rest on the surface of the soil.

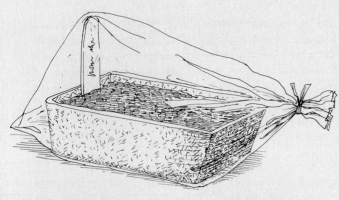

A plastic bag around your container of just-planted seeds holds in essential moisture until the seedlings emerge from the soil.

3. Place planted containers in a warm spot; the cooler it is, the longer it will take for plants to emerge. Never put containers in direct sun, however; the plastic holds in the heat and you'll cook your seeds to death. Some warm spots include the top of the refrigerator and the television, but be careful with water around electrical appliances. You can also buy heat mats or cables at garden stores. Check containers periodically to make sure soil is still moist. If you see signs of mold, loosen the covering to let air in.

Until seedlings emerge from the soil, light is unnecessary, with the exception of lettuce and celery seeds. Sow these seeds by pressing them into the soil or covering them very lightly with ⅛ inch of fine soil, then keep containers in a bright spot or put a 40-watt incandescent light over them.

4. Check the containers daily. As soon as you see the first green shoots emerging, remove the covering. Your seedlings now need a spot with plenty of light and proper growing temperatures.

Light and Temperature

The light your plants receive is one of the most important factors in good growth. A south-facing window is one option, but not the best one. Even on a sunny windowsill, plants receive only a fraction of the light they would get outside. Windowsill plants often become tall and spindly because they get too warm in relation to the light they receive. It's best to keep your seedlings on the cool side (60 to 65°F, 75° maximum) to encourage slower growth; this will give you sturdy, stocky plants that transplant well. While a 10 to 15° drop in temperature at night is beneficial, a windowsill can get pretty chilly at night when it's still wintry outside. Several layers of newspapers placed between the glass and the plants will keep windowsill plants warmer on frosty nights if you must grow your plants there.

Growing seedlings under fluorescent lights is a better way to keep light-hungry plants happy. If possible, set up your lights near a window so that plants receive both natural and artificial light.

Ordinary cool-white, 40-watt fluorescent bulbs are fine for starting seedlings. The more expensive grow lights produce the broader light spectrum that plants need for flowering and fruiting, but your seedlings will be out in the garden before they are ready to flower. Use one pair of bulbs for every 1-foot width of growing area. Lights should be kept on for no more than 16 hours a day so plants can rest. Inexpensive timers are available to turn the lights on and off automatically.

Check the temperature at plant level under the lights with a thermometer. If it is too warm for good seedling growth, a small fan may help keep plants cooler. Optimum temperatures and growing requirements for seedlings are listed in the table on page 46.

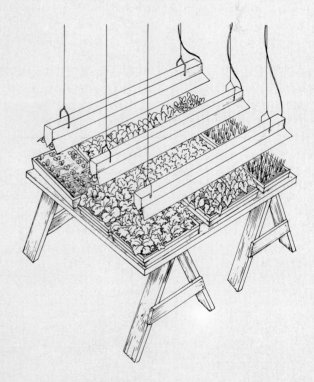

Here's a good small system for growing seedlings under lights. Put plant trays on a sheet of plywood supported by sawhorses. Light fixtures should be adjustable so that the bulbs are 2 to 4 inches from the tops of the seedlings at all times. If you can't adjust the level of your lights, use pieces of wood to raise trays closer to the lights when seedlings are small, lowering the trays as plants grow. Because light is strongest near the center of the bulbs, you should rotate the trays periodically.

Watering

Water fragile young seedlings carefully. Mist them with a gentle spray, or water from the bottom by setting the container in a pan of water just long enough for the soil surface to feel wet (sitting in water longer than this can damage plants' roots). Then remove the container from the pan and let it drain. Keep the soil surface moist but not soggy. Always use lukewarm water.

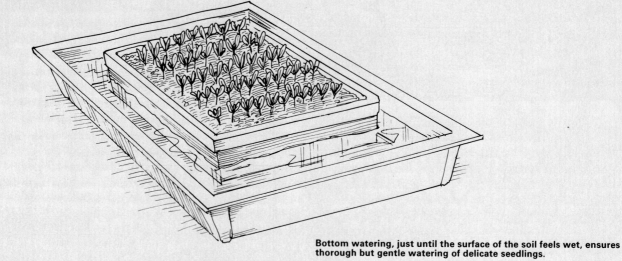

Bottom watering, just until the surface of the soil feels wet, ensures thorough but gentle watering of delicate seedlings.

Germination and Growing Requirements for Seedlings

	Number of weeks from seeding to transplant	Optimum soil temp. for germination	Optimum growing temp.*		Average germination time** (days)	Sowing depth	Pot size or distance between thinned plants
			Day	**Night**			
Broccoli	5–7	75°	60–70°	50–60°	5	¼–½"	2–3"
Brussels sprouts	5–7	75°	60–70°	50–60°	5	¼–½"	2–3"
Cabbage	5–7	75°	60–70°	50–60°	4–5	½"	2–3"
Cauliflower	5–7	75°	60–70°	50–60°	5–6	¼–½"	3" pot
Celery	10–12	70°	65–75°	60–65°	14–21	⅛"	2–2½" pot
Cucumbers	3–4	85°	70–75°	65–70°	3–5	¾–1"	3" pot
Eggplant	6–8	80°	70–75°	65–70°	6–8	¼–½"	2–3"
Leeks	8–10	75°	60–65°	55–60°	4–6	¼–½"	½–1"
Lettuce	3–6	75°	55–65°	50–55°	2–3	⅛–¼"	1½–2"
Muskmelon	3–4	85°	70–75°	60–65°	3–4	¾–1"	3" pot
Onions	6–8	75°	60–65°	55–60°	4–5	¼–½"	½–1"
Parsley	6–8	75°	NA	NA	14–21	⅛–¼"	1–1½"
Peppers	6–8	85°	65–75°	60–65°	8–10	¼–½"	2–3"
Squash, summer & winter	3–4	85°	70–75°	60–65°	4–6	½"	3" pot
Tomatoes	6–10	85°	65–75°	60–65°	6–8	¼–½"	2–3"
Watermelon	3–4	95°	70–75°	65–70°	4–6	½–1"	3" pot

*Choose the lower range of temperatures if your lighting conditions are less than optimum.
**At optimum germination temperature. If soil temperature cooler than optimum, germination may take longer.

As plants get sturdier, you can water with a sprinkling can with a rose, a nozzle that breaks the water into many fine streams. Once plants get their first set of true leaves and have bigger root systems, you should let the soil surface dry out slightly between thorough waterings. Apply enough water at one time so that some runs out the drainage holes in the bottom of the container, but never leave the container sitting in water. Overwatering promotes damping off disease (see box) and decreases the amount of air in the soil, resulting in a weaker root system. With soilless mixes it is sometimes difficult to tell when to water, because they may look dry on the surface when they still have plenty of water. Take a pinch of the top half-inch of mix and squeeze it between your fingers. If you can squeeze out any water, hold off watering. The difference in weight of the container when the soil mix is moist or dry can also indicate when to water. Water plants in the morning, if possible, so foliage dries quickly to avoid disease problems.

Certain containers require more frequent watering than others. Soil in clay pots dries out faster than that in plastic pots. Peat pots also dry out fast. Try putting your peat pots or growing cubes together in a tray and packing moist peat moss between them to keep them from drying out too rapidly.

Damping Off

One day you are admiring your strong, healthy seedlings; the next you're gaping in dismay at the sight of them toppled over and dying. The attacker was damping off, a fungus disease that infects young seedlings, sometimes even before they have a chance to emerge from the soil. If you examine infected seedlings closely, you'll usually see that the part of the stem near the soil line is sunken and water-soaked.

Damping off is one of the most common problems that seed starters face, but fortunately it can be controlled through good sanitation and cultural practices. Sterilizing containers (see page 44) and using pasteurized soil go a long way toward preventing problems. Wet growing media and high nitrogen encourage this fungus, so avoid overwatering and use a well-drained germinating mix that is low in nitrogen, or don't use fertilizer until seedlings have developed their first true leaves. Sowing seed thinly so there is good air circulation can also help.

If you notice seedlings in one portion of the container beginning to damp off, remove them as quickly as possible and do what you can to make the growing conditions less favorable for the fungus. With luck, you'll be able to save the rest of the batch.

A rose at the nozzle of a watering can breaks up the gush of water into a gentle rain, fine for watering larger and sturdier seedlings.

Cold Frames and Row Covers

Cold Frames

A cold frame is essentially a mini greenhouse, a box with a cover of glass, plastic, or fiberglass that lets sunshine in. Inside the box, light waves are converted to heat waves. This trapped heat allows your plants to thrive even when the weather outside the box is quite cold. With a cold frame you can start seedlings of hardy plants when it's still too cold for them in the open garden. You can also use the frame to harden off seedlings grown indoors. Seeds of certain crops such as lettuce and spinach can be sown directly in the soil inside the frame in spring for early harvests and late in the season for harvests long after frosts have come.

A cold frame can be as simple or as fancy as your budget and inclination allow. Scrap lumber is fine for the sides of the frame and old sash windows can be used as a cover. If you treat wood with a preservative, be sure it's one that is safe for use around plants, such as copper naphthenate.

The size of the cold frame depends on your needs, but it should be at least 3 × 6 feet to retain a sufficient amount of heat. The best spot for your frame is on well-drained soil, in full sun, facing south. The top should slant, preferably toward the south, to allow more light to enter when the sun is still low in the sky and to shed rain. Slope the top about 1 inch for every foot of width. For example, if the back wall of the frame is 18 inches high (a good height for most frames), the front wall of a 4-foot-wide frame would be 14 inches high.

You should construct your frame so that it is tight enough to keep out wind and cold. Weatherstripping around the cover is a good idea, as is insulating the walls of the frame. There are a number of ways to do this: cover the sides with rigid foam insulation, pile hay bales around the outside of the frame, mound soil up around the sides, or excavate a spot for the frame and bury it halfway in the ground.

Depending on the weather, you may also need to insulate the top of the frame at night. Rigid foam insulation, tarps and blankets (although these get wet), loose hay, or leaves held down with a piece of snow fencing can help hold in heat on frosty nights.

Even in cold weather, too much heat can accumulate in the frame, so it needs to be ventilated. This is the one big drawback of a cold frame. You must be able to check the frame frequently and adjust the opening to make sure plants are neither too hot nor too cold. One bad decision can ruin a lot of plants! It may be too cold to open the frame when you leave for work in the morning, but if the sun breaks through the clouds at noon, you may arrive home to cooked seedlings.

For gardeners who can't check on their cold frames regularly, an automatic cold frame opener can be a plant saver. Solar-powered openers that close at 65°F and open at 75°F are available.

A thermometer that records minimum and maximum temperatures is a big help in monitoring conditions within your cold frame. With a min-max thermometer you will be able to decide when to plant certain crops in the frame (see the table on page 46 for optimum day and night growing temperatures for various crops).

Row Covers

Row covers are good for protecting large numbers of plants in the garden. While they don't offer as much protection as a cold frame, they gather heat during the day and provide some protection from cold at night. They can be a big help in getting warmth-loving plants such as eggplant and peppers off to a good start early in the season.

A row cover might be a frame made of sturdy wire covered by clear plastic with slits cut in it for automatic ventilation. Or you may have to roll it up during the day to prevent plants from overheating.

Reemay is a type of commercial row cover that needs no frame. Made of a lightweight fabric that traps heat while letting light and moisture in, it is laid over the row or bed and held down at the edges with soil. Emerging seedlings push up the material as they grow. Reemay also helps keep some insects away from young plants.

Individual Plant Covers

These range from such simple devices as plastic milk jugs with the bottoms cut out to hinged plastic or glass covers, or cloches. Most individual plant covers are best for providing frost protection on a cold night. If they don't let light in or can't be ventilated, be sure to remove them in the morning so plants don't overheat.

Wall O'Water is a unique plant protector consisting of a ring of clear plastic tubes which are filled with water. The water absorbs heat from the sun during the day and releases it slowly at night to keep plants warm. Because the top is open, you don't need to worry about plants getting too hot during the day.

Thinning and Transplanting Indoors

When seedlings have three leaves, or when onions and leeks, which send up a single blade, are 2 inches tall, it's time to thin them or move them from shallow flats to larger quarters. This is an important step in which timing is crucial. If you let seedlings get too large while they're in small containers, they'll be set back in their development; if you don't space them out at all, you'll end up with weak plants.

To thin plants that will continue growing in the same container, snip out the extra seedlings at the soil line with a pair of scissors. If you try to pull these extras out, you may disrupt the roots of the plants that are staying. Snip out any weak or misshapen plants. Refer to the table on page 46 for correct spacing between seedlings.

Prick out seedlings when you transplant by holding the leaves and using a small utensil to loosen the roots. This way you will avoid injury to the fragile roots and stem.

To move seedlings, first fill the new container with moist growing medium. Poke holes in the medium large enough for the seedlings' roots (the eraser end of a pencil is a good tool for this). Prick out the plants carefully, using the blade of a table knife or a small, flat stick such as a plant label to lever the seedling out of the soil. Always hold the seedlings by the tips of their leaves; otherwise it's easy to crush delicate stems or injure the growing point. Set plants slightly deeper than they were growing before. Firm the soil gently around the roots, water well, and keep them out of direct sun for a day to recover.

Fertilizing

Regular fertilization helps produce strong, healthy plants. After seedlings have been transplanted or thinned, dilute a water-soluble fertilizer to one-third strength and add it to your watering can. Water with the solution once a week.

Transplanting

Buying starter plants. If you don't grow your own transplants at home, you'll probably buy them at a nursery, farmstand, or garden center. Seedlings of eggplants, peppers, tomatoes, broccoli, cabbage, and cauliflower are normally offered at planting time. At some nurseries you may also find lettuce, onions and leeks, collards, celery, and a few other crops.

Whatever ones you buy, choose healthy-looking plants. Tomatoes, for example, should have a stocky

The true leaf seedling stage when seedlings have three leaves is the critical point for you either to thin or to transplant to a larger container. If you fail to do one of these, the seedlings will be set back.

stem, be about 6 inches tall, and sport dark green foliage. Avoid crowded, large plants in small containers because the roots are often bound up and have no further room to grow. The older plants are, the more likely they are to have suffered some kind of stress.

Hardening Off

Seedlings grown indoors at home or those purchased from a greenhouse need to get acclimated gradually to the brighter light and cooler temperatures of the outside world. This process, called hardening off, checks plants' growth, causing them to store more food and to increase the thickness of the outer leaf layer.

A week or two before you plan to set plants in the garden, stop fertilizing and allow more time between waterings. Take plants outside for a half-hour of filtered sunlight in the warmest part of the day. If it's windy, erect a windbreak. Gradually increase the amount of time the plants spend outside and the intensity of the light they're exposed to, bringing them in at night. Or move the plants to a cold frame (see page 48), opening it more each day and closing it at night. Plants that have been raised in a cold frame all along will need much less hardening off.

Blocking is a hardening-off technique that you can use for seedlings grown in a common container. Two or three days before transplanting, cut down through the soil between the plants. This gives the seedlings a chance to recover from the disruption of their root systems before they are set out in the garden.

Don't harden everything. With the exception of tomatoes, it is best not to harden off those plants that are very susceptible to frost such as cucumbers, squashes, melons, and eggplant. Wait to set these plants out when the soil and weather are warm, and shade them for a few days after you've set them out.

Don't overharden your plants. Certain crops such as cabbage and broccoli can bolt quickly in the garden if seedlings over 3 weeks old are repeatedly exposed to temperatures lower than 40°F for a couple of weeks.

Setting Plants Out

Transplants can be set in the garden in rows or beds as described in the following chapter. Choose a calm, cloudy day, if possible. Late afternoon is a good time for transplanting so plants have a chance to recover from the shock of transplanting out of the midday heat and sun. Garden soil should be moist, not soggy. Water the planting area the day before planting if the weather has been dry. Moisten the soil in the pots or flats so it holds together around the plants' roots when they're removed from their containers.

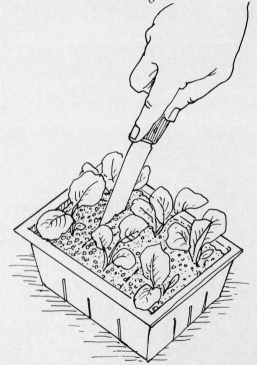

Blocking, or cutting down through the soil between plants, is a hardening-off technique for seedlings started in a flat. Give the seedlings two or three days to recover before setting them out in the garden.

It's sometimes hard to get a plant out of its pot. Turn the plant upside down, cupping the pot with your hand. Rap the edge of the pot sharply against the edge of a table, tap on the bottom of the pot, and the root ball should slide out intact. If not, rap again. Don't yank on the stem in an effort to get the plant out of the pot or you may damage its roots.

When setting out plants in biodegradable peat pots, make a few slits down the sides of the pot first to help roots push through. Also tear off the lip of the pot so it does not stick up above the soil surface where it will act like a wick to pull moisture out of the soil. With premade growing blocks encased in netting, cut off the netting before planting.

When you set out seedlings or transplants started in peat pots, be sure to tear off the top edge flush with the soil so the pot won't wick moisture away from the seedling roots. Then set out the plant without disturbing the roots.

Loosen the soil and dig planting holes so that plants are set at the same depth that they were growing in their flats or containers. (Leeks and tomatoes are exceptions; they are often set in deeper.) Don't add any fertilizer directly under plant roots when you're putting a transplant into the ground. The roots will burn and die off if they come in contact with a high-nitrogen material.

Firm the soil gently around the roots, leaving a small depression around the stem to hold water, then water immediately. You can water with a dilute starter solution (a soluble fertilizer high in phosphorus) to help plants recover from transplant shock more quickly.

Set up a windbreak if necessary so plants don't dry out too fast. Use heavy cardboard, old wooden shingles, planks or other objects set firmly next to each transplant. Keep them in place for a week or so.

If you didn't get an ideal transplanting day and it's hot and sunny, shade plants until the sun goes down. Don't be too alarmed if your plants look a little droopy after you set them out. If the root system is strong, they'll soon recover. Cabbage seedlings can lie down and look almost dead, for example, and be up and growing in a day or two.

Planting Seeds Outdoors

While you may need to give your eggplants and tomatoes a jump on the season by starting them early indoors, there are many vegetable seeds that can be sown directly in the garden. If you are direct-seeding, wait until your soil has dried out sufficiently before you work it and be sure that it is warm enough for the seeds you plan to plant. Pea seeds, for example, will germinate in soil as cool as 40°F and may be planted as soon as the soil can be worked in the spring. Squash seeds, on the other hand, need warmth. If the soil temperature is much below 65°F, the seeds are likely to rot in the ground before they sprout. The table on page 46 lists the appropriate soil germination temperatures for different kinds of seeds. The surest way to determine the temperature of your soil is to use a soil thermometer, available at many garden stores.

The chart on pages 54–55 gives the general range of planting dates for different sections of the country. These dates are general guidelines; if your soil is heavy and wet or your garden slopes to the north it will take longer to warm in the spring than a lighter, well-drained soil or a garden on a south-facing slope.

Planting Methods

Seeds can be planted in a variety of patterns: using single rows, wide rows, beds, raised beds, or hills. The method you choose depends on your climate, your tools and resources, and your taste. Whichever way you choose, there are a few basic principles to follow for planting seeds.

Immediately before sowing seeds, loosen the soil where you will plant with a hoe or shovel to a depth of 6 inches. Rake over the area to create a smooth planting surface. Do not walk over the area where you will be sowing seeds, stay in the pathways; compacting the soil will make it difficult for any seedlings to emerge or send down their small roots.

Sowing seeds at the proper depth is important. A seed planted too deeply will use up its supply of stored nutrients before the seedling can push its way to the surface, while one planted too shallowly may dry out. A general rule is to plant seeds at a depth two to three times their diameter. The chart on pages 26–27 gives the recommended planting depth for different kinds of seeds. Try to sow at a uniform depth, too. Seedlings

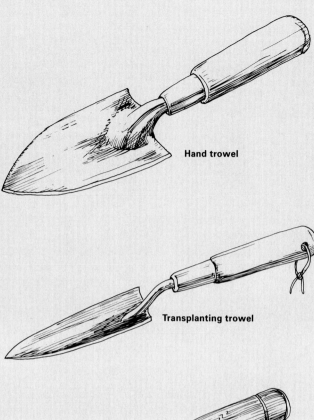

Hand trowel

Transplanting trowel

Hand fork

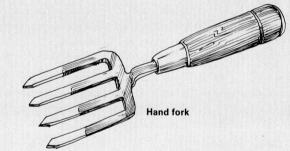

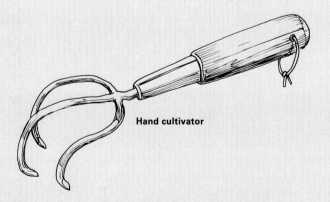

Hand cultivator

A basic hand trowel is an indispensable tool for the gardener, but there are many other specialized hand tools for specific jobs such as transplanting, mixing composts into a planting hole, or hand cultivation and weeding. Wood handles are pleasing to hold, but many brands have metal or plastic handles molded for an easier grip.

are more likely to emerge at the same time if you do, and you'll be able to see where all your plants are when you do your first weeding.

Water newly planted seeds carefully. Use a watering can with a rose or a hose with a breaker attachment. A strong stream of water can wash the seeds out of the bed or too deeply into the ground. Keep the seedbed moist but not soggy until seeds germinate. Heavy soils often form a crust as they dry out, making it difficult for seedlings to break through. A moist surface will help prevent crusting, as will covering seeds with vermiculite or a mixture of vermiculite and soil, instead of soil alone. If the weather is dry after sowing seeds, you should gently water the seeded area every 2 days or so.

Row Planting

The first step in row planting is to mark the placement of the row within the garden. A planting line, or simply string and stakes, makes it easy to lay out rows. Make a furrow, or trench, of the correct depth along the row. To make a shallow furrow, lay a rake or hoe on the ground underneath your string marker, and press the handle into the soil. You can make deeper furrows by dragging the corner of your hoe across the soil surface, using the string as a guideline.

Sow seeds more thickly than you want the final spacing of the crops to be to insure an adequate number of plants in case some seeds fail to sprout. Thinning a row will be less of a chore if you space seeds as evenly as possible. Large seeds of peas and beans are easy to space at precise intervals, but even spacing of small seeds like carrots can be a real challenge. One trick is to mix these tiny seeds with some fine sand, then sprinkle this mixture in the furrow.

Cover seeds with fine soil, then firm them with the back of a hoe to make sure all the seeds are in contact with the soil. Water gently.

Wide Row Planting

First choose the width of your row, usually from 10 to 16 inches. You may want to run strings along the outside edges of the row to clearly designate the planting area. Smooth the soil until it's level. Sprinkle seeds over the entire bed — with most crops, try to land seeds ½ to 1 inch apart (for peas and beans, 1½ to 2 inches). Pat them down with the back of a hoe.

Use your rake to lift soil from outside the planting area up onto the seeds. Pull soil up in large clumps and then smooth it over the seeds to the same depth every-where — about ½ inch for small seeds, 1 inch for peas and beans. Pat the soil down again to bring the added soil into firm contact with the seeds. Water.

Bed Planting

Planting in beds is about the same as planting a wide row. (To prepare your beds, refer to pages 40–41.) If you do not have permanent beds, mark off the dimensions and smooth out the soil. You can broadcast seeds, sow in single rows with a few inches of space separating the rows, or plant them individually the proper distance apart.

Hill Planting

Planting seeds in hills or groups is often recommended for vining crops like cucumbers and squash that spread out. Loosen the soil well in a 3-foot-diameter area, add fertilizer if required, and level the area. Then plant five or six seeds close together. Keep the two strongest seedlings and thin out the remainder.

If your soil is heavy, planting in a raised hill (sometimes called a mound) is a good idea. The raised soil warms up more quickly than the surrounding soil and drains better. Be careful in midsummer not to let the mound dry out.

Thinning Outdoors

Soon after seedlings put out their second set of leaves, it's time to space them out. Don't neglect this important step; crowded seedlings turn into weak, spindly plants that don't produce well. Separate plants by hand or with a narrow hoe according to the distances in the chart on pages 26–27 or refer to the individual vegetable chapters.

When you thin plants, either discard the extra seedlings or move them to another part of the garden. The newly transplanted seedlings will need extra attention until they get established. Shade them from the hot sun for a day or two and be sure to keep them well watered. Root crops such as beets and carrots transplant poorly, as do beans and peas. Lettuce is one of the easiest vegetables to move when small.

Thinning can be done in stages with some crops, with delicious results. If you've never tasted beet greens cooked up with tender, marble-size beets still attached, you've missed a real treat. Start by thinning seedlings to an inch or two apart. As the plants get to be 6 to 8 inches tall, pull up every other one and enjoy the small beets. Leave a final 4 - to 6-inch spacing for larger beets to develop. Carrots and lettuce are other good candidates for gradual thinning.

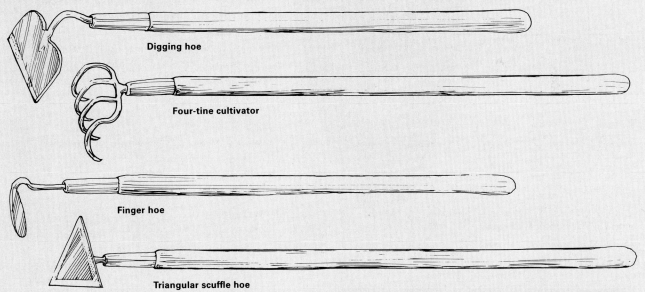

Digging hoe

Four-tine cultivator

Finger hoe

Triangular scuffle hoe

In addition to a spade, fork, and shovel, at least one hoe belongs in every gardener's tool shed. The familiar digging hoe is useful for every phase of gardening, but there are numerous specially designed hoes for bed building and weeding. Long handles on these tools help prevent backache or even injury and make garden work more pleasurable. The cultivator weeds and loosens soil; the finger hoe is for fine weeding; and the scuffle hoe has sharp edges for skimming just below the soil surface to cut weeds from their roots.

Average Dates of the Last Spring Frost

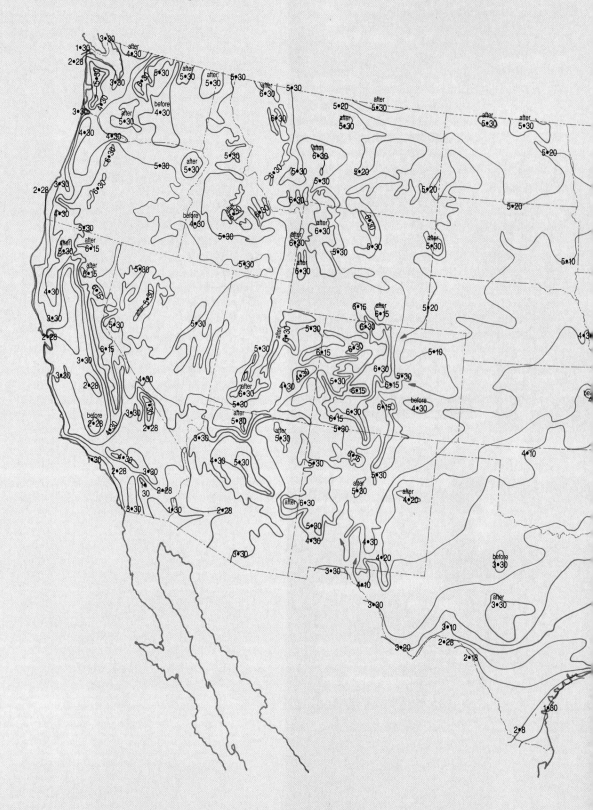

The average last spring frost date is a key date in a garden plan, as many vegetable plants can be safely set out in the garden only after the danger of frost has passed.

This map presents a *general* outline of the last spring frost date ranges across the country. If you don't know the date for your area, locate your region on the map. Please understand that the actual average may be different by a week or so in your area, depending on such factors as the altitude of your property, slope of land, type of soil, vegetative cover, nearness to bodies of water, air drainage, and urban heat effects.

Spring freezes are assumed to occur between January 1 and June 30. "Before" or "after" is entered on most small areas of this map to show more readily whether the mean frost date in the area is before or after the date noted on the line.

Range of Safe Planting Dates According to Average Last Spring Frost Date

Crop	February 8	February 28	March 20	April 10	April 30	May 20	June 10
*Asparagus			2·1–3·10	3·10–4·10	3·20–4·15	4·20–5·15	5·5–6·1
Beans, lima	2·10–5·1	3·15–6·1	4·1–6·15	4·1–6·30	4·1–6·30	5·15–6·15	
Beans, snap and dried	2·1–5·1	3·10–5·15	3·15–5·25	4·10–6·3	5·10–6·30	5·15–6·30	
Beans, Southern pea	2·15–5·15	3·10–6·20	4·1–7·1	5·1–7·1	5·15–6·1		
Beans, soybean	3·1–6·30	3·20–6·30	4·10–6·30	5·1–6·30	5·15–6·15		
Beet	1·10–3·15	2·1–4·15	2·15–5·15	3·10–6·1	4·1–6·15	4·25–6·15	5·15–6·15
*Broccoli	1·1–1·30	2·1–3·1	2·15–3·15	3·15–4·15	4·1–5·1	5·1–6·15	5·20–6·10
*Brussels sprouts	1·1–1·30	2·1–3·1	2·15–3·15	3·15–4·15	4·1–5·1	5·1–6·15	5·20–6·10
*Cabbage	1·1–2·10	1·15–2·25	2·1–3·1	3·1–4·1	3·15–4·10	5·1–6·15	5·20–6·1
Cabbage, Chinese						5·1–6·15	5·20–6·1
Carrots	1·1–3·1	2·1–3·1	2·15–3·20	3·10–4·20	4·10–6·1	5·1–6·1	5·20–6·1
*Cauliflower	1·1–2·1	1·20–2·20	2·10–3·10	3·1–3·20	4·10–5·10	5·10–6·15	6·1–6·15
*Celery and celeriac	1·10–2·10	2·1–3·1	3·1–4·1	4·1–4·20	4·15–5·1	5·10–6·15	6·1–6·15
Chard	1·10–4·1	2·1–5·1	2·20–5·15	3·15–6·1	4·15–6·15	5·10–6·15	6·1–6·15
*Collards	1·1–2·15	1·15–3·15	2·15–5·1	3·1–6·1	4·1–6·1	5·1–6·1	5·20–6·1
Corn, sweet	2·10–4·1	3·1–4·15	3·15–5·1	4·10–6·1	5·10–6·15	5·15–6·1	
Cucumber	2·15–4·1	3·1–4·15	4·1–5·1	4·20–6·1	5·15–6·15	6·1–6·15	
*Eggplant	2·10–3·15	3·10–4·15	4·1–5·1	5·1–6·1	5·15–6·10	6·1–6·15	
Garlic			2·1–3·1	2·20–3·20	3·15–4·15	4·15–5·15	5·15–6·1
Kale	1·10–2·1	2·1–2·20	2·20–3·10	3·10–4·1	4·1–4·20	4·20–5·10	5·15–6·1
Kohlrabi	1·10–2·1	2·1–2·20	2·20–3·10	3·10–4·10	4·1–5·10	4·20–5·20	5·15–6·1
Leek	1·1–2·1	1·15–2·15	2·1–3·1	3·1–4·1	4·1–5·1	5·1–5·20	5·1–5·15
*Lettuce, head	1·1–2·1	1·15–2·15	2·15–3·10	3·10–4·1	4·1–5·1	5·1–6·30	5·20–6·30
*Lettuce, leaf	1·1–2·1	1·1–3·15	2·1–4·1	3·15–5·15	4·1–6·1	5·1–6·30	5·20–6·30

*Plants
Source: R. E. Wester, USDA Home Garden Bulletin 202, 1972.

Range of Safe Planting Dates According to Average Last Spring Frost Date *(continued)*

To use this chart, find the average date of the last spring frost in your area by referring to the map on pages 54–55, or contact your local Extension Service office. The dates at the top of the columns in this chart are the average dates of the last spring frost. If the last frost date in your area falls on February 8, the safe dates for planting lima beans are February 10 through May 1. If the last frost date falls between the dates listed in the chart, you'll need to extrapolate. For example, if the last frost in your area occurs around February 15, you'd probably figure March 1 as the earliest safe date for planting lima beans.

Blanks indicate that the crop may not mature when grown in zones with that average last spring frost date. However, plantings may be successful if weather is favorable or early-maturing varieties are used.

Bear in mind that these are general guidelines. Local variations in topography influence frost dates. Keeping records of the specific conditions in your garden from year to year will help you plan more precisely.

Crop	February 8	February 28	March 20	April 10	April 30	May 20	June 10
Melons	2·15–4·1	3·1–4·15	4·1–5·1	4·20–6·1	5·15–6·15		
Mustard	1·1–3·1	2·1–3·1	2·20–4·1	3·10–4·20	4·1–5·10	5·1–6·30	5·20–6·30
Okra	2·15–4·15	3·10–6·1	4·1–6·15	4·20–6·1	5·10–6·1	6·1–6·20	
*Onion plants	1·1–1·15	1·1–2·1	2·10–3·10	3·1–4·1	4·1–5·1	4·20–5·15	5·10–6·10
Onion, seed	1·1–1·15	1·1–2·15	2·10–3·10	3·1–4·1	3·15–4·15	4·20–5·15	5·10–6·10
Onion, sets	1·1–1·15	1·1–3·1	2·1–3·20	3·1–4·1	3·10–4·10	4·20–5·15	5·10–6·10
Parsnip		1·15–2·15	2·15–3·15	3·10–4·10	4·1–5·1	5·1–5·20	5·20–6·10
Peas, garden	1·1–2·15	1·15–3·1	2·1–3·15	2·20–3·20	3·20–5·1	4·15–6·1	5·10–6·15
*Pepper	2·15–4·15	3·15–5·1	4·10–6·1	5·1–6·1	5·15–6·10	5·25–6·15	
Potato	1·1–2·15	1·15–3·1	2·10–3·15	3·10–4·1	3·20–5·10	4·15–6·15	5·15–6·1
Pumpkin	2·15–4·1	3·1–4·15	4·1–5·1	4·20–6·1	5·15–6·15		
Radish	1·1–4·1	1·1–4·1	1·20–5·1	3·1–5·1	3·20–5·10	4·15–6·15	5·15–6·1
*Rhubarb				3·1–4·1	3·20–4·15	4·15–5·10	5·15–6·1
Rutabaga		1·1–2·1	1·15–3·1		5·1–6·1	5·1–5·20	5·20–6·1
Salsify	1·10–2·10	1·15–3·1	2·15–3·1	3·10–4·15	4·1–5·15	5·1–6·1	5·20–6·1
Shallot	1·1–2·10	1·1–3·1	2·1–3·10	3·1–4·1	4·1–5·1	4·20–5·10	5·10–6·1
Spinach	1·1–2·15	1·1–3·1	1·15–3·15	2·15–4·1	3·20–4·20	4·10–6·15	5·1–6·15
Spinach, New Zealand	2·15–4·15	3·15–5·15	4·1–5·15	4·20–6·1	5·1–6·15	5·20–6·15	
Squash, summer	2·15–4·15	3·15–5·15	4·1–5·15	4·20–6·1	5·1–5·30	5·20–6·15	6·10–6·20
Squash, winter	2·15–4·1	3·1–4·15	4·1–5·1	4·20–6·1	5·15–6·15		
Sweet potato	3·1–5·15	3·20–6·1	4·10–6·1	5·1–6·1	5·20–6·10		
*Tomato	2·20–4·10	3·10–5·1	4·1–5·20	4·20–6·1	5·10–6·15	5·25–6·15	6·15–6·30
Turnip	1·1–3·1	1·20–3·1	2·10–3·10	3·1–4·1	3·20–5·1	4·15–6·1	5·15–6·15

*Plants
Source: R. E. Wester, USDA Home Garden Bulletin 202, 1972.

Average Dates of the First Fall Frost

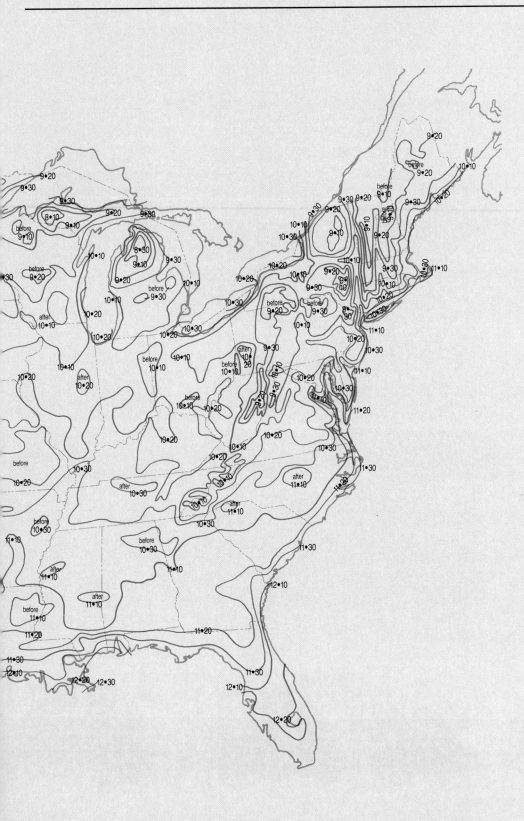

The average first fall frost date can help you figure out when to plant vegetables that will mature in the fall. For example, Iceberg-type lettuce should ideally be harvested before any frosts. If you know your expected average first fall frost date and you want to grow an 85-day lettuce variety, you can determine the safe planting time by counting back from that frost date.

Bear in mind that the actual average may be different by a week or so in your area, depending on such factors as the altitude of your property, slope of land, type of soil, vegetative cover, nearness to bodies of water, air drainage, and urban heat effects.

Fall freezes are assumed to occur between July 1 and December 31. "Before" or "after" is entered on most small areas of this map to show more readily whether the mean frost date in the area is before or after the date noted on the line.

Range of Safe Planting Dates According to Average First Fall Frost Date

Crop	September 10	September 30	October 20	November 10	November 30	December 10
*Asparagus			11·1–12·15	12·1–1·1		
Beans, lima		6·1–6·15	6·15–6·30	7·1–8·15	8·1–9·15	9·1–9·30
Beans, snap	5·15–6·15	6·1–7·10	7·1–8·1	7·1–9·1	8·15–9·20	9·1–9·30
Beans, Southern pea			6·1–7·1	6·15–8·15	7·1–9·10	7·1–9·20
Beans, soybean		5·25–6·10	6·1–7·5	6·1–7·25	6·1–7·30	6·1–7·30
Beet	5·15–6·15	6·1–7·10	7·1–8·5	8·1–10·1	9·1–12·15	9·1–12·31
Broccoli	5·1–6·1	6·1–6·30	7·1–8·1	8·1–9·1	8·1–10·1	8·1–11·1
Brussels sprouts	5·1–6·1	6·1–6·30	7·1–8·1	8·1–9·1	8·1–10·1	8·1–11·1
*Cabbage	5·1–6·1	6·1–7·10	7·1–7·20	9·1–9·15	9·1–12·31	9·1–12·31
Cabbage, Chinese	5·15–6·15	6·1–7·15	7·15–8·15	8·15–10·1	9·1–11·1	9·1–11·15
Carrots	5·15–6·15	6·1–7·10	6·15–8·1	8·1–9·1	9·15–12·1	9·15–12·1
*Cauliflower	5·1–7·1	5·10–7·15	7·1–8·5	8·1–9·1	8·15–10·10	9·1–10·20
*Celery and celeriac	5·15–6·15	6·1–7·5	6·1–8·1	7·1–8·15	8·1–12·1	9·1–12·31
Chard	5·15–7·1	6·1–7·5	6·1–8·1	6·1–9·15	6·1–11·1	6·1–12·1
*Collards	5·15–6·15	6·15–7·15	7·15–8·15	8·15–10·1	9·1–12·1	9·1–12·31
Corn, sweet		6·1–7·1	6·1–7·20	6·1–8·15		
Cucumber		6·1–7·1	6·1–7·15	6·1–8·15	7·15–9·15	8·15–10·1
*Eggplant		5·20–6·10	6·1–7·1	6·1–7·15	7·1–9·1	8·1–9·30
Endive	6·1–7·1	6·15–8·1	7·15–9·1	8·1–9·1	9·1–11·15	9·1–12·31
Garlic				8·1–10·1	9·1–11·15	9·15–11·15
Kale	5·15–6·15	6·15–7·15	7·15–8·15	8·1–9·5	9·1–12·1	9·1–12·31
Kohlrabi	6·1–7·1	6·15–7·15	7·15–8·15	8·15–9·15	9·1–12·1	9·15–12·31
Leek	5·1–6·1				9·1–11·1	9·1–11·1
*Lettuce, head	5·15–7·1	6·15–8·1	8·1–8·30	8·15–10·15	9·1–12·1	9·15–12·31
*Lettuce, leaf	5·15–7·15	6·1–8·1	7·15–9·1	8·25–10·1	9·1–12·1	9·15–12·31

*Plants
Source: R. E. Wester, USDA Home Garden Bulletin 202, 1972.

Range of Safe Planting Dates According to Average First Fall Frost Date *(continued)*

Many vegetables such as broccoli and iceberg-type lettuce have a better quality and fewer insect problems when grown for a fall harvest. This chart will help you determine when to start these and other crops in order to have them mature before the harsh cold of late fall or early winter stops their growth.

To use this chart, find the average date of the first fall frost in your area by referring to the map on pages 58–59, or contact your local Extension Service office. The dates at the top of the columns in this chart are the average dates of the first fall frost. If the first frost date in your area falls on September 10, the safe dates for planting snap beans are May 15 through June 15. If the first fall frost date falls between the dates listed in the chart, you'll need to extrapolate. For example, if the first fall frost in your area occurs around September 15, you'd probably figure June 30 as the last safe date for planting snap beans.

Blanks indicate that the crop often does not have ample time to mature when grown in zones with that average first fall frost date. However, with favorable weather or special early varieties, plantings can be successful.

Bear in mind that these are general guidelines. In mild climates, you may be able to grow certain crops during the winter. Local variations in topography influence frost dates. Keeping records of the specific conditions in your garden from year to year will help you plan more precisely.

Crop	September 10	September 30	October 20	November 10	November 30	December 10
Melons		5·15−6·1	6·15−7·20	7·15−7·30		
Mustard	5·15−7·15	6·15−8·1	8·1−9·1	8·15−11·1	9·1−12·1	9·1−12·1
Okra		6·1−7·1	6·1−8·1	6·1−8·20	6·1−9·20	8·1−10·1
*Onion plants	5·1−6·10			9·1−10·15	10·1−12·31	10·1−12·31
Onion, seeds	5·1−6·10				9·1−11·1	9·1−11·1
Onion, sets	5·1−6·10			10·1−12·1	11·1−12·31	11·1−12·31
Parsley	5·1−6·15	6·1−7·15	7·15−8·15	9·1−11·15	9·1−12·31	9·1−12·31
Parsnip	5·1−6·15	6·1−7·1			9·1−11·15	9·1−12·1
Peas, garden	5·1−7·1	6·1−8·1		9·1−11·1	10·1−12·31	10·1−12·31
*Pepper		6·1−7·1	6·1−7·10	6·1−8·1	6·15−9·1	8·15−10·1
Potato	5·1−6·15	5·1−6·15	6·15−7·15	7·25−8·20	8·1−9·15	8·1−9·15
Pumpkin		5·15−6·1	6·15−7·20	7·15−7·30		
Radish	5·1−8·1	7·1−9·1	8·1−10·1	9·1−11·15	9·1−12·31	8·1−9·15
*Rhubarb	9·15−10·15	10·1−11·1	10·15−12·1			
Rutabaga	5·1−6·15	6·1−7·1	7·10−7·20	7·15−8·15	9·1−11·15	10·1−11·15
Salsify	5·10−6·10	6·1−6·20	6·1−7·1	6·15−7·20	8·15−9·30	8·15−10·15
Shallot				8·1−10·1	8·15−10·15	9·15−11·1
Spinach	6·1−7·15	7·1−8·15	8·20−9·10	9·5−11·1	10·1−12·31	10·1−12·31
Spinach, New Zealand		5·15−7·1	6·1−8·1	6·1−8·15		
Squash, summer	6·1−6·20	6·1−7·1	6·1−7·20	6·1−8·10	6·1−9·1	6·1−9·15
Squash, winter		6·1−6·15	6·1−7·1	6·20−7·20	7·15−8·15	8·1−9·1
Sweet potato			6·1−6·15	6·1−7·1	6·1−7·1	6·10−7·1
*Tomato	6·10−6·20	6·1−6·20	6·1−7·1	6·1−7·15	8·1−9·1	8·15−10·1
Turnip	6·1−7·1	6·1−8·1	7·15−8·15	9·1−10·15	9·1−11·15	10·1−12·1

*Plants
Source: R. E. Wester, USDA Home Garden Bulletin 202, 1972.

Care

It must have been a very meticulous and perhaps overly ambitious gardener who gave us the stern maxim: "To live *off* a garden, live *in* it." Certainly, the prospect of spending all your free time keeping up with your garden's demands is *not* inviting. But it doesn't have to be that way.

Pulling weeds and cultivating the soil can be done in a few minutes if you understand weeds and anticipate their arrival. The process can be even less time consuming if you use an appropriate mulch.

If you've planned your garden well — its size, especially — caring for it can be a pleasurable routine. A few minutes a day spent inspecting (and admiring) your plants for signs of insect or disease problems, loosening hard-packed soil, or hoeing away small weeds, is all it takes. When you must water, it'll take a bit longer, since most vegetables and fruits require slow, deep soakings for best results.

Controlling Weeds

Weeds are the bane of just about every gardener. They compete with crops for water, nutrients, and light, and sometimes harbor insects and diseases. As with other pests, a knowledge of their life cycle and growth habits will help you come up with an efficient plan for keeping weeds at bay. Plan your weed control strategy well and you'll spend more time enjoying your garden and less time battling intruders.

Different types of weeds have different survival strategies. The most important distinction is between *annuals* and *perennials*.

Annuals grow from seed to mature plant to flower to new seed all in one year. Pigweed is a good example of this group. Its thousands of seeds can live for years just waiting for the right conditions for germination. A few will come up every year for some time; it's one way the species assures its survival.

Nutsedge (perennial)

so prolific it takes over whole garden beds in very little time. It spreads underground by means of rhizomes and tiny tubers. When you pull up the tuft of leaves that appears above ground, the bits of rhizome and the tubers stay behind, busily making new plants. One of the most infuriating things about this plant is that it can poke its way through black plastic, and will even find its way through tiny cracks in pavement.

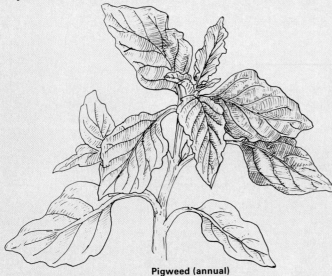

Pigweed (annual)

Once the seeds of annual weeds germinate, the roots grow rapidly, providing plenty of nourishment to the green tops. Many will produce seed stalks by midseason if you let them. Some, like the galinsoga, will even produce seed after you've uprooted them.

Perennials survive from year to year and spread by any means possible. They may send out roots, tubers, rhizomes, runners — anything that keeps them from being eaten, dug, pulled, or chopped. Some have so perfected their methods that efforts to get rid of them can end up producing more plants.

Nutsedge is a good example of a troublesome perennial weed especially common in the South. Nutsedge is

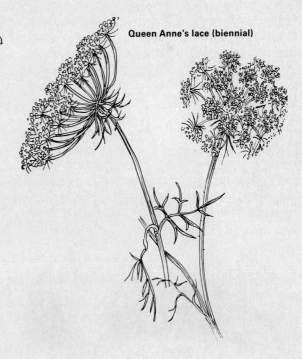

Queen Anne's lace (biennial)

Biennials take two years to produce seeds. During the first year they produce lots of leaves, and the second year send up a flower stalk. The root stays in the ground over the winter. Queen Anne's lace is a biennial. It looks much like carrots the first year, then produces a flat-topped cluster of white flowers the following summer. If you've ever watched carrots go to seed, you can see how closely related these two plants are.

Try to identify your weeds because you'll have to use slightly different methods to get rid of annuals and perennials. Perennials, for instance, must be removed carefully, roots and all, or they'll be that much tougher next year. To help you identify the weeds in your garden check your library for a guide to the local flora or a weed identification book.

Weeds aren't in your garden just to annoy you; they've chosen a spot that feels like home. One way to discourage them is to make your garden less inviting. Though some weeds like the most fertile ground you can give them, many take advantage of soils that are less than ideal.

So to start with, do everything you can to increase the humus content of your soil and make it the best possible growing environment for your crops. This will help your vegetables grow quickly and keep ahead of the weeds.

Most weeds like sunlight, and many of their seeds germinate best near the soil surface where there's plenty of light. That's why black plastic will keep seeds from germinating. Or you can pile on a deep layer of organic mulch (weed-free straw or hay or any other materials you have handy) on paths and around your vegetables. You'll have to put down 2 to 6 inches — any less and you'll just be pulling weeds through the mulch. Or plant so that the leaves of the crops will touch when mature, shading the ground below them.

Think about weed control when you plant. When you put in onion sets, for instance, place them in a grid pattern so you can pull a hoe between rows in either direction to uproot weeds. If you plant in wide rows, try placing several parallel rows close together instead of broadcasting; weeding will be much easier.

Don't plant until the soil is warm enough to let your vegetable seedlings germinate and grow quickly. In cold soil, the weeds will surely beat them to it. If weeds have been a real problem in your garden and your season is short, use transplants whenever possible. That way you can cultivate and rake the area thoroughly before planting and your plants will be visible

when the weeds take off (they might even outgrow the weeds).

Paths are favorite weed habitats. Instead of running the tiller through them every week or spending a day or two a month laboriously pulling weeds, try mulching them.

Some crop diseases and pests overwinter on weed residues. Till them in thoroughly or pull them and compost or burn. In mild-winter areas where weeds can keep on growing all winter, you can till, then plant a fast-growing cover crop to crowd them out or cover the area with black plastic until you're ready to plant the next crop. If the weeds have already gone to seed, you're better off pulling up the plants carefully to minimize spreading the seeds throughout the soil.

Annual Weeds

There are probably staggering numbers of weed seeds lying in wait in your garden. They'll germinate when conditions are right. The simplest and best way to stay in control, if you can possibly discipline yourself to do it, is to hoe them religiously every week or so, whenever a new batch appears (many will germinate a day or two after a rainfall). At this stage they're easy to

Don't cultivate for weeds too deeply. That way you will neither harm the roots of your vegetable plants nor bring new weed seeds to the surface where they can sprout.

kill. After a year or two of this treatment, your garden will have far fewer weed seeds.

Unless you need to destroy deep-rooted perennials, hoeing should always be shallow, disturbing no more than about the top half-inch of soil. (Scuffle hoes that cut weeds just below the soil surface are excellent.) That way you will neither bring new weed seeds to the surface nor harm the roots of your vegetable plants.

If you've had a serious weed problem, consider leaving the garden, or a section of it, idle for a few months or a whole season, and hoeing or tilling it repeatedly to kill off the unwanted plants. A fast-growing cover crop like buckwheat can choke out many weeds. Two crops of buckwheat in a summer, tilled in before they go to seed, can clear many weeds from an area and simultaneously add loads of organic matter to your soil.

If you've missed the early stage of control, at least try to get rid of the annuals before they go to seed. To pull, wait until the ground is moist and loose; otherwise you'll end up pulling off the tops, perhaps allowing the roots to regrow. Remember also that some of these plants will continue to mature their seed even after being pulled, so if you leave them lying in the garden you may be adding to next year's gardening chores. Weeds around the edges of your garden will be producing seeds, too, so mowing or clearing that area will also help.

Perennials

The best control for perennials is prevention. When you start a new garden, don't be fooled by the appearance of freshly tilled soil. If perennials have been there, rake out all roots and other plant parts thoroughly, and if at all possible wait a few months to plant. A full season may sound like a long time to get going, but when you consider the time you'll save later in pulling out weeds, it isn't so bad.

When you transplant any trees or shrubs from a friend or neighbor (or even a nursery), you may be bringing in perennial weeds. Watch the area around the plants carefully that first season and remove any weeds that show up.

Mint, comfrey, horseradish, and some other invasive plants can turn into weeds very quickly. If you want them contained, use some sort of liner below ground when putting them in the garden to keep their roots in place. Sunken pots, cans with the ends removed, or foot-deep hunks of drainage tiles will slow them down.

Any perennials sprouting from seed during the growing season will be taken care of by the same methods you've followed for annuals. Once they've made a good start and have an established root system, though, they're harder to kill off.

The best time to attack many perennials is just after they've flowered, as the seeds are starting to set. Then the weeds have used up most of their food reserves and if you whack off the top the roots are least likely to resprout. If you do it too early, though, before the seeds are setting, they might just respond like a hydra and come back at you with two flower stalks. Biennials can do the same — in late summer you can often see Queen Anne's lace in recently mown lawns, sporting short white clusters of flowers close to the ground. If you can't bear to wait that long, you can start tilling earlier, either in the fall or early spring, but you'll have to plan on repeated treatment every few weeks for several months at least before the plants will finally give.

Another solution is to smother perennials with heavy black plastic for a season. Make sure it's heavy, not the cheaper light types, or it will weaken after a while and the plants will push their way through. Summertime, when the sun is hot, is best for this since the ground will heat sufficiently to kill off the roots and many seeds of annuals as well. This is a good method for weeds with persistent roots, such as quack grass. Perennials sometimes have unbelievable root systems, so pulling or digging out individual plants can pose a real challenge.

For young weeds near crop plants, hold the crop down with one hand while pulling the weed up with the other to prevent pulling the crop out with the weed. For digging larger ones, pick a day when the soil is moist (not wet), loosen the area with a fork, then dig down to get the whole thing. Try to fish out as many rhizomes and tubers as possible from weeds that reproduce in that way.

Weeds are good compost material, but if you're composting perennials they need to be heated thoroughly to prevent their reinfesting the garden. Put them near the center of your compost pile to be sure they cook thoroughly, or burn them.

Mulches

One of the best ways to keep weeds at bay in the garden is by using a mulch which shuts out sunlight and stops their growth. The range of mulching materials runs from organic substances such as straw, grass clippings, sawdust, and peat, through mineral, such as

A Scavenger's Guide to Mulches

Material	Type	Thickness	Advantages	Disadvantages	Comments
Pine needles	D*	3–4 inches	Light, usually free of weed seeds; absorbs little or no moisture; can be used more than once; does not pack down.	Decompose very slowly.	Add extra nitrogen fertilizer for faster decomposition; slightly acidic.
Polyethylene (black or clear)	WND**	One layer	Can be used more than once; absorbs no moisture; black plastic very effective weed control, even with perennial weeds.	Weeds will grow under clear plastic; difficult to apply properly; is not penetrable so rain cannot get through easily; may make soil too warm; not always attractive.	Warms soil in spring; effective with warmth-loving crops such as melons; ground must be moist before applying; does not add any nutrient or organic matter to soil.
Aluminum foil or foil-backed paper	WND	One layer	Good for shady gardens, as it increases the light around the plants; aphids and other insects avoid foil-mulched plants; can be used more than once.	Foil can tear if handled roughly; can be expensive.	Keeps ground very cool so it's better for misdummer than spring; apply only after ground has warmed up.
Bark chips	D	2–3 inches	Attractive; can be used more than one season; good for permanent mulch.	If untreated, it may attract carpenter ants or termites; redwood bark may resist water penetration.	Decomposes very slowly unless composted first; redwood bark chips decompose slower than others; can be raked at the end of season and reused; redwood chips may repel insects.
Compost	D	1–2 inches	Good feeding mulch; partially decomposed compost will continue decomposing quickly into humus.	Must have had sufficient heating period to kill weed seeds, bacteria, or disease.	Plan and start ahead so compost will be ready when you need it.
Corncobs and cornstalks	D	3–4 inches	Readily available in many areas; good weed inhibitor.	Water cannot penetrate easily; corncobs may begin to generate heat.	Add extra nitrogen fertilizer to aid decomposition; don't use stalks or cobs that have been infested by disease, borers, or worms; work best if ground or chopped.
Cottonseed hulls	D	2–4 inches	Readily available in areas of the South; fertilizer value similar to cottonseed meal.	Very light, so wind can scatter.	Can be sifted down between plants in double or triple rows to keep down weeds; cover with very thin layer of other mulch to prevent scattering by wind.
Grass clippings	D	2–3 inches	Improves soil by adding organic matter; readily available almost everywhere.	Absorbent, may carry weed seeds.	May be mixed with other materials to prevent packing down; may decompose rapidly so add more layers as necessary; dry for a few days after cutting to prevent rotting; don't use clippings from lawns treated with herbicides.
Hay	D	6–8 inches	Obtainable in large quantities; legume hays such as alfalfa add large amounts of nitrogen to soil.	First-cut hay is usually full of weeds.	Second- or third-cut hay more likely to be free of weed seeds; may not have to add more during season—just fluff up what is there.

*D—decomposes
**WND—will not decompose

A Scavenger's Guide to Mulches *(continued)*

Material	Type	Thickness	Advantages	Disadvantages	Comments
Leaves	D	2–3 inches	Readily available to most people; contain many trace minerals; best food for earthworms.	May become soggy and pack down, making it hard for water to penetrate to soil.	Chipping or mixing with other materials will prevent packing down, matting; best to compost before using or may inhibit seed germination.
Paper (newspaper or scrap paper, no color pages)	D	5–6 pages, 4–6 inches if shredded	Usually readily available; may add trace minerals to the soil.	Sheets may pack down and slow water penetration; not always attractive; wind can scatter.	Hold down edges with rocks or dirt to protect from wind; shredded paper decomposes more readily; often used to protect against unexpected frost; slightly alkaline.
Peanut hulls	D	2–3 inches	Contain considerable amounts nitrogen, phosphorus, and potassium; decompose rapidly into rich humus.	Not readily available outside the southern states.	May be attractive to rodents if not completely free of peanuts.
Peat moss	D	1–2 inches	Clean and free of weed seeds.	Extremely absorbent so water will not readily penetrate to soil; can be expensive; adds little or no nutrients to soil.	Very good as soil conditioner to loosen up heavy soil and improve water retention; acidic; long decomposition time.
Rock, crushed gravel, or marble chips	WND	1–2 inches	Relatively inexpensive; not absorbent; water penetrates easily; nonflammable.	Not best for weed control; not readily available; adds no organic matter.	Should be considered permanent decorative mulch.
Salt marsh hay	D	4–6 inches	Usually weed-free; easy to gather in marshy areas or along marshy coast; long-lasting and can be reused.	Not widely available; expensive if purchased.	Can be tilled under at end of season; chopping may make more attractive and easier to handle; does not decompose rapidly.
Sawdust	D	2–3 inches	Readily available from lumber yard or workshop.	Takes very long to decompose unless weathered or aged outdoors first; water penetration only fair; may encourage crown rot in some plants by holding moisture against stem.	Add extra nitrogen fertilizer to speed decomposition; hardwood sawdust rots faster than pine or cedar, especially if weathered or aged outdoors first.
Seaweed	D	3–4 inches	Can be used more than once; available at little or no cost to those along coast; water penetrates to soil easily.	Not readily available inland unless sold (packaged) at store; may have excess salt content; not necessarily attractive.	Salt can be washed out if left outside in a number of rains; decomposes slowly.
Straw	D	6–8 inches	Readily available in some areas.	Can be difficult to handle; can be fire hazard.	Chopping may make more attractive and easier to handle; add extra nitrogen fertilizer to aid decomposition unless straw is weathered or aged outdoors first.

* *D*—decomposes
** *WND*—will not decompose

Critical Period of Water Needs for Vegetables

Bean, lima	Pollination and pod development
Bean, snap	Pod enlargement
Broccoli	Head development
Cabbage	Head development
Carrots	Root enlargement
Cauliflower	Head development
Corn, sweet	Silking, tasseling, and ear development
Cucumber	Flowering and fruit development
Eggplant	Uniform supply from flowering through harvest
Melon	Fruit set and early development
Onion, dry	Bulb enlargement
Pea	Flowering and seed enlargement
Pepper	Uniform supply from flowering through harvest
Potato	Tuber set and tuber enlargement
Radish	Root enlargement
Squash, summer	Bud development and flowering
Tomato	Uniform supply from flowering through harvest
Turnip	Root enlargement

Source: University of Illinois Cooperative Extension Service.

stones and gravel, to manmade items such as plastic film. In addition to suppressing weeds, mulches help retain soil moisture, and organic materials improve the soil as they decompose. Plastic mulches help warm a cool soil in the spring, while a thick organic mulch can help keep soil and roots cool through the heat of the summer.

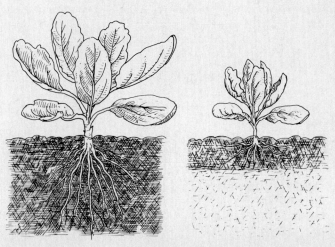

The key rule for watering established plants is to water well, to a depth of at least 6 inches. This encourages roots to penetrate deeply where they will be less susceptible to drought.

Watering

You will need to water your crops at different rates depending on their stage of growth. In the 2 weeks after transplants are put in the garden, frequent watering is recommended to help the roots recover from transplant shock. Germinating seeds benefit from frequent, gentle watering, which enables them to sprout and emerge quickly; as do seedlings with small root systems near the soil surface.

For established plants, water well when you do water, then give the soil a chance to dry out slightly before watering thoroughly again. Try to apply enough water at each irrigation to wet the soil at least 6 inches deep; dig down with a trowel to see how far the water has penetrated. Frequent, shallow waterings do more harm than good because they cause roots to develop mainly in the upper few inches of the soil, where they are susceptible to drying out.

If your garden has heavy clay soil or is on a slope, you may find that water begins to run off before the soil is wet 6 inches deep. Try watering at intervals to

Watering Methods

Soaker hoses. These are hoses that slowly ooze water. Lay them along the soil at the base of plants. Plastic and rubber soaker hoses last longer than canvas ones. Many gardeners leave them in place all season.

Watering with a hose. Few gardeners have the patience to stand holding a hose long enough to wet the soil thoroughly at each watering. A better solution is to attach a breaker or bubbler to the hose, then lay it on the ground and let the water either flood the bed or fill furrows in the bed.

Drip/trickle irrigation. This method of watering puts water exactly where it is needed and uses the least amount of water. Various kinds of emitters or tubes with holes in them put out a small, steady amount of water directly to the root zone. Systems may be above ground or permanently installed below ground. Drip irrigation kits are available or you can build your own.

Sprinklers. When using sprinklers, water in the morning to lessen loss by evaporation and so leaves are dry before nightfall. Don't buy a sprinkler that puts out water faster than your soil can absorb it or you'll lose a lot as run-off. If you have heavy soil that absorbs water slowly, or if your garden is on a slope, choose a sprinkler that puts out a low volume of water.

avoid this problem. Water for 10 to 15 minutes, let the water soak in for 15 to 20 minutes, then water again.

Because roots need air as well as water, it is important to keep the soil from becoming water-logged. Your finger is the best indicator of when the soil has dried sufficiently to rewater. Dig down several inches into the soil; if it is dry to your touch 3 to 4 inches down, it's time to irrigate.

Wilting can be a sign that your soil is in need of water, but it's best for your crops to water them before they reach this stage. Wilting can be a misleading symptom at times. Some plants, like tomatoes, peppers, and eggplant, tend to wilt slightly during the heat of the day in warm climates, even if the soil has enough moisture. Check the soil before irrigating to make sure you don't overwater. Overwatering can even cause plants to wilt. If the soil is water-logged, roots die from lack of air. With fewer roots, the plant can no longer take up the water it needs from the soil and it wilts. Root damage from insects and disease can also cause wilting.

Different crops have different water needs. Some, like celery, are real water lovers and prefer to have moist soil around their roots at all times. Shallow-rooted crops like onions and cabbages need more careful watering during dry spells than deeper rooted crops like tomatoes that can pull water from greater depths.

In general, most vegetables use about 1 inch of water per week; 1½ inches in hot, dry climates. If you don't get 1 inch of water as rainfall you will have to supply it yourself. A good way to tell if you've watered enough is to partially sink some inch-marked cans or plastic containers here and there in the garden to collect water from your hose or sprinkler. You can also measure flow by purchasing an inexpensive flow meter from the hardware store to attach to the outdoor spigot. To figure out the flow rate at the spigot yourself, turn off all spigots and read the water meter. Then turn on the spigot serving the hose line for one minute. Re-read the meter to find out how much water flows through the hose in 1 minute. You'll need about 60 gallons per 100 square feet of garden to get 1 inch of water.

The time of day you water will make a difference mainly if you are using a sprinkler. Less water is lost to evaporation (an important consideration in hot, dry climates) if the garden is watered in the cool of the morning rather than the heat of the afternoon. It also gives leaves a chance to dry off before evening; foliage

that stays wet all night can set the stage for fungus diseases.

If you have a zeolite-type water softener that works by exchanging sodium ions for the calcium ions causing hardness in the water, irrigate your garden from a faucet installed on the line before it reaches the water softener. Long-term watering with water high in sodium leads to breakdown of soil structure, causing soil compaction and poor drainage.

Side-dressing

Depending on the type of fertilizer you are using, the crops you are growing, and the type of soil you have, it's a good idea to add repeat doses of fertilizer throughout the growing season, a practice called side-dressing. For example, sandy soils do not hold onto nutrients well; giving plants regular, small applications of fertilizer insures a steady supply. If you use a slow-release fertilizer, you may not need to side-dress until late in the season or not at all.

Both chemical and natural fertilizers can be used for side-dressing. A 5-10-10 fertilizer is a good choice for many crops. Use 1 to 2 tablespoons per plant, or 1 to 2 pounds per 25 feet of row, depending on the size of plants. Sprinkle the fertilizer around the base of the plant, a few inches from the stem, or spread it down the length of the row, several inches from plant stems.

Depending on plant spacing, side-dress either in a narrow furrow down the row (*above*) or around each individual plant (*opposite*). In each case the fertilizer should be several inches from the plant stem.

Rake it lightly into the soil, then water. Dry natural fertilizers such as blood meal can be used in the same manner, adjusting the amount applied to the strength of the fertilizer.

Adding liquid fertilizers to your watering can is an easy way to side-dress plants. Either natural (fish emulsion, manure tea) or chemical soluble fertilizers can be used. (Follow the directions on the label.) Pour the fertilizer around the base of the plants. To make manure tea, fill a pail half full of manure, then top off with water. Stir, let it sit until the mixture is tea colored, then strain it.

Too much fertilizer can be more harmful than too little. Fertilizer salts accumulate in the soil and damage plant roots. Be sure that growing conditions allow plants to use the fertilizer that you apply. Don't add fertilizer during a dry spell if you can't irrigate the garden, since roots can't take up nutrients without adequate soil moisture. If plants are growing slowly because of cool weather, go easy on fertilizer until temperatures warm up.

The kind of plants you are growing makes a difference. Plants that take a long time to mature, such as tomatoes and eggplant, and plants that are heavy feeders, such as corn, generally benefit more from side-dressing than quick-maturing crops such as lettuce or legumes such as peas and beans that fix their own nitrogen. The box at right gives some general guidelines for side-dressing various crops.

Recommended Times to Side-dress

Beans, green	Not necessary.
Beet greens	2 weeks after leaves appear.
Beets	When tops are 4–5 inches high; go light on nitrogen, which encourages leaf growth.
Broccoli	3 weeks after transplant; go light on nitrogen.
Brussels sprouts	3 weeks after transplant; again when sprouts begin to appear.
Cabbage & cauliflower	If your soil was well fertilized, no need to side-dress.
Carrots	3 weeks after plants are well established.
Celery	3 weeks after setting out; again 6 weeks later.
Sweet corn	3 weeks after planting; again when plants are 8–10 inches high; again when tassels appear.
Cucumbers	When they first begin to run; when blossoms set.
Eggplant	3 weeks after setting out plants.
Kale	When plants are 6–8 inches high.
Lettuce, head	3 weeks after transplant; as heads form.
Melons	When they begin to run; a week after blossom set; again 3 weeks later.
Onions	3 weeks after setting out; when tops are 6–8 inches tall; when bulbs start to swell.
Peas (English)	No need to side-dress.
Peppers (sweet)	3 weeks after transplant; after first fruit set.
Potatoes	When plants bloom.
Pumpkin	When plants start to run; at blossom set.
Radishes	No need to side-dress.
Spinach	When plants are about 1/3 grown.
Squash, summer	When plants are about 6 inches tall; when they bloom.
Squash, winter	When plants start to run; at blossom set.
Tomatoes	2–3 weeks after transplant; before first picking; 2 weeks after first picking; go light on nitrogen.

Keeping Animals Out of the Garden

In addition to insects and diseases, gardeners must keep an eye out for two- and four-footed pests. Whether or not one of the critters listed below will cause problems in your garden depends a lot on where the garden is located. If woods adjoin your property, squirrels and raccoons may become pests; if you're surrounded by fields, mice and woodchucks may invite themselves in to dine on your tender young plants.

As you read the control suggestions listed below, you'll notice that fencing is one of the most common recommendations. Although it can be expensive, it is the most reliable means of keeping most animals out of the garden. Even a sturdy fence is not a 100-percent guarantee, however; sometimes trapping may be the only solution to an especially persistent woodchuck or raccoon. (Check first with your state Fish and Wildlife Department to find out if there are any regulations governing trapping of the animal you have in mind.) Live traps can be purchased in most hardware stores; get the appropriate size for the animal you hope to catch. When you have the animal in the trap, be sure to take it several miles away before letting it loose so it cannot find its way back to your garden again.

Mice

A fence of ¼-inch mesh hardware cloth 12 inches high, with another 12 inches buried underground, will keep mice out. Keep the garden free of weeds and keep the area around the garden mowed; mice do not like to cross an open area and expose themselves to predators. You can also set traps in the garden, but make careful note of where they are so you don't catch an unsuspecting human harvester.

Moles

These pests do not feed on plants. They eat insects such as grubs and earthworms, but may damage the roots of plants with their tunneling. In gardens, traps set in tunnels are most effective in controlling moles. To find active tunnels, tamp down the raised soil, which indicates tunneling. The tunnels that are raised a day later are active.

Woodchucks

Also known as groundhogs, these pests will happily feed on just about everything in the garden. A fence at least 3 feet high, with another 12 inches bent underground (as recommended for mice), is the best way to keep them out. Leave the top 18 inches of the fence unattached to the support posts. This way, as the woodchuck attempts to climb over the fence, it will bend back down under the animal's weight. A strand of electric fence at the top of a woven wire fence will also discourage them.

Gophers

In the western part of the country, gophers can raise havoc with gardens, eating roots and the underground parts of plants. Trapping is the most practical solution in most cases. Find an active runway by probing the soil near a fresh mound of dirt with a crowbar. Set two traps in the runway, one facing each direction. Tie the two traps together, then cover them with soil to keep out all light. If your garden is small, you may want to erect a gopher barrier. It's a lot of work, but it will do the trick.

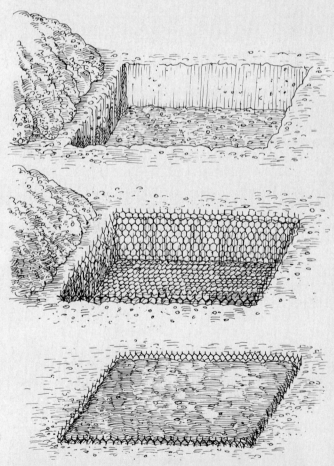

A gopher barrier of 1-inch chicken wire will keep this western pest out of permanent beds. Roll out a panel of wire along the bottom of a dug-out bed and another around the sides. Carefully attach the chicken wire with baling wire along the lower edge. The wire should last about five years.

Rabbits

A fence with 1½-inch mesh that is at least 2 feet high should keep rabbits out of the garden. Make sure the bottom is tight to the ground or bury the bottom edge as recommended for woodchucks. Dried blood sprinkled in the garden will repel rabbits, although it will need to be renewed frequently.

Raccoons

A fence similar to the one recommended for woodchucks, but 4 feet high instead of 3, will usually keep raccoons out. A strand of electric fencing on top will act as an added deterrent. Some gardeners claim that planting squash vines solidly around the perimeter of the garden (or at least the corn patch) will keep raccoons out; they don't like to cross over the prickly leaves.

Cats and Dogs

Fences work best to keep both your pets and the neighbors' out of the garden. Cats are a problem mainly early in the season when they like to dig in the newly tilled ground; laying chicken wire or hardware cloth over the seedbed until plants sprout will encourage them to dig elsewhere.

Birds

Starlings and crows have an uncanny sense of where you planted your corn seeds. To keep birds from eating seeds or pulling up newly sprouted plants, protect the seedbed with a tunnel of hardware cloth. By the time the plants have outgrown the tunnel, they are no longer at a stage that is appetizing to birds.

Deer

A slanted fence is a good way to keep deer out of the garden since their instinct is to try to crawl under a fence before jumping it, and they are less likely to jump a fence that is wide. A slanted fence can be 4 to 5 feet high, while a vertical fence must be at least 8 feet high to keep deer from jumping over it. Deer are also repelled by bags of human hair hung along the edge of the garden, or dried blood sprinkled on the ground, although both need to be renewed frequently.

4-5'

45°

4-5'

A slanted wire fence is an effective solution to keeping deer out of the garden. Deer are less likely to jump a fence that is wide; a vertical fence would have to be much taller.

Harvesting

Your first harvests, a month or so after outdoor planting begins, are often small — a handful of lettuce leaves for the first straight-from-the-garden salad, a few scallions and radishes. In midseason, as the early crops mature and the first of the warm-season vegetables like beans are ready, you'll be so busy you may forget the thrill of your first haul. Now, whichever direction you turn, there seems to be something that needs picking or processing right away. Finally, at the end of the season you can harvest for out-of-season eating. This might mean some late-season freezing or canning or, if you have the space, bringing produce to a root cellar or cold storage room to keep for several months.

Whenever you harvest, it is an exciting and rewarding process. On the following page we've offered a few ideas for getting earlier produce, evening out peak harvest, and savoring more of your harvest for a longer time.

When to Harvest

One of the chief reasons people garden at home is to have fresh produce (supermarket produce travels an average of 1,300 miles before you get it). For the freshest produce, harvest your crops when they are tender. This may mean harvesting before plants, roots, or fruits reach full size. A 15-inch zucchini is impressive, but it tastes better at 6 or 8 inches. Carrots and beets easily grow woody or bland.

A good rule for many of your early crops is to start harvesting when there's enough for one serving at a meal. Spinach, chard, scallions, radishes, lettuce, and cabbage family crops certainly fit the bill here. They don't grow as well in warm weather, so it's wise to make the most of your spring and pick some of these crops when temperatures are cooler.

Once you start harvesting, try to visit the garden regularly and pick something on each visit.

Some plants need harvesting to keep them productive. Snap beans, summer squash, lima beans, snow- and snap peas, broccoli, okra, parsley, spinach, and lettuce are crops that, if kept harvested, will continue to produce more pods, shoots, and leaves.

How to Harvest

When you head to the garden to harvest, bring a good harvesting knife, paper bags or buckets, and possibly a wire basket for easy washing of produce with a hose.

If you can avoid it, don't harvest when plants are wet, especially beans. Many fungus diseases spread in moist conditions, and brushing the plants with your tools or pantlegs can carry disease organisms down the row.

Also avoid the heat of the day for harvesting if your schedule permits. Try to harvest early in the day when moisture levels in the vegetables are highest, refrigerate the produce, and prepare it later in the day.

In the fall, wait as long as you can to dig up root crops such as carrots, rutabagas, and beets if you intend to store them in a root cellar or cold storage room. They can take frosts, but harvest them before the ground freezes. They'll come out of the ground easily if it is lightly moist.

Don't wash crops that are going into the root cellar; just gently brush away clumps of soil. Use any blemished or cut vegetables in the next few days.

Saving Seeds

Most gardeners find that no matter how carefully they plan, they usually end the gardening year with extra seeds of a number of different crops. Fortunately, most seeds are still usable for a year or more if kept under the proper conditions.

Seeds keep longest if they are stored under cool, dry conditions that slow their life processes down. Room temperature is acceptable for many vegetable seeds, but keeping them in the refrigerator will prolong their storage life considerably. The freezer is an even better place to store seeds (be sure to warm them for a day or two at room temperature before planting). To keep seeds dry, place a couple of tablespoons of powdered milk *from a freshly opened container* in a packet made of cleansing tissues, then place the milk and seeds in a glass container with a rubber-sealed lid (such as a canning jar) to keep out moisture. The milk will absorb any moisture from the air. Replace with fresh milk every 6 months.

The approximate storage times for vegetable seeds stored without any special moisture or temperature controls are as follows:

1 year — sweet corn, onion, parsley, parsnip

2 years — beet, pepper

3 years — asparagus, bean, celery, carrot, lettuce, pea, spinach, tomato

4 years — cabbage, cauliflower, eggplant, okra, pumpkin, radish, squash

5 years — cucumber, endive, muskmelon, watermelon

If you have a favorite variety that is suited to your tastes or growing conditions, or individual plants that thrive in your garden, you can save their seeds and gradually alter the variety to best fit your needs. The Resources section beginning on page 406 lists sources for obtaining detailed information on saving seeds.

Saving your own seed is a way of keeping heirloom varieties alive. Many of the heirlooms, which are difficult or impossible to obtain from commercial sources, have something special to offer, such as adaptation to the growing conditions in a particular area, certain types of disease resistance, or especially good flavor.

Heirloom varieties represent a reservoir of genes that plant breeders can use to improve present and future crops. There are several organizations listed in the Resources section dedicated to the preservation of heirloom vegetable and fruit varieties. Contact them for more information on finding and preserving heirlooms.

Asparagus

The 5-year-old asparagus bed at left will send up thick, delectable spears for 4 to 6 weeks each spring. Female plants *(above)* produce berries and seeds but yield slightly less than male, pollen-producing plants.

A temperate climate crop that must go dormant in winter, asparagus will succeed just about anywhere except in the mild-winter areas of the Gulf Coast states. Tender springtime spears grow into towering ferns that die in late fall, to be replaced by new spears the next spring. The perennial cycle will repeat twenty times or more if you invest the time and effort to give the plants a healthy start.

Preparing an asparagus bed is hard work, but if you do it right, maintaining it will be a breeze. Asparagus is most often grown from young *crowns*, the pencil-thin storage roots attached to an underground stem called a rhizome. With extra care, though, you can sow seeds directly in your garden or raise your own transplants from seed.

Creeping weeds have been the downfall of many an asparagus patch. But if you work hard to keep weeds out of your garden right from the start, you'll have fewer problems.

Until very recently, there have been few varieties to choose from. New developments in breeding promise improved vigor, yield, and disease resistance — but for home growers, the old standards are still excellent.

Planning

Once asparagus is well established, it will yield dependably for 20 years or more. The worst problem is with perennial weeds creeping into the asparagus beds. So take the time to prepare the beds well and be vigilant about weed control.

The easiest and most rewarding way to start a new bed of asparagus is from crowns. Asparagus plants generally take three growing seasons to get fully established. Each year the roots develop further and send up increasing numbers of spears. If you start from crowns, you can expect a light harvest in the spring of the second year. If you start with seeds or seedlings, the first cutting will come in the third year. (Plants started from 2-year-old crowns will not produce much faster than 1-year-olds; both need at least one full growing season before they can be harvested without damage to the plant.)

Asparagus is most often grown from crowns, pencil-thin storage roots attached to an underground stem. Drape the roots of one crown around each mound and firm them in before covering the crowns with 2 inches of soil.

Many garden centers sell roots; they don't have to be ordered. Allow about ten to twenty plants for each asparagus lover in your family. Check the crowns carefully before buying or when they arrive by mail to see that they are fleshy and firm, not mushy and withered. Trim torn or broken roots back to healthy tissue, then refrigerate until you're ready to plant.

Whether you're starting from seed, seedlings, or crowns, the best time to plant is early spring, as soon as the soil can be worked. To perform well, the new plants need to get growing before hot, dry weather sets in. If the days are warm and the nights are cool, your seeds will sprout and crowns will send up shoots within a couple of weeks of planting.

Preparation

Select the site for your asparagus bed carefully. The fernlike foliage may grow to 5 feet tall, so keep it far enough away from other crops to avoid shading them out.

Asparagus doesn't need full sun and it's not fussy about the type of soil (although sandy loam is ideal). It does best in slightly acid soil (about pH 6.5), but can tolerate alkaline conditions, often found in the West, even up to 9.0. Asparagus requires adequate drainage to keep the roots from rotting.

Take the time to eliminate as many weeds as possible before planting by repeated tilling or by growing a cover crop (see pages 35–37) a year in advance. Since asparagus is a perennial crop, you won't get another chance to till the soil and destroy weeds for 15 to 20 years.

To prepare your bed, we recommend the method used by Bob Thomson, host of the "Victory Garden" television show.

Dig a trench 12 inches wide and 15 inches deep and set the topsoil to one side (see box on page 81). Add 4 inches of rich organic matter, preferably aged manure (compost or peat moss will do), then toss on about 2 inches of the topsoil and mix together in the bottom of the trench. Spread superphosphate fertilizer or bone meal to provide phosphorus — the key ingredient for strong root systems — at the rate of 5 pounds per 100 square feet. Add another inch or so of topsoil and mix it all together again. The planting bed should now be 6 inches or more below ground level with plenty of topsoil waiting on the sidelines.

Planting

When you're ready to plant, soak the crowns briefly in lukewarm water.

Draw a hoe along each side of the trench to form a mound in the center running the length of each trench. Set your crowns 18 inches apart atop the mound, draping the roots over the sides so they can feed through a broad layer of soil. Mix more aged manure with the topsoil you set aside (1 part manure to 3 parts topsoil), bury the crowns 2 inches deep, and tamp the area gently. Water the beds thoroughly and leave the leftover topsoil/manure blend piled up alongside the trenches to use later.

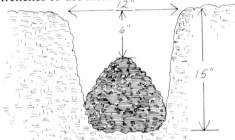

Care

Keep the beds hand-weeded as the crowns get established. Periodically add more soil/manure around the emerging shoots, an inch or two at a time until the trench is filled. Then spread a 4- to 8-inch-thick layer of mulch to keep weeds down throughout the growing season.

Water regularly to provide at least an inch a week. In early fall, pull back the mulch and apply a dose of balanced fertilizer such as 10-10-10 at the rate of 2½ pounds per 100 square feet. Cut down the dead ferns late in the fall and burn them to prevent harboring any insects and disease. Scatter some superphosphate over the bed at a rate of 2½ pounds per 100 square feet and put the mulch back around the plants.

In the spring of the second year, cultivate the bed lightly by hand until the new spears are several inches tall, then keep it thickly mulched. Apply more balanced fertilizer at the same rate as above, once in

Essentials

Planning

- *The easiest way to start asparagus is from crowns.*
- *Plant in the spring as soon as the soil can be worked.*
- *Plants will take three growing seasons to become established.*
- *Allow ten to twenty plants per person (15 to 30 feet of row).*

Preparation

- *Select a well-drained site; full sun is not necessary.*
- *Asparagus will thrive in slightly acid soil (pH of about 6.5), but will tolerate alkaline conditions up to 9.0.*
- *Eliminate all weeds by repeated tilling or by growing a cover crop a year in advance.*
- *About 1 week before planting, prepare trenches for crowns. (See page 78 for details.)*

Planting

- *Soak the crowns briefly in lukewarm water before planting.*
- *Draw a hoe along each side of the prepared trench to form a mound in the center running the length of the trench.*
- *Set the crowns 18 inches apart on the mounds in the trench, draping the roots over the sides.*
- *To cover the crowns, mix 1 part manure to 3 parts topsoil and bury the crowns 2 inches deep.*
- *Water the bed thoroughly.*

Care

- *First year: Weed the beds carefully. Periodically add more topsoil/manure around emerging shoots until the trench is filled. Then spread a 4- to 8-inch layer of mulch — such as hay or leaves — or a 3- to 4-inch layer of aged manure, compost, or shredded bark around the base of the ferns. Water regularly. In the early fall, pull back the mulch and side-dress with 2½ pounds of a balanced fertilizer per 100 square feet. Cut down dead ferns in late fall and side-dress with 2½ pounds superphosphate per 100 square feet.*
- *Second year: Cultivate lightly by hand until the new spears are several inches tall, then keep the bed thickly mulched. Side-dress with a balanced fertilizer such as 10-10-10 at the rate of 2½ pounds per 100 square feet in the spring and early fall. Follow first year instructions for late fall.*
- *Third year and beyond: Maintain as for the second year, but apply the spring side-dressing after the harvest.*

Harvesting

- *Plants started from crowns can be harvested lightly in the spring of the second year; plants started from seeds in the third year.*
- *Harvest only those spears that are thicker than a pencil.*
- *Cut or snap off the spears at or just above ground level when they are 6 to 8 inches tall.*

Starting Asparagus from Seed

Although starting from crowns is probably the easiest way to establish an asparagus patch and the fastest way to reach the first harvest, there are some drawbacks to this method. Crowns lose vigor in the cutting process and are apt to deteriorate somewhat in transit from the nursery. If you're not ready to plant them the day they arrive, they may deteriorate further in storage.

To avoid these problems, you can start a new stand directly from seed, but it is a delicate enterprise that requires a lot of expertise. Success depends on exceptionally good soil preparation, soil temperature, adequate moisture, and thorough weed control. The variety may also make a difference; *Brock* is said to be good for direct seeding.

Start your transplant seedlings just as you would start a tomato or any other plant for transplanting. Sow seeds in small pots, move the seedlings to larger pots, and then transplant them to the garden when they are large enough.

Here is a system developed by horticulturists for starting a bed from homegrown transplants:

1. Soak the seeds in tepid water for 24 hours to hasten germination.
2. Fill small peat pots with moist potting soil mixed with well-aged manure or compost if available.
3. Plant three seeds in the center of each pot, ½ inch deep and ½ inch apart.
4. Place the pots in a warm, partially sunny location and keep the soil moist. With a soil temperature of 75° to 80°F, the seeds will germinate within 2 or 3 weeks.
5. When the seedlings are 2 to 3 inches high, thin to one per pot.
6. Before the seedlings outgrow the peat pots, prepare larger pots to receive them. (Note: This intermediate transfer may not be necessary if 6-inch-diameter pots were used for the initial planting.) Fill the pots with a moist planting medium, as above. To stimulate growth, add 1 teaspoon of balanced fertilizer such as 10-10-10 to each pot.
7. Make a hole in the middle of each pot to accommodate the seedling, peat pot and all. (If the initial pots were not peat, be careful not to disturb the roots when making this switch.) Firm the soil around the seedling to ensure good contact with the roots.

The seedlings should be ready for transplanting to the garden about 8 to 10 weeks after they first emerged, preferably during the spring or early summer. When the time comes, gently scoop the seedlings out of their pots along with the soil, leaving the roots and foliage intact, but otherwise following the same procedure as for planting crowns: set the seedlings 18 inches apart in a deep, well-prepared trench, cover with rich topsoil, and then gradually back-fill the trench as they grow.

Asparagus started from seed takes a year longer to become well established than plants grown from crowns, so hold off on the first harvest until two full growing seasons have passed. Pick lightly for no more than 2 weeks in the spring of the third year, then 3 or 4 weeks the year after that, and 6 weeks or more every year thereafter.

This seeded asparagus is beginning its third season of growth. Allow two full growing seasons to pass before harvesting lightly in the spring of the third year.

late spring and again in early fall. Cut and burn the dead ferns and add superphosphate in late fall.

From then on, take care of your asparagus bed as you did in the second year, but expect increasingly heavier harvests. (Apply a balanced fertilizer such as 10-10-10 just after you've finished harvesting.) In time, the plants will fill in the bed.

Keeping the asparagus bed free from weeds is an important chore. However, one popular remedy that we do not recommend is the practice of spreading salt between the plants. That may indeed kill weeds, but it can also dry up your asparagus. Furthermore, salt will break down the soil structure and leach to other crops.

Asparagus plants are very hardy once established and are rarely bothered by insects or disease. Although asparagus beetles and Japanese beetles may damage some spears, you probably won't need pesticides to keep them in check.

Rust is a common disease. Choose rust-resistant varieties to avoid problems.

Harvesting

If you started your bed from crowns, you should be able to harvest lightly for a week or two in the spring of the second year. The third year should bring a moderate harvest for 3 or 4 weeks and then heavy picking for 6 weeks or more every year thereafter. If you live in the South or any region where summer nights stay warm (above 70°F), wait an extra year to begin harvesting so the plants can build up energy reserves before you cut the spears.

Always gauge the length of your harvest by the previous season's growth. Select only those spears that are thicker than a pencil; anything thinner should be allowed to grow into ferns. Cut or snap off the eligible spears at or just below ground level when they are not more than 6 to 8 inches tall. If they're tough to snap, they'll be tough to eat.

When the emerging spears get progressively thinner, it's time to stop harvesting.

Tips for Digging an Asparagus Trench

Many years ago, Bob "Victory Garden" Thomson learned a valuable lesson from his father while preparing an asparagus patch.

"We were to dig a neat, straight-sided trench, 12 inches wide and 15 inches deep," he recalls, "using strings to keep it in proper alignment. To a lad of nine or ten, digging that trench looked like a monumental task — and it was a big job all right.

"I started digging right in the middle, moving down the proposed trench, scraping off an inch or two of soil at a time and tossing it off to one side. I made good progress until I hit hard soil about 5 inches down that I simply couldn't budge. But it wasn't long before my father's trench was finished — the sides straight up and down and the bottom flat as a pancake. He generously suggested that I just watch him for a while.

"I soon realized that while I had scraped off the loose topsoil along the top of the entire trench, he had gone down to the 15-inch depth right away, clearing an area about 3 feet long and a foot wide. This was tough going, but now he could stand in the trench and use his sharp heavy spade to slice away. As the soil fell back into the excavated trench, he would easily scoop it out and toss it to the side. The process was simple, it was done with an easy rhythm, and within half an hour the trench was completed.

"It was, in all honesty, quite a few years down the road before I could do the job as well, but I had learned a valuable lesson.

"It's almost always tempting to shortcut a given task, and with a short-term crop you can even appear to get away with it — at least for a time. But with a crop like asparagus, where the bed can last a lifetime if it's properly prepared and cared for, the few hours of hard work spent digging and back-filling the trenches will be but a fond memory — every time you enjoy a plate of tender spears."

Asparagus Sources

*Brock (seeds) 6, 35, 105
*Jersey Giant (crowns) 7
Martha (seeds and crowns) 16, 64, 74
Mary (seeds and crowns) 37, 40, 42
Viking (seeds) 39, 128

*hybrid

Harvest spears that are thicker than a pencil. Cut or snap them off at or just below ground level when they are 6 to 8 inches tall.

Beans

With care, beans can produce for many weeks. Note the blossoms and ready-to-pick beans on the same plant above.

Entire cookbooks have been devoted to beans, and there are as many tempting recipes as there are cooks with imagination — and almost as many varieties of beans. Perhaps that's the reason two-thirds of all gardeners raise beans, and many raise all three basic types: snap, shell, and dried.

For eating fresh in early summer, crispy snap beans — green, purple (they turn green when cooked), and yellow wax — are a hands-down favorite. Later in the season, plump buttery shell beans such as limas and Southern peas are sure winners. Dried beans are a no-fuss crop, harvested late and allowed to dry for cooking up into hearty soups and chilies in the winter.

Although you harvest each of these different types of beans at different stages of their development, many of the soil preparation, planting, and maintenance techniques are the same, no matter what variety you plant. Many beans such as soybeans and limas are just as tasty to eat at the green shell stage as at the dried stage. You can find varieties of beans that grow as a bush crop or that climb up space-saving poles and trellises. So no matter what you like to eat or how much space you have in your garden, we think you will find a bean variety — or several — just right for you.

Planning

Whether you decide to plant snap, shell, or dried beans, you'll find beans easy to grow. Although there are some differences among them, particularly when it comes to harvesting, all three types of beans have the same requirements of warm soil and a light application of fertilizer. They are all bothered by the same pests. Here are several tips to help you raise better, higher-yielding beans.

First, ignore the rules and plant a few seeds early. Beans are a warm-season crop, and the common advice over the years has been to wait until the soil temperature is above 60°F before planting — that's usually just after the last expected spring frost. Germination is lower in the cool, moist soils of a rainy spring. However, gambling a handful of seeds on an extra-early row may bring that first harvest of fresh pods 7 to 10 days earlier. Select the driest part of your garden and plant seeds 2 weeks before the last frost date.

It's hard to predict the weather, but many earlier-than-usual plantings pay off handsomely. Early crops are often less likely to be bothered by insects. If the plantings are late, on the other hand, the plants blossom in high temperatures (above 80°F), causing some blossoms to drop and reducing overall yields.

Preparation

Gardeners often think of beans as "light feeders" when it comes to nitrogen. Although nitrogen is important for their good growth, beans are legumes and can "fix" nitrogen from the air (change it into a form that plants can use) through the action of *Rhizobium* bacteria that live in nodules on their roots. This means that a nitrogen-rich soil is not necessary for a thriving bean crop.

Coating your bean seeds before planting with an inoculant containing the proper type of *Rhizobium* will insure that the bacteria are present in the soil. Although these bacteria may be in the soil already,

the cost of the inoculant is small and it's probably worth the expense, especially in a new garden where beans have not been grown before. Never inoculate seeds that have been treated with fungicides since they will kill these nitrogen-fixers. (See "Fungicide-treated Seed," page 27.)

There is little benefit in adding inoculant and fertilizing heavily at the same time, but light doses of nitrogen, especially on sandy soils that leach nutrients quickly, should not interfere much with the formation of *Rhizobium*-containing nodules on the roots and may improve growth. The recommended application of fertilizer is 1½ pounds of 5-10-10 or equivalent per 100 square feet, mixed in before planting.

Many gardeners use fertilizers to meet most of the beans' nitrogen needs rather than depending on *Rhizobium* bacteria. A high-nitrogen, slow-release commercial fertilizer applied a week or so before planting guarantees that some nitrogen is available for plants as soon as they need it. Then it's available slowly throughout the season. However, too much nitrogen has been shown to promote excessive vegetation and delay pod production.

Though some gardeners might recommend it, don't soak the seeds before planting to speed germination. Too often seeds will crack and germinate poorly.

Trellises, supports, and tepees should be set up before planting. Supports are necessary with pole bean varieties. Stakes and strings or coated wires can also be used with bush snap beans to improve yields and make harvesting easier.

Planting

The optimum spacing for bush snap bean plants is 3 to 4 inches in a single row with 18 inches between rows. The plants fill in the open areas quickly, weeds are blocked out, and the yields are high. Planting three or four close single rows in 3- or 4-foot-wide beds results in smaller harvests because only the plants on the outside

Leave about 18 inches between your bean rows *(top right)* to make early-season weeding easy; the plants will fill the open area quickly *(bottom right)*.

would yield well. However, if you live in a dry climate you might consider wide-row planting. Since the seeds are commonly 2 or 3 inches apart in all directions, the young seedlings manage to block sun from the soil around them after just 1 or 2 weeks of growth. Shading the soil this way brings the same benefits as mulching: less water is lost to evaporation and weeds are kept in check.

Essentials

Planning

❧ All beans, except cool-weather fava beans, are sensitive to frost and cold soil temperatures. Plant your main crop when the soil is warm and all danger of frost is past.

❧ Plant fava beans 2 to 3 weeks before the last spring frost date. On the West Coast, plant fava beans in the fall or late winter.

❧ In the far North, grow large late-maturing lima beans by starting seeds in individual pots about 3 weeks before the average last spring frost date.

❧ Rotate the location of your bean crops from year to year to discourage disease.

Preparation

❧ Beans grow well in a wide range of soils without fertilizer. Where fertility is low, it's advisable to mix a complete fertilizer into the top 3 or 4 inches of soil before planting.

❧ Set up trellises or pole tepees before planting climbing beans.

Planting

❧ See the chart on page 91, Planting Guide for Beans, for spacing and seeding rates. Generally, planting extra seeds and thinning out plants to the recommended spacing is best.

Care

❧ Mulch snap and dried beans to help keep the soil cool and retain moisture.

❧ Mexican bean beetles (page 279) and Japanese beetles (page 278) are perhaps the most worrisome insect pests. Aphids (page 276), leafhoppers (page 279), and seed corn maggots (page 280) may appear.

❧ Possible diseases include anthracnose (page 282), bacterial blight (page 282), nematodes (page 285), powdery mildew (page 286), viruses (page 287), and white mold (page 287).

Harvesting

❧ Snap beans: Pods should be firm and crisp at harvest; the seeds inside should be undeveloped or very small. Hold stem with one hand and pod with other to avoid pulling off branches that will produce later pickings. Pick all pods to keep plants productive.

❧ Shell beans: Pick these varieties when the pods change color and the beans inside are fully formed but not dried out. Pods should be plump, firm, and young. Quality declines if you leave them on the plant too long. They can be kept in the refrigerator for a few days before cooking if necessary.

❧ Dried beans: Let the pods get as dry as possible in the garden. Before cold weather hits or when plants have turned brown and lost most of their leaves, pick all the dry pods (or pull the plants up if more drying time is needed) and store. Pods, when thoroughly dry, will split readily, making seeds easy to remove. Store dry beans in tight-lidded jars or cans in a dry, cool place.

Building a Sturdy Pole Bean Trellis

National Gardening Association member David Cavagnaro grows his beans in Santa Rosa, California, close enough to the Pacific coast so that ocean winds sometimes threaten to topple a bean trellis laden with heavy vines and pods.

Over the past 7 years, David has grown and evaluated over 200 varieties of beans. He has found that the strongest structure to support a massive pole bean vine is a "conical tepee."

David's bean tepees are much bigger and tougher than the commonly seen ones that have only three or four poles driven a few inches into the ground and lashed together at the top. He makes his tepees with twelve poles that are 10 to 15 feet long. While most gardeners use saplings to build their tepees, David makes ingenious use of reed grass, which is prevalent in his area. (Reed grass is similar to bamboo: straight and round and perhaps ⅓ inch or 1 inch in diameter.) You can save reed-grass poles from year to year. If you don't have reed grass in your area, any kind of bamboo or sturdy pole should work.

Each tepee takes about 10 minutes to put together at planting time. First, set up the 12 poles in a tepee that's about 6 or 8 feet in diameter. David recommends large, walk-in tepees with a gap between two poles just big enough to allow you to wiggle through at harvest time to get the pods from inside.

To provide plenty of support for the pole bean vines, tie a string at the bottom of the tepee, looped around each pole. Then tie another loop up near the top. Between those two strings tie two longitudinal strings between pairs of poles. The strings are 3 or 4 inches apart to correspond with the seed spacing of the plants. Plant one seed near each string. If you have a lot of seeds, plant two in each location and later thin to one.

With this ingenious pole tepee, you can cut the strings and slide the poles out at the end of the season. This leaves a mass of string and vines for the compost pile and a set of poles that can be used next season.

David Cavagnaro's sturdy conical tepees allow pole beans to be harvested from the inside and the outside.

Care

Watch for the Mexican bean beetle. Check the underside of the bean leaves regularly for clusters of yellow eggs ⅓ inch long. They will hatch into ⅓-inch-long yellow grubs that mature into adult beetles. These pests can multiply tremendously during the summer if you don't kill them.

Bean diseases don't generally ruin a backyard harvest, but it's worth taking some precautions. Don't work among wet bean plants — you'll spread disease organisms from plant to plant. Remove all bean debris from the garden when the crop is finished. This will reduce the threat from bean diseases and eliminate breeding grounds for some insects.

Beans (especially snap) are susceptible to a condition called bald-heading, which causes plants to emerge from the ground only to arrest growth and not put out any leaves. It is caused by injury to the seeds when they are picked, stored, or handled. Unfortunately, there isn't much you can do about it.

Snap Beans

Succession plantings of bush snap beans will provide a longer, easier-to-manage harvest. Most gardeners count days or weeks to time their succession plantings, but you can also take your cue from the size of the last-planted bean row. Try waiting until the second level of leaves forms on the plants, then sow your next row. You can plant seven or eight rows each season in most climates.

Snap beans come in both pole and bush varieties. To save space in small gardens, late bush beans can be planted as soon as early-season crops, such as peas, turnip greens, or scallions, are harvested. Plant bean seeds immediately after pulling out or thoroughly spading in the debris of the old crop, but add dehydrated manure or other fertilizer with nitrogen because decomposing roots and crop residues can temporarily tie up the nitrogen supply in the soil.

Side-dressing will extend the harvest of pole beans. One planting of a vigorous climbing variety of snap bean should last all season if properly tended, though bearing will usually begin later than with bush types. Harvest all pods before seeds begin to bulge in the pod and side-dress with a balanced fertilizer, such as 5-10-10 or dehydrated animal manure, every 3 or 4 weeks to assure continued production. A tablespoon of commercial fertilizer per plant (or a generous scoop of manure) is a good guide for side-dressing amounts. Pole beans, at least those pods maturing on the upper portion of a trellis or bean tepee, may even live through the first fall frost, while bush beans growing close to the ground will be killed.

To increase yields and simplify harvesting of your snap beans, try supporting the plants with a trellis system. Use 3-foot stakes and set strands of light string or coated wire 8 inches apart.

To improve yields and make harvesting of bush snap beans easier, support the plants with 3-foot stakes and light string or coated wire. Run the wire close to the plant stalks when the plants are a foot high. The first wire should be 8 inches above the ground. As the plants grow, add strands of wire 8 inches apart. The system promotes upright growth and keeps branches from sagging from winds, heavy rains, or a heavy crop of pods.

For the best snap beans, harvest them when they are young and tender, before the seeds inside have a chance to develop.

Shell Beans: Limas, Southern Peas, and Soybeans

The growing requirements of shell beans are similar to those of snap beans. As with snap beans, you can find both bush and pole varieties of shell beans. A critical difference is that shell beans tend to need higher soil temperatures for germination. Also, shell beans have a longer growing season (60 to 80 days, depending on the variety), since the beans are harvested when the pods are fully mature but not dried out. Then you "shell" out the beans and eat them fresh.

Many shell bean varieties can be left to dry and harvested as dried beans. French

Here's a very productive row of *Fordhook 242* lima beans nearing the harvest point. Harvest shell beans when the pods are bright green, plump, and fresh looking.

Horticultural beans, soybeans, and lima beans are frequently raised by gardeners as both shell beans and dried beans.

Most gardeners, however, don't bother to let their lima beans dry. The special flavor of freshly shelled and cooked lima beans — so different from the starchy, mealy beans you buy at the store — delights thousands of devotees in all regions of the country.

Though gardeners are often impatient for the first lima bean pods to mature, patience is the order of the day near planting time. For good germination of lima bean seeds, soil temperatures must be 65° to 75°F, warmer than for snap beans. If the soil temperature is below 60°F, few seeds will come up.

To assure warm soil, plant at least 2 weeks after the average last spring frost date in your area. If you don't plan to use an inoculant, purchase seed pretreated with a fungicide or coat the seeds yourself with a recommended fungicide powder at planting time to help protect germinating seeds from fungal attacks in case the soil cools down from rains or unexpected low temperatures.

Because lima beans need a longer growing season than snap beans, some gardeners, particularly in northern states, sow their seeds in pots indoors and then set the plants in the garden when the soil warms up and the plants are 4 to 5 inches tall.

Even in central and southern states, starting at least a few plants indoors is a kind of insurance that some plants will bloom before summer temperatures get too high. Lima bean blossoms will often abort on sunny days with temperatures in the low 90s if the plants are not heavily watered.

Short-season gardeners can sow seeds a bit earlier than usual on beds raised 6 to 8 inches; soil temperatures can often be 4 or 5 degrees warmer in raised beds.

Bush varieties are better for gardeners with short seasons. Small-seeded lima beans are earlier than the big-seeded kinds. *Henderson Bush Lima, Baby Bush,*

Thorogreen Early Bush Lima, and *Jackson Wonder* are bush types that yield within 75 days of planting.

Pole limas should be side-dressed with a balanced fertilizer, such as 10-10-10 or dehydrated manure, every 3 or 4 weeks. Lima beans, especially the pole types, which require more growing time and bear larger beans over a longer period, need more nitrogen and other basic nutrients than snap beans.

Harvest shell beans when the pods are plump but still bright green and fresh looking; the beans should be tender and not dried out or too starchy.

Despite their name, Southern peas are a member of the shell bean family. If you have a climate suitable for lima beans, you can grow Southern peas. They'll do especially well where the summers are long and hot, and will yield well on poor soils because, of all the beans, they produce the most nitrogen via bacterial fixation on root nodules.

Southern peas (among them the famous California black-eyed pea) go by many different — and colorful — names, such as *Blue Goose, Six Weeks Browneye, Mississippi Silver,* and *Knuckle Purple Hull.* Some northerners know Southern peas as cowpeas because they've been planted as forage crops; but in the South where they are more of a fixture in backyard gardens, you can call them field peas, crowders, or cream peas.

New Southern pea varieties such as *Colossus* and *Queen Anne* are noted for productivity, compact growth, and flavor. Traditional favorites such as *Purple Hull Pinkeye* still yield well and have good disease resistance. Like other types of beans, some varieties will vine extensively, making them good candidates for growing on poles or trellises. Southern peas don't have tendrils, so if you choose a vining variety for trellising, you'll have to tie the vines to the structure.

Although you can grow Southern peas to the dried stage, many people harvest earlier at the shelling stage. Watch the color of the pods — when it changes (from deep green to yellow, red, brown, etc., depending on variety), it's time to harvest. The peas inside should still be soft and ready for cooking.

Soybeans are a versatile member of the shell bean family. They will probably attract converts with the recent introduction of newer, more flavorful varieties developed for harvesting in the fresh, green shelling stage. Though highly rated for protein and vitamin A content, soybeans have been a frustrating crop for many gardeners because of their long growing season, limited variety selection, bland flavor, and lengthy cooking time.

Now, flavorful soybeans can be harvested just 2 months after the bean plants emerge. *Envy* and *Butterbeans* are two recent introductions that are adapted to a wide growing area.

Plant soybeans at the same time as snap beans — just after the last spring frost dates. If you have a long season, you can plant a second crop 10 to 14 days later or save seeds to fill in areas of the garden that become bare. Like other beans, soys have a low nitrogen requirement, but you may have to add more phosphorus and potassium.

Recommended Bean Varieties

If you haven't already settled on your favorite bean varieties, you might want to try some of the National Gardening Association favorites. These beans are all proven high yielders and they taste wonderful.

Blue Lake Pole (Bush) Bean: A green snap bean noted for retaining excellent flavor and texture as a frozen bean. These beans tend to mature all at the same time unless you use succession plantings.

Christmas Lima: This large bean lima is vigorous, very beautiful, and one of the more productive large-lima types. You can eat it green shelled or dry.

Jacob's Cattle Bean (Trout, Dalmatian): An heirloom bush dried bean noted for excellence in baked beans. Seeds are pure white with maroon splashes. Named after the streaked and striped markings of the cattle raised by Jacob in the biblical story.

Kentucky Wonder Pole Bean: A standard with many gardeners, especially in central and southern states. Yields a large harvest of fine-tasting fresh green beans; flavor and crispness remain even when pods get large.

Queen Anne Blackeye Pea: A bush variety of Southern pea; very productive and good for canning or freezing.

Romano Bean: Some say this is the tastiest bean of all, no matter whether they are harvested as snap beans, shell beans, or dry beans. This is a seed you can get almost anywhere. It is extremely prolific and the pole varieties produce for a long period.

Scarlet Runner Bean: This runner bean is one of the biggest beans you can grow and is a good soup bean. When cooked they swell up to an inch in diameter — quite meaty and delicious.

Vermont Cranberry Bean: An early and very popular shelling bean; the pods hold five or six large, flavorful beans. The beans are also good dried.

Shell beans need a longer growing season than snap beans because they are harvested when the pods are fully mature. The *Cranberry* shell bean at left is prolific and flavorful.

Regional Notes

East and South

Saving your own bean seeds may result in diseased crops. Bacterial blight (signs are bright yellow or brown spots on the pods) is carried by seeds from the previous crop. East of the Mississippi, weather conditions for the spread of this disease — plenty of moisture and high humidity — are often favorable. Don't rely totally on saved seeds; purchase some commercial seed which is usually grown in dry climates of the West.

West

In many mild-winter areas of the West (lowest winter temperature in the mid-20s), the *Scarlet Runner* bean can be grown as a perennial. Cut the plant back in late fall and cover it well with a mulch. The vines are quite vigorous, and will require a very sturdy trellis.

Bean Sources

Baby Bush 5, 17
Blue Goose 23, 98, 104
Blue Lake Pole or **Bush** 75, 98
Butterbeans 20, 51
Christmas Lima 23, 75, 98
Colossus 17, 98, 104
Envy 20, 45
Fordhook 242 Lima 23, 43
Henderson Bush Lima 17, 23, 104
Jackson Wonder 17, 23, 104
Jacob's Cattle (Trout, Dalmatian) 20, 45, 71
Kentucky Wonder Pole 71, 75, 98
Knuckle Purple Hull 17, 23, 98, 104
Low's Champion 20
Maine Yellow Eye 20
Purple Hull Pinkeye 17, 23, 98, 104
Queen Anne Blackeye Pea 23, 104
Red Kidney 17, 75
Romano 23, 75
Scarlet Runner 23, 45, 71
Six Weeks Browneye 98, 104
Soldier 20, 71, 75
Sulphur (Taratsumara azufrado) 65
Thorogreen Early Bush Lima 17, 104
Vermont Cranberry 45, 75

If you're going in heavily for soybeans, use the bacteria inoculant specific to soybeans, *Rhizobium japonica,* to insure that nitrogen fixing can occur on root nodules.

To harvest soybeans in the green shelling stage, look for plump pods containing fully formed seeds. Begin to harvest when the pods start to lose their bright green color. They should average two or three beans per pod.

After picking the fuzzy soybean pods, put them in a saucepan, cover with water, and boil until some pods begin to open (as little as 3 minutes). Put a pod under cold water to cool it, then squeeze it. If the beans pop out easily, the pods are ready for shelling. Shell out all the beans into a colander or strainer and cool them under running cold water. They are now ready to be cooked.

Dried Beans

For many gardeners, the joy of growing dried beans might be that there's no harvest to keep up with during the summer. Watering in a dry spell or watching for insect or disease signs every few days is the routine instead.

Some gardeners prefer bush varieties of dried beans because they require less labor than the pole types. Plant when the ground temperature warms to 60°F or more. If you have ample garden space, keep 4 to 5 feet between bean rows to make cultivation easier; some varieties will spread a foot or more to each side. Plant seeds an inch deep, 4 to 6 inches apart.

To save space, some gardeners plant bush dry beans between rows of sweet corn. After the corn is harvested, cut down the cornstalks. The beans will be ready to harvest, dry in the pod, after several more weeks.

You can let your bean pods dry until the leaves of the plant drop off and begin harvesting when there's just one or two green pods to ten dry ones. Then let them dry for a few weeks in a dry place with good air circulation. Put the pods in bags and walk on them to separate out the beans. To be sure the beans are dry enough to store, let them dry another week or two. Putting all the beans in the freezer for 36 hours will kill any bean weevils that could damage the crop in storage. The beans might collect some moisture in the freezer, so it's a good idea to give them extra drying time before packing them away in glass jars.

To test for dryness, put a few beans in a tightly capped glass jar and set it in the sun. If no drops of moisture appear inside, the beans are dry. Color-splashed beans should not be left out in sunlight as the colors will fade.

Planting Guide for Beans

Type	Pounds of seed per 50-ft. single row	Depth of planting (inches)	Spacing between rows (inches)	Spacing in rows (inches)		Days to first harvest
				Seeds	Plants	
Snap						
Bush	¼–½	1–1½	18–30	1–2	2–4	50–60
Pole	¼–½	1–1½	24–48	3–6	4–8	60–70
Shell						
Lima, bush	¼–½	1–1½	18–30	2–4	4–8	65–75
Lima, pole	¼–½	1–1½	36–48	3–6	6–8	70–90
Southern peas	¼–½	1–1½	30–54	2–4	2–4	55–80
Fava beans	½–1	1½–2½	24–30	2–4	4–6	65–110
Soybeans	¼–½	1–1¼	15–30	2–3	2–3	60–100
Dried						
Bush	¼–½	1–1½	18–30	1–2	2–4	71–102
Pole	¼–½	1–1½	24–48	3–6	4–8	81–112

Beets

Golden beets *(left)* have the same fine taste as red varieties *(above)*, but have a lower germination rate and should be sown more thickly.

Beets are a vegetable for all seasons. Fast-growing, they do best in cool, moist weather, and so are a two-crop-a-year vegetable in most areas. They are easily frozen, canned, pickled, or stored for year-round eating.

Nutritionally, beet greens are even better than the delicious roots. With half the calories, cooked greens provide more vitamin A, vitamin B_1, vitamin B_2, vitamin C, calcium and iron than beet roots. One nice thing about greens is that they can be grown without the sometimes painstaking task of thinning required for growing good roots. Surplus beet greens can be frozen like spinach and enjoyed throughout the year.

There are many beet varieties available. Two varieties, *Golden* and *Albino White*, are ideal for the cook who dreads the inevitable red sink, cutting board, and countertops that follow preparation of ordinary beets. *Albino White* and *Golden* are also good if you want to add the familiar beet flavor to a dish but don't want to turn the rest of the ingredients red. One drawback of these non-red varieties is a somewhat low germination rate, but that can be overcome with closer plantings. Before you get too carried away, though, remember that a dish like borscht just wouldn't be itself if it weren't bright red. So do plant traditional red varieties as well.

Planning

There are as many different varieties of beets as there are uses — each offering the gardener or cook a unique trait for different purposes. If you freeze or can beets, you might try *Cylindra* and *Formanova*, cylindrical beets up to 8 inches long that can be grown closer together than regular beets. Because of their shape, cylindrical beets yield more slices per beet than round varieties and make slicing easier.

If you are more interested in flavor than uniformity, try *Lutz Green Leaf* (also known as *Winter Keeper* and *Long Season*). Though rough in appearance and irregular in shape, its flavor remains sweet no matter how large the root. (With enough space, moisture, and food, the *Lutz* beet can reach volleyball size.)

Sweetheart, another flavorful variety, boasts the genetic parentage of a sugar beet. It's nothing much to look at, but it tastes extra sweet. The smaller and better-looking *Little Ball* is a sweet, tasty beet that does best when planted in early spring and fall.

Cylindrical varieties are an option for cooks who prefer uniform slices. They yield more slices per beet and can be grown closer together than regular varieties.

Most varieties grown for cultivation ease are not extraordinary in flavor. *Ruby Queen* is grown commercially for its large yields in a short season, but it is of average flavor. Most varieties that claim early maturity, such as *Red Ace Hybrid*, are not worth the loss in flavor since they mature only 5 to 10 days sooner than other, tastier beets.

If the greens excite you more than the beet roots, try *Green Top Bunching*. Its leaves are greener than those of other varieties, but the root is not as good for eating. *Crosby Green Top* and *Lutz Green Leaf* are two other often-recommended varieties for good greens.

Preparation

Beets thrive in humus-rich soil with a pH close to 7.0. An acid soil (pH below 6.0) is often the culprit when a crop seems stunted and slow-growing, even when other conditions are perfect and the soil is fertile.

Phosphorus and potassium are two key nutrients essential to good beet yields. If you haven't done a soil test recently, add 2 to 4 inches of well-aged manure over the planting area and work it deeply into the soil to be sure the crop gets these essential nutrients. Do not use fresh manure. Root crops fertilized with fresh manures tend to develop rough, prongy side shoots and sometimes lush top growth at the expense of the roots. If aged manure is not available, work 3 to 4 cups of 5-10-10 or equivalent fertilizer per 20 feet of row into the top 4 to 6 inches of soil before planting.

While you're adding manure, compost, or fertilizer to the planting area, remove any hunks of wood, bark, clods, or sizable rocks; these obstacles could cause misshapen roots.

Planting

For a single row of beets, plant seeds about ½ inch deep and 1 inch apart. Allow 18 to 24 inches for a walkway between single rows or beds. To conserve space, you can also put two single rows together, about 8 inches apart, with the walkway between double rows.

Keep the soil moist throughout the germination period. Seedlings will emerge in about 2 weeks in 50°F soil temperatures; 6 days at 68°F.

In areas with low rainfall, consider planting a band of seeds in a 6- to 8-inch-wide furrow. Dig the furrow 2 to 3 inches deep, level the area, soak it well, and let the water sink in for a few minutes. Then scatter the seed as close to 1 inch apart as you can, tamp the seeds gently, and cover with about ½ inch of soil. The shallow furrow should catch a bit more rainwater and retain more moisture since it is out of the wind.

If you are planting a fall crop for winter storage (or simply because fall plantings fare better in your area), you may run into a problem with germination due to hot, dry weather. You can avoid this dilemma by soaking the seeds before planting, saturating the soil in the furrow before planting, and keeping the soil covering the seeds damp until the seedlings emerge.

Soak the seeds for at least 24 hours, swishing them around in the container several times to break up air bubbles that cling to the seed coat. The seeds will not germinate until this coat is thoroughly saturated.

Care

Each so-called beet seed is actually a dried fruit containing several seeds enclosed in a tough coating. There may be as many as five or six seeds inside — a puzzle to some new gardeners who swear they placed seeds exactly 1 inch apart.

Because the interior seeds may all sprout, thinning the crop is a standard step. Pulling out the seedlings disturbs the other plants, so most gardeners take the time to get down on their knees and pinch off competing seedlings when they are 1 or 2 inches tall, leaving plants 1½ to 2 inches apart. If you'd like to save time, try rake-

Essentials

Planning

❧ *For sweet, tender beets grow the plants in cool, moist weather.*

❧ *In the North, plant throughout the spring and in mid- to late summer. Start planting 30 days before your last spring frost date and continue with successive plantings at 3- to 4-week intervals into July, depending on how hot your summer is.*

❧ *In the South, plant in the fall and early spring.*

❧ *Beet roots are ready to harvest in 45 to 65 days; greens can be harvested as soon as they are large enough to eat.*

Preparation

❧ *Work aged manure or compost into the top 8 inches of the soil. If manure is not available, mix 3 to 4 cups of a general fertilizer, such as 5-10-10 or its equivalent, 4 to 6 inches deep for every 20 feet of row.*

Planting

❧ *Sow seeds ½ inch deep (1 to 1½ inches in hot weather), 1 inch apart.*

❧ *In dry climates, plant in a well-soaked, 6- to 8-inch-wide furrow about 3 inches deep. Cover seeds with ½ to ¾ inch of soil.*

❧ *For greens only, sow seeds ½ inch apart in all directions. No thinning is necessary.*

Care

❧ *Thin seedlings to stand 1½ to 2 inches apart 10 to 14 days after emergence. A month later thin plants to about 4 inches apart. Eat thinnings for greens.*

❧ *If growth is slow, side-dress with a high nitrogen fertilizer when the beets are half grown. Apply 2 cups of 10-10-10 or its equivalent per 20 feet of row and water it in well.*

❧ *Watch for the larvae of the leaf miner (page 279), which feed within the leaves. Leafhoppers (page 279), Mexican bean beetles (page 279), and wireworms (page 281) may appear. Also, watch for mice and other rodents (page 72) that nibble on roots above the soil line.*

Harvesting

❧ *For greens, pick entire plants when leaves are 4 to 6 inches long.*

❧ *Beet roots generally reach most tender size (between golf ball and tennis ball dimensions) in 40 to 50 days.*

❧ *Harvest late fall beets for the root cellar after a short dry spell. Let the beets dry in the sun for a few hours, top them leaving 2 inches of stem (roots intact), and store only solid, unblemished beets. They'll keep best at 32° to 35°F and 95 percent humidity. Don't let beets freeze.*

Regional Notes

West and Southwest

Gardeners in these areas may have trouble with curly top virus, spread among beet plants by leafhoppers (page 279). The most noticeable signs of the virus diseases are stunted plants and leaf edges that curl up and feel brittle.

Southwest soils may lack boron, which results in beet roots with bitter black spots. Keep the soil pH in the 6.0 to 7.0 range and provide adequate moisture and routine additions of organic matter. If necessary, add boron to the soil: mix household borax with water (1 tablespoon to about 12 quarts of water per 100 feet of row).

thinning the seedlings when they are about ½ inch high; because seedlings sprout so close together, a little hand thinning might still be necessary.

About a month after the initial thinning, beets will need a second thinning, only this time there should be plenty of delectable greens and some small, tasty roots to cook afterward. Pull plants up completely to leave remaining beets about 4 inches apart. A little closer spacing is all right if you have the ingredients beets need: correct soil pH, constant moisture, and humus-rich soil.

If you're growing beets strictly for greens, they won't need thinning. Sow seeds about ½ inch apart in a row or bed and start harvesting them when they are eating size.

Beets need plenty of water through the growing season, too, especially when the roots are forming rapidly. If the soil dries

Far right: **If you grow beets strictly for greens, they won't need thinning. Beet greens with small bulbs are all the better for cooking.**

Each beet seed is actually a dried fruit containing several seeds. Because all these interior seeds may sprout, thinning is a standard step. Thin early by hand when seedlings are 1 or 2 inches high, leaving plants 1½ to 2 inches apart.

out appreciably, expect some stringy fibers through the beet; they'll be quite apparent when the beets are sliced. Water if the top few inches of soil are dry. Beets are shallow-rooted, so in hot climates an organic mulch 2 to 3 inches thick will help conserve soil moisture.

Harvesting

You can harvest beets for the roots any time you think they are large enough. After 40 to 50 days most varieties will be about 1½ inches in diameter and tender, but they'll still be tasty if left to grow 1 or 2 weeks more to reach full size. If conditions are right (cool weather, moist soil), beets can be left in the ground past maturity and still retain their flavor.

If you store beets in a root cellar, harvest in late fall, but before the ground freezes. If you can, pull the roots after a short dry spell; brush off the soil gently, cut the tops off, leaving about 2 inches of stem, and dry them in the sun for a few hours. As with other vegetables, set aside any bruised, nicked, or damaged beets for immediate kitchen use.

Beets keep best in a dark area at 32° to 35°F and 95 percent humidity. If you don't have a root cellar, double-bag them in plastic bags closed with a twist tie. Punch some airholes into each bag and put the bags in a cold, but not freezing, place.

Where the winters are mild, the crop can be kept in the ground. Insulate the beet row with a layer of mulch about 8 inches thick and extending 1 foot on either side of the row to prevent the ground from freezing. Pull beets as needed. They won't last very long, so use them within a couple of days of harvesting.

100 Beets per Square Yard

This method will yield an abundant harvest of beets in just 1 square yard.

1. Rake a well-prepared square-yard area smooth and poke twenty-five equidistant holes in an 18-inch block. Plant one block and sow others at 5- to 10-day intervals. Do not use raised beds, as plants on the edge will suffer from moisture stress and soil loss in weeding.

2. Put two seeds ½ inch deep in each hole and cover with soil. Tamp down over the block. Keep the area moist until plants emerge.

3. When the seedlings are 2 inches tall, pinch out all but the strongest plant at each hole.

4. Weed by hand or with a narrow-bladed hoe.

5. When the beets are golf ball size, start harvesting every other one. Let the remaining beets get larger.

Beet Sources

Albino White 12, 39
Crosby Green Top 16
Cylindra 18, 29, 62
Early Wonder 11, 12, 29
Formanova 25, 39, 46
Golden 12, 29
Green Top Bunching 39
Little Ball 39, 43, 63
Lutz Green Leaf (Winter Keeper, Long Season) 18, 39, 62
***Pacemaker II** 33, 39, 74
***Red Ace Hybrid** 12, 18, 25
Ruby Queen 12, 16, 29, 43
Sweetheart 11, 20

***hybrid**

Broccoli

Romanesco (above) is an old-time type of broccoli. For regular broccoli heads as large and luscious as the one at left, variety considerations are important.

Broccoli is becoming more and more popular with home gardeners — 53 percent more gardening households have added it to their gardens in the last few years — for good reason. It is rich in vitamins C and A and it has been found to contain cancer-preventing substances. Broccoli is also versatile in the kitchen; it has fine flavor raw or cooked and it's one of the easiest vegetables to freeze.

With careful timing you can get months of continual broccoli harvest. If your soil is rich in nutrients, you can set broccoli plants as little as 6 inches apart. So it's an excellent choice for gardeners with little space.

Planning

Broccoli loves cool weather, so it's safest to plan for a fall harvest. To time your fall planting, work backward from the average first fall frost date. If you start the crop in flats for later transplanting, try to plant your seeds about 100 days before the frost date. If you direct-seed, do it about 85 days before the frost date.

Direct seeding is best for a fall crop. The plants are usually more vigorous since they can quickly develop a deep taproot. There's no pot or flat to constrict them, no transplant shock when you set them out. That extra vigor translates into a better yield.

In some cases, setting out transplants is better than direct seeding. It depends on whether you are planting for a spring or fall crop and what your climate is like. Generally, transplants are a good idea for a spring crop. You can set the transplants out early so they mature while the spring temperatures are still cool. However, in the far northern states where summers are cool, you can sow seeds directly, starting about May 15.

Gardeners who buy the 6- or 12-plant starter flats at a nursery or garden center won't have a wide choice, if any, of broccoli varieties. However, if a choice is available, selecting the right variety for your garden — and your kitchen — has a lot to do with how successful you'll be.

Here are some instances where variety choice is crucial:

1. If you're planning to freeze broccoli you will want a variety that produces large uniform heads, that is, most or all plants heading up at the same time. This makes for efficient processing. Good choices are *Premium Crop, Green Comet,* and *Green Hornet.*

2. Broccoli heads will flower quickly in warm weather and lose quality, so gardeners in southern or central areas where hot weather is common in late spring might want the earliest-maturing variety possible or a variety known to withstand some

The plastic cones at right will protect early-season broccoli transplants from strong winds by reducing moisture loss and transplant shock. Young transplants can survive a light frost, but should be protected when a hard frost threatens.

heat. Good choices are *Emperor, Bravo,* and *Green Duke* (heat tolerant).

3. Growers wanting a long, steady harvest of the smaller broccoli shoots that form after the main head is harvested should look for a variety noted for good side-shoot production. More and more of the new varieties don't have this trait. Good choices are *De Cicco* and *Calabrese.*

4. If you live in humid or coastal areas, we recommend a variety where the main head protrudes above the foliage, rather than forms under a canopy of leaves. When heads are high, air circulation will dry out the head after a rain, thus reducing the chance of disease. Dusting for insects is also easier. Good choices are *Prominence* and *Paragon.*

Preparation

Broccoli has a relatively high demand for phosphorus and potassium. Before planting apply 3 to 4 pounds of 5-10-10 fertilizer (or its equivalent) to each 100-square-foot area. Rake or rototill it into the top few inches of soil a day or two before planting.

Planting

Sow seeds about ¼ inch deep, 2 to 5 per foot of row, and keep the area moist until seedlings emerge, usually in 5 to 7 days. Later, thin the plants to stand 6 to 18 inches apart.

Seed packets will tell you to space broccoli rows 24 to 36 inches apart and to put another 18 to 36 inches between plants in the row. But if space is limited, try setting your plants closer to one another. Individual head size is smaller as plant density increases, but overall you'll get more broccoli from more plants. Diseases are more likely to erupt during a wet spell with close planting, however, so keep your eyes on the broccoli. (Plants dry off more easily when air can circulate around them.)

Whether you direct-seed or start seeds in flats, growing a fall crop means you'll be starting broccoli in the summer when soil and air temperatures can be very hot.

Broccoli is very sensitive to moisture stress, so water young seedlings well.

If you want a spring crop, it's important to set transplants out early — up to 3 or 4 weeks before the last spring frost date. Protect plants against harsh winds with a windbreak to reduce moisture loss and transplant shock. Young broccoli plants can take a light frost, but you should cover them if a hard frost is predicted.

Care

The tastiest broccoli will come from a fast-growing plant, one that has a steady supply of nitrogen and a good foundation of other key nutrients.

In addition to applying fertilizer before planting day, apply a second helping of nitrogen fertilizer about 3 weeks after transplanting or 5 weeks after direct seeding. Apply about 1 tablespoon of a balanced fertilizer per plant, gently mixing it into the soil 4 to 5 inches from the main stems. Use less if you have rich soil.

Use a thick layer of mulch around the plants to retain water and keep soil tem-

Essentials

Planning

ᶫ *Two crops a year are possible in many areas.*

ᶫ *Start spring transplants indoors 5 to 7 weeks before the last spring frost date, or buy nursery transplants 3 weeks before the last spring frost date.*

ᶫ *Plan to seed fall crops 85 to 100 days before the average first fall frost date.*

ᶫ *Where the weather is warm, select a variety that is bolt resistant.*

Preparation

ᶫ *Add 3 to 4 pounds of 5-10-10 or its equivalent per 100 square feet before planting.*

Planting

ᶫ *Set out transplants 3 to 4 weeks before the last spring frost.*

ᶫ *Set the transplants 6 to 18 inches apart, with 20 to 36 inches between rows, depending on the fertility of the soil.*

ᶫ *Protect transplants from hard frosts with newspapers, plastic cones, paper bags, or baskets. Provide a windbreak to reduce transplant shock and moisture loss.*

ᶫ *For fall crops, direct-seed the broccoli in the garden. Sow the seeds ¼ inch deep, 2 to 4 seeds per foot of row, leaving at least 20 to 36 inches between rows, depending on soil fertility.*

Care

ᶫ *Thin direct-seeded seedlings when they are 4 inches tall. In rich soil, thin seedlings to stand 6 to 12 inches apart. Where soil is of average fertility, thin seedlings 12 to 18 inches apart.*

ᶫ *Side-dress each plant 3 weeks after setting out transplants or 5 weeks after sowing from seed with 1 tablespoon of fertilizer high in nitrogen.*

ᶫ *Flea beetles (page 278) may bother young transplants. Cabbageworms (page 278), cabbage loopers (page 276), and aphids (page 276) can feed on leaves and heads. Root maggots (page 276) may cause sudden wilting.*

ᶫ *Clubroot (page 283) can stunt or wilt plants. Other possible diseases are black rot (page 283), downy mildew (page 284), and white mold (page 287).*

Harvesting

ᶫ *Harvest for peak quality when the buds of the head are firm and tight. If buds start to separate and the yellow petals inside start to show, harvest immediately.*

Purple Head Cauliflower

Purple cauliflower performs well as a fall-maturing crop and is easier to grow than the white variety. When cooked, the heads turn bright green like regular broccoli.

Gardeners who have had trouble growing cauliflower will find the purple head far easier to grow than the white variety.

Early in the season purple cauliflower tastes like broccoli. As cold weather sets in, and particularly after a frost, it has a sweet cauliflower flavor. It's listed under the Latin name *Brassica oleracea botrytis,* the scientific name for cauliflower. Yet the plants are tall and produce delicious side shoots like broccoli as well as large central heads.

The plants are relatively pest resistant and hardy. They don't need blanching like most varieties of cauliflower. The florets are more tender than those of white cauliflower and resemble a very fine-budded broccoli.

Purple head cauliflower takes up to 110 days to mature, so we recommend growing it as a cool-weather fall crop, which also reduces the threat of insect damage.

Harvest the heads just when they're fully developed, but before the buds start to open. Then, in a few weeks, you can get a second harvest of side shoots. When cooked, the heads turn bright green like regular broccoli.

This young broccoli plant has wilted because of maggot damage to its roots. Place mats around the base of transplants to minimize damage by this pest.

peratures down. Make sure the mulch is loose enough to allow rain and irrigation water to seep through.

Water well throughout the season. Try to avoid sprinkler irrigation when heads are maturing because water sitting on the heads can lead to disease. A soaker hose or drip irrigation system is a better method.

Pest problems vary widely around the country, but after growing broccoli a few seasons you'll most likely meet flea beetles, aphids, imported cabbageworms, cabbage loopers and cabbage root maggots. You can use *Bacillus thuringiensis*, a biological control, for imported cabbageworms and cabbage loopers up to 3 days before the harvest. For aphids and certain other pests, use insecticidal soap.

If young plants wilt in the heat of the day, you may have cabbage root maggots, a serious pest in the northern United States. Physical barriers such as mats over the soil near broccoli plants can minimize damage by this pest.

Broccoli Sources

Bravo 20, 39
Calabrese 9, 13, 46
De Cicco 7, 9, 13
Emperor 20
Green Comet 7, 16, 35
Green Duke 1, 9, 35
Green Hornet 39
Paragon 39
Premium Crop 1, 7, 20
Prominence 1

*hybrid

If you're growing a broccoli variety that produces side shoots, harvest the main head 5 to 10 inches down the stalk to promote the growth of large side shoots. Whether harvesting main heads or side shoots, cut them while they are firm — before the buds begin to open and show their yellow flowers.

Harvesting

Broccoli heads are actually immature flower clusters. Cut the large central heads while they're a deep green and the tiny flower buds are tight. If the buds have begun to yellow, you've waited too long. Two or 3 days can make the difference between tender, tasty broccoli and tough, half-open buds.

If you're growing a variety that produces side shoots, harvest the mature central head about 5 to 10 inches down the stalk to encourage production of large side shoots. Keep an eye on those side shoots

and harvest them before the flower buds open, just as you do with the main head.

Even if you've watched carefully for insect problems and dealt quickly with them, we recommend a quick rinsing of broccoli heads just in case. Soak them for 10 minutes or so in a basin of water that has some salt and vinegar added to flush out possible insect debris.

Use broccoli quickly to get the most nutrition from it. Though you can keep broccoli in the refrigerator for about a week, a lot of its vitamin C is lost. Using it fresh in salads or with dips rather than cooked will preserve valuable vitamins.

Brussels Sprouts

One or two healthy plants will provide enough sprouts to fill your basket at harvest time. Removing leaf branches at the proper time will allow sprouts to grow larger.

Although Brussels sprouts are a popular crop in England, gardeners in the United States don't seem to appreciate them — only about one gardener in ten grows them. Perhaps too few gardeners have picked fresh, frost-sweetened sprouts in late fall, cooked them just to the fork-tender stage, and served them with melted butter. They are delicious! And the harvest can extend well into the winter months, making this a rare fresh vegetable for northern growers to enjoy during the cold months.

Brussels sprouts thrive in cool weather. For a good fall crop, the sprouts' maturity needs to coincide with the first few frosty days of the year. If you plant them too early, their flavor may be too strong; too late and heavy frost followed by thaw can make them rot. But plant them to mature just after the first frost and you'll enjoy fresh, crispy Brussels sprouts for months. If you live in the Southeast, a spring crop may also be possible.

Right: Starting from the bottom of the plant, break off the leaf stems when the sprouts are half the size you desire. *Below:* To force the plant to put its energy into maturing the sprouts, you can snip off its terminal bud.

Planning

The key to success with Brussels sprouts lies in timing your planting just right. If you live in the Southeast where the weather is mild throughout the winter, you may be able to have both a spring and a fall crop. In the North, only one crop of Brussels sprouts sweetened by light frosts is possible. The challenge is to extend the harvest as long as possible while preventing the plant — and the surrounding soil — from being hit by a hard freeze.

For a fall crop of Brussels sprouts, count back 90 to 100 days from the date of your first fall frost to determine when to set plants in the ground. If you live in the North and are willing to put extra effort into mulching and protecting the plants from hard freezes, you can time your planting even later. Sow seeds so the plants are two-thirds to three-quarters mature at an average first frost date; add 2 weeks to seed packet maturation dates for your sprouts to allow for the shorter days in the fall. Then count backward to figure out when to start plants.

Occasionally you'll find started Brussels sprout plants in garden centers. Often these plants are available so early in the spring that if you were to set them out, they would mature in the heat of the summer and produce unpleasantly strong-tasting sprouts.

When you purchase seeds, you can select a variety that suits your growing season. *Prince Marvel* needs a long growing season. Dwarf forms, such as *Jade Cross* and *Long Island Improved*, do best in areas with short growing seasons.

For a southern spring crop, select an early variety and plan to seed directly in the garden. You want the plants to grow as quickly as possible so they will mature before the heat of summer sets in. You can plant as early as February, providing extra water and fertilizer, and harvest by May.

Preparation

If you start your own transplants, 4 to 6 weeks before your set-out date, sow your seeds in a light potting mix in small flats with good drainage. Keeps the flats indoors under lights.

In about 2 weeks, when the first two leaves appear, transplant the seedlings into 2½-inch peat pots where they can grow for another 2 to 3 weeks or until the roots are well established.

Before setting out the seedlings, work the soil well and add plenty of aged manure. If manure is not available, work a balanced fertilizer such as 5-10-10 into the soil at the rate of 2 to 4 pounds per 100 square feet. Add the same amount of fertilizer if you are seeding directly.

Planting

When setting out transplants, space them 14 to 24 inches apart. Water well, ensuring that the soil is settled.

Sow seeds directly in the garden to a depth of about ¼ inch, four to five seeds per foot.

Care

Direct-seeded Brussels sprouts will require thinning. When the plants are 4 to 5 inches tall, thin to leave the healthiest plants standing 14 to 24 inches apart.

Water is important for smooth growth. It is crucial for spring crops that must mature fast.

Side-dress once a month with a balanced fertilizer such as 5-10-10 at the rate of 1 to 2 tablespoons per plant.

The plant matures the sprouts from the bottom up. When the bottom sprouts are about half the size you want, break off the leaves under them so they'll have more growing room. Repeat in later weeks as the sprouts higher on the plant grow.

If you live where the growing season is short or if the sprouts have been slow to mature, snip off the terminal bud of the plant to force the plant to stop growing and put its energy into maturing the sprouts already there. Don't do this if your plants have ample time to mature because it will reduce your total yields.

Harvesting

Harvest sprouts from the bottom of the plant up as you need them. The sprouts will keep best if left on the plant. They will taste best if they have been exposed to a few light frosts.

You can continue the harvest well into the cold weather if you protect the plants with mulch. Apply the mulch after the first hard frost but before the ground freezes. We recommend piling very dry hay or straw around the base of the plant. If possible, cover the entire plant.

Then cover the beds with polyethylene weighted down at the ends and sides against the wind. From beneath this cover of plastic and hay, you will be able to harvest cold-sweetened Brussels sprouts even after the rest of the garden is buried in snow. Although the typical late January thaw can finish off the plants, some gardeners using this system can harvest Brussels sprouts as late as March.

Essentials

Planning

❧ *Fall crops are generally more successful than spring crops. Brussels sprouts improve in flavor after a light frost. Date of maturity varies, depending on variety, location, and season. Count backward from the first fall frost date to figure out the best time to start plants.*

❧ *Plan to start seeds in flats or pots 4 to 6 weeks before planting in the garden, or buy nursery transplants if available. You can also sow seeds directly in the garden 4 months before the average first fall frost date.*

Preparation

❧ *To reduce the threat of pests and diseases, plant where other members of the cabbage family have not grown for at least 3 years.*

❧ *Work a balanced fertilizer such as 5-10-10 into the soil at the rate of 2 to 4 pounds per 100 square feet.*

❧ *Raised beds can help avoid the freeze-thaw cycle that rots plants.*

Planting

❧ *In flats sow seeds 1 inch apart. Transplant into 2½-inch pots after the first two true leaves appear. When roots are established, transplant to the garden, spacing the plants 14 to 24 inches apart.*

❧ *To sow seeds directly in the garden, plant 4 to 5 seeds per foot to a depth of ¼ inch.*

Care

❧ *Thin the healthiest direct-seeded plants to stand 14 to 24 inches apart when they are 4 to 5 inches tall.*

❧ *Side-dress once a month during the growing season with a balanced fertilizer.*

❧ *Mulch to retain moisture in summer heat and to control weeds.*

❧ *When sprouts reach half the desired size, remove the lowest leaves on the plant to enable the sprouts to attain maximum size.*

❧ *Watch out for cabbage root maggots (page 276), aphids (page 276), flea beetles (page 278), imported cabbageworms (page 278), and cabbage loopers (page 276).*

❧ *Possible diseases include black rot (page 283), clubroot (page 283), downy mildew (page 284), and white mold (page 287).*

Harvesting

❧ *The best harvest is after a fall frost.*

❧ *Harvest sprouts from the bottom of the plant up when they are 1 to 1½ inches in diameter.*

❧ *Harvest as needed. Plants are tolerant of light frosts.*

Cabbages

New varieties of cabbages head up very quickly; the one at left will be ready in a week or so.

It's hard to know which cabbage variety to grow. With green, red, and Chinese to choose from, not to mention new high-yielding, early-maturing varieties, it's no wonder many gardeners prefer to start their own plants from seeds rather than rely on the limited selections at most nurseries.

There are new, fast-growing sweet green cabbages available for spring planting. These mature in 65 days, leaving plenty of time to grow another crop in the same spot for a fall harvest.

The thick-leaved red cabbage is a good fall crop because it keeps well and tastes terrific. The more tender, flavorful, crinkle-leafed savoy cabbage can be grown for an early summer or fall harvest. Both the red and savoy types usually command a premium price at the market over green cabbage. Of course, regular green cabbage has always been a favorite for cole slaw, sauerkraut, and other dishes. No matter which cabbage you grow, you will be harvesting a crop rich in vitamins A, C, and K and several essential minerals.

Chinese cabbage is a tasty green with wide, crunchy stems that are delicious in stir-fries and other specialties. Chinese cabbage thrives in the cool fall garden and is very productive; you need only 10 square feet to have plenty of this crispy, sweet vegetable.

Planning

Heat diminishes the quality of cabbage heads, so plan to grow and harvest early cabbage before the hot spells of late spring (in the South) and early summer (in the North).

If you follow three steps to growing spring cabbage, you can get it to mature before the onset of high temperatures. First, choose the right variety for quick maturation. Second, start your transplants early. Finally, set the transplants in the garden 2 to 3 weeks before the average last spring frost date, preferably with protection.

Some of the newer hybrids produce good-size heads under 65 days after transplanting, including *Salarite* (57 days) and *Emerald Cross* (63 days). *Copenhagen Market* (65 days) and *Early Jersey Wakefield* (63 days) are traditional early, open-pollinated choices with good flavor. Early varieties are very good for cole slaw, salad, and lightly cooked dishes. Later types make better sauerkraut. Select both early and midseason varieties to stretch out your harvest.

Preparation

Determine your last spring frost date and sow seeds indoors 50 to 60 days before. Cabbage will germinate in 4 to 5 days if the temperature is near 75°F. As soon as the crop emerges, put the flats in a cooler place (at 55° to 65°F); heat will cause cabbage seedlings to grow too fast and become very leggy. Keep fluorescent lights 1 inch from the plants. Transplant the seedlings into new containers about a week after they get their first true leaves, putting them in the soil slightly deeper than they grew before to check legginess.

If possible, set the plants in a cold frame 1 or 2 weeks after their first transplanting to accustom them to outdoor weather and help prevent legginess. Where late winter weather is mild, cold frame life won't present many problems. But in some northern states, take care. On cold nights,

To grow short, stocky transplants keep lights just 1 inch from the leaves. Leggy seedlings *(right)* are often quite fragile and are damaged easily when transplanted.

throw a heavy tarp over your cold frame.

If you don't have a cold frame, start hardening off your plants about 3 weeks after the indoor transplanting. Seedlings set out early respond better to transplanting and have less time to get leggy.

About a week before transplanting the seedlings into the garden, mix three or four shovelfuls of aged manure or compost into the soil for each transplant you'll set out. If aged manure is not available, use a balanced fertilizer such as 5-10-10 at a rate of 3 to 4 pounds for every 100 square feet.

Planting

Transplant your seedlings or buy nursery plants and set them out 2 to 3 weeks before the average last spring frost date. If possible, choose an area of the garden with light-textured soil, as it warms up early in the season and won't be overly wet. It's best to transplant on a calm, cloudy afternoon to avoid the stress of wind or bright sun. Set plants 12 to 15 inches apart in well-fertilized soil either in beds or single rows. If young transplants have been hardened off well, they'll take a spring chill down to 22°F. If you have hot-caps (commercially made caps of strong waxed paper that resemble little hats), place them over the transplants to ease shock, promote a quick takeoff, and keep flea beetles out for a while. Remember to watch out for the build-up of heat on hot, sunny days. Remove the hotcaps after about 2 weeks.

Care

About a month after transplanting, side-dress cabbage plants with about 1 pound of balanced fertilizer such as 10-10-10 or its equivalent for every 25 feet of row.

Moisture is very important for even growth of early cabbages. When the temperature starts rising, apply a thick organic mulch around the plants to conserve soil moisture and keep the soil cool. (Soil temperatures trigger cabbage bolting, or going to seed, more than do air temperatures.)

Watch for flea beetles early in the season, and later, cabbageworms and cabbage loopers. Cabbage root maggots are another pest to be on the lookout for. These pests are the larvae of small flies that lay eggs in the soil at the base of small cabbage plants in the spring. Barriers such as mats placed over the soil tight to the plant stem can keep many flies from laying eggs. Mats are not foolproof, however. Cabbage root maggot damage should be suspected if one or more plants in a row suddenly slow down their growth and wilt when others seem strong.

Planting anise or marigolds in cabbage rows will reduce the number of imported cabbageworm eggs. The aromatic flowers and herbs somehow offend the white butterflies that lay their eggs on cabbage leaves. However, these plants steal nutrients and moisture from the cabbages, resulting in smaller heads. A better control for worms is *Bacillus thuringiensis*, a bacterial control sold under the names Thuricide and Dipel, among others. Start spraying when you see the moths beginning to land on your cabbages.

Essentials

Planning

🍂 *Cabbage is best when the heads mature in cool weather, so plan to harvest before the onset of hot weather or in the fall.*

🍂 *For a spring-planted crop, buy transplants at a nursery or start seedlings indoors 50 to 60 days before the last spring frost date.*

🍂 *Late-maturing varieties are best for fall harvests. Plant them in early summer in the North, mid- to late summer in central and southern areas.*

🍂 *Plant Chinese cabbages for a fall harvest.*

Preparation

🍂 *A week or so before planting, mix three or four shovelfuls of aged manure or compost into the planting bed for each transplant you'll set out, or use a balanced fertilizer such as 5-10-10 at the rate of 3 to 4 pounds per 100 square feet.*

Planting

🍂 *For spring crops, set out well-hardened cabbage transplants in the garden 2 or 3 weeks before the last expected frost date. Space early-maturing cabbages 12 to 15 inches apart, either in beds or single rows; later types, 18 to 24 inches apart.*

🍂 *For fall crops, sow seeds directly in the garden. Plant seeds ¼ inch deep, 1½ to 2 inches apart.*

🍂 *Sow seeds for Chinese cabbage in the fall ¼ to ½ inch deep and 3 inches apart.*

Care

🍂 *When cabbages are 4 to 5 inches tall, thin or transplant to stand 18 to 24 inches apart; Chinese cabbages should be thinned to 12 to 15 inches apart.*

🍂 *About a month after transplanting, side-dress cabbages with about 1 pound of 10-10-10 or its equivalent per 25 feet of single row. Side-dress Chinese cabbages with ½ pound of 10-10-10 or its equivalent per 25-foot single row when plants are 4 to 6 inches tall, and every 3 weeks thereafter.*

🍂 *Apply a thick layer of mulch to retain moisture.*

🍂 *Watch for aphids (page 276), imported cabbageworms (page 278), cabbage loopers (page 276), flea beetles (page 278), and cabbage root maggots (page 276).*

🍂 *Cabbage diseases include black rot (page 283), clubroot (page 283), downy mildew (page 284), and white mold (page 287).*

Harvesting

🍂 *Start harvesting when cabbage heads are firm and softball size.*

🍂 *Cut the head from the stem with a sharp knife and discard the outer leaves.*

🍂 *Begin harvesting Chinese cabbage when the leaves are 10 inches tall and still loose or wait until the heads are formed.*

🍂 *To keep cabbage as long as possible, harvest late in the season before hard freezes and keep heads in a cold, moist area.*

Cabbage heads may crack and split open from the pressure of excessive water taken up after the heads are solid. Cutting the roots by spading 6 to 8 inches deep in a semicircle 6 inches from the plant can reduce the problem.

Harvesting

Harvesting can begin as soon as some heads reach softball size and are firm to the touch. The grocery store size is about 2 to 3 pounds, but many garden varieties can develop heads of 6 to 8 pounds. After the center head is removed, small heads may develop where the base leaves meet the stem. Let one of them grow and you'll often get another head weighing 1 or 2 pounds.

Fall Cabbages: Green, Red, and Chinese

Variety selection and timing are the key points for raising a good fall crop of cabbage. If you live where fall weather is mild, you may be interested in the later "wintergreen" varieties; they keep their quality longest in the garden and store well, too, when you finally pick them.

Fall is the best time to grow red cabbage, as most varieties are late. Many growers report that red cabbage isn't plagued by cabbageworms and loopers to the extent that green types are. Watch for insect problems, nevertheless. *Lariat* (125 days) is a new, medium-size, extra-late cabbage developed for long-term storage. It's also resistant to late-season frost damage and has a very dense interior.

Fall cabbages can be very sweet. Studies show that late-maturing cabbages such as *Danish Ballhead* (110 days) contain more glucose and fructose than early-maturing types. Other studies show that the amount of these two sugars is increased by using organic fertilizers, such as manure, rather than commercial fertilizers.

If you choose late-maturing varieties, give them enough time to mature before fall frosts arrive. (If for some reason you miss the planting date, you can grow a so-called early spring cabbage that matures quickly.) Heads of early varieties won't keep as long after harvesting, however. Late types are better keepers because of their densely packed leaves and high dry-matter content.

The crinkly-leafed *Savoy* cabbage *(left)* is often more tender and flavorful than regular types. At right is *Michihli* Chinese cabbage. Both are rich in vitamins A, C, and K.

Seeds of the fall crop can be started in flats or directly in the garden in a bed or row. Sow seeds in early summer in the North, mid- to late summer in central and southern regions. If you are seeding where you want the crop to mature, sprinkle two or three seeds per foot, ¼ to ½ inch deep, cover with soil, tamp down, and keep moist. After the seedlings are up and have developed four or five leaves, thin or transplant the crop to 18 to 24 inches between plants.

Since fall crops must get their start in the garden in hot weather, use mulch, water often, and keep a watch out for such insect pests as the imported cabbageworm.

In mild-winter coastal areas, grow fall and early winter cabbages in raised beds to assure good drainage in case of heavy fall rains. Cabbage plants thrive in heavy soils that hold moisture, but they will develop problems in overly wet soils.

To keep fall cabbages as long as possible, harvest them late in the season before the first hard frost. If kept in a cold (just above 32°F), moist area, the heads can last for 3 to 4 months. The higher the temperature, though, the shorter the storage period. In a dry, cold area wrap heads in waxed paper to create humidity. Store only solid, blemish-free heads.

Chinese cabbage, a sweet, crunchy vegetable, is best grown as a fall crop. There are two basic types — heading (*Pe-tsai*) and nonheading (*Pak Choi*). Heading varieties can be short or round (*Wong Bok*) or tall and torpedolike (*Michihli* or *Chihli*). The nonheading type forms loose, upright leaves. Varieties include *Lei-Choi* and *Crispy Choy*.

Sow Chinese cabbage seeds ¼ to ½ inch deep and 3 inches apart. When the seedlings are 4 to 5 inches tall, thin or transplant them to stand 12 to 15 inches apart. Then side-dress with ½ pound of 10-10-10 or its equivalent for every 25 feet of single row, and every 3 weeks thereafter.

You can begin harvesting heading types when the leaves are 10 inches tall and still loose, or you can wait until the heads are fully formed. Cut the heads at soil level. Begin harvesting the nonheading types when there's enough to eat. Cut off a few outside stalks at a time or harvest the entire plant.

Cabbage Sources

Copenhagen Market 15, 29, 39

Danish Ballhead 15, 29, 60

Early Jersey Wakefield 29, 33, 60, 66

*Emerald Cross 29, 33, 39

Lariat 20

*Salarite 15, 34, 66

Chinese cabbage

Chihli 23, 107

Crispy Choy 6

Lei-Choi 6, 28

Michihli 6, 28, 35

Wong Bok 66

See also Oriental Vegetable seed sources (77–81) for less common varieties.

*hybrid

Variety selection and timing are crucial for raising a good crop of cabbage. Red cabbage is often planted for a late fall (or early winter) harvest.

Carrots

Good-tasting carrots come in many sizes. Thinning the row to the correct spacing is essential for producing roots worth harvesting.

Carrots will grow in almost any garden — no matter what type of soil you have. We've found the key to success with carrots is to find the variety that performs best in your garden.

In clay soil, you might try *Royal Chantenay*. Their strong tops are less likely to break off as you pull them out of the soil, leaving the carrot still in the ground — a real problem at harvest time in heavy soils. In very heavy soils, beet-shaped varieties such as *Golden Nugget* do especially well.

If you have loose soil to a depth of 10 or 12 inches, you might want to try *Orlando Gold* or *A-Plus*, new hybrids that offer 40 percent more vitamin A than old favorites such as *Nantes*. These and other new hybrids have a darker color and richer flavor than the traditional varieties.

Planning

Refer to the variety chart on page 121 and choose a variety that matches your soil conditions. Plan successive plantings of carrots, starting 3 to 4 weeks before the average last spring frost date.

Preparation

Carrots grow best in soils that are deep and friable and have few clumps or large stones, which cause branching and forking of roots. If the developing taproot meets a rock or impenetrable clay, it will branch or simply stop growing.

Right top: Carrots won't sprout and become well established without steady moisture. Right bottom: When carrots are still quite small, thin them to stand about 3 inches apart.

The soil should drain well, otherwise the carrots may develop cavity spots — black spots near the crown of the root that break down, leaving unsightly, rotting cavities.

We've found that planting carrots in beds rather than rows makes for easier soil preparation and thinning. Till or spade the beds to a depth of at least 6 inches.

Carrots need fertilizer, so it's a good idea to mix a healthy amount of compost into your seedbeds before planting. Fine, decomposed compost helps lighten the soil, retain moisture, and remedy boron or manganese deficiencies. Don't use manure unless it is well rotted; fresh manure adds excess nitrogen, which can cause branching and hairy, fibrous roots. Potassium, however, promotes solid, sweet carrots. Wood ashes contain highly soluble potassium that reaches the plants quickly. Sprinkle a very thin layer of ashes over the seedbed and work them into the top 4 inches of the beds, where the carrots' feed roots will thrive. Then rake the beds smooth of rocks and soil clumps.

If you use a commercial fertilizer, mix 1 pound of 5-10-10 or its equivalent into every 50 square feet of garden area.

Planting

Although carrot seeds will germinate in soil temperatures that range from 40° to 95°F, they sprout fastest in warm (80°F), moist soil. Plant some seeds early in cooler soils for an early harvest, but plant the bulk of your seeds when the soil temperature is warm. The later, fast-sprouting carrots will reduce your early weeding woes and extend your harvest. Also, early seeded carrots lose vitamin A as they mature in midsummer heat. Later carrots will be richer in color and contain higher vitamin levels.

Carrot seeds won't germinate unless you keep the soil surface moist. It takes 10 days or more for the carrots to emerge. Some gardeners cover their carrot beds with wet burlap bags after planting. Beginning 5 days after planting, check every day for emerging seedlings. Once the seedlings are up, remove the burlap and water the beds daily until the seedlings are well established.

Another way to encourage good carrot germination is to cover the planted row with clear plastic. This will both warm the soil and conserve moisture. Using this method, the first shoots will appear in 5 to 7 days, at which time the plastic should be removed, as a long, sunny day could create enough heat under the plastic to burn the young plants.

Essentials

Planning
- Choose a variety that matches your soil conditions.
- Stagger your carrot seeding starting 3 to 4 weeks before the average last spring frost date.
- Plant additional areas at 3-week intervals as the soil temperatures rise.

Preparation
- Mix 1 pound of 5-10-10 or its equivalent into every 50 square feet of garden area.
- Work the carrot seedbed well with a tiller or hoe to break up any soil clumps. Remove all rocks and stones.
- Sprinkle a thin layer of wood ashes over the seedbed to add potassium to the soil for sweeter carrots. Work the ashes into the top 4 inches of the bed. Then rake the beds smooth.

Planting
- Make furrows ¾ inch deep, spaced 4 inches apart.
- Put a ¼-inch layer of sifted compost or peat moss in the bottom of each furrow and sow the seeds, about 3 per inch, on top. Cover with a ½-inch layer of the same material.
- Lightly mulch the seedbed to retain moisture and prevent soil crusting.

Care

Thin carrots to stand 3 inches apart when they are 1 to 2 inches tall. Many gardeners find getting down on their hands and knees and pulling tiny seedlings time consuming and tiring, but there are easier strategies for getting the job done. Thinning options are discussed on page 119.

Care
- Thin carrots to stand 3 inches apart. (See page 119 for various thinning strategies.)
- Weed carefully and cultivate lightly near the plants.
- Add mulch about 6 weeks after sowing to prevent exposing the roots to the sun, which gives them a bitter taste.
- When the carrot tops are about 6 inches tall, side-dress with a sprinkling of a natural fertilizer such as dried cow manure. If the bed is mulched heavily, use a liquid fertilizer such as fish emulsion, seaweed, or other general-purpose plant food.
- Carrots are rarely bothered by pests or diseases; however, wireworms (page 281) may appear.
- Aster yellows disease (page 282) may strike, causing tops to turn rusty red or yellow and the roots to have poor taste and color.

Harvesting
- Carrots are generally ready for harvest in 2 to 3 months, when they are about ½ inch in diameter. Leave them in the ground until you need them.
- Drench the bed with water for easy harvesting.
- Pull the carrots by grabbing the greens at their crowns and gently tugging with a twisting motion.
- Harvest carrots for the root cellar after the first hard frosts but before the ground freezes.

Carrots can be planted in single rows *(top)* or wide rows *(bottom)*. Single rows can be easier to weed and thin than wide-row or bed planting.

Water or wind can wash soil away from around your plants. Carrots develop "green shoulder" and become bitter when their crowns are above ground and exposed to the sun. A 3- to 4-inch layer of mulch will prevent this problem.

With a hand tool, cultivate the soil around the plants carefully to kill any weeds that have started to germinate. Carrot seedlings are weak and grow slowly while young, so it's important to keep weeds down during the first few weeks. Mulch the carrot bed to prevent exposing the crowns of the carrots to the sun, which causes green shoulder and makes them bitter.

Give the carrots a fertilizer boost when they are about 6 inches tall. Sprinkle dried cow manure alongside the row and let the next rain or watering feed your crop, or apply a liquid feeding such as fish emulsion or seaweed.

Poor color in carrots is usually the result of the crop ripening in hot weather.

Most carrot pests and diseases can be controlled by promptly removing any diseased plants and by rotating the crop. Try this method of rotation:
• Year 1: Carrots
• Year 2: Peas, to fix the nitrogen in the soil
• Year 3: Lettuce or spinach, to use the nitrogen

Harvesting

Begin harvesting carrots when they reach eating size — about ½ inch in diameter — usually 2 to 3 months after planting. Pick only what you need, as even mature carrots will retain their quality in the ground unless the weather is extremely hot.

Four Thinning Methods

Carrots must be spaced about 3 inches apart, otherwise excessive competition for space will produce lovely green tops on small, hardly-worth-harvesting carrots. Unfortunately, since carrot seeds are so tiny and light, it's difficult to control the density of the seeds as you sow unless you buy the pelletized seeds, which are available at only a few outlets. The solution for most gardeners is thinning. Here are four approaches to the task of thinning carrots:

1. Plant carrots in a square-foot format and snip — don't pull — extra seedlings. Mel Bartholomew, author of *Square Foot Gardening,* plants his carrots and other crops in separate square-foot areas of his garden. He keeps thinning to a minimum by carefully planting his seeds in exact spacings.

With carrots, Mel divides his well-worked, compost-rich, square-foot areas into four parts by drawing a line in the soil with his finger. Using two fingers, he pokes sixteen holes, each about ½ inch deep, in the soil. He then puts three or four seeds in each hole and covers them with soil or compost and keeps them watered with a gentle spray. When the seedlings emerge, he pinches off all but one plant in each hole. Ideally, this leaves sixteen carrots per square foot.

A disadvantage to the square-foot method is that poor germination of seeds will leave skips. Also, we find that careful spacing isn't very easy to accomplish.

2. Thin early by hand — it's slow but reliable. If you have just a small row of carrots, thinning by hand is probably the easiest method, but be sure to thin when the plants are no more than an inch or so high. Thin the carrots to stand at least 1 inch apart. This is also a good time to cultivate the soil close to the plants to kill weeds that have started to germinate.

After a month or so, you'll need to thin again — and this time there should be some finger-size carrots to eat. Leave about 3 inches between plants. Whenever you pull some of the smaller, more tender carrots, you'll free up space, moisture, and fertilizer for nearby roots.

3. Plant carefully and thin late. Some gardeners hate to thin — unless they can eat their thinnings. If you wait until your plants are about 12 inches tall, you can thin out many delectable finger-size carrots. The key to this method is not to crowd the seeds in your furrows. While this method makes plenty of sense, the seeding must be done very carefully. Also, the competition for space probably slows the development of large carrots.

4. Rake-thinning saves hours of work in a large garden. If you're tending a large carrot crop, try your first thinning with a regular 14- to 16-inch garden rake. It usually takes longer to work up the courage to try this method than to actually go through with it.

Timing is important — the plants should be no more than ¼ or ½ inch tall when you rake them. Drag the rake across the row or bed, rather than down it (that would pull out too many plants). The tines of the rake should penetrate the soil just about ¼ inch. You'll notice the rake tines are spaced so they pull out about the right number of plants.

Once you master the technique — and it shouldn't take too long — you'll be able to thin a long row quite quickly, and you can do it standing up.

Rake thinning should be done when plants are about ¼ or ½ inch tall. Drag the rake across the width, rather than down the length, of the row.

It's possible to harvest tasty carrots throughout the winter. In areas where the ground freezes during the winter, cover your carrot bed with hay before the ground freezes.

In areas where the ground freezes during the winter, gardeners have a choice of strategies for keeping carrots. One system is to bury your carrot bed completely under a foot or more of dry hay late in the fall, before the ground freezes. Cover the hay with 4- or 6-mil polyethylene plastic film and weight the ends and sides securely with rocks, planks, and earth to keep winter winds from tearing it loose. Without the plastic, rain or snow would trickle down through the hay and rot the vegetables. You can harvest from the ends of the bed periodically through the winter, being careful to re-cover the opening.

Another method is to dig the carrots late in the fall, brush them off gently, cut the tops about ½ inch from the carrot, and double-bag them in large, food-safe plastic bags punched with a few airholes. Then store the carrots in a root cellar or any area where temperatures are cool — 32°F — and humidity is high. Carrots will keep well under these conditions for up to 6 months without losing much vitamin A.

Carrots can be sliced and dried in home dehydrators, but we don't recommend this procedure, as it robs them of vitamin A. A better alternative is to freeze small, tender carrots whole. Large carrots do not freeze well unless they are sliced into sticks or pennies.

Many southern, southwestern, and Pacific northwestern gardeners can store their carrots in the ground through the mild winter months and always have easy access to a few freshly dug carrots for a meal. Keeping carrots in the ground through the winter does, however, give pests, such as the carrot rust fly maggot and wireworm, more opportunities to get at the crop. If you notice signs that insects are feeding on the carrots, dig the rest of the crop and store it.

Use this guide and the chart on the facing page to help you select carrots that will do well in your garden.

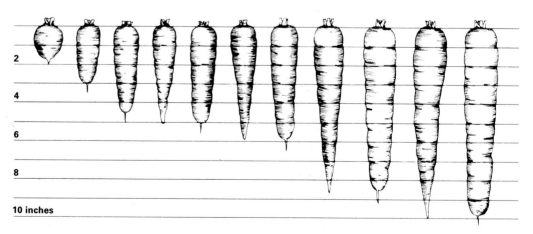

2

4

6

8

10 inches

Carrot Varieties by Soil Depth

The depth of your topsoil will determine which varieties of carrots will do well in your garden. Before ordering your seeds, be sure to read the seed catalog descriptions.

Names of varieties change from one catalog to another. Also, carrots that do well in one climate may not flourish in another.

The carrots in this chart are categorized by their shape. The stubby carrots are wide with rounded tips, the tapering carrots produce narrow, pointed roots, and the round carrots resemble beets.

Soil Depth	Type	Variety Name	Sources
10 inches	Stubby	Lindoro	35
10 inches	Tapering	A-Plus	21, 52
		Canuck	39
		Orange Sherbet	39
		Orlando Gold	28, 39, 99
		Spartan Fancy	39
		Tendersweet	15, 23, 35
		Waltham Hi Color	33
8–9 inches	Stubby	Cutlass	26
		Danro RS	106, 108
		Imperator	6, 7, 11, 99
		Nantes Tip Top	8, 72
		Kuroda	51, 108
		Royal Cross Hybrid	35
		Spartan Winner	23, 43
8–9 inches	Tapering	Berlicummer	8
		Camden	39
		Candy Pack	21, 52
		Dominator	24
		Gold Pak	6, 11, 15, 17, 21
		Hybrid Sweet & Crisp	12
		Nandor Hybrid	35
6 inches	Stubby	Dess Dan	21, 26, 39
		Forto	48
		Gold King	28, 40
		Hybrid Chrisna	17, 29
		Nantes Strong Top	43, 99
		Pioneer	7, 16
		Scarlet Nantes	15, 28, 45, 108
		Spartan Bonus	6, 7, 8, 33
		Touche Hybrid	26
6 inches	Tapering	Amsterdam Forcing	8, 45, 108
		Danvers Half Long	6, 7, 8, 33, 35
		Minicor	15, 21, 39, 47
		Toudo Hybrid	6
5 inches	Stubby	Early Scarlet Horn	45, 62
		Early Chantenay	9, 11
		Red Cored Chantenay	6, 8, 45, 66
		Royal Chantenay	6, 15, 26, 29, 108
5 inches	Tapering	Nantes Coreless	9, 11, 12, 35
		Nantes Half Long	6, 8, 23
		Touchon	12, 47, 62
4–5 inches	Stubby	Amstel	63
		Goldinheart	11
		Kinko	20, 51, 63
3 inches	Stubby	Baby Finger	26, 63
		Lady Finger (Little Finger)	11, 28, 35
		Minicor	20, 21, 26
		Short and Sweet	6, 11
		Sucram	66
1–2 inches	Round	Glowing Ball	9, 12
		Golden Ball	35, 36
		Gold Nugget	15
		Kundulus	35, 74
		Parisian Ball	8, 48
		Planet	39, 47, 63

Celery

From indoor-grown seedling to full-size plant about 100 days later, celery likes plenty of moisture. It's a challenging vegetable to grow but well worth the effort.

Although celery is a challenging plant to grow, many gardeners get two fine crops a year, a feat that should inspire and encourage other celery growers. A productive patch of those crisp and scrumptious green stalks is something any gardener would take pride in.

Celery does best where the growing season is long with moderate temperatures, such as coastal regions or in towns near large lakes and rivers. It can't tolerate high heat, so it grows quite well during the mild winters of the South and the cool summers of the North, which is why Florida and Michigan are two leading commercial areas. On the other hand, a string of night temperatures below 55°F can make the plants go to seed prematurely. Despite this fussiness about temperature, you can grow great crops of celery in most regions of the country with some modifications in growing techniques. You don't have to skip celery because it's "too hard to grow."

Two Crops of Celery in One Season

National Gardening Association member Frank Campobasso of Arlington, Massachusetts, routinely grows not one but two crops of delicious celery per year. We've outlined his annual production schedule below. (Note: The last spring frost date in Arlington is early May.)

For the summer harvest
- Sow seeds indoors in flats in late January or early February.
- Transplant seedlings to outdoor cold frame in early April.
- Move from cold frame to row in mid-May.
- Start blanching rows in late July.
- Begin harvest in early August.

For the fall harvest
- Sow seeds in flats or pots in early May.
- Move seedlings to garden in early June.
- In early July set plants 1 foot apart in rows.
- Start blanching in mid-September.

Frank prefers *Tendercrisp* for both summer and fall crops. Plants grow about a foot tall and have dark green stalks. Though celery needs a relatively cool season with no extreme temperatures, Frank recommends warming up the soil for spring transplants or they may not get established quickly. He assembles an easy-to-build cold frame over the young celery plants made from wood and old storm windows.

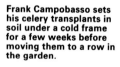
Far right: **These sturdy seedlings are ready for the garden. Because celery requires a long growing season, most gardeners either start their own plants early or buy transplants.**

Frank Campobasso sets his celery transplants in soil under a cold frame for a few weeks before moving them to a row in the garden.

Planning

Celery needs a long growing season of 120 to 150 days, so most gardeners start the plants indoors under fluorescent lights about 3 months before the final spring frost date. (A few nurseries will offer transplants, but availability is uncertain from year to year.)

When starting your own transplants, buy fresh seed every year, since old seeds often aren't viable. Soak the seeds in warm water overnight before planting. This will reduce the normal 15- to 20-day germination period.

Preparation

Soil preparation is essential for successful celery. Because the plant's taproot is unavoidably broken during transplanting, celery winds up with a shallow root system, reaching only 4 or 5 inches deep and spreading about 6 inches around the plant. Thus the top few inches of soil must retain moisture and supply all the nutrients the plants need.

Lots of organic matter is the best way to ensure necessary moisture in the soil, so every fall till as much compost, leaves, and well-rotted manure into the bed as possible. In the spring, after the fall additions have begun to decompose a bit, work more compost into the top 3 inches.

Planting

Because celery needs such a long growing season, most gardeners either start their own plants early or buy transplants. To start plants indoors, drop the seeds sparingly into small pots or flats filled with a sterilized commercial seed-starting medium. Press the seeds into the soil or cover them with a 1/8-inch layer of fine peat moss or more commercial mix. Keep the mix moist and set the flats where the temperature is about 65°F.

When the seedlings are about 2 inches tall, transplant them to individual peat pots. Keep them under lights and make sure the soil remains evenly moist until the seedlings can be moved into the garden. A

week before transplanting, harden them off by cutting back on water and introducing the plants gradually to outdoor conditions.

In areas with a long growing season, celery can be direct-seeded. Soil temperature should be at least 60°F before seeds are sown outdoors.

Plant the celery in beds measuring about 3 feet square. This makes it easy to prepare the soil for the crop's special needs. It also saves space, important for a crop that's in the ground for such a long time.

Celery does not do well in the cold. A string of night temperatures below 55°F can make plants go to seed prematurely. However, you can transplant celery outside a week or so before the average last spring frost date. Considering its long growing season, risking low night temperatures is a chance worth taking. If you're squeamish about risking the plants, consider covering them with a plastic cloche for a few weeks to protect them from the cold, and try *Golden Self-Blanching*, a standard variety that is slow to bolt.

Transplant the seedlings 8 to 10 inches apart in all directions in the bed. Water thoroughly, then mulch the bed with any material that won't mat and prevent water

Essentials

Planning

🌿 *Celery requires about 125 days of a long, relatively cool growing season. For a summer harvest, start plants indoors 10 to 12 weeks before the last spring frost date.*

🌿 *Where the fall climate is mild, try a midsummer seeding in the garden.*

🌿 *Some gardeners prefer to blanch celery for a milder taste when eaten raw. If you're pressed for time, try a self-blanching variety.*

Preparation

🌿 *Enrich the soil by tilling in plenty of organic matter and fertilizer to provide a steady supply of nutrients and moisture.*

Planting

🌿 *Presoak seeds to speed germination, whether you're starting them indoors or sowing directly in the garden.*

🌿 *Sow seeds indoors in small pots or flats. Move to individual containers when they are 2 inches tall.*

🌿 *In areas with a long growing season sow seeds in the garden at a depth of 1/8 inch in rows 30 to 36 inches apart after soil temperature reaches 60°F.*

🌿 *Set out transplants 8 to 10 inches apart in rows 10 inches apart a week or so before your last spring frost date.*

Care

🌿 *Thin direct-seeded plants to stand 8 to 10 inches apart when they are 4 to 5 inches tall.*

🌿 *Apply a heavy layer of mulch immediately after planting and provide a regular supply of water.*

🌿 *Celery is a heavy feeder, so side-dress with a liquid fertilizer every 2 to 3 weeks.*

🌿 *Blanch varieties that require it when the plants are 12 inches tall.*

🌿 *Earwigs (page 278) are a possible pest.*

🌿 *Early blight (page 284) and late blight (page 285) may trouble plants. Other possible diseases are nematodes (page 285) and viruses (page 287).*

Harvesting

🌿 *Start harvesting outer stalks when they are 6 to 8 inches tall.*

🌿 *Harvest stalks in fall as needed before the ground freezes. Celery can tolerate light frosts.*

Regional Notes

Midwest and South Central

Frequent dry spells and high summer temperatures make growing celery in this region very challenging. Try these special techniques: plant in partial shade; use 3 or 4 inches of organic mulch around plants; fertilize and water twice as often as other crops and mist frequently in a drought as well; pick outer stalks early and regularly so they have less time to become tough and strong flavored.

North

Transplant celery seedlings to the garden a week or so before the average last spring frost date to extend the growing season.

A heavy mulch, like this salt marsh hay, is a tremendous help in growing good celery. It retains much-needed moisture, eliminates weed competition, and keeps the roots cool.

from reaching the roots. Straw is a good choice. Tuck the mulch around the celery so only the leafy tops are exposed to the sun. As the plants grow, add layers of mulch to hinder weeds, retain moisture, and keep roots cool.

Care

Celery plants need a constant water supply to produce crisp, juicy stalks. If their growth slows down for lack of water or for any other reason, the stalks turn tough and stringy and the flavor becomes bitter.

Regular watering will prevent a disorder known as black heart, where the center of the plant turns black, decays, and dies off. It can be triggered by dry soil, fluctuating moisture conditions, or a rapid surge of growth caused by too much nitrogen.

Pascal celery is shown here afflicted with black heart, a disorder caused by erratic watering. You can avoid black heart by watering regularly.

Even if your garden has rich soil, side-dress every 2 or 3 weeks. Use manure tea or a teaspoon of 5-10-10 or its equivalent per plant.

With many varieties, blanching, or blocking out light, will produce pale, mild-tasting, tender stalks. You certainly can blanch celery if you prefer, but newer varieties such as *Golden Self-Blanching* make that time-consuming ritual unnecessary. The self-blanching golden types are popular in Europe where they are grown primarily for eating fresh, while the darker green (and stronger tasting) types are used for cooking. The standard green varieties for U.S. home gardeners are *Tendercrisp* and *Giant Pascal.*

There are many ways to blanch celery. Some gardeners set planks tightly along both sides of the celery row when the plants are a foot high. This forces the plants up a bit and makes the stalks a little pale, giving them a mild flavor. You can also wrap pieces of roofing paper around each plant and secure them with large rubber bands, slip large fruit juice cans over the plants, or push straw up to the top leaves of the plant.

Home gardeners usually don't have problems with diseases, but two should be mentioned. Early blight can occur in all regions when days are warm and night temperatures are in the 60s. A fungus attacks wet or dew-laden leaves, causing enlarging yellow spots on the leaves and stalks.

Late blight can be troublesome in the East and in the Pacific Northwest. The fungus responsible thrives in cool, rainy weather. Yellow spots appear on older leaves and turn darker, speckled with tiny black dots. Severely infected plants die.

For both problems, a fungicide can be applied at 7- to 10-day intervals starting when damage is first noticed. Residues of diseased plants should be removed from the garden, not dug in after the harvest, as fungus spores survive in debris left in the garden.

Another protective measure is to buy treated seeds or, before planting, to soak seeds in hot water (118°F for 30 minutes) and dry at room temperature.

Harvesting

When the plants get large enough — about 6 to 8 inches tall — start harvesting some of the outer stalks as you need them. The hearts of the plants will continue to grow. Remove any "suckers," or small shoots, that form at the base of the plants to keep the main plant growing vigorously. Harvest celery before the ground freezes. It can tolerate a light frost.

Celery Sources

Giant Pascal 5, 13, 35
Golden Self-Blanching 6, 67
*Tendercrisp 6

*hybrid

To give celery stalks a milder flavor, begin blanching them about 2 weeks before harvest. You can set planks tightly against both sides of the celery row when the plants are a foot tall, or you can slip a large can over each plant.

Corn

The supersweet corn at left, *Early Extra Sweet,* can retain its sweetness for 7 to 10 days after picking.

Within the last several years many new, outstanding varieties of sweet corn have been introduced. Although some of the older varieties such as *Golden Bantam* and *Silver Queen* are still highly rated by home growers, the "supersweet" varieties are what many people are talking about.

If you have not yet tried them in your garden, you are in for a culinary delight. The genetic make-up of supersweet varieties makes the kernels twice as sweet as standard varieties and prevents the sugar in them from being converted to starch as quickly as in standard sweet corn. Ears of supersweet corn can be left on the stalk or stored in the refrigerator for 7 to 10 days and still have excellent flavor — no more starting the water to boil before you go out to the garden to harvest just enough ears for dinner. Because of the higher sugar-to-starch ratio in their kernels, supersweets tend to be less vigorous than other varieties. As a result, germination conditions must be optimal.

Some home gardeners have complained that supersweet varieties do not have a true corn taste. We recommend performing a taste test in the summer to determine your preference.

Sweet Corn

Planning

If you want to try a supersweet corn this year look for varieties listed in catalogs as "shrunken two" (Sh$_2$). Along with sweeter flavor and longer storage life, another advantage of these varieties is that they are more compact than standard sweet corn — they usually grow only 4 to 5 feet tall. Where gardening space is limited, you can plant a block of four rows in an 8-by-10-foot area. This will yield about sixty ears of corn.

Some people don't like the taste of the supersweet varieties but they appreciate being able to store ears for a few days in the refrigerator. If you are among this group, you may be more satisfied with hybrid varieties such as *Sugar Loaf* or *Honeycomb*, which have only 15 percent more sugar than the standard types and are judged by some to be creamier. These hybrids have a sugar enhancer sweet gene, "se," listed in some catalogs as SE, or by the registered trademark Everlasting Heritage or EH. They have their own special taste because they contain two kinds of sugar (maltose and sucrose). These hybrids are usually more tender than the supersweets and will keep their excellent flavor for 4 or 5 days. When picked at the perfect stage, they practically melt in your mouth. Varieties in this group include *Kandy Korn, Tendertreat, White Lightning,* and *Miracle.*

Despite all the excitement about the new sweet corns, don't forget the many outstanding regular hybrids such as *Silver Queen, Butter and Sugar,* and *Early Sunglow,* or the long-time, open-pollinated (not hybrid) favorites such as *Country Gentlemen.*

Preparation

All types of corn will grow best in fertile, well-drained soil on a sunny site. If your soil is less than ideal, you can improve it by adding organic matter or by planting cover crops of annual ryegrass, soybeans, or hairy vetch the previous season.

Since corn is gluttonous and must grow quickly to produce well, you must fertilize at planting time. In soils with low to moderate fertility, broadcast and mix in 10 pounds of a commercial fertilizer such as 10-10-10 for every 500 square feet of growing area before planting. At planting time, side-dress (5 or 6 inches away from row) with about 3 to 4 pounds of the fertilizer per 100 feet of row. This extra band of fertilizer is not necessary if your soil is very fertile.

Planting

To insure good pollination it's best to plant corn in blocks of four to six rows at least 10 to 15 feet long; rows should be spaced 2 to 4 feet apart. Different types of corn — open-pollinated, standard hybrids, sugar enhancer, supersweet, and also corn-meal and popcorn — shouldn't be allowed to cross-pollinate. Plant each variety of each type of corn in a separate block.

If you are planting several varieties of the same *type* of sweet corn — standard, sugar enhancer, or Everlasting Heritage — you can plant the blocks near each other. Plant the supersweet corn (shrunken-two, or Sh$_2$) at least 250 feet or more away from regular hybrid or open-pollinated sweet corn since cross-pollination will result in tough, starchy corn. The sugar enhancer (SE), or Everlasting Heritage (EH), types can cross-pollinate with standard sweet corn with less dire results — the corn won't be starchy, but it will be less sweet.

Plant seeds 6 to 8 inches apart and thin the seedlings to 10 to 12 inches apart when they are 4 to 5 inches tall to allow adequate room for each plant. You will need about 4 ounces of seed to plant four 25-foot rows. Don't skimp on seed. It's much better to sow thickly and have to thin later than to be faced with spotty rows because of poor germination. One hundred feet of row will yield about 100 to 125 ears of corn.

Far right: Succession planting will produce a continuous supply of sweet corn over several weeks.

The soil should be 60° to 65°F when you sow. When it's much cooler than this, seeds may rot in the ground unless they have been treated with a fungicide. For gardeners in climate zones 5 and 6, sweet corn can usually be sown from mid-April to early July. The old farmer's adage that the time to plant sweet corn is when oak leaves are as large as squirrels' ears (about ½ inch) is fairly reliable. In the Deep South, where corn is planted in more gardens than in any other region, gardeners can sow seeds as early as late January and early February.

To insure a steady harvest of fresh sweet corn, you should sow blocks of one variety at 2-week intervals or blocks of several varieties with different maturing dates at one time.

Care

Corn grows fast and needs lots of water to grow and mature properly. When it does not receive enough it will be stunted and yield small, partially filled ears. When the leaves of corn look limp, dull green, and curl at the edges, it's time to water.

Essentials

Planning

🍂 *Plant corn directly outdoors after all danger of frost has passed and the soil temperature is about 60°F.*

🍂 *Seeds can be started indoors, two seeds per peat pot, 3 to 4 weeks before the last frost date.*

🍂 *Plan the garden to prevent cross-pollination between incompatible types of corn and to prevent tall varieties from shading nearby crops.*

Preparation

🍂 *Work plenty of manure into the soil the previous fall.*

🍂 *Just before planting, sprinkle 3 to 4 pounds of 5-10-10 or equivalent fertilizer per 100 feet of row along the side of each row and work it into the soil.*

Planting

🍂 *Plant corn in blocks of at least four rows with 2 to 4 feet between rows (the closer spacing is for short varieties). Sow the seeds 1½ to 2 inches deep, 6 to 8 inches apart.*

Care

🍂 *Thin the corn to stand 12 to 16 inches apart when the plants are 4 to 5 inches tall.*

🍂 *Provide at least 1 inch of water a week.*

🍂 *Control weeds with frequent shallow cultivation until the plants are knee high. Then apply a 3- to 5-inch layer of mulch.*

🍂 *Side-dress with a high-nitrogen fertilizer, such as 2 pounds of ammonium nitrate per 100 feet of row, when the plants are 8 to 10 inches tall and again when the silks appear.*

🍂 *Watch for signs of nitrogen deficiency (yellowing leaves) and respond with quick side-dressings of fish emulsion, manure, commercial fertilizer, or a combination of the three.*

🍂 *Watch for damage from birds (page 73), raccoons (page 73), corn earworms (page 277), and European corn borers (page 278). Minor damage may be caused by flea beetles (page 278), earwigs (page 278), Japanese beetles (page 278), corn rootworms (page 277), seed corn maggots (page 280), wireworms (page 281), and aphids (page 276).*

🍂 *Bacterial wilt (page 282) is a common disease problem; also watch for corn smut (page 284), corn leaf blight (page 283), and maize dwarf mosaic virus (page 287).*

Harvesting

🍂 *Sweet corn should be harvested when its ears are completely filled out and a pierced kernel shows a milky white liquid.*

🍂 *Sweet corn varieties (except for supersweets) lose their sweetness soon after harvest. Immediately after picking prepare the ears for eating or preserving.*

🍂 *Harvest corn for meal or popping as late as possible and dry on the cob, then store.*

Techniques for Early Sweet Corn

William John Park, president of Park Seed Company in Greenwood, South Carolina, boasts of getting the earliest ripe corn in his area — in June. His secret is to start it indoors so the seeds can germinate in warm soil. Because corn roots suffer if they are disturbed during transplanting, he starts the seeds in individual 3-inch peat pots in mid-March (a month before his last frost date) and sets the seedlings out on April 15 or so. The soil isn't warm enough then to germinate seeds, but it's good for healthy young seedlings. He sets out 150 pots for each variety he raises, setting them 12 to 14 inches apart.

In June he starts eating *Early Extra Sweet.* This is followed by *Seneca Chief,* then *Silver Queen* — a continuous harvest.

Planting in trenches is a good technique for early corn in hot, dry areas. The trenches channel water straight to the seeds, encouraging speedy germination.

Dig the trenches as narrow as possible, 5 inches deep and 15 inches apart. Cover each trench with a sheet of 4-mil clear plastic cut with slits to let in air and rain. The combination of plastic and trench provides a good, quick rise in soil temperature and protection from frost.

Plant your seeds 3 weeks before the average last spring frost date. For the best germination rates, soften your seeds by soaking them between warm, damp paper towels for about 3 days before planting.

Raised beds are the way to an early crop in places where sun and heat are at a minimum and rain is overabundant. Raised beds dry out and warm up early, shed excess water, and provide corn seedlings with the conditions needed for good, rapid growth.

Where spring soil temperatures are cool, presprouting seeds is another way to get an early crop going. When you sow seeds directly in your garden in the early spring, most sweet corn, especially the super-sweet varieties, will rot because the soil temperatures are too cool. Presprouting seeds prevents this problem.

To presprout your corn, put the seeds in a jar filled with warm water and let them soak overnight. The next day, rinse the seeds with fresh water and put them in a plastic bag. Lay the plastic bag on its side and open it ½ inch for ventilation. Put the bag in a warm spot, such as the top of the refrigerator or under a fluorescent light. Rinse the seeds each morning by filling the bag, then drain it several times. After about 4 or 5 days, the seeds should start to sprout.

To sow presprouted seeds, plow or till trenches 4 to 6 inches wide and deep, or make furrows where the rows are going to be. As mentioned earlier, work in fertilizer at the side of these furrows. Lay the sprouted seeds in this trough at 6- to 8-inch intervals. Cover the presprouted seeds with about ½ inch of soil and water them.

By following these techniques, you can have early maturing varieties of sweet corn on the table by the end of June or early July in many areas.

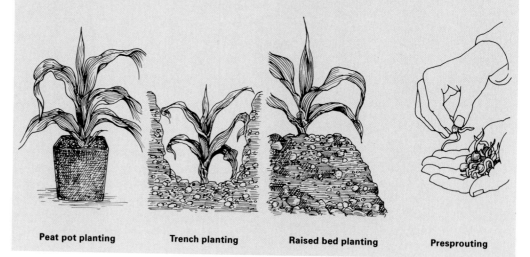

Peat pot planting   **Trench planting**   **Raised bed planting**   **Presprouting**

For most growing conditions an inch of water per week is adequate for corn. In extremely hot, dry, windy weather, provide 2 inches or more per week.

Control weeds with frequent shallow cultivation and mulching. When the plants are 6 to 8 inches tall, push up a mound of soil around each stalk to bury and kill small, hard-to-reach weeds near the plants. (Hilling will also make plants sturdier in the face of strong winds.) Don't do any cultivating after the corn is knee high to avoid root damage. Apply a 3- to 5-inch layer of organic mulch after the soil has warmed up in late spring or early summer.

Side-dress corn with a fertilizer high in nitrogen such as urea or ammonium nitrate at the rate of about 2 pounds per 100 feet of row when the plants are 8 to 10 inches tall and again when the silks appear. Or use dehydrated manure. Nitrogen from urea and other organic sources is most available to plants when the soil is warm. If the weather is cool and damp, it's better to use ammonium nitrate.

Corn needs a substantial amount of nitrogen. If growth is stunted and the bottom leaves of the young corn plants turn yellow, suspect nitrogen deficiency. Normal, healthy corn plants should be vigorous with dark, shiny green leaves. Remedy nitrogen deficiency by side-dressing at the above amounts.

Probably the most common and destructive insect pest you will encounter, especially with late-season corn, will be the corn earworm. It feasts on young corn kernels at the tip of the ear.

A few other insect pests that may attack corn include flea beetles (they transmit bacterial wilt), Japanese beetles, corn borers, corn rootworms, and aphids. Aphids are seldom a severe problem, however. Usually lady beetles reduce their numbers, but if they are bothering the crop, you could apply an insecticidal soap for quick, safe results.

Corn suffers from several different diseases, including bacterial wilt, smut, northern and southern leaf blights, and maize dwarf mosaic virus. The best control measures are to plant disease-resistant varieties, remove stalks of corn that have been infected, and rotate crops.

Insects and diseases aren't the only pests when it comes to corn. Squirrels and raccoons relish the first sweet corn of the season. Squirrels can be especially troublesome pests in suburban or city areas.

Corn requires plenty of water to grow and mature properly. Curled leaves *(left)* are a sign of water stress. Drip irrigation *(below)* is ideal for corn because it delivers water only where it is needed.

Keeping Raccoons Out of the Garden

Raccoons have a finicky sense of touch. Greasy, prickly, or leafy things put in and around the corn patch tend to discourage visits. For example, National Gardening Association member Ray Fowler of Wenham, Massachusetts, puts rose bush trimmings on the ground around the corn patch and then leans some thorny branches against the corn stalks so that his patch has a natural "barbed wire" enclosure.

A more productive method based on the prickles theory is to plant members of the squash family with their rough, spiny leaves and stems between the corn rows.

Emily and James Hickey of Barley's Harbor, Wisconsin, discovered that raccoons don't like getting their feet caught in black plastic netting. After the corn has formed ears, the Hickeys wrap netting around the corn patch and over as much corn as possible.

James Hoeft of Nebraska City, Nebraska, has had luck for the past seven years with scattering newspapers down his corn rows. (You will probably need to weigh them down if your area is windy.) He thinks it may be the rattling of the papers that scares them off. Another member claims that the answer to raccoons in corn is a flashing light in the middle of the corn field.

You can also use electric wires, which are very effective but more expensive than other methods. James Hoff of Worden, Montana, puts two wires around his garden, one 6 inches and another 16 inches above the ground. One wire, a foot above the ground, surrounding his corn patch, seems to do the trick for Albin Anderson of Plymouth, Indiana.

Pick sweet corn when the husks are dark green and the silks are brown but not brittle.

Some gardeners are successful in keeping squirrels out of the garden by using 6-foot-long inflatable snakes (sold at various garden supply stores).

Harvesting

Sweet corn is ready to pick when the husks are dark green; if they have yellowed you probably have waited too long. With supersweet corn, if you harvest when the corn is too mature, it will still be sweet, but tougher than if it had been picked at the right time.

Ripe corn silks should be brown but not brittle. Look for rounded, full ears with blunt tips (although shape will vary somewhat depending on the variety grown). Puncture a few of the kernels with your thumbnail. The juice should be milky; if it's clear, it's not ripe.

For best flavor, cooking time is also critical. Boil your supersweet corn for 4 to 6 minutes only; standard sweet corn, if fully mature but not overripe, may need to be boiled 6 to 8 minutes.

Cornmeal Corn

Just as home grown corn on the cob is much better than the store-bought variety, home-grown, home-ground cornmeal is far superior to that found in the stores. It has more taste, minerals, protein, and fiber than the flat-tasting, refined meal usually sold by stores.

Grow it just as you would sweet corn, leaving more room between the plants and rows because the plants can get large. Plant it 100 feet or more away from your sweet corn, if possible, to avoid cross-pollination.

Cornmeal corn, when dry, stores well for a long time and needs no freezing, canning, or pickling. Young immature ears of some varieties — "dent" corns — can be eaten like sweet corn; and delicious cornbreads, pones, muffins, and mush can be made from the dried meal.

Cornmeal corn needs to be thoroughly dry so it won't mold or spoil in storage. It often looks drier than it is. Let it dry on the stalk as late in the fall as is practical, then pick and shuck the ears. Dry them further indoors over a heat register or by a stove. Really dry corn shells off the ear by hand much more easily than partly dried corn, which can be difficult to remove from the cob. To shell, wrap your hand tightly around the ear and twist, forcing the kernels sideways and off the cob.

You can leave the kernels on the ear as long as you want and shell only as much as you need from time to time. Store the ears in a cool, dry place. The dried kernels can be ground into meal in a food blender or grain mill.

Although any late-season variety of corn can be dried and ground into meal, special cornmeal varieties in the following list have a harder starch in their kernels that makes them more suitable for grinding. (Variety descriptions are followed by sources.)

Reid's Yellow Dent: Tall (up to 9 feet) corn with large ears, often two to a stalk.

Birds and Corn Seedlings

Though fun to look at, scarecrows in the corn field rarely do much to prevent birds from getting at young corn seedlings. So you'll have to use other tactics.

The birds are interested in eating the corn seed at the bottom of the tiny plant; they usually leave the larger corn plants alone. Any technique that protects very young seedlings from the birds will work.

Many gardeners start seedlings indoors in peat pots and put the pots out only after the plants have had a good start. Or you can plant directly in the garden and cover the seedlings. National Gardening Association member Joseph Brumfield of Worthington, Ohio, has designed his own device.

He made seedling guards from 1-inch lumber strips, 8 feet long, 5 inches wide, and 4 inches deep, nailing them together at the corners to form a rectangle. Each rectangle is covered with ¼-inch hardware cloth. He places the guards over his rows of corn, pressing them 1 inch into the soil. Once the corn tips start growing through the holes in the hardware cloth, it is time to remove the guards. The seedlings continue to grow, bird-free, since they are no longer of appetizing size. A simpler version of this technique is to put chicken wire over the small plants and roll it up when the plants are about 4 inches tall.

It's been called the most popular variety of open-pollinated corn. It stands hot weather well and is good for the central and southern corn belts. Matures in 85 to 95 days. *12, 17, 35*

Hickory King: A white corn good for hominy, grits, and cornmeal. It can be used for roasting ears or for making masa harina to use in corn tortillas. Matures in 85 to 110 days. *3, 15, 17, 104*

Blue Corn: Open-pollinated, it often has two or more ears, 8 to 11 inches long, on 5- to 6-foot-high stalks. The meal has a blue-gray tint. Matures in about 100 days. *12, 68*

Mandan Bride: A multicolored flour corn for corn flour or hominy. Ears are 8 to 9 inches long. Matures in about 98 days. *20, 51*

Longfellow Flint: The kernels are orange, the ears 10 inches long on 10-foot stalks. It makes a sweet cornmeal and is high yielding. Good for northern gardens. Matures in 117 days. *20*

Rhode Island White Cap: Said to come from the Narragansett Indians. White ears with an occasional red one. Good for making Rhode Island johnnycake. Matures in 115 days. *20*

Popcorn

The popcorn we grow today bears a close resemblance to an archaic type called pod corn and to corn's wild relative, teosinte, which also pops when heated. Popcorn supplies carbohydrates, dietary fiber, and small amounts of protein, minerals, and vitamins — all for 25 calories per cup.

Grow popcorn as you do sweet corn. However, popcorn will cross-pollinate with sweet corn, so you must keep them separate — by 250 feet, if possible. Sweet corn won't hurt popcorn if the two cross, but popcorn can make sweet corn starchy and toughens the outer skin on the kernels.

Popcorn does need a slightly longer growing season than sweet corn, and it should be left to mature fully and dry on the stalk before harvest. Normally a few frosty nights won't hurt popcorn. Harvest by twisting the ear from the stalk. To complete the drying indoors, pull back the husks but don't detach them so you can hang them to dry. Or you can peel off the husk completely and put the ears in a basket to dry in a dark, warm, airy place.

Popcorn pops because the seed coat around each kernel dries hard and seals out air while the inner portion (endosperm) retains some moisture. When you heat popcorn, the moisture expands rapidly, causing the whole kernel to explode.

Blue corn was once a staple among Indians of the Southwest. It can be ground to make tortillas, tamales, or cornbread.

After harvest it's important to cure popcorn for 3 or 4 weeks to let the seed coat harden and reduce the moisture level in the kernels. Store popcorn in airtight containers in a dark, cool place. In most climates, it is rare for popcorn to get too dry, but if your kernels don't pop, try putting some in a glass jar, sprinkling them with water, and letting them sit for half an hour before popping.

Strawberry-colored popcorn will pop out white.

Corn Pollination

Sweet Corn Varieties by Type

Some of the many popular varieties for each type of sweet corn are listed in this chart, which includes sources.

Plant blocks of similar types of corn together, isolated from other types, for best pollination. For example, keep shrunken-two (Sh₂) supersweet corns separated from standard hybrids or open-pollinated types by 250 feet, if possible, to avoid cross-pollination, which makes for starchy corn. If space is limited, separate as much as practical and put supersweet upwind of the others. Supersweet can be planted nearer to the sugar enhancer (SE) corns with fewer ill effects.

If your space is limited, consider planting only one type of corn.

Types of Corn	Open-Pollinated	Source	Standard Hybrids	Source	Sugar Enhancer (SE or EH)	Source	Supersweet (Sh₂)	Source
Early 60–70 days	*Trucker's Favorite White* (65 days)	35	*Seneca Star* (65 days)	43	*Stardust* (70 days)	43	*Party Time* (63 days)	43
			Early Sunglow (63 days)	35, 43			*Early Extra Sweet* (70 days)	17, 35, 75, 105
Midseason 70–85 days	*Improved Golden Bantam* (75 days)	23, 45	*Butter and Sugar* (73 days)	16, 35, 43	*Honeycomb* (79 days)	28, 105	*Great Time* (78 days)	43
			Quicksilver (75 days)	16	*Pride and Joy* (70 days)	43		
			Seneca Chief (82 days)	35, 104	*Earliglow* (75 days)	35, 43		
					Platinum Lady (78 days)	6, 43		
Late season 85 or more days	*Reid's Yellow Dent* (85 days)	12, 17, 35	*Golden Bantam* (85 days)	12, 15, 20, 51 104	*Miracle* (85 days)	26, 105	*Florida Staysweet* (84 days)	16
	Country Gentleman (89 days)	20, 23, 24, 66	*Silver Queen* (94 days)	15, 26, 28, 35, 105	*Sugarloaf* (83 days)	26, 28, 105	*Dinner Time* (85 days)	43
	Hickory King (85 days)	3, 15, 17, 104			*Symphony* (86 days)	16	*Illini Chief* (85 days)	43
	Blue Corn (100 days)	12, 68			*Kandy Korn* (89 days)	15, 26, 75, 105		
	Mandan Bride (98 days)	20, 51			*Tendertreat* (95 days)	29, 75		
	Longfellow Flint (117 days)	20			*White Lightning* (86 days)	1, 29, 35, 105		
	Rhode Island White Cap (115 days)	20						

*Hybrid

Cucumbers

The slender, tasty, European-type cucumbers, so productive when grown on a trellis, are becoming more popular in American gardens.

You don't need much space to harvest a bumper crop of cucumbers. New varieties promise more tasty pickling and salad cucumbers from each plant. One well-tended salad cucumber plant can yield a startling 30 to 40 pounds of cucumbers.

In addition to the new extra-productive hybrids there are scores of standard "picklers" and "slicers" that have proven themselves over decades. There are some exotic types worth growing, too, like the tender Oriental climbing varieties, the lemon cucumbers that are easily eaten out of hand like an apple, and sweet Armenian fruits that are tasty at 18 inches long.

All cucumbers love the most invigorating subtropical conditions: warm soil and long, hot, humid days with plenty of sunshine and balmy nights. But if your climate doesn't deliver these ideal conditions, don't worry. Many varieties are fast growers, delivering a bountiful harvest in 60 days, and produce well even in the short summers of the northern states.

Planning

There's a cucumber variety for every garden. Even if your garden is very small, you can have an abundant crop of cucumbers.

A new variety of home garden cucumber will set fruit without pollination. Plant breeders are now introducing a line of mild-flavored, thin-skinned, slender, seedless cucumbers that are very productive in the home garden. These new hybrids are parthenocarpic, which means that they will set and enlarge fruit *without* pollination. With the standard cucumber varieties, pollination is performed by bees, but they will not visit the short-lived cucumber flower in bad weather. The result can often be poor fruit set and low yields. Parthenocarpic varieties will set fruit with or without bees.

With fruit set assured, you can grow a profusion of cucumber fruits in a cramped space. One plant can do handsomely for a small family's fresh use; two can provide extras for relish and pickles. You will need at least a square foot of land (or a big container) for each plant, and it's helpful to have a 6-foot-high trellis.

Sweet Success does well in all regions of the country, has resistance to cucumber scab and tolerance to cucumber mosaic virus, downy mildew, and powdery mildew. This parthenocarpic variety and others normally have only female blooms, which are earmarked by miniature fruits at their bases. But male blooms may occasionally develop if plants are stressed by lack of water, extreme temperatures, or insufficient nutrients. Pollination may occur from either the occasional male bloom or from other nearby cucumber varieties, producing some fruits with a seed-filled bulge at one end. (This is a good reason to put *Sweet Success* on the opposite side of the garden from standard cucumbers.)

The standard varieties are monoecious — they produce both male and female flowers and need bees to serve as pollinators to have a good fruit set. As sunny weather does not guarantee the arrival of bees, try encouraging more bees to the cucumber patch by planting a few marigolds in the row or one at the center of each hill.

Generally classed as pickling and slicing cucumbers, there are many excellent standard cucumber varieties that produce very well for backyard gardeners.

Treat picklers pretty much the same way as the larger, salad-type slicers; they tend to start bearing a bit earlier but often do not spread as far as slicers. Highly recommended picklers are *Saladin, Wisconsin SMR 18,* and *County Fair.*

Of the many different slicing varieties available, *Marketmore 70* holds its quality very well on the vine after it is mature. This variety produces firm, crisp, dark green fruits that are usually 6 to 9 inches long. *Burpeeana Hybrid II* can grow a bit larger than *Marketmore 70,* but is still firm and crisp, and the plants are vigorous growers. *Straight Eight* is a popular and prolific slicing type. Many slicing varieties offer excellent disease resistance, so read the seed packets and catalog descriptions carefully when choosing which slicer to plant. When picked small, slicers make good picklers, too.

Gynoecious cucumbers are special pickling or slicing hybrids that have only female flowers; however, they still need pollination. Seed companies usually include a few seeds, coated with an identifying colored dust, of a standard variety (having male blooms) for use as pollinizer. Plant one of the colored seeds for every seven or eight gynoecious seeds. The benefit of a gynoecious cucumber is an earlier, heavier harvest because the plant's first blooms will be female, fruit-bearing ones, rather than male, nonbearing blossoms as in standard varieties.

You may find the term "burpless" used in plant descriptions to describe long, slender cucumbers with tender skin and mild flavor. Usually burpless types are less bitter than other cucumbers and can be eaten unpeeled, fresh from the vine.

Although trellises aren't necessary for growing cucumbers, they do save space and promote the growth of uniformly shaped fruit. The cucumber trellis at right folds together for easy storage at season's end.

Essentials

Planning

❧ *Cucumbers grow best with long, hot, humid days with maximum sunshine and warm nights. Plants are extremely susceptible to frost.*

❧ *Sow seeds outside only after danger of frost when soil has warmed. Make a second sowing 4 to 5 weeks later for a late summer or early fall harvest. Cucumbers are ready to harvest in 65 to 105 days, depending on the variety.*

❧ *For an earlier harvest and to reduce the threat of insect damage to seedlings, start a few plants indoors in individual pots (or trays with separate compartments) about a month before your last spring frost date.*

❧ *Select disease-resistant varieties.*

Preparation

❧ *Choose a fertile site with well-drained soil; yields suffer in soil that stays wet.*

❧ *Set up trellises.*

Planting

❧ *To seed in rows, plant seeds 1 inch deep and about 6 inches apart.*

❧ *To plant in hills, plant four or five seeds in 1-foot-diameter circles set 5 to 6 feet apart.*

Care

❧ *Thin plants in rows to 1 or 2 feet apart, depending on the variety, when 3 to 4 inches tall. Thin plants in hills to the healthiest two plants when plants have two or three leaves.*

❧ *Keep soil evenly moist to prevent bitterness in cucumbers.*

❧ *Side-dress cucumbers about 4 weeks after planting, just as vines begin to run. Apply 2 handfuls of good compost or a tablespoon of 5-10-10 or similar fertilizer per plant in a narrow band along the vines of each plant.*

❧ *Apply a thick layer of mulch about 4 weeks after planting.*

❧ *Cucumber beetles (page 277) are the most common insect pest. Also possible are pickleworms (page 279), squash vine borers (page 280), and whiteflies (page 281).*

❧ *Watch for bacterial wilt (page 282), which is spread by cucumber beetles. Also watch for mosaic virus (page 287), powdery mildew (page 286), downy mildew (page 284), anthracnose (page 282), bacterial blight (page 282), and fusarium wilt (page 285).*

Harvesting

❧ *Once cucumbers reach pickling or slicing size, harvest every couple of days to prevent cukes from getting overly large or yellow and to keep plants productive. Pickling varieties seem to go by their peak the fastest.*

Preparation

Cucumbers are shallow-rooted and require ample soil moisture at all stages of their growth. Before planting, mix plenty of compost or well-rotted manure into the soil to hold in moisture. Be sure the soil drains well or yields will be reduced.

After the soil has been well prepared, set up trellises to support the vines. By setting them up now, you will avoid stepping on plants or compacting the soil later. Although trellises aren't necessary for growing cucumbers, we recommend them to save space and promote the growth of uniformly shaped fruit. The long fruits of *Sweet Success* will particularly benefit from growing on trellises. They will grow well on the ground, but many of the long fruits will be curved because one side of the fruit is restricted by the soil.

Planting

Sow seeds outdoors 1 inch deep and about 6 inches apart, when the soil has completely warmed and all danger of frost has passed.

Cucumbers can be planted in rows or hills. Hills are not raised mounds of soil but planting circles about 1 foot in diameter. You should set your hills 5 to 6 feet apart. Sow seed at a rate of 4 to 5 seeds per hill. With rows spaced 4 to 6 feet apart, the seeds should be sown about 6 inches apart. The advantage of hills is that you can thin according to which plants

Out-of-the-Ordinary Cucumbers

Bush Varieties

Several compact varieties, such as *Pot Luck* and *Bush Champion,* are ideal for gardeners with only a tiny space for cucumbers. (Standard varieties may easily spread 6 to 10 feet.) The bush plants usually vine about 2 or 3 feet at most; per plant yields, however, are lower than standard types.

Armenian Cucumbers

Armenian cucumbers originated in southern Asia and have been grown in India for many years. Also called snake or serpent cucumbers, they are actually part of the melon family. The fruits are long and skinny, crisp, thin-skinned, and never bitter. They have few seeds and spines and are burpless. It's best to pick them after they are 18 inches long. They'll grow to 3 feet, one reason they are sometimes called "yard-long" cucumbers. They're 2 to 3 inches wide throughout their length, so they're great for slicing.

Gherkins

You can make gherkin pickles using small standard cucumbers (the method used for supermarket gherkins) or by using fruits of the so-called true gherkin, a plant of a different species. The true gherkin doesn't vine as much as regular cucumbers and its leaves resemble those of watermelon plants. The gherkin fruit is 2 to 3 inches long, oblong, and grows on a long stem.

Lemon Cucumbers

Lemon cucumbers don't taste like lemons, but are yellow and look like them. Unavailable in most stores, they're sweet and crisp, great in salads and for pickling. Some gardeners eat them out of hand like apples. *Lemon* cukes don't become bitter on the vine with age. They store well in a cool, dark place or in the refrigerator.

Suyo Long Cucumbers

This is one of several Oriental burpless cucumbers that is easy to digest, quite slender (averaging about 1½ inches in diameter), and long (up to 17 inches). *Suyo Long* is highly ridged with spiny skin, but is still fine for fresh eating. These cucumbers are exceptionally sweet, with seeds so small they are scarcely noticeable.

The *Suyo Long* is widely adapted, grows well in hot weather, and sets fruits early. It is resistant to powdery mildew.

Bush cucumber

Armenian

Gherkin

Lemon

Suyo Long

look healthiest, rather than which ones are the proper distance apart.

Care

Cucumbers will benefit from side-dressing with compost or a general fertilizer about 4 weeks after planting. Apply the fertilizer in a narrow band alongside each vine, two handfuls of compost or 1 tablespoon of 5-10-10 per plant.

Mulch (if you use organic materials, you'll need a thick layer) at this time to maintain moisture and keep the fruits off the soil.

Cucumbers have few insect problems; the most troublesome may be the cucumber beetle, a chewer that in certain areas of the Midwest, North, and Mid-Atlantic states can feed heavily on small plants and spread an uncontrollable bacterial wilt that causes plants to die out before giving a harvest.

Harvesting

You should harvest picklers when they are 4 to 5 inches long; *Liberty* is one pickling variety that can grow larger and be harvested later as a slicing cucumber.

When you're going to make a batch of pickles, harvest the cucumbers in the morning as soon as the leaves dry off, and put them in the refrigerator or a very cool place. They'll be in their firmest condition at this point.

Slicing cucumbers can be harvested whenever they are big enough to use, but before they begin to turn orange or yellow. If your vines bear more than you can use at one time, pick the cukes anyway. Allowing them to ripen to the orange stage on the vine will cause the plant to stop producing.

Cucumbers contain mostly water, so the key to storing them after the harvest is to keep that water in, a reason many cucumbers in supermarkets are waxed. Wrap fruits in plastic wrap or bag them and they'll keep a week or more in the refrigerator. The best storage temperature is 45° to 50°F.

How to Control the Cucumber Beetle

Young cucumber plants are especially vulnerable to attacks by cucumber beetles. Adult beetles emerge from the soil in the spring and begin to nibble on the leaves and stems of the emerging plants. Adults also lay eggs at the base of the plant and then the larvae gnaw on the roots. The beetles spread a bacterial wilt carried in their feces; this disease will cause plants to wilt and die before bearing fruit. There are two kinds of cucumber beetles, one spotted, one striped; both are ¼ inch long, greenish-yellow with dark markings.

Here are some basic control strategies:

1. Stagger your planting dates. Start some seedlings early indoors and set them out at normal planting time. If the plants are big enough they will avoid much damage. Sow different hills a week or 10 days apart so your plants won't all be at the most vulnerable stage at the same time.

2. Cover up. If you have just one or two hills of cucumbers, try covering each hill area with a fine netting (anchored with soil at the edges) right after seeding to fend off adult beetles.

3. Trap them. If your plants are in the blooming stage, you can trap some inside spent blossoms. They gather there after the blooms have been pollinated and begin to wither and close. Check the blossoms in late evening. If you see any beetles inside, pick the flowers and drop them into a bucket of ammonia water to dispose of them.

4. Mulch well. A thick straw mulch may reduce the number of adult beetles laying eggs at the base of the plants.

5. Interplant. In a small garden, interplanting cucumbers with onions, tomatoes, and chives might help keep beetles from harming your cucumbers.

6. Watch for later beetle hatches. In most areas you'll get more than one generation of cucumber beetles hitting the garden. Be on the alert. Also, be sure to till or spade the garden late in the season to expose adults feeding on plant debris and weeds.

7. Home gardeners should not need to use poison sprays for most problems. However, the ultimate means of control for cucumber beetles is to spray regularly with a recommended pesticide as soon as plants emerge from the ground. Be sure to apply spray around the base of the plants.

Cucumber Sources

Armenian 6, 73
***Burpeeana Hybrid II** 6
***Bush Champion** 6
***County Fair** 21, 39
Gherkins 25
Lemon 6, 21, 39
***Liberty** 6, 21
Marketmore 1, 6, 39, 70
***Pot Luck** 25, 29
***Saladin** 6, 29
Straight Eight 6, 29, 39
Suyo Long 51, 69, 73
***Sweet Success** 6
Wisconsin SMR 18 1, 39

***hybrid**

Eggplant

There are easily twenty or more eggplant varieties to choose from. The *Dusky Hybrid* eggplant at left is a reliable, short-season variety ideal for central and northern gardeners.

For a long time, eggplant, a staple of many Middle Eastern countries, was a low-ranking crop on the list of vegetables popular in the United States. In fact, in the USDA's 736-page 1959 yearbook, which was devoted entirely to food, eggplant was not even mentioned. But today, gardeners grow eggplant more frequently than they do strawberries, asparagus, pumpkins, and a host of other crops.

It may be that higher food prices have led cooks and gardeners to look for vegetable substitutes for expensive meats. Eggplant fits that bill admirably. Also, breeders have introduced plants that yield more eggplants earlier, so it's getting easier for a family (even in northern climates) to garner enough for the season from just three or four plants.

The origin of eggplant is a bit obscure, but whether it came from India or China, it appears that enterprising Arab traders carried it west on their travels. By the middle of the fourth century A.D. it was established in Middle Eastern as well as Far Eastern countries. The first varieties bore brightly colored, egg-shaped fruits of white, green, brown, yellow, and purple. You can still grow colorful eggplants today.

Far right: If you live in a region with a short growing season and want to encourage early fruiting, you can pinch off the bottom three or four suckers about a month after transplanting. If left on, these suckers will develop late flowers, which may set fruit that won't ripen before a frost.

Eggplants are available in a wide range of colors. Novelty white eggplants grow smaller than regular purple varieties but taste just as good.

Planning

It is just about impossible to raise eggplants by direct seeding in the garden, but plants are available in the springtime just about anywhere tomato starts are sold. If you are buying plants, look for the short, stocky ones with healthy-looking foliage. Each plant, if tended well, can yield ten or twelve fruits during the season.

You can also grow your own "six pack" of plants. Plan to sow eggplant seed in flats or peat pots at least 60 days before the ground warms up (about a week earlier than your tomatoes). Germination takes about a week if room temperature is over 65°F (longer in cooler rooms).

There are easily twenty or more eggplant varieties available from mail-order companies to tempt gardeners. Most common in the United States are *Black Beauty, Burpee Hybrid, Early Beauty,* and *Jersey King.* These will normally produce the first large harvest about 70 or 75 days after transplanting. *Dusky Hybrid* matures its first fruits in 62 days or so and is a good choice for northern growers.

If you'd like to investigate the thinner, longer eggplants, try *Early Long Purple, Long Tom Hybrid,* or *Ichiban. Ichiban* is a dependable hybrid Oriental eggplant with slender fruits up to 12 inches long, 2 to 3 inches in diameter. As for the novelty types, we've found the *Easter Egg* variety delightful in the garden and as easy to prepare in the kitchen as the purple varieties. If you'd like to try a small eggplant said to be truly round and perfect for stuffing, get seeds of the *Ronde de Valence* or *Small Round Italian* eggplant.

Preparation

Soil requirements are the same as for related vegetables, such as peppers and tomatoes. Choose a fertile, well-drained spot in full sun. Thoroughly prepare the soil with a combination of rotted manure and compost or a general commercial fertilizer such as 5-10-5 a week or so before planting time. Apply 2 to 3 pounds per 100 square feet.

Eggplant is tender and needs hot weather for growth. Don't set it out too early without protection; wait until the last spring frost date has passed.

If spring comes late in your area and soil temperatures stay cool, you can increase your production of eggplants by using black plastic mulch.

Planting

Set the plants 1½ to 2 feet apart in rows or beds. Add to each transplant hole a tablespoon of balanced fertilizer such as 5-10-10, mixed with and topped with 2 or 3 inches of soil. If you live in the South, you may want to give the plants more space.

Care

Over the long growing season, your eggplants will grow quite large. Many southern gardeners stake the plants for extra support when they get tall.

Though eggplant is somewhat drought tolerant, try to give it the 1 inch of water a week it needs if rainfall is insufficient.

An organic mulch will help retain moisture, but don't spread it until the soil has completely warmed up, usually about 4 weeks after transplanting.

If you live in the North, prune the bottom three or four suckers on your eggplant when they are still small to encourage earlier fruiting. They appear about 4 weeks after transplanting when the plant is about 15 inches high, forming

between the main stem and existing branches (just like the ones on your tomato plants). If you leave the suckers they will develop late flowers, and these may set fruit that won't ripen before frost.

A 3-year crop rotation for eggplant and other members of the tomato family is recommended to discourage verticillium wilt and phomopsis blight (also called fruit rot). *Florida Market* is a variety resistant to phomopsis blight.

One early-season foe is the flea beetle. It often arrives right after transplanting, leaving many shotgun holes in the leaves at a critical time in the plant's growth. If spider mites attack in dry weather, plants may be hosed daily to knock the mites off the leaves. Later in the season you can handpick larger bugs, such as Colorado potato beetles, if they become a problem.

Harvesting
Start harvesting eggplants when they're about half grown (usually 4 to 5 inches long with standard varieties, a bit smaller with mini types). If you let some grow to full size, harvest them when the skin is still glossy; when it dulls, the flesh is getting tough and losing flavor. Overripe eggplant also has black seeds forming inside. Use a sharp knife to cut fruit off with an inch of stem so you don't damage the plant.

Essentials

Planning
🍂 *Eggplants are a warm-weather crop.*
🍂 *Start plants indoors in flats or peat pots about 2 months before the soil warms up in your region, or buy nursery transplants just before planting.*

Preparation
🍂 *A fertile, well-drained soil is required for best results.*
🍂 *Use a covering of black plastic mulch to warm heavy clay soils before setting out transplants.*
🍂 *Mix an inch or so of well-rotted manure or a general fertilizer such as 5-10-5 throughout the planting bed about a week before planting. Apply 2 to 3 pounds per 100 square feet.*

Planting
🍂 *Set out the transplants when all spring frost danger is past. Space plants 18 to 24 inches apart.*
🍂 *Mix a tablespoon of 5-10-5 or a shovelful of rotted manure or good compost with the soil in the bottom of each planting hole and cover with more soil.*

Care
🍂 *Add an organic mulch to retain moisture and control weeds after the soil has completely warmed up, about 1 month after setting out transplants.*
🍂 *Side-dress with 1 tablespoon of 5-10-5 or 10-6-4 per plant when the plants have set several fruits. In southern regions where the growing season is long, side-dress every 3 to 4 weeks.*
🍂 *Watch for flea beetles (page 278), Colorado potato beetles (page 277), and spider mites (page 280). Tomato hornworms (page 281) may also be troublesome.*
🍂 *Anthracnose (page 282), phomopsis blight (page 285), and verticillium wilt (page 287) are potential disease problems.*

Harvesting
🍂 *Start harvesting when the eggplants are 4 to 5 inches long. The skin should be shiny; dull skin is a sign that the eggplant is overripe.*
🍂 *Use a sharp knife and cut the eggplant from the plant, leaving at least 1 inch of stem attached to the fruit.*

Herbs

Dill *(left)* is one of ten herbs recommended for a small, easy-to-manage herb garden. The flavor of its leaves peaks when the flower heads are opening.

Herbs, with their multitude of uses, enhance gardens by adding color, interesting forms, and rich or subtle fragrances. An essential addition to many recipes, herbs are easy to grow and well worth the effort.

Plant your herbs where you can get to them easily for frequent harvesting. You can keep them in your vegetable garden or plant them in a special show-off bed of their own. If you plant perennial herbs in the vegetable garden, set them off so they'll be easy to avoid during spring and fall tilling.

Herbs may be annuals (started from seed each year, as is basil), biennials (like parsley), or perennials (like chives). Despite these basic differences, most herbs require the same growing conditions: a minimum of 6 hours of sunlight per day, excellent soil drainage, and moderately rich, friable soil.

All herbs will benefit from a little fertilizer added to the soil. Use 1½ to 2 pounds of 5-10-10 or its equivalent per 100 square feet during soil preparation a day or two before planting. Many herbs will get tall and leggy with higher fertilizer amounts; compact, bushy plants usually produce more essential oils for herb flavor.

Growing herbs, like cooking with herbs, is often a process of trial and error. If a plant is not growing well in a particular location, dig it up and try it in a new location. Early spring, just as new growth begins, is a good time to move many perennial herbs.

Basil should be pinched back slightly at 6 weeks to spur side growth and delay flowering. If flowering stalks do develop, cut them off.

Basil

If you do any Italian cooking at all, you'll want to include basil in the herb patch. Basil can't be planted until after the last frost date, but in the heat of summer it will produce abundantly.

There are several types of basil to choose from; the one offered by most garden supply stores and in seed racks is bush or sweet basil, a compact plant growing to 18 inches or so during the season. Purple basil (*Dark Opal*) adds a splendid burgundy color to the garden. It can be used like common basil, though it's a little less sweet. The purple leaves create a beautiful color when steeped in white vinegar. Recently rediscovered by many cooks, lemon basil adds a lemony-basil fragrance to both the garden and the kitchen.

Start seeds indoors 6 weeks before the last frost date (70°F soil temperature preferred) or seed directly in the garden (about ¼ inch deep) after the last frost date when soil is warm. Set transplants or thin seedlings to stand at least 10 to 12 inches apart; more room (16 to 24 inches apart) will encourage low, bushy plants to develop. Plant in full sun.

Pinch the center stalk of basil after it has grown for 6 weeks to force side growth and prevent early flowering. If flower stalks do develop, cut them off. Mulch is recommended in hot areas since basil likes a steady moisture supply. Basil is generally pest-free. Early cold weather as the plants mature may ruin the crop, so be sure to harvest if temperatures threaten to dip into the 30s.

Basil is at its most pungent when fresh. The best time to harvest is just as the plant starts to bud, well before flowers bloom. Snip leaves or branches at this time and pinch off flower buds to keep the plant productive. You can also cut the entire plant about 6 to 8 inches above ground, leaving at least one node with two young shoots intact. The plant should produce a second but smaller harvest several weeks later.

Since the leaves lose some of their flavor when dried, freezing is the best method for winter storage. To quick-freeze basil, clean and dry whole sprigs and pack them in plastic bags with the air pressed out.

To dry basil, pinch off the leaves at the stem and dry them in a shady, well-ventilated area. Check in 3 or 4 days, and if they are not totally dry, finish drying in the oven, otherwise the leaves may turn brown and black. (Use the lowest heat possible with the door slightly open, turn leaves for even drying, and check frequently.)

Chives

Once you plant chives in your garden, chances are you'll always have them. Chives are hardy perennial plants — one of the first harvests each year — and can be easily dug up, divided, and moved as your garden evolves over the years.

Common chives (*Allium schoenoprasum*) grow to a foot tall and have narrow, hollow green leaves and spherical pink or purple flowers. The leaves are used in all kinds of sauces and salads to lend a delicate onion flavor. The flowers, when added to white vinegar, impart a lovely pink or purple color.

Garlic chives (*Allium tuberosum*) are a close relative of chives but differ slightly in flavor and appearance. Garlic chives have flat leaves, and white flowers, highly attractive to bees, appear in the summer. Although the seed heads are excellent for decorating wreaths, be careful not to let the seeds fall, as garlic chives could become a nuisance. As the name indicates, their flavor combines the tastes of garlic and chives. Sometimes called Oriental chives, they are used in soups, salads, sauces, and meat dishes.

Start plants from seed, purchase a plant or two, or dig up part of a clump from a neighbor's garden. If seeding, plant in mid- to late spring in a sunny or slightly shady area. Chives prefer rich soil and will tolerate either moist or dry conditions. Sow in clusters 1 to 1½ feet apart. Small clumps of chives potted in the fall will grow indoors.

Remove flower stalks after they bloom. Divide the plants every 3 or 4 years.

You can begin harvesting about 6 weeks after planting or as soon as established plants resume growth in the spring. As you need leaves, cut the outer ones right back to the base. Use them fresh or frozen; they do not retain their flavor well when dried.

Dill

Common dill grows to a height of about 3 feet; *Bouquet* dill is a smaller variety that generally produces fewer seedheads.

Dill does poorly when transplanted, so start the crop from seed in the garden. The plants thrive in rich, loose soil and a very sunny location. Plant 1 or 2 weeks before the last spring frost date if you want the seeds to mature when you are doing your first cucumber pickling.

Sow seeds ¼ inch deep in rows 18 to 24 inches apart or broadcast over a bed 2 feet square and gently rake the seeds into the soil. Plants should emerge in 10 to 14 days; let them grow for 10 to 14 more days and then thin them to 12 to 18 inches apart.

Make small sowings a few weeks apart until midsummer to get a season-long supply of fresh leaves.

The plants are very spindly so you may have to stake the tallest plants to keep them from bending over in strong winds. Let a few plants mature their seed; if the area is not disturbed very much they will provide many new plants next season.

You can start harvesting the fernlike leaves about 8 weeks after planting. Pinch off outer leaves close to the stem. Leaves have the highest flavor just when flower

The hollow green leaves of chives can be used in many sauces and salads. Chives are one of the first harvests in the spring and can be easily dug up, divided, and moved.

heads are opening. Dry leaves in a dark place on a screen and seal them in an airtight jar; freeze leaves to retain more of their flavor.

For pickling, cut off the seedheads when they're light brown, dry them for a few days in paper bags with air holes in the sides, then shake seeds loose to the bottom of the bag.

French Tarragon

French tarragon is an essential herb for many cooks, but one that can cause some confusion to the first-time grower.

You must know exactly what you are buying when you purchase a plant because French tarragon is often confused with Russian tarragon, a weedy plant with little value in cooking. French tarragon is a hardy perennial that can only be grown from tip cuttings of new growth, root cuttings, or division. If tarragon seed is for sale, it's probably the Russian variety.

French tarragon is a hardy perennial. One or two plants should be sufficient for a family. Young leaves and stem tips are best used fresh or to flavor vinegar.

This herb does well in full sun or partial shade, but it needs well-drained soil. Purchase plants, or if you have a friend with an established tarragon bed, get plants in early spring by dividing each established plant into two or three. New plants can also be derived from stem cuttings of new growth or from root cuttings in the spring or fall. Space plants about 2 to 3 feet apart to give them room to spread.

Prune the plants to prevent flowering and to keep the height down to 2 feet so they don't flop over. In central and northern states, mulch plants in late fall to protect the roots over the winter. Divide the plants every 3 to 4 years to keep them healthy and vigorous.

Leaves are best used fresh in early summer or frozen for later use. Tarragon's aniselike flavor makes it a wonderful addition to salads, fish, chicken, sauces, and vinegars. Drying some of the harvest is also an option, but the leaves can lose a lot of their flavor if left to dry too long. Pack them in airtight containers as soon as they are dry.

Marjoram

A very popular herb, marjoram goes by several names: sweet marjoram, garden marjoram, and annual marjoram. A tender perennial, sweet marjoram rarely survives even mild winters, so seeds or cuttings must be started each year. The herb, a close relative of oregano, will grow in an upright bush form up to 2 feet tall. Creeping golden marjoram is smaller and makes an attractive border plant.

Seeds are quite small and are best started indoors about 6 weeks before the last frost date. They can be set out after that date in full sun and in slightly alkaline soil rich in organic matter. Place plants about 6 to 8 inches apart or in several clumps of two or three plants set 12 to 14 inches apart. Six to ten plants will supply a household's normal use.

Keep the soil slightly moist around plants. Try to cultivate often to prevent weed competition and aerate the soil. Add 1 inch of compost in a 12-inch circle around the plants after each harvest to nourish them.

When flowers appear, cut the plants to several inches above the soil line. Cut again later in the season when more flower heads form. Use leaves fresh or dry them for winter use. To dry, tie the stems together and hang bunches upside down in a ventilated, dark area. Leaves dry quickly and retain their flavor well. After drying, crush the leaves, toss out the stems, and store in airtight containers.

Mint

The mint family offers a tremendous diversity of refreshing scents and tastes for cooking, in beverages, and in potpourris.

Mint is terribly invasive, particularly in a rich, moist soil, so plan to control it by growing it either in a pot or with some sort of confinement such as metal or plastic (to a depth of 14 inches) in the garden.

Spearmint (*Mentha spicata*) is used most commonly in the kitchen for mint juleps, sauces, jellies, teas, or to highlight flavors in a fruit salad. It's very fragrant and grows 2 to 3 feet tall with pale violet blooms in mid- to late summer. Peppermint (*Mentha x piperita*) is another popular mint with a strong aroma; it grows to 3 feet tall with smooth leaves 1 to 3 inches long. Another dozen or so mint varieties, including some interesting fruit-scented types, are available from garden centers or herb plant companies.

Start with one or two purchased plants and set them about 2 feet apart in a sunny location. They'll quickly fill in the open area between plants. Use a light mulch to retain moisture and keep leaves clean. Harvest young or mature leaves.

Don't let the plants get too thick. Cut them back frequently to promote fresh growth. A rust fungus infection may appear on some leaves; pick and destroy blemished leaves and move roots to a new location.

Garden Plan

This 3-by-10-foot herb plan is for a bed in a vegetable garden. There are perennials in the bed, but they are grouped together for ease in maintenance. The mints should be planted in lumber containers to restrain their roots. There is no dill in the bed because dill does best planted in a single row or in groups of rows. It is not easily mixed with other herbs.

Harvesting and Drying Herbs

Harvest herbs throughout the growing season, as most plants benefit from being cut back. For leaf herbs the best time to harvest is just as the plants begin to bud, when they'll have maximum flavor and fragrance. Cut herbs in the morning, when the dew has dried but before the sun becomes very bright. (Many herb oils will volatilize into the atmosphere during the heat of the day.) Once cut, wash the herbs, pat them dry, and hang or lay them in a warm, dark, well-ventilated spot until they are dry. Label and store them in glass or plastic containers out of direct sunlight.

To freeze herbs, wash and pat them dry. Then chop them by hand or in a food processor. Put the chopped herbs into labeled plastic containers and freeze. A good quick method is to add a bit of water to the herbs in the food processor and then pour the mixture into ice cube trays and freeze. When you need herbs for soups, stews, or sauces, just pop out an herb cube.

The mint family offers a tremendous range of scents and tastes. Spearmint, shown here, grows 2 to 3 feet tall and is very fragrant.

Pick leaves throughout the summer as you need them. Mint leaves can be dried easily for winter use on trays or by hanging bunched branches upside down in a dark, well-ventilated, warm area. Leaves are easy to freeze, too.

Oregano

There are several types of oregano, and while we recommend only one for kitchen use, others can be used as attractive border plantings or for wreath-making.

The oregano most often used in cooking is *Origanum heracleoticum* and goes by the common names Greek oregano, winter sweet marjoram, and Italian oregano. It's a hardy plant that establishes quickly, getting no taller than 6 to 8 inches. Be sure not to buy the common oregano (*Origanum vulgare*) if you want to cook with it. Common oregano has no real flavor, though it is covered with ornamental lavender flowers in summer, which dry well and are often used in wreaths. Golden oregano can be used for a ground cover or in container plantings. For culinary oregano, purchase a plant or plants from a reputable herb nursery to insure a flavorful, hardy plant.

Oregano is easily started from seed after the last spring frost; you can also divide

Oregano is easily started from seed after danger of frost has passed. Its leaves dry easily, store well, and can even be frozen.

an established bed to get new plants. Rich, fertile soil is best. Thin plants to stand 8 to 10 inches apart.

Trim back before flowering (approximately 5 to 6 weeks after planting) to stimulate a denser, bushier growth habit. Plants will seed easily so you can thin out 3- and 4-year-old plants to keep the bed quality high.

Harvest leaves as you need them; the optimal flavor period is just before flowers bloom. Leaves dry easily and store well; they can be frozen, too.

Parsley

Parsley deserves recognition for more than its role as a garnish — it is very rich in iron and vitamins A and C and is a good breath freshener.

Although parsley is a biennial, it is best sown every year because the leaf flavor is diminished in the second season. Growing it from seed requires patience, as the seedlings can take up to 4 weeks to emerge from the soil. Soaking the seeds overnight in warm water before planting will help speed germination.

The curly leaf parsley (var. *crispum*) is the most common type because it makes such an attractive garnish. For cooking and chopping, the flat-leaved parsley (var.

neapolitanum) is preferable; it's easier to work with and has a better flavor.

Sow in individual pots indoors or start outside in the garden. Plants do well in sun or partial shade, and prefer a rich, moist soil. Choose as weed-free an area as

Parsley is an excellent herb for indoor or container growing. Even though it's a biennial, sow parsley each year; second-year sprigs have less flavor.

possible for garden sowing — you don't want a jungle to develop while you're waiting for seeds to germinate. The crop can handle cold weather, so start seeding 2 to 3 weeks before the last spring frost. Thin plants to stand 6 to 10 inches apart. Provide an even supply of water all summer. The cabbage looper may nibble on plants in some areas.

To harvest, cut entire leaves from the outer portion of the plant as you need them. To dry parsley, cut the plant at soil level and hang it in a shady, warm, well-ventilated area. Once thoroughly dried, crumble the parsley and store it in an airtight container.

To keep fresh parsley for as long as possible, store it in the refrigerator with the leaf stalks in water.

A few plants can be dug up, set in large pots with extra soil, and brought indoors to a sunny window for light winter harvests.

Sage

Sages encompass a large group of plants, although just a few are really considered to be good culinary herbs.

First and foremost is garden sage (*Salvia officinalis*), a hardy perennial recognized by its gray-green foliage and beautiful blue flowers in the spring. Plants can get quite tall and leggy, so the dwarf form (*Salvia officinalis* var. *nana*) is a better, more compact specimen. It has an equally good flavor but is not as hardy as its standard counterpart.

There are several cultivars of garden sage that are highly ornamental because of their leaf color. Purple sage (*Salvia officinalis* cv. Purpurescens), golden sage (*Salvia officinalis* cv. Aurea), and tricolor sage (*Salvia officinalis* cv. Tricolor) can add great variety and accent to the garden although all tend to be less hardy than regular sage.

You can start plants easily indoors from seed or in the garden in early spring. However, plants grown from seed may not have the same leaf shape and color as the parent plant. A better way to grow true-to-form, high-quality sage is to get cuttings from a friend's best-looking plants. Set plants or thin seedlings to stand 24 to 30 inches apart. Sage thrives in a sunny garden location and, while plants are young, needs a steady moisture supply in well-drained soil.

Each spring, prune the heavier, woody stems from the plants. The quality will drop off after 4 or 5 years, so dig up older plants and replace them with new ones started from seed or by cuttings.

Don't harvest too heavily the first year; give the plants time to get established. The leaves can be harvested at any time. They keep well dried or frozen.

Thyme

The thyme group of herbs is aromatic, versatile, and plentiful — over fifty varieties are judged beneficial for culinary or garden uses.

The thyme most often used in cooking is known as English thyme (a form of *Thymus vulgaris*). Like the other thymes, it has woody stems with small oval leaves. It will grow 8 to 12 inches high (many other thymes are smaller). Creeping varieties are good as edging plants or in rock gardens.

Loved for its lemon scent, lemon thyme (*Thymus x citriodorus*) is a delightful plant for both garden and kitchen. A cultivar of lemon thyme with variegated yellow leaves and a prostrate habit is known as Doone Valley. It makes a beautiful ground cover, particularly in winter when it turns strong shades of yellow, red, and green. Caraway thyme (*Thymus herba-barona*) is a low-growing plant combining the fragrances of caraway and thyme; it has dark green leaves.

Seeds are troublesome to start because of slow, uneven germination. Buy a plant or two of the variety you want from a good nursery and plant it in the spring in full sun where the soil is light and well drained. You can also start plants from cuttings if you have a friend willing to share. Space the plants 9 inches apart.

Where winters are very cold, mulch the plants after the ground freezes with a light mulch such as pine needles. Trim the plants back a bit in the spring and summer to contain growth and prevent them from developing too much woody growth.

Leaves and sprigs can be harvested all summer. In the early fall cut and tie sprigs together and hang them upside down in a dark, well-ventilated, warm area to dry. You can also dry stemless leaves on a tray or freeze them.

Herb Sources

Catalogs specializing in herbs may offer plants and/or seeds. Park and Nichols vegetable catalogs also offer large herb selections.

Basil

Chives
Common chives
Garlic chives

Dill

French Tarragon
(var. sativa)
plants only

Marjoram

Mint
Spearmint
Peppermint

Oregano
Common oregano
Origanum heracleoticum (Greek oregano, winter sweet marjoram, Italian oregano)

Parsley
Curly Leaf (var. crispum)
Flat leaved (var. neapolitanum)

Sage
Dwarf garden sage
Garden sage
Golden sage
Purple sage
Tricolor sage

Thyme
Caraway thyme
English thyme
Lemon thyme

Herb Basics

Herb	Season	Spacing (inches)	Height (inches)
Basil, Sweet *Ocimum basilicum*	Annual	10–12	18–24
Chives *Allium schoenoprasum*	Perennial	12–18	12
Dill *Anethum graveolens*	Hardy Annual	12–18	24–36
French Tarragon *Artemesia dracunculus* var. *sativa*	Perennial	24–36	30
Marjoram, Sweet *Origanum marjorana*	Tender Perennial	6–8	24
Mint *Mentha,* various species and cultivars	Perennial	24	18–24
Oregano *Origanum heracleoticum* (syn. *Origanum hirtum*)	Perennial	8–10	8
Parsley *Petroselinum crispum*	Biennial	6–10	8–12
Sage *Salvia officinalis*	Perennial	24–30	24
Thyme *Thymus,* various species	Perennial	24	18–24

Lettuce

A tight mulch keeps soil cool and helps loose-headed lettuce *(left)* retain its crispness and flavor. Red-leafed lettuce *(above)* stands out in the garden and in the salad bowl.

With the proper growing schedule, you can have an extended salad season of lettuce far superior to anything you find in the supermarkets. Home-grown head lettuce such as *Iceberg* can have thirty times the vitamin A as supermarket heads, and it will always be fresh when you pluck it out of the garden at its peak.

The key is to plant small amounts of lettuce, not one big crop, beginning as early in the season as possible and extending through the summer into early fall. We recommend direct seeding or transplanting lettuce seedlings into the garden every 2 weeks or so.

Growing your own lettuce allows you to experiment with lots of different types besides the familiar *Iceberg* types. There are many tasty looseleaf varieties, as well as tall, rich-flavored cos or romaine types, buttery, soft-headed types such as *Bibb* or *Boston,* not to mention special varieties that are heat-resistant to give you good crops into the summer.

Top: Sow extra seeds of romaine-type lettuces because of their low germination rate. *Middle: Iceberg*-type or crisphead lettuces produce well as a fall crop. *Bottom:* Several good red or *Ruby*-type leaf lettuce varieties are now available.

Planning

Lettuce is one of the easiest crops to grow if you have fertile garden soil. The challenge is in the timing — keeping fresh leaves and heads coming for as long as possible without having all of them reach maturity at the same time.

The season starts in the North during the cool, moist weather of spring, and during winter in the Deep South and parts of the Southwest. (Lettuce can be grown year-round in some Pacific coastal areas.) Once the season begins it's a matter of sowing more seeds or setting out small numbers of transplants at regular intervals, every 2 weeks or so in most areas.

Even for gardeners with little space, continually sowing small amounts of lettuce is a good idea because lettuce fits in just about everywhere in a small garden — between broccoli and other cabbage family members, where peas don't come up in the row, or intercropped with tomatoes, for example.

There are four major lettuce groups to choose from — crispheads, loose heads, cos or romaine types, and leaf lettuces.

Crispheads form solid, round, firm heads — the familiar *Iceberg* variety belongs here. Most varieties do poorly in heat, so we recommend growing your first *Iceberg*-type crop for a fall harvest — the cool weather is much more conducive to good head formation. Timing is important for fall harvest of mature heads. Plan to have the crop mature around the time of the expected first frost. Use the days-to-maturity rating of the variety (85 days for *Ithaca MI*, for example), add 10 days to compensate for declining light conditions, and then count back from the frost date.

The loose-head or Bibb lettuce types (also called butterhead) don't ever get as firm as *Iceberg* types. Instead they form loose heads with tender, dark or medium green leaves; with some varieties the outer leaves fold around delicate yellow-to-white leaves at the center of the plant. A few varieties tolerate some summer heat without losing quality.

Cos or romaine lettuces form taller, upright heads with longer leaves and thick midribs. Cos types generally take longer to mature than leaf or loose-head types and their seeds are slower to germinate.

Looseleaf lettuces do not form heads at all and reach eating size very quickly, in 30 to 40 days.

All lettuces do best in cool weather; the high temperatures of early summer tend to produce bitter leaves and trigger bolting in many varieties. Plan to sow or transplant lettuce for the summer season in partly shaded areas such as behind a cucumber trellis or shed, near the corn patch, or under a pole bean tepee.

Preparation

Work the soil in the earliest-drying section of the garden as soon as possible in the spring for your first sowing. Nitrogen is a key nutrient for a successful crop because greens must grow quickly to be of good quality. Nitrogen is especially important in the spring when soil microorganisms can't make nitrogen from available organic sources due to cold soil temperatures. Work 1 pound of 10-10-10 or its equivalent into the top few inches of soil for every 25 square feet of planting area.

Lettuce is a good crop to follow summer-harvested crops such as cabbage or green beans. To prepare a planting area, dig under the old crop, chopping it as best you can in the process. Mix twice the fertilizer recommended above, water the area heavily, and wait a few days before planting.

Planting

To make the most of the spring lettuce season, start some plants indoors 6 to 8 weeks before the last spring frost date. Try to space seeds about ½ inch apart, ¼ inch deep, in flats about 4 inches deep. There's no need to thin out the plants when they come up.

After 3 weeks of growth you can set them into the garden following a short hardening period. Space leaf types 3 to 4 inches apart, loose-heading types 6 to 8 inches apart, and cos and crispheading varieties 12 to 16 inches apart.

Cos and crisphead crops need plenty of space to develop nice, well-shaped heads. Lettuce roots are shallow and compete for food if they are spaced too closely. With regular water and side-dressings, you could space heading types closer, about 8 inches apart, and harvest some of them before they reach full size.

To start seeds in flats later in the season for setting out in late summer or early fall, follow the steps above. In warmer weather you can grow the plants on a protected porch or patio area instead of indoors.

Plant seeds well before the last spring frost date and make additional sowings every 10 to 14 days; keep them about ¼ to ½ inch deep, about an inch apart, in beds or rows.

Care

Immediately after setting out transplants, spray or water them with a mixture of seaweed and fish emulsion to help them overcome transplant shock and to give them some immediate nourishment. In cold, harsh weather, a windbreak will ease the shock.

When direct-seeded plants are about 2 inches tall, thin them according to type: leaf lettuce, 3 to 4 inches apart; loose-head lettuce, 6 to 8 inches apart; cos and crisphead types, 12 to 16 inches.

Side-dress plants 3 to 4 weeks after planting; use 1 teaspoon of 10-10-10 per plant sprinkled in a circle 3 to 4 inches from the plant, or water the plants thoroughly with another mixture of fish and seaweed emulsion.

When temperatures start climbing in late spring and early summer, consider mulching deeply around your lettuce to keep the soil cool and help maintain a high-quality harvest.

A steady supply of water is critical if you want crispy, tender leaves. Don't let the soil dry out at any time. Moisture is especially important in helping the lettuce

Essentials

Planning

🍃 *Lettuce is a cool-weather crop. Sow seeds as soon as the ground can be worked in the spring and follow with small sowings at 10- to 14-day intervals until late spring in warm summer areas or early summer in the North.*

🍃 *For earliest harvest, start seeds indoors 6 to 8 weeks before the last frost date and set them out after 3 weeks.*

🍃 *Plant heat-resistant varieties for late spring sowings.*

🍃 *Start fall crops in flats or directly in the garden in midsummer in northern states and in late summer in central and southern gardens.*

Preparation

🍃 *Work the earliest-drying part of the garden first for a spring crop.*

🍃 *Add 1 pound of 10-10-10 or its equivalent per 25 square feet of growing area before planting in early spring.*

Planting

🍃 *Sow seeds indoors ½ inch apart, ¼ inch deep, in 4-inch-deep flats.*

🍃 *Plant seeds outdoors in beds or rows ¼ to ½ inch deep.*

🍃 *Set out transplants spaced 3 to 4 inches apart for leaf lettuce, 6 to 8 inches for cos and loose-headed types, and 12 to 16 inches for firm-headed types.*

🍃 *Sow in late spring in semishaded areas to extend the harvest into the summer.*

Care

🍃 *Thin seeded lettuce outdoors when plants are 2 inches tall to stand 3 to 4 inches apart for leaf lettuce, 6 to 8 inches for cos and loose-headed, and 12 to 16 inches for firm-heading types.*

🍃 *Mulch in early summer to keep the soil cool.*

🍃 *Side-dress plants 3 to 4 weeks after planting; use 1 teaspoon 10-10-10 or its equivalent per plant or water with a mixture of fish and seaweed emulsion.*

🍃 *Insects and diseases are rare in home lettuce plantings. Slugs (page 280) may be a problem in cool, wet areas. Other insects that may infest lettuce include earwigs (page 278), leaf miners (page 279), and whiteflies (page 281).*

🍃 *Possible diseases include aster yellows (page 282), downy mildew (page 284), powdery mildew (page 286), and white mold (page 287).*

Harvesting

🍃 *Harvest leaf lettuce as soon as leaves are big enough to eat.*

🍃 *For a steady harvest, cut heading types before they reach full size.*

🍃 *Harvest in early morning when leaves are crisp and full of moisture.*

Regional Notes

Southwest

Grow lettuce in the fall and the spring, and even through the winter if it's mild. Start seedlings in flats and be sure to irrigate regularly to avoid bitterness. Recommended varieties are *Bibb, Buttercrunch, Black Seeded Simpson, Oakleaf, Ruby, Salad Bowl,* and *Romaine.* Choose the most heat-resistant types you can find, except in winter, and as temperatures rise, plant in partly shaded spots.

Hot soils (over 80°F) may cause thermodormancy in lettuce seed, preventing germination. Dampen seeds and refrigerate for 3 to 5 days before planting.

Northwest and California

In coastal areas you can probably grow lettuce most of the year. Mosaic virus can be a serious problem, though, so buy seed with the letters *MI* after the variety name, which indicate that the variety has a low incidence of mosaic virus.

Southeast

Gardeners in the Southeast often have a hard time growing lettuce because they may have a very short spring. Although lettuce can endure some heat during the day, if it remains hot at night the plants begin to produce a bitter-tasting substance.

Avoid the heat by growing lettuce very early or late. Start head lettuce 4 weeks before you usually can get out to work the soil; plant outdoors as soon as possible. Sow leaf lettuces outside at this time, too.

For fall crops, put seeds or plants in the ground in late summer when night temperatures begin to cool. Use maturity dates to time plantings so they're well grown just about the time of the first killing frost.

Good performers in southern gardens are *Mission* (crisphead) and *Augusta* (butterhead).

Seaweed and fish emulsion fertilizer added to the watering can will help new plants get off to a good start. A steady supply of water is critical for maintaining a high-quality lettuce harvest.

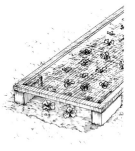

Lettuce is a cool-weather crop; high temperatures can produce bitter leaves and trigger bolting. To shade your crop, tack cheesecloth or a shade film to a wooden frame and set the frame 3 to 4 inches above the plants.

plants you set out in late summer get off to a good start. Shading small plants during hot weather is a good idea — use cheesecloth or a shade film tacked to a light wooden frame, and set the frame 3 or 4 inches above the plants.

Since lettuce is so shallow-rooted, weed around the plants with care to avoid disturbing any important feeder roots.

It's rare that you'll have an insect problem in home garden lettuce patches. In some parts of the country, slugs may appear, especially in a long wet spell or if plants are too close together.

Harvesting

With leaf lettuces, begin harvesting when leaves reach a usable size, about 4 to 5 inches long. You can pick the large outer leaves or slice the whole plant off about an inch above the soil line, prompting the plant to send out new growth, which will reach eating size in another 3 to 5 weeks.

If you plant enough heading plants, you can start harvesting when they reach half size. With *Iceberg* types, for example, that means when the plants have large leaves but before they form a head. This way you won't have all your heads full size during the same week. For those heads you allow to mature, harvest them promptly when they are ready; mature heads will deteriorate quickly. Use a sharp knife and cut the whole plant off right at the soil line. Handle the heads gently.

Leaves or heads will keep for a week or more in a loosely fastened plastic bag in the refrigerator.

Lettuce Varieties

Crisphead

Crispheads resemble familiar *Iceberg,* form a solid head with white, crunchy, densely packed inner leaves.

Great Lakes: Medium green, small, firm, flattened heads, fringed outer leaves. Holds well in warm weather. 70 days. 6, 33, 66

Montello MI: Recent new release from University of Wisconsin forms large heads. Resists root rot, tolerant to tip burn and rib blight; mosaic tested. 60–85 days. 33, 39

Ithaca MI: Medium-size, solid heads; an early, rapid grower. Resists tip burn, premature bolting; good throughout season. 60–85 days. 20, 39

King Crown: Similar to *Great Lakes* but earlier; large heads (to 8 inches). Good in range of soil types, weather conditions. Resists bottom rot, tip burn. 64 days. 20

Burpee's Iceberg: Medium-size heads, few outer leaves, silver-white hearts. 85 days. 6

Premier Great Lakes: Heads large, solid, uniform dark green. Heat and drought resistant, slow to bolt. 75–93 days. 17, 39

Mission: Dense, tight, 6- to 8-inch heads, sweet taste. Exceptional heat resistance. 74 days. 35

Vanguard: Outer leaves dark green, inside cream. Hot-weather type developed by USDA resists tip burn and sunscald. 90 days. 35

Calmar MI: Great Lakes strain; large, solid, medium green heads. Standard variety of West Coast lettuce industry for years. Resists most mildews, tolerant to tip burn. 70–75 days. 108

Montmar MI: Similar to *Calmar* but slightly earlier, more heat tolerant. Recommended for interior of southern California. 73 days. 108

Loose Heads

Also known as bibbs or butterheads; dark or medium green, smooth, thick, outer leaves folded around yellow-to-white center.

Buttercrunch: Leaves thick, juicy. Good early cold-frame crop, bolt resistant for summer crop. 50–65 days. 16, 20, 35, 39

Augusta: Extra-large, medium green leaves; smooth, buttery, with sweetest flavor of those tested by Park Seed Company. Disease resistant, heat tolerant. 57–68 days. 35

Tom Thumb: Leaves medium green and crumpled, center creamy white, heads tennis ball size. Good in window boxes. 65 days. 6, 35

Dark Green Boston: Dark green, smooth, waxy leaves, excellent flavor. 63–80 days. 6, 35, 39

Bibb: Dark green; the old standard of this type. 57 days. 35, 39, 66

Burpee Bibb: Small heads, dark green outer leaves, sometimes tinged brown, yellow inside. Slow to bolt, less subject to tip burn than other Bibbs. 65 days. 6

Kagran Summer: Light green, large firm hearts. Most bolt-resistant Bibb in hot weather; resists tip burn. Early midsummer harvest. 55 days. 20

Resistant: Medium-size *Boston* type, darker green than *Kagran Summer.* Resists tip burn, mosaic virus. 56 days. 20

Tania: Boston type, deep green, beautiful regular heads, smooth, tender. English strain with resistance to four types of mildew. Best as early or late crop; does not tolerate heat well. 65 days. 16

Cos or Romaine

Cos, or romaine, lettuces form tall, upright heads with long leaves and thick midribs.

Parris Island Cos: Leaves dark green, vigorous. Mosaic resistant. 75 days. 16, 17

Paris White Cos: Crisp, sweet, crunchy, 10-inch-tall heads. 63–83 days. 6, 33, 66

Valmaine Cos: Similar to Paris White, but dark green and larger. Mildew and heat tolerant, mosaic indexed. 68 days. 35, 39, 108

Erthel Crisp Mint: Like a typical cos in early stages, later developing savoyed leaves. Crisp and sweet, early; very slow to bolt, can be harvested for 3 months. Mildew, mosaic tolerant. Cos 65 days, mature 85 days. 74

Wallop: 1¼-pound heads, tender and sweet, like a cross between a crisphead and a cos. 80 days. 74

Lobjoit's Green Cos: 12-inch-tall, dark green heads, mild, good flavor. English strain, one of the earliest romaine types, a week ahead of Parris Island. 62 days. 20

Looseleaf

Looseleaf lettuces do not form heads; they are best harvested by picking off larger outer leaves or cutting plant back to an inch and letting it grow back.

Black Seeded Simpson: Crinkly, juicy, light green leaves. Earliest. 42 days. 6, 20, 33

Grand Rapids: Similar to previous two, slow to bolt. Standard for winter greenhouses, early spring outdoor crops. 45 days. 6, 17, 39

Salad Bowl: Leaves deeply cut, frilly, good flavor. Not as early as *Black Seeded Simpson,* but stands heat better. 46 days. 6, 17, 20, 66

Prizehead: Light green frilled and curly leaves, tinged with bronze or red. 48 days. 20, 33

Oakleaf: Tender, light green, oakleaf-shaped leaves. An old variety that stands the heat well. 46 days. 17, 20, 66

Ruby: Bright green and red ruffled leaves, sweet. 47 days. 6, 17, 35, 66

Melons

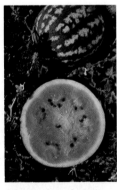

A home crop of muskmelons or watermelons will yield for several weeks in many areas. At left, note the near-ripe muskmelon and its still-developing neighbor.

Although we think of melons as fruits, they are grown like vegetables and need to be replanted each year.

Melons are a lot easier to grow than many people think. All melons, whether muskmelon, watermelon, or honeydew, have four requirements for high sugar content and flavor: lots of moisture, plenty of space, bright sun, and warm temperatures.

Three to four months of temperatures between 55° and 80°F is the usual requirement to grow good melons. For areas with shorter growing seasons, a couple of season-extending techniques that require very little labor guarantee sweet melon enjoyment for everyone.

The trick is to select early varieties, start seeds indoors, and use black plastic mulch and plastic row covers to provide plenty of heat for this warmth-loving crop. With these season-lengthening techniques, all backyard melon growers — in the North and the South — can know the joy of harvesting a tender, vine-ripened, annual fruit from the garden, one that doesn't require pruning or take the long wait for a fruit tree to yield.

Most melon lovers agree that the best way to eat any melon is straight out of hand, with spoon or without. "Eating a watermelon," an old saying goes, "is the only way to eat, drink, and wash your face at the same time."

Special Soil Enrichment Recipe for Melons

Here's a preplanting fertilizer recipe used by Marshall Richards, a retired market gardener and author of *Marvelous Melons*. His mixture can be placed under rows or hills a few days or a week before planting, whenever it is convenient.

Combine the ingredients below in a wheelbarrow and mix well. This amount will supply enough fertilizer for two or three melon plants.

    3 shovels of soil
    1 shovel of compost
    2 shovels of manure
    1 shovel of peat moss
    1 cup bone meal
    2 cups alfalfa meal
    1 cup cottonseed meal
    1 cup wood ashes
    1 cup dolomitic limestone

Put the mixture in a deep trench for row planting or in a hole for hill planting. Water well and add enough soil to make the surface level. Mark the hills and trenches with stakes and plant when the weather and other conditions are right.

Muskmelons

Planning

Many muskmelon varieties mature within 75 to 90 days, so if you want to grow melons in an area with a short growing season, they're the best melon to try. (Muskmelon is the correct term for what many gardeners and produce managers call cantaloupes. The true cantaloupe is a green-fleshed melon with a very hard, warty rind and is rarely grown in this country.)

There are three keys to growing muskmelons where a cloudy, cool summer or a short, frost-free season makes the crop risky: choose early varieties, start plants indoors, and use black plastic mulch and slitted row covers to warm up the soil.

Muskmelon varieties developed specifically for shorter seasons are *Earli Sweet* (68 days), *Sweet Granite* (75 days), *Delicious 51* (70 days), and *Ambrosia* (85 days). Muskmelons highly rated for sweetness are *Harper Hybrid* (90 days), *Supermarket* (an 85-day hybrid), and *Israel (Ogen)* (70 days), an open-pollinated type. Market gardeners might also choose *Mainstream* (80 days), a midseason crop with excellent flavor. It holds quality very well after the harvest.

The novelty *Banana* muskmelon (90 to 95 days) is actually shaped like a banana. It's very sweet and grows to be about 2 feet long and weigh 4 to 5 pounds. The outer rind is yellowish, the flesh juicy, highly sweet, and salmon-colored.

If you start plants indoors, sow seeds only 3 to 4 weeks before your average last frost date. Starting them any sooner will not help — large plants don't transplant well. Plant seeds in 3-inch peat pots, two or three seeds per pot. Try to keep pots at a constant temperature of 70°F for best germination.

Once the seedlings are 2 inches high, thin to one healthy plant per pot. Since melon seedling roots should not be disturbed, thin by snipping, rather than pulling, the unwanted plants.

After the last frost date, start exposing well-grown seedlings to outdoor temperatures and direct sunlight to harden them off. A cold frame helps.

Preparation

At least several days before transplanting, prepare your melon rows. Enrich the soil underneath the planting area with aged manure and/or compost. Add about ½ cup of bone meal (or its equivalent) per foot of row as a source of phosphorus to help early root development. Cover the rows tightly with black plastic for soil warmth — it can bring you a harvest as much as 1 to 2 weeks earlier and keeps weeds to a minimum. Even in the South, melon growers are turning to plastic mulches.

Planting

If you start transplants, set them in the garden a week or so after the last frost date or later when temperatures will go no lower than 55°F. If you use black plastic, cut slits every 18 to 24 inches and set transplants into the soil through the slits. Do not disturb the transplants' roots in the process. Transplants can be planted in rows, which are easier to weed than the hills traditionally used for direct seeding.

After transplanting, water the seedlings with a soluble fertilizer high in root-strengthening phosphorus. Then for maximum benefit, cover the rows with clear plastic slitted row covers. These are usually stretched over wire hoops to create a greenhouse that keeps plants warm and protects them somewhat from insects. Once female flowers appear, usually after the male flowers, remove the row covers. (Female flowers are attached to small, round, green ovaries, whereas male flowers are attached directly to the stem.)

If you are seeding directly, you can either plant melons in hills (groups, actually) or in rows. For hills, plant half a dozen seeds at a depth of 1 inch and thin to the two healthiest plants. Otherwise plant seeds 1 inch deep and 4 inches apart

Essentials

Planning

🐛 *Melons need 80 to 100 days to reach maturity. If your season is long enough, you can sow seeds directly in the garden after all danger of frost is past and the soil is warm. Otherwise, start seeds indoors in separate peat pots 3 to 4 weeks before the average last spring frost date.*

🐛 *Melons need lots of space. Plan on leaving 6 to 8 feet between rows or beds.*

Preparation

🐛 *Choose a site in the warmest part of your garden — preferably a south-facing slope.*

🐛 *Enrich the soil with aged manure or good compost at least a few days before planting.*

🐛 *To increase soil temperature and hasten growth, cover the planting area tightly with black plastic mulch just before planting.*

Planting

🐛 *Add ½ cup of bone meal to each foot or so of row at planting time.*

🐛 *Set transplants 1½ to 2 feet apart in rows 6 to 8 feet apart. Keep the plants in their peat pots so as not to disturb roots. Water transplants with a starter solution high in phosphorus.*

🐛 *If seeding directly, plant seeds 1 inch deep and 4 inches apart. Thin when plants touch each other, leaving healthiest plants about 2 feet apart.*

🐛 *If desired, cover rows with slitted row covers to maintain warmth and promote fast growth.*

Care

🐛 *When fruits have formed, side-dress. Use liquid fertilizer such as manure tea or fish emulsion for side-dressing when you mulch with plastic. Side-dress unmulched plants with approximately ½ cup of 5-10-10 or similar balanced fertilizer for every four to five plants. In sandy soils, side-dress again 3 to 4 weeks later.*

🐛 *Watch out for the cucumber beetle (page 277), a common pest. The pickleworm (page 279) and squash vine borer (page 280) may also appear.*

🐛 *Possible diseases include anthracnose (page 282), bacterial wilt (page 282), and downy mildew (page 284).*

Harvesting

🐛 *Allow melons to ripen on the vine.*

🐛 *Ripe muskmelons develop a crack at the point of attachment to the stem and slip off the vine with little help.*

🐛 *A ripe watermelon's underside turns from white to yellow and tendrils nearest the melon turn brown and dry; the melon's skin also becomes dull and is difficult to penetrate with your fingernail.*

Left: Male flowers of the melon plant *(top)* are attached directly to the straight stem, whereas female flowers are attached to small, round ovaries. *Right:* Melons get more heat and are less prone to ground rot when they are allowed to ripen on an overturned coffee can.

If raised on a trellis, melons should be supported with a nylon or fabric sling shortly after they form on the vine.

in rows 6 to 8 feet apart and thin plants to stand 1½ to 2 feet apart when they are 4 inches tall.

Plant melons in the warmest part of your garden — preferably a south-facing slope. If space is a problem, train your muskmelons to grow up a sturdy fence or trellis. Erect the trellis before planting.

Care

When the fruits have formed, give the plants extra fertilizer. If your rows are covered with black plastic or if the plants are heavily mulched, water around the stem of the plants with manure tea or fish emulsion. For unmulched plants use about ½ cup of 5-10-10 or its equivalent for every four or five plants. Be careful not to overfertilize. Too much nitrogen may give the melons poor flavor, poor texture, and a greenish appearance. In sandy soils, side-dress a second time 3 to 4 weeks later.

Keep the melons off the soil to prevent rotting. Pieces of cardboard, old cottage cheese containers, or upside-down coffee cans work fine. If you grow your melons on a trellis, support the large, heavy fruit with nets or fabric slings shortly after they

form on the vine. Animal visits can be curtailed by covering the ripening melons with milk-carton-type crates or wire cages of some kind.

Harvesting

Picking muskmelons when they are just ripe is crucial to getting good flavor since the plants provide the fruit with much of the natural sugar during the last few days of ripening. Melons that ripen off the vine (i.e., most store-bought melons) just don't taste as sweet. Most commercial growers pick muskmelons, for example, at the "half-slip" stage before ripening is complete.

Knowing when your muskmelons are ripe is no mystery. The rind of a ripened melon will be tan rather than green between the surface netting. Many will have a strong muskmelon fragrance. The surest sign that the fruit is ready is a crack that forms on the stem right near the point of attachment with the melon. This crack signals the "slip" stage, and in a few days the melon will slip off the vine with minimal pressure. If you have to struggle to separate a melon from the vine, chances are the fruit is not ripe.

Once the first melon ripens, look over the patch every day or two so you won't miss any. When a muskmelon is overripe, the outer skin softens, making it easily penetrable by birds and bees. Bees drill a pencil-thick entry hole into melons. When you pick up a melon, you may be surprised by a couple of angry bees!

Watermelons

Planning

Choosing the right variety is also important in growing watermelons, especially up North where many of the larger melon varieties haven't enough time to mature. Even if there are enough frost-free days (80 to 100) for watermelons to reach maturity, cool temperatures or cloudy skies may prevent some varieties from developing enough sugar to taste sweet.

Muskmelons and Clear Plastic

New Hampshire market gardener John Mayer uses transparent, rather than black, plastic mulch in his muskmelon patch to get a quick start and early harvest. The 4-mil clear plastic collects more heat than black, but also spurs weed competition. John raises the plastic periodically and scoops the weeds away.

Later in the season, still-ripening melons can be protected from early frosts with 6-mil plastic covers. Be sure to remove them once the sun comes up. Melons will continue to ripen, assuming the frost is not severe and good weather returns.

This muskmelon is at the full slip stage — ripe and ready. If you have to struggle to separate a melon from its vine, chances are the fruit is not ripe.

If you live in a cool climate with a short growing season, select early varieties adapted for these conditions. Plenty exist, but the fruits are smaller than a main season crop.

Yellow Doll (65 days) and *Yellow Baby* (70 days) are early small melons with yellow flesh. *You Sweet Thing* (80 days) and *Sugar Baby* (75 days) are popular early red-fleshed melons. The *Sugar Baby* melon has a relatively thin rind, thus yielding more of an edible portion than you'd expect from the 6- to 10-pound fruits. *Sweet Favorite* (75 days) is a red melon that, though early, can grow up to 20 pounds.

The standard watermelon in many gardens in recent years has been *Charleston Gray* (85 days), noted for its disease resistance, dependability, and pale green 20- to 30-pound fruits. Rivaling *Charleston Gray* is *Crimson Sweet* (85 days), a roundish, very sweet melon with redder, finer-textured flesh. It has fewer and smaller seeds than *Charleston Gray*. If you like an intensely red-colored flesh in your melons, try *Dixielee*, a 90-day green-striped melon averaging 20 to 30 pounds.

Home gardeners might also enjoy *Willhite's Tendergold* (80 days), a golden-fleshed variety that is becoming quite popular in southern markets because the melons hold their flavor and quality up to 3 weeks after ripening. The flesh of these 25-pound melons turns more orange as it matures.

If you live in a central or southern state and can raise later, larger varieties, try *Tom Watson* (30 to 40 pounds), *Cobb Gem* (50 to 60 pounds), or *Garrisonian* (30 to 40 pounds). They need 110 to 115 warm days.

You can also try some of the seedless varieties such as *Hybrid 313*. Seedless melons don't get very big (10 to 12 pounds) but provide good, effortless eating. There are two things to keep in mind about seedless varieties: the seeds germinate at 80° to 85°F, so indoor sowing under warm conditions is recommended; and the plants must be grown next to a seeded variety in order for fertile pollen to pollinate the flowers and set fruit.

Planting

Grow your early watermelons the same way you grow muskmelons. Timing and temperature requirements are the same, though watermelon seeds take a bit longer to germinate. Like other melons, watermelon seedlings should not be grown indoors for more than 3 or 4 weeks before transplanting, and their roots should not be disturbed. Watermelons also benefit from a high-phosphorus transplanting solution. Black plastic mulch and clear plastic row covers are helpful with this crop as well.

Care

In cool or short-season areas, pick off watermelon blossoms after three or four fruits have formed. This helps generate a ripe harvest before cold weather sets in. You can also limit each melon runner to one fruit, thus directing more of the plant's energy to fewer melons and upping your chances of getting sweet melons by the

Far right: A casaba melon ripens in the California sun. Most casaba melons require a long growing season with warm, fairly dry weather.

The dull skin and yellow area on the watermelon on the right are signs of ripeness.

variety's maturity date. Keep the melon closest to the hill — it's usually larger than any later-developing ones.

Harvesting

Thumping on a melon with your knuckles and listening for a telltale hollowness is the traditional way to see if a watermelon is ripe, but there are more accurate ways: the tendrils on the stem near the melon should be brown and dry, the bottom of the melon will be yellow, rather than green, and the melon's skin will be dull and difficult to break with your fingernail.

Other Melons

In addition to the large number of watermelon varieties to try, there are all kinds of other, more unusual melons just begging to be planted and tasted — by southerners and northerners alike.

Golden Crispy (85 days) is one of a number of small, Oriental melons similar in taste to honeydew. It has a thin, edible yellow skin. Slice the fruit in half, scoop out the seeds, and eat it whole like an apple. Each fruit weighs about a pound.

Honeydew melons are available from earlier-maturing varieties such as *Limelight Hybrid* (96 days), with sweet, juicy, pale green flesh. Honeydews do not ripen very much off the vine and the chief home garden mistake is picking them too early. Keep a record of your variety's maturity date and keep the melons on the vines at least until then, a bit longer if you've had a cool spell during the season. They will improve for a few days after picking if kept at room temperature.

Most casaba melons need 110 to 115 days of warm, fairly dry weather to produce well. *Casaba Golden Beauty* develops a rich golden color when mature, weighs 7 to 8 pounds, and has thick, tasty white flesh and a small seed cavity.

Crenshaw melons also require long seasons, around 115 days. They have salmon-colored flesh; when the outer dark green rind turns a mottled yellow, the melon is ripe.

Persian cantaloupes (110 days) are fairly distinct from muskmelons, with firm skin and no ribbing. They have very dark green rinds and dark orange flesh like a sweet potato. They can be grown along a trellis or fence.

Okra

Once production starts, the okra pods mature rapidly; note the developing pods at left. Blooms *(above)* are short-lived but exquisite.

Okra has long been a delight in the South, where it is sometimes called gumbo by enthusiasts. It is easy to grow and even easier to use. Okra pods are high in vitamin A and low in calories. As a bonus, throughout the growing season, okra produces a steady stream of showy flowers like those of hibiscus, with cream-colored petals around a purple heart. Each flower represents a potential pod.

This is one hot weather crop that can be grown in all but the coldest climes. Okra doesn't take long to grow (about 50 to 60 days to harvest), but it can't be planted before warm weather has truly settled in. All it takes is a little patience — and some ingenuity if warm weather is in short supply.

Harvested young and tender, immature pods can be used in soups or stews (also called gumbo), boiled, broiled, steamed, roasted, or fried. They can be frozen, canned, pickled, or even eaten raw. If you want to be really efficient, you can even eat the nutritious leaves, which are high in vitamins A and C, as well as protein, calcium, and iron.

Planning

Okra is a warm weather crop. Surprisingly, it takes only 50 to 60 days to mature, so it can be grown in most regions. Okra will not do well during fickle spring weather, so don't rush it. Wait until the nights stay above 55°F and the soil has warmed to 65° to 70°F. Okra planted after the weather has stabilized and the soil and air have warmed sufficiently will easily overtake a premature planting. Patience pays! For example, okra seeds can often be planted in late April in Alabama; in New Hampshire, you'd best wait until late June to plant seeds or even set transplants outdoors.

In regions where summer comes slowly, you can give your okra a jump on the season. Start the seeds indoors in peat pots 3 to 4 weeks before the average last spring frost date. Give the plants a few days' hardening off first, then transplant outside when your garden soil warms up (a soil temperature of about 65°F is best).

Alternatively, you can start okra a few weeks early directly in the garden 3 to 4 weeks before the last frost date if you cover the young plants with some sort of cold frame or grow tunnel until warm weather arrives. Make sure the covering you erect is 2 to 3 feet tall so the stalks have room to grow.

Select the okra variety that is right for you. If you have plenty of space, grow the standard varieties, which can reach well over 6 feet in height. In small gardens, dwarf varieties are the best bet; they peak at 3 feet. The leaves and pods of okra are

Pods of many varieties will get quite large; quality will depend on the variety and other factors such as soil moisture.

usually covered with tiny spines that will make you itch (when harvesting the okra, not when eating it), but plant breeders have created several spineless alternatives. Most varieties will yield green pods, but decorative reds and whites have also been developed.

Year-old okra seeds may not sprout at all, so to be on the safe side, buy a new supply each year.

Preparation

Put the plants in full sun, ideally on a southern slope for maximum warmth. The soil should drain well and yet be able to retain enough moisture to prevent wilting.

Any fertile garden soil will do, but fast-growing, high-producing okra can always put some extra nutrition to good use. Prepare the soil a week or so before planting by working in a balanced fertilizer such as ½ pound of 10-10-10 or its equivalent per 25 feet of row. Water generously.

Planting

Because okra seeds are tough and slow to sprout, you can hasten germination by soaking them overnight in tepid water before planting.

Sow seeds in a row, 3 or 4 inches apart and about ½ inch deep. Okra grows tall (some varieties top 6 feet), so space rows far enough apart so they won't shade each other. Your best bet is to plant one long row, or intersperse rows of okra with other vegetables.

Care

When the seedlings are about 3 inches tall, thin them to stand anywhere from 1 to 2 feet apart. We recommend the wider spacing to let in more light and allow each plant to grow without competition. If failed seeds leave a bare spot in the row, you can transplant some of the extras at thinning time; just scoop them up, roots and all, and water them well in their new location.

Keep the plants well watered. About 1 inch per week is ideal; more if you live in an especially hot, arid region.

Essentials

Planning
🌰 *In most parts of the country, plant okra directly in the garden when the nights stay above 55°F and the soil has warmed to 65° to 70°F.*

🌰 *In the most northern areas, start seeds indoors in peat pots several weeks before the soil warms up. Or direct seed through black plastic and cover the rows with grow tunnels.*

Preparation
🌰 *Choose a site in full sun, preferably on a southern slope for maximum warmth.*

🌰 *A week or so before planting, work into the soil ½ pound of 10-10-10 or its equivalent per 25 feet of row.*

Planting
🌰 *To hasten germination, soak seeds overnight in tepid water or freeze them to crack their coats.*

🌰 *Sow seeds ½ to 1 inch deep, 3 to 4 inches apart.*

🌰 *Set out transplants to stand 1 to 2 feet apart in rows 3 to 4 feet apart.*

Care
🌰 *When the seedlings are about 3 inches tall, thin to stand 1 to 2 feet apart.*

🌰 *Provide at least 1 inch of water per week; more in hot, arid regions.*

🌰 *When plants are young, cultivate lightly to eliminate weeds. Then mulch heavily (4 to 8 inches) to keep weeds down and conserve moisture.*

🌰 *Side-dress with 10-10-10 (½ pound per 25 feet of row), aged manure, or rich compost. Side-dress three times: after thinning, when the first pods begin to develop, and at least once midway through the growing season.*

🌰 *Hand-pick stinkbugs (page 281) and Japanese beetles (page 278). Watch for aphids (page 276), corn earworms (page 277), and flea beetles (page 278).*

🌰 *Okra is susceptible to verticillium wilt (page 287) and fusarium wilt (page 285).*

Harvesting
🌰 *The first pods will be ready in 50 to 60 days. Harvest the pods when still immature (2 to 3 inches long).*

🌰 *Pick at least every other day to encourage production.*

🌰 *Wear gloves and long sleeves to avoid coming in contact with the irritating spines on the leaves and pods. Use a knife to cut the stem just above the cap.*

Pods will first appear near the base and then progressively higher up the stalk. After the initial harvest, remove the lower leaves to boost production. Depending on the variety, the stalks can grow so tall that by the end of the season you may be bending them over to reach the pods.

Okra's consistency varies with recipes and cooking times, so experiment to find out how you prefer your pods. Probably the most popular way to prepare okra is to batter dip and fry the pods whole. Gumbos and pickled okra are also favorites among connoisseurs.

There are as many ways to freeze okra pods as there are ways to use them. Some people slice them beforehand; others leave them whole. Some bake or blanch them; other freeze them uncooked. We recommend just tossing unwashed, uncut, and uncooked pods into freezer bags. They won't stick together and you'll be able to prepare them any way you like once you thaw them out. This is certainly the quickest and easiest way to deal with a flood of okra during peak harvest season.

Cultivate lightly to eliminate weeds when the plants are young, then mulch heavily with 4 to 8 inches of organic mulch to keep weeds down and retain moisture.

To boost and prolong production, side-dress with a small amount of fertilizer (5-10-10, aged manure, or rich compost) several times: once after thinning, again when the first pods begin to develop, and at least once more midway through the remainder of the growing season. If your soil is especially sandy and/or the rains are frequent and heavy, side-dress more often.

These three steps — watering, mulching, and side-dressing — will prevent the plants from slacking off. In the Deep South, plants can get overly large. Cut them back near the soil surface and allow them to resprout. Then gently hoe 1 pound of 10-10-10 per 25 feet of row into the soil near the plants to get them growing rapidly.

There aren't many potential insect or disease problems with okra, especially up North. Southern growers are more likely to encounter a few insects and diseases, but these can usually be prevented or controlled. Some stalks or pods may be damaged, but rarely is an entire planting of okra devastated.

If stinkbugs are in the neighborhood, they may stop by to suck the juice from developing pods; hand-pick and destroy them. Aphids, corn earworms, and flea beetles can also be a nuisance.

Okra is susceptible to verticillium wilt and fusarium wilt, which are best controlled by rotating your crops.

Red-podded okra varieties are available. The tender pods can be cooked, canned, frozen, pickled, and even eaten raw.

Harvesting

The first pods will be ready for the table about 2 months after planting (assuming you waited for warm weather). Harvest them when they're tender and still immature — about 2 to 3 inches long for most varieties. If they grow longer than 4 inches, they're apt to be tough and woody.

You'll have fresh okra until the first frost if you keep the pods harvested. Pick them faithfully — every other day during the peak season — and you'll have some at all stages of development all the time. If some unnoticed pods grow too large, pick them for the compost pile or production will slow to a trickle.

The leaves and pods of most varieties are covered with tiny spines that will irritate your skin, so wear gloves and long sleeves (or select a spineless variety). Use a knife to cut the stem just above the cap. If the stem is hard to cut, the pod is probably too old to enjoy; pitch it into the compost pile.

Okra Varieties

Most varieties of okra can be successfully grown throughout much of the United States. Some grow taller than others; some bear slightly earlier than others (an advantage for northern growers); some produce spineless pods; some produce pods that are not green. Here is a partial list of available varieties and their sources.

Variety	Days to Maturity	Description	Sources
*Annie Oakley	52	The first hybrid okra; spineless pods; 5 feet tall.	17, 100
Clemson Spineless	58	The standard for many years, accounting for 90 percent of U.S. commercial production; spineless pods; 5 feet tall.	17, 99, 100
Clemson Spineless 80	60	Available since 1983, expected to replace Clemson Spineless; it yields earlier and more heavily.	99
Dwarf Green Long Pod	54	Grows to 3 feet tall; heavily ribbed.	17, 100
Emerald	58	Spineless round pods; may grow over 6 feet tall.	98, 100
Lee	53	New variety; spineless pods; grows to 5 feet tall.	35, 100, 103
Louisiana Green Velvet	60	Large, vigorous, 6-foot-high plants; smooth, spineless, light green okra retains its color when processed.	17, 98
Park's Candelabra Branching	50–60	First base-branching okra; open habit makes picking easy; 4 to 6 bearing spikes per plant.	35
Red River	60	Bright red pods, leaf veins, petioles, and stems.	99
Spineless Green Velvet	58	Pods 7 inches long, ¾ inch in diameter; smooth, round, and spineless.	35, 100
White Velvet	60	White pods.	17, 98, 99

*Hybrid

Onions

A small area of garden can yield zesty onions of many shapes and colors (*left*). The less-than-ordinary Egyptian onion (*above*) sprouts year after year.

Yellow cooking onions, sweet onions, bunching onions, pickling onions, shallots, garlic, leeks — each adds a unique flavor to foods, from subtle to bold. How can anyone do without them in the kitchen?

If you want to grow bulb onions such as yellow cooking onions or sweet onions, be sure to buy seeds or sets for varieties that will do well in your area. Many onions are classified as "short-day" or "long-day onions." These classifications could easily be "South" (short-day) and "North" (long-day).

You can start seeds indoors or you can start most types from easy-to-plant bulbs, or sets, early in the spring. With onion sets, you get a quick start with no germination problem — and there's no thinning.

Keeping weeds under control through shallow cultivation is about the only gardening task required. There aren't too many pests or diseases that plague onions; some people even plant garlic with other crops to control pests.

Onions are one of those relatively care-free crops that everyone should make space for in their vegetable gardens — or even mix in with a flower or ornamental garden.

Planning

Although all of the onions in this chapter belong to the same genus, *Allium*, three types require slightly different handling — garlic, shallots, and leeks. Storage onions, sweet onions, pickling onions, and bunching onions can be started from seeds or sets, small bulbs harvested the previous season and stored through the fall and winter. Sets are hardy; you can plant them anytime after the soil can be worked in late winter or early spring. Yellow onion sets are the most common at garden centers, but you may find white and red ones, too. Buy sets that are firm (not sprouting) and about the diameter of a dime.

If you want big bulbing sweet onions, we recommend that you start the seeds indoors about 2 to 3 months before your average last spring frost date. You can sow sweet onion seeds directly outdoors in early spring, but often the resulting bulbs are not as large. The size of the bulb is directly related to the amount of green top leaves the plant has when the bulbs begin to develop. Most varieties will begin bulbing when day length and temperature reach certain levels, not at a certain number of days after planting. So an earlier start will normally yield bigger onions.

To grow pickling and bunching onions, it's easiest to start by planting seeds outdoors.

Preparation

For the largest sweet onion bulbs, start seeds in flats 2 to 3 months before the average last frost date. Plant them ¼ inch deep and thin the young seedlings to stand ½ inch apart when plants are 1 to 2 inches tall. You won't have to transplant the seedlings to another container if you use a 4- to 6-inch-deep flat. Keep the plants well watered and fed; keep the tops of the onions trimmed to a height of 3 inches.

If possible, choose the most weed-free part of your garden for onions, whether you plant seeds, sets, or set out transplants. Onions perform poorly in weedy areas. An area that grew beans last year or one that was mulched is likely to have fewer weed problems.

A day or two before planting, work the area to get rid of any weeds starting to germinate. Apply 1 pound of 10-10-10 fertilizer or its equivalent for every 20 feet of row. If you are planting wide rows, add a bit more fertilizer for the same row length. Work it into the soil to a depth of 2 to 3 inches.

Planting

If you started plants indoors, gradually harden off the seedlings and move them to the garden when danger of heavy frosts

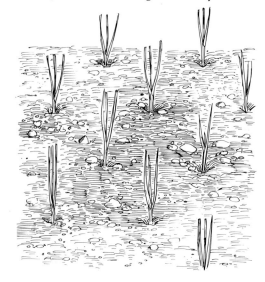

If you want to start onions from seed, it's best to sow seeds in a deep flat. Keep the onion tops trimmed to about 3 inches in height.

To grow the largest bulbs, set out your plants (right) or sets (far right) about 4 inches apart. Keep weeds in check and side-dress the plants at least twice.

has passed. Set each onion plant about 4 inches apart.

Plant sets 1½ to 2 inches below the soil surface, flat or root end down. Place them 4 inches apart, closer if you will be thinning some out to eat as scallions. Be sure to firm the soil down with the back of a hoe to bring the sets in good contact with the soil around them.

Care

Since the more top growth an onion plant develops the more energy it will be able to direct to bulb-making, fertilize regularly and water often. Onions that are water-stressed often produce more pungently flavored bulbs. The critical time for water is when the bulbs begin to swell. Keep the beds well weeded.

Side-dressing onions is essential for good growth. Timing is critical, too. Side-dress when the leaves are 4 to 6 inches tall and again when the bulbs start to swell. Apply 1 pound of 10-10-10 or its equivalent per 20 to 25 feet of row. Sprinkle it in a shallow trench about 3 inches from the plants. If you've planted in a wide row, it may be easier to sprinkle a natural fertilizer such as composted manure throughout the bed and let rain or irrigation water take it to the roots. Use about 3 pounds of composted manure for every 15 feet of wide row.

Essentials

Planning

🌿 *Onions are usually started from seeds or bulbs (sets). For the largest bulbs, sow seeds indoors in flats 2 to 3 months before your average last frost date. Or sow directly outdoors as soon as the soil can be worked in early spring. Plant sets any time from early spring to early June. You can also buy started plants.*

🌿 *In mild-winter areas of the South and the Pacific Coast, plant in the fall for winter and early spring harvests.*

Preparation

🌿 *Choose a fertile, well-drained, weed-free area of your garden to plant onions, especially if you are planting from seed.*

🌿 *In the fall before planting, work manure or compost into the soil, or fertilize right before planting, using a balanced fertilizer such as 10-10-10 applied at a rate of 1 pound per 20 square feet.*

🌿 *Sow seeds indoors in flats ¼ inch deep, 4 seeds per inch in narrow rows. Keep the onion tops clipped to 3 inches tall.*

Planting

🌿 *Transplant plants started from seed when danger of heavy frost is past. Set the transplants 4 inches apart.*

🌿 *To direct-seed, sow seeds ¼ to ½ inch deep, 1 to 3 seeds per inch.*

🌿 *To plant sets, push each bulb into the soil almost to its full depth, 4 to 5 inches apart, pointed end up.*

Care

🌿 *Thin direct-seeded onions to stand 4 inches apart for bulb onions; 1 to 2 inches apart for scallions.*

🌿 *Control weeds with frequent shallow cultivation.*

🌿 *Provide at least 1 inch of water each week.*

🌿 *Side-dress with 1 pound of 10-10-10 or equivalent fertilizer per 20 to 25 feet of row when plants are 4 to 6 inches tall and the bulbs are just beginning to swell.*

🌿 *To develop scallions, leeks, or bunching onions with long white stems, keep the soil hilled up around the stems.*

🌿 *If a plant sends up a flower stalk, pull the onion and use it.*

🌿 *The onion maggot (page 279) is a common pest.*

🌿 *Downy mildew (page 284) is a potential disease problem.*

Harvesting

🌿 *Begin harvesting scallions when they are 6 to 8 inches tall.*

🌿 *Harvest bulb onions when about a quarter of the tops have fallen over and the bulbs have begun to develop papery skin. Gently knock over the rest of the tops with a hoe or by hand, bending but not snapping them. Leave the onions in the ground for another few days. Then pull the bulbs and let them dry in a warm, airy place out of direct sun or rain for a week or two.*

🌿 *When storage onions are dry, hang them in mesh bags, old panty hose, or as braids in a cool, dry place.*

Harvesting

When about a quarter of the onion tops have fallen and the bulbs have begun to develop a paper skin, it's time to harvest. Gently knock over the rest of the tops with a hoe or by hand, bending, not snapping, them. Let the onions stay in the ground for a few days, then dig up the bulbs. Gently brush off the soil; don't wash them. Spread them out on a screen or pallet that allows air to circulate and let them dry in a warm, airy place out of direct sunlight or rain for a week or two. Then store in a cool, dry place out of direct light. Storage onions will keep for several months, but sweet onions will store for only a few weeks.

Storage Onions

Storage onions, or keepers, are the most familiar onions sold in stores. The keepers you harvest in summer or fall will stay firm and flavorful through winter and often into spring.

Whether you store your onions in braids or bags, it's a good idea to leave them in a cool, fairly dry storage area until you're ready to use them. Bringing them into a warm kitchen will cause many of the bulbs to sprout, which will greatly decrease storage time.

Because of their hard outer skin, the papery yellow keepers such as *Yellow Globes, Stuttgarter,* and *Orbit* are recommended for their storage qualities. *Capable* is suggested for northern gardeners because it matures early, dries quickly, and keeps well into the spring.

Sweet Onions

All onions have about the same sugar content, but pungent onions contain more sulfur compounds, which give them their characteristic bite. When tissues of pungent onions are cut or bruised, enzymes in the onion react with the compounds and sulfur is released; that's what stings your tongue. Cooking destroys these compounds and thus sweetens the onions.

How much sulfur compound is in an onion depends on its genes. Sweet onion varieties such as *Walla Walla, Grano, Granex, Sweet Spanish,* and *Bermuda* all have low sulfur potential, but they need to have specific environmental conditions to develop their full sweetness potential. That's why growing sweet onions may be an uncertain process. They must have the right number of daylight hours, the appropriate amounts of heat and light, and suitable soil and moisture conditions.

The *Walla Walla* variety has been finely tuned to the climate of the Northwest. These onions are planted in late August or early September, kept out in the fields over the winter, and harvested the following summer. The bulbs are huge, usually 5 to 6 inches in diameter. The onions must be eaten within a month of harvest as they deteriorate rapidly.

Some catalogs list *Walla Walla* onion seed but, grown outside of Washington state, they are reported to be of lower quality. Start the plants inside early and get them into the garden as soon as possible in the spring. This will give your *Walla Wallas* enough time to develop large leaves before the bulbs start growing.

Grano or *Granex* are mild onions developed for the South and grown over a large area. When these varieties are grown in the counties around Vidalia, Georgia, they are especially sweet. It is thought that the reason Vidalia onions, as they are known, are so sweet is because the soils in the Vidalia area are low in sulfur. The same *Grano* or *Granex* grown in parts of Hawaii also produces a remarkably sweet onion, the *Maui Sweet*. In this case, it's probably the volcanic soils that are responsible.

Growing *Vidalia* onions poses a different challenge from growing the *Walla Walla* since Georgians claim the sulfur content of the soil is an important factor. There's also the problem of day length. *Vidalias* are short-day onions, bred to do well in the South (see box), so growing them north of Virginia (or north of Sacramento in the West) is likely to be disappointing.

The reason breeders are not working to provide more kinds of sweet onions, ones that will grow in a variety of climates, is that sweet onions don't store well, so they are economically unattractive to large-scale producers. The sulfur-containing compound that makes an onion pungent also seems to protect the onion from decay organisms.

Sweet Spanish onions are sweeter than most onions, but they store fairly well. Because of their storability, you can be sure they're not as sweet as the *Walla Walla* or *Vidalia* onions. Some varieties marketed as *Sweet Spanish* are actually hybrids with some *Yellow Globe* genes to improve their keeping ability.

The true *Sweet Spanish* is pretty sweet, though, and it can be grown as far north as Minnesota. Seeds should be started indoors 2 to 3 months before your average last frost date, then put out in the warmer days of spring.

Sweet Sandwich is a new long-day variety that doesn't go by the usual rules. It's pungent when harvested and becomes sweeter during storage. Its sweet flavor (which many claim beats that of *Sweet Spanish*) and greater storability make it a likely candidate for northern gardens.

The *Bermuda*, also famed for mildness, at one time actually came from Bermuda. Like *Vidalia* growers, *Bermuda* lovers claim the onion has to be grown on native soil to taste like the real thing. Grown in the South, *Bermudas* are short-day onions.

Bunching Onions

Bunching onions, green onions, scallions, spring onions, green tails — all are different names for the same type of onion. Though you can get scallions by harvesting just about any onion early, there are certain varieties that never form large bulbs and are grown specifically for their delicate stems and juicy green tops. Hardy

Long-Day and Short-Day Onions

Onions form bulbs in response to the number of daylight hours. Seed catalogs and packets often describe onions as "short-day" or "long-day" varieties. Short-day onions begin to bulb up when the day is 12 to 14 hours long. Long-day varieties do not start forming bulbs until the day is 14 to 16 hours long.

The farther away you get from the equator, the greater the variation in the length of days from one season to another. In the North, day length changes dramatically from winter to summer as the earth tilts back toward the sun. Winter days in Minnesota can be as short as 8 hours in December, while a day in June can be as long as 16 hours. The longest day is around June 21, the summer solstice. In the South there is much less variation in day length from summer to winter; day length is in the neighborhood of 12 hours all year long.

It is important to know the day length requirement of the onion varieties you are planting. Northern gardeners should choose long-day varieties. If you plant short-day varieties in the North, the critical day length to initiate bulbing will occur early in the season while plants are still small. Since the size of an onion depends on the number and size of leaves when bulbing starts, short-day onions grown in the North will produce only small bulbs.

Short-day onions are adapted to Southern growing conditions. If you plant long-day onions in the South, the days never get long enough to initiate bulbing and the plants never bulb up.

Temperature also plays a role in controlling the formation of onion bulbs. If the weather is cool enough, bulbing will be delayed even if the day length is suitable. This is why gardeners in the South can plant onions in the fall for a harvest the following spring.

and quick-growing, these onions can be grown directly from seed.

Sow seeds in early spring for summer use, in summer for fall use, or in the fall to overwinter and use in the spring. Plant seeds ½ inch deep, ½ inch apart, in a bed, row, or shallow trench. Don't thin these plants — the scallions need little room since they're mature and ready for harvest when ⅜ inch or less in diameter. Be sure to keep the bed free from weeds. For long white stems, hill the plants with loose soil when tops are 4 inches tall.

To grow bunching onions as perennials, try *Evergreen White*. Plant seeds in the fall and let the plants overwinter — even if your winters are severe. The following summer, dig up groups of plants, divide the clumps, set them 4 to 6 inches apart, and begin the cycle anew. A good plan is to keep the plants in a bed 2 feet by 3 feet, in a section of the garden where you won't be tilling (near asparagus, for example). Thin out the plants each summer to keep the bed from getting too crowded.

For areas with hot, dry weather, *Beltsville Bunching* is recommended, although it has a tendency to form larger bulbs than other scallion varieties. Other suggested varieties for all areas are *Ishikira Long* for long, single, nonbulbing stalks; *White Lisbon* for mild flavor; and *Long White*, which produces clusters of stalks that overwinter well.

Pickling Onions

If you find yourself searching out the tiny onions in your bread-and-butter pickles, try growing pickling onions from seed. Harvested early, these pearl-sized white onions can be cooked with your fresh peas. Harvested later in the summer, the larger "boilers" can be served creamed or in stews. Since the skin doesn't form until late summer, these onions make preparation a breeze.

Seed these onions much more closely than the larger varieties, about ½ inch or less apart, in 4-inch-wide bands. No thinning is needed, but do keep the bed well weeded.

Try *Quicksilver* for small, attractive bulbs that get no larger than Ping-Pong balls; *White Portugal* and *Silver Queen* are other favorites.

"Pearl" or pickling onions should be planted quite thickly so that bulbs will remain small.

Garlic

Garlic has been hailed as an insect repellent, cold fighter, fever cure, pain killer, and evil spirit deterrent. Whether you believe in any of its reputed powers or not, you should still grow garlic for its one characteristic that needs no proof: flavor.

Garlic can be planted either in early spring, as soon as the ground can be worked, or in the fall. Fall planting is recommended for northern gardeners and those with very hot summers. Planting in late fall for a harvest the following summer usually produces larger bulbs than a spring planting. Northern gardeners should cover the garlic with straw or hay mulch for overwintering. If seed stalks appear in the spring, pick them off promptly, or you can let a few plants go to seed and save the tiny bulbs that form at the top of the seed stalk for fall planting.

Garlic needs full sunlight and well-drained soil that is rich in organic matter. Plant the individual cloves flat end down, 3 to 4 inches apart, 1 to 2 inches deep. Water every 3 to 5 days until stalks come up through the ground. Harvest is usually in 90 to 100 days. Using a pitchfork, harvest the bulbs when the leaves turn brown and begin to collapse. Let the bulbs dry outside in the sun for a few days, then store in a cool, dry place. You can braid the dried leaves for attractive, handy storage.

Shallots

Though closely resembling garlic in appearance, shallots have a more delicate flavor that has earned them a reputation for continental elegance. They are more tender and cook more quickly than regular onions, making them perfect for sauces. Though expensive in stores, shallots are easy to grow at home. Don't be intimidated by their gourmet mystique — they'll fit right in with any cooking style.

You can grow shallots in any well-drained soil that has been worked with aged manure or compost. Plant the cloves,

Planting garlic in the fall for a harvest the following summer usually produces larger bulbs than a spring planting. The *Elephant* garlic above was planted in Oregon in the fall and harvested in early July.

like garlic, either in early spring, as soon as the ground is workable, or, if your summers are very hot, in the fall. Northern gardeners can plant in the fall and mulch the plants for winter.

Plant individual cloves broad end down, 1 to 2 inches deep, 4 inches apart, in rows or beds. Sprouts will appear in 1 to 2 weeks. Keep shallots well watered throughout the growing season and fertilize them as you would onions.

Shallot bulbs are ready for harvest when the spearlike leaves start to wither but haven't yet completely collapsed. Dig the shallots when the weather is dry so you can cure them outside, out of direct sun, for a few days. Once dried, they can be braided and stored in a cool, dry place.

When choosing shallot sets for planting, be sure to select the variety most appropriate for your cooking needs. *French Shallots*, with slightly pink skins and pink flesh, are the traditional cooking shallots used by the French. Yellow shallots such as *Brown Shallots*, often called multiplier onions, are used mostly for greens, as well as for flavoring soups and other dishes.

In most areas leeks can be harvested in the fall or early spring after wintering over. Don't use too much force pulling them out of the ground — a slow, twisting motion is best.

Leeks

Judging from market prices, you'd think that growing leeks is a difficult, if not impossible, task. Yet leeks are a hardy, pest-free, easy-to-grow crop. Their creamy texture and unique flavor — more delicate than any other onion — are too good and versatile to be relegated to the rare and precious category. Grow your own and make leeks as much a staple in your kitchen as they are in most European households.

Leeks require deep, rich soil. They're fairly heavy feeders, so be sure your soil has plenty of nitrogen. Work in manure and/or rich compost before planting time and side-dress like onions 50 days or so after planting.

Leeks can be grown from seed in both the North and the South. Since their growing season is relatively long — from 90 to 130 days — they should be started indoors in the North. In February or March, sow seeds ¼ inch deep, 4 seeds per inch, in 6- to 8-inch-deep flats. In the South, sow seeds directly outdoors in the fall. Space seeds ¼ to ½ inch deep, ½ inch apart, in rows or beds. Thin the seedlings to stand 6 inches apart, using your thinnings as scallions. Start thinning when plants are 2 inches tall.

Whether you sow your leeks directly or transplant seedlings from indoors, you will have to hill soil around the leek stem two or three times during the season to create the blanched, edible part. One method is to grow plants 6 inches apart in rows 2 feet apart, hilling soil or soil and mulch up around the stem. The other is to set the transplants 6 inches apart in 12-inch-deep trenches containing 3 inches of compost. As the plants grow, fill in the trench, covering the bases of the stems with soil.

If you're concerned about getting soil into the leaves, place a cardboard toilet paper roll over each seedling when they're transplanted in a trench, keeping the roll in place with soil. As the leek grows and you fill in the trench, raise the roll. The roll eventually disintegrates and the mature leeks come out relatively clean.

Leeks can be harvested and used at any size. Small thinnings make great salad additions. Pencil-thin leeks can be steamed whole and eaten much like asparagus. But surely the best leeks are those whose diameters are between ¾ and 1½ inches. These are ready in the North a few weeks before the first fall frost. In the South, it's usually January to February when the leeks are fully mature. Some northern gardeners like to extend their harvest through the winter by covering the leeks (still in the ground) with mulch. Then they can harvest the leeks at any time. Plants larger than 1½ inches in diameter, however, are usually too tough for good eating, though they can be used in soup. Some suggested varieties for overwintering are *Giant Musselburgh* and *Elephant*.

When you harvest your leeks, don't use too much force — a twisting, easing motion is best. While the leeks are still in the ground, cut around each plant with a trowel to trim the underground roots. This will make harvesting easier.

To wash leeks, cut them vertically, most of the way through, down to, but not through, the base. Holding it by its base, swish the leek up and down in a pail of clean water. Be sure to drain thoroughly.

Multiplying Onions

Multiplying onions usually reproduce not by blooming and producing seeds but by dividing underground. Three unusual multipliers are now much more available to home gardeners than in years past — the yellow potato onion, the white multiplier, and the Egyptian top onion (or "tree onion").

The yellow potato onion was popular in home gardens up until the 1940s when the starter sets for the onion disappeared from mail-order catalogs. Many home and market gardeners kept growing the onion, however, and now sets are once again available.

Both large and small onions should be planted in the fall. Each small onion will usually grow to produce a single large onion by next midsummer. Save some of these large bulbs in a cool, dry place to replant in the fall. Use the rest as your stock of delicious cooking onions. If you leave the large bulbs in the ground too long in midsummer they will resume growth and their quality as cooking onions will deteriorate.

Each large bulb planted in the fall will produce a spring harvest of five to twenty scallions. Don't harvest all the clumps of scallions at once. Leave some clumps alone; the green tops will die down and a number of small sets will be produced on the bottom. Harvest those small sets, store in a cool, dry place, and plant them in the fall. They'll each continue the cycle and grow a large potato onion by the next summer.

As long as you plant a mixture of sizes in the fall, you'll have onions for eating and sets for more planting. The fall planting gets roots established before the ground freezes. Sets will survive temperatures of $-25°F$ or colder with a mulch. Spring planting is satisfactory, but to get large individual onions, plant in the fall.

Plant potato onion sets, large or small, about 8 to 10 inches apart and only 1 inch deep. A light application of balanced fertilizer at fall planting time gives them a good start. In cold winter areas, use a heavy organic mulch or a few inches of soil from beyond the row. Where winter drainage can be a problem, it's best to plant in raised beds.

In the spring, as the onions begin to grow, remove the mulch or soil and fertilize. Later, as the onions develop, pull away the remaining soil to let the new bulb clusters form on the soil surface.

Harvest, dry, and store potato onions like regular onions. Don't break the clusters until you cook or plant them.

White multiplier onions may have the best flavor of the multiplying onions. The long green leaves harvested in spring are sweet and mild, like chives. The bulbs won't grow much larger than 1 inch in diameter, but when they mature in early summer to midsummer, they can be used fresh or pickled as pearl onions. These onions keep well; some bulbs can be dried and stored for fall planting. In the Deep South, they provide scallions from November to early spring.

Egyptian top onions are the most carefree onion of all. The Egyptian top onion forms a cluster of sets at the tip of a flower stalk and divides underground. The top sets can be used to plant new areas.

Since they do not form large bulbs, Egyptian onions are harvested primarily as green onions in the spring and again in the fall when new growth resumes in milder areas. Cold-hardy, they are the first sign of green in the garden. As Egyptian onions get older, the number and size of the top sets increase.

Onion Sources

Onions
Beltsville Bunching 1, 71, 93
Bermuda
Yellow 9, 23, 100
White (Crystal Wax, Eclipse) 9, 17, 99, 100
Red 23
Evergreen 9, 17, 20, 23, 99
Granex
Red 100
White 17, 99, 100
Yellow 17, 28
Grano
New Mexico White 28, 105
New Mexico Yellow 93, 105
Texas 17, 28, 99, 100
Ishikira Long 20, 71
Long White (Tokyo) 1, 29
Maui Sweet (see **Grano** or **Granex**)
*****Orbit** 20
Quicksilver 20
Silver Queen 39
Spartan Sleeper 39
Stuttgarter Reisen (seeds) 39; (sets) 16, 20
*****Sweet Sandwich** 1, 26, 28, 66
Sweet Spanish 1, 29, 38
Yellow 17, 100, 105
White 9, 28, 39, 93
Vidalia-type onions (see **Granex** or **Grano**)
Walla Walla Sweet 20, 66, 71, 105
White Lisbon 28, 71, 105
White Portugal 16, 39
Yellow Globes 1, 20, 38

Shallots
Brown Shallots 84
French Shallots 83

Leeks
Elephant 8, 36
Giant Musselburgh 9, 23, 39, 46

Multiplying Onions
Egyptian top onions 9, 83, 84
White multiplier 83
Yellow potato onion 83, 84

*****hybrid**

Parsnips

All parnsips taste better when dug after a cold spell. Parsnips harvested in the spring *(above)* will be sweet and flavorful. At left are well-shaped *Hollow Crown* parsnips.

The secret to parsnips is to let them grow late in the fall so they can take on that sweet, nutty flavor and crispness that comes from exposure to cold and a few frosts. The starch in parsnips turns to sugar at temperatures between 40° and 34°F. Many gardeners keep parsnips in the ground through the winter and harvest supersweet roots in the spring.

Parsnips may not be the most popular vegetable on the supermarket produce shelves, but gardeners who raise this slow-growing root crop know that home-grown parsnips usually taste much better than store-bought ones — they're sweeter, crunchier, and more flavorful.

The thinner, more tender parsnips harvested in fall can be steamed or sautéed in butter. Larger parsnips harvested later can be sliced and then steamed, sautéed, or added to soups, stews, or casseroles. Cooked with butter, parsnips provide their own sugar for caramelizing. Sliced and fried as chips, or boiled and puréed, parsnips make sweet substitutes for potatoes; in fact, food historians tell us that parsnips reigned supreme in Europe before the introduction of potatoes in the sixteenth century. Shredded raw parsnip makes a nice addition to salad; raw parsnip slices are excellent with dips.

Planning

Choosing a variety of parsnips is not much of a problem since seed catalogs rarely offer more than two. *Hollow Crown* and *Harris Model* are two common varieties, both producing smooth, white roots; *Harris* is a bit longer and narrower.

Parsnip seeds are slow to germinate and the plants are slow growing. Plants need about 175 days to develop decent-size roots. But since parsnips are relatively pest-free and disease-free, they are easy to grow.

Preparation

The seeds are slow to germinate, so pick as weed-free an area of the garden as possible for your parsnips. They'll have trouble competing with weeds in an area that was recently sod, for example. A good choice for a parsnip location is where your bush snap beans grew the previous season, since the broad foliage of that crop shades out weed growth.

Work the soil deeply and be sure to stir up the planting area immediately before marking your row or bed. This will kill many small weeds that are germinating just under the soil surface.

Because the crop is in the ground a long time, consider mixing some slow-release fertilizer into the soil before planting. Used properly, the fertilizer should feed the crop for 2 or 3 months. If you have some, a healthy dose of broken down, aged manure will provide the same service.

Planting

Since the seeds take 2 to 3 weeks to germinate, it is easy to forget exactly where you planted them. And weeds can get a stronghold in the planting bed before the parsnips are well established. So we recommend mixing radish seeds in with the parsnips (about ten radish seeds per one hundred parsnip seeds) when you sow them. The radishes will germinate within a few days, breaking up the soil and marking the rows for you. They will be ready

Cover seeds with horticultural-grade vermiculite to help germination; the material does not harden after watering as some soils do. It's an ideal medium for retaining moisture until the seedlings emerge 2 to 3 weeks after planting.

for harvest just as the parsnips begin to require more space.

You can speed up the germination process by about 5 days by soaking the seeds in warm water for 24 hours before planting.

Drain off the water from the seeds and then dig 3-inch-deep furrows 12 to 18 inches apart. Dampen the bottom of each furrow with a liquid fertilizer mixed according to package directions. Plant the seeds about 3 inches apart in the bottom of each furrow and cover them with an inch of horticultural grade (medium-size) vermiculite. Vermiculite holds moisture well; it will not harden up and form a crust when the surface starts to dry out, as heavy soils will do. Water the rows and keep the soil damp until the seedlings emerge.

In heavy soils you might need to dig individual holes rather than long furrows. Using a crowbar or pipe, dig cone-shaped holes 16 to 18 inches deep, 5 inches wide at the top, 6 to 9 inches apart. Fill each hole with compost or rich, well-worked soil. Plant 3 or 4 seeds ½ inch deep in each hole. Vermiculite can be used to cover the seeds. Water gently and keep moist until seedlings show through. When seedlings are well established (3 to 4 inches high), thin to one per hole.

For either planting method, mark the rows with radish seeds.

Care

Once the parsnips are up, they require very little care. Pests and diseases will rarely bother the crop. For good-size roots, thin plants when 3 to 4 inches tall to stand from 3 to 6 inches apart. Wider distances between plants will encourage fatter roots. Maintain good moisture after that so the roots won't get woody. If you did not add slow-release fertilizer, water once a month with a liquid fertilizer or side-dress every month or so with about 1 cup of complete fertilizer such as 5-10-10 or its equivalent per 25 feet of row. Keep the weeds under control with shallow cultivation.

Harvesting

Wait until a few frosts have sweetened the parsnips before harvesting. If you want to leave the parsnips in the ground over the winter, apply a layer of heavy mulch about 18 inches deep. If you live in the North or where the ground does freeze, a heavy mulch will keep the plants from thawing out in a midwinter warm spell and then refreezing, which lowers the quality of the vegetable. In the South, mulching may keep the ground from freezing, which will allow you to easily dig up the parsnips all winter long.

Harvest overwintered parsnips in the spring as soon as the ground thaws and use them quickly. Do not allow the parsnips to start growing in the ground again or they will become tough and woody.

Essentials

Planning

🍂 *Parsnips require a long growing season (100 to 130 days). They tolerate frosts and can be harvested just before the ground freezes or left in the ground over the winter.*

🍂 *Time seed sowing for harvest just after the average first fall frost date. In areas with mild winters, you can also sow seeds in the fall from September through November.*

🍂 *Purchase fresh seeds each year.*

Preparation

🍂 *Work soil at least a foot deep to remove rocks, clods, and other obstructions.*

🍂 *In heavy soils, form raised beds about 4 to 6 inches high.*

🍂 *Add commercial slow-release fertilizers or aged manure.*

Planting

🍂 *Soak seeds for 24 hours before planting directly outdoors.*

🍂 *Sow the seeds ½ inch deep, 2 seeds per inch in rows or beds. In heavy soil, cover with vermiculite so the seedlings can emerge easily.*

🍂 *Because parsnips seeds are slow to germinate, it's a good idea to mix some radish seeds in with them to break the soil and mark the rows.*

🍂 *Parsnip seedlings will emerge in 2 to 3 weeks.*

Care

🍂 *Thin well-established seedlings to stand 3 to 6 inches apart, depending on how large you want your roots.*

🍂 *Keep the rows weeded with shallow cultivation.*

🍂 *If you haven't used a slow-release fertilizer, side-dress 1 to 2 months after planting with 1 cup of 5-10-10 per 25 feet of row or its equivalent. (Slow-release fertilizers will be used up in 2 to 3 months.)*

🍂 *Parsnips are fairly pest-free and disease-free.*

Harvesting

🍂 *For the best-tasting parsnips, harvest before the ground freezes but after a few frosts, or leave them in the ground through the winter.*

🍂 *If you store parsnips in the ground, cover them with a thick organic mulch. Harvest immediately after the ground thaws in the spring.*

Peas

Sugar snap peas *(left)* have been a boon to gardeners — they're easy to grow and a cinch to prepare for the table. Let pods get plump before picking them.

There's a reason you rarely find fresh peas of distinction in a supermarket — they start losing their sweetness and quality right after harvest. Because they keep so poorly, it takes a backyard pea patch to satisfy real pea lovers.

There are now three main types of peas to select from, thanks to breakthroughs in plant breeding in recent years.

First is the traditional *garden pea* with delicate, sweet, tender peas inside tough, usually inedible, outer pods.

Next are the *edible-podded peas,* called snowpeas by growers in southern China who found they weren't bothered by a light snow. These plants produce tender, flavorful pods that are harvested when the peas inside them are quite small and undeveloped.

Newest to the pea family are the sweet, crunchy *snap peas,* which have both a delicate edible pod and full-size peas inside with the sweetness of the best garden peas. The new snap peas, available in space-saving dwarf varieties, as well as pole types that will surpass 8 feet if you let them, make shelling peas a chore of the past, although some varieties need destringing before use. They are as wonderful eaten raw, lightly steamed, or stir-fried.

Planning

The best way to plant peas depends in part on when you are planting and what your spring soil conditions are. The earlier you plant, the higher your yields will be. Where spring soils are often wet and soggy, you can try using raised beds for early planting. If your soil is sandy, planting in trenches will keep the pea roots cool, which will also promote higher yields. Trench planting also works well for fall crops.

If you are planting a dwarf variety, the peas can be sown in labor-saving wide rows, where they will support themselves so you don't have to erect a support trellis. In a good wide row, the plants won't need thinning or much weeding because fast-growing peas form a shade mulch with their foliage that keeps out weeds. The shade also helps the soil hold moisture, which peas like. Wide rows are a good idea in southern gardens where high air and soil temperatures in the spring often spoil peas before they mature. Dwarf peas that are planted in single or double rows, however, should have some kind of support to grow on.

Pole or climbing pea varieties produce up to five times as many pods per plant as the dwarf bush varieties, so choose tall types for highest yields. The taller-growing varieties such as *Alderman* or *Sugar Snap* are easy to mulch, fertilize, harvest, and nurture through a long bearing season when they're trellised properly. The vines have better air circulation around them on a trellis, which helps prevent disease problems.

Many types of wire fencing or nylon netting can be used to train tall-growing peas; small mesh fencing may be hard to clean of dead vines at the end of the season because the plants weave through the mesh so many times. Besides fencing or netting, gardeners can use brush cuttings about ¼ to ½ inch thick at the base. Push the cuttings solidly into the ground in a dense row and then plant on both sides.

Whatever type of support you choose, make sure it's a bit taller than the height your variety will reach, and set it up before planting to avoid stepping on small plants later.

Peas can germinate in a wide range of soil temperatures, starting as low as 40°F. However, the cooler the soil, the slower the germination time. Coating seeds with a fungicide will protect them where soils are moist and cool.

Use bacterial inoculant to help peas fix nitrogen only when you are planting peas

Far right: **Mix bacterial inoculant with pea seeds just before planting. Stir in a little molasses or honey so the powder will stick to the seeds.**

These illustrations show four good ways to plant peas.

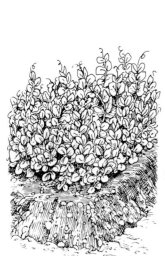

Wide-row planting works best with dwarf varieties.

Trench planting captures more moisture — an asset in low-rainfall areas.

Plant on both sides of a sturdy wire trellis. Put posts about 6 feet apart.

Brush cuttings support bush peas well.

in a new garden area that's never been cultivated. Do not mix inoculant with treated seeds (see "Fungicide-treated Seed," page 27) or the inoculant won't work.

Preparation

Peas, like most legumes, do best in deep, rich soil that is well drained. If the seeds sit in the wet ground too long before sprouting, they may be lost to rot organisms. Seed rot is more likely in early spring, especially if you're working a heavy clay soil that is slow to drain.

The solution is to prepare raised beds the fall before you plant your peas (see "Raised Beds," pages 40–41). A raised planting area will get soil temperatures of 50°F or higher quite early in the spring, which leads to faster germination.

Add organic matter to the beds in the fall, then in the spring when the soil is thawing out and starting to warm up, gently rake the top of the bed to break open the hard-packed surface formed over the winter. Depending on the weather and your soil type, you may be able to sow pea seeds in just a few days, well before other areas of the garden are ready.

Peas need a good supply of phosphorus and potassium at planting time and only a small dose of nitrogen. Phosphorus is key for root development, potassium aids flower development, and nitrogen promotes good growth of vines and leaves.

Essentials

Planning

❧ Plant peas early in spring as soon as the soil can be worked, and harvest before hot, early summer days.
❧ Plant dwarf varieties to save space and produce early harvests. Plant tall or pole varieties for bigger harvests over a longer period of time.

Preparation

❧ For early spring planting, select a well-drained site that dries out quickly after the winter.
❧ Mix into the soil 1 to 1½ pounds of 5-10-10 fertilizer or its equivalent per 100 square feet before planting.
❧ Where spring soil stays wet for extended periods, build raised beds in the fall and mix in manure and compost for fertilizer.
❧ Erect trellis or supports for all varieties before planting.

Planting

❧ Sow seeds in the early spring 1 to 1½ inches deep and 2 inches apart; for summer plantings where soils are drier, plant 2 inches deep. Plant raised beds in double rows, 6 inches apart with a support structure or trellis in the middle. Allow 24 to 30 inches between double rows. Plant single rows 3 feet apart with supports alongside each row.
❧ Water summer-planted rows often to prevent the sprouts from drying out.

Care

❧ Start training the tendrils onto the supports when the plants are about 6 inches tall.
❧ When pods are maturing in a hot spell, water daily if necessary to keep up quality.
❧ Avoid deep hoeing around peas — the roots are tender and damage easily.
❧ Side-dress trellised plants when they are about 6 inches tall at a rate of ½ pound of a 1:1 mixture of ammonium sulfate and dehydrated manure per 25 feet of row.
❧ Watch for pea aphids (page 276), seed corn maggots (page 280), and slugs (page 280) in early-planted crops in cool weather.
❧ Possible diseases include fusarium wilt (page 285), powdery mildew (page 286), and viruses (page 287).

Harvesting

❧ Harvest pods carefully. Use your fingernail to pinch off the pods or use scissors.
❧ Pick garden peas when pods are well filled but before they begin to harden or fade in color. Harvest snowpeas when the pods are young and tender and the peas inside are undeveloped. Snap peas are ready when the pods are plump but still crisp and well colored.
❧ Pick peas every day during the harvest period.

A Superior Trellis

An A-frame trellis works well for tall-growing peas or beans sown in double rows. Use 8-foot lengths of cedar (or substitute) and two-by-twos for the uprights. The legs of the frame should straddle the bed and sink into the ground on either side. A good base width is 3 or 4 feet.

Nail the lower horizontal member of the frames 12 inches above the bottom of the legs. Nail the upper horizontal member 9 inches from the top.

The length of your bed will determine the number of frames you need to build and the length of the pieces that join them. For 25-foot beds, use four frames connected at the top with two-by-twos a little over 6 feet long.

Screw hooks into the connecting pieces at 3- to 4-inch intervals. On the lower horizontal piece, about 3 inches from each end, screw in large metal eyes. Set the frame in the garden. Attach support wires to the metal eyes on each frame. We recommend using re-bar, a concrete reinforcing rod. Even heavy wire will pull up and out of shape when you attach strings to it.

Tie string or twine from the re-bar up and around the hooks on the top connecting member, back down around the re-bar, and so on until one side is strung. Repeat on the other side.

In China farmers say they must "teach the vine." When the vines are 5 to 6 inches tall, the tendrils start looking for something to hold on to. Pea vines are much more tender than beans, and not as self-sufficient. You have to help them attach themselves to the trellis strings so they can begin to climb.

"Teaching" must start early. Vines left to grow any which way become a big mess, all twined together. If you do manage to find the tendrils and try to get them to hold on to the strings, you may break or damage them.

To prevent strong winds from blowing the grown vines down, you can use additional horizontal string about 4 feet up along the sides of the A-frame.

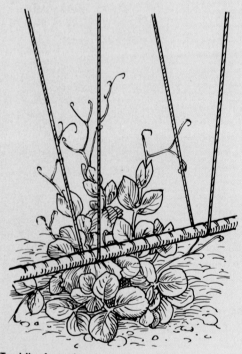

Tendrils of pea vines must often be placed by hand around the support when the plants are small. Training must start early; you can damage the fragile tendrils if you try to disentangle them.

Too much nitrogen reduces pod production, so be careful. Apply 1 to 1½ pounds of 5-10-10 or equivalent fertilizer per 100 square feet a few days before planting.

Just before planting, set up your trellises in double rows — two single rows 6 inches apart, with the fence or trellis set between them.

In gardens that receive a lot of sun or have light, sandy soils and limited rainfall, the soil may dry out too quickly and heat up too much as the crop nears maturity. We recommend trench planting for these conditions. With your hoe, make a 3- or 4-inch-deep trench, 5 or 6 inches wide. Set up your trellises and supports right alongside the trench. Soak the trench and let the water drain into the soil. While the plants are small, the trench collects and holds rain or irrigation water to provide a steady moisture supply.

Where the soil is neither too wet nor too dry, you can plant in double rows or wide rows. To prepare a wide row bed, spade or till your planting area deeply — a row 20 inches wide by 10 feet long is a good size for experimenting with wide row planting. Fertilize with 1 to 1½ pounds of 5-10-10 or its equivalent per 100 square feet, then create a smooth planting surface by lightly grading the area with the back of a garden rake.

Add the same amount of fertilizer if you are planting double rows.

Planting

To sow seeds in raised beds, trenches, or double rows, space the seeds 1 to 1½ inches deep and 2 inches apart. (Put double rows 6 inches apart.)

To seed a wide row, sprinkle the seeds as evenly as you can throughout the bed. Most should land about 1½ to 2 inches apart. Tamp the seeds down with the back of a hoe; they must be in good contact with soil for germination. Then scoop up soil with a hoe or rake from outside the planting area onto the bed and gently spread it evenly over the seeds to a depth

Planting presprouted peas in a trench may be worth trying if you are planting in hot summer weather for a fall harvest. Be sure to keep the soil lightly moist until seedlings emerge and get established.

of 1 to 1½ inches. Once the soil surface is smooth and level, tamp it down again with the hoe.

Care

When plants growing in a trench are 5 or 6 inches tall, feed them a small amount of natural fertilizer (2 cups of dehydrated manure per 10 feet of trench, for example), and then fill the trench halfway with soil. This will insulate pea roots and keep them cool. After another week or so, top off the trench with more soil.

Although peas are known as a light-feeding crop (they have a low need for added nutrients), we recommend side-dressing tall-growing trellised peas such as *Sugar Snaps*. You can harvest from tall varieties for a long period under good conditions and they need extra nutrients to remain vigorous. Side-dress when the plants are about 6 inches tall. (If you wait until they're taller, the fertilizer could cause a delay in flower formation.) A good fertilizer to use is a 1:1 mix of either

Pea Varieties

In this list varieties are grouped by season—early, midseason, and late season. We also include comments on characteristics and the sources for buying the varieties.

Key to chart:

G—garden pea (needs shelling)
E—snowpea-type edible pod (harvest when peas are small)
S—snap type (pod and large peas edible)

Variety	Type	Days	Height (inches)	Comments	Sources
Early Varieties (first harvest 55–64 days after planting)					
Alaska	G	55	26–36	Old standard, often grown for dried peas for soups; smooth seeds; 6–8 peas/pod. Not the sweetest, but good fresh for early crop.	6, 52, 75
Blue Bantam	G	64	15–18	Pods 4", 7–9 peas/pod; good bearer.	6, 97
Burpeeana Early	G	63	18	Sweet; 3" pod, 8–10 peas/pod; medium to large size.	6
De Grace	E	55	12–14	Very dwarf, early snowpea. Plant early.	8
Freezonian	G	63	24–30	Dark green pods; 7–8 peas/pod; excellent for freezing. Productive.	6, 16, 97
Frosty	G	60	24–30	Good freezing pea; 3–3½" pods, 6–8 peas/pod. Wilt resistant.	11, 16
Grenadier	G	61	14–18	Plump, 4" pods; resistant to powdery mildew; good fall crop choice.	6, 52
Lacy Lady	G	64	18	Novella-type with few leaves. 2½–3" pods, 6–8 peas/pod. Pods set on top portion of plant.	8, 33, 75
Little Marvel	G	65	18–20	3" pods, tightly packed with 7–8 large peas. Good for freezing; reliable yielder.	6, 16, 28, 52, 75
Maestro	G	61	24–28	Highly resistant to powdery mildew; resistant to other diseases. 9–12 peas/pod. Heavy producer; good fall choice.	6, 13
Norli	E	50	18	Snowpea type; very sweet and very early. Good producer.	8, 71
Progress #9	G	62	16–20	Very early long-podded pea. 7–9 peas/pod; resistant to fusarium wilt; good flavor.	21, 28, 75
Recette	G	55	30	Sets two pods at each node. Baby peas, 8–9 peas/pod. Small and sweet.	8
Snowbird	E	58	16–18	Very early—no support necessary; 3" pods; high yields.	6, 109
Snowflake	E	58	24–36	Oriental snowpea type. Straight, flat pods, 4" long, 1" wide. Grow with or without support.	20, 24
Sparkle	G	55	18–24	Good early, short-vined variety. Sets a concentrated crop of 3" pods with 6–8 peas/pod.	11, 16, 24, 97
Sugar Ann	S	56	24–28	Very early, short-vined snap pea; 1984 All-America Selections winner.	16, 52, 75
Sugar Bon	S	56	18–24	Compact, bushy vines. Pods 2–3", 6–7 peas/pod. May be grown without support.	6, 28, 52
Sweet Snap	S	64	36–40	Heavy producer; 2–3" pods, 6–7 peas/pod.	6, 8, 52, 75
Thomas Laxton	G	58	36–44	Veteran early variety. Yields a large pea good for freezing. Long bearer.	51, 75, 97

ammonium sulfate or ammonium nitrate with dehydrated cow manure. A half-pound for every 25 feet of row is sufficient in most gardens.

In the spring when the peas first come up in the garden, slugs may try to feast on the tender vines and leaves. Slug traps, slug bait, and hand-picking can keep them from doing too much harm.

The fall crop is bothered mostly by aphids, especially when the vines are 4 to 5 feet tall. Usually a cold water spray in the early morning will control them.

Harvesting

Pick peas each day during the harvest season to harvest them at top quality and encourage more production, especially with pole types. The best time to pick is early morning because the pods are crispest then and will store better and stay fresh longest. At midday and in the after-

Pea Varieties *(continued)*

Variety	Type	Days	Height (inches)	Comments	Sources
Midseason Varieties (first harvest 65–70 days after planting)					
Dark-skin Perfection	G	65	30	Tolerant to heat; 3½″ pods, 7–9 peas/pod. Pods set in clusters, easy to pick.	*12*
Green Arrow	G	70	24–28	High yielder; pods set in pairs at top of plant; 9–11 peas/pod. Resistant to downy mildew and fusarium wilt.	*6, 16, 21, 52*
Lincoln	G	66	18–30	An old-timer, still a favorite. 7–9 peas in medium-size pods.	*11, 16, 75*
Mammoth Melting Sugar	E	68	48–60	Thick pods 4½″ long, ¾″ wide. Productive, wilt resistant.	*6, 33, 75*
Novella (Bikini)	G	65	20–28	Large, medium green peas, 8–10 peas/pod; broad, straight pods; little foliage so harvest is easy.	*6, 21, 28*
Novella II	G	65	28	Nearly leafless type; grows well in double rows with no staking; 8–9 peas/pod.	*6*
Oregon Sugar Pod II	E	68	28	Good for fresh stir-fries or freezing; pods 4½″ long, ¾″ wide.	*6, 33, 66*
Sugar Rae	S	68	30	Slightly later than *Sugar Snap*; produces up to 5 vines per plant, so plant seed less thickly. Resistant to powdery mildew.	*26, 51, 75*
Sugar Snap	S	70	60–72	Sweet, crunchy 3″-round pods, good served raw. Wilt resistant vines.	*6, 16, 21, 28*
Wando	G	68	28–32	A productive, hot-weather pea; good yielder; 7–8 peas/pod.	*6, 16, 52, 75*
Late Season Varieties (first harvest 70–80 days after planting)					
Alderman (Telephone Dark Podded)	G	74	60–70	Plump, curved pods, 8–10 peas/pod.	*28, 52*
Giant Stride	G	73	18	Very large, dark green peas. Stocky plants, large pods, 8–10 peas/pod. Very good flavor and good producer.	*21, 28*
Morse's No. 60 (Dwarf Telephone Dark Podded)	G	75	28	Pointed pods, 4–5″ long, 8–10 peas/pod; excellent for market garden. Sweet flavor, resistant to fusarium wilt.	*28, 75*
Rondo	G	74	28–30	Broad, plump pods, 8–10 large peas/pod. Heavy bearer. Very sweet flavor.	*28*
Sugar Daddy	S	74	24–30	A stringless snap pea, pods similar to *Sugar Snap*, but slightly narrower.	*6, 35*

noon, the pods become softer and don't seem to keep as well. The cool of the evening is another good picking time, but morning is best.

To keep pods in the refrigerator, put 1-pound batches in brown paper bags and then put them into a plastic bag and seal with a twist tie. The paper bag absorbs any extra moisture so that peas aren't actually sitting in water, and the plastic bag holds in enough so the peas stay fresh.

Snowpeas got their name in southern China when growers discovered that these edible-podded peas were not bothered by a light snow. Pick snowpeas before their pods fill out.

Peppers

Golden Bell (left) is one of several new yellow sweet bell peppers. At the other end of the flavor spectrum is the popular *Jalapeno* hot pepper, shown above at mature size.

Peppers make the garden brighter for gardeners, the kitchen more exciting for cooks, and the dinner table more memorable for everyone. There's a staggering range of pepper colors, sizes, shapes, and flavors available to today's home gardeners and cooks, while supermarket shoppers often have to settle for just green or red bell peppers.

With their passion for peppers, it's no wonder American gardeners rank the crop second in popularity, right behind tomatoes. In spite of their high vitamin C content, it's probably not the pepper's nutritional value that entices gardeners. Rather, it's the many uses of peppers, from the salad bar to zesty taco sauces and sweet and flame thrower–hot pickled delights, that excite home growers.

The kitchen is, perhaps, the best place to start your pepper-growing adventure. All pepper varieties sound tantalizing in catalogs. But before succumbing to those glowing phrases and ordering too many seeds of peppers you "can't live without," think first about how you'll use them in the kitchen.

If you're satisfied with just green bell peppers, a good nursery will have some variety choices. But to grow a sampling of more interesting varieties, you will have to grow your own starter plants.

Once you've set the plants out in the garden, a moderate amount of care — proper side-dressing and a steady supply of water — will result in a long, rewarding season of pepper harvesting.

Planning

To enjoy some of the great diversity of pepper types, you'll want to grow your own transplants from seed and then set them out in the garden. Starting plants indoors is the norm in all regions since the seeds are slow starters and many varieties need 80 or more warm days to yield well.

Peppers are quite sensitive to cold weather and cold soils; the best outdoor planting time is usually a week to 10 days after the last spring frost date. Sow your seeds 8 to 10 weeks before this date.

Peppers need warmth for good germination. Keep the flat or pots where it's warm (75°F). Seeds will come up fastest when the soil temperature is 80° to 90°F. In a cold seed-starting room (under 65°F), the peppers might take 2 or 3 weeks to emerge.

Some gardeners hang a light bulb over the flats to warm up the area. You can also use an electric heating coil under the flats to keep the soil warm. Be sure to mark all your varieties clearly from the start so you don't mix up sweet and hot peppers.

A soil thermometer can indicate precisely the optimum time to set out peppers. The soil 4 inches below the surface of the planting bed should measure 65°F or higher at 8 A.M. If set out too early, peppers will produce poorly all season.

Preparation

Vigorous plants may grow to be 6 to 8 inches tall a week or two before your planting date. Transplant these peppers to a larger pot where the roots will have more room. The best pepper yields are possible only if the roots are never constricted.

About a week before planting, broadcast 1 to 1½ pounds of 5-10-10 or its equivalent per 100 square feet.

Starting from about 2 weeks before your planting date, gradually harden the plants by setting them outside for a few hours on warm days. As your planting date gets closer, give them more time outdoors, but don't let them suffer through a windy, cold day until they're well prepared for it.

Planting

Peppers will never completely recover from a cold shock; they'll produce poorly all season if set out too early. Use a soil thermometer to measure soil temperatures. It's time to set out peppers when the soil 4 inches below the surface of the planting bed measures 65°F or higher at 8 A.M.

Space plants close enough so that leaves of full-grown plants will touch those of their neighbors to prevent sunscald and promote higher overall yields. Bell pepper plants should be spaced farther apart than hot pepper types.

Peppers require a good dose of fertilizer at transplanting time to put on enough vegetative growth to support large yields of good-size fruits. Without it, plants may be small or spindly, unable to support many peppers. If any peppers set fruit before they are a foot tall, pick off the peppers and side-dress the plants with a fertilizer containing nitrogen.

Mix a teaspoon of 5-10-10 or its equivalent with soil in the hole where the pepper transplant will be set. Be careful not to overfertilize. Too much nitrogen can reduce pepper yields.

Care

Good pepper yields are influenced by many factors; one important factor is the amount of nitrogen the plants get after planting. Side-dress 2 months after transplanting seedlings with a natural fertilizer such as composted manure, or use a commercial fertilizer such as 5-10-10. Apply 5 cups of 5-10-10 for every 100 square feet of pepper area. With light, sandy soils, it's a good idea to add an additional 1 to 2 cups after the first harvest over the same area. Always be ready to fertilize if your plants turn pale green or yellowish, usually a sign they need more nitrogen.

Peppers also respond well to magnesium, an element not adequate in many soils. A tablespoon of Epsom salts (magnesium sulfate) in a gallon of water will supply young plants with this nutrient.

Because they help retain soil moisture, mulches are highly recommended for pepper growing. To warm the soil at planting time, you can mulch with plastic or, once the soil is sufficiently warm, use an organic mulch around plants.

Extensive testing in Alabama has shown that a new type of plastic — brown polyethylene — helps peppers yield 20 percent more than do black plastic or clear plastic. (All the plastic mulches boosted pepper yields significantly over control crops with no mulch.) Brown plastic doesn't build up as high a soil temperature as either black or clear plastic. The heat from black and clear materials works well early in the season; but later, it can actually hinder growth. Brown plastic is a good choice in all regions that have very hot summers.

If you use straw or hay mulches don't use them too early. It's best to wait until the very hottest days of summer when the peppers really need moisture conservation.

If you spray-paint black plastic with aluminum reflective paint it will repel aphids, which spread cucumber mosaic virus. Aluminum foil stapled on cardboard mats also works well. The aphids are apparently confused by the reflected light

Essentials

Planning

⁍ Plan to set out home-grown or purchased transplants after the last spring frost date.

⁍ Start plants indoors in flats or pots 8 to 10 weeks before the average last frost date.

Preparation

⁍ One week before setting out transplants, broadcast 1½ pounds of 5-10-10 or its equivalent per 100 square feet.

Planting

⁍ Set hot pepper plants 12 to 15 inches apart, larger bell types 15 to 18 inches apart.

⁍ Place a teaspoon of 5-10-10 fertilizer or its equivalent into each planting hole and cover with an inch of soil before setting in transplants.

⁍ Provide windbreaks.

Care

⁍ Provide deep waterings weekly for pepper plants.

⁍ Side-dress monthly with about 1 tablespoon of 5-10-10 or its equivalent for each plant.

⁍ Support bushy, heavy-yielding plants with 2-foot-high cages, or stake them.

⁍ Apply heavy organic mulches when summer heat begins to peak.

⁍ Temperatures over 90°F can cause buds and blossoms to drop; the condition is more serious if humidity is low also.

⁍ Pests are not a serious concern. Possible pests include the Colorado potato beetle (page 277), corn borers (page 278), flea beetles (page 278), and leaf miners (page 279).

⁍ Uneven watering can trigger blossom end rot (page 283).

⁍ Sunscald (page 286) may develop with varieties that have sparse foliage.

⁍ Diseases you may encounter include cucumber mosaic virus (page 287), anthracnose (page 282), fusarium wilt (page 285), verticillium wilt (page 287), bacterial spot (page 282), and leaf spot (page 285).

Harvesting

⁍ Begin harvesting when peppers reach a usable size.

⁍ Leave some peppers on the plant to ripen fully. The peppers will change color and develop greater levels of vitamin C. Don't let all peppers stay on the plant as this will cut off further blossoming and fruit set.

Extra-Early Peppers

To get an extra-early pepper harvest, or to grow some varieties that normally might not mature in your area, you can try growing peppers under tunnels.

Dr. Arthur Pratt, a horticultural researcher from Cornell University in New York, investigated tunnel growing for three seasons. He found that tunnels improve the microclimate around pepper plants, increase air temperature around the plants on cold days, and offer moderate frost protection. Plants grow taller and wider faster; they set fruit earlier and yield more peppers.

Slitted row covers, which offer good ventilation on hot sunny days, allow gardeners to set out transplants 2 to 4 weeks before the last spring frost date.

Heat build-up is the biggest danger when using plastic coverings over peppers. Excessive temperatures — over 90°F — can cause blossoms to drop. It's best not to use black plastic in conjunction with slitted row covers; peppers might actually overheat. Remove the tunnel soon after the last spring frost when the weather warms up and no more cold spells are expected.

An aluminum foil mulch works well in southern gardens. It maintains a steady soil temperature during the hot summer months and also disorients some flying pests when they try to land.

and don't land on peppers. This effect diminishes through the season as foliage growth shades the mulch.

Water peppers well, providing about an inch of water weekly. In southwestern states irrigation is essential to a good pepper harvest. In very hot weather, gardeners in this region might need to water their peppers every day.

You may need to support bell and banana pepper varieties. Small, 2-foot-high cages prevent strong winds or heavy rains from bending plants. If you don't have cages handy, stake the plants or run a tough cord along your row for branches to hang on.

Some buds and blossoms may drop when the temperature goes above 90°F, especially if the humidity is low, or when temperatures are too low (below 55°F). When the weather is hot and plants are in the bud-and-blossom stage, water is very important. If the plants are hurting for water, many buds and blossoms will drop. Peppers produce more blossoms than the plants can maintain and develop, so losing just a few is not serious.

Fruit exposed to intense direct sunlight can develop sunscald — light-colored, soft, slightly wrinkled areas that deteriorate and become discolored. Growing plants close together and choosing foliage-rich varieties such as *California Wonder 300* will reduce the incidence of sunscald.

There are several viruses that can bother pepper plants. Chief among them is the cucumber mosaic virus, which is spread by aphids. Choose virus-resistant varieties. Other diseases that may occur include bacterial spot and leaf spot. Blossom end rot may be a problem if watering is erratic.

Insects are not usually a serious concern for most home gardeners.

What Makes Hot Peppers Hot?

Cayenne Long Red Slim

The hotness or pungency of chili peppers is derived from a natural chemical substance called capsaicin, which is present in almost all peppers. Of course, it's present in much greater quantities in hot peppers. It's so strong to the human taste bud that it's been reported that even a dilution of one part per million can be detected. Very pungent peppers — like the *Jalapeno* — might have 3,000 or so parts per million of capsaicin. (Note: in some areas of the country a chili pepper might refer to a favorite local variety, but often the term is a catchall for any kind of hot pepper.)

The capsaicin is found in tiny blisterlike sacs between the lining and the inner wall of the pepper. If you cut a pepper in half lengthwise, you can see the inside partitions that divide each pepper into lobes and surround the seed cavity. The clear membrane covering these partitions also covers the capsaicin sacs. These sacs are easily broken if a pepper is handled at all roughly, releasing the capsaicin throughout the inside of the pepper and spreading the hotness. Seeds of the hottest peppers cause a burning sensation if they come in contact with your eyes or mouth, so wear rubber gloves to remove the stem and seed core when preparing these peppers.

Irrigation is essential for a good pepper harvest in many regions. Trickle irrigation puts out a small, steady amount of water directly to the root zone.

Hungarian Sweet Wax

Pick Your Peppers

Here's a list of possible pepper uses and some variety selections to match:

To stuff with rice, meat, or pasta filling, use thick-walled, large bell peppers such as *Big Bertha* or *Park's Whopper*. (Grow thick-walled types if you must peel peppers for a recipe.)

To make a sweet pepper sauce to garnish vegetables, fish, or poultry, try *Hercules Sweet Red,* a large one, ready about 70 days after transplanting.

For best flavor in fresh salads, try the *Green Boy* bell pepper, which won taste tests in New York State research. It is a thick-walled pepper.

Making your own cayenne pepper? Use *Cayenne Long Red Slim,* a narrow, 6-inch-long pepper that can be dried and powdered. It can be used fresh in hot sauces as well.

For making pepper vinegar, try *Small Chili,* an oblong hot variety that matures about 80 days after transplanting.

If you plan to pan-fry, roast, or make pepper relish, we suggest *Sweet Banana* (also called *Long Sweet Hungarian* or *Yellow Banana*) or *Italian Sweet.*

For red color and sweet flavor in garden and pasta salads, in Spanish omelets, or for canning, try *Pimiento Perfection*. This flavorful, bright crimson, crunchy pepper is tasty enough to eat out of hand. First harvest is 80 or so days after transplanting. (Pimientos are the red peppers used to stuff olives.)

We recommend *Tam Mild Jalapeno* for hot sauces, or salsas, nachos, picante sauce, and pizza topping. It's a hot pepper with one-third the bite of the standard *Jalapeno*. The *Serrano Chili* (2¼ inches long) has a candle-flame shape and is extremely pungent, a favorite in many southwestern gardens.

You can pickle many sweet and hot peppers. The *Jalapenos* and *Serranos* are very hot when pickled with their seeds. *Hungarian Yellow Wax Hot* (6 inches by 1½ inches) and the pungent *Cascabella* (1½ inches by ¾ inch) are two other traditional pickling favorites.

Try the very productive and quick-maturing *Gypsy* for container growing. It's relatively thick walled, sweet, wedge shaped, and yellow or green. Fruits grow to be 4 to 5 inches long.

For making Tabasco sauce, it has to be the *Tabasco* pepper, which is a different species from all the others on this list. It takes 100 to 120 days after transplanting until harvest, producing very hot, ¾-inch-long fruits. Wear rubber gloves when handling.

If your summer is short, try early bell peppers such as *Ace* or *Canape*. These are very reliable bearers, often weeks ahead of standard types such as *California Wonder* or *Yolo Wonder,* which are sold by many nurseries and garden centers.

For gift giving, try one of the small (12- to 14-inch-high) ornamental peppers such as *Tequila Sunrise* or *Candlelight,* which can be potted and grown indoors. They're good as flower bed or border plants, too.

The *Chocolate* pepper has an unusual and delectable color. It ripens from green to rich chocolate and has a spicy-sweet flavor.

Harvesting

The first peppers can be harvested as soon as they reach usable size. Steady harvesting after that will keep plants producing new fruits. You may want to let some ripen fully to their red or orange color. The longer a fruit stays on the vine, the greater its vitamin C content will be. The vitamin C in a deep red bell pepper is nearly double that of a green one of the same variety. (Peppers have the highest vitamin C content per pound of any common food, including citrus.)

When harvesting peppers use care not to break the branches. Cut bell peppers with a sharp knife. Some gardeners use scissors to harvest tiny hot peppers so they don't disturb the delicate plants.

Ripening will continue after harvest. Keep your peppers in a cool place; in a warm room, the peppers may ripen too quickly. Bell and banana peppers keep well for 2 weeks in plastic bags in the refrigerator.

Remember that hot peppers require special care in the kitchen. Use rubber gloves to handle and prepare them. Many beginners have "burned" their hands, mouth, nose, and even eyes by touching peppers without protection.

Hot peppers are good to dry for a long-lasting supply. Pick them after they turn

Peppers are quite sensitive to cold weather. A Wall O'Water plant protector is being filled after a pepper plant has been set out in the spring.

red or orange and dry them anywhere that's warm and has good air circulation. Don't stack them up, though. Many gardeners thread peppers onto a string and hang them in the kitchen where they look decorative as they dry. Later you can remove stems and seeds from dried peppers and grind the peppers to the consistency you want. (Use gloves for both of these processes.) To slow down their loss of pungency, keep ground peppers in airtight containers.

Potatoes

Freshly dug potatoes *(left)* should sit in the sun for only a few hours before heading to the kitchen or to storage. Blue potatoes *(above)* are one of many old-time varieties available from seed exchanges.

The best return on potatoes may well be with early-harvested, golfball-size potatoes that sell in the markets for a price five times what potatoes will cost by autumn. New potatoes, boiled in their jackets and served with a pat of butter, are one of the delights of the garden — sweet, tender, and utterly unlike any other potato.

Potatoes are often neglected in the home garden because they are so easily available and take up quite a bit of space. But new potatoes aren't that easily available, and certainly they aren't inexpensive. An early harvest of new potatoes leaves space in the garden for later crops.

If you have only a small garden, we recommend that you grow new potatoes. You'll want to plant them early (a month before the last expected spring frost date) and harvest them early (about 10 weeks after planting) when they are small and tender so you can use the garden space twice in the season, not just once.

If you have the space, there's no reason not to grow some midseason and late storage potatoes. You'll be able to grow varieties you can't find in the store with flavors that store-bought potatoes can't match.

Planning

Potatoes are treated differently from most other garden vegetables. First, they are not planted from seed, but from pieces of potatoes, called seed potatoes, containing buds, or eyes. They are planted in trenches. As the potato plants grow, soil is pushed up around the stem of the plant in a process called hilling to provide underground room for potatoes to form. Periods of harvest are generally midsummer through fall in the North, and April through June in the South.

In the North, plant potatoes from mid-April to mid-June. Plant early-maturing potatoes very early in the season — as soon as the frost is out of the ground and you're able to work the soil. In most areas, this can be 6 to 8 weeks before the expected last frost date.

In the South, planting times range from January to the end of March for spring planting, mid-August to September for a fall crop. Potatoes do not grow well in the South in the heat of midsummer. Where winters are relatively mild, as in central Florida, you can plant potatoes in January. February is planting time in many parts of Texas and Oklahoma.

The soil, not the calendar, will tell you when it's time to plant. The soil should not be so wet that it sticks together and is hard to work. Let it dry out a bit first. Potato seed pieces, like other seeds, can rot if planted in ground that is too wet.

Preparation

Potatoes will grow in just about any well-drained soil. They need loose, loamy soil to expand. Heavy clay soils compact, making it harder for plant roots to get air and water. If you have clay soil, try to add lots of aged manure or good compost to the soil before planting.

Nearly everyone who gives advice about growing potatoes says that soil pH — the measure of soil acidity or alkalinity — is an important factor, but home growers shouldn't take it too seriously. Commercial growers monitor their soil pH as carefully

as cardiologists track heartbeats; they try to keep the soil pH in the range of 4.8 to 5.4 to inhibit the growth of the bacteria-like organisms that cause potato scab, a disease that leaves raised, scabby marks on potato skins.

But most backyard gardeners need not be that particular about the soil pH for potatoes. Potatoes will grow better where the pH ranges from 6.0 to 6.5, the slightly acid condition suitable for most vegetable crops. A little scab on some potatoes won't hurt them — just peel the affected potatoes before cooking.

For a rewarding potato crop, plants must make a rapid, healthy start and develop lots of top growth. To assure a good start, use a balanced fertilizer, such as 5-10-10, at planting time. You can broadcast it over the planting area (about 1½ pounds for every 100 square feet), or you can sprinkle it in the planting trenches (1 pound per 25 feet of trench) and cover with 2 inches of soil. It's fine to use well-rotted manure or good compost instead of commercial fertilizer.

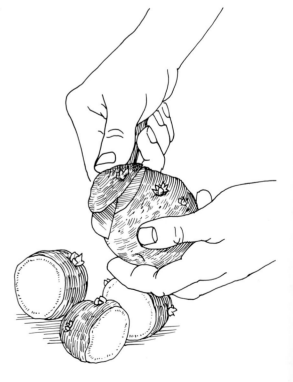

Potatoes are grown not from seeds but from pieces of potatoes, called seed potatoes. Cut seed pieces to weigh approximately 1½ ounces each with at least one "eye," or recessed bud.

A seed potato is a piece of the tuber or a small whole potato. Cut larger ones into pieces that have at least one "eye," or recessed dormant bud. The pieces should be about the size of a large ice cube and weigh about 1½ to 2 ounces.

Larger seed pieces produce plants that yield a high number of small to medium-size potatoes. Planting pieces that are smaller than recommended may give you fewer, but larger, potatoes. It may be tempting to plant smaller pieces in the hope of getting big potatoes, but stick to middle-size pieces. Small ones have less starch stored up to nourish a young plant; their food supply is quickly exhausted. A larger piece has more energy, which can help a young plant recover from an early-season injury.

Cut your potatoes into pieces about 2 days before you intend to plant them. This lets them "cure," or heal and develop a protective covering. Cured pieces retain their moisture when planted, but will have a hardened surface to resist rot organisms. The process is quickest if you can keep them indoors at about 70°F in a very humid place.

Later in the spring when the soil is warmer and drier, rot is less likely, so seed pieces can be planted immediately after being cut.

There's an advantage to planting small, whole potatoes as seed. Without cut surfaces, they are less apt to rot in the ground. Small potatoes have more eyes too, which results in more stems and a heavier set of tubers per plant.

As an extra measure to protect cut seed pieces from rot organisms in cool, moist soils, dust them with sulfur powder before planting. Sulfur is a natural, inexpensive fungicide available at most drugstores and many garden centers. One ounce will cover about 10 pounds of seed potatoes. Put seed pieces in a paper bag, add 2 tablespoons of sulfur, and shake the bag. The powder will stick to the pieces and protect them in the ground.

Essentials

Planning

☙ Buy seed potatoes of early varieties for planting as soon as soil can be worked in the spring.

☙ In the North, plant seed potatoes of later varieties from mid-May to early mid-June, 4 to 5 weeks after planting early varieties. In the South, plant seed potatoes of late varieties 1 to 2 weeks after early varieties.

Preparation

☙ Cut seed potatoes into small pieces with two to three eyes per piece a few days before planting.

Planting

☙ Dig trenches 6 inches wide, 8 inches deep, and 30 to 36 inches apart. Spread 5-10-10 at a rate of 1 pound per 25 feet or its equivalent along the bottom of the trench and cover with 2 inches of soil.

☙ Plant small whole seed potatoes or cut seed pieces 10 to 15 inches apart in the trench and cover with about 4 inches of soil.

Care

☙ Protect emerging plants with soil or other cover in case of a hard late spring frost.

☙ Hill the soil up against the plants about a week after leaves emerge from soil. Repeat 2 to 3 weeks later.

☙ Side-dress when you hill for the second time with compost, seaweed, or fish emulsion, or about 1 pound of 5-10-10 per 25-foot row.

☙ Be sure to provide adequate water 6 to 10 weeks after planting, when the potatoes start to form.

☙ Watch for flea beetles (page 278), the Colorado potato beetle (page 277), aphids (page 276), and wireworms (page 281). The European corn borer (page 278), leafhoppers (page 279), and leaf miners (page 279) may also cause problems.

☙ Possible diseases include early blight (page 284), late blight (page 285), potato scab (page 286), fusarium wilt (page 285), verticillium wilt (page 287), and mosaic virus (page 287).

Harvesting

☙ Harvest small, new potatoes about 10 weeks after planting.

☙ Harvest storage potatoes after the vines have died and tubers have developed tough outer skins. In the North, harvest before fall frosts arrive.

Regional Notes

South

Gardeners in the Gulf Coast states have the climate for two potato crops — spring and fall — but seed potatoes are unavailable in the fall. Saving your own from the spring crop is a good option.

Timing is important because a freshly dug potato will not sprout until it goes into a dormancy period for about 90 days. So start by planting part of your spring crop as early as possible — February 10 to 15 in Louisiana, for example. If light frosts are predicted, cover small plants with soil or burlap bags.

The potatoes should mature in about 90 to 100 days. Select about fifty small potatoes, approximately 1½ inch in diameter, for fall seed potatoes. Store them in a well-ventilated area where the temperature is about 65° to 75°F. When it's time to plant the fall crop — around mid-August — many of the potatoes will have sprouts. Plant them carefully in prepared trenches, covered by 3 inches of soil. Tamp the soil around them firmly but gently to avoid damaging the tender sprouts. (It's all right if long sprouts extend above ground a bit.)

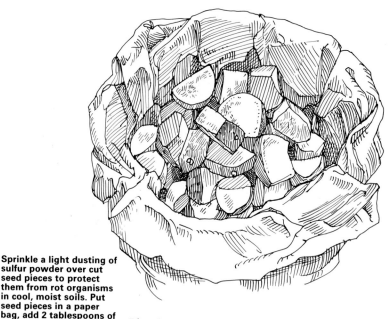

Sprinkle a light dusting of sulfur powder over cut seed pieces to protect them from rot organisms in cool, moist soils. Put seed pieces in a paper bag, add 2 tablespoons of sulfur, and shake the bag.

Planting

Dig the planting trenches with a hoe. They should be about 6 inches wide and 8 inches deep. Space the trenches 36 inches apart. To help potatoes develop roots quickly, you might add some superphosphate (0-20-0). Place a handful every 10 inches or so in the trench and cover with more soil.

Place small whole potatoes or potato seed pieces cut side down in the planting trenches. Space them 10 to 12 inches apart in the trench, optimum spacing for both early harvests of new potatoes and later ones of larger storage potatoes. At 8 or 9 inches apart, you may get too many undersized tubers; at 15 or 18 inches, the tubers may be larger than average, but fewer in number. The pieces or whole potatoes should be about 4 inches below the soil surface (slightly deeper for loose, sandy soils in hot climates).

Fill the entire trench with 3 to 4 inches of soil and tamp it down with the back of a hoe to press soil tightly around the potato piece.

Care

Potato plants are sensitive to frost. If the leaves of the plants have emerged from the

Left: Place seed pieces about 10 to 12 inches apart, cut side down, in the planting trench. Then cover them with 3 to 4 inches of soil. *Right:* Hilling, pulling soil up around the stems of the plants, allows the tubers to develop underground. Potatoes should be hilled twice — the first time soon after plants have emerged and again 2 to 3 weeks later.

ground and you expect a hard frost, cover them with soil to protect them. They'll be able to grow back through the added soil.

As the plants grow, you must pull additional soil up around the potato plant stems to enable the tubers to develop and expand easily. This hilling will prevent the potatoes from poking through the soil and turning green from exposure to sun. (Greening is a sign that poisonous solanine has developed; always cut away green sections before cooking.) A hilled row of potatoes will also have fewer weed and drainage problems — a big help for those with heavy, compacting soils.

Start hilling potatoes about a week or so after the plants poke through the soil. Use a broad hoe and pull up plenty of soil around the stems. If you cover a few leaves, don't worry about it. They'll push through in a few days.

Hill a second time about 2 to 3 weeks later, before the potato vines are tall enough to spill out into the walkways. This is a good time to put additional fertilizer in the soil. Use compost, seaweed, fish emulsion, or about 1 pound of 5-10-10 fertilizer or its equivalent per 25 feet of row, laying it in a band about 6 inches from the plant stems before you hill.

Potatoes need a steady, season-long supply of water, but water is most important when the plants start to develop their tubers, about 6 to 10 weeks after planting, depending on the variety.

When plants don't get enough water, the tubers grow very little and their cells start to mature. If you water them after a drought, they start a second, new growth spurt and develop cracks or odd shapes. Water thoroughly to moisten the soil to a depth of 8 to 10 inches.

The weather plays a big part in the health of a potato crop; you may have a disease problem one year and none the next. Moisture and temperature conditions may trigger certain diseases that spread rapidly through the potato patch.

To protect your crop, rotate the potato plot each year. Plant certified seed potatoes, not old tubers rescued from the root cellar or supermarket vegetable bin. Certified seed potato stock has been inspected during growth and storage and is free of disease.

Consider using an approved "potato dust" or spray regularly through the season. Potato dust is a chemical mixture of fungicide and insecticide that prevents some diseases, such as late blight, and thwarts some pests, too, such as the Colorado potato beetle. To be most effective, dusts and sprays must be applied to the potato foliage every 7 to 10 days, beginning when the plants emerge from the ground.

Early blight and late blight can be two of the most serious diseases for backyard growers. Late blight, caused by the fungus *Phytophthora infestans,* triggered the Irish potato failures of 1845 to 1848.

You can't be a potato grower for too many seasons without meeting Colorado potato beetles. They're present in just about every state. As soon as the weather warms, take regular walks through the rows and look for the adults. The first arrivals will be near the ground since adult beetles overwinter in the soil. Mulching deeply with materials like loose straw or shredded newspaper may help prevent these emerging beetles from climbing stems to lay eggs.

Later, check on the underside of leaves for orange egg masses and rub them out to help keep the population in check. Adults and larvae feed heavily on the foliage.

Other insects to keep a watch out for are flea beetles, aphids (which can spread the viruses that cause mosaic), and wireworms.

Harvesting

The first harvest is generally ready about 10 weeks after planting. Harvesting those early, small tubers is easy; just reach into the potato hill, feel for golfball-size tubers, and gently pull them out. Leave smaller tubers to continue maturing. If you pack the soil back around the plant, in 2 or 3 weeks more potatoes will be ready for harvesting in that hill.

Red Norland spuds don't get overly large, but they are prized as a first-of-the-season "new" potato. Digging potatoes is easiest when the soil is light and dry.

If you have enough plants, dig up one or two completely for each meal. The next day you can remove any plant residues, work the soil, mix in a handful of fertilizer, and plant a different vegetable.

Don't dig storage potatoes until the tops of the plants have died down and frost is approaching. By then the potatoes will be large with a thick skin that won't slough off easily.

Digging will be easier after a few rainless days when the soil is light and dry. Dig with a five- or six-tined spading fork if you have one. The potatoes are generally at the same level in each hill, so after digging a few hills you'll be able to dig under the potatoes at the right spot and not spear or bruise any by accident.

Leave the potatoes outdoors for an hour or two to dry off on the ground. There's no need to wash or brush them before storing, although you can wipe away any clumps of soil. Keep the potatoes in complete darkness after they've dried in the open for a short time. Don't leave them in any container light can penetrate or they'll begin to turn green.

Storage potatoes benefit from a short drying or curing period of 1 to 2 weeks. Keep them in a dark place with high humidity and temperatures around 55° to 60°F. Curing allows for rapid healing of any cuts or bruises on the potatoes.

For long-term storage, potatoes belong in a much cooler, dark place. Experts recommend 40°F, with moderate to high humidity and ventilation. If you can provide these conditions, you can keep mature potatoes for up to 8 months. Higher temperatures mean quicker sprouting, shriveling, and rotting.

A root cellar requires good air circulation because potatoes have to breathe in storage. They still carry on normal life processes, using oxygen and giving off carbon dioxide, heat, and moisture. Store potatoes in bins with slatted sides and bottoms; never pile them higher than 6 to 8 inches.

Potato Varieties

When choosing potato varieties, search locally first. It's more expensive to order the following potato varieties from mail-order sources. Most heirloom varieties are not widely available; try the seed exchanges if you're interested in them.

Butte: These handsome, long, russet-shaped potatoes are noted for their uniform size and are especially good for baking. *12, 32*

Explorer: Now available to grow from seed, this Irish potato can be harvested as new, boiling potatoes in 90 days and as big, 4- to 6-inch bakers a month later. *17, 35, 52, 108*

Irish Cobbler: Introduced in the 1870s, this early-maturing cream-colored variety is still popular. It's more susceptible to scab than some other varieties, but it produces well and is versatile in the kitchen. Some cooks find its texture is mealier than other early potatoes. *33, 98*

Lady Finger (Fingerling): Introduced to the United States by early German settlers, the little yellow-fleshed fingerlings grow 1 inch across, 4 to 5 inches long. They melt in your mouth. *15, 33*

Katahdin: This late season, round white potato is a good all-purpose variety, widely adaptable to soil, climate, and cultural conditions. It is not scab resistant. *24, 42, 87*

Norland: A red-skinned potato with oblong, smooth tubers and shallow eyes, it is widely available in the United States and has moderate resistance to scab. Though tastiest when small, large *Norlands* will develop if you let them, and they'll be fine for cooking, too. *32, 33, 87*

Red LaSoda: A good red-skinned variety, this potato is popular in the South, perhaps because it's known to tolerate some very high temperatures. *33, 98*

Red Pontiac: Another widely adapted red-skinned variety that can tolerate some high heat, it's actually listed as a midseason potato, but many tiny red potatoes will form early. If the crop is left to enlarge and mature, the potatoes keep well in storage. *24, 32, 87*

Superior: This white-skinned variety, grown along the east coast, has excellent yields and cooking qualities. It is somewhat less tolerant of severe drought. *42*

Pumpkins

Small Sugar **pumpkins**
(left) **are one of several**
multi-use varieties. In a
small garden ***(above),***
pumpkins can be planted
on the border with vines
trained out over the lawn.

Strictly speaking, a pumpkin is just another member of the squash family. But for all practical purposes, it's a vegetable in its own right. Because pumpkins are so versatile, they deserve their own place in the garden. Use them in delicious soups, casseroles, muffins, and pies and save the seeds for tasty snacks. You might also want to grow your own jack-o'-lantern or enter a competition at a county fair. There are varieties of pumpkins suited to each of these uses, so it's worth growing a few different kinds.

Once one of America's most popular vegetables, the pumpkin gradually fell from favor, perhaps because of a lack of space in gardens. Thanks to a broad selection of new varieties for any size garden, pumpkins are on the rise again — for good reason. Few crops are easier to grow or more reliable.

Pumpkin Seeds

All pumpkins produce edible seeds — if you want to take the time to remove the hulls. However, it's a tedious job. So if you like to munch on pumpkin seeds, choose a variety bred to produce thin, edible seed coats (see variety chart on page 221). Rinse the seeds, spread them on a cookie sheet, and roast in a 250°F oven for 20 to 40 minutes, turning frequently so they don't burn.

Don't expect to save the seeds produced by this year's crop for growing next year's pumpkins unless you are sure that the nearest close relatives (other pumpkin varieties and certain winter squash) were at least ¼ mile away from your pumpkin patch. Otherwise, the plants may have cross-pollinated and the resulting seeds will not grow true to their variety. Invest in new seeds each year.

Seed pumpkin varieties tend to have large seed cavities and smaller areas of usable pulp.

Planning

When choosing a pumpkin variety, keep in mind that some pumpkins are more suited to eating while others are better for jack-o'-lanterns, and some varieties are perfect for both (see variety chart, page 221).

The phrase "when the frost is on the pumpkin" is quaint but misleading when it comes to growing pumpkins. Pumpkins are actually quite susceptible to frost damage and must be harvested before a hard one strikes.

People who live in the coldest, northernmost extremes where the growing season is shortest should start seeds indoors to get any pumpkin harvest at all. At the other extreme are those who can comfortably grow two pumpkin crops — and even take time out in between.

Wherever you live, the general rule is to plant seeds or set out transplants as soon as all danger of frost has passed and the soil has begun to warm a bit. If your growing season is short, start plants indoors in individual peat pots 3 or 4 weeks in advance, so by the time they go out they have half a dozen leaves.

Preparation

The soil should be well worked and fertilized. We recommend mixing in both composted (or dried) cow manure and a handful of 5-10-5 fertilizer under each hill.

Planting

Whether you're planting seeds or seedlings, we suggest you grow pumpkins in hills. By hills we mean level circles, not mounds, which would drain moisture away from the roots during summer dry spells. Set the plants in a slight dish or depression where the hill, or planting circle, is located to keep roots moist.

Space your hills about 6 to 8 feet apart. If you're starting with young plants, put two or three close together in each hill; otherwise set five or six seeds in a circle about 1 inch deep and thin to the healthiest two or three plants a few weeks later when several true leaves have appeared.

Care

To promote steady growth and high quality, make sure your plants receive a thorough soaking each week, perhaps twice a week in times of drought. Mulch to control weeds and retain moisture. If you're growing jack-o'-lanterns and want symmetry, rotate the pumpkins from time to time so they don't flatten on one side under their own weight. Turn them gently and take care not to damage the stems.

In addition to their main roots, most pumpkin vines have a second root system. Wherever there's a leaf and the vine touches the ground, there's the potential for sending out a root right there. These side roots increase the plants' ability to absorb water and nutrients. While it's normally not necessary, you can side-dress these secondary roots for extra-large pumpkins. Take care not to overcultivate; the roots are shallow and easily damaged.

To keep the vines from overrunning neighboring vegetable beds and to encourage larger fruit, periodically pinch off their fuzzy ends after a few pumpkins have formed. The optimum number of pumpkins per vine depends on the natural size of the variety and the size you're trying to encourage. The smaller the pumpkin is, the more the vine can support. With some of the really gigantic varieties, you are lucky to get one fruit on one vine. With a variety like *Mini Jack,* you might have seven or eight to a vine.

To conserve space, you can direct the vines back in on themselves — up to a point, that is. Some varieties are bushier and will be content to stay within 4 or 5 feet of the hill, but most pumpkin vines simply like to sprawl. If you let them grow around your corn patch, you may be able to stave off raccoons.

If space is really tight in your garden, you might try trellising the vines. Pumpkins have eager tendrils, but when the fruits begin to put on weight, they'll need to be supported with slings. (Old panty hose works well.) Trellises are best for

Essentials

Planning
≈ *Pumpkins require a long growing season — from 75 to 100 frost-free days.*
≈ *Plan to sow seeds directly in the garden after all danger of frost has passed and the soil has warmed. In the far north start seeds indoors 3 to 4 weeks before the last frost.*

Preparation
≈ *Work organic material (composted manure is ideal) and a handful of 5-10-10 fertilizer into the top 6 to 8 inches of soil for each hill.*

Planting
≈ *Plant pumpkins in hills (circles 6 inches across, not raised mounds) 2 to 3 feet apart in rows 6 to 8 feet apart.*
≈ *Plant six seeds 1 inch deep in each hill. Cover the seeds with soil, leaving a slight depression in each hill (about 1 inch below the surrounding soil surface) to encourage water to soak into the roots.*
≈ *Set out two to three transplants per hill after all danger of frost has passed and the plants have about six leaves.*

Care
≈ *When several true leaves have appeared, thin each direct-seeded hill to the healthiest two or three plants.*
≈ *Mulch to keep weeds down; do not overcultivate or the shallow roots may be damaged.*
≈ *Pinch off the fuzzy ends of each vine after a few pumpkins have formed.*
≈ *To grow extra-large pumpkins, side-dress the hill or the side roots that develop along each vine after several small pumpkins form on the plant.*
≈ *Cucumber beetles (page 277) may attack just as the leaves first appear; squash bugs (page 280) may arrive later.*
≈ *Watch out for mosaic virus (page 287) and bacterial blight (page 282). Powdery mildew (page 286) and downy mildew (page 284) can be especially serious problems in the South. Other possible diseases include blossom end rot (page 283) and fusarium wilt (page 285).*

Harvesting
≈ *Unless frost threatens, don't harvest until the vine dies.*
≈ *Don't hold pumpkins by the stem. If a stem breaks, use that pumpkin as soon as possible because it will soon rot.*
≈ *Before storing pumpkins whole, cure them in a warm (75° to 80°F), well-ventilated room for a week or two.*

Regional Notes

South

Because of mildew problems, it's best not to grow pumpkins in the hottest, wettest part of the summer. But southern growers can still get two crops.

The first crop can be a spring crop, with transplants set out in the fields about the end of February. The pumpkins will be ready for harvest before the heaviest rainfall and the worst of the summer heat.

For the second crop, transplant 2- or 3-week-old plants to the field by the beginning of July for Halloween harvest. For a really late crop, you can plant seeds in late August or early September. You should be able to harvest just before the first freeze.

smaller pumpkins, such as *Spookie, New England Pie, Mini Jack,* and *Triple Treat.*

Watch out for cucumber beetles which attack plants when a few young leaves have formed. Cucumber beetles can wipe out a crop, so control them quickly. Also look out for squash bugs which suck the sap from leaves and stems.

Harvesting

After the growing season ends but before the first frost in your area, bring pumpkins inside. If possible, let the vines die first, then harvest.

The first rule in handling pumpkins is not to pick them up by the stem because, once the stem is broken, this weak spot becomes open to decay.

Cure the pumpkins in a warm (75° to 80°F), dry place for a week or so. Then dip them in a weak chlorine bleach solution (10 parts water to 1 part bleach) to kill fungi and bacteria on the skin, and store at 50° to 60°F. Don't store in a damp root cellar. Unheated attics are ideal. If you're lucky, the pumpkins will last right through the winter.

Pumpkins just before the harvest. To grow extra-large pumpkins, side-dress the hill or the side roots that develop along each vine after several small pumpkins have formed.

Pumpkin Varieties

Variety	Days	Pounds	Skin			Flesh		Comments	Source
			Red-orange	Orange	Cream-green	Coarse	Sweet		
Atlantic Giant	120	300–400	●					Excellent for competition; not for eating.	15, 39, 66, 75
Big Max	120	100	●					Competition and jack-o'-lantern variety; O.K. for pies, but a bit watery.	5, 6, 12, 15, 17
Big Moon	110	100–200		●				A competition type.	12, 15, 35, 43
Cinderella	95	5–15		●				Bush type, needs only 6 sq. ft. per plant. For pies and jack-o'-lanterns. Does not keep as well as other varieties.	6
Connecticut Field (Big Tom)	110	20–25	●			●	●	Jack-o'-lantern type; O.K. for baking.	6, 11, 15, 21, 39
Cushaw Golden	120	12		●		●	●	Nice size and flesh for pies or canning.	32, 71
Cushaw Green Striped	100	12			●		●	Canning type; sweet flesh.	12, 17
*Funny Face	95	10–15		●			●	Hybrid, good North and South. Semibush, compact vines. For jack-o'-lanterns and pies. Keeps better than most bush types.	4, 12, 43
Half Moon	105	14–18		●				Good for carving; O.K. for pies. Uniform.	43
Howden	115	8–12		●				For jack-o'-lanterns and pies.	16
Jack-o'-Lantern	110	12–18	●					Just what the name implies.	5, 16, 17, 35
*Jackpot	100	10–18		●				Hybrid. Semibush, compact vines. Good for jack-o'-lanterns and pies.	16
Little Boo	105	4–10						White skin when mature; for decoration, you can paint a face on it instead of carving, and it will last much longer.	1
Luxury Pie	100	5–15	●					Excellent winter keeper; for pies. Golden skin with a cantaloupelike net on it.	21
Mammoth Gold	110	60–100		●				Yellowish, coarse flesh; irregular globe shape. Used for pies or novelty.	5, 21, 66
Mini Jack	95	1–2		●				Very small, perfectly round (4–5″ dia.) fruit; Halloween novelty; good for pies.	21
Pankow's Field	115	5–11		●				For pies and jack-o'-lanterns.	16
Small Sugar (New England Pie)	95	6–8	●				●	Rich orange flesh; good for pies and general cooking purposes.	6, 11, 15, 35, 75
*Spirit	110	15–20		●				Hybrid. Semibush, compact vines. Great for jack-o'-lanterns and pies.	1, 4, 6, 43, 66
Spookie	105	3–6	●				●	Small fruit (5–7″ dia.); high yields. For jack-o'-lanterns and pies.	1, 16, 39
*Trick or Treat	100	10–12		●				Hybrid. Semibush, compact vines; tall plants. Hull-less seeds; also for pies.	11
Triple Treat	110	6–8	●					Good for hull-less seeds, jack-o'-lanterns, and pies. Smaller fruit (6–8″ dia.); keeps well.	6

*Hybrid

Radishes

There's a great variety of radish types — and flavors — to choose from. Because they sprout so quickly, radishes *(top)* can be interplanted to mark rows of slow-to-emerge seedlings.

To many gardeners, radishes are tools that just happen to be edible. They plant radishes to mark the rows of slow-to-emerge crops, to loosen up the soil, to attract insects away from other crops, and to satisfy their impatience to see some results after planting (the 18-day variety really does mature in 18 days). Other gardeners just love their sharp flavor and juicy texture and feel that a garden would not be complete without them.

Radishes mature in 2½ to 6 weeks, depending on the variety. If you mix in some radish seeds along with a crop such as carrots (about 1 part radish seeds to 9 parts carrots, or more if you pick radishes when small), harvesting the radishes will loosen up the soil, as well as uproot some small carrots. The remaining carrots will respond favorably by growing quickly to fill in the newly available space.

Radishes may protect other vegetable crops by attracting and diverting insects, especially cabbage root maggots. The insects go for the radishes, leaving more vulnerable young plants alone.

For anxious gardeners, spring radishes provide tasty eating at a time when not much else is ready for harvest, and flavorful winter radishes extend the season for radish lovers who find the spring harvest season just too short.

Radish Sources

Le Marché (62) carries many unusual radish varieties not listed.

Cherry Belle 6, 21, 35, 100
French Breakfast 6, 21, 39, 100
Long Black Spanish 62
Round Black Spanish 6, 21, 39
White Chinese 6, 39

Right: White radishes are grown here as row markers for parsnip seedlings. They should be pulled soon to give space to the main crop of parsnips.
Far right: Let a few plants go to seed and you'll be able to try radish seed pods in salads.

Planning

Growing different varieties can change your whole radish outlook. There are several types of lesser-known radishes that can add variety and interest to your garden and your menus.

Radishes fall into two general groups — the early spring types and the winter radishes (including the long, thin, white Oriental daikons). Varieties in the early spring group should be planted as early as possible as they mature quickly in cool weather. Varieties in this group include *French Breakfast* and *Cherry Belle*.

The winter radishes are more diverse in flavor, size, and color. They are larger and mature more slowly than spring varieties, and they keep longer in storage than the spring types. They range in pungency from mild to very hot; the *White Chinese* variety is mild, the *Round Black Spanish* is medium hot, and the *Long Black Spanish* is quite hot.

Winter radishes are usually planted in early summer for fall harvest. In warmer areas we recommend planting winter radishes in midsummer for late fall and winter harvest. Most need cool weather at the end of their growing season and shorter day lengths to discourage them from forming seeds. Winter varieties mature in 45 to 70 days.

Spring radishes can be counted on to provide the fastest harvest of any vegetable in the garden. The plants germinate in 3 to 10 days and are ready for crunchy eating in 4 to 6 weeks.

Since there are season-long opportunities for radish seeding, we recommend buying seeds "by the scoop," if you can find a garden store selling seeds in bulk. You can also order seeds in ounce size packages from mail-order seed companies (average price $1.50), rather than buy 2 or 3 seed packets with much less seed. Stagger small plantings of radishes at 1-week intervals.

Preparation

No special soil preparation is necessary for planting radishes. We recommend sowing radishes in rows with crops that are slower to germinate, such as carrots and parsnips.

Planting

Sow radish seeds directly in the garden. Plant spring varieties ½ inch deep and about 1 inch apart. Plant the larger winter varieties 2 to 3 inches apart.

Care

When seedlings are an inch high, thin spring radishes to stand 2 to 3 inches apart. Thin winter varieties to stand 4 to 5 inches apart.

If you want good-tasting radishes, provide regular even watering. Moisture stress can result in hot tasting radishes with a woody texture.

A common and very damaging insect pest of radishes, both spring and winter types, is the cabbage root maggot, which attacks all members of the cabbage family.

You can repel the flies that lay the maggot eggs with hardwood ashes worked into the soil and spread on top of the new plantings. Other suggested methods are planting radish seeds mixed with diatomaceous earth or coffee grounds.

Harvesting

Spring radishes will not hold their quality for very long, so begin to harvest them as soon as there is something big enough to eat. Before the radishes become tough and pithy, harvest the entire crop. With their tops trimmed off, they can be stored in plastic bags in the refrigerator. Winter radishes can be left in the ground and harvested as needed if the weather is cool.

Do allow some of your spring radishes to go to seed. According to Rob Johnston of Johnny's Selected Seeds in Maine, the young seed pods are edible. They are green and juicy, up to 1½ inches long, and ¼ to ½ inch thick. Try them pickled or raw in salads.

The seeds themselves make sprouts that are very much like cress, with a tangy, peppery flavor more interesting than the usual alfalfa sprouts. If you are feeling adventurous, try collecting the seeds for some unusual eating. Wait until the whole radish plant dries and the pods are brown and papery on the inside. Put the pods in a bag, then walk on the bag to break open the pods. You can then screen out the seeds from the pods or, as Rob suggests, put them in a jar of water. The seeds will sink and the pods will float and can be poured off. Dry the seeds immediately or your whole crop will sprout at once.

Essentials

Planning
&· *Plant short-season or spring varieties in spring or fall, depending on local temperatures. Ideal growing temperature is 60° to 65°F. Cooler or warmer weather results in harsher-tasting radishes. Plants will mature in 18 to 45 days, depending on variety.*
&· *Plant winter types in the summer or fall, depending on the variety; they mature in 45 to 70 days.*

Preparation
&· *Spring radishes can be planted right next to rows of larger, slower crops — no need to create a separate radish bed.*

Planting
&· *Sow radishes directly in the garden. Plant spring varieties 1 inch apart, ½ inch deep.*
&· *To get larger spring radishes, plant seeds 1½ inches deep, 1½ inches apart, in rows 24 inches apart.*
&· *Plant winter varieties 2 to 3 inches apart.*

Care
&· *When young radishes are 1 inch tall, thin to 2 to 3 inches apart.*
&· *Provide even watering. Heat and too little or uneven watering can result in tough, pithy, very hot radishes.*
&· *The most damaging insect pest, the cabbage root maggot (page 276), may be repelled by hardwood ashes in the soil. Flea beetles (page 278) may pester the crop; the younger the plants, the more vulnerable they are.*

Harvesting
&· *Pick spring varieties as soon as they reach the size you prefer.*
&· *Before they become tough and pithy, pull all the radishes, trim off the tops, and store in plastic bags in the refrigerator.*
&· *Winter varieties will keep adequately in the ground for a few weeks after maturity, in cool weather. Store these radishes through the winter as you would carrots or beets, in sawdust or peat moss.*

Rhubarb

Rhubarb is a traditional — and still quite popular — spring-harvested perennial. It emerges early *(top)* and in several weeks offers the first of many tender, tart stalks.

Unlike most other vegetables, rhubarb is a perennial plant that can be kept in production for at least a decade. Also, it is grown from roots, not seeds. But the most unusual feature of rhubarb is that its leaves are poisonous; you eat only the juicy, tangy stalks and discard the leaves.

Rhubarb needs cool weather. It does best where the winter temperatures fall below 40°F. Northern growers can plant rhubarb and raise bountiful crops with very little effort. But we've also found gardeners in the West and South who grow great rhubarb in spite of their climates. So rhubarb lovers will be happy to know that they can grow this crop just about everywhere in the United States.

Rhubarb's rich tart flavor always gets a response. Some people eat it raw without grimacing, but most prefer it softened to a pleasant tang with sugar or maple syrup cooked into a sauce or baked into an aromatic pie. Mixed with strawberries, sugar, and a little cornstarch, and topped with a thick, flaky crust, a deep-dish rhubarb pie has no competition.

Far right: **Divide rhubarb crowns every 3 or 4 years; it's best done in late fall or early spring.**

Seed stalks consume much of the plant's energy which could be better spent producing the edible stalks. If seed stalks develop, cut them off.

Planning

Rhubarb is easy to grow, where the climate permits. The plant requires a certain amount of chilling over the winter in order to break dormancy and resume vigorous growth in the spring. It does best where the average daily temperature falls below 40°F in the winter and below 75°F in the summer. Fortunately for rhubarb aficionados in the South and West, the higher elevations are often cool enough for rhubarb to thrive. If you live in a questionably warm area, plant your rhubarb in the coldest spot you've got — perhaps a north-facing slope or some other cold pocket.

There are green, pink, and red varieties of rhubarb to choose from. In general, redder stalks are more tender. Beware of catalog descriptions of rhubarb. Some supposedly red varieties may be reddish on the outside of the petiole (leafstalk), but green in the center. Redness is also somewhat dependent on climate. The same variety may be redder if grown in a cool climate than in a warmer one.

For rhubarb that is red all the way through the stalks, buy varieties such as *Valentine, Crimson Cherry,* or *Canada Red* (also called *Chipman* or *Chipman's Canada Red*). *Valentine* hardly ever produces seed, and *Chipman* does so only about 10 percent of the time. Seed stalks use up much of the plant's energy that could be used to produce edible stalks. Some varieties are more prone to sending out seed stalks than others, but any plant will produce them if they are crowded, old, or if soil fertility is low.

When you purchase rhubarb, you'll be buying a section of root with one or more growth points — called buds or eyes. Avoid small root sets; they're apt to be less vigorous and will take longer to reach maturity. Three to five mature plants should be plenty for an average family with an average appetite for rhubarb.

Plant as early in the spring as possible.

Preparation

A rhubarb plant will remain productive for a decade or more if you prepare the soil well before planting. Select a fertile, well-drained site, preferably in full sunlight. Rhubarb leaves will shade out annual weeds, but it competes poorly with hardy perennials such as quack grass, so choose a weed-free site — or diligently create one.

Rhubarb is a heavy feeder. Work in plenty of organic matter before planting, such as compost, leaf mold, or rotted cow manure.

Planting

Root sets should be spaced about 4 feet apart. Position the buds 1 to 2 inches below the soil surface. Mulch generously with a heavy layer of straw and cow manure to provide nutrients to the plant, retain moisture, and discourage weeds.

Don't harvest from your rhubarb plant during its first growing season. Give it a chance to grow large roots and become well established.

Care

Rhubarb is a hardy vegetable and even neglected plants will produce a crop — but just the same, be sure your plants get sufficient moisture during the summer and a side-dressing of some sort at least once a year.

Remove seed stalks as soon as they appear. In late spring or early summer each year, mulch with a generous layer of straw and cow manure to provide additional nutrients, retain moisture, and keep a check on weeds. Insects and disease will not disturb your crop if you keep the rhubarb patch weed-free.

After a few years, split each crown with a spade in late fall or early spring. Depending on the size of the crown, you can split up to 10 sections from each one. Leave one section in place; then replant, discard, or give away the extras.

Frost rarely harms growing rhubarb. But if it ever does get hit especially hard late in the spring, the petioles may lose their healthy appearance. You can test the severity of the damage by pinching a petiole between your thumb and forefinger: if the petiole collapses readily, it's best to cut the damaged ones down to ground level and let them grow back — which they will do eagerly.

Harvesting

If your plants do well, you can harvest lightly the spring after the first full growing season. Each leaf is crinkly when it first appears, and gradually becomes smoother as it expands. Just before the crinkles disappear and the leaf begins to resemble an elephant's ear, the petiole is at its peak quality. Grab the base of the leafstalk and pull it away from the plant with a gentle twist, or cut the stalk at the base. Always discard the leafy portion — it contains toxic amounts of oxalic acids.

You can prolong your harvest throughout the summer. Choose your strongest plants and keep harvesting the stalks as they approach full length. Always leave at least 2 stalks per plant to ensure continued production. Keep these plants watered and side-dress with manure, manure tea, or whatever you feed your garden, and you can have fresh rhubarb until fall frost. Stop harvesting when the plant begins producing thin stalks — a sign that the plant's energy is low. The next year, choose different plants for your extended harvest so the previous year's can restore their vigor.

Essentials

Planning

๏ *Rhubarb is a perennial; put it where it won't be disturbed.*

๏ *Purchase and plant rhubarb roots (not seeds) in early spring as soon as the soil can be worked.*

๏ *Three to five plants should provide enough for an average family.*

Preparation

๏ *Select a well-drained site in full sun.*

๏ *Eliminate all perennial weeds before planting.*

๏ *Dig large bushel basket-size planting holes and add a mixture of equal parts garden soil, sand, and rotted manure or compost.*

Planting

๏ *Space rhubarb roots 4 feet apart. Set roots so buds are 1 to 2 inches below the surface of the soil, cover with soil, and firm the area.*

Care

๏ *Mulch with straw and cow manure if possible to provide nutrients and retain moisture during the summer.*

๏ *Remove seed stalks as they form.*

๏ *Fertilize in the early spring each year with 2 to 3 shovelfuls of well-rotted manure per plant (or ½ cup of 5-10-10 or similar fertilizer). Side-dress at the same rate in early summer after the main harvest period.*

๏ *Dig and split roots every 3 to 4 years. Expand your patch or give root sections away.*

๏ *If you keep your rhubarb patch weed-free, it is not apt to be disturbed by insects or disease, but hand-pick stray Japanese beetles (page 278).*

๏ *Crown rot (page 284) is a potential disease problem.*

Harvesting

๏ *Start harvesting the year after planting in early spring when the stalks are 12 to 18 inches long.*

๏ *When the plants are established (after 3 years), the harvest period should run 8 to 10 weeks, or until the stalks become thin, a sign that the plants' food reserves are low.*

๏ *At least one third of the stalks should be left on the plant after the harvest.*

๏ *The petioles (leafstalks) are edible; the leaves are poisonous.*

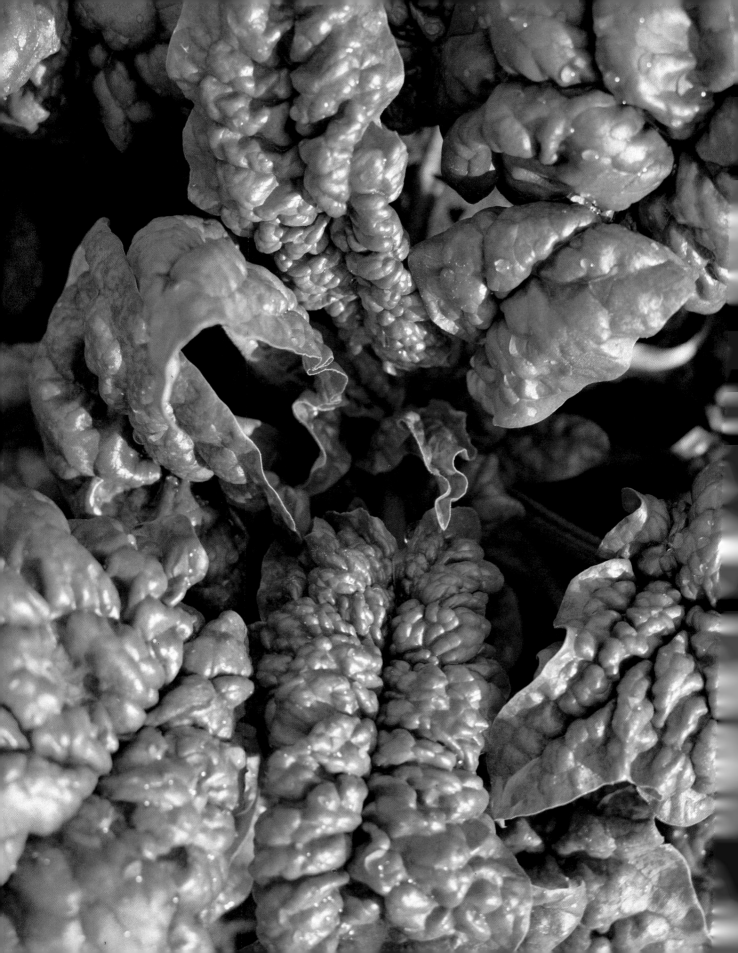

Spinach

Follow the lush spring harvest *(left)* with a small planting of New Zealand spinach *(above)* for a summer of spinachlike fare.

The fresh green leaves of spinach are a welcome sign of spring. Spinach is a rich source of vitamin A and minerals. It is just as delicious raw in salads as it is cooked. Surplus spinach can be frozen to provide vitamin-rich cooked greens all winter long.

With the right growing conditions, spinach is amazingly easy to grow. It's not a summer crop, though. Most spinach varieties can't stand heat and long days. They bolt at once, producing small leaves and tall heads of seed. Spinach thrives in cool weather, and should be planted early in the spring or late in the fall. In fact, home gardeners in the far northern United States will sometimes find that the remnants of last year's fall spinach have survived sub-zero winter temperatures to burgeon again in the spring.

Where the weather is warm, don't give up on raising spinach altogether. There are delicious spinach substitutes that actually prefer the heat. Spinach can be a year-round, coast-to-coast crop.

Planning

Plant your spring crop as early as the soil can be worked, in many areas 4 to 6 weeks before your last spring frost date. You'll be enjoying spinach as early as 6 weeks after planting. The spinach will bolt (go to seed) as soon as the warm weather arrives. Till your spinach bed under and plant a heat-loving crop in its place.

For your spring plantings, select bolt-resistant varieties such as *America, Melody,* and *Bloomsdale Long Standing* for a prolonged harvest in warmer weather. These varieties will do best where the spring temperatures are quite warm, too; but don't expect them to continue to produce in hot weather.

After the peak summer heat has passed, plant again and you can enjoy more fresh spinach in the fall. A good time to plant is 4 to 6 weeks before your average first fall frost date.

Some gardeners plant a final crop of spinach late in the fall to winter over and produce an extra-early crop in the spring. Wintering over spinach is something of a gamble. A good variety to try this with is *Cold Resistant Savoy.* If you don't have a heavy snow cover, mulch the spinach bed to prevent thawing and refreezing.

Preparation

It doesn't take a lot of effort to grow spinach, but you should start with the right soil conditions. Spinach needs fertile, well-drained soil with a high nitrogen content in order to produce large, healthy, delicious leaves. Just before planting the seeds, mix some compost, manure, and/or fertilizer (10-10-10) into each row for good measure.

Planting

Sow spinach seeds ½ inch deep, about a dozen seeds per foot of row, or sprinkle

Pick and destroy leaves damaged by the tunneling leaf miner larvae. Sprays are not effective once the leaf miner eggs have hatched and larvae are inside the leaves.

them about 1 inch apart over a wide row or bed. When the plants are 1 inch tall, thin them to 4 inches apart.

Care

Spinach is 96 percent water and shallow-rooted, so provide ample water throughout the season. In a dry spell, you need to water every few days. In a single-row planting you can mulch plants at any size to retain precious moisture and cut down on weeds.

Spinach is susceptible to two common diseases: downy mildew and spinach blight, also known as cucumber mosaic virus. Select disease-resistant varieties such as *Melody* or *Dixie Market*.

Just about every gardener who has grown beets, spinach, or chard is familiar with the damage done by the wide-ranging spinach leaf miner. The first signs of an infestation — which can occur just about anywhere in the United States and Canada — are irregular, light tan blotches on the leaves. If you peel these blisterlike areas apart, you'll find black specks of insect waste and, possibly, the maggot itself, chomping away. The maggot is the immature stage of a tiny fly that lays small white eggs in clusters on the undersides of the leaves beginning in early spring and continuing throughout the season.

Unfortunately, by the time you notice the damage, leaf miners are safely inside the leaf and cannot be controlled with insecticides. All you can do is pick and destroy the infested leaves. If you spot their egg clusters before they hatch (perhaps last year's experience has alerted you to the danger), immediately apply an approved insecticide.

You can avoid insecticides and discourage leaf miners before they get established by regular weeding, cleaning up your garden in the fall, and planting when the insects are not active — very early spring or late fall.

Essentials

Planning

🖙 *Spinach must have at least 6 weeks of cool weather from seeding to harvest.*

🖙 *Plant seeds outdoors 4 to 6 weeks before your last spring frost date, and again 4 to 6 weeks before the first fall frost date.*

🖙 *Spinach bolts when days are 14 to 16 hours long; warm weather makes it bolt even faster.*

Preparation

🖙 *Mix compost, manure, and/or fertilizer into each row or plot before planting.*

Planting

🖙 *Sow seeds ½ inch deep, about 12 seeds per foot of row, or sprinkle them over a wide row or bed.*

Care

🖙 *When seedlings are 1 inch tall, thin to stand 4 inches apart.*

🖙 *Water every few days during dry spells; mulch spinach planted in rows to retain soil moisture.*

🖙 *Watch for the spinach leaf miner (page 279). Other possible pests are aphids (page 276) and flea beetles (page 278).*

🖙 *Also watch for two common spinach diseases: downy mildew (page 284) and spinach blight, which is the same as cucumber mosaic virus (page 287). Nematodes (page 285) can also infect spinach.*

Harvesting

🖙 *To harvest early, cut individual leaves as soon as they are big enough to eat. When the weather warms up, cut the whole plant close to the ground, below the lowest leaf. Harvest again after a few new leaves reappear. Repeat as necessary.*

A Bug-Baffling Tunnel

Leaf miners are probably the most common insect problem with spinach. You can eliminate the threat of leaf miners altogether by constructing a protective cage and covering the susceptible plants. Here's a description of one such device.

Rudy Perkins maintained the Victory Garden for the popular national PBS show of the same name. Working with fellow gardeners, he developed a simple, sturdy, wide-row cloche that performs a double function. When covered with plastic, the cloche gives plants a head start on the growing season. Then, by replacing the polyethylene with mosquito netting or cheesecloth, it becomes a screened-in growing area ideal for keeping the troublesome leaf miner out of beets and spinach.

To build a bug-baffling tunnel like the one pictured, follow these steps:

1. Use flexible plastic conduit (such as ABS or Polybutylene, available from home improvement and piping supply stores). To create arches large enough to span a 3½-foot-wide growing bed, cutting the tubing into 7-foot lengths with a hacksaw. The number of arches you will need depends on the length of your row; space them about 4½ feet apart.

2. Drive 12-inch lengths of 1-inch galvanized metal pipe into the ground on either side of the row, spaced 4½ feet apart to receive the arches.

3. Flex the 7-foot lengths of tubing and anchor the arches in the sunken pipes.

4. Cover the tunnel with wide sheets of plastic or netting (allow 4 to 6 inches of extra material on either side). Tie a piece of string tightly over each arch on top of the tubing and fasten it to the base of the tubes at each end of the arch. This holds the cover in place on a windy day, but allows you to slide it up and out of the way for watering, weeding, and harvesting.

5. Hold down the edges of the covering with earth or stones and continue along the length of the row.

6. Cover the ends of the tunnel — and frustrate every leaf miner.

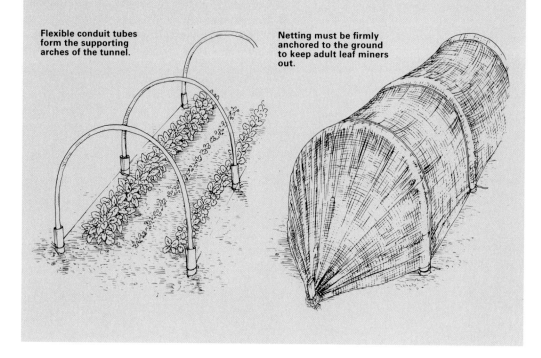

Flexible conduit tubes form the supporting arches of the tunnel.

Netting must be firmly anchored to the ground to keep adult leaf miners out.

Harvesting

Start harvesting spinach as soon as there is something big enough to eat. If you wait for the leaves to grow too large, the plant may bolt. Once it starts to bolt, cut the whole plant down close to the ground, below the lowest leaf. More leaves will grow back rapidly and the plant won't bolt as soon the next time. When three or four new leaves reappear, cut the plant back again.

Spinach Substitutes: Another Way to Extend the Season

Spinach lovers can't get enough of their favorite greens when the weather turns warm. That's why many gardeners are turning to New Zealand and Malabar spinach to meet their cravings.

Actually neither New Zealand nor Malabar are related to true spinach — they come from totally different plant families and have very different growth habits. But when cooked or frozen for later use, many people say they can't tell the difference between true spinach and these substitutes. (They don't taste at all like true spinach raw, so cook before judging!)

Plant New Zealand spinach when warm weather arrives; it thrives under summer heat. Because this spinach is very bushy, space the rows almost 2 feet apart. Plant seeds 4 inches apart and thin them to about 8 inches when they get crowded. The seeds are slow to germinate, so it's a good idea to soak them for a day before planting.

Side-dress the rows in midsummer with a few handfuls of 10-10-10 or its equivalent. Plants will continue to produce leaves as you harvest them.

An import from India and the tropical regions of the Far East, Malabar spinach thrives in hot weather. It grows much like a philodendron: long stems run along the ground from the base of the plant. Its thick, succulent leaves grow up from the stems. If you want to put Malabar on a trellis, you will have to tie it because it has no tendrils to attach. An advantage to growing the vines on a trellis is that the leaves are never gritty with soil, as spinach leaves frequently are.

To harvest, pick the leaves off at random when they get big enough to eat. Some of them will get as big as a dinner plate.

Start seeds inside 6 weeks ahead of planting time to give them a good head start. First soak them for 2 hours to hasten germination. Transplant the young plants to individual 4-inch pots when they are 2 inches tall.

Set Malabar spinach outside when the mean 24-hour temperature is about 65°F. Even light frost will wipe it out. Space the plants 3 feet apart in well-loosened, compost-rich soil. They'll spread like vines. Mulch heavily to retain moisture and to keep the dirt off the leaves.

Harvest spinach close to the ground. Often the plants will produce new, tender growth for a later harvest.

Malabar spinach thrives in hot weather. Harvest leaves individually when they are big enough to eat.

Squash

At the peak of the season, zucchini summer squash develops from flower to fruit in a matter of days.

Summer and winter squash may look and taste entirely different, but they're really just two more vegetables in the cucurbit family, which also includes pumpkins, cucumbers, and melons.

All squash are considered vine crops. However, some are less inclined to vine and are more bushy than others. These days, virtually all summer squash varieties are bush types that can be grown in close quarters. Although some bush winter squash varieties are available, most are vine types.

All squash thrive under the same growing conditions (rich soil and warm weather) and suffer from the same pests. The real differences come at harvest time and at dinner time. Summer squash is harvested while still tender and immature; winter squash is harvested only after the rind has hardened completely, as much as two months later. Winter squash are more richly flavored and sweet tasting than summer squash.

Zucchini is a big favorite among summer squash growers, but more and more gardeners are discovering the delicate scallop, or patty pan, squash. Crookneck and straightneck yellow squash are also popular. Favorite varieties among winter squash are *Butternut, Buttercup,* and *Hubbards.* And *Delicata* and *Gold Nugget* are appearing in more and more gardens.

Summer squash is very prolific; one plant per household member is usually adequate. As this garden harvest shows, there's a wide array of summer squash shapes and colors.

Scallop (or patty pan) squash is aptly named for its shape. Popular varieties are *Early White* bush and *Peter Pan*. If you can spare the space, grow lots of *Peter Pan* scallops so you can afford to pick them when very young — less than 3 inches across.

The consensus seems to be that if you like winter squash at all, you'll love *Buttercup*, which grows to about 4 pounds in 100 days. *Buttercup* yields quite well, it's relatively early, and it has great flavor. An uncommon but related squash called *Green Hokkaido* (95 days) is high in dry matter and sweet flavor.

These days, *Butternut* (1 to 3 pounds in 75 to 90 days) is even more familiar than *Buttercup*. It has a small seed cavity and a neck that is solid squash. There are larger varieties, such as *Hercules*, which have a much bigger neck, where most of the fruit is. The so-called *Neck Pumpkin* is an even larger butternut relation. If you haven't got room for these vining varieties, *Butterbush* produces the smallest fruit of this type in about one-quarter the space.

At 15 to 40 pounds apiece, *Blue Hubbard* is the heaviest winter squash and the slowest to mature (about 120 days). These traditional giants, including *Green* and *Golden Hubbards*, are less common in today's gardens.

Acorn squash often grow on bush or semibush plants and reach 1 to 3 pounds mature weight in 70 to 80 days. *Ebony Acorn*, *Table Queen*, and *Table King* are all good quality. A newer one called *Jersey Golden Acorn* has a slightly stringy texture and is extra sweet.

There are several more winter squash with miscellaneous merits. *Gold Nugget* is a small butternutlike squash that grows on small bush-type plants. It's beautiful to look at and the fruit is solid with few seeds and thick, sweet flesh. *Vegetable Spaghetti* squash boils down to long fibers that taste great with meat and cheese sauces. The cream and green striped *Delicata* is perfect for stuffing, with a large,

Planning

Virtually all summer squash now on the home garden market grow on bush plants. With few exceptions, the fruit are ready to eat about 50 to 55 days after planting. Hybrid varieties generally produce more, earlier, and better-quality fruit than the open-pollinated ones. All can be classified into three basic types.

Constricted neck squash (including both crookneck and straightneck varieties) are commonly known as yellow squash. Popular varieties include *Early Summer Crookneck*, *Seneca Prolific*, *Goldbar*, and *Early Prolific Straightneck*.

Zucchini types are usually club-shaped with dark green skin. *Chefini*, *Ambassador*, and *Aristocrat* are just a few of the many reliable hybrids. Unusual selections include *Greyzini*, green-gray and praised by many for its flavor and texture; *Gold Rush*, a yellow zucchini; and *Gourmet Globe*, which yields round fruit best picked at about the size of a large orange.

hollow center and uniform, ½-inch-thick walls of flesh. Its pale flesh is very sweet and smooth textured. Rounding out the assortment are *Banana* squash, *Red Kura, Little Gem,* and the monster *Tahitian* squash, but unless you have plenty of room to spare, don't experiment with too many varieties at once.

Consider when to plant. Whether you're planting seeds or transplants, put nothing into the garden until all danger of frost has passed and the soil is warm and only mildly moist. Wait until nighttime temperatures are above 55°F. It's unusual to find started plants at a garden store, but it's easy to start seeds in individual pots 3 to 4 weeks before the last frost date.

Preparation

Perhaps no other crop responds to fertile soils as much as squash does, so work in plenty of rich organic material before planting. The traditional preparation technique for vining types is to work a bushel of rotted cow or horse manure beneath each hill and cover with 2 to 3 inches of soil before planting seeds. This works very well. If you don't have a source of manure, work in plenty of compost and a handful of 5-10-10 or its equivalent into the top 5 to 6 inches of soil for each hill.

Planting

Bush types will grow comfortably in rows; vining types are better off grouped in hills or planting circles.

When planting squash in rows, allow about 4 feet of space on either side of a row (or hug the edge of your garden on one side). Plant two to four seeds per foot, 1 inch deep. When true leaves appear a week or two later, thin to one plant per 18 inches. If you're starting with transplants, put them in 18 inches apart.

This may seem awfully tight, but our experience has shown this to be the optimum spacing for maximum yield — per given area, if not per plant. It will restrict

Essentials

Planning

🦋 *Wait until all danger of frost has passed before planting seeds or started plants.*

🦋 *Start seeds indoors in individual pots 3 to 4 weeks before the last frost date.*

🦋 *If you don't have much space, grow bush varieties.*

🦋 *Summer squash is very prolific. One plant per person in the household is usually adequate.*

Preparation

🦋 *Work into the soil plenty of good compost or aged manure to a depth of about 1 foot.*

🦋 *Set up trellises for small varieties of winter squash, if desired.*

Planting

🦋 *Plant summer squash 1 inch deep, 2 to 4 seeds per foot. Set transplants 18 to 36 inches apart at the same depth as their container.*

🦋 *Group vining winter squash in hills about 6 feet apart. Plant half a dozen seeds 1 inch deep in each hill.*

Care

🦋 *Thin plants in rows to 1 plant per 18 to 24 inches, or in hills to the best 2 or 3 plants per hill, when the first true leaves appear.*

🦋 *When the first five leaves appear, mulch to eliminate weeds and retain moisture.*

🦋 *Provide about 1 inch of water per week.*

🦋 *Periodically pinch off the fuzzy ends of winter squash vines after a few fruit have formed.*

🦋 *Watch for the most common squash pests: cucumber beetles (page 277), pickleworms (page 279), squash vine borers (page 280), squash bugs (page 280), and stinkbugs (page 281).*

🦋 *Fusarium wilt can be a problem (page 285), along with downy mildew (page 284) and powdery mildew (page 286), bacterial wilt (page 282), and blossom end rot (page 283).*

Harvesting

🦋 *Harvest summer squash when immature and still tender, about 50 to 55 days after planting or within one week of flowering. For best eating, pick elongated types (yellow squash and zucchini) when not more than 6 to 8 inches long and 2 inches in diameter. Harvest scallop, or patty pan, types when they are 3 or 4 inches in diameter. To prolong production, keep each plant harvested.*

🦋 *Harvest winter squash before the first frost when fully mature and hardened, from 70 to 120 days, depending on the variety. Leave 2 inches of stem attached and handle carefully.*

🦋 *Before storing winter squash whole, cure in a warm, well-ventilated place for a week or two.*

More Squash in Less Space

To keep ambitious squash vines from taking over your garden, try these strategies:
- Diligently pinch off the growing ends of vines after enough fruit have set.
- Direct the vines back in toward the plant.
- Plant squash along the edge of your garden and let the vines run onto the lawn.
- Weave the vines around your corn patch where they can be useful: raccoon hate to cross the prickly leaves.

For those with extremely limited space, trellises may be the answer. This is impractical for the largest winter squash, but worth considering for the smaller ones. You have to construct a sturdy trellis unless you can use a fence, the side of your garage, or some other convenient support. As each fruit puts on weight, secure it to the trellis in a cloth cradle so it won't break loose. Since the vines will be off the ground, be sure to keep the plants well mulched and watered to compensate for the moisture they lose to the wind.

Summer squash and the few bush-type winter squash demand far less elbow room, but they can be restricted further if space is really tight. As mentioned, the plants can be spaced 18 inches apart within their rows. If you want a more drastic measure, keep them out of the garden altogether by growing them in containers. Fill buckets with a mix of good soil and compost and raise a couple of plants in each one. Keep them well watered and add some liquid fertilizer now and then as you would for a houseplant.

To protect young plants from the cucumber beetle you can cover the hills with Reemay cloth immediately after planting. Reemay, anchored well on the edges, keeps beetles out but allows light and rain to penetrate.

the size of the plants but not of the individual fruit. The common complaint is an overwhelming abundance of summer squash; bear this in mind and allow just 1 or 2 plants per person in your household.

Hills — for vining types — are something of a misnomer. Not necessarily mounds, hills are merely several seeds grouped in a circle. Allow about 6 feet between hills, and plant half a dozen seeds 1 inch deep in each. Later, thin to the best two or three plants in each hill (or, again, start with that many if you're putting in transplants).

If you have prolonged summer dry spells or light, sandy soil that dries out quickly, design your rows or hills as basins, 1 to 2 inches below the surface of the surrounding soil, so moisture will collect where it's needed. Plant on mounds 3 to 5 inches high only if you have heavy soil or plenty of wet weather.

Care

Several weeks after planting there will be lots of bright yellow flowers on your summer and winter squash plants. If you're up for a treat, pick some open blossoms before fruit develop, dip in a batter, and deep fry.

Female flowers, naturally, bear the fruit; you will recognize them by the swelling at the stem beneath the blossom. All the earliest flowers are male, but females will follow within a week or so. Squash pollen is too heavy to float on the wind, so bees perform the pollinating rituals. Continued cold, wet weather will delay their activity, perhaps even a week or two, but any flowers that die unfulfilled will be followed by plenty more. All in all, it's difficult to prevent squash pollination.

Different squash varieties can readily cross-pollinate. That won't affect this year's crop at all, but the mixed parentage seeds that result are apt to produce astonishing, and often inedible, fruit next time around. It's better to buy new seeds each year to avoid any unpleasant surprises.

Weed young plants, being careful not to damage their shallow roots; eventually the squash plants will shade out competing weeds as they grow. Water deeply and regularly throughout the summer, about 1 inch per week. In very hot and dry areas, 2 to 3 inches of water may be necessary. To conserve moisture and eliminate weeds all in one motion, put down a layer of mulch. As a bonus, you'll be encouraging earlier and larger harvests. A combined program of black plastic mulch and trickle irrigation can be especially beneficial.

If you added enough rich organic matter before planting the squash, side-dressing is not necessary. Overfertilization will promote the growth of stems and leaves at the expense of fruit. Be conservative if you do decide to give your plants a fertilizer push. Side-dress summer squash when plants are about 6 inches tall and again when they bloom. Use approximately 1 tablespoon 5-10-10 or its equivalent per plant each time. Side-dress winter squash at the same rate when the vines start to run and also when small fruit form.

Winter squash vines require a little extra attention during the growing season to keep them from taking over the garden. Where space is limited or the season is

The Beauty of Black Plastic Mulch

It's not pretty to look at, but black plastic mulch can be functionally beautiful. A recent study by the USDA's Research Service in Vincennes, Indiana, confirmed that it benefits zucchini tremendously, especially when used in combination with drip irrigation. Plants pampered in this way produced more and better zucchini significantly earlier. (There's nothing unique about summer squash in this regard; winter squash and all other vine crops stand to gain just as much.)

Black plastic mulch warms the soil, traps moisture, and eliminates weed competition. Drip irrigation complements these actions by supplying water gradually and directly to the roots. Slow and steady watering also keeps nutrients from being washed away.

While drip irrigation adds a nice touch, especially in parched areas of the West and Southwest, it's not the determining factor for raising superior squash. For home gardens, black plastic mulch can make the difference on its own. You can easily water the plants where they come up through the plastic, and if you get enough rain to saturate the soil, water will soak in beneath the plastic, too. The plastic itself also reduces evaporation and surface run-off, so you're not going to lose too much moisture.

The system is easy enough: prepare the soil, spread out the plastic, anchor it tightly to the soil, and cut holes for the seeds or transplants. If you decide to go all out, stretch a soaker hose alongside the planned rows of squash before spreading the plastic.

Black plastic mulch typically helps you grow more and better squash. It warms the soil, traps moisture, and hinders weeds.

Thin hills to the best two or three plants when seedlings are a few inches tall. Hills are not really mounds but merely several seeds planted in a circle.

ing on young plants. By the time the squash outgrow their protection they will be far less vulnerable.

Squash vine borers are a problem everywhere east of the Rockies. The larvae tunnel into the stalks, making them wilt and eventually die. Small piles of grainy, yellowish frass (excrement) are often the first signs of an infestation.

One way to keep moths from laying eggs on the leaves without using insecticides is to spread aluminum foil under the plants. It reflects the sunlight, which "discombobulates" the borers. The foil must stay shiny to be effective, so don't throw dirt over it when you cultivate. And don't laugh until you've tried it.

You can also wrap the stem itself with aluminum foil to physically prevent the moths from laying eggs there. In any case, watch for, scrape off, and destroy egg clusters on the stems and undersides of leaves.

Squash bugs suck the sap from leaves and stems, causing the plants to wilt and die. Look for clusters of shiny red eggs on the underside of leaves. Crush the eggs or pick the whole leaf and dispose of it.

Most squash are susceptible to several diseases, including fusarium wilt, powdery mildew, downy mildew, bacterial wilt, and squash mosaic virus. Whenever possible, select disease-resistant varieties.

Harvesting

Your winter squash will be barely halfway along by the time your summer squash is ready to eat — about 50 to 55 days after planting and usually within a week of flowering. Cut the stem with a knife when the fruit is small and tender. Most elongated types — yellow squash and zucchini — are best harvested when not more than 6 to 8 inches long and 2 inches in diameter; scallop (patty pan) types are at their peak quality when 3 or 4 inches in diameter.

If given half a chance, summer squash will grow to mammoth proportions, zucchini in particular. Bigger is not better;

short, periodically pinch off the fuzzy end of each vine after a few squash have formed so the plant will redirect its energies toward maturing those fruit. The number of fruit per vine to expect varies with the size of the squash. The largest varieties, such as *Hubbards,* may yield no more than one squash per vine; the smaller ones, such as acorns, may produce half a dozen.

Both summer and winter squash are vulnerable to attack from certain insects and diseases. Cucumber beetles are harmful to very young plants, and they may also nibble away on developing vines and fruit throughout the season.

Controls include starting seeds or transplants under some sort of cold frame or grow tunnel to keep the beetles from land-

smaller is generally tastier. Stay abreast of your plants or fruit quality will decline and, in the long run, so will plant productivity. If some fruits grow huge when you're not looking, pick them right away.

Anywhere from 3 to 4 months after planting, your winter squash will ripen. You want them to ripen before a freeze because they're quite susceptible to frost damage. Nothing tastes flatter than unripe winter squash, and they won't ripen after picking, so it really pays to be patient. A winter squash acquires a deep, solid color when mature; the stem and rind are hard. Most fruit on a vine will ripen at the same time. To be safe, wait until the vine dies or frost threatens. If they're not quite ready and an early frost is predicted, cover the squash overnight. You may still have an Indian summer later.

When the time comes to cut them loose, use a sharp knife and leave a 2-inch piece of stem attached. It is important to handle the squash carefully and not by the stem. A single bruise or a broken stem can cause the fruit to rot in just a few weeks. If the stem breaks or the squash gets bruised, use it right away.

Undamaged winter squash can be stored for several months after curing, which allows the rinds to harden and dry completely. If you can maintain a long-term storage temperature of 50° to 55°F, skip the curing process. Otherwise, leave them in a warm place — as warm as 80°F if possible — on a sunny porch or near the furnace or woodstove for a week or two.

After curing, dip each squash in a weak solution of chlorine bleach (about 10 parts water to 1 part bleach) to kill surface bacteria and prolong storage. Allow them to drip dry and then store them in a cool (anywhere from 45° to 60°F), dark, dry, well-ventilated area. An unheated attic is ideal. Spread the squash out singly or, if you must stack them, do so no more than two deep. Be sure to check the squash from time to time and remove any that are beginning to soften.

Luffas and Other Gourds

Gourds are just another member of the squash family except that they're generally grown for fun, not food. They're grown just like winter squash, but the larger ones can take even longer to mature (some as long as 140 to 150 days). For this reason, gourd growers throughout much of the country will have to start their plants inside several weeks in advance of the last spring frost date. Seeds take up to 2 weeks to sprout, but will emerge faster if presoaked for 48 hours in tepid water.

You may want to try trellising some gourds so they'll grow straight and unblemished; let others rest on a hard, flat surface — to create jugs that won't roll over, for example. Developing gourds can be confined to square containers to create square bowls.

Like winter squash, gourds should ripen on the vine if they're to last long. Mature fruit will have hard, glossy, solidly colored shells and tough, dry stems. Luffas will have turned from green to light yellow to brown and will be 1 to 2 feet long.

After harvesting hard-shell gourds, gently wipe off surface dirt. Cure them in a warm, dry spot. Smaller ornamental varieties will be ready in a week or two; the largest bottle gourds must cure until the seeds rattle inside, which can take up to 6 months. When cured, dip them in a weak chlorine solution (10 parts water to 1 part chlorine) and drip dry. If you like, polish the shells with furniture wax (not shellac; it alters the color). Wait until your gourds are dry before you open them with a drill.

Instead of curing luffas, soak the gourds in tepid water for several days until the skins can be peeled off easily. Wash the fibrous interior under a strong stream of water, squeeze out loose pulp and seeds, and set it in a sunny spot to dry for a week or so. Shake out any remaining loose seeds, then allow the spongy interior to bleach in the sun a while longer, or soak it in a mild bleach solution (10 parts water to 1 part bleach).

When wet again, a homegrown sponge will soften up like any other, but it will stay rough enough to give you or your dishes a good rubdown.

Squash Sources

Ambassador 33, 43, 67
Aristocrat 43, 66 ·
Banana 9, 15, 33
Blue Hubbard 1, 6, 15, 20, 23
Bottle gourds 6, 99
Butterbush 6, 67
Buttercup 6, 9, 15, 20, 43, 67
Butternut 1, 15, 23, 43, 68
Chefini 17, 53
Delicata 15, 20, 66, 68
Dipper gourds 6, 15, 53
Early Prolific Straightneck 1, 6, 9, 17, 33
Early Summer Crookneck 6, 9, 23, 24, 33
Early White 6, 17, 23, 24
Ebony Acorn 1, 15, 24, 67
Golden Hubbard 23, 33
Gold Nugget 9, 15, 20
Gold Rush 1, 6, 17, 43, 66
Gourmet Globe 1, 17, 43
Green Hokkaido 20
Green Hubbard 23, 43
Greyzini 6, 33
Jersey Golden Acorn 6, 20, 66, 99
Little Gem 53, 59
Luffa 6, 17, 20, 53
Neck Pumpkin 1
Peter Pan 6, 17, 33, 99
Red Kura 20, 67
Seneca Prolific 20, 24, 43
Table King 6, 24, 67, 99
Table Queen 1, 9, 15, 66
Tahitian 5, 15
Vegetable Spaghetti 15, 24, 43, 66, 67

*hybrid

Luffa gourds yield well when grown on a trellis. Plants need from 110 to 120 days to mature their spongelike fruits.

Sweet Potatoes

It's easy to grow your own starter plants or "slips" *(above)* and assure an abundant harvest of plump sweet potatoes like the ones at left.

The sweet potato is overdue for a resurgence in popularity. Fifty years ago the per capita annual consumption of sweet potatoes in the United States was 30 pounds; now the figure is under 5 pounds. Many of us think of it only as a holiday dinner extra.

Perhaps today's gardeners think of the sweet potato as a space-consuming, subtropical, long-season crop that is usually reasonably priced at the supermarket. This is all true, to a point. But sweet potato culture is changing. There are new, highly improved varieties with vines that don't spread far. Specialty companies offer varieties not found in supermarkets, such as the delicious white sweet potato. And horticultural researchers well north of sweet potato country have harvested bigger yields than the best southern growers by using black plastic mulch on raised beds.

All this, coupled with the sweet potato's ease of growing, its drought and heat tolerance, its lack of serious pests or diseases, and its superior flavor when freshly harvested, make it a likely candidate for many more vegetable gardens all over the country.

Planning

Sweet potatoes are started from "slips" or "draws," which are sprouts that grow out of stored sweet potatoes and develop roots and leaves.

In the South and some parts of the Midwest it's easy to find certified disease-free seed potatoes to use in growing your own slips. It's also easy to find the slips at garden centers, local farmers markets, or nurseries at planting time. The slips are usually sold in bunches of twenty-five or fifty.

But where commercial sweet potato growing is rare, you may not be able to find a source from which to buy seed potatoes or slips at planting time. So to try your hand at sweet potato growing, you'll have to order slips from a plant company (a convenient way to experiment with the crop) or produce your own slips. Growing slips is an annual rite for many veteran gardeners who have developed techniques to grow vigorous, sturdy slips quite inexpensively. They either have a local source for stock potatoes or they save some of the best-shaped, blemish-free roots of favorite varieties over the winter to grow sprouts from in the spring. You don't always know which varieties you're getting when you buy slips at nurseries or from local growers. The best way to insure that you grow varieties you enjoy is to save potatoes and grow slips yourself.

For gardeners without potatoes to save, an alternative is the local supermarket. Most commercial potatoes are harvested in September and October, so start scouting the supermarkets in early November for the best of the new harvest. (Don't buy starting potatoes in February because they may be lower grade or have suffered from overhandling.) Look for unblemished, uncracked, medium-size sweet potatoes, allowing one potato for every 12 plants you want, plus a few extras just in case some don't sprout. Many times the potatoes are sprayed with a sprout inhibitor that wears off slowly.

Store the stock potatoes in a warm (65° to 70°F), well-lit area until about 90 days before your last spring frost date, when it's time to pot them. Many will have sprouted slightly by this time at one end. If the frost date is May 15, pot them around February 15. They'll need about 90 days bedded in soil, kept continuously warm and moist to produce slips large enough to plant outdoors.

In the South, growers can use outdoor beds and cold frames to produce plantable slips, but in central and northern states it's better done indoors. Use a 1½-gallon potting container for every two seed potatoes. Poke drainage holes in the bottom of the container and put in 3 inches of mulch, such as wood chips or well-shredded

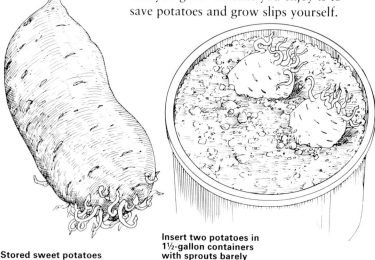

Stored sweet potatoes beginning to sprout.

Insert two potatoes in 1½-gallon containers with sprouts barely above the soil surface.

When slips are 6 to 12 inches tall, cut them 1 inch above the potato.

leaves, then add garden or potting soil. No fertilizer is needed — the potato has enough nutrients to support sprouts.

Insert the stock potatoes in the soil at about a 45-degree angle so the sprouts at the tip stick up above the soil surface. Pack soil around the potato. Don't break those tender sprouts — each one will become a plant.

A room temperature of 65° to 70°F is just right for sprouting sweet potatoes. They don't need grow lights; just put them near a sunny window.

When the slips are about 6 to 12 inches tall, they're ready to plant, but don't plant outside until after all frost danger has passed and the garden soil has warmed. Sweet potato plants thrive in hot weather; they will hardly grow at all at temperatures of 60°F or lower.

Preparation

Because sweet potato *roots* are harvested, the soil must be well tilled and loose to a depth of 8 to 10 inches, giving the roots room to expand. A fertile, well-drained soil yields the best crops.

After you have thoroughly tilled the soil, make raised beds or ridges 6 to 8 inches high and a foot or so wide. This gives the roots more room and helps production, unless the soil is extremely sandy, in which case moisture stress is possible in hot weather.

Planting

When you are ready to plant, cut the slips off 1 inch above the surface of the potato. If you pull the slip up with its roots intact you risk transferring diseases the stored potato may have. Cut slips recover more slowly from transplanting but catch up to the pulled rooted slips by the sixth week.

Set the slips 12 to 18 inches apart along the ridge. Set them deep enough to cover the roots and ½ inch of the stem. Firm the soil and make a shallow depression around each plant to catch moisture. Water with a starter solution high in phosphorus, and water generously for a few days to help the plants root well.

Essentials

Planning

▸ *Most varieties require at least 4 frost-free months to grow big potatoes. Plants thrive in hot weather.*

▸ *Start the crop by setting out 6- to 8-week-old slips or draws, available at nurseries in southern states. If you are growing your own slips, begin sprouting them about 8 weeks before planting.*

▸ *Expect about a pound of sweet potatoes for each foot of row under average growing conditions.*

Preparation

▸ *Add about 3 pounds of 5-10-10 (5 pounds in sandy soils) or its equivalent per 100 feet of row and work it into the soil before planting. Also add fine compost or aged manure to provide a long release of nutrients.*

▸ *Till the soil to a depth of 8 to 10 inches.*

▸ *Unless the soil is very sandy, raise the planting bed 6 to 8 inches to make a ridge a foot or so wide.*

Planting

▸ *After danger of frost is past and the weather is warm (nights above 55°F), set slips 12 to 18 inches apart along ridges or in rows that are 36 to 48 inches apart. Set the slips in the soil to the depth of the first leaves with several nodes (joints) underground. Firm the soil and make a shallow depression around the plant.*

▸ *Water with a starter solution high in phosphorus. Water generously for a few days.*

Care

▸ *Control weeds by hoeing or mulch the area 4 to 5 weeks after planting.*

▸ *Side-dress 3 to 4 weeks after transplanting with 3 pounds (5 pounds in sandy soils) of 5-10-10 per 100 feet of row.*

▸ *Provide deep watering in hot dry periods to increase yields. If you plan to store part of the crop, don't give the plants any extra water late in the season.*

▸ *Mice and other rodents may travel in mole runways to feed on roots.*

▸ *Watch for flea beetles (page 278), sweet potato weevils (page 281), and wireworms (page 281).*

▸ *Sweet potato scurf (page 287) is a common disease problem, especially in heavy, wet soils.*

Harvesting

▸ *In most central and southern states harvest in late September to mid-October, or dig up small potatoes at any time. In the North, harvest before any impending frost.*

▸ *To harvest, dig roots carefully. Handle storage potatoes carefully, they bruise easily and won't keep well if bumped around. Gently put them in baskets or crates in a warm, humid location for curing.*

Regional Notes

North

Order slips by mail in late winter. *Centennial* is a proven winner in northern climates. The company will ship near your planting time — indicate about a week after the last frost date in your area.

If you can't work the soil and plant on the day the slips arrive, put them in 1 inch of water in jars. They'll keep for about a week.

Grow the plants on raised beds 6 to 8 inches high and about 20 inches wide. To get top yields, consider using black plastic mulch on the planting beds. Researchers at the University of Massachusetts found the combination of raised beds and black plastic yielded more than two times the harvest of standard growing practices. Use 36-inch-wide plastic and cover it solidly with soil at the edges to retain maximum heat. Cut slits in the plastic, and slide the slips into the soil below. Keep the soil moist until transplants take hold and begin growth.

Set slips 12 to 18 inches apart in a raised ridge of soil. Water heavily for a few days until they get established.

Some of the slips may wither when you set them in the garden. Don't worry. Just keep them watered, and in about 2 weeks, new growth will let you know a cutting has rooted successfully.

Here's a way to give your cut slips a better chance for survival. A week or two before planting time, cut the slips 1 inch above the potato and root them in buckets of moist sand in a shady spot. An occasional misting during the day will protect plants from drying out while rooting. The root growth will help the plants resume growth faster when they are transplanted to the garden.

Care

To keep weeds down while the plants get established, hoe occasionally, being careful to reshape the ridges with soil, or mulch the area. Once the vines start to spread out, they'll cover the area quickly and serve as a mulch. Don't prune the vines because they should be vigorous for good harvests.

Side-dress 3 to 4 weeks after transplanting with 3 pounds of 5-10-10 (5 pounds in sandy soils) per 100 feet of row.

Although the sweet potato's deep root system resists drought, deep watering in hot, dry periods will increase yields. But if you are going to store part of the crop, do not give the plants extra water late in the season. Fast growth near the harvest period may create growth cracks and tender skins on the roots, which can cause them to bruise easily in handling or storage.

Few serious insect or disease problems bother a home crop of sweet potatoes. Mice and other rodents may travel in mole runways to feed on the roots. Some diseases only show up after months of storage and may just be surface problems.

Harvesting

To harvest, start digging up roots as soon as there is something big enough for a meal. Harvest the main crop before the first frost.

For long-term storage, sweet potatoes must be cured. Keep the roots in a warm (80° to 80°F) location at high humidity levels for 10 to 14 days after harvest. A small closet or basement room with an electric heater works well for small plantings.

The curing process allows the formation of a second skin over scratches and bruises that occur when digging and removing roots from the vine. Curing also converts starches to sugars, improving the flavor of the roots as well. For best curing, don't allow the potatoes to touch each other.

After the curing period, inspect the potatoes carefully and take out any bruised ones. Wrap each one in newspaper and pack them carefully in a box. Sweet potatoes must be kept at 55°F or higher. The best range is 55° to 60°F. Cold storage is bad; the flesh darkens and potatoes shrivel or rot.

Don't overhandle the potatoes. Gently remove the ones you need from the top of the boxes. Don't go looking through the boxes for a different size.

At no time should the sweet potatoes be washed or cleaned; just break away the dirt carefully when harvesting.

Scurf, also called soil stain, causes a dark freckled appearance on the skin of storage potatoes. The fungus attacks only the skin and causes no loss in eating quality.

Sweet Potato Varieties

Moist-fleshed varieties convert much of their interior starches to sugar during cooking, becoming sweet and soft. Types that convert less starch are known as dry-fleshed.

Check with your local Extension Service or Agricultural Experiment Station for information about new varieties that may be available.

Allgold: High-yielding potato with orange skin and moist, salmon-orange flesh. Good canning quality; stores well. Susceptible to nematodes. *88, 89*

Bunch Porto Ricos: Also called bush or vineless. A good choice for gardeners with limited space. Copper-colored skin and light red flesh; flavorful. 100 days to first small harvests. *17, 88, 89, 90*

Centennial: Variety released by the Louisiana Experiment Station and one of the most popular types. High yields of smooth roots with orange skin and carrot-colored flesh. Storage life good, canning quality only fair. Moist-flesh type. A reliable producer for northern growers as well. 10 days earlier than *Porto Ricos. 88, 89, 90*

Jewel: Popular variety with copper-orange skin and orange flesh. Flesh type is moist, storage quality good. Has good disease resistance. *17, 35*

Nancy Hall: An old-time favorite. Light skin, yellow flesh. Juicy, waxy, and sweet when baked. Also called *Yellow Yam. 17, 88, 90*

Vardaman: Bush-type sweet potato. Golden-yellow outside skin that darkens after digging. Deep, bright orange flesh. Heavy yielder. *35, 75, 90*

White Yams: White dry flesh with white outer skin. Very good flavor. *88, 89, 90*

The best part is digging up the treasure. Carefully break away the dirt, then cure the roots for 10 to 14 days.

Tomatoes

A lush, productive plant is shown at left trained to a single stem. In short-season areas, consider planting varieties bred to bloom in cool weather.

Many home gardeners are paying more attention to the flavor of the tomatoes they grow. That's because today's off-season supermarket offerings tend to be tomatoes in name only — red, but with a thick, tough, outer wall (to withstand shipping trauma), not much juice, and in most cases, little flavor (owing to green-stage harvesting and gas ripening in warehouses). For tomato lovers, juiciness, tender meaty interiors, little or no inner cores, and above all, that full, rich tomato flavor are best had by tending a crop at home.

Tomatoes are the number-one garden plant when it comes to popularity. So it is no wonder that there are literally hundreds of varieties available. Most gardeners choose a few different types of tomatoes to grow — some meaty slicing tomatoes, a few paste tomato plants, and some tiny cherry tomatoes for salads. If you do have the space for a few different plants, it's always a good idea to select plants with different maturation dates so you can extend your harvest.

Even gardeners with limited space should have no trouble raising plenty of tomatoes. Varieties are often labeled "determinate" or "indeterminate." A determinate variety will grow only to a certain height and produce a set amount of tomatoes, while the growth of an indeterminate has no limits. If you are limited in space, tuck a few plants of a determinate variety anywhere in your garden — even with your ornamentals. Or consider raising tomatoes in patio pots. No one should do without the fresh, rich taste of home-grown tomatoes.

Planning

Whether you are skimming through the pages of your seed catalogs or checking out the stock of tomato plants at your nursery, you should consider several factors when selecting varieties: dates to maturation, disease resistance, and how you will use the tomatoes in the kitchen. Also consider how much space you want to devote to your tomatoes. They are high yielders; one well-tended tomato plant can yield twenty-five to fifty tomatoes.

If you are starting your own plants, sow seeds for all but extra-early varieties about 6 weeks before the last spring frost date; sow the extra-early varieties, which should be set out under protection, 10 to 12 weeks before the frost date. In southern Florida, mild winter parts of California, and the Southwest, tomatoes can be planted in the fall for a winter harvest.

When shopping for tomato transplants, look for short, stocky plants with dark green foliage and thick stems. Avoid blossoming plants; they are probably rootbound or under some kind of stress. Plants in individual pots usually have larger root systems than those in 6-packs or 12-packs and should rebound faster from transplanting.

Preparation

To start seeds indoors in flats, sow seeds about ¼ inch deep and at least ½ inch apart. If you are using pots, sow only two or three seeds in the individual containers and thin to the strongest plant about a week after the plants emerge.

The seedlings need 12 to 14 hours of light a day or they'll get very spindly. A sunny windowsill will not provide enough light early in the season, so hang fluorescent lights within 1 or 2 inches of the seedlings. The light is stronger at the center of the tubes than at the ends, so rotate your flats and pots once a week.

When the seedlings develop four leaves, transfer them to deeper flats or individual pots. Set them deeper than they originally grew to check any tendency toward legginess.

Feed growing plants regularly with soluble fertilizers added directly to regular waterings. All-purpose houseplant fertilizers can be used if they're diluted to one-quarter strength.

Take 10 days to harden off your plants before they're set in the garden. Do not fertilize or water heavily during this time or you'll promote tender new growth. Set the plants outdoors in a protected, shady spot for a few hours at first, lengthening the time each day.

You can harden plants much earlier if you have a cold frame. Plants get plenty of sunshine in a cold frame and the cooler temperatures promote thick, sturdy stems. Daytime heat can build up on a sunny day, so be sure to open the frame and give the plants fresh air.

Location is critical for tomatoes. In most areas of the country, the sunnier the spot the better. However, where summers are extremely hot — in the Deep South and South Central states, for example — plant in a slightly shady area to reduce the number of blossoms that drop off when temperatures climb over 90°F. This precaution improves fruit set and results in better yields.

About a week before planting, add 1 to 1¾ pounds of 5-10-10 fertilizer or its equivalent per 100 square feet of growing area. On lighter or more sandy soils, add 2 to 4 pounds.

Planting

Trellised, staked, and caged plants generally should be set 18 to 24 inches apart in rows about 3 feet apart; unstaked plants, 3 feet apart in rows 4 to 5 feet apart. Determinate varieties, those which grow to a certain height and then stop, can be set closer together than indeterminate tomatoes, which keep growing all season.

A teaspoon of 5-10-10 applied to the planting hole and mixed with soil before setting in the plants will help the young tomatoes get off to a good start.

Plants should be set deeper in the garden than they were growing in pots. Pick off some of the lower leaves and set the plant deep into the soil to force the plant to grow additional roots along its stem.

Horizontal or trench planting encourages the development of a strong root system near the surface of the soil, which warms up quickly and provides what heat-loving tomato plants need. To plant by this method, pinch off all the lower leaves of the tomato plant and lay it in a shallow trench, about 4 to 5 inches deep. Cover the stem with 2 or 3 inches of soil and bring the top cluster of leaves above the surface. Roots will form along this buried stem. If you're going to stake these tomatoes, drive the stakes at planting time to avoid cutting any roots later in the season.

Protect the stems of your transplants against cutworms and shield the tomato transplants from the wind for 10 to 14 days after you set them out. Wind compounds transplant shock; a steady, harsh wind can whip young plants and dry them out.

Twelve-inch-wide strips of black roofing paper set in a circle around the plants will cut down wind and trap heat, improving production as much as 50 percent.

Care

Most gardeners use some kind of support system for their tomatoes. There are definite advantages (along with a bit of work) to caging, staking, or trellising tomatoes. Plants grow upright, making them easy to work around, to spray, and to harvest. The fruits on upright plants don't touch the ground where they would be exposed to soil rot organisms and disease.

Still, there are very good gardeners who pick beautiful tomato harvests from plants that run free. They feel that staking or trellising is not worth the effort. Below is a look at the pros and cons of the four popular tomato-growing techniques.

Essentials

Planning

🍂 Select several varieties that mature at different times to extend your harvest.

🍂 If you don't purchase plants, start seeds indoors in flats or pots 6 to 7 weeks before the average last frost date, and set out transplants when the soil is warm and all danger of frost is past.

Preparation

🍂 Select a site in full sun (except in very hot climates, where some shading will be desirable to prevent blossom drop).

🍂 A week or so before planting, fertilize with 1 to 1¾ pounds of 5-10-10 or its equivalent per 100 square feet. Increase the amounts for sandy soils.

Planting

🍂 Set up trellises, cages, or stakes at planting time.

🍂 Dig planting holes 18 to 24 inches apart if you plan to stake or trellis the crops, 36 to 48 inches apart if the plants aren't trained.

🍂 Mix a teaspoon of 5-10-10 fertilizer or its equivalent and 1 tablespoon ground limestone with soil at the bottom of the planting hole. Pinch off two or three of the lower branches on the transplant and set the root ball of the plant well into the hole until the remaining lowest leaves are just above the soil surface.

🍂 Water generously and keep the plants well watered for a few days.

Care

🍂 Provide an even supply of water all season.

🍂 If staking or trellising, prune suckers to allow one or two central stems to grow on staked plants, two or three central stems for trellis systems.

🍂 Apply a thick organic mulch 4 or 5 weeks after transplanting.

🍂 Side-dress tomatoes initially when the first clusters of fruit have formed and every 3 weeks thereafter. Two cupfuls of 5-10-10 or its equivalent are generally adequate for 20 plants.

🍂 The most likely pests are tomato hornworms (page 281), tomato fruitworms, also known as corn earworms (page 277), and stinkbugs (page 281). Other possible pests are aphids (page 276), Colorado potato beetles (page 277), flea beetles (page 278), cutworms (page 277), and whiteflies (page 281).

🍂 Watch for blossom end rot (page 283), catfacing or growth cracking (page 283), blossom drop (page 259), and sunscald (page 286).

🍂 Serious diseases include fusarium wilt (page 285), verticillium wilt (page 287), late blight (page 285), nematodes (page 285), and curly top virus (page 259). Other diseases are anthracnose (page 282), bacterial spot (page 282), and early blight (page 284).

Harvesting

🍂 For best flavor, harvest tomatoes when firm and fully colored.

Caging

Advantages:

- Easy to use. Plants can be left alone. Little need to remove suckers, prune, or tie branches.
- Plants grow naturally and support themselves as they get big.
- Good ones are reusable for many years.
- Caged tomato plants develop enough foliage to protect developing fruits from sunscald.

Disadvantages:

- May cost some money. A popular material for caging is concrete reinforcing wire. You may be tempted by short, light, inexpensive metal cages. Don't buy them. Get something sturdy that stands 6 feet high.
- Cages need to be pushed into the ground about a foot or lashed to a few short stakes; they're bulky — storing more than a few is a problem for some gardeners.
- Plants in cages can develop quite a lot of foliage; northern gardeners might need to prune some branches late in the season to allow warm air in around the plant to hasten the ripening.

Staking

Advantages:

- Saves space, so it's a good option in limited space gardens. (Set plants as little as 12 inches apart.)
- Keeps vines and tomatoes off the ground so the harvest is cleaner with less rotting.
- Promotes earlier harvest of bigger tomatoes. Staked plants need pruning and that forces more of the plant's energy into ripening the fruit.
- Easy to pick tomatoes, spray plants, and watch for insects and diseases.

Disadvantages:

- Takes time and effort for setup, pruning, and training. (For example, a vigorous-growing plant with two main leaders may need to be tied in twenty places by the time it's fully grown.)
- Tomatoes are more prone to cracking, water stress, blossom end rot, and sunscald because they are more exposed.
- Generally produces the lowest yields of the systems outlined here.
- Plants may need a 6- or 8-inch organic mulch in warm weather.

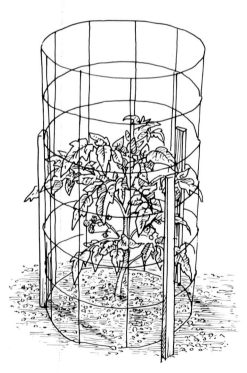

Trellising

Advantages:

▪ Like staking, trellising holds the tomatoes off the ground for cleaner, easier-to-pick harvests.

▪ Allows plants to be grown very close together.

▪ Allows two or three main stems to be grown.

▪ Fruits ripen a bit earlier than those on ground-grown tomatoes.

Disadvantages:

▪ Can be hard work, especially for a large number of plants. Poles, wires or string, and braces are usually needed.

▪ Requires maintenance once or twice a week when plants are growing vigorously to keep them running up the trellis. Often the plants need to be tied to trellis wires or strings.

Allowing Tomatoes to Sprawl

Advantages:

▪ Saves work; there's little or no pruning, no staking and training, no supports to build, buy, and set up.

▪ Yields are generally higher than with staked, trellised, or caged plants.

▪ Foliage protects fruits from sunscald, shades the soil, and conserves moisture.

Disadvantages:

▪ Wet, humid weather may trigger rotting and slug and snail problems for tomatoes on the ground. A light mulch under the fruits may be necessary.

▪ Requires more space for each plant, 1 square yard or more.

▪ Tomatoes may sometimes be difficult to find and harvest; some stems on the ground send out roots, making it hard to pick up the branches to get tomatoes.

Regional Notes

Pacific Northwest

Due to the cool summers and soil conditions of the Pacific Northwest, some special steps are recommended for good tomato crops.

Choose early, proven varieties such as *Fantastic, Early Cascade,* and *New Yorker.*

Many soils are too acidic and lack calcium and magnesium, so test to see if agricultural lime is needed.

Use black plastic to warm up the soil at planting time. Consider raised bed planting to encourage early, warm soil temperatures and faster drainage after rain.

To encourage early ripening, stop watering a few plants early in August or root prune several plants. You may also pick off blossoms and small tomatoes that develop after mid-August.

Pruning tomato plants is not necessary unless you're growing tomatoes up stakes or on some kind of trellis. Then it's convenient to restrict the growth to one or two main stems for staking or two to three stems for trellising. Controlling the growth of the plant requires pinching off the suckers or side shoots that sprout at the intersection of the main stem and a leaf branch.

If, besides the main stem, you want additional stems to develop, allow the suckers closest to the bottom of the plant to grow. These will have more flower blossoms and are easier to train to the outside of the plant than suckers that sprout higher up.

Prune suckers of staked or trellised plants to keep the crop manageable. The suckers or side shoots sprout between the main stem and leaf branches.

To reduce sunscald problems, let two or four leaves on suckers develop before pinching off the growing tips. They will offer some shade but won't blossom or need tying up.

Some gardeners prune off the growing tip of the plant when it reaches the top of the stake to stop further vertical growth.

Caged plants, or those running loose on the ground, don't have to be pruned. However, some northern gardeners and those in cool, coastal areas may want to remove blossoms and any small tomatoes late in the season to force the plant to ripen its larger tomatoes faster. Removing some branches when cool fall weather arrives might also allow warm air to speed ripening of fruits that are hidden by heavy foliage.

Tomatoes need quite a large food supply. So in all but the most fertile gardens, side-dress at least one or two times during the season. (In general, side-dressings should follow every 3 weeks after the first application.)

Choose a complete commercial fertilizer such as 5-10-10 or 10-10-10, or an organic fertilizer such as dried manure or cottonseed meal. High-nitrogen concentrated fertilizers such as ammonium sulfate are easy to use — but be careful not to overdo it. A small amount packs quite a wallop; overfertilizing may produce tall, dark green plants with very few blossoms and fruits.

Side-dress when the first tomatoes have just formed and they're about golf-ball size. A pound (2 cups) of 5-10-10 should be enough for all the plants in a 30-foot row (about 20 plants). Put a small handful of the fertilizer in a 1-inch-deep circular furrow 5 or 6 inches away from the stem. Don't get any of this fertilizer on the leaves or stem because it can burn them.

Getting Earlier Tomatoes

If you want to pick the first certified, vine-ripened, home-grown tomato in your neighborhood, plant a few extra-early tomato plants and pamper them. You should never bet the whole crop, but you might devote a small area to this pursuit.

1. Select a tomato variety that matures fruits in 50 to 60 days after transplanting and can set fruit in cool weather. *Pixie, Fireball, Jung's Improved Wayahead,* and *Early Cascade* are good choices.

2. Plant the seeds indoors in flats 10 to 12 weeks or more before the average last spring frost date.

3. Repot each seedling into a separate deep container when 3 or 4 inches high. Large pots at this stage — 4 inches square, for example — will result in better early yields. Pick off all the lower leaves and insert the plant up to its top leaves. If the plants grow to stand 8 to 10 inches high, consider repotting again.

4. Harden off the plants well. Get the plants into the ground 2 or 3 weeks before the average last frost date.

5. Set the plants in the ground vertically, only as deeply as they were growing in the pot; you want to place the roots near the surface where they will warm up fastest. Soak the area after transplanting. Use only black plastic mulch, which can be laid down tightly before planting.

6. Gather heat around each plant with hotcaps, plastic jugs, or old tires. The warmer the air temperature, the sooner the harvest. Also block winds to lessen transplant shock. Cover on cold nights.

7. Spray flower clusters twice a week with a commercial hormone spray such as Blossom Set (usually available at garden centers) to help the plants retain blossoms that otherwise might drop in cool weather.

8. Side-dress the plants with a balanced fertilizer when they have formed several small tomatoes, and repeat every 2 weeks.

9. Root prune a couple of tomato plants when three or four clusters of tomatoes are ripening. Take a long knife and slice in the ground halfway around the plant 6 or 8 inches deep, and about a foot away from the stem; you are actually slicing through some of the roots. This will shock the plant and force it to ripen the tomatoes faster.

10. To gain a few extra days, pick the tomatoes when they are red but not fully ripe and finish ripening them indoors.

Tomatoes are heavy feeders. Side-dress plants every 3 weeks once small tomatoes appear. Place a small handful of 5-10-10 fertilizer in a circular furrow about 6 inches from the stem.

Cover the fertilizer with about 1 inch of soil. The next rain or watering will start carrying the nutrients down into the root zone of the plants. If you are using ammonium sulfate, use only a tablespoon per 2 feet of row (about 1 pound for 30 feet of row) and sprinkle it in a furrow 8 to 12 inches from the stem.

Foliar fertilizing — spraying side-dressing nutrients on the plant — gets the nutrients to the plant faster than by adding them to the soil and waiting for the roots to take them up. Staked tomatoes have shown excellent results from foliar feeding in some tests. Fish or seaweed emulsion, as well as magnesium-rich Epsom salts, can be sprayed on the foliage in the home garden.

Tomatoes need an even supply of water through the season; erratic watering will cause problems such as blossom end rot. Like most other garden crops, tomatoes need at least 1 inch of rain or irrigation water per week for steady growth. In the hotter, drier parts of the country, 2 inches of water per week are needed during the summer months. Soak the soil to a depth of at least 6 inches. A thorough soaking every 4 or 5 days on light, sandy soils and every 7 to 10 days on heavy soils is a good general guide for irrigating tomatoes if you don't get enough rain.

Use a thick organic mulch to help retain moisture in the soil. Mulches reduce the fluctuation of soil moisture, which helps the crop avoid blossom end rot. Don't apply mulch until after the transplants have been growing for 5 to 6 weeks — a time when the soil has usually warmed up adequately.

Tomatoes are subject to a number of diseases and disorders. Practicing good garden sanitation and rotating your tomato crop each year are good preventative measures. However, some disorders are caused by weather.

Blossom end rot shows first on the bottom of the tomato; it appears as a large, dry, brown or black sunken area and affects both green and red tomatoes. It is caused by a fluctuating moisture supply that results in a lack of calcium in the plant.

Staked and pruned plants are more likely to suffer from blossom end rot than unstaked tomatoes, and it's most likely to affect the earliest fruits of the season. The rot often starts as the plants are putting on some quick growth and a hot dry spell hits. They suffer moisture stress and the roots are unable to take up enough calcium to satisfy the needs of the fast-growing plant.

Keep the water supply even through the season, mulch, and try spraying calcium on the leaves and fruits to check further damage. You can buy the calcium in the form of calcium chloride, which is sold as deicing salt at hardware stores. Mix 2 tablespoons to a gallon of water and spray two or three times a week.

Catfacing, or growth cracking, can occur during warm, rainy periods, especially if this weather follows a dry spell. The fruits simply expand too fast. The

Yellow tomatoes have a rich taste. To harvest tomatoes at their peak, pick the fruits when they are firm and fully colored.

best way to avoid the problem is to keep the moisture supply as steady as possible throughout the season. Some varieties, such as *Early Girl, Jet Star,* and *Roma,* are crack tolerant.

Blossom drop may occur in both cool and very hot weather. Early in the season, night temperatures below 55°F will encourage blossom drop. Some varieties, such as *Pixie,* will keep their blossoms and set fruit in cool weather, but most will not. Some blossoms may drop when summer temperatures reach about 75° at night or over 100°F during the day — partly why it's difficult to get a summer-long crop of tomatoes in the hot southern and southwestern states. Blossoms may also fall when plants don't get enough water, when the crop is planted in too shady an area, or after an overdose of side-dressing fertilizer has been applied.

Sunscald occurs when green or ripening tomatoes get too much sun exposure. A yellowish-white patch appears first on the side of the tomato facing the sun. Sunscald often hits after leaf diseases have robbed the plant of some foliage. Growing tomatoes in cages without pruning them is a good way to avoid the problem. You can also use straw, shredded newspapers, or other material to cover the tomatoes while they're ripening.

Don't smoke in the garden or when working with tomato plants. There's a danger of passing the tobacco mosaic virus, one of several serious viruses that can infect tomatoes and other crops.

Fusarium wilt and verticillium wilt are serious; the plant's lower leaves turn yellow, wilt, and die. There are no remedies for these diseases, which are caused by soil-borne fungi that remain in the soil and on plant residues for many seasons. It's best to destroy diseased plants immediately and to plant only varieties resistant to the diseases.

Curly top is a disease that can affect tomato crops in the West. It is a virus disease spread by the beet leafhopper (found west of the Mississippi). Leaves will curl and the plant will turn a dull yellow and stop growing. If leafhoppers can be kept in check, there is much less likelihood of a problem.

Other serious diseases are early blight, late blight, bacterial speck, and leaf spot.

Tomatoes can be bothered by many of the same insects that afflict other vegetable crops. See pages 276–287 for information on cutworms, flea beetles, Colorado potato beetles, whiteflies, spider mites, and aphids, as well as the insects described below.

Tomato hornworms eat tomatoes, leaves, and stems. Hand-picking these creatures is the best bet in the home garden because you usually discover them at harvest time when it's unwise to spray chemicals. However, the nontoxic bacterial control *Bacillus thuringiensis* (available as Dipel, Thuricide, and BT, among others) is very effective and requires no waiting time before harvesting.

Tomato fruitworms, also known as corn earworms, do their damage by chewing deep holes in the fruits. If you spot damaged fruits, get rid of them and spray the plants with Dipel or another approved control.

Stinkbugs suck sap from the tomato plant and fruits, leaving behind many young deformed tomatoes. The stinkbug is a pest mainly in southern states; it gives off a strong odor when crushed.

Harvesting

For best flavor, harvest tomatoes when they are firm and fully colored. When temperatures are high (air above 90°F) softening occurs rapidly and color development is hindered. In these conditions, tomatoes can be picked before the fully ripe stage and ripened at temperatures between 55° and 72°F. Some light will increase the color of house-ripened tomatoes, but it is not essential. Fruits ripening in direct sun indoors may get too much heat, resulting in poorer flavor.

Tomato Varieties

Some of the more popular and widely adapted tomato varieties available from mail-order seed companies are listed here, along with seed company sources. Your local retail garden centers and nurseries should be able to recommend other varieties for your area.

Our division of varieties—early, midseason, and late season—should help you plan your garden to extend the harvest season. One or more varieties from each category planted at the same time should produce a continuous tomato harvest starting from around 60 days after transplanting. If you have space, choose one or two new varieties to grow each year along with your traditional favorites. You may find a tomato that will outperform your trusted standby.

Key to chart:
V—Resistant to verticillium wilt
F—Resistant to fusarium wilt
T—Resistant to tobacco mosaic virus
N—Resistant to nematodes
I—Indeterminate
D—Determinate
SD—Semideterminate
H—Hybrid variety

Variety (days to harvest)	Disease Resistance	Growth Habit	Comments	Sources
Early Varieties				
Big Early (H) (62)		I	Rugged hybrid; large, thick-walled fruits; good in cages.	15, 32, 91, 92
Early Cascade (H) (63)	VFN	I	Early, but bears well into season; tall plant, needs strong staking; 4–6 oz. fruits.	23, 91, 92, 105
Early Girl (H) (62)	V	I	Tasty, full-flavored tomato; widely adapted; 4–5 oz. fruits	29, 35, 91, 92
Fireball (60)		D	Good early choice in many areas; 4–6 oz. fruits.	16, 23, 92
Floramerica (H) (65)	VFN	D	Widely adapted, with multiple disease resistance; deep red color, large fruits; All-America winner; can be caged or staked to short poles.	26, 35, 91, 92
Improved Wayahead (63)		D	Round, smooth fruits; sets well in cool weather.	21, 92
New Yorker (60)	V	D	Recommended for northern short-season areas; small plants, 3–5 oz. fruits.	16, 51, 91, 92
Pixie (H) (55)		D	Popular, successful container variety or early garden choice; sturdy, upright habit; good flavor; 1¾-inch-diameter fruits.	6, 91
Spring Giant (H) (65)	VFN	D	High-yielding; concentrated, early harvest; 8–10 oz. fruits.	23, 29, 91, 92
Springset (H) (65)	VF	D	Heavy but short harvest period; thin foliage, susceptible to sunscald; 5–6 oz. fruits.	33, 67, 91, 92
Midseason Varieties				
Better Boy (H) (70)	VFN	I	Great in flavor and quality, by many accounts; produces large, meaty fruits, 12–16 oz.	6, 26, 91, 92
Big Girl (H) (78)	VF	I	Very popular "main crop" tomato; large, globe-shaped, deep red fruits.	6, 91, 92
Burpee's Long-Keeper (78)		I	Best harvested at partially ripe stage for storage up to 12 weeks; orange color, medium to large fruits.	6
Burpee's VF (H) (72)	VF	I	Very popular; good in cages or on trellis; 6–8 oz. fruits, meaty and firm.	6, 32, 91
Celebrity (H) (70)	VFNT	D	Large, stocky plants; well-adapted; steady bearer; very productive; 1984 All-America winner; fusarium race 1 & 2 resistant; 8 oz. fruit.	26, 35, 92
Champion (H) (70)	VFNT	I	Vigorous, early-ripener; excellent flavor and quality; 8 oz. fruits.	26, 33, 91
Delicious (77)		I	Small seed cavities, large fruits, good for slicing; world record tomato—6 lbs. 8 oz.—was a Delicious.	15, 91, 92
Fantastic (H) (70)		I	Sturdy hybrid, high yields of 6–8 oz. fruits; good fall bearer.	29, 35, 92
Heinz 1350 (72)	VF	SD	A popular canning type with thick, meaty-fleshed fruits.	26, 39, 91
Hybrid 980 (H) (75)	VF	I	Deep red, mild flavor; 4–6 oz. fruits.	1, 23
Jet Star (H) (72)	VF	I	Popular in western states, though adapted to wider area; large, firm fruits.	3, 16, 92

Variety (days to harvest)	Disease Resistance	Growth Habit	Comments	Sources
Marglobe (75)	VF	D	A traditional favorite with many gardeners; good foliage; smooth and firm; 8–10 oz. fruits.	23, 33, 91, 92
Monte Carlo (H) (75)	VFN	I	Widely adapted variety, praised in South for nematode resistance; smooth, 9 oz. fruits.	11, 39, 91
Park's Whopper (H) (70)	VFNT	I	Large, round, and flavorful fruits; long bearing.	35
Pink Delight (H) (77)		I	Tolerant to cracking and blossom end rot; good size and widely adaptable.	43, 91, 92
President (H) (68)	VFNT	D	Widely adapted bush type with good disease resistance; very flavorful; 6–8 oz. fruits.	29, 92, 105
Sunray (70)	F	I	Has outstanding mild flavor; medium to large fruits, bright golden yellow color. Good yielder.	16, 29, 92
Walter (75)	F	D	Popular in Southeast; resistance to blossom end rot, cracking, and leaf diseases; stake culture preferred.	23, 43, 92

Late Season Varieties

Variety (days to harvest)	Disease Resistance	Growth Habit	Comments	Sources
Beefmaster (H) (80)	VFN	I	Continuous producer, large (up to 2 lbs.), deep oblate fruits, deep red color.	26, 35, 91, 92
Beefsteak (90)		I	Vigorous vine—cages recommended; large, slightly ribbed fruits; good rich flavor.	23, 32, 91
Big Boy (H) (80)		I	Large, deep globe, thick walls; excellent flavor; fruits 12 oz. and up.	32, 35, 91
Oxheart (86)		I	Large, heavy, round, smooth fruits; heart-shaped, with solid interior and thick, firm walls.	23, 33, 91, 92
Ponderosa Pink (90)		I	Old-time variety, with huge fruits (up to 2 lbs.); solid fruit, small seed cavity; use cages to increase foliage protection.	16, 39, 92
Rutgers (80)	VF	SD	An old name in tomato growing, now with disease resistance; late bearing; 8–10 oz. fruit.	23, 29
Super Beefsteak (H) (80)	VFN	I	Good flavor, very large fruits, and good yielder.	6

Cherry Tomato Varieties

Variety (days to harvest)	Disease Resistance	Growth Habit	Comments	Sources
Red Cherry (75)		I	Half-dollar diameter fruits; steady bearer.	16, 29, 33
Small Fry (H) (65)	VFN	D	All-America winner; excellent taste; compact bush plant; fruit in clusters of 8 or 10.	26, 35, 91, 92
Sugar Lump (65)		D	Early, heavy producer, rich sweet taste; good salad choice.	35, 52, 105
Sweet 100 (H) (70)		I	Long-bearing, very productive, delicious sweet flavor borne in large clusters.	35, 91, 92, 105
Sweetie (79)		I	Very sweet; vigorous grower.	17, 66, 91, 92
Tiny Tim (55)		D	Very small plant, good for small deck or patio planters.	35, 91, 105
Toy Boy (H) (75)		D	Ping-Pong-ball-size fruit; small plants, so double up in containers.	35, 91, 92, 105
Yellow Pear (75)		I	Mild flavor; clusters of 1-inch-wide pear-shaped fruits.	29, 32, 91, 92

Paste Tomatoes

Variety (days to harvest)	Disease Resistance	Growth Habit	Comments	Sources
Bellstar (74)		D	Recent introduction; large-fruited plum shape with 4–6 oz. fruits.	20, 39, 92
Chico III (72)	F	D	Sets fruit at high temperatures; good choice for juice-making; vigorous, compact plant; pear-shaped fruits, 2½–3 inches in diameter.	21, 61
Nova (65)	VF	D	Early, deep-red fruits; good for short season areas; 1¼ by 3 inches in size.	20, 39, 92
Roma VF (76)	VF	D	Compact plant bearing heavy crop of plum-shaped tomatoes; few seeds; good for canning whole.	29, 32, 91
San Marzano (80)		I	Highly praised; good for purees and tomato paste; rectangular shape; 4-oz. fruits.	6, 33, 91

Turnips

Good earth and cool weather create the ideal growing conditions for tasty turnips.

Turnips aren't exactly America's favorite vegetable, though we're not sure why. These tasty roots can be eaten raw, boiled like potatoes, or added to soups and stews. They're versatile, they're flavorful, and they keep well.

In the South, turnip greens are very popular. They are delicious steamed with a bit of bacon or ham. As a bonus, they provide calcium, potassium, iron, small amounts of other nutrients, and a large supply of vitamin A.

Rutabagas are closely related to turnips. They are larger, starchier, and sweeter. They take longer to grow than turnips; but to compensate, they store well for longer periods of time. Another relative, the kohlrabi, looks like a cross between turnip and cabbage.

It's easy to grow turnips. Just about all you need to supply is good earth and cool weather. In much of the country, you can raise both spring and fall crops. Though the quality of the early crop is often uncertain, we think you'll find the reward worth the risk.

Kohlrabi *(right)* is often called "the aboveground turnip." When the plants are small, thin them to stand 6 to 8 inches apart.

Turnip Greens

To hear some growers tell it, you'd think the turnip itself was just a bonus of greens production.

National Gardening Association member Alice Yeager of Texarkana, Arkansas, is one such green grower. She makes two plantings: once in early spring and again in late fall. Sure, she enjoys the turnips, but the "delectable" greens are the real treat.

Alice considers the popular *Purple Top White Globe* a good source of greens only when its leaves are young and tender. According to her, the flavor alters with each passing frost until it borders on quinine. The turnips also take on a strong flavor and become pithy.

Alice thinks *Tokyo Cross Hybrid* outdistances *Purple Top White Globe* in a number of ways: its leaves are tasty and tender and the round, white turnips are mild and crisp enough to be eaten raw or sliced for salads.

Alice's delicious turnip green recipe starts with frying some bacon or ham beforehand to make drippings. Then stuff plenty of greens in a good-size pot. Remember that greens cook down quite a bit. Add some turnips cut into bite-size pieces. Then add the meat and some of the drippings along with about 2 cups of water — or more, depending on how much broth you want. Cover and cook over low heat for 20 to 25 minutes, stirring the greens occasionally so they don't wilt together in a mass.

Authentic, Southern-style turnip greens are best appreciated when served with homemade, piping hot cornbread, according to Alice. "And don't forget to dash a little hot pepper sauce on your plate of greens. That's the gourmet touch!"

Planning

Turnips love cool weather from seeding to harvest, about 2 months later. They can withstand cold temperatures, so even if the nights bring frosts to your spring crop, the turnips won't be harmed. If you can plant your spring turnips quite early, you will be rewarded with sweet turnips, unless a heat wave sets in before the turnips are mature, in which case they are likely to become bitter. If your garden stays too muddy to let you plant early, perhaps you should wait for a fall crop.

For a good fall crop, you want the roots to form after the summer heat has passed so they'll stay sweet. Again, a little frost doesn't hurt them at all, but harvest the roots before the ground freezes. Regardless of which season you plant in, you'll find that turnips are easy to grow and fairly trouble-free.

Other than taking a month longer to mature, rutabagas are grown, used, and stored just as turnips are, though we recommend only a fall crop. In addition to being larger and firmer, rutabagas are a lot sweeter. Many people think they taste better raw, too.

In central and southern areas rutabagas need not be planted until midsummer or harvested until Thanksgiving.

Preparation

Bed planting is the most efficient way to grow turnip greens or roots. Select a fertile spot with well-worked soil — the looser the better. Fertilize with 2 pounds of 10-10-10 or its equivalent per 50 square feet.

Planting

Turnip seed packet directions tell you to plant seeds ½ inch deep, anywhere from three to twenty seeds per foot of row, depending on how much thinning you intend to do. We think there is a much simpler method. After you thoroughly till the soil, broadcast the seeds over the bed so they land about ¼ to ½ inch apart. To cover the seeds with soil, set your tiller on shallow and run it lightly over the seedbed. This will save you the trouble of raking the soil over the seed. If you don't have a tiller and are only planting a small bed of turnips, broadcast the seeds, then rake the bed gently to cover the seeds with a shallow layer of soil.

Care

For roots, thin the seedlings to stand 2 to 4 inches apart when they are about 4 inches high. Space them even farther apart if you want to nurture really big turnips — but bigger is not necessarily better.

To ward off strong taste and stringy texture, water deeply once a week (about 1 inch of water at a time) rather than a little bit every day. Shallow and erratic watering can cause turnips to bolt and form only a tiny, inedible root.

Cabbage root maggots can be a problem. Cover the seedbed with cheesecloth or a similar covering, or dust around the bases of the plants with diatomaceous earth or wood ashes to repel adult flies from laying eggs.

Harvesting

If you want, you can leave your fall turnips in the ground until just before it freezes. Depending on your climate, heavy straw mulch can extend the harvest right into winter. Just check the roots periodically and harvest them as necessary.

Turnips aren't too particular about their storage conditions. They will keep for several months in a Styrofoam cooler in a cool room or in a spare refrigerator. Put the roots in plastic bags with holes for air circulation.

Essentials

Planning
- *Turnips mature in about 2 months.*
- *Fall crops are usually sweeter and more tender than spring crops, and insects are less of a problem late in the season.*
- *For best results, sow spring crops as soon as the soil can be worked.*

Preparation
- *Before planting add fertilizer at the rate of 2 pounds of 10-10-10 or its equivalent per 50 square feet.*
- *Prepare beds rather than rows.*

Planting
- *Broadcast seed over a well-tilled bed. Rake to cover seeds with ½ inch of soil or use a tiller set on shallow to bury the seeds.*

Care
- *Do not thin if growing turnips for greens only.*
- *For turnip roots, thin seedlings to stand 2 to 4 inches apart when they are 4 inches high.*
- *Water deeply once a week (about 1 inch of water at a time) so the roots don't become tough and bitter.*
- *Mulch heavily.*
- *Watch for cabbage root maggots (page 276).*

Harvesting
- *Harvest turnips at any eating size during the growing season.*
- *In the fall, dig mature roots before the ground freezes and store in a cool place.*

Other Vegetables

Green Globe artichokes **(left)** prefer damp, mild, coastal areas, but can thrive inland with some extra watering. Mustard **(above)** is a fast-growing, early- or late-season green.

Tomatoes and peppers may be the vegetable crops most popular with American gardeners, but we don't want to ignore less widely grown crops that are also delicious and high in nutritive value.

Kale and collards may not be big items at the supermarket, but if you are looking for high-nutrition produce, you will certainly want to include them in your garden plan. A cup of cooked kale, for example, contains more vitamin C than 8 ounces of orange juice.

Chard is another underrated green; it does well in both cool and warm temperatures and, like spinach, can be cooked or used raw in salad when the leaves are young and tender. And if you are careful to harvest the entire top of the chard plant about 2 inches above the soil line, new tender leaves will begin to grow and provide a second harvest.

Mustard greens grow very quickly and have a fine flavor when harvested in cool weather. Seeds of this crop should be among the first sown in the spring and the last sown near the end of the season for a second harvest.

Celeriac and salsify are two lesser-known root crops that many chefs prize in the fall when they are first dug. They need a few light frosts before the starch in the roots begins to turn to sugar, improving the flavor remarkably. In many areas, both crops may overwinter easily, providing additional harvests in late winter.

Watercress and globe artichokes require special growing conditions, but their flavor and high price at the market make them worth growing if you are up to the challenge.

Ruby chard

Kale

Red mustard

Chard

Planning

Both white and ruby varieties of chard are available, but whether there is much difference in flavor between the two is a matter of some disagreement. The ruby variety, with its red stalks and dark green leaves, certainly makes a colorful addition to the garden, even if some growers claim that the green varieties are more tender.

Chard is a green that can tolerate some heat during its growing season, which makes it an excellent succession crop for spinach. Plant it in the early spring 2 to 3 weeks before the last spring frost date and at 10-day intervals for a month. Plant again in late summer (40 days or more before the first fall frost date) for a fall or early winter harvest.

Preparation

Chard thrives in well-drained, rich, crumbly soil with a pH between 6.0 and 6.8. Before sowing seeds, mix into the soil 1 cup of 5-10-10 or its equivalent for every 20 feet of single row.

Planting

Sow seeds ½ to ¾ inch deep in single rows 18 to 24 inches apart or in wide rows 10 to 18 inches apart. Sow 8 to 10 seeds per foot of row.

Care

When the plants are 3 to 4 inches tall, thin them to stand 4 to 6 inches apart, 9 to 12 inches apart for larger individual plants.

Chard requires an even supply of water to grow well. Mulch plants to conserve moisture, and, during summer heat spells, water often.

Although chard does not bolt as spinach does, don't let it get overgrown or it will become tough and less flavorful. For best quality, cut plants back when they get a foot tall — harvest or compost the cut plants.

Chard is relatively problem-free. Watch out for leaf miners (page 279) and slugs (page 280).

Harvesting

Start harvesting chard by cutting off the outer leaves or the entire plant 1½ inches above the ground when the plants are 6 to 8 inches tall. New growth will sprout after a week or two.

Cook the leafy portion like spinach; use the midribs or stalks in stir-fries or steam like asparagus.

Kale

Planning

Kale is a very hardy green that can tolerate fall frosts. It stays green in the garden long after other plants have died back from the cold. It is also rich in minerals and vitamins C and A, another reason to try this succulent green. For best results, plant in early summer to midsummer for fall harvests.

Preparation

Kale does best in loamy soil with a pH of 5.5 to 6.8. Fertilize before planting by mixing 1½ cups of 5-10-10 or its equivalent per 25 feet of single row into the top 3 to 4 inches of soil.

Planting

Sow seeds ¼ to ½ inch deep in rows or beds.

Care

Not much care is required for raising a bumper crop. Thin the seedlings to stand 8 to 12 inches apart after 2 weeks. Mulch the soil heavily after the first hard freeze; many plants will overwinter and produce more leaves before going to seed in early spring.

Watch for imported cabbageworms (page 278), flea beetles (page 278), and aphids (page 276).

Harvesting

Begin harvesting when leaves are the size of your hand. Avoid picking the terminal bud at the top center; this will keep each plant productive.

Harvest about one fistful of leaves per serving. Small, tender leaves can be used in salads. Cut and cook larger leaves like spinach. Before cooking large leaves, remove the tough ribs.

Collards

Planning

Collards are a cool-season vegetable, rich in vitamins and minerals, and closely related to kale.

Transplants are often available in the South for spring plantings. But if you can't find started plants in garden centers, don't worry. This crop is easily raised from seed sown directly in the garden. Sow seeds 4 to 5 weeks before the last spring frost date. Sow again in midsummer (in the North) to late summer (in the South) for fall harvests.

Preparation

Collards thrive where kale thrives — in loamy soil with a pH of 5.5 to 6.8. Fertilize before planting by mixing 1½ cups of 5-10-10 or its equivalent for every 25 feet of single row into the top 3 to 4 inches of soil.

Planting

Plant seeds ¼ to ½ inch deep, 4 to 5 seeds per foot of row. Allow 3 feet between rows — since the plants get large — or plant in wide rows.

Care

Thin plants after 3 weeks to stand 6 to 12 inches apart. Collards are heavy feeders so side-dressing is necessary. Side-dress plants about 1 month after planting using approximately 1 pound of 5-10-10 or its equivalent for every 25 feet of row or provide large amounts of composted manure.

Flea beetles (page 278), imported cabbageworms (page 278), aphids (page 276), and cabbage root maggots (page 276) may bother the crop. Plants are susceptible to diseases affecting the cabbage family.

Harvesting

All the green parts of the plant are edible, though many gardeners cut only the inner rosette of young growth. You can also wait until the plants are a foot high and then pick the largest leaves, allowing the younger leaves to develop.

Wait until after the first fall frost (when the flavor improves) to begin harvesting the fall crop.

Mustard Greens

Planning

This fast-maturing, easy-to-grow vegetable has the highest quality when it matures in cool seasons. Many varieties can be harvested in 50 days or less.

Preparation

Mustard greens thrive where kale thrives — in loamy soil with a pH of 5.5 to 6.8. Fertilize before planting by mixing 1½ cups of 5-10-10 or its equivalent per 25 feet of single row into the top 3 to 4 inches of soil.

Planting

About 3 weeks before the last spring frost date, sow seeds ½ inch deep in rows 18 to 24 inches apart. Seeds can also be broadcast in wide rows 15 to 20 inches wide.

Sow again in late summer or early fall, 35 to 45 days or more before the first fall frost date.

Care

Thin plants to stand 4 to 8 inches apart. Since mustard is a fast grower, water well, especially in a dry spell.

Aphids (page 276), flea beetles (page 278), and imported cabbageworms (page 278) can pester the crop. Downy mildew (page 284) is one disease threat.

Harvesting

The young leaves are the best flavored and most tender. Cut the entire plant or pick off individual leaves. The flavor becomes strong in summer heat.

Salsify

Celeriac

Planning

Celeriac is sometimes called celery root. You harvest the large, knobby roots, which do taste remarkably like celery.

This root crop requires a long, 120-day growing season. The roots attain full flavor after fall frosts. Transplants are generally not available, so plan to start this crop indoors 8 to 12 weeks before the last spring frost.

Expect about 1 pound of celeriac roots per foot of row.

Preparation

To start seeds indoors sow seeds thickly in pots (8 to 10 seeds per pot). Thin seedlings to 1 plant per pot. The seeds germinate best at 70°F; keep night temperatures at 60° to 65°F, with daytime temperatures 5 to 10 degrees warmer.

Celeriac needs deep, fertile soil. Spade or till to a depth of 8 to 10 inches. Mix in liberal amounts of old manure. Use a bushel or so for every 20 feet of row; the manure will help retain moisture for the crop through the season.

Planting

Set out transplants when seedlings are 2 to 2½ inches high. Set them 6 to 7 inches apart.

Care

Provide ample water during hot spells. The root quality drops in drought unless the plants are watered regularly.

Remove side shoots when they develop at the base. In mild-winter areas, mulch the row heavily for winter harvesting.

Harvesting

Wait until after the first fall frosts to begin harvesting. The bulbs should be about 2½ inches in diameter.

Use peeled roots grated or sliced in salads, cooked in soups and stews, or separately for a side dish.

Salsify

Planning

Widely grown in Europe and prized for its 8- to 10-inch-long roots, salsify needs at least 100 days' growth before freezing weather in the fall, so plant accordingly. It is similar in culture to parsnips.

Preparation

Salsify thrives where celeriac does — in deep, fertile soil — so spade or till the soil to a depth of 8 to 10 inches. Mix in a liberal amount of dried or composted manure. Use a bushel or so for every 20 feet of row; the manure will help retain moisture for the crop through the season.

Because the seeds are slow to germinate, it's best to select a weed-free site so weed competition won't slow the growth of the salsify seedlings.

Planting

Plant seeds in the spring ½ to ¾ inch deep. Sow 10 to 12 seeds per foot of row. If soil crusting is a problem, lightly mulch the seed bed.

Care

Salsify is a slow-starter, so hoe small weeds near the row carefully. Thin after a week or two of growth to stand 2 to 4 inches apart.

The crop can withstand a dry spell and still maintain quality. Diseases and pests are rarely a problem.

Harvesting

Harvest salsify after light fall frosts have improved its flavor. In mild-winter areas plants overwinter well and roots can be harvested until growth resumes in spring.

Harvest the roots as you need them; they wither quickly, although they may be kept for 3 to 4 days in open plastic bags in the refrigerator.

Small, tender shoots will grow from overwintered plants in early spring. When the shoots are 5 inches tall, cut and cook them as you would asparagus.

Watercress

Planning

Watercress is a perennial, cool-season salad vegetable with pungent flavor. It needs very moist growing conditions or almost daily irrigation. In harsh winter areas it can be grown as an annual.

The plants can be started as cuttings from bunched watercress at the supermarket or from seed sown in the spring.

You can grow watercress in containers or on a patio; however, container plantings require even more watering and misting than in-ground crops.

Preparation

Select a weed-free site. Before planting, shallowly till or spade the planting bed at 3- or 4-day intervals a few times. Work in lots of manure and organic matter to hold water. Mix in well with the soil.

Planting

In the spring, two or three weeks before the last frost date, sow seeds shallowly and thickly in beds of three or four rows, each 12 to 18 inches apart. Or set cuttings from bunched watercress 8 inches apart in rows 12 to 18 inches apart.

Care

Never allow the soil to dry out; mist plants regularly.

Thin plants to stand 8 inches apart. When the plants are 6 inches tall, pinch the leading shoot to encourage branching. Don't let the plant flower. If you see flower buds, prune the plants back.

Fertilize with soluble plant food such as a seaweed mix every 3 weeks or so.

Aphids (page 276) and flea beetles (page 278) may occasionally bother the crop.

Harvesting

The crop should be ready for harvest in 60 to 70 days. Harvest by cutting off about 6 inches of the leading shoots or side shoots.

Cut shoots can be kept for a few days in water or in the refrigerator wrapped in plastic.

Globe Artichoke

Planning

Globe artichokes are a perennial crop best grown in damp, mild coastal areas; they can also be grown in mild-winter areas inland if watered heavily during spring and summer hot spells.

In cold-winter areas, plants are best grown in large tubs and protected through the winter to keep roots alive. A few varieties, such as *Grand Beurre* and *Green Globe*, produce early enough to be grown as annuals in the North.

Plants grow 3 to 6 feet tall and just as wide, resembling a coarse thistle. Big flower buds form at the top of stalks; these buds are the artichokes.

Preparation

The plants are heavy feeders, so add plenty of good compost or manure to the planting areas. If you don't have manure, use ½ cup of 5-10-10 or its equivalent mixed thoroughly with the soil.

Planting

Plant dormant roots from a local nursery (or seedlings from containers) in early spring. Set the roots in the ground with the buds just above the soil surface. Space the plants 4 to 6 feet apart in rows 6 to 8 feet apart. Keep the planting bed moist until growth starts.

Care

Mulch when the plants are 6 to 8 inches tall. Side-dress every 3 to 4 weeks with 3 tablespoons of 5-10-10 or its equivalent around each plant.

Cut the plants back to the ground in the fall. In cooler areas, cut the plants back to 15 to 20 inches above ground, bend the stalks over, mulch heavily with leaves, and secure them with a rain-proof tarp or basket.

Harvesting

Harvest buds, or artichokes, when they are green, unopened, and about the size of an orange. Cut with 1 to 2 inches of stem.

Other Vegetable Sources

Most are widely available except watercress (6, 35, 47), salsify (6, 9), and globe artichoke (109, 129). Some catalogs may list mustard with herbs.

Vegetable Insects and Diseases

Insect and disease problems are sure to confront most gardeners sooner or later. Luckily, while there are many possibilities for problems, relatively few of them occur in a particular garden. Well-watered, well-fed plants will be less susceptible to pests and diseases, and good garden sanitation will go a long way toward keeping the garden trouble-free.

Monitor weather conditions to head off potential problems; a long stretch of rainy weather encourages the growth of many fungus diseases, while a hot, dry spell may lead to a spider mite explosion. Keep a vigilant eye on your plants when conditions that promote a pest or disease are present. It's much easier to nip a whitefly infestation early or prevent the spread of a fungus disease than to deal with a full-blown infestation or infection.

Insects

The array of sizes, shapes, colors, and life cycles in the insect world is mind-boggling. But despite their diversity, most insects cause damage in one of three ways: by chewing on plants, sucking out their sap, or spreading disease.

Most insect life cycles can be divided into two broad categories. In one, insects go through a complete metamorphosis; that is, the immature stages look completely different from the adult insect. An egg hatches into a larva (plural: larvae). The larva feeds for a period of time, then changes into a pupa (plural: pupae), a resting stage during which the insect changes into an adult with a completely different form. A classic example of an insect with this type of life cycle is the butterfly.

In the second category, insects go through a series of gradual changes before reaching adulthood. In their early stage these insects are called nymphs. They look like adults, only smaller and perhaps different in color.

Although just one stage of the life cycle of an insect may damage plants, you may need to control another. For example, leaf miners are the larval stage of certain flies. The adult flies do no direct damage but, since their maggots feed inside the leaf, safe from pesticides, the only control is to kill the adult flies or prevent them from laying eggs.

Not all stages of the life cycle are equally susceptible to pesticides. The egg and nymphal or pupal stages are often resistant. If you are spraying for whiteflies, you may kill any adult flies present, but not the eggs and nymphs. You will have to spray at intervals to catch the survivors as they reach a susceptible stage.

An insect may have more than one generation each year, which means you'll need to maintain your vigilance longer, perhaps throughout the entire season. For specific information on the life cycle and number of generations per year, refer to the individual pest descriptions that follow.

Diseases

Disease-causing organisms in plants are divided into a number of broad categories: fungi, bacteria, viruses, nematodes, mycoplasmas, and viroids. Many kinds of fungi produce spores, minute pieces of fungal tissue that are carried to plants by wind, water, soil, insects, or contaminated tools. Bacteria spread by similar means. Viruses are often carried by sucking insects as they feed. Chemical fungicides can be used to control the spread of fungus diseases. Other diseases, such as many bacterial diseases, viruses, and mycoplasmas, have no chemical controls and must be kept in check with cultural and other nonchemical controls or by controlling the insects that carry them from plant to plant.

Controlling Insect and Disease Problems

For many gardeners, a combination of chemical and nonchemical controls works best to keep plants thriving. Some gardeners choose not to use any chemical pesticides at all. One can often have a healthy, productive garden without resorting to chemical sprays, but it does take more effort in some cases. For example, hand-picking Colorado potato beetles daily is more labor-intensive than spraying periodically.

To decide which pest control method and which pesticide to use for a particular problem, start with the least toxic control strategy. Read through the descriptions of the individual problems to get an idea of which insects and diseases are most likely to be problems in your area. Prevention is the best way to control pests whenever possible. Try nonchemical controls if you can. If these are not sufficient, then move on to chemical controls, choosing the least toxic pesticides recommended.

Nonchemical solutions include physical methods (putting up barriers around plants, traps, destroying diseased plants), planting resistant varieties when available, and cultural controls such as good sanitation.

Practice good housekeeping in your garden. Don't work among your plants when they are wet to avoid inadvertently spreading disease-causing organisms from plant to plant. Water plants early in the day so the foliage is dry before nightfall. Clean up all plant debris in the garden at the end of the season and keep weeds down in and around the garden. Both can harbor insects, eggs, or diseases that can spread to your vegetables and fruits. Don't compost obviously infected or infested plant material.

You can try biological controls such as releasing or encouraging beneficial insects and parasites and the use of microbial insecticides such as *Bacillus thuringiensis* and milky spore disease powder, which cause disease only in the specific target pests (in the case of *Bt*, caterpillars; in the case of milky spore, Japanese beetle grubs). These types of insecticides are very safe to use because their effects are so specific.

Chemical controls in general are referred to as pesticides, those that control insects are called insecticides, those that inhibit the growth of fungi, fungicides. Other terms you may run across include miticides (to kill mites), bactericides or antibiotics (to kill bacteria), and fumigants (poisonous gases that kill a wide range of organisms). Plant-based insecticides such as rotenone, sabadilla, ryania, and pyrethrum are less toxic than many synthetic pesticides and generally break down quickly after they have been applied. Insecticidal soaps are quite safe to use and are effective against a number of pests.

Pesticides come in many forms, including dusts, powders or liquids that are diluted with water and sprayed on plants, and granules. The equipment used to apply dusts is often less expensive than a sprayer to apply liquids, but it may be easier to cover the plant thoroughly with a spray. Granular forms are useful for mixing into the soil.

Most fungicides act as protectants to keep infections from getting started. An established infection cannot be cured, but it can be prevented from spreading. This is why it is important to begin applying a fungicide at the very first sign of disease and make repeat applications at the recommended intervals as long as the weather is favorable for the spread of the disease. This protective barrier must be maintained intact over the susceptible parts of the plant to keep new infections from beginning. If a heavy rain occurs soon after you have sprayed a plant with a fungicide, you may need to make a repeat application sooner than usual to renew the fungicidal barrier.

You'll notice that we do not usually recommend any specific pesticides. Pesticides are carefully regulated by the government. Their registrations — what pesticides can be used on what plants to control particular insect and disease problems — may vary from state to state and from year to year. No matter what you read in a book, hear from a neighbor, or are told by a garden store clerk, the only legal way to apply a pesticide is according to the directions on the label.

Use the following section to identify problems and time controls. Then go to your local garden store and *read labels* to find out what specific products can be used to control the insect or disease that is causing trouble in your garden. Your county Extension Service agent can make specific recommendations for current pesticides.

Many pesticides have both trade and generic names. For example, Ortho Vegetable Disease Control contains the fungicide chlorothalonil. Sevin is the trade name for the insecticide carbaryl. The generic name is listed as the active ingredient on the pesticide label. Some products may contain several different pesticides. All of them will be listed as active ingredients on the pesticide label.

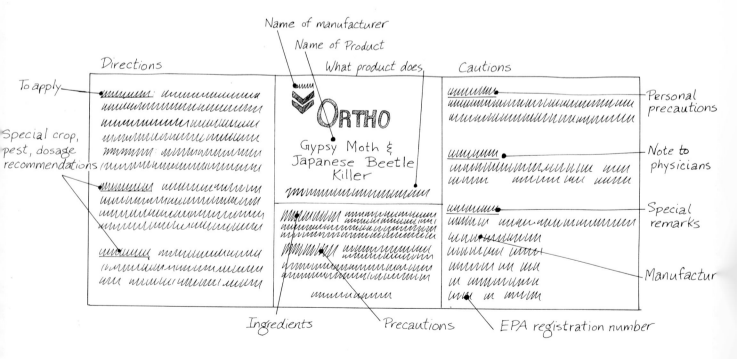

Using Pesticides Safely

If you follow two basic rules, you'll probably never go wrong. First, read the entire label before using any pesticide and follow directions exactly; second, use common sense. Most pesticides are poisons and should be treated with respect. The label will tell you the toxicity rating of the pesticide (see box) and recommend specific precautions where necessary.

For safe use, we recommend that you:

1. Mix pesticides outdoors, if possible, in a well-ventilated spot. Always wear rubber gloves; make sure there are no holes in them. When mixing a powder with water or applying a dust, avoid inhaling it; the best advice is to wear a dust mask. An unmixed powder or undiluted liquid is more concentrated than a prepared spray; be especially careful handling it. Wear long pants, a long-sleeved shirt, and leather or rubber shoes when applying pesticides.

2. Avoid getting the pesticide on your skin, in your eyes or mouth, or inhaling it. If any of these happen, follow the first aid instructions on the label. If you have any doubts about proper treatment, contact your local poison control center. Don't eat, drink, or smoke while applying pesticides. Wash the clothes you wore in hot water after each use.

3. Be sure to observe any waiting period listed on the label — the amount of time to wait between the last application of a pesticide and harvest — to make sure that no harmful residues remain on the crop.

4. Many insecticides are harmful to bees, especially carbaryl (Sevin), diazinon, and malathion. Avoid spraying plants in bloom, if possible, or spray in the evening after bees have stopped flying.

5. Store pesticides safely out of reach of children and pets. Keep them in their original containers with labels intact. Store away from food or animal feed.

6. Buy only the amount of pesticide you need for one season, if possible. Mark containers with the date of purchase. Most pesticides have a shelf life of at least 2 years. Store containers away from light, moisture, and excessive heat (over 100°F) and (for liquids) freezing temperatures. Even if a pesticide is old and no longer fully active against its target pests, it is still a toxic waste. Don't dump it down the drain or toss it in the trash. Contact your county Extension Service agent or state environmental agency to find out the recommended way to dispose of a particular product.

7. Dispose of empty pesticide containers properly. Don't reuse them for *any* purpose. Rinse out the containers three times; dispose of the rinse water by using it to mix up your last batch of spray. Wrap empty containers in several thicknesses of newspaper and put in the trash.

Explanation of Signal Words

Signal Word	Degree of Toxicity
Caution	Low toxicity or relatively free from danger; it would take from an ounce to more than a pint to kill an adult human.
Warning	Moderately toxic; one to three teaspoons can kill an adult human.
Danger	Extremely toxic; less than a teaspoon can kill an adult human.

Vegetable Insects

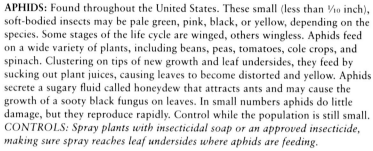

APHIDS: Found throughout the United States. These small (less than ¹⁄₁₀ inch), soft-bodied insects may be pale green, pink, black, or yellow, depending on the species. Some stages of the life cycle are winged, others wingless. Aphids feed on a wide variety of plants, including beans, peas, tomatoes, cole crops, and spinach. Clustering on tips of new growth and leaf undersides, they feed by sucking out plant juices, causing leaves to become distorted and yellow. Aphids secrete a sugary fluid called honeydew that attracts ants and may cause the growth of a sooty black fungus on leaves. In small numbers aphids do little damage, but they reproduce rapidly. Control while the population is still small.
CONTROLS: Spray plants with insecticidal soap or an approved insecticide, making sure spray reaches leaf undersides where aphids are feeding.

ASPARAGUS BEETLE: Found throughout the United States. Adult beetles are ¼ inch long. Larvae are greenish-gray, hump-backed grubs with dark heads. Adult beetles emerge in early spring to lay numerous shiny, black eggs on spears; eggs hatch out into larvae in about a week. Both adults and larvae feed on developing spears, and later in the season, on ferny foliage. There are two to five generations per year, depending on the part of the country.
CONTROLS: Spray with an approved pesticide at the first sign of infestation, making repeat applications as needed. Spray ferns in late summer or early fall to kill overwintering beetles. Clean up plant debris and trash in the garden to reduce the possibility of beetles overwintering.

CABBAGE LOOPER: Found throughout the United States. Loopers are the larvae of night-flying moths. The 1¼-inch-long caterpillars double up their bodies into loops as they push themselves along; hence, their name. Ragged holes chewed in the leaves of cabbages, broccoli, Brussels sprouts, and cauliflower are the first signs that these caterpillars are at work. Later in the season, they bore into developing heads. Loopers can also attack lettuce, spinach, beets, peas, celery, parsley, potatoes, and tomatoes. There may be three to four generations per year.
CONTROLS: Spray with Bacillus thuringiensis *when loopers are small. Be sure to direct spray to leaf undersides. Cover plants with netting to prevent moths from laying eggs.*

CABBAGE ROOT MAGGOT: Primarily found in northern parts of the country. The adult fly lays eggs in the soil at the base of the stem. White, legless maggots, ⅓ inch long, hatch and feed inside the roots. Root maggots attack all cole crops, as well as turnips and radishes. Infested plants are stunted and lack vigor and may wilt during the heat of the day. Damage is usually greatest in spring, early summer, and fall, when the weather is cool and moist. There are two to three generations per year.
CONTROLS: Place mats around the base of transplants to prevent flies from laying eggs. Dust around the base of the plant with diatomaceous earth or cover plants with netting to prevent egg-laying. Drench the soil with an approved insecticide before planting or transplanting.

COLORADO POTATO BEETLE: Most commonly found in the eastern half of the country. These ⅜-inch-long beetles feed on the leaves and stems of potatoes, tomatoes, eggplant, and peppers. Their fat, soft-bodied, hump-backed larvae, red with two rows of black dots down each side, are equally voracious feeders. The adult beetles overwinter in the soil, emerging in the spring to lay yellow egg clusters on leaf undersides. There are one to three generations per year, depending on the part of the country.
CONTROLS: A thick organic mulch makes it hard for emerging beetles to reach plants in spring. Hand-pick beetles and larvae and crush egg clusters. Sprinkle wet plants with bran; beetles eat bran, which expands inside their bodies, killing them. Apply approved insecticides.

CORN EARWORM: Found throughout the United States. This 1½-inch caterpillar with alternating light and dark stripes may be green, pink, or brown. In spring, yellow eggs are laid on leaf undersides by a night-flying moth. This first generation of caterpillars feeds on the leaves. Eggs of later generations are laid on the silks; the emerging caterpillars feed on the silks and the kernels at the tip of the ear, just inside the husk. The earworm attacks a variety of plants, including tomatoes, beans, peas, peppers, potatoes, and squash.
CONTROLS: Apply Bacillus thuringiensis *before caterpillars enter ears or fruits. Squirt half a medicine dropper of mineral oil into the tip of each ear after the silks have wilted and begun to turn brown (any earlier may interfere with pollination). Plow garden in fall to kill overwintering pupae.*

CORN ROOTWORM: There are two types of rootworms. The northern rootworm is a pest mainly in the upper Midwest; adult beetles are greenish-yellow, ¼ inch long. The southern rootworm is the same as the spotted cucumber beetle (see cucumber beetle entry) and is found all over the United States east of the Rockies. White worms, ½ to ¾ inch long, tunnel into and feed on the roots of corn plants, making them stunted, yellow, and unstable. Adult beetles feed on silks, pollen, tassels, and occasionally, leaves.
CONTROLS: Rotate corn crops in the garden. Apply an approved insecticide to the soil at planting time to control worms and one to the tops of plants to control adults. Keep down nearby weeds.

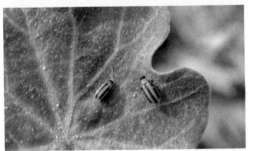

CUCUMBER BEETLE: Found throughout the United States. These ¼-inch-long, striped or spotted beetles are a triple threat to all cucurbits. The adult beetles feed on leaves, the white, wormlike larvae feed underground on the roots, and the adult beetles carry two serious cucurbit diseases — bacterial wilt and mosaic virus. Adults overwinter on weeds and plant debris, emerging in early spring. In the North there is only one generation per year; in the South there may be two or more.
CONTROLS: Dust plants with approved insecticides as soon as they are set out or emerge from the soil, or at the first signs of beetle damage. Make repeat applications weekly as needed. Cover young plants with netting to keep beetles away. Clean up plant debris and nearby weeds at the end of the season.

CUTWORM: Various species are found throughout the United States. The larvae of night-flying moths that lay their eggs in the soil, cutworms feed at night, hiding in the soil during the day. They curl up tightly like a spring when disturbed. These pests chew through the stems of young seedlings at or just below ground level. There are also climbing cutworms that feed on leaves, buds, and fruits. Damage is usually most severe on plants set out early in the season, such as cabbage family members, tomatoes, and peppers, although they can attack just about all garden vegetables.
CONTROLS: Make cutworm barriers for transplants. Sprinkle wood ashes or diatomaceous earth around the base of plants to discourage egg-laying by adults. Spray with Bacillus thuringiensis.

EARWIG: Found all over the United States. These reddish-brown, 1-inch-long nocturnal creatures feed primarily on decaying organic matter or other insects, hiding in dark, damp places during the day. When their populations are high, they may cause damage in the garden by feeding on a variety of plants such as lettuce, corn, celery, tender young seedlings, and blossoms and ripening fruits. *CONTROLS: Trap earwigs by filling a flowerpot with crumpled paper. Invert it in the garden propped up with a stick. Earwigs will crawl into the paper during the day to hide, at which point they can be destroyed.*

EUROPEAN CORN BORER: Common everywhere except for the far West and Southwest. After overwintering as caterpillars in old corn stalks, adult moths emerge in early summer. Clusters of white eggs laid on leaf undersides hatch into caterpillars that chew small holes in leaves and feed on tassels. Later they bore into the stalk and the base of the ear. There is usually one generation per year in the North; in the South there may be several and the borer is more likely to infest other crops, such as tomatoes, potatoes, and peppers, along with corn. *CONTROLS: Pull out or plow under old stalks after harvest. Make a slit in the stalk and remove the borer. Apply an approved insecticide to the shoots and centers of leaf whorls at the first sign of infestation.*

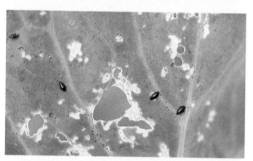

FLEA BEETLE: Various species found throughout the United States. These tiny, 1/16-inch-long beetles feed on leaves, riddling them with small "shotholes." They jump rapidly when disturbed, like fleas; hence, their name. Various species feed on just about any plant in the garden, including eggplant, tomatoes, cabbage, corn, potatoes, spinach, peppers, and sweet potatoes. Adult beetles can spread diseases such as early blight to potatoes or bacterial wilt to corn, and larvae feed on roots. Adults overwinter in the soil and on garden debris, emerging in early spring. Beetles can destroy small plants rapidly with their feeding. *CONTROLS: Control them promptly. Use garlic and hot pepper sprays, diatomaceous earth/pyrethrum blends, or other approved insecticides, making repeat applications as needed. Clean up garden debris at the end of the season.*

IMPORTED CABBAGEWORM: Found throughout the United States. The cabbageworm is the larval stage of a white, day-flying butterfly with three to four black spots on its wings. Caterpillars may get 1½ inches long. The damage done by these caterpillars is similar to that of the cabbage looper — large, ragged holes are chewed in the leaves of cabbages, broccoli, Brussels sprouts, and cauliflower, and the caterpillars may bore into the heads, leaving trails of dark green frass. There are several generations per year. *CONTROLS: Spray with* Bacillus thuringiensis *when caterpillars are small. Be sure to spray leaf undersides where they are feeding. Cover plants with netting to prevent moths from laying eggs on plants.*

JAPANESE BEETLE: Found primarily in the eastern half of the country. Female beetles lay eggs in the soil in late summer. White, C-shaped grubs hatch and feed on the roots of grasses. Adult beetles emerge a year later in late spring or early summer. These beautiful, ½-inch-long beetles are extremely destructive, feeding voraciously on a wide variety of plants, including beans, asparagus, rhubarb, okra, and the leaves and silks of sweet corn. They chew out the leaf tissue between the veins, leaving a lacy skeleton. *CONTROLS: Use an approved insecticide. Adults can fly up to 5 miles. To control new invasions, spray at 10-day intervals. Treat sod areas with milky spore disease powder to control grubs. Set up scent traps away from the plants you are trying to protect.*

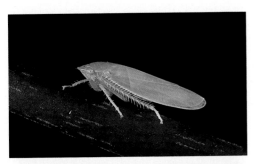

LEAFHOPPER: Different species found all over the United States. These tiny, ⅛-inch-long, wedge-shaped insects fly or hop away quickly when disturbed. They feed on a variety of plants, including beans, beets, and potatoes, by sucking out the plant's juices, weakening the plants and causing leaves to become stippled, yellow, and distorted. Leafhoppers may also transmit diseases from plant to plant, such as aster yellows and viruses. Eggs are laid on leaf undersides of vegetable plants and nearby perennial weeds.
CONTROLS: Get rid of nearby perennial weeds such as thistles, plantains, and dandelions that may harbor leafhopper eggs. Spray leaf undersides with approved insecticides. Dust plants with diatomaceous earth.

LEAF MINER: Found throughout the United States. Irregular, winding trails or blisters within the leaf tissue (called "mines") are signs that leaf miners are at work. The larval stage of certain flies, these tiny maggots tunnel through the inner layers of the leaf to feed. If you peel away the papery top layer of the mined area, you'll see black specks of maggot excrement inside. Various species of leaf miners attack a number of plants, including beets, spinach, lettuce, peppers, and potatoes. Adult flies lay eggs inside leaf tissue or on leaf undersides.
CONTROLS: Once miners are inside leaves, they are safe from applied insecticides. Approved sprays should be applied to control adult flies during the egg-laying period. Pick and destroy infested leaves.

MEXICAN BEAN BEETLE: This relative of the ladybug is found throughout the United States. The adult beetle is about ¼ inch long, with sixteen black spots on its back. Larvae are fat, hump-backed, spiny, yellow grubs about ⅓ inch long. Both adults and larvae feed on foliage, leaving a skeleton of veins. Adults overwinter on plant debris, emerging in late spring or early summer to lay clusters of yellow eggs on leaf undersides. There are one to four generations per year.
CONTROLS: Hand-pick adult beetles and larvae. Crush egg clusters on leaf undersides. Spray with an approved pesticide. Clean up plant debris in the garden at the end of the season to reduce the number of overwintering adults.

ONION MAGGOT: A problem mainly in the northern part of the country. This ⅓-inch-long maggot burrows into the underground part of the stem of young onion plants or into the developing bulb of larger onions. After overwintering as pupae in the soil, adult flies emerge in late spring to lay eggs at the base of young onion plants. There may be three generations per year. The last generation often attacks onions just before they are harvested, causing many to rot in storage. Cool, wet weather favors the maggots.
CONTROLS: Dust soil around onions with wood ashes or diatomaceous earth to discourage adult flies from laying eggs. Treat soil at planting time with an approved insecticide. Clean up plant debris at the end of the season to reduce the number of overwintering insects.

PICKLEWORM: Found mainly in the southeastern United States. These ¾-inch-long caterpillars feed on the blossoms, stems, and, later, developing fruits of summer squash, cucumbers, and muskmelons. The adult moths emerge in spring after overwintering as pupae in semitropical areas such as southern Florida. They migrate northward to lay eggs on leaves, buds, stems, and fruits of susceptible plants. There may be four or more generations per year.
CONTROLS: After harvest, pull up and destroy vines, leftover fruits, and nearby weeds in areas where the insect overwinters. Plant early, if possible, to harvest crops before late summer, when damage is usually greatest. Spray with approved insecticides, making repeat applications as necessary.

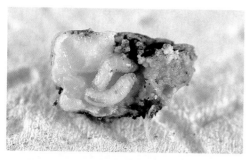

SEED CORN MAGGOT: Found all over the United States. This ¼-inch-long maggot burrows into the seeds of corn, peas, and beans. Seeds may never sprout or, if they do, plants are stunted and weak. The adult flies lay eggs in the soil in early spring. There are three to five generations per year in most parts of the country. Cool, wet soil encourages this insect.
CONTROLS: Plant seeds shallowly in warm, well-prepared soil so that seeds germinate quickly before maggots get to them. Flies are attracted to soils high in organic matter. If maggots are a problem, add manure in the fall rather than the spring. Treat seeds with an approved insecticide before planting.

SLUGS: Found throughout the United States. Not true insects, these pests are mollusks, related to shellfish. They feed on a wide variety of plants, chewing large, ragged holes in leaves, fruits, and stems. Other signs that slugs are at work include trails of slime on leaves and soil near plants. Slugs feed at night.
CONTROLS: Set out old shingles, boards, and cabbage leaves in the garden. Slugs will crawl under these for shelter during the day; check traps in the morning to collect and destroy them. Set out shallow pans of stale beer in the garden; slugs will crawl in and drown. Sprinkle wood ashes, lime, or sand around the edge of the garden; slugs don't like to crawl across rough particles. Make 2-inch-high protective barriers of metal or screen bent out at an angle.

SPIDER MITES: Found throughout the United States. These tiny, pin-head-size pests are not true insects, but are closely related to spiders. They attack many kinds of plants, feeding on leaf undersides by sucking out the plant's juices, causing leaves to become stippled, yellow, and dry. Fine webbing may run between leaves and across leaf undersides. If you suspect mites, hold a piece of white paper under a leaf, tap the leaf sharply, and see if any reddish specks fall to the paper. Mites are encouraged by hot, dry conditions. They reproduce rapidly and there are many generations per year.
CONTROLS: Spray plants with a forceful spray of water to knock mites from leaves. Spray leaf undersides with insecticidal soap or other approved insecticide; repeat at least three times at 5- to 7-day intervals.

SQUASH BUG: Found throughout the United States. Adult beetles are flat-backed, brown, about ½ inch long; the immature nymphs look like small adults but are whitish with black legs. This insect attacks all kinds of cucurbits, but is usually most severe on squashes and pumpkins. Adults and nymphs feed by sucking out the juices from leaves, causing leaves to wilt, dry up, and turn black. Adults overwinter under plant debris or in the soil. They emerge usually about the time vines begin to "run" to lay clusters of reddish-brown eggs on leaf undersides. There is one generation per year.
CONTROLS: Lay shingles or boards in the garden at night; bugs will hide under them during the day. Collect and destroy hiding bugs first thing in the morning. Crush egg clusters.

SQUASH VINE BORER: Found east of the Rockies. The adult moth lays its eggs on the stems near the base of the plant in late spring to early summer. Fat, white caterpillars with brown heads hatch out and tunnel into the stems to feed, causing sudden wilting of all or part of a squash vine. If the stem of the wilted vine is cut open lengthwise, it will be filled with sawdustlike frass and often one or more caterpillars. The borer attacks squashes primarily, but will occasionally infest cucumbers and melons as well. In the Deep South there may be two generations per year; in the North, only one.
CONTROLS: Spray with an approved insecticide during the egg-laying period; direct spray to base of plant. Slit open wilted vines and take out borer; cover cut with moist soil to encourage the vine to reroot.

STINKBUGS: Various species of this pest are found throughout the United States; they are more common in the South. Stinkbugs are shield-shaped, about ⅝ inch long, and may be green, brown, or bluish-gray. They give off an unpleasant odor when crushed. Stinkbugs feed on okra, squash, beans, tomatoes, and a number of other plants by sucking out the plant's juices. New shoots may wilt; fruits are distorted with hard, dimpled areas where mouth parts are inserted into them. Adults overwinter in garden debris and in nearby weedy areas. There are several generations per year.
CONTROLS: Spray or dust with approved insecticides. Keep weeds down around the graden. Clean up the garden at the end of the season. Hand-pick early in the morning when bugs are slow to escape.

SWEET POTATO WEEVIL: A problem in the southern United States. Sweet potato roots and vines are tunneled through by ⅓-inch-long, white, legless grubs with dark heads. The adult weevil, a ¼-inch-long antlike insect with a long snout, feeds on the tops of the plant, but usually does little damage. Eggs are laid in cavities in the potato or on the vine near the soil surface. Weevils overwinter in stored sweet potatoes or on nearby weeds such as wild morning glory. There may be as many as eight generations per year.
CONTROLS: When buying slips or seed potatoes, make sure they are certified weevil-free. Mound soil around the base of stems to make it difficult for larvae to enter roots. Clean up all weeds and leftover sweet potatoes at the end of the season. Rotate crops.

TOMATO HORNWORM: Found throughout the United States. These large (up to 5 inches long), fat caterpillars feed voraciously on the leaves and fruits of tomatoes, peppers, eggplants, and potatoes. Adults are rather spectacular sphinx moths, grayish-brown with orange spots on the body and a 4- to 5-inch wing span. After overwintering in the soil in 2-inch, brown, spindle-shaped pupal cases, moths emerge in late spring to early summer to lay greenish-yellow eggs on leaf undersides. Caterpillars feed for about a month, then go into the soil to pupate. There is one generation per year in the North; two or more in the South.
CONTROLS: Use Bacillus thuringiensis when caterpillars are small. Hand-pick (caterpillars cannot sting with their "horn").

WHITEFLIES: Found throughout the United States. These tiny, 1/12-inch-long insects feed in large numbers on leaf undersides of tomatoes, cucumbers, lettuce, and other plants by sucking out plant juices. They secrete a sticky, sugary substance called honeydew that may cause the growth of a sooty black fungus on leaves. Eggs laid on leaf undersides hatch into larvae that look like flat, oval, semitransparent scales, which change into adult flies in about a month.
CONTROLS: Spray with insecticidal soap or other approved insecticides. Make at least two repeat sprays at weekly intervals since different stages of the life cycle are not susceptible to insecticides. Whiteflies cannot survive freezing temperatures; in northern gardens they are reintroduced on infected plants each spring. Check purchased plants carefully before setting in the garden.

WIREWORMS: Found throughout the United States. These jointed, hard-shelled worms that may be up to 1½ inches long feed on the underground stems, roots, seeds, and tubers of a wide variety of plants, including corn, potatoes, beets, carrots, and sweet potatoes. They are generally more of a problem on land that has recently been in sod. The adult beetle is brown, ½ inch long. It lays eggs in the soil in spring. The worms may take from 2 to 6 years to reach the adult stage, depending on the species.
CONTROLS: Spear pieces of potato on a stick and bury them 2 to 4 inches deep in the garden. Dig up the pieces after a week and destroy them, along with the wireworms that are feeding inside. Set the potato traps at 3- to 10-foot intervals. Treat the soil with an approved insecticide before planting.

Vegetable Diseases

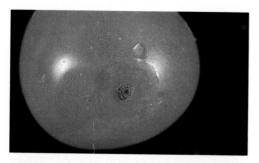

ANTHRACNOSE: This fungus occurs mainly in the eastern part of the country. Beans develop round, black, sunken spots on pods and stems. Veins on leaf undersides turn black. Cucumber and muskmelon leaves develop yellow spots that dry up and fall out; spots on watermelon leaves are black. Infected fruits are covered with sunken spots with dark borders. Tomatoes develop sunken spots on ripe fruits, the central parts of which turn dark. Wet weather encourages the disease to spread. The fungus overwinters in plant residues in the soil.
CONTROLS: Apply an approved fungicide every 7 to 10 days when weather conditions are favorable for disease spread. Don't work with plants while they are wet. Rotate crops yearly. Keep ripening fruits out of contact with soil.

ASTER YELLOWS: This disease, caused by a mycoplasma, affects carrots over most of the United States and lettuce over most of the country except for the Southwest. The inner leaves of carrot tops are stunted and yellow, the outer leaves reddish at their margins. The taproot is stunted and "hairy," with many fine side roots. The inner leaves of lettuce are stunted, curled, and yellow; the lettuce may fail to form a head. Aster yellows is spread from plant to plant by leafhoppers as they feed.
CONTROLS: Control leafhoppers (see page 279). Mow nearby weeds in which the disease can overwinter and which may host leafhopper eggs.

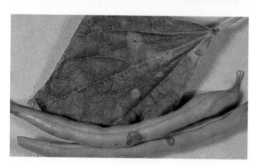

BACTERIAL BLIGHT: Found over most of the United States. Several different bacterial blights can infect both snap and lima beans. Leaves of plants infected with halo blight (pictured here) have many small dead spots with yellow halos around them. Spots on pods produce a cream-colored ooze when the weather is humid. Cool, wet weather promotes the spread of this disease. Common blight causes large, water-soaked, light green spots on leaves that later turn brown. Water-soaked spots appear on pods and may produce a yellowish ooze in wet weather. Brown spot blight, more common on limas, causes small, reddish-brown spots with distinct margins on leaves and pods.
CONTROLS: Use a 3-year crop rotation for beans. Don't work in the garden when plants are wet. Don't save seeds from infected plants.

BACTERIAL SPOT: Found mainly in eastern parts of the country. This bacterial disease affects tomatoes and peppers. Small, dark, corky, raised spots with slightly sunken centers appear on green fruits. Rot organisms may enter at the spots and decay the fruit. Infected blossoms drop; small, dark spots form on leaves, which yellow and drop. This defoliation weakens plants and exposes developing fruits to sunscald. Very warm, wet weather encourages the development of the disease. The fungus overwinters in plant residues in the soil.
CONTROLS: Apply an approved fungicide every 10 to 14 days as long as weather is favorable for disease spread. Destroy infected fruits. Keep plants well watered and fertilized. Use a 3- to 4-year crop rotation. Avoid overhead watering.

BACTERIAL WILT: This disease occurs over most of the United States. It affects cucumbers and muskmelons and, not as commonly, pumpkins and squash. Individual leaves wilt during the heat of the day, but recover overnight initially. Later all or part of the vine wilts and dies. To test for the disease, cut a wilted stem near the base of the plant. Squeeze the sap out of the stem. If it is sticky and white and forms a thread when the tip of a knife is touched to it and drawn away, bacterial wilt is probably present. (This test works best with cucumbers.) This disease is spread by cucumber beetles as they feed; the fungus overwinters in their bodies.
CONTROLS: Control the cucumber beetles that spread this disease (see page 277).

BLACK ROT: This bacterial disease affects all members of the cabbage family over most of the United States, but is more common in the East. Infected young seedlings turn yellow and die. On older plants, yellow, wedge-shaped areas occur at the leaf edges and spread toward the center of the leaf. The veins within this dead tissue turn black. Older leaves at the base of the plant are affected first. Sometimes symptoms occur mainly on one side of the plant at first. As the disease progresses, the head may begin to rot. It is spread by insects, splashing water, and contaminated tools. Warm, humid weather encourages this disease, which can persist on residues in the soil for 2 years.
CONTROLS: Destroy infected plants. Avoid wetting the tops of plants when watering. Use a 2-year crop rotation between susceptible plants.

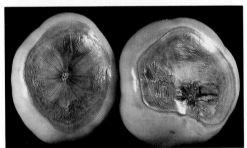

BLOSSOM END ROT: This physiological disorder of tomatoes, peppers, and cucurbits is caused by a calcium imbalance within the plant. If there are large fluctuations in soil moisture, if the soil is excessively wet or dry or high in salts, the roots cannot take up enough calcium. The result is a water-soaked spot at the blossom end of the plant that enlarges, turning dark brown and leathery. Rot may set in at the spot. Blossom end rot is common when plants grow rapidly in the beginning of the season, then set fruit during dry weather.
CONTROLS: Keep plants uniformly watered throughout the season. Water deeply; wet the soil at least 6 inches down. Use a mulch to conserve water during hot weather.

CATFACING AND GROWTH CRACKS: Catfacing is a tomato disorder that causes fruits to become distorted and puckered; bands of tan scar tissue run across the surface. Symptoms are often most pronounced at the blossom end. Catfacing occurs when conditions such as cold weather (below 55°F), hot weather (above 85°F), or drought interfere with flower and fruit development. Growth cracks are circular cracks in the skin of tomato fruits at the stem end. Rot may set in at the cracks or they may heal over with corky, brown tissue. It is often more of a problem when weather is wet or plants are watered heavily as the fruits ripen, especially after a period of dry weather.
CONTROLS: Keep plants uniformly watered throughout the growing season. Choose crack-resistant varieties.

CLUBROOT: This fungus disease occurs on all members of the cabbage family everywhere in the United States. Plants wilt during the heat of the day and recover at night, older leaves yellow and drop, roots become swollen and distorted, and the plants are stunted and may eventually die. The disease-causing fungus can live in the soil for many years. Acid soil and warm, moist weather encourage the disease.
CONTROLS: There is no way to cure infected plants. To protect new plantings, keep the soil pH above 7.2, protect transplants with an approved fungicide drench when they are set out, and use at least a 7-year rotation between susceptible crops, if possible.

CORN LEAF BLIGHTS, NORTHERN AND SOUTHERN: Northern corn leaf blight causes large (½-inch by up to 6-inch) grayish-green to tan spots on corn leaves. Southern corn leaf blight causes small (½-inch by ¼-inch) tan spots with reddish-brown borders on the leaves. Corn leaf blights occur in the eastern part of the country. The infection does not usually kill the plant, but weakens it, making it more susceptible to other diseases. Young plants are most susceptible. These blights are favored by warm, wet weather. The fungus overwinters on infected plant debris in the soil.
CONTROLS: Spray with an approved fungicide every 7 days as needed. Clean up garden debris at the end of the season. Plant tolerant varieties.

CORN SMUT: This fungus disease occurs on corn over most of the United States. It can infect any aboveground part of the plant, causing galls that are white and spongy when young, which later become gray-brown and filled with powdery spores. Spores are spread by wind and splashing water. Hot, dry weather encourages the development of the disease, which is more common on younger plants.

CONTROLS: *There are no chemical controls. Cut off the galls as soon as you notice them, before the masses of spores are released. Clean up all plant debris in the garden at the end of the season. Grow tolerant varieties.*

CROWN ROT: This fungus disease is a problem mainly in the northcentral and northeast states. Sunken spots form on the crown and the bases of stems, leaves wilt and turn yellow, and stalks collapse and die. The fungus thrives in warm temperatures and heavy, poorly drained soil.

CONTROLS: *Destroy infected plants. Drench the base of the plant with an approved fungicide. Plant in well-drained soil.*

DAMPING OFF: This fungus disease attacks seeds and seedlings of all kinds of plants all over the United States. Plants may never emerge from the soil if seeds or seedlings just beginning to germinate and grow are infected. Young seedlings that have emerged from the soil are susceptible until they are a couple of inches high. Seedlings topple over and die suddenly. The base of the stem near the soil line is pinched and shriveled. The fungi that cause damping off are common in most soils, but they cause problems only if the soil is overly wet.

CONTROLS: *Plant in well-drained soil and don't overwater. Dust seeds with an approved fungicide before planting. When starting seeds indoors, use a pasteurized soil mix (see page 44).*

DOWNY MILDEW: Various types of downy mildew fungi cause disease in a number of plants all over the United States. Irregular brown or yellow spots develop on the upper leaf surface; the lower leaf surface beneath these spots is covered with a hairy white or purple mold during humid weather. Severely infected leaves die. The fungus that attacks cucumbers and muskmelons (and less frequently squash and pumpkins) occurs mainly in the East. Fruits of infected plants are small and bitter. Cabbage family members are often infected as seedlings, which rapidly yellow and die. Mature plants may have sunken black spots on their heads. Moist weather encourages the spread of this fungus.

CONTROLS: *Plant resistant varieties. Spray with an approved fungicide every 7 to 10 days. Avoid wetting tops of plants when watering.*

EARLY BLIGHT: This fungus disease attacks tomatoes and potatoes over most of the United States. Plants under stress or with a heavy load of fruit are most susceptible. Dark brown spots with concentric rings in them form on older leaves first. Infected leaves turn yellow and die. Potato tubers are covered with brown, corky spots. Tomato fruits may sometimes be infected; a black, sunken, leathery spot forms at the stem end. Warm, moist conditions encourage disease development. The fungus overwinters in plant residues in the soil.

CONTROLS: *Apply an approved fungicide every 7 to 10 days as needed. Don't wet foliage when watering. Keep plants well fertilized. Use certified disease-free seed potatoes.*

FUSARIUM WILT: This soil-borne fungus disease is most severe during hot, dry weather and is more of a problem in the warmer parts of the country. It affects tomatoes, potatoes, peppers, cucurbits, asparagus, and peas. Lower leaves turn yellow, curl and wilt during the heat of the day, recovering overnight initially. Eventually the entire plant wilts and dies. Often the wilt only affects one side of the plant at first. If you cut the stem, there will be a brown ring inside the green outer layer. The fungus persists indefinitely in the soil.
CONTROLS: Fumigate the soil before planting. Plant resistant varieties. Destroy infected plants. There are no chemical controls.

LATE BLIGHT: Found over most of the United States. This fungus disease attacks tomatoes and potatoes at any stage of growth. Irregular gray spots form on leaves. White mold grows on the undersides of these spots. Infected leaves turn brown and dry up. Gray, water-soaked spots on infected fruits later turn dark brown and corky. Infected tubers are covered with brown spots where rot begins. Wet weather with cool nights and warm days favors the spread of the disease. The fungus overwinters in infected plant debris.
CONTROLS: Spray with an approved fungicide every 7 to 10 days as long as weather is favorable for the spread of disease. Avoid overhead watering. After potato vines die at the end of the season, wait a week before digging tubers to prevent infection while digging.

LEAF SPOTS: Different fungi and bacteria cause leaf spotting on many plants throughout the United States. Spots form on leaves, which yellow and die if severely infected. Warm, humid weather can promote their development. With septoria leaf spot of tomato, common in the northeastern United States, many small brown spots with dark borders form on lower leaves first. Plants defoliated by septoria leaf spot are weakened and their developing fruits exposed to sunscald. The fungus survives in plant debris in the soil for 3 years.
CONTROLS: Remove garden debris at the end of the season, avoid overhead watering, or water in the morning so plants are dry before nightfall, and don't work in the garden when plants are wet. Consult your county Extension Service agent for help identifying and controlling specific leaf spots.

NEMATODES: Various species of these microscopic worms are found all over the United States, but they are a more severe problem in the South. They feed on the roots of a wide variety of plants, including tomatoes, celery, beans, and spinach. Infected plants are stunted, yellow, may wilt during hot, dry weather, or die if severely infected. Roots may have many small, round nodules on them, and taproots, such as carrots, may develop many small side roots. They are spread by infected soil, water, tools, and plants. Damage is similar to that caused by other stresses that injure roots; have your soil tested for nematodes.
CONTROLS: Fumigate the soil before planting. Plant resistant varieties. Keep the soil's organic matter level high to encourage nematode predators. Plant marigolds as a trap crop (see page 300).

PHOMOPSIS BLIGHT: This fungus disease infects eggplant in the eastern part of the United States. It can attack all the aboveground parts of the plant. Infected spots on young seedlings may girdle stems, killing the plant. On leaves, the fungus causes clearly defined, 1-inch, circular brown spots, the centers of which later turn gray with tiny black spots. Infected leaves turn yellow and die. Large spots may spread to cover most of an infected fruit, which is soft and watery at first, later turning dry and shriveled. The fungus is most prevalent in warm, wet weather. It overwinters on plant residues, soil, and seed, and is spread by insects, splashing water, and contaminated tools.
CONTROLS: Spray with an approved fungicide every 7 to 10 days as needed. Destroy infected plants and fruits. Use a 3-year crop rotation.

POTATO SCAB: This disease, caused by a bacterialike organism, affects potatoes all over the United States. Brown, corky areas or pits cover the outside of the tubers. Neutral and alkaline soils encourage the development of scab. Other susceptible crops include beets, turnips, carrots, rutabagas, and parsnips, although scab is usually not a serious problem on these.
CONTROLS: Plant resistant potato varieties. Keep the soil pH below 5.2 (see page 31 for information on changing soil pH). Use a 3-year rotation between susceptible crops. Avoid using fresh manure in the potato patch because it may carry scab-causing organisms.

POWDERY MILDEW: This fungus disease occurs all over the United States and infects a wide variety of plants, including beans, cucurbits, lettuce, and peas. A powdery white growth covers the upper surface of leaves, which eventually turn yellow and dry. Older leaves are usually infected first. The fungus competes with the plant for nutrients, reducing yields and weakening — or even possibly killing it — if infection is severe. Fruits and pods may also be covered with mildew. This disease usually develops late in the season on mature plants and thrives in both dry and humid weather. It can spread rapidly.
CONTROLS: Spray with an approved fungicide every 7 days as needed. Plant resistant varieties where available.

ROOT ROT: Various species of fungi cause root rots of a wide variety of plants all over the United States. Plants are stunted, yellow and wilt, especially during hot, dry weather. The roots of infected plants are black, soft, and rotting. Root rots are usually only a problem on poorly drained or overwatered soils.
CONTROLS: Prevention is the best control. Plant in well-drained soil. Let soil dry out slightly between waterings. Consult your county Extension Service agent for help identifying specific root rots; fungicide treatments may be effective in some cases.

SEPTORIA BLIGHT: Also called celery early blight, this fungus disease is a problem on celery, mainly in the East and Pacific Northwest. Yellow spots up to ½ inch in diameter appear first on older leaves. Spots later turn dark brown, with tiny black dots in the center. Infected leaves and stalks may die, as may the entire plant if conditions are cool and moist for long enough. The fungus overwinters in infected plant debris and seeds, and is spread by splashing water and contaminated tools.
CONTROLS: Spray plants with an approved fungicide every 7 to 10 days from the first sign of disease until weather is no longer favorable for its spread. Plant tolerant varieties such as Emerson Pascal. *If saving your own seeds, place in 118°F water for 30 minutes to kill fungus.*

SUNSCALD: This disorder occurs on the fruits of peppers and tomatoes when they are suddenly exposed to direct sun. Light, blistered areas form that later become sunken and covered with a papery surface. Rot may invade the scalded areas. Sunscald is most common on the green fruit of plants that have been heavily pruned or that have lost a lot of leaves due to disease.
CONTROLS: Keep plant well fed and disease-free to encourage good leaf cover. If foliage is sparse, cover plants with light netting to shade fruits. Fruits need warmth, rather than direct sun, to ripen.

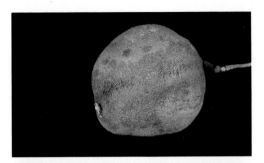

SWEET POTATO SCURF: This fungus disease affects sweet potatoes in the southern United States. It causes dark brown stains on the skins of roots. However, the flesh inside the roots is not affected and the roots are still edible. This disease is most common in poorly drained soils with a high pH and lots of organic matter. Infected roots dry out quickly in storage.
CONTROLS: Plant in well-drained soil. Keep the soil pH above 7.0. Buy certified disease-free slips or seed potatoes. Use a 3- to 4-year crop rotation. Use infected roots immediately rather than store them.

TOMATO LEAF ROLL: This is not really a disease but a disorder caused by poor environmental conditions. The edges of the older leaves on tomato plants roll up, a sign that the plant is under some kind of stress. Excessively wet soil, high temperatures, drought, or a heavy load of fruit all promote leaf curl.
CONTROLS: Once the underlying cause has been remedied, the leaf symptoms disappear with no lasting effects. Some varieties such as Floramerica, Big Boy, *and* Beefsteak *are more susceptible to leaf curl than others.*

VERTICILLIUM WILT: This soil-borne fungus occurs all over the United States, but is more common in the cooler parts of the country. It infects many plants, including eggplant, tomatoes, potatoes, peppers, and okra. Symptoms start on lower leaves, with yellowing between leaf veins and wilting. Leaves may die and drop from the plant without wilting first. Young leaves at the tip of the plant may curl up but remain green. Fruit production is poor, but usually the entire plant does not die. If you cut into the lower stem, you will find a brown ring inside the green outer layer. The fungus can persist in the soil for many years.
CONTROLS: Fumigate the soil before planting. Plant resistant varieties. Destroy infected plants. Use a 3-year rotation for susceptible crops.

VIRUSES: There are many kinds of viruses that can infect a wide variety of plants all over the United States, including beans, celery, cucurbits, peas, peppers, corn, and tomatoes. Symptoms vary with the specific virus, but include mottling, streaking, puckering, or curling of leaves. An example is mosaic virus, which infects cucurbits, causing green and yellow mottling of leaves, curled leaves, stunted plants, and fruits with light splotches and warty bumps on them. Many viruses are spread from plant to plant by sucking insects such as aphids and leafhoppers as they feed. Consult your county Extension Service for help with a specific diagnosis.
CONTROLS: Control insects that spread disease. Destroy infected plants. Choose resistant varieties when available. Buy certified virus-free seed potatoes.

WHITE MOLD: This fungus disease occurs all over the United States and can attack a wide variety of plants such as beans, lettuce, and members of the cabbage family. Symptoms on beans begin as water-soaked spots on blossoms, stems, leaves, and pods that enlarge rapidly and become covered with a cottony white mold. Infected leaves wilt, yellow, and die. Infected pods may rot. The fungus overwinters in plant residues in the soil.
CONTROLS: Destroy diseased plants as soon as you notice them. Don't wet tops of plants while watering, or water early in the day so plants are dry before nightfall. Use a 3- to 4-year crop rotation with nonsusceptible plants such as corn, beets, or spinach. To prevent infections, spray with an approved fungicide just as buds open and again a week later.

FRUITS & BERRIES

Planning Fruit Trees

Planning a small orchard of fruit trees should take more time and research than planning your vegetable garden or berry patch. Fruit trees are expensive, and they are a long-term investment. You'll be living with your choices for your orchard for quite some time.

But sufficient research and planning now will enable you to make well-considered choices of which fruits and then which varieties and rootstocks to grow. The result will be a fruit tree collection best suited for your needs and climate, and fruit tree gardening success for many years to come.

Choosing Fruit Trees

Fruit trees are a long-term investment. Don't let tempting catalog pictures and descriptions lure you into quick decisions on which ones to plant. Instead, spend some time planning. Call your county Extension Service agent to find out what weather problems and fruit diseases are troublesome in your area, and which types of fruits, varieties, and rootstocks are best adapted. Consult the planting guide on page 303 and the variety information in the individual fruit chapters. Carefully assess your soil conditions, choose the best sites in your yard for fruit trees, and sketch a landscape plan.

Consider the following questions when choosing the types of fruits and varieties you'll grow:
- Do your favorite fruits grow well in your area? Can you count on a crop almost every year, or much less often due to frequent weather problems?
- When do the varieties you're considering ripen in your area? It's nice to have fresh fruit ripening continuously from early summer to late fall.
- How will you preserve some of the harvest? Some varieties are better than others for cooking, canning, or freezing.
- How much space do you want to devote to fruit trees? Remember that fruit trees are beautiful flowering trees as well. You can plant beds of flowers and herbs underneath and around them, or *espalier* them (train them along a fence or trellis) to save space.
- How many varieties of each type of fruit do you need? Some fruits are self-pollinating so only one variety is needed; others require a second variety nearby in order to set fruit.
- How much time do you want to devote to tree care? All fruit trees require yearly pruning and some pest control, and all large fruits require some fruit thinning.
- What tree qualities are important to you? Dwarf size? Quick fruit production? Long life? Disease resistance? All these vary with the species of fruit tree, the variety, and the rootstock.

Anatomy of a Fruit Tree

Fruit tree varieties are not grown from seed because they possess a great deal of genetic variability. Only rarely do seeds of fruit tree varieties produce offspring that are identical or even similar to the tree from which the seed was taken.

Every fruit tree you buy consists of two or more different plants that were joined together by *grafting* (see box). The named variety such as a *McIntosh* apple or

How Fruit Trees Are Grafted

Grafting involves placing a *scion,* a stem section from the desired fruit variety, into close contact with the trunk of a *rootstock* tree, so the two will unite and grow together. If the scion contains several buds, the operation is termed *grafting;* if it contains just one bud, it's called *budding.* The scion is cut from the desired variety during the dormant season and kept dormant in cold storage until grafting time, so it will have a few weeks to join with the rootstock before the buds begin to grow.

The rootstock and scion are carefully cut and placed so that they fit together and their *cambium* layers match. The cambium is the layer of actively dividing cells between the bark and the wood which produces new food-conducting tissues and wood each year. The cambium is the only tissue that will grow together, producing the new tissue that is connected across the graft union.

The graft is wrapped tightly to hold it in place until the cuts have healed and the cambium layers united. Once the graft has taken and the scion buds begin to grow, the top of the rootstock is cut back. The new variety becomes the top half of the new tree. The tree then grows for a year in the nursery before it is dug and sold as a grafted fruit tree.

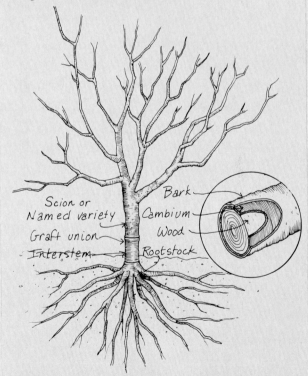

Virtually all fruit trees you buy consist of a scion, a tree top producing a named variety of fruit, grafted onto a rootstock, the root system of another tree. There may be an additional piece of stem called an interstem grafted between the scion and the rootstock. The graft union(s) appears as a scar on the trunk.

Bartlett pear is propagated by cutting a bud or stem piece from its branches, and grafting this onto a *rootstock* — a young tree, whose top is later cut off, that provides the root system for the new tree. Grafting assures that the top half of the new tree, the fruit-producing part, is exactly like the tree from which the bud or stem piece was taken, while the rootstock controls tree size and affects qualities such as cold hardiness and disease resistance.

Sometimes, an *interstem,* a stem piece of a third type of tree, is grafted between the variety and the rootstock. The interstem may be used between a rootstock and a variety that do not graft together well because of genetic differences, or it may help dwarf the tree or increase its cold hardiness.

Standard versus Dwarf Fruit Trees

A *standard* fruit tree is a variety grafted onto a rootstock of the same or a closely related species. Standard trees grow 15 to 35 feet tall depending on the species — and take up a rather large amount of yard space. The taller species — apple, pear, or sweet cherry — can double as shade trees, which can be an advantage if you have the space. You'll need a ladder to prune and harvest these trees.

Dwarf fruit trees grow about 8 to 12 feet tall, and *semidwarfs* grow 12 to 20 feet tall, depending on the species. Dwarf trees produce less fruit per tree than full-size trees, but they produce more per amount of yard area and start bearing a year or two sooner. Dwarf trees make it possible to grow more varieties of fruit trees in a given amount of space, take less time to prune and spray, and allow most work to be done without ladders.

While dwarf trees are perfect for many gardeners, they have some disadvantages. Most dwarf and semidwarf trees are grafted onto rootstocks that are also small-growing. The dwarfing rootstock stimulates the tree to begin flowering and fruiting at a younger age, which reduces vegetative growth. Often, the rootstock also dwarfs the tree by reducing water and nutrient uptake. The most serious drawback is that many dwarfing rootstocks are shallow-rooted and poorly anchored; therefore, trees will require staking, extra fertilizer, and irrigation during drought.

Sometimes, as with apples and sweet cherries, the dwarfing rootstock is a member of the same fruit species. Most dwarf peaches, plums, and apricots offered today are kept small by using a related species as the rootstock. For example, most dwarf pears are grafted onto quince rootstocks. Generally, varieties dwarfed by grafting onto rootstocks that are closely related will be more healthy than those that aren't.

A few dwarf fruit trees are *genetic dwarfs;* that is, the variety itself is naturally small-growing and is

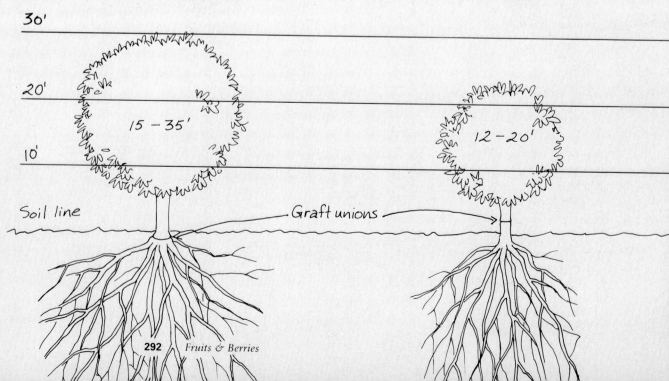

Standard variety on standard rootstock

Semi-dwarf

30'

20'

15 – 35'

10'

12 – 20'

Soil line

Graft unions

grafted onto a standard rootstock of the same or a closely related species. The standard rootstock provides better tree anchorage and water and nutrient uptake than most dwarfing rootstocks, and the tree will probably live as long as full-size trees if the variety is adapted to the area where it's planted. The problem with genetic dwarfs is that variety selection is limited, and many aren't very winter hardy or disease resistant.

You can also keep fruit trees small by choosing a site with less fertile soil (if possible), by spreading or bending down branches to induce earlier fruiting, and by summer pruning (see page 307).

Each rootstock, whether dwarfing, semidwarfing, or standard, has its own particular climate and soil adaptation, susceptibility to various pests, and management needs. Home growers should consider rootstock choice as carefully as variety choice.

Fruit Pollination and Bearing

Fruit growth begins with the pollination of flowers. Flowers of tree fruits contain both male and female parts. Pollen from the anthers (the male flower parts) must be transferred to the stigma (tip of the female flower part), grow down the style, and release sperm, which unite with the egg in the ovary. This union of sperm and egg develops into the seed.

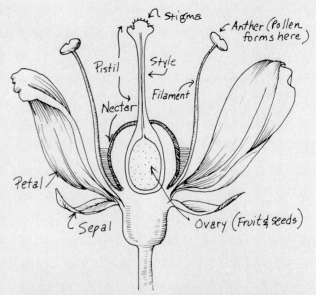

Fruit trees may be self-fertile, partially self-fertile, or self-infertile, which means they may or may not require pollination by another variety to set fruit. Be sure to check this when you choose varieties, so that you buy two varieties if necessary.

There are several possible combinations of rootstocks and tree sizes. A standard variety on a standard rootstock produces a standard-size tree. The same variety on a dwarfing rootstock or interstem will produce a semidwarf or dwarf-size tree. There are advantages and disadvantages to any combination, so remember that rootstock selection is as important as variety selection.

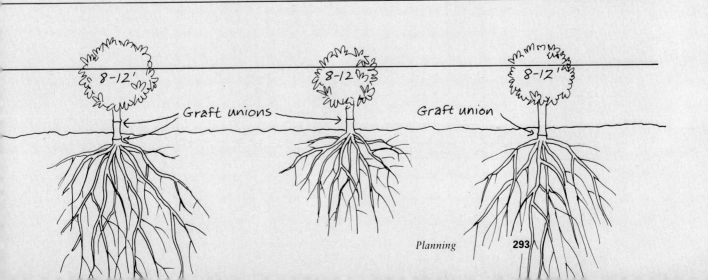

Standard variety on dwarfing rootstock

Standard variety on dwarfing interstem on standard rootstock

Genetic dwarf variety on standard rootstock

Graft unions

Graft union

8-12'

Pollination and seed growth stimulate the ovary walls and surrounding tissues to grow into the fleshy fruit we eat. Because the fruit develops solely from maternal tissues, the source of pollen does not affect the fruit characteristics of the variety being pollinated.

The showy petals and scent of fruit tree flowers attract insects, mostly bees, which feed on nectar and pollen. Pollen sticks to the insect's body and is brushed against the stigma. The insect — the agent of pollination — is called the pollinator, and the tree that provides the pollen is called the pollinizer.

Fruit tree varieties fall into one of three pollination classes:

1. *Self-fertile* varieties set a good fruit crop when pollinated by other flowers on the same tree, so only one variety is needed.

2. *Partially self-fertile* varieties set some fruit when pollinated by other flowers on the same tree, but will set better crops if pollinated by a different variety.

3. *Self-infertile* varieties must be pollinated by a different variety in order to set fruits, so two different varieties in close proximity are necessary.

The fruit tree planting guide on page 303 will give you an idea of the general pollination needs of each kind of fruit. There are exceptions, so check the variety information in the individual fruit chapters and nursery catalogs.

When choosing varieties for cross-pollination, make sure their bloom times overlap. Most varieties of the same type of fruit will bloom at about the same time, but a very early bloomer may be finished before a late bloomer begins.

Varieties

Choosing a variety that is well adapted to your climate is perhaps the most important decision you'll make. The hardiness zone map on pages 296–297 and the zone adaptations for different varieties listed in the individual fruit chapters provide a general guideline for selecting varieties that will do well in your part of the country. Choose the hardiest varieties only if you live near the northernmost limits for that type of fruit. Superhardy varieties are often adapted to prolonged, steady cold but not to the fluctuating winter temperatures that occur over most of the country.

All deciduous fruit trees (those that lose their leaves in winter) go through a period of rest, or dormancy. Dormancy is broken when the tree has been exposed to temperatures between 32°F and 45°F for a certain number of hours. This is the chilling requirement of the tree. Gardeners in zone 9 often need to choose "low-chill" varieties — those which require less winter cold to break dormancy in spring.

Cold hardiness takes three forms: wood hardiness, flower bud hardiness during winter, and flower bud hardiness during spring when buds swell and bloom. Some varieties are very hardy in wood, but tender in bud. Others have only moderate bud hardiness while dormant but are hardy longer into spring than other varieties, and even have some frost resistance during bloom. In the coldest areas, choose varieties very hardy in both wood and bud. Resistance to spring frosts is less important because very cold winters slow flower bud development, so trees bloom late and usually escape spring frosts. In moderate-winter areas such as the lower Midwest, Southeast, and areas near large bodies of water, varieties need not be superhardy in wood, but buds should resist both winter cold and spring frosts.

Many varieties of apricots, peaches, sweet cherries, and Japanese plums have cold-susceptible buds and bloom early. In most areas it's important to choose varieties that bloom late or have buds and blossoms that can tolerate frosts well.

You should also consider disease resistance when choosing a fruit tree variety. Some of the worst diseases, such as fire blight of pears and apples and bacterial canker of stone fruits, can kill the tree and can't be controlled solely by spraying. Other diseases, such as apple scab or cherry leaf spot, can be controlled with fungicides, but resistant varieties eliminate the need for them. If you select resistant varieties you'll still have to control insects and possibly some other diseases, but you'll need far fewer sprays.

No variety is immune to every disease, but only a few diseases cause significant damage most years in any particular location. Don't just look for varieties resistant to as many diseases as possible — ask your Extension Service agent which diseases are serious in your area and choose accordingly.

You don't have to limit your selection to already-proven varieties. Many of the newer disease- and frost-resistant varieties have not been widely planted yet, but if they have done well in areas with a similar climate, they are probably a good bet.

Rootstocks

Choose rootstocks as carefully as varieties. The rootstock is literally the bottom half of every fruit tree you buy, and the tree's life depends upon it being well adapted to your climate, soil type, and pest conditions.

Buying a dwarf fruit tree without knowing which rootstock is used to dwarf it can invite disappointment. Some dwarfing rootstocks cause early tree death, others aren't as winter hardy as standard rootstocks for that type of fruit, and others are very susceptible to certain diseases or soil insect pests.

Unfortunately, it is often difficult to find out what rootstocks have been used on the trees you buy. Mail-order nurseries may not list this information in their catalogs, and garden centers generally can only tell you the variety of the fruiting part of the tree. When ordering trees by mail, try to choose a company that lists rootstock information or write for specific information before ordering. If the garden center can't give you the information you're looking for, you can ask them to find out from the wholesale nursery where they purchased the trees.

Sources for Trees

Fruit trees are sold either balled-and-burlapped, bare-root, or in containers. We recommend buying bare-root trees (which can be purchased through most mail-order nurseries) because they transplant very well. Some bare-root trees come with their roots packed in a ball of peat moss covered with plastic. Container and balled-and-burlapped trees are more expensive than bare-root trees but do not transplant any better or grow any faster, and have some serious drawbacks. Most container trees are dug bare-root by the wholesale nursery, then just potted by the retail nursery or garden store. They may be left in the container to grow for a year, resulting in trees with very poor branch structure that should be cut back severely when planted, and won't be as easy to train. The root ball of balled-and-burlapped trees have more secondary roots, but these trees aren't dug as deeply as bare-root trees, so the main roots are cut off shorter.

One-year-old trees, 4 to 5 feet tall, are the best buy. Those less than 3 feet tall are too weak growing, and those over 6 feet tall are too vigorous and will be hard to train. Apples and pears will be branchless; apricots, sweet cherries, and European plums may contain a few branches; and peaches, tart cherries, and Japanese plums will have a number of branches. Two-year-old trees have bigger tops and more branches, but the roots are dug at the same depth, putting more stress on the roots in transplanting. Most of those branches will have to be cut off anyway because they'll arise from the trunk at too narrow an angle.

Buying fruit trees from the nursery that grew them, whether local or mail-order, is usually best. These nurseries generally offer wider selections, more information on varieties and rootstocks, and their trees are usually stored properly.

Reputable nurseries guarantee that their fruit trees are true-to-name (the variety you order is the variety you get), healthy, and disease-free when purchased. They often offer certified virus-free trees for the fruit trees most troubled by viruses.

Beware of bargain-priced ($3 or $4) fruit trees. You may get a variety that's mislabeled, highly disease susceptible, or not at all suited to your climate. Fruit trees are a long-term investment. The true bargain is a certified disease-free tree, of carefully chosen variety and rootstock, that was grown, dug, and stored properly.

Hardiness Zones

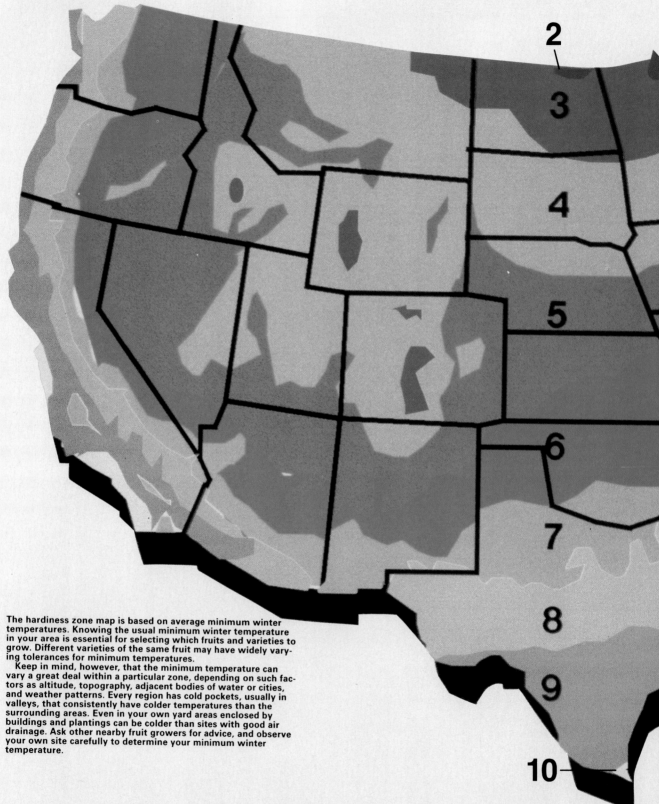

The hardiness zone map is based on average minimum winter temperatures. Knowing the usual minimum winter temperature in your area is essential for selecting which fruits and varieties to grow. Different varieties of the same fruit may have widely varying tolerances for minimum temperatures.

Keep in mind, however, that the minimum temperature can vary a great deal within a particular zone, depending on such factors as altitude, topography, adjacent bodies of water or cities, and weather patterns. Every region has cold pockets, usually in valleys, that consistently have colder temperatures than the surrounding areas. Even in your own yard areas enclosed by buildings and plantings can be colder than sites with good air drainage. Ask other nearby fruit growers for advice, and observe your own site carefully to determine your minimum winter temperature.

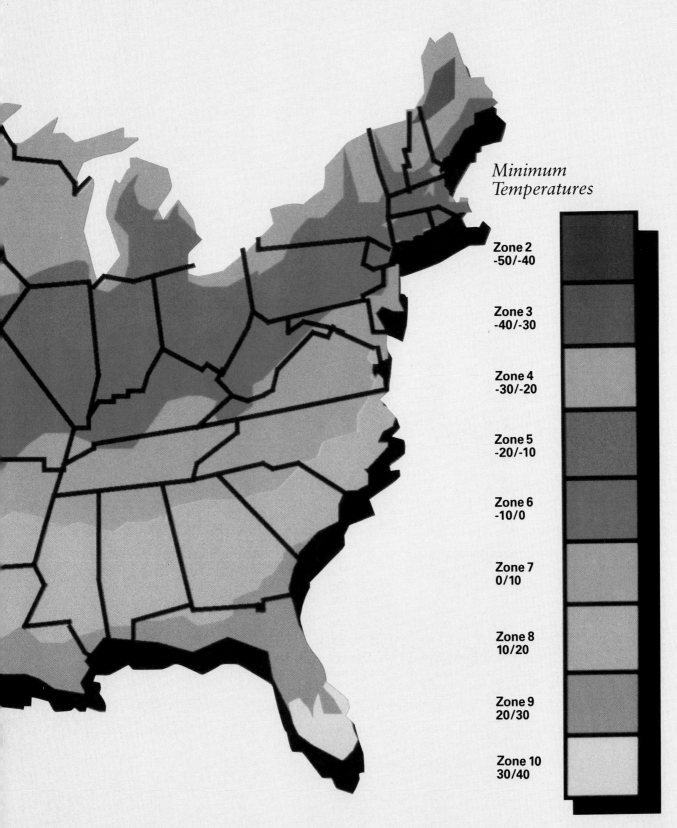

Minimum
Temperatures

Zone 2
-50/-40

Zone 3
-40/-30

Zone 4
-30/-20

Zone 5
-20/-10

Zone 6
-10/0

Zone 7
0/10

Zone 8
10/20

Zone 9
20/30

Zone 10
30/40

Preparation for Fruit Trees

Choosing the optimal site or sites for your fruit trees is the most important part of preparation. Considerations include amount of sun, protection from deep cold, late spring frost and wind, water drainage, soil, and what has been previously grown at that site.

Moving a tree is a great deal of trouble and may irreparably harm the tree, so choose your site carefully and take care of any soil improvements well ahead of planting.

Selecting a Planting Site

Try to choose a planting site in full sun; fruit trees require a minimum of 8 hours of sun per day during the growing season. Early morning sun dries dew off the foliage quickly and minimizes diseases; midday and early afternoon sun improves fruit flavor. Plant fruit trees far enough from shade trees to provide adequate light and to minimize root competition.

Your site should have good air drainage. Avoid low spots and areas enclosed by buildings or shade trees, where cold air settles, causing trees to suffer from winter cold and spring frost injury.

A north-facing slope or north side of a building is a good site for frost-sensitive crops such as peaches, Japanese plums, sweet cherries, and apricots. The shadow cast by the slope or building in the winter keeps the plant cooler, which delays bud development and bloom in the spring, while the higher summer sun angle provides enough light during the growing season. Fruit ripening will also be delayed on a north slope. A south-facing slope or wall hastens both bloom and harvest and requires extra protection from frosts as well as from winter sunscald. In areas with short or frequently cloudy growing seasons, the hardier fruits (apples, pears, tart cherries, European or American hybrid plums) do better on a south-facing slope or wall, which receives more intense light. Where summers are very hot and dry, avoid south or southwestern slopes, or give the trees plenty of irrigation. East- and west-facing slopes have intermediate effects.

In areas with strong winds, choose a site protected by existing plantings or buildings, or plant a windbreak (see box). Windbreak trees can also serve as border plantings or screens, provide shelter and nesting sites for insect-eating birds, and may lure pest birds away from your fruit trees.

In addition to the right amount of sun and air, soil type should be a major consideration in choosing a site. Once you plant a fruit tree, it will remain in the same spot for many years, so it pays to examine and prepare soil carefully before you plant. Even if this means delaying tree planting by a year, you'll gain back that year in increased tree growth and health. Your Extension Service agent can provide useful soil survey information.

Fruit trees do not like wet feet — well-drained soil is a must for a healthy tree. Avoid low areas where water puddles during rains. Well-drained soils are generally uniform in color with no streaks. Poorly drained soils

Planting a Windbreak

Strong winds increase the trees' moisture needs and can whip trees around in their planting holes, weakening them and leaving them vulnerable to pest attack. Heavy spring winds can interfere with pollination by desiccating blossoms and hindering bee movement. Strong summer or fall winds can knock fruit off trees; winter winds can increase cold damage.

If you live in an area with high winds, decide whether summer or winter winds are more important to control, and plant your windbreak accordingly. Summer windbreaks for fruit trees can be just one row of fast-growing but long-lived, drought-tolerant trees. Small (15- to 25-foot) windbreak trees, such as redbud, Russian olive, white (Chinese) or black mulberry, or serviceberry, will provide enough protection for dwarf or semidwarf fruit trees. Medium-size (35- to 50-foot) windbreak trees, such as thornless honey locust, red mulberry, or lacebark (true Chinese) elm, will be needed for standard-size fruit trees. Winter windbreaks should contain a row of evergreens (usually pines or spruce).

Avoid trees that could spread diseases in your fruit planting, such as Eastern red cedar (alternate host of cedar-apple rust), scab- or fire-blight-susceptible crab apples, hawthorn, mountain ash, or ornamental cherries. Also avoid overly competitive, brittle-wooded, or short-lived trees such as Lombardy poplar, hackberry, green or white ash, osage orange, cottonwood, silver maple, catalpa, or Siberian elm (often erroneously called Chinese elm).

Plant your windbreak at least as far from the fruit planting as its ultimate height. Also, don't box in your fruit trees with windbreak plantings on all sides that stop air movement, which can aggravate disease problems.

have grayish or bluish streaks in the top 3 feet. (To determine whether your soil drainage is adequate, see page 15.)

If you don't have *any* well-drained sites you can install drainage tiles or build raised mounds or beds (6 to 8 inches high and as wide as the mature tree's spread) where you'll plant the trees. To make mounds, mix equal parts soil from other areas of the yard with compost. If you bring in topsoil of a different texture, mix it into your own soil very well. Don't add sand; that would improve drainage only in the top layer where it's mixed in, but hurt drainage below because of the textural change.

You will also need to build raised beds if your soil is not deep enough for the trees' roots — at least 3 feet of soil for trees on dwarfing rootstocks, and at least 5 feet of soil for standard-size trees. If you think your soil is shallow, dig a hole or use a soil auger to the necessary depth. While digging, look for an abrupt change in soil texture. Watch for soil that suddenly becomes very clayey; this type of soil will restrict water drainage and root growth into the soil below.

Although good soil drainage is one of the most important factors for fruit trees, soil texture will influence their growth. Loam soils, clay loams, or sandy loams are better for fruit trees than very sandy or heavy clay soils. However, different fruit tree rootstocks are adapted to different conditions — some rootstocks tolerate clayey soils well and others withstand sandy soils. In general, peaches, sweet cherries, Japanese plums, and apricots do better in sandy soils; apples, pears, tart cherries, and European plums do better in heavier soils.

Have your soil tested, preferably the season before you intend to plant your trees. If necessary, add lime or sulphur to correct the pH to a range of 5.5 to 7.0, suitable for most trees. Add phosphate or potash fertilizers if phosphorus or potassium levels are low.

All fruit plants will be healthier if the soil contains high levels of organic matter, so turning under a green manure crop or two before planting helps a great deal. Plant nematode-susceptible stone fruits (peaches, plums, cherries, and apricots) where a grass cover crop or lawn grew for the previous 2 years. Two years without broad-leaved plants almost completely eliminates the most troublesome nematodes, root knot and lesion, as well as verticillium wilt. Nematode- or verticillium-infected fruit trees are stunted and unproductive, and once infected, there is no cure.

Many vegetables and small fruits are susceptible to verticillium wilt. Try not to plant fruit trees where susceptible plants have grown in the last 2 years.

If you must plant stone fruits where vegetables grew recently, choose an area where corn has grown. Have the soil tested for nematodes before planting. If high levels of root knot or lesion nematodes are found, plant the ground with a *trap crop* of marigolds, which will attract nematodes to their roots, the season before planting the fruit trees. Don't bother planting marigolds around the trees once they're set out to get rid of nematodes; you need to get nematode levels down *before* tree-planting time.

Choose a marigold variety proven to be a good trap crop, such as *Tangerine* or Park Seed Company's *Nemagold* blend. Plant them 6 to 7 inches apart so they form a solid stand, and keep them weeded. In early fall, pull up the marigolds — roots included — and destroy them. Then plant a winter rye cover crop for additional protection against nematodes, and till it in early next spring before planting trees.

Planting fruit trees in a lawn is fine; just remove the sod in a circle 3 or 4 feet out from each fruit tree, and mix some compost or other organic matter into the whole area. If the lawn contained many broad-leaved weeds, test the soil for nematodes and follow the instructions above for planting marigolds. Eliminate any noxious perennial weeds such as quack grass. Remove competitive grasses such as Bermuda or zoysia from the entire area that the fruit trees will ultimately occupy, and replace them with less competitive groundcovers (see page 305).

It's a good idea not to replace an old fruit tree with the same or a closely related type of fruit. Not only have nematodes and other soil-borne diseases built up, but the roots of certain fruit trees, such as peaches, exude a toxin that inhibits the growth of new peach roots. Don't place new stone fruit trees right next to older ones, to prevent the spread of noncurable diseases such as X-disease or cherry yellows.

Planting Fruit Trees

Advice on planting fruit trees has changed in the past few years. Until recently it was generally accepted practice to dig an enormous hole, fill it with layers of topsoil and compost, and put in the tree. It has been found, however, that the result is often a pot-bound tree, with roots going around and around in the hole instead of penetrating the surrounding soil. Needless to say, such a tree never grows or yields as it should.

Planting practice now is to change the soil texture as little as possible in a hole only a bit larger than the tree's pruned root system. This is why it is important to improve the soil in the whole area ahead of time. The roots will then grow downward and outward as they should, reaching nutrients and moisture, firmly anchoring the tree to the earth, and giving the tree its best start on a long and fruitful life.

In most parts of the country, fruit trees should be planted in early spring. Where winters are mild (zone 7 and south), you may plant in late fall, enabling roots to become better established before the trees leaf out the following spring. It's a little risky, however; winters may cause damage.

Plant the trees the day you get them, if possible. If weather conditions delay planting, keep the roots moist until you can plant. Bare-root trees will be wrapped in moist peat or a similar material when you get them; leave this intact when you open the package and add water as needed. Water balled-and-burlapped or container trees as needed. Soak bare roots in a bucket of water for a few hours before planting, keeping them in water until planting.

Dig planting holes a few inches deeper and wider than the roots spread. Be sure to match the hole size with the type of rootstock. Set trees on standard rootstocks (including genetic dwarf varieties) with the graft union a few inches *below* soil level to reduce root suckering. (If the tree is budded high — a foot or so off the ground — set it just a few inches deeper than it grew in the nursery.) Set trees on dwarfing rootstocks with the graft union several inches *above* the soil; if the union is buried, the variety could root and overcome the rootstock's dwarfing effect. Set interstem trees with the interstem piece *half above and half below* the soil. In all three cases, set the trees a little bit higher than you ultimately want them. Mound the soil up slightly (3 to 4 inches high and 1 foot in diameter) around the trunk to help drainage and reduce problems with crown rot.

Don't add fertilizer of any kind to the planting hole or drastically change the soil texture. *Never* add any materials that might burn the roots, such as chemical fertilizers, fresh manure, or moth balls. Compost can be mixed into the planting hole, but don't add more than a few shovelfuls — it can change the soil texture and cause poor drainage. Compost is best mixed into the entire area around the tree before planting and can also be used as mulch on top of the soil.

Cut off, rather than bend, any broken roots and any extra-long roots. Spread out the roots in the hole and tamp the soil around them firmly. Air pockets around the roots can kill the trees. Surround the trunk of each tree with a 14-inch mouse and rabbit guard (see page 306) before filling the hole completely. Place the guard so that the bottom 2 inches will be below ground when the hole is filled with soil. Pour 2 gallons of water around each newly set tree to thoroughly soak the soil.

Pruning at planting time is a simple but essential step and should not be overlooked. Pruning back the top prevents too much demand on the root system which was pruned when the tree was dug up. A straight whip should be cut back to about 30 inches from the ground, just above a bud. Remove any branches that are less than 18 inches off the ground.

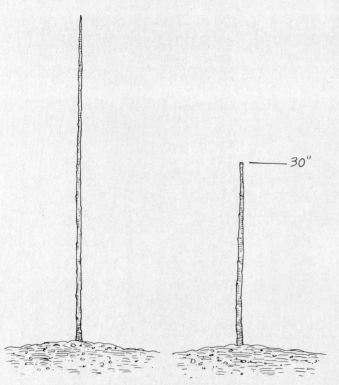

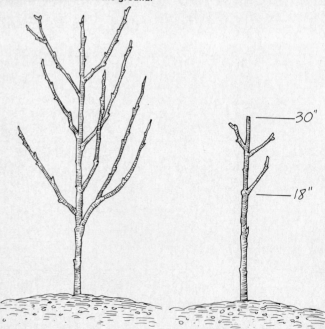

30"

30"

18"

Prune spring-planted trees immediately, but wait until early spring to prune fall-planted trees. Cut the trees off at about 30 inches from the ground, just above a bud. This pruning helps adjust the tops to the reduced root system, which was pruned in transplanting, and avoids stressing roots too much.

If the tree has branches, remove any that are less than 18 inches off the ground. If any strong branches above this height arise from the trunk at a wide angle and in desired positions (see page 310), you can leave them, but cut them back by one-half. Cut all narrow-angled branches off, even if you're left with few or no side branches. Buds on the trunk will grow into side branches that you can train to better angles. Begin training trees in early summer.

Tie trees on dwarfing rootstocks to a sturdy stake. Trees on standard rootstocks do not require staking unless the site is extremely windy.

Planting Guide for Fruit Trees

Kind of fruit	Zones of adaptation	Pollination require-ments*	Mature height (ft.)**	Mature spread (ft.)**	Year of bearing after planting	Yield/tree at maturity	Bearing season	Years of expected life	Fruit bud hardiness
Apple									
dwarf	4–9	SS or PSF	6–14	8–12	3rd–4th	3–5 bu.	July–Oct.	12–25	hardy
semidwarf	3–9	SS or PSF	14–20	14–18	4th–5th	5–10 bu.	July–Oct.	15–30	hardy
standard	2–9	SS or PSF	22–30	20–25	5th–7th	10–25 bu.	July–Oct.	30–40	hardy
Apricot	3–9	PSF	20–25	18–20	4th–5th	2–4 bu.	July	20–30	very sensitive
Sweet Cherry									
semidwarf	5–7	SS	14–20	14–18	4th–6th	20–40 qt.	June	20–30	very sensitive
standard	5–7	SS	25–35	20–25	4th–6th	30–60 qt.	June	20–30	very sensitive
Tart Cherry									
genetic dwarf	3–8a	SF	6–12	8–12	3rd	10–25 qt.	June	12–15	hardy
standard	4–8a	SF	16–18	16–18	4th	30–50 qt.	June	15–20	hardy
Peach and Nectarine									
genetic dwarf	5–9	SF	6–10	6–10	3rd	1–1½ bu.	July–Sept.	8–10	sensitive
standard	5–9	SF	15–18	18–20	4th	3–5 bu.	July–Sept.	10–15	sensitive
Pear									
dwarf	5b–9	SS	10–15	10–12	3rd–4th	1–3 bu.	Aug.–Oct.	10–15	hardy
standard	3–9	SS	25–40	20–25	5th–7th	4–6 bu.	Aug.–Oct.	30–40	hardy
Asian Pear	6–9	PSF	25–35	20–25	4th–5th	4–6 bu.	Aug.–Sept.	30–40	sensitive
Plum									
dwarf			8–14	10–14	3rd–4th	1–2 bu.		10–15	
standard			18–22	18–20	4th–5th	3–5 bu.		15–20	
European	4–8	PSF					Aug.–Sept.		mod. hardy
Japanese	5–9	SS					July–Aug.		very sensitive
American	2–9	SF or PSF					Aug.–Sept.		hardy

Note: The values listed are approximations and may vary with varieties, locations, and care given to fruit plants.

*Abbreviation key:
SF—self-fertile. Only 1 variety needed for pollination.
PSF—partially self-fertile. Generally sets heavier fruit crop with two or more varieities planted nearby.
SS—self-sterile. Two varieties needed for pollination; occasional exceptions with some varieties.
**Tree height and spread can be limited somewhat by summer and winter pruning.

Compiled by Brenda Olcott-Reid.

Care of Fruit Trees

Fruit trees will need some special care every season, but it needn't be too time-consuming. Most trees need some pruning twice a year; if done regularly, pruning will never be a chore simply because excess growth has not been allowed to continue unchecked for several seasons.

Pruning instructions may sound complicated to first-time growers, but after you have pruned your trees for a season for two, pruning will probably become second nature. The important point is to begin early in your tree's growth to create the best structure.

There's more to tree care than pruning, of course. Proper fertilizing, watering, and prewinter maintenance are essential, too, for healthy, productive trees.

Water, Mulch and Groundcovers

During the first two growing seasons, water the trees deeply (6 to 8 gallons of water per tree) about once a week if there's been little or no rain. Don't apply less water more frequently — it encourages shallow rooting. Spread 4 to 6 inches of mulch around the trees to their dripline to conserve moisture and control weeds. You can use bark mulch or other attractive mulches and plant noncompetitive flowers (spring bulbs and shallow-rooted annuals) around the trees. Before spreading straw mulch, let it sit out and wet it several times to encourage weed seed germination.

You can grow a lawn or other groundcover between the mulched areas around the trees, and the mowings can be used for mulch. You might plant quick-growing annual cover crops such as buckwheat and annual rye during the first few years to provide organic matter, but as the trees get older you'll need to establish a permanent groundcover. Legumes such as bird's-foot trefoil (with yellow flowers) or crimson clover (with red flowers) make attractive groundcovers where they are adapted. Mow grasses to reduce competition, and mow legumes frequently to reduce stinkbug injury. Groundcovers that don't require mowing include wildflowers and noncompetitive evergreens such as *Vinca minor* and creeping phlox. Avoid warm-season grasses such as Bermuda or zoysia, and competitive groundcovers such as pachysandra. Ask your nursery for other recommendations for your area.

Irrigate bearing fruit trees if they receive less than 2 inches of rain during any 2-week period between bloom and early fall. If no rain has fallen for 2 weeks, this means you need to add 1 gallon of water per square foot of rooting area, which extends several feet farther out than the tree's dripline. Measure rain and sprinkling systems with open containers on the ground. The most critical time to water is during fruit expansion, but don't apply more than 2 inches. Excessive watering can cause fruit to expand too much and be more prone to rot.

Fertilizing

Supply fertilizer and abundant organic matter during the first few years to get the trees off to a good start, but keep in mind that heavy or careless applications of fertilizer can damage the trees. To avoid burning the new root system, wait 6 weeks after planting to fertilize. Then apply a fertilizer containing $1/10$ pound of *actual nitrogen* in a wide band 1 foot out from the trunk. It's best to apply a nitrogen source separately and adjust phosphorus and potassium according to soil test results, although a complete fertilizer can also be used. You can apply nitrogen in any form as long as it equals the specified amount.

Don't plan on supplying all of a young tree's nitrogen needs with compost or manure. If you added enough to do that, nitrogen would still be released in early fall, inducing the tree to grow too late in the season and predisposing it to winter injury.

During the summer, check the amount and color of growth to guide you in fertilizing next year. Leaves should be dark green and *terminals*, the shoot growth from the sides or end of a branch, should grow 16 to 20 inches during the season. If trees received adequate water but leaves are yellowish and terminals didn't grow that long, add more fertilizer next year. If terminals grow 22 inches or more, cut down on fertilizer.

During the second growing season, make two fertilizer applications: one when growth begins in spring and one in early summer. Apply about $1/8$ pound of actual nitrogen each time, if growth was in the desired range last year.

Established fruit trees require little fertilizer other than organic matter. From the third season on, apply only enough nitrogen to produce the desired amount of growth. Bearing trees that produce crops on 1-year-old branches (peaches, apricots, and Japanese plums) should make 15 to 18 inches of terminal growth per season. Those which bear mainly on spurs (apples, pears, cherries, and European plums) should make no more than 10 to 14 inches of terminal growth per season. Excess nitrogen can cause poor fruit bud set, poor fruit color, delayed fruit maturity, and softer fruit, which is more prone to rot and doesn't store well. Time fertilizer applications so that nitrogen will be released when growth is starting in spring, and when fruit buds are forming in early to midsummer.

Established trees usually don't benefit from phosphorus applications in most soils, and excess phosphorus can cause zinc deficiency. Potassium may be deficient on alkaline soils high in calcium and magnesium. Potassium deficiency reduces fruit size, sugar content, and storage time; it can be recognized by small, bluish-green leaves with yellowed or dying edges.

Zinc and boron must be applied frequently on western, alkaline soils. These are best applied as foliar sprays; ask your county Extension Service agent for details. You can apply liquid seaweed emulsion throughout the growing season to provide small amounts of trace elements and *cytokinins*, growth hormones that reduce stress on the tree. Foliar nutrient sprays can be added to pesticide sprays.

Fall and Winter Care

Each fall, fruit trees begin to harden up in preparation for winter. Growth slows and metabolic changes take place that enable plants to withstand much lower temperatures without damage. Help the plants harden by allowing their growth to slow. Don't apply too much fertilizer or apply it past midsummer because high nitrogen levels will cause continued growth. Don't water from early fall on, except when less than 1 inch of rain has fallen during a 2-week period. Mow around the fruit trees less often in early fall to allow the lawn or groundcover to compete and help slow tree growth. Do not prune in the fall, so as not to stimulate growth or leave fresh cuts open to winter injury.

During the winter, desiccation can cause as much injury to plants as cold temperatures. Water trees well in *late* fall (not early), after they are dormant, but before the ground freezes, if the weather has been dry.

Rake fallen leaves. Compost them only if you're sure they are disease-free.

Paint tree trunks white in late fall to prevent winter sunscald. This damage, often worse than that from absolute cold, occurs when the unshaded trunks heat up to high temperatures during the day, then rapidly cool to very low temperatures at night. Combine 1 part interior white latex paint to 3 parts water, and spray or brush this mixture on trunks up to the first main limb. Rabbit and rodent repellents can be mixed into the paint to prevent these animals from feeding on the bark in the winter. Or place 1/4-inch mesh hardware-cloth cages around your trees, making sure the guards reach above the expected snow level. You can also use white plastic tree guards to prevent both sunscald and rodent damage. Pull mulch away from the tree trunks in the fall to avoid attracting rodents.

Deer feeding on the tender twigs and branches in the winter can cause a lot of damage. The most effective deer repellent, according to those troubled by them, is an egg spray. Blend three raw eggs with two or three cups of water in a blender, then dilute this mixture with more water in a 3-gallon sprayer. The spray must be reapplied at monthly intervals.

Thinning

Fruit trees may produce ten times more flowers than they need for an optimum crop. Due to the uncertainty of weather, it's best to encourage maximum fruit bud formation, survival, and pollination, but when conditions are favorable trees will set more fruit than they can support. The tree partially compensates for a heavy fruit set by dropping some of the excess fruit while they are small. About 2 weeks after the petals and unpollinated flowers fall, a heavy "first drop" of undeveloped fruitlets occurs. A couple of weeks later (5 to 8 weeks after full bloom), a slightly larger fruit drop occurs. This is often called June drop because it occurs in early June in northern states; it occurs in May in southern states. Don't be alarmed by natural fruit drop; it reduces stress on the tree. A tree with a heavy fruit set can afford to lose up to 90 percent of its tiny fruit.

Most years, you'll need to take nature a step further by thinning the fruit — removing those which are still too crowded. The remaining fruit will get bigger and sweeter. Thinning will decrease yields somewhat, but it's better for the tree. Fruit thinning reduces branch breakage and stress on the tree, making winter injury

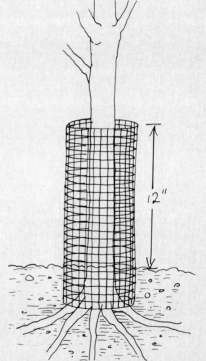

To protect young fruit trees, put a cylinder of 1/4-inch mesh hardware cloth around the trunk, extending it several inches below the soil and at least 12 inches above.

less likely. It also prevents *biennial bearing* — a heavy crop of small fruit one year, then very few fruit the next — by stimulating increased fruit bud formation for next year's crop.

You should thin fruit early, soon after the first drop and between 4 to 6 weeks after bloom, for the greatest benefit. The tree will still be dropping some fruit at this time, but the fruit that will fall naturally are very easy to knock off, so don't worry about removing too many. For specific information on thinning see the individual fruit chapters.

Keep the largest fruit and remove those which are diseased, insect-infested, or damaged. Thin the fruit so they don't touch to reduce fruit rots and other diseases. Rake up and destroy thinned fruit and natural drops.

Young trees on poorly anchored dwarfing rootstocks may also require fruit thinning. Excess early fruiting, induced by the rootstock, reduces root growth much more than shoot growth. It can lead to extremely poor anchorage, causing trees to lean even though they've been staked.

Pruning Fruit Trees

All fruit trees should be pruned every year. You should be as dedicated to keeping the trees strong and healthy by removing excess branches as you are eager to enjoy high-quality fruit.

Unpruned trees develop branches that arise from the trunk at narrow angles and break under the weight of a fruit crop. Too many branches crowd each other, reducing air circulation and increasing the chance of disease. The tree grows too tall and wide, and fruit is borne only around the outside of the tree where sunlight is adequate. At the center of the tree is a mass of tangled, unfruitful branches.

Beginning fruit tree growers often think that pruning is too complicated for them to learn, something only experts can do well. But the basics of pruning are really quite simple. So don't miss out on a good crop of fruit by neglecting to prune regularly.

When to Prune

Prune fruit trees twice a year: late in the dormant season and again in summer. Dormant pruning shapes the tree and encourages new growth. Undesirable branches are easier to spot during the dormant season. Wait until late winter or early spring to prune; trees pruned in early winter are more susceptible to damage from subzero temperatures. Wounds on trees that are pruned just before growth begins will heal quickly. Wait until after buds begin to swell or bloom to prune trees with winter-tender fruit buds or those which bloom early.

Pruning young trees again in early summer channels that new growth in desired directions. Prune mature trees in mid- to late summer to control tree size and allow better light penetration. The later in the growing season you prune, the less regrowth will occur. In areas with cold winters, prune no later than midsummer to give new growth a chance to harden before winter. In the summer, prune the current season's shoot growth, but don't cut into older wood.

Pruning Tools

Proper tools, kept sharp, are essential to pruning. A tool that is dull or not strong enough to make a certain cut can tear the bark or leave a jagged surface that heals slowly or becomes diseased. You will need the following tools:

1. Hand pruners — scissors type, used to prune small branches up to ¼ inch in diameter.
2. Loppers — long-handled, used for cuts of ¼ to ½ inch in diameter.
3. Pruning saw — teeth set so saw cuts on pull rather than push stroke, making it easier to cut from below; used for cuts larger than ½ inch; or a fine-toothed saw that makes a smoother cut than a coarser-toothed pruning saw, but requires more effort to use.

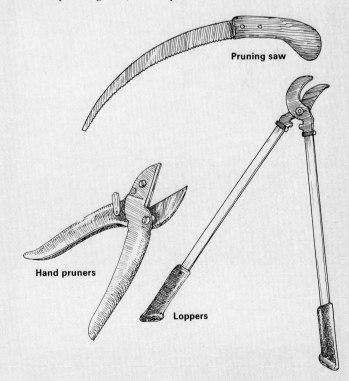

Pruning saw

Hand pruners

Loppers

Pruning Terms

Shoot — new growth developing during the current growing season.

Branch — a mature shoot that has passed through one or more dormant seasons.

Terminal shoot — growth from the sides or end of a branch.

Lateral shoot — growth from the sides of a branch.

Trunk — the main central stem of the tree.

Leader — an upright-growing branch in the center of the tree, selected as the continuation of the trunk.

Scaffold branch — one of the main branches arising from the trunk and growing outward, forming the tree's basic framework.

Crotch angle — the angle at which a branch arises from the trunk or scaffold branch.

Branch bark collar — the raised ridge of tissue in the crotch of a branch, where it comes out from the larger branch.

Fruit spurs — short, thick growth upon which flowers and fruit develop, growing on branches 2 years old or older, and continuing to produce fruit for many years.

Watersprout — vigorous, unfruitful shoot or branch growing straight up from a larger branch.

Crown — the juncture of the top of the tree and the root system; the part of the trunk right around the soil line.

Sucker — shoot or branch growing from the roots or crown of the rootstock.

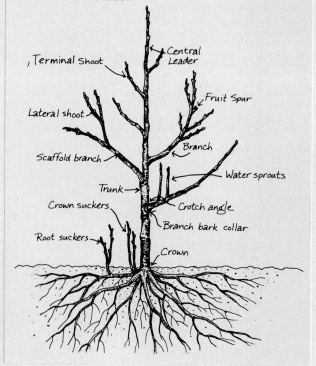

4. Ladder — 10- or 12-foot stepladder, not a leaning type.

5. Orange shellac — for painting cuts larger than 2 inches immediately after pruning (available at hardware stores).

Treating with shellac isn't necessary for preventing disease but it helps prevent cold damage and invasions by borer insects. Asphalt-base wound dressings are too thick and can encourage decay, while oil-base materials or dressings containing creosote or Bordeaux mixture may injure the tree. Cuts smaller than 2 inches in diameter heal quickly and do not need a wound dressing in most areas. Where borers are severe problems, paint all pruning wounds.

If you prune your trees each year, you can remove undesirable branches while they're still small, eliminating the need for saws and wound dressing.

To prune tops of trees always stand on a ladder. Standing on tree limbs to prune can damage the bark. With tall trees, you may need pole pruners — loppers on very long handles — in addition to a ladder.

Making Pruning Cuts

There are only two types of pruning cuts: thinning and heading. *Thinning*, or thinning out, excess branches means cutting them off completely where they arise from the larger branch. *Heading*, or heading back, a branch means cutting it back but not removing it entirely. You will usually head back to a specific part of the tree, such as a strong or weak lateral. If you head back to a lateral branch, it means that you are removing all of the branch from the outside of the tree up to the point where the lateral branch is growing. *Pinching* — removing part of a new shoot in summer while it's still growing — is a form of heading.

Thinning and heading produce opposite effects: thinning decreases the production of new shoots; heading encourages it. Late-summer thinning cuts have a strong dwarfing effect, whereas dormant-season heading cuts invigorate the tree. Before deciding whether to remove a branch or just to cut it back, consider whether you want to reduce or stimulate new shoot production in that part of the tree.

Make thinning cuts as close as possible to the bark branch collar, but do not cut through the collar. If you leave a stub or cut through the collar, the branch will heal poorly and may be invaded by disease and insects. Make heading cuts just above a bud growing in the direction you want the new terminal to grow.

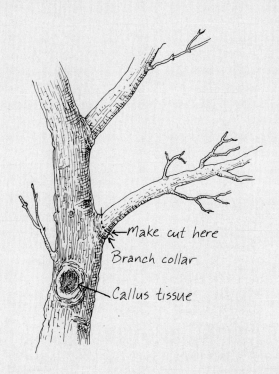

Make cut here
Branch collar
Callus tissue

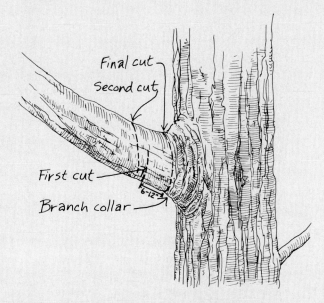

Final cut
Second cut
First cut
6-12"
Branch collar

To prevent tearing a large branch, remove it with three cuts. First, saw up the branch from the bottom about 6 to 12 inches from its base. Then saw completely through it from the top. The final cut should be almost flush with the remaining branch. If you don't cut into the branch bark collar, callus tissue should form and the cut should heal properly.

Large branches should be removed in three steps to prevent tearing the branch. First, at a point about 6 to 12 inches from the base of the branch, saw halfway up the branch from the bottom, then saw through from the top, removing most of the branch. Finally, remove the remaining stub, sawing it off almost flush with the branch but not cutting into the branch bark collar.

Removing Diseased Wood

When removing diseased wood, sterilize pruning tools after each cut to prevent spreading disease from branch to branch. Use a solution of 1 part household bleach to 9 parts water. When you're finished, wash tools, then oil them to prevent rusting. You can avoid spreading disease with pruning tools by breaking off rather than cutting infected twigs. Remove and destroy diseased tissues as soon as you see them, no matter what time of year. Prune branches off at least 4 inches below where the disease is visible.

Fungi or bacteria that can rot wood enter winter-injured areas on the trunk or near the base of scaffold limbs, forming *cankers*, sunken areas on the bark. Try

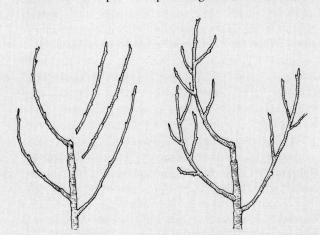
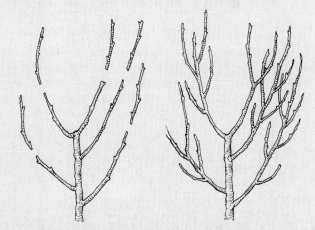

There are two types of pruning cuts. Thinning cuts (*left*) remove branches completely where they arise from a larger branch. Heading cuts (*right*) remove a portion of the branch.

to prevent winter damage, but if cankers form, cut out cankered branches, if possible. If the canker is on a main framework branch that you can't remove without destroying the structure of the tree, cut back the edges of the canker to live bark with a knife and scrape out the dead bark and wood in the center. Then cover the injured area with orange shellac. Destroy the infected wood you remove.

Pruning and Training Systems

Training is the art of selecting and developing branches to become the main bearing framework of the tree. It begins at planting time and includes both heading and thinning cuts, pinching new growth, and limb spreading or tying. Training develops a limb structure that's strong and open enough to support heavy crops of high-quality fruit that have minimal disease problems. Proper training also encourages the tree to begin bearing fruit at an early age.

The branches of nonbearing (or not-yet-bearing) fruit trees tend to grow too upright because they don't have the weight of fruit pulling them down. Arising from the trunk at too narrow an angle, they are very susceptible to winter injury and structurally weak, often breaking under heavy crop loads.

Branch spreading develops a strong bearing framework, reduces the amount of pruning needed later, and promotes the formation of flower buds. Early fruiting in turn takes some of the tree's energy away from vegetative growth, so is a powerful dwarfing agent.

Fruit trees can be trained into many different shapes, according to your needs. Where space is very limited or a formal screen of trees is desired, dwarf fruit trees can be espaliered into various patterns. The branches of espaliered trees are forced to grow along one plane

Branches of young fruit trees tend to grow too upright unless they are forced outward. Branch spreading develops a strong bearing framework.

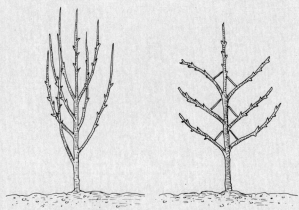

and tied to a supporting trellis. This produces a flat "tree fence," which can be grown against a wall or divide two areas of the yard.

Free-standing fruit trees are trained according to one of two basic systems: the *central leader* or the *open center*. The ideal *central leader* tree is shaped like a Christmas tree: a dominant central trunk continuing straight up to the top of the tree, with scaffold branches coming out from it. No branch should be directly above another. The uppermost branches are pruned back closer to the trunk than the lower branches to allow light to reach the lower branches.

An *open center* tree is shaped like a vase: the central trunk has been cut off above the point where three scaffold limbs arise from it. These scaffold limbs grow upward and outward, forming the walls of the vase, while the center is kept free from branches to allow better light penetration.

A *modified leader* tree is a compromise between the two. Training begins like that for a central leader, but after four or five main scaffold limbs have formed, the central leader is cut back above the top outward-growing scaffold limb. The center is kept open from that point up.

The training system you use depends in part on the fruit you grow. Train dwarf trees to a central leader for best light penetration and yields. Dwarf apples, pears, plums, and cherries are easy to train to this system, since one branch tends to grow dominantly over the others. Semidwarf or standard-size trees of these fruits or apricots also yield best when trained to a central leader, but home gardeners usually train them to a modified leader because it is easier to maintain with a larger tree. Peaches, nectarines, and Japanese plums are more easily trained to an open center because they don't have a dominant upward-growing branch. All other tree fruits can be trained to an open center, if desired.

The basic framework of the tree should be in place by the fourth or fifth season. Most trees will begin bearing between the third to seventh years. Young bearing trees need little pruning. Remove diseased or damaged branches, those which grow upright, water-sprouts, and root suckers. As the tree fills its allotted space, prune to keep it in bounds, thin out crowded branches, and maintain and renew fruiting wood. The types of pruning cuts you make depend on the way the tree grows and where the fruit is borne. For specific pruning information, see the individual chapters.

Keep in mind that pruning is a little like cutting hair: things always grow back. Short of cutting down the entire tree, it's hard to make a really irreparable mistake.

Central Leader Training and Pruning

These instructions are for training and pruning dwarf fruit trees to a central leader. Standard and semidwarf trees can also be trained to a central leader. Allow a maximum of ten scaffolds on these larger trees, and space them farther apart along the trunk.

Early summer of first year: Choose the most vigorous upright shoot arising from one of the uppermost buds on the trunk as the central leader. Prune off any trunk stub above this shoot. Remove the next two shoots below the central leader so they don't compete with it.

Remove any shoots arising within 18 inches of the ground. If possible, select several strong-growing side shoots for scaffold branches. The lowest branch should be 18 to 20 inches off the ground, and each successive branch should arise 5 to 8 inches above the one below and grow out in a different direction. When these selected shoots are 3 to 4 inches long, spread them with clothespins so they develop a wide crotch angle.

Other shoots should be kept weak growing, so they don't compete with the selected ones, and encouraged to bear fruit. One way to do this is to repeatedly pinch these shoots back to about 4 inches long, once a

Left: The central leader system features a dominant central trunk with scaffold branches that spiral out every 5 to 8 inches; no branch is directly above another. *Right:* Training begins in early summer of the first year. Branches lower than 18 inches are removed and the first scaffold branches selected.

New shoots that would make desirable branches but are growing too upright can be spread before their crotch angle hardens. A clothespin or piece of wood with notches cut in each end can be placed between the branch and the trunk, or the branch can be tied to the trunk or a stake in the ground. A weight fastened to a shoot will pull it down into the right position. Four-mil-thick grafting tape is good for tying branches; it's inexpensive and won't girdle the branches.

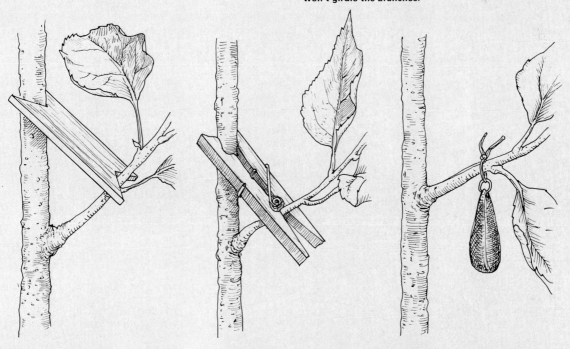

month during June, July, August, and (where growing seasons are long) September. Pinching induces the formation of fruit buds and fruit-bearing spurs. As an alternative you can severely bend down these shoots in mid- to late summer, when they are long enough, by looping them down and tying them to the trunk.

Early spring of second year: Make final selections of lower scaffold branches, and pull these down to an almost horizontal position by tying them to the trunk or to stakes in the ground. Head back the central leader at about 16 or 18 inches above the top scaffold branch to induce more scaffold branches to develop above the first set. Without this severe heading back of the leader, lower vegetative buds will not grow and the next set of scaffolds will be too far above the first. Make the cut just above a bud.

Head back the scaffold branches until the tree conforms to a Christmas tree shape, wider at the base and narrowing to the central leader tip. If the scaffolds' growth was thin and weak, head them back severely; cut only a few inches off strong-growing scaffolds.

Make cuts to a bud on the side of the branch; cutting back to a top bud will produce a shoot that grows straight up, and heading to a bottom bud leads to weak growth. Heading the scaffolds back will strengthen them and induce more secondary branches to form. This is necessary to develop a strong tree framework, but it delays fruiting on the scaffolds.

Encourage early fruiting and reduced vegetative growth on nonscaffold branches arising from the trunk. If not already pinched back or tied down, bend these down to *below* horizontal and tie to the trunk. Do not head these branches back during the dormant season; that would encourage vegetative growth. Thin, weak branches can be left alone.

Early summer of second year: Again choose the strongest-growing upright shoot near the top of the tree as the central leader, and prune off any trunk stub above this shoot. Remove the next two shoots below the central leader.

Similarly, choose a single shoot to continue the outward growth of each scaffold branch chosen last year,

In early spring of the second year, select lower scaffold branches and head them back. The central leader should also be headed back to induce new, higher scaffold branches to form.

In early spring of the fourth and following years, cut back the leader and scaffolds only slightly; work for a Christmas-tree shape. Continue standard pruning of dead or diseased wood, crossing or crowded branches, and so on.

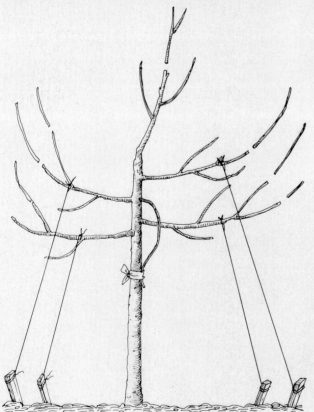

and remove the next two shoots below this shoot. When the terminal shoot of each scaffold is about 10 to 12 inches long, pinch out the growing tip to encourage more lateral branching.

Select well-spaced, strong-growing side shoots on the trunk for the next set of scaffolds, and spread them with clothespins. Pinch back or tie down other side shoots arising from the main trunk and overvigorous shoots arising from the scaffold branches chosen last year. Remove any root suckers.

Early spring of third year: Follow the same instructions as for the spring of the second year. Very little, if any, thinning of secondary branches on the scaffolds is needed at this time — remove only branches that are crossing, diseased, or damaged. Tie down secondary branches that grow vigorously or upright.

Early summer of third year: Follow the same instructions as for the summer of the second year. Your trees may bear some fruit this year. If the fruit load starts to bend the central leader, support the leader in an upright position with a temporary stick (½-by-½ inch will work) tied to the trunk and extending to the top of the leader.

Early spring of fourth and subsequent years: Continue this training until the tree has developed six to eight scaffold limbs and reached the desired height. At that time, during early spring of the fourth or fifth year, cut the leader back only slightly to a weak lateral branch. When the scaffolds reach the desired length, cut them back slightly to weak laterals also. Retain the Christmas tree shape — the higher the branches are in the tree, the shorter they should be.

Continue to remove dead, diseased, or damaged wood each year. Remove vigorous, upright branches or head them back to laterals. Thin out crossing or crowded branches, paying special attention to the upper and outer parts of the tree to admit adequate light into the center.

Branches that have borne crops for several years will be pulled down under the weight. Do not remove all drooping branches or you will lose fruit production in the lower part of the tree. Head drooping branches after they have fruited for three or four years, cutting them back to an outward-growing side branch.

Summer of fourth and subsequent years: Continue to select a new leader and scaffolds, and pinch or tie down other shoots, each year until the tree is trained.

Continue to remove root suckers and watersprouts each year in midsummer; this produces much less

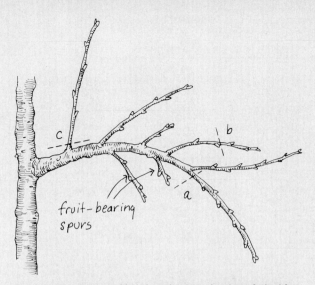

fruit-bearing spurs

Pruning a bearing tree. After drooping branches have fruited for 3 or 4 years, head them back to an outward-growing lateral (a). Select a new replacement lateral and head it back (b) to stimulate its growth. In a few years the drooping branch will be headed back to this lateral. Remove upright growth (c).

regrowth than sucker removal during the dormant season. Retain the established tree shape by pinching back shoots that are growing too vigorously.

After the scaffold branches begin bearing heavy crops in the fifth or sixth season, remove the weak temporary branches or cut them back to fruit-bearing spurs in midsummer. When the tree has filled its allotted space, keep it in bounds by pinching or cutting about ½ inch off of all new shoot growth in midsummer. This pinching also allows more light into the tree canopy, increasing formation of spurs and flower buds for next year's crop, and producing larger, sweeter fruit with better color. Do not summer-pinch trees that have lost many leaves to diseases.

Open Center Training and Pruning

Here are year-by-year instructions for training and pruning fruit trees to an open center.

Summer of first year: By early June most buds on the tree will have developed into leaves or growing shoots. The most vigorous shoots, arising from the top two or three buds, will have narrow crotch angles that are unsuitable for scaffold limbs. Cut these vigorous shoots back to two or three buds. Below these there should be wide-angled shoots, which you want to encourage. If you have no lower shoots, this severe pruning will usually cause lower buds to grow. If the new shoots from these lower buds start growing too upright, spread them with clothespins before the crotch angles harden.

About a month later, check the trees and cut the top shoots back again if necessary. As soon as the tree has three wide-angled branches spaced about equally around the trunk and arising from the trunk at 2- to 4-inch intervals, 18 to 26 inches off the ground, cut other branches back to a few inches of growth. If one of these scaffold branches is overly vigorous, cut it back to bring it into balance with the other two.

Early spring of second year: You will need to choose three scaffold branches if you didn't select them the summer before. If only two good scaffold branches have developed, you can train a third from a strong side branch coming from the base of one of the scaffolds. If one scaffold has grown much more than the other two, cut it back to bring it into balance with the others. Otherwise, do not head back the scaffolds; doing so will delay the onset of fruiting.

Cut the branches remaining in the center of the tree, above the three scaffolds, back to short stubs. A small cluster of shoot growth will develop from these stubs; this will help keep the scaffold branches growing outward and the center of the tree open.

Completely remove all growth arising from the trunk below the scaffold branches and any growth on the scaffold branches within 6 inches of the trunk. Remove any broken side branches and those with poor crotch angles, winter injury, or insect damage. Allow all other side branches on the scaffolds to remain.

Early summer of second year: Cut back the shoots arising from the stubby growth above the scaffold branches to 3 to 5 inches. Remove any growth arising from the trunk below the scaffold branches. If necessary, lightly prune the scaffold branches to maintain tree balance.

Early spring of third and subsequent years: Completely remove the stubby growth above the three scaffold limbs. The shape of the tree should now be well established.

The tree should have some flower buds by this time, if you have cared for it properly. If you prune between the time the buds swell and bloom occurs, you will be able to assess the winter damage to the flower buds, prune off branches with dead buds, and keep those with live blossoms. If bloom is light, leave as many blossoms as possible, but if it is heavy, cut longer branches back to lighten the crop load.

Continue to cut out dead, diseased, or damaged wood each year. Remove upright growth or cut it back to outward-growing branches. Thin out crowded branches and remove crossing or drooping branches.

As the tree grows, head back older branches to encourage the growth of new fruiting wood close to the trunk. Otherwise you will end up with long, unfruitful scaffold limbs bearing fruit only around the edges of the tree.

Summer of third and subsequent years: If the tree is vigorous and leaf cover is dense, pinch or cut the new growth back by an inch or so once or twice in mid-summer. This will keep the tree from putting too much energy into leaf growth instead of into developing flower buds, and will help keep the tree smaller. Be sure to leave enough leaf cover to prevent sunburn of newly exposed fruit. Also, if your tree is weak or has

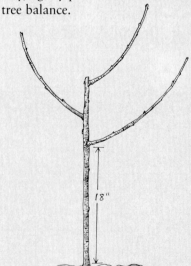

Basic first-summer scaffold structure of a tree being trained to an open center shape.

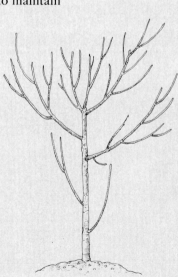

Early in the second year, cut branches in the center of the tree back to short stubs; prune any shoots developing below scaffolds.

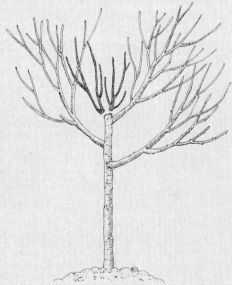

Remove growth in the center of the tree in the third and subsequent years to keep an open shape.

lost many of its leaves to disease, you shouldn't cut off new growth.

Modified Leader Training and Pruning

Modified leader training begins like central leader training, with well-spaced scaffold limbs radiating out in spiral-staircase fashion from a central trunk, instead of just three scaffolds arising from close to the same point as in the open center. In the modified leader system you will allow four or five scaffold limbs to develop, then cut back the leader to the top scaffold branch, rather than to a weak lateral branch as in the central leader system. This leaves the center of the tree open above the scaffolds.

Follow the same instructions as for central leader training, but lightly head back the scaffold branches each spring to encourage lateral branching, and keep them all about the same length. Once four or five well-spaced scaffolds have developed, cut the leader off above the top one. When the scaffolds reach the desired length, cut them back to a weak lateral branch as in the central leader system. Subsequent pruning is the same as for the central leader system, except that you keep the center open. Undesirable branches can again be temporarily retained, severely pinched back, or tied down to provide some fruit while the scaffolds are developing.

If you want a shade tree, a modified leader is a good choice. (Trees trained to a central leader or an open center must begin branching too close to the ground to make them suitable as shade trees.) Head the tree higher at planting time, at about 4 feet off the ground, and remove all laterals. During early summer of the first year, select a central leader shoot and remove the next two shoots below it. Pinch all other laterals back to invigorate the central leader. During early spring of the second year, head the leader back to 5 or 6 feet to induce scaffold branches to develop at the desired height of about 4 or 5 feet off the ground. Remove all lateral branches below this height. From this point on, follow the system for modified leader training — choosing and spreading scaffold branches, heading back the central leader and the scaffold branches each spring, and cutting back the leader to the top scaffold branch after four or five scaffolds have been chosen. The permanent bearing structure of these large trees will not fruit until the fifth to eighth season. If you want fruit a few years earlier, temporarily keep some undesirable branches and pinch them back or severely tie them down.

Renovating Neglected Mature Trees

Fruit trees that have not been pruned in several years are overly dense, unproductive throughout much of the tree canopy, too tall and wide, and probably contain many diseased and dead branches. You can reinvigorate these trees by careful dormant-season and summer pruning. If the tree has been neglected for many years or if many large cuts are needed, complete rejuvenation may take 2 or 3 years of rather severe pruning.

Up to half of the total wood can be removed from peaches or Japanese plums, so you can often renovate these trees in a single year. On the other hand, you should remove no more than one-third of the total wood during one pruning season of apples, cherries, apricots, or European plums. Don't remove more than one-tenth of the total wood of pears each year to avoid stimulating vigorous new growth susceptible to fire blight.

To renovate a tree by dormant-season pruning:

1. Remove all root suckers and watersprouts from the lower trunk to enable you to see the tree better.

2. Remove undesirable large limbs from the center of the tree, if necessary. Limbs that are entirely dead or diseased, or those which have split or have very narrow crotch angles, should be removed. Up to four large limbs may be removed in one year.

3. Remove large secondary branches with these same problems, and thin out crowded branches.

4. Lower the height of the tree where necessary. Up to 4 or 5 feet of growth can be removed in one year. Make cuts to outward-growing lateral branches.

5. Reduce the tree's spread by heading to lateral branches. Prune upper branches to shorter lengths than lower branches.

6. Remove all dead, diseased, and broken branches.

7. Remove most watersprouts and upright-growing branches entirely, or if they are needed to replace removed branches, head them back to a lateral branch or outer bud. Work from the outside of the tree in for better visibility.

8. Head back very weak drooping branches, and those which grow too long, to a strong lateral branch. Do not remove or head back all drooping branches, or the tree's fruiting zone will remain far off the ground. Drooping branches will become productive once they are no longer shaded from above, and are willowy enough to resist breaking under fruit loads.

9. If the remaining branches are still too dense, thin out those which are too close or cross each other. Make more thinning cuts in the outer parts of the tree to permit adequate light penetration into the center.

This heavy pruning will stimulate new growth, including root suckers and watersprouts. Remove these in midsummer. Also pinch or cut back the growing tips of all shoots around the outside of the tree. Continue renovating the tree the following dormant season, if needed.

Harvesting Tree Fruit

It may seem that there could be nothing simpler than plucking a ripe, luscious peach or apple off a tree. There is a trick to picking fruits properly, however. Don't pull down or straight away from the fruit spur. Instead, lift up each fruit with a slight twisting motion. This will prevent injury to the fruit spur and will ensure that the stem remains attached to the fruit. Handle fruits gently. Soft fruits like peaches and cherries bruise easily.

Cool ripe fruits in the refrigerator soon after picking, if possible. If you pick some fruits such as apricots and peaches before they are completely ripe, let them sit at room temperature to soften up.

Berries

For a gardener just venturing into the world of fruit growing, berries — including strawberries, raspberries, blackberries, and grapes — can be a good place to start. If you are intimidated by the intricacies of pruning and caring for fruit trees, take heart. Berries, in general, are less complicated and easier to grow. You can get started with a relatively modest investment and in a short time be enjoying a delicious harvest.

If you're gardening in a limited space, berries will pay you back handsomely for your efforts. Ten raspberry plants should bear up to 20 pints of delectable, jewel-like fruits once they are established, while a 10-by-12-foot patch of strawberries will provide the makings for many shortcakes. Grapevines can be trained along trellises to save space, or do double duty when grown on an arbor, providing both shade and fruit.

Controlling insect and disease problems on berries is usually less of a chore than on tree fruits. While none of the fruits is guaranteed problem-free, it is possible to enjoy many of the berries without resorting to sprays if they are properly planted and cared for.

Perhaps the biggest advantage of berries is how soon you'll be enjoying a harvest. Most of these small fruits begin to bear by the second year after planting. And, once planted, most will go on producing a bountiful crop for a decade or more with a minimum of care.

Growing your own allows you to enjoy fruits that may not be available in local markets. Blackberries are often hard to find, and raspberries are usually offered only at an exorbitant price. In addition, fruits fresh from your garden can be picked at the peak of ripeness and flavor.

So if you've put off growing fruits because you thought they were too difficult or took up too much space, think again! The following chart gives the basics for planting berries; see the individual chapters for detailed growing information.

Planting Guide for Berries

Kind of fruit	Zones of adaptation	Spacing (feet)	Year of bearing after planting	Yield/plant at maturity	Bearing season	Years of expected life	Fruit bud hardiness
Blackberry							
erect	4–8	7 x 3	2nd	1½–2 qt.	June–Aug.	10–12	sensitive
trailing	6–9	8 x 5	2nd	1½–2 qt.	June–Aug.	10–12	very sensitive
Grape	3–10	8 x 8	3rd	10–20 lbs.	Aug.–Sept.	25–30	mod. hardy
Raspberry							
red and yellow	2–9	6 x 2½	2nd	1½ qt.	July–Oct.	8–10	very hardy
black and purple	4–9	7 x 2½	2nd	1½ qt.	June–July	8–10	hardy
Strawberry							
June bearing	3–10	4 x 2	2nd	1 qt.	May–June	3–5	hardy
everbearing	3–10	3 x 2	1st	1 qt.	May–Sept.	2–4	hardy

Note: All berries are self-pollinating, so only one variety is necessary.
The values listed are approximations and may vary with varieties, locations, and care given to fruit plants.

Compiled by Brenda Olcott-Reid.

Apples

The beauty of apple trees — springtime blossoms and tasty fresh fruit in summer and fall — is easier to achieve today with the introduction of disease-resistant varieties and improved dwarfing rootstocks.

If you were told about Johnny Appleseed as a schoolchild, you may hope to grow apples as easily as he did, dropping seeds in the ground and leaving a trail of apple-laden trees across the continent.

Unfortunately, it's not that easy. Apples require a fair amount of patience and planning. If you want a choice crop, you'll have to control insects, diseases, and other pests, worry about the weather, prune every year, keep up with the harvest — which won't start for 3 years or more after planting — and gather drops before they clog the lawn mower.

Horticulturists have been working to help the home gardener simplify the task. They have developed disease-resistant varieties, strategies for defeating insects with far less spraying, easier ways to prune, and dwarfing and semi-dwarfing rootstocks that keep trees to a manageable size.

Apples can be grown almost everywhere in the United States. Good for eating out of hand, storing in the root cellar, preserving in jars as applesauce, and baked into innumerable desserts, apples are well worth the work.

Planning

When setting up a home orchard, you will find there are dozens of apple varieties to choose from. Talk to local nursery people, your county Extension Service agent, or other growers to help you select varieties that do well in your area.

Rootstock choice determines whether a tree is a dwarf, semidwarf, or standard size. Dwarf trees grow to be 8 to 12 feet tall and just as wide; semidwarf trees grow to be 12 to 18 feet tall and wide; and standard trees grow to be 18 to 22 feet tall and wide. In general, we recommend semi-dwarfing rootstocks for apples, if space permits, as true dwarfs are somewhat less hardy and therefore less suited to the coldest parts of the country. Dwarfs also need more fertile soil and must be staked for their entire life as the roots do not provide enough anchorage. Full-size, standard trees are big for home gardens, but because they are the most hardy, they may be the only choice in the far North.

The same rootstock combined with different varieties will produce trees of different sizes with differing degrees of vigor. Spur-type strains of a variety (for example, *Winespur* is a spur-type strain of *Winesap*) produce more fruit-bearing spurs and less

vegetative shoots than their parent variety. This dwarfs the tree by about 25 percent yet increases the yield.

Not all rootstocks, nor the apple varieties grafted onto them, will be successful in every region. Most varieties survive well in zones 5 to 7; there's a smaller, but still excellent, group of cold-hardy choices for zones 2 to 4. There are several low-chill varieties for the mild-winter areas of zones 8 to 10.

Some of the new disease-resistant varieties such as *Freedom, Liberty, Prima,* and *Priscilla* do *not* have to be sprayed for the first 3 or 4 years after planting. Once the trees begin bearing, sprays or special tactics must be used against insects attacking fruits. With all other varieties, a series of fungicide as well as insecticide sprays are required every season to control insects and diseases.

Apple blossoms need pollen from another variety to be fertilized. It's best to plant at least two varieties within 100 feet of each other. (You can set bouquets of another variety near a poor-setting tree to improve the fruit set.) If your trees are near other apple trees, cross-pollination is less of a concern since bees are sure to carry apple pollen to your trees. A few popular varieties don't produce good pollen, though they set well when pollinated. These include *Jonagold, Mutsu, Baldwin, Winesap,* and *Gravenstein.* If you grow any of these varieties, plant two others as well to ensure good cross-pollination.

Try to pick pairs of different early, mid-season, or late varieties to ensure that pollen of two varieties is available at the same time. Depending on your variety selection, you can have fresh apples from early July until early November in many areas.

Some apple varieties are best for cooking, others are good for eating fresh, and some are delicious for both. Varieties highly rated for eating fresh are numerous, including *McIntosh* and other "Mac" types such as *Jonamac* and *Jerseymac,* which bear fruit earlier than *McIntosh.*

Spur-type varieties such as this *Yellow Delicious* bear heavy crops at an early age because they have more fruit-bearing spurs and fewer vegetative shoots.

Prima, *Empire*, and *Macoun* are excellent for early, midseason, and late harvests, respectively, and are enjoying increasing popularity.

Golden Delicious and *Red Delicious* are two well-known, sweet-tasting varieties; *Lodi*, *Ozark Golden*, and *Rome Beauty* are examples of tarter fruits.

If you enjoy baked apples, consider *Cox Orange Pippin* or *Duchess*, old favorites, or more recent choices such as *Mutsu*, *Melrose*, and *Jonagold*, which are excellent for cooking as well as eating fresh.

Buy dormant, bare-root trees, at a local nursery. Get 1-year-old whips, if possible; if not, be sure the trees are not more than 3 years old. Younger trees will become established more quickly, are less costly, and allow you more control in the development of a good framework of branches.

Preparation

Apple trees will tolerate a wide range of soil conditions. While you can improve your soil with fertilizer and mulch, other factors — full sun, good water drainage, the right varieties, and loving care — will go a long way toward overcoming less-than-perfect soil.

Planting

In the North, plant as early in the spring as possible. In the South where fall and winter weather is moist and mild, fall planting works well; it gives the roots a good headstart on spring.

Dig a hole a foot wider and a foot deeper than the root ball, then partially fill it with topsoil or compost. Space standard trees 30 to 35 feet apart, semidwarfs 20 to 25 feet apart, and dwarfs 15 to 20 feet apart. Pound in a stake on the downwind side for support. Support is not essential for semidwarfs, but it is still a good idea for the first few years.

Place your tree in the hole and spread the roots carefully. With dwarf or semidwarf trees that have only one graft, make sure that the graft union (a small swelling

Essentials

Planning

🐦 *Select resistant varieties to minimize apple scab and other disease problems.*

🐦 *Apple trees are not self-fertile; plant at least one other variety that blooms at the same time. Flowering crab apples that bloom at the same time will work.*

🐦 *Spring planting is recommended in central and northern areas. Where fall and winter weather is generally mild and moist, fall planting is successful.*

🐦 *Buy dormant, bare-root, 1-year-old trees, if possible.*

🐦 *Dwarfs and semidwarfs will bear in 3 to 4 years, yielding 1 to 2 bushels per year. Standard-size trees will start to bear in 4 to 8 years, yielding 4 to 5 bushels of apples.*

Preparation

🐦 *Choose a site with full sun, moderate fertility, and good air circulation and water drainage.*

🐦 *Apples will tolerate a wide range of soil types.*

Planting

🐦 *When planting trees on dwarfing and semidwarfing rootstocks, be sure the graft union stays at least 1 inch above ground.*

🐦 *Space standard trees 30 to 35 feet apart, semidwarfs 20 to 25 feet apart, and dwarfs 15 to 20 feet apart.*

🐦 *Surround each tree with a mouse guard before filling the hole completely.*

🐦 *Water, prune, and mulch young trees right after planting.*

Care

🐦 *Water young trees regularly, especially those on semidwarfing or dwarfing rootstocks, to ensure that the root system becomes well established.*

🐦 *Renew the mulch periodically, but pull it away from the tree in the fall so mice don't nest over the winter and eat the bark.*

🐦 *Begin training trees to their permanent framework in the first season.*

🐦 *Prune bearing trees annually.*

🐦 *Apple maggots (page 400), plum curculios (page 401), green fruitworms (page 326), and codling moths (page 401) are pests that can trouble the crop. Annual spray programs are usually necessary.*

🐦 *Fire blight (page 404) and powdery mildew (page 405) are potential disease problems.*

Harvesting

🐦 *The harvest season ranges from midsummer to late fall, depending on the variety.*

🐦 *To avoid pulling out the stem when you harvest, cup the apple in your hand, tilt it upward, and twist to separate it from the spur at the point of attachment.*

near the base of the trunk) remains at least 1 inch above ground, or the upper variety will take root and override the desired influence of the rootstock.

Deep planting of both rootstock-dwarfed and interstem-dwarfed trees results in better tree anchorage and fewer suckers growing up from the roots. However, planting trees much deeper than they grew in the nursery can increase problems with crown rot. Plant trees on MM106 or M26 rootstocks just slightly deeper than they grew in the nursery. Plant trees on other dwarfing rootstocks deeper, and plant M7 as deeply as possible, taking care to keep the bud union a few inches above ground. With interstem varieties, the interstem section should be half above and half below the ground.

Before you fill the hole, place a mouse guard around the trunk to extend about 10 inches or so above the ground.

Water your fledglings thoroughly. Then mulch with clean straw or some other weed-free organic material to keep the soil moist and to control weeds. (For more detailed planting instructions, see pages 301–303.)

Care

Train dwarf apple trees to the central leader system (see pages 311–313). In the early years of growth it's important to create a strong framework of scaffold branches because apples can bear heavy crops year after year.

Semidwarfing trees can be trained to a central leader shape, but are more easily

Characteristics of Commonly Used Apple Rootstocks and Interstem/Rootstock Combinations

Rootstock	Tree height (ft.)	Bears fruit early	Staking needed	Soil drainage needed	Adaptation to		Winter hardiness	
					Sandy loam	Clay loam		
M27 (EMLA 27)	4–6	yes	yes	good	yes	maybe	tender	
M29 (EMLA 9)	8–12	yes	yes	good	no	yes	hardy	
M26 (EMLA 26)	10–14	yes	yes	very good	yes	no	hardy	
M7a	12–16	yes	maybe	good	no	yes	mod. hardy	
MM106 (EMLA 106)	16–20	yes	no	very good	yes	no	mod. hardy	
MM111 (EMLA 111)	18–22	no	no	good	yes	yes	hardy	
Antonovka	22–28	no	no	good	yes	yes	very hardy	
Novole	24–30	yes	no	good	yes	yes	hardy	
Interstem/Rootstock								
M27/MM106	8–10	yes	no	very good	yes	no	slightly hardy	
M27/MM111	9–11	yes	no	good	yes	yes	slightly hardy	
M9/MM106	10–12	yes	no	very good	yes	no	mod. hardy	
M9/MM111	12–14	yes	no	good	yes	yes	hardy	
M8s/Antonovka	10–14	yes	no	good	yes	yes	very hardy	
M8s/K-14 Seedling	10–14	yes	no	good	yes	yes	very hardy	

trained to a modified leader system. Standard trees should also be trained to a modified leader. Larger trees need more pruning and you'll eventually have to use a ladder to get the job done. Spur-type apples require less pruning than other trees because they produce more fruiting spurs and less vegetative growth. *Delicious* types have a strong vertical growth habit, so scaffold branches should be spread in the first few years and beyond, if necessary, to force them to grow more horizontally.

Apples are often grown without any thinning other than what nature provides in the annual spring drop. However, to avoid potential disease and insect problems, you might want to thin after the natural fruit drop (about 4 to 6 weeks after bloom) to one fruit per cluster, or about 6 to 8 inches between fruit.

Home gardeners who wouldn't dream of using pesticides on other crops may have to consider this option with apples. The fruit are subject to many insect and disease attacks that twist, perforate, and mangle them; most caretakers must spray to get an acceptable crop. But there is an alternative.

You can avoid using fungicides by selecting disease-resistant varieties such as *Prima, Priscilla, Liberty,* and *Freedom.* These have been field tested for many years and require no spraying for apple scab, cedar-apple rust, and other common diseases, while most other varieties require periodic spraying every spring and summer after planting.

	Susceptibility to		Fire Blight		Tendency to Grow		
Drought	Crown Rot	Woolly Aphids	Suckers	Variety	Burr Knots	Root Suckers	Sources
VS	R	VS	S	more S	mod.–high	mod.–high	120, 137
VS	R	VS	VS	more S	mod.–high	mod.–high	116, 133, 134, 148
VS	S	VS	VS	more S	high	low	116, 119, 120, 133, 137, 142, 149
S	MS	VS	MR	slightly more S	mod.–high	high	116, 118, 119, 120, 133, 154
MS	MS	VR	S	more S	moderate	moderate	119, 120, 132, 133, 137, 156
R	MR	VR	MR	no effect	moderate	moderate	119, 120, 131, 133, 134, 137, 157
R	R	MS	MR	no effect	low	moderate	118, 119, 133
R	R	MS	MR	no effect	very low	moderate	Check locally
MS	MS	VR	S	more S	mod.–high	moderate	132
R	R	VR	MR	more S	mod.–high	moderate	119
MS	MS	VR	VS	more S	mod.–high	moderate	131, 133, 142
R	R	VR	S	more S	mod.–high	moderate	116, 131, 133, 142
R	R	MS	MR	slightly more S	moderate	moderate	154
R	MR	MS	MR	slightly more S	moderate	moderate	154

R—resistant; *MR*—moderately resistant; *VR*—very resistant; *S*—susceptible; *MS*—moderately susceptible; *VS*—very susceptible.
Compiled by Brenda Olcott-Reid.

Dwarfing Rootstocks for Apples

Up to nine different varieties on dwarfing rootstocks can be grown in the space devoted to one standard-size apple tree. Quite a few dwarfing rootstocks are used for apples, each with its own degree of dwarfing, soil adaptation, pest susceptibility, and management needs.

The dwarfing rootstocks in current use were developed in East Malling, England, or cooperatively between scientists in East Malling and Merton, England. The Malling series are identified by *M* followed by a number, and the Malling-Merton series by *MM* followed by a number. The numbers have nothing to do with how dwarfing the rootstock is, but of those commonly propagated, Mallings are fully dwarfing and Malling-Mertons semidwarfing.

All of these dwarfing rootstocks, except the semidwarfing MM111, induce the variety to bear fruit at a younger age than do standard seedling rootstocks. However, all but MM111 are much less drought-tolerant than seedlings and require irrigation. The most dwarfing rootstocks are poorly anchored, and trees must be supported by a sturdy stake.

All of these rootstocks require well-drained soil, but M26 and MM106 are especially sensitive to wet conditions and should only be planted on raised mounds in very well drained spots. These two rootstocks perform well in sandy loam soils but not so well in clay loams, while M9 and M7 do the opposite. Loam soil suits them all.

All the Malling rootstocks are highly susceptible to woolly apple aphids, a soil pest that attacks the roots. A large woolly apple aphid population on these rootstocks can stop tree growth, so do not choose them if this pest is a problem in your area. The Malling-Merton rootstocks are very resistant to woolly aphids.

Root suckers of M9, M26, and MM106 are susceptible to fire blight, which spreads easily to the variety. Varieties on these rootstocks also tend to be more blight-susceptible than the same varieties on other rootstocks. Avoid using these rootstocks with highly blight-susceptible varieties, such as *Granny Smith, Golden Russet, Jonathan, Jonagold, Sir Prize, Spigold,* and *Tydeman Red.*

Winter hardiness of the rootstocks varies. MM106 keeps the variety actively growing later into the fall, which can prevent proper tree hardening. This can lead to winter damage, especially to the crown, and subsequent crown rot. Delayed hardening of trees on MM106 is accentuated when the fruit ripens late in the season, so MM106 should not be used with late-ripening varieties.

One way to have a fully dwarfed apple tree, yet avoid the problems of the Malling rootstocks, is to buy a tree with an M9 or M27 interstem. The interstem dwarfs the tree and induces early bearing, while the Malling-Merton rootstock provides some additional dwarfing, good anchorage that doesn't require staking, and high resistance to woolly apple aphids.

The MM111 is an excellent rootstock choice in this situation as it also provides drought tolerance, resistance to fire blight, moderate resistance to crown rot, and adaptation to either sandy loam or clay loam soils. MM106 as the rootstock will produce a slightly smaller tree, but should be planted only on very well drained soil, and more summer irrigation should be provided. Again, do not choose MM106 for a late-maturing variety or one that's very susceptible to fire blight. M27 as an interstem produces a smaller tree than M9, but is less winter hardy, and is often killed in the lower Midwest.

The dwarfing rootstock M27 induces this *Empire* apple tree to bear fruit at a younger age than would a standard seedling rootstock.

You can also reduce the need for insecticides from the usual 10 or 12 annual sprayings if you combine them with other controls. The entire crop may not be flawless, but home growers can afford to be less finicky than commercial orchardists about the appearance of their fruit.

The apple maggot is one of the most troublesome pests to apple growers in Eastern North America. The female fly punctures the skin of the apple and injects an egg into the fruit. The larva, commonly called a railroad worm, tunnels within the flesh of the apple, creating long, brown, winding paths as it goes.

If you're troubled by apple maggots, you can trap them by coating balls with a sticky substance called Tangle Trap, available at garden stores. (As always, be sure to pick up and destroy immediately all infected fruits that drop.) Proper timing of the traps is crucial for success. They should be hung out in time to catch the earliest apple maggot flies, which begin to emerge from mid-June to early July (south to north, respectively). Once the traps are up, leave them in place throughout the growing season.

One or two traps will help you monitor your apple maggot flies, but it takes many more to control them effectively. Use one trap per 100 apples, or one per bushel of large apples and one per half-bushel of small apples. As a general guideline, hang one trap for each fully dwarfed tree, two to four traps for a semidwarf, and six or more for a standard tree.

Position the traps carefully. There must be abundant fruit and foliage below and beside the trap, but the trap must remain visible. Leave a 6- to 12-inch open area all around it.

How often the traps will have to be cleaned depends on the insects in your area. If the traps get cluttered with large insects, you can pick them off with a stick about once a month.

The sticky Tangle Trap coating will most likely last through the season unless

Apple maggots can be troublesome pests, but they can be trapped. The rule of thumb is to use one trap per 100 apples. Position the traps above abundant fruit and foliage, but leave enough space around them to keep them visible.

you have especially heavy rainfall, in which case you might have to recoat the traps once during the summer. Instructions for coating are included in the product package.

To clean the traps off completely at the end of the season, first cut a piece of stiff but flexible plastic from a milk jug. Cup it in your hand and, letting the edge follow the curve of the ball, scrape off the insects. At the beginning of the next year, recoat with Tangle Trap.

Another troublesome pest is the plum curculio. Unfortunately, to control this insect, pesticides are the only recourse (see page 380). Try Imidan, a broad-spectrum insecticide with mild residual activity that is least harmful to the natural predators of mites and aphids. Spray when you notice the first crescent-shaped egg-laying scars on fruits and again 7 to 10 days later. As a bonus, Imidan used against plum curculio can eliminate several other unwelcome insects such as codling moths and green fruitworms. (Check with your Extension Service to make sure Imidan is approved for use in your state.)

Green fruitworm moths emerge in early spring and begin laying eggs about the time apple trees are in the ½-inch green leaf stage. The young larvae feed on new leaves and flower bud clusters; as they grow older, they chew holes in young fruit. Worms are active for about a month after bloom. They may take only a few bites from a fruit or consume it entirely. Severely injured apples will drop. Those that mature are often misshapen by large, indented, corky areas. Apply Imidan at petal fall, which should control this worm in most areas. If not, spray with *Bacillus thuringiensis*, a biological insecticide, as required.

The codling moth larva burrows into the flesh of the apple and feeds near the seed core. A grainy mass of brown frass leaking out of the entry hole is a sure sign of an active codling moth. If you are already using Imidan for plum curculio, your last spray may have taken care of codling moth problems. If not, you may have to spray once in the summer.

Use pheromone traps to time an Imidan application specifically for codling moths (see page 398). The traps catch only male moths so they will not provide adequate control, but they will tell you when the moths are active.

The tarnished plant bug is not too much of a problem for backyard growers because it doesn't destroy a lot of fruit. But it does suck juices from the developing buds and young fruit and inject a toxic substance that creates a dimple on the apple skin. Don't worry about the blemish — it's purely cosmetic.

Scales, mites, and aphids should be controlled by natural parasite and predator populations if you haven't used a lot of

To harvest apples such as these *Golden Russets*, twist the fruit upward with a rotating motion. If it separates easily from the tree, it's ready to pick.

sprays. For problem areas, you can try an anti-insect oil (for example, Superior Oil, 60-second viscosity), usually available where pesticides are sold. Spray it in the spring when your apple trees are in the tight cluster stage: after the leaves have unfolded from the fruiting cluster, but before the buds begin to show pink.

Harvesting

Most apples are ready to pick when they separate easily from the tree. With some varieties, you may notice the fruit softening a bit or apples may start dropping.

Another indicator is the color of seeds in the core — when they turn dark brown, the apples are ready.

Don't yank on the apple to pick it; instead, twist the fruit upward with a rotating motion.

Early-season apples tend to start bearing at a younger age; but they generally don't keep long after harvesting them. Many late-season types have good keeping qualities — they'll keep for a few weeks in a cool place. In a good root cellar, storage apples can keep 5 months or so.

Special Apple Varieties

Variety	Zones	Comments	Sources
Disease-Resistant Varieties			
Beacon	3–6	Red; early to midseason; resistant to scab and fire blight.	119, 133
Freedom	5–8	Highly resistant to apple scab, good resistance to cedar-apple rust and fire blight; very productive, ripens with *Delicious*; flavor is slightly subacid, good fresh or for sauce or juice.	134, 148, 153, 156
Liberty	4–6	Deep red; early fall; resistant to fire blight, cedar-apple rust, powdery mildew, scab.	130, 141, 142, 154
Prima	5–8	Dark red; midseason; fair to good quality for fresh use; keeps well; resistant to scab, fire blight, powdery mildew; tends to have bitter pit early in life.	119, 133, 154
Priscilla	5–8	Bright red blush on yellow; midseason; good keeper; good pollinizer for *Prima*; resistant to scab, fire blight, powdery mildew.	134, 152, 154
Sir Prize	5–8	Yellow; not a pollinizer for other apples; tends to bruise; resistant to fire blight, cedar-apple rust, powdery mildew, scab.	138
Sweet Sixteen	4–6	Good cooking apple with high sugar content; red striped; late; good keeper; resistant to fire blight, scab, cedar-apple rust.	142
Low-Chill Varieties			
Anna	8–10	Yellow with slight red blush; requires pollinizer such as *Dorsett Golden*; early; keeps for a couple of months at cool temperatures.	17, 125
Dorsett Golden	8–10	Like *Golden Delicious*; good pollinizer for *Anna*; suitable where temperatures stay above 45°F.	17, 125
Winter Banana	5–10	Pale yellow with pink blush. Aromatic; tangy taste. Good keeper.	130, 141, 142, 153
Cold-Hardy Varieties			
Honeygold	3–5	Similar to *Yellow Delicious*; late; stores well; good for cooking and eating.	133
McIntosh	3–5	Red with sweet, white flesh; midseason; somewhat disease-prone.	119, 133, 135, 141, 142
Regent	3–5	Red; good keeper; good for cooking and eating.	133
Yellow Transparent	2–7	Yellow; early; poor keeper; good for cooking and eating; scab resistant.	133, 152, 153

Apricots

Luscious apricots are ready for picking when they develop that rich apricot color and the skin gives slightly when pressed. In heavy-harvest years, fruits can be sliced and dried easily.

Apricots are beautiful to look at and wonderful to eat, but many people still don't fully appreciate them. Fresh apricots are difficult to find in many markets because they don't ship well. And although dried apricots are delicious, they are expensive.

The commercial growing range for apricots is limited, but home gardeners can grow them successfully in many parts of the country by selecting the right variety and location for the tree. Genetic dwarf varieties can be grown in containers. In areas with severe winters, you can wheel them into the garage or other sheltered area until spring warms things up outdoors.

Apricot trees can be a lovely centerpiece in a yard: their blossoms are white or pink; their foliage is bronze in the spring, deep green in the summer, and yellow in the fall.

Apricots in the North

Apricots are much hardier than most people think. The trees can take bitter temperatures, sometimes down to −20°F. However, because they have a low chilling requirement (400 to 900 hours), they respond to any warm period in late winter or very early spring by bursting forth with blossoms that are then easily killed by a frost. The longer you keep the trees from blooming, the more likely it is they'll escape a late frost.

To encourage your trees to bloom late, plant them where they'll stay cool in the spring. The north side of a building is a good location. Set the tree where it is shaded in the spring; as the sun gets higher in the summer, it will get plenty of light. You can also delay blooming by mulching the roots heavily in late winter so the soil will thaw later.

Some years it may be too cold for bees to be out pollinating when apricots bloom, which could limit the crop. Some smaller insects do come out and pollinate blossoms whenever temperatures rise even for a short period. Because these insects don't fly very far, you may consider planting a few apricots closer to each other than the 25-foot distance usually recommended.

Although most apricots are considered self-fertile, some, especially several of the hardier ones such as *Moongold* and *Sungold,* are not, so check carefully when buying or ordering trees. You may need another variety for cross-pollination.

Standard trees can grow 20 to 30 feet tall and can live up to 75 years or more in ideal climates. In the North, where the trees are under unusual stress, they'll probably survive about 15 years (more if the climate is favorable) and grow to be about 20 feet tall.

Planning

Apricots bloom earlier in the spring than other fruit trees and have only a limited tolerance of high summer heat. While the tree is fairly hardy (some varieties withstand winter lows down to −20°F), it can bloom too early — if you get a warm spell in late February or early March. In areas that have late frosts, you can choose some of the newer varieties developed in the North that bloom later and produce well in harsh climates.

When choosing a variety, select one recommended for your zone and climate that will flower after the last spring frost in your area and that will live through your winter. In preferred apricot growing areas such as Santa Clara and San Benito counties in California, you will want to consider the ripening period — early, midseason, or late.

Most varieties are self-fertile; that is, one variety is all you need for trees to set fruit. The full-size trees generally grow to be between 20 and 30 feet tall and live

The *Floragold* tree at right is trained to a vase shape, or an open center. Train apricot trees to an open center in mild climates, to a modified central leader in harsher climates.

Under good growing conditions, apricot trees produce too many fruits. Thinning the fruits in each cluster guarantees you'll get large and healthy apricots.

about 75 years. Most will start bearing in their third or fourth year.

According to the International Dwarf Fruit Tree Association, there are no satisfactory dwarfing stocks for apricots (though current research may turn up a good one soon). If you really want a dwarf tree, try a genetic dwarf such as *Stark Golden Glo* or *Garden Annie* apricot. These trees are naturally small, so they don't need to be grafted onto dwarfing stock.

To find the best variety for your garden, match your climate to the zones outlined on pages 296–297. Unfortunately, the best quality fruit seems to come with the least hardy trees. If you live in a warm portion of your zone, you may want to take a chance from the next less hardy group.

Plant trees in early spring in the North and East; in California and other mild-winter areas, you can plant in the fall.

Essentials

Planning

❧ *Plant new trees in early spring. Fall planting in mild areas can be successful if trees are dormant.*

❧ *Buy dormant, bare-root, 1-year-old trees, if possible.*

❧ *Although most varieties are self-fertile, fruit set is better when planted with one or two other varieties nearby.*

❧ *Trees will start bearing in the third or fourth season.*

❧ *Expect 3 to 4 bushels of fruit from a standard-size tree, 1 to 2 from a dwarf variety.*

Preparation

❧ *Choose a site in full sun. Northern growers should put trees on the north side of a building so trees warm up as late as possible in the spring.*

❧ *Apricot trees do well in a wide range of well-drained soils.*

Planting

❧ *Space standard-size trees about 25 feet apart; plant genetic dwarfs 8 to 12 feet apart.*

Care

❧ *Apply a small amount of nitrogen fertilizer each spring.*

❧ *Where apricots are easily grown, train to an open center. For colder areas use a modified central leader.*

❧ *Prune bearing trees annually to encourage new fruiting spurs.*

❧ *When fruits are 1 inch in diameter, thin to 3 to 4 fruits per cluster to increase the size of remaining apricots and prevent over-bearing one year, little the next.*

❧ *Apricots may be bothered by codling moths (page 401), peach tree borers (page 401), and plum curculios (page 401).*

❧ *In humid areas, watch for brown rot disease (page 404).*

❧ *Gophers (page 306) are attracted to the roots.*

Harvesting

❧ *Harvesting peaks in July in mild areas and in August in colder ones. The picking season is short.*

❧ *Pick when fruits are fully colored and skin gives slightly when pressed.*

Regional Notes

Far North (colder parts of zone 5 and beyond)

Manchurian types are truly hardy apricots that grow more as bushes than trees. Since they're most often grown from seed, their quality varies a lot. Many have a sort of woody flavor, others are tasty. *Moongold* and *Sungold* are recommended for the far North. They both have medium-size fruit. *Moongold* has a tough skin, but good quality flesh; *Sungold* is mild and sweet. Plant them together to insure pollination.

Zone 5

Alfred produces a medium-size, juicy, freestone fruit with a sweet, rich flavor. It is self-fertile and a reliable producer. *Sundrop* ripens just before *Alfred*. Its fruit is bright orange, juicy, sweet, and has a medium-firm texture and a mild flavor. The pit clings slightly some years. *New York 544* produces deep orange, sweet, rich, freestone fruits. It is as hardy as *Alfred* and ripens 4 days later.

Zone 6

Harcot, Harglow, Hargrand, Harlayne, and *Harogem* are all introductions from the Harrow, Ontario, research station. They should produce reliably in zone 6 and may do well in parts of zone 5. *Harglow* blooms late, an advantage in areas with late frosts. *Hargrand* produces large fruits (up to 2½ inches in diameter). *Veecot* has very firm flesh and is excellent for canning, jam, or drying, although it is not as good as some of the others for fresh eating. *Stark Sweetheart* has deep orange fruits with edible almondlike kernels (most peach and apricot seeds should never be eaten).

Zone 7

Any variety will grow well in this zone.

Zones 8 and 9 (low-chill varieties)

Gold Kist has early yellow fruit with a red blush and is a heavy bearer. *Katy* produces a large, vigorous tree with large, red-blushed, early fruit. *Royal (Blenheim)* is an old European variety of high quality. The fruit is large if thinned, and the tree is highly productive. *Early Golden, Moorpark,* and *Hungarian* are also good choices for these zones.

Far right: By espaliering, or training a tree to grow flat, it's possible to grow a mini apricot orchard along a fence. The fruit is easy to harvest, and pest and disease problems are easier to control because of good ventilation and sunlight infiltration.

Preparation

Choose a site in full sun. In cold climates, set trees on the north side of a building, if possible, so that trees will warm up later in the spring and blossoms will be delayed until the danger of frost has passed. Apricots are not very particular about soil type as long as it is well drained.

Planting

Plant standard-size trees about 25 feet apart; space genetic dwarfs 8 to 12 feet apart. Apricots have the same planting requirements as other fruit trees (see pages 301–303).

Care

Apricots need water consistently throughout the growing season. Lack of moisture in early summer will result in small fruits; later in the season, it can interfere with bud set for next year's crop. You will probably need to water deeply every 10 to 14 days if there is no rain. Where there is plenty of moisture in the winter and spring, you may need to water only three or four times during the summer. Mulch around the trees to retain moisture and keep grass down.

Many growers in western states train young apricot trees to a vase shape (open center). In harsher climates a modified central leader is a better idea. Fruit develops on spurs of 1-year-old branches; the spurs live for 3 or 4 years. Weak branches require thinning or heading to strong lateral branches to encourage new fruiting wood and expose more of the inner parts of the tree to sun and air. Remove fruiting wood that is 6 years old or older. Since apricots bloom very early and many flowers may be killed by frost, wait until after petal fall to prune.

If the fruit set appears heavy, you will also need to thin the fruit. Under good growing conditions trees produce too many fruits. If all the fruits are allowed to stay on the trees, your apricots will be small, and the weight of the fruits could break the branches. Thin out the weakest

fruits to the three or four healthiest apricots per cluster.

The best time to thin is when fruits measure about 1 inch across. If you have only one or two trees, hand-pick the excess fruits. If you have several trees, you can take a broom handle and knock the fruits off the branches, although this method may injure them.

Apricots are relatively free of pests and diseases. However, in areas where humidity tends to be high, brown rot disease can pose serious problems. Aside from the plum curculio, few insects bother these trees. Protect trees from gophers when planting (see page 306).

Harvesting

The harvest season for apricots is July in mild climates and August in colder ones, though different varieties can be slightly earlier or later. Expect 3 to 4 bushels of fruit from a full-size tree, 1 to 2 from a dwarf. Pick the fruits after they attain a rich apricot color and give slightly when pressed. The apricot season is short, so try to plan around it. If you leave for a 2-week vacation at the crucial time, you may come back to bushels of spoiled fruit on the ground.

Apricot Rootstocks

Buy varieties propagated on apricot seedling rootstocks, not peach rootstocks, such as *Lovell* or *Halford,* or plum rootstocks, such as *Myrobalan,* which many nurseries use. Apricots on peach or plum roots may not live as long or produce as well because of genetic differences. Furthermore, most apricot seedlings are immune to root-knot nematodes, resistant to lesion nematodes, and moderately resistant to peach tree borers. Peach seedlings are susceptible to all of these, and *Myrobalan* plum is susceptible to borers and lesion nematodes. Peach rootstocks do offer moderate resistance to bacterial canker, which may be worth a reduction in tree longevity in some areas.

In the coldest parts of the apricot's range, choose the closely related Manchurian apricot or Siberian apricot as rootstocks for their extra hardiness and resistance to trunk splitting during winter. These rootstocks also dwarf the tree somewhat. Seedlings of both types are also offered by nurseries as fruiting bushes or small trees, but the quality of the fruit is inferior.

Do not purchase apricots dwarfed by Nanking cherry or sand cherry rootstocks.

Apricot Sources

Alfred *142*
Early Golden *17, 125, 158*
Garden Annie *144*
Gold Kist *144*
Harcot *119, 133, 142*
Harglow *142*
Hargrand *133, 142*
Harlayne *133, 142*
Harogem *119, 133, 142*
Hungarian *158, 159*
Katy *144*
Moongold *128, 129, 141*
Moorpark *17, 125, 158*
New York 544 *142*
Royal (Blenheim) *120*
Stark Golden Glo *154*
Stark Sweetheart *154*
Sundrop *142*
Sungold *129, 141*
Veecot *133, 142*

Rootstock Sources

Apricot seedling *142*
Halford peach *12, 119, 124, 134*
Lovell peach *124, 129*
Manchurian apricot *15, 154*
Myrobalan seedling *129, 141*
Standard American plum *135*
St. Julien plum *154*

Blackberries

Trained to a wire trellis like the *Marion* blackberries at left or to a post (*above*), a few blackberry plants will give you a prolific harvest.

The great tangles of thorny blackberry vines that sprawl over abandoned farmland in some parts of this country are a far cry from the tamer types that, with a little coaxing, grow tidily in even a small backyard.

Blackberries are among the easiest fruits to grow at home. Cultivated varieties have larger berries than the wild types. They'll start to bear the second year after planting and continue for about 15 years. Trained properly, four plants, each with a 3-by-3-foot growing area, can supply enough berries for a family of four. Where winters are not too severe, the new thornless varieties do well.

Blackberries are classified botanically as *Rubus,* a genus that also includes raspberries. Blackberries may be called dewberries in some areas. Boysenberries, marionberries, or loganberries are not separate species, just common names for the blackberry varieties *Boysen, Marion,* and *Logan.*

Compared to the wild types that gardeners grew years ago, today's blackberry varieties are superior strains, with a more erect growth habit, more and larger berries with smaller seeds, and greater disease resistance.

Planning

You may be tempted to start your blackberry patch with plants from a neighbor; blackberries are prolific and tend to spread widely, so people often give plants away. It's easy to do, too. The upright types form suckers up to 10 feet from the parent so you can just dig up the well-rooted young shoots in the spring and move them. Trailing blackberries will root where the tip of a cane touches the ground, making a new plant in no time. But don't accept donated plants unless you're sure your neighbor's patch is healthy.

Viruses are a widespread problem with blackberries. Symptoms aren't dramatic, so early detection may be difficult. Plants decline gradually, producing less and less until you're left with berryless brambles. There's no way to cure such infections.

If possible, purchase certified virus-free plants from a reputable nursery. Once you have a few good plants you can multiply them by digging up suckers or by rooting cane tips.

Preparation

Blackberries need full sun. They aren't fussy about soils, although good drainage is important. If the soil has a good amount of humus, so much the better, but average fertility is all they need.

Do not plant blackberries where any other brambles have been growing; diseases can build up over time and one of the easiest ways to avoid problems is to start fresh on a new site. Because wild blackberries and raspberries can harbor diseases and pests, try to keep your garden plants at least 300 feet from any wild relatives. Also avoid planting where any nightshade family members — tomatoes, potatoes, eggplants, peppers — grew in the last 2 years, as they can transmit verticillium wilt to blackberry plants.

Planting

Plants should be set out in early spring. If you get your plants from a mail-order company, order them at least a month or two before planting time and indicate the week you'd like the plants to arrive. If you can't plant the day they arrive, keep plants, well wrapped, in a cool place. If they are loose and unpacked, set them temporarily in a shallow trench at the edge of the garden and fill it with soil so the roots don't dry out.

Nursery plants may have a 6- or 8-inch dormant cane extending from the root ball. You can use it as a handle in moving the plants and later as a row marker.

Set the plants in the ground 1 inch deeper than they were grown in the nursery, then firm moist soil around the roots. Plant upright varieties at least 3 feet apart in the row, with 8 feet between rows. For trailing types, allow 5 to 8 feet between plants and 6 to 10 feet between rows.

The plants are relatively drought tolerant, but they'll need a steady supply of water to get them established. In the second and subsequent years, plants need 1 to 2 inches of water per week during fruit development, especially if the weather turns dry and windy, a bit less once the crop is harvested. Drip irrigation is a good watering method for blackberries.

Care

Each year blackberry plants produce new canes from the crown just below the soil surface, and from roots that extend some distance out. Each cane lives for 2 years. The first year a cane produces only leaves, the second year it bears fruit. It won't fruit again, so old canes should be pruned out as soon as possible after the harvest to prevent disease from attacking the plant.

Pruning reduces stress on the plants. Keep enough fruiting canes to have a good crop and remove the rest along with undesired root suckers each year.

That sounds simple enough, and it is, except that there are two different types of blackberries, upright and trailing, and each requires a different pruning method. The upright ones produce arching canes that can just support themselves. Included

One-year-old thornless berries trained to a wire system. Fruits are similar to regular blackberries, but are often a bit seedier. Taste will vary, though many varieties have a slight tang to them.

The illustrations at right show the growth habits of upright (*top*) and trailing (*bottom*) blackberries. Most thornless varieties are trailing types with fruit all along the vine. Upright types bear fruit at the tips of the canes.

in this group are the semi-uprights, which flop a bit but can be treated just like the uprights. The trailing types sprawl and must be supported on wires.

The two groups also bear their fruit differently: upright kinds have fruit at the tips of the canes, trailing kinds have berries all along their length. The trailing types tend to be less hardy than the uprights, but they are usually more productive. Most thornless types have a trailing habit. Uprights take less space and are a bit easier to manage. Your choice depends on where you live, how much space you have, and the variety of fruit you prefer.

Essentials

Planning
🍂 *Choose virus-free plants.*
🍂 *Plan a training system to match the growth habit of your variety — either upright or trailing.*
🍂 *Plant in early spring in most areas; in mild-winter areas of the South and Pacific Coast, plant in fall or winter.*

Preparation
🍂 *Choose a well-drained site in full sun at least 300 feet from any wild blackberries.*
🍂 *Construct trellises for trailing varieties before planting.*

Planting
🍂 *Plant upright varieties at 3-foot intervals in rows 8 feet apart. Set trailing varieties 5 to 8 feet apart in rows 6 to 10 feet apart.*
🍂 *Set plants 1 inch deeper than they were grown in the nursery.*

Care
🍂 *Cultivate shallowly; the roots are near the surface.*
🍂 *Mulch with a thick layer of shredded bark, wood chips, leaves, or hay.*
🍂 *Plants usually don't require pruning the first year. Prune out fruiting canes as soon as berries are harvested each summer, and select replacement canes for the following year.*
🍂 *Fertilize early each spring with ½ to ¾ cup of a complete fertilizer such as 5-10-10 or 8-8-8 per plant. Sprinkle it in a band 12 to 24 inches from canes and hoe it lightly into the soil.*
🍂 *To prevent chilling injury in the winter, lay the canes of trailing types on the ground in winter and cover with a thick layer of mulch.*
🍂 *Viruses (page 336) may result from using diseased stock or setting out new plants near wild, diseased specimens. Aphids (page 400) suck the juice from plant foliage and transmit several virus diseases as well. Orange rust (page 404) is another problem disease.*
🍂 *Mites (page 397) and raspberry crown borers (page 402) can be problem pests.*

Harvesting
🍂 *Berries should be harvested every 2 to 4 days when ripe.*
🍂 *Pick berries in the cool of early morning. Refrigerate berries immediately after harvesting.*

Regional Notes

South (zones 7, 8, 9)

Plant root cuttings or plants in the winter, November through February. Choose one of the low-chill varieties such as *Brazos,* a thorny upright type, or *Cheyenne,* recommended for Arkansas and surrounding areas. *Olallie* is a newer hybrid trailing type. If diseases are a problem in your area, cut all the canes to the ground after harvest — they'll have plenty of time to grow back by the end of the season.

West (zones 7, 8, 9)

Choose low-chill varieties in mild-winter areas. Favorites on the Pacific Coast include *Boysen, Marion,* and *Logan* (a red-fruited variety). *Boysen* has extra-large fruit and a full flavor. The trailing types are more productive than the uprights and especially suited to this region. Provide water during dry spells, especially when fruit is forming.

North (zones 3, 4, 5)

Upright-growing varieties are the most reliable. *Darrow* is a good choice, as it bears large, consistent crops of good-tasting fruit, but it can fail to survive the winter where temperatures fall lower than $-20°$ to $-25°F$. Put canes of trailing types on the ground in the winter and cover to prevent chilling injury.

Training Blackberries

Post system. If you want to support upright-growing blackberry plants, you can train them to grow neatly around posts. Space plants 3 feet apart in rows. Each plant should be attached to a 6-foot post about the thickness of a wrist or to a 2-by-2-inch board sunk about 1 foot into the ground.

When the new canes (the leafy ones) are about hip high, pinch back the growing tip of each one. This encourages the canes to branch out during the rest of the season; the tip of each new side shoot will bear a cluster of fruits the following year.

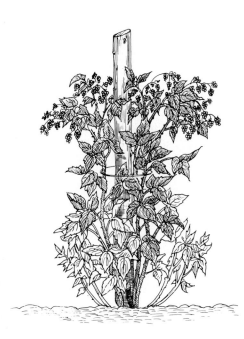

The next summer the leafy canes become fruiting canes, bearing amazing clusters of fruits at a height where they're easy to pick.

Later in the summer, immediately after you've harvested the blackberries, cut off the fruiting canes close to the ground. New leafy canes will have sprouted up around the fruiting canes. Choose three or four of the strongest and healthiest leafy canes to replace the canes that fruited and tie them loosely to the post, about 3 feet from the ground. The rest of the canes and any suckers popping up between plants should be cut off and discarded.

Wire trellis system. Give trailing plants a wire trellis or fence to grow on instead of a post, and spread the canes out as much as possible. How much the canes will grow in 1 year varies; one way to handle the very long ones is to wrap them around two strands of wire (see illustration). British gardeners sometimes train these types of canes by fanning them out along separate wires so they get maximum light. The fruit dangles within easy reach, minimizing scratches while harvesting. Thornless varieties can also be trained this way.

In northern areas, where winter protection is necessary, set the canes on the ground for the winter, cover them with clean straw or leaves if you don't get much snow, then carefully place them up on the wire in early spring before they start growing again.

In milder climates, train the new canes on the wire as soon as you've cut out the fruiting canes and leave them right there through the winter. Each year remove the canes that have fruited and allow several leafy canes to replace them.

In areas with long growing seasons, the vines may get extremely long and require a dormant-season pruning. Cut them back to about 8 to 10 feet in late winter. Fruiting is heaviest near the base of the canes, so you won't be losing much of the crop and the resulting berries will be larger.

Harvesting

Berries will ripen over a period of several weeks and should be harvested every 2 to 4 days. Pick berries in the cool of early morning and avoid bruising them. Refrigerate the berries immediately; they'll keep for 4 to 5 days at 35°F; if picked when warm, berries don't keep as long.

Blackberry Sources

Boysen 12, 107, 128, 158
Brazos 125, 128, 158
Cheyenne 125, 162
Darrow 12, 125, 128, 161
Dirksen 12, 128, 161
Hull Thornless 128, 161, 162
Logan 107, 128, 149
Marion 107, 141, 155
Olallie 131, 146
Thornfree 128, 155, 158, 162
Thornless Evergreen 131

Cherries

If you decide to grow tart cherries, consider the *Montmorency* variety (*left*); it yields heavy crops of large cherries. Sweet *Bing* cherries (*above*) are a good choice in dry western areas, but not in humid, rainy areas.

The cherries sold fresh in most markets are sweet cherries — they have a thick, rich, almost plumlike texture and sweet taste. If you like your cherries cooked, then you have probably eaten tart cherries, which are juicier and slightly sour. While sweet cherries certainly have their virtues, tart cherries are delicious in preserves and pies and are much easier to grow.

Although sweet and tart cherries have very similar growing requirements and are subject to the same pests, tart cherries are more tolerant of cold winters and long, hot, humid summers and have fewer disease problems. The trees are smaller so they are easier to harvest, prune, and spray. Tart cherries are self-fertile, so you can plant just one tree and still harvest fruit. Why not start with one beautiful tart cherry tree to enhance your edible landscape? In time, perhaps you'll want to add more tart cherries or, if you have the right growing conditions, some of the more finicky sweet cherries.

Planning

If you've never grown cherries before, we recommend starting with tart cherries. The trees are ornamental, and the fruit makes wonderful pies, cobblers, and toppings. To get the most from your trees, start with varieties suitable for your climate and look for certified virus-free trees. Tart cherries are hardy in zones 4 through 6.

The standard-size *Montmorency* has been the leading tart cherry variety for many years. It yields heavy crops of large, bright red, high-quality tart cherries in mid- to late June (in zone 6). The tree is available on semidwarfing *Colt* rootstock, which produces a tree two-thirds standard size, as well as on standard-size rootstock.

Several genetic dwarf varieties are available. These are naturally small and can be grafted onto the standard rootstocks. They include several spur-type *Montmorency* sports (varieties that arise from a bud mutation) and *Meteor*, all semidwarfs, and *North Star*, a full dwarf.

The spur-type sports of *Montmorency* — *Montmore*, *Starkspur Montmorency*, and *Galaxy* — produce more fruiting spurs and less vegetative growth, so they are three-quarter-size trees (12 to 14 feet tall) which start to bear at a younger age and yield more heavily. Their fruit is similar to *Montmorency* and ripens at the same time.

Meteor is a genetic semidwarf growing 10 to 12 feet tall. It's hardy to zone 3, productive, and highly resistant to cherry leaf spot. Fruits are slightly larger than *Montmorency* with comparable flavor and quality. It blooms and ripens about a week after *Montmorency*, which may help avoid spring frost damage to developing buds.

North Star, a genetic full dwarf that grows just 6 or 7 feet tall, is also hardy to zone 3. Fruit quality is not quite as good as the others, but it can be grown in very cold areas and where space is extremely limited. It's also resistant to both leaf spot and brown rot.

Kansas Sweet, a cross between a sweet and a tart cherry, is more like a tart. The fruit is sweeter than other tarts, though, with a crisp tart texture, not the plumlike texture of true sweet cherries. Tree characteristics are similar to those of tarts but it needs a nearby tart cherry to cross-pollinate it. Ripe in late June, the fruits can be used as a sweet cherry substitute where true sweets are too difficult to grow.

Duke, another sweet-tart cross, is similar and better for canning than either sweets or tarts.

Sweet cherries aren't for everyone, but for those willing to choose varieties carefully, prune and spray regularly, and deal with marauding birds, the rewards are great. Choosing varieties adapted to your area and resistant to its major diseases is critical. Most sweet cherry varieties are hardy in zones 5 through 7; in colder zones, choose varieties with the hardiest wood and buds.

A few sweet cherry varieties resist the problems that plague most sweet cherries — fruit cracking, brown rot, and cherry leaf spot. Some are very hardy, a few are only mildly attractive to birds, and a couple are self-fertile and genetically dwarfed. Some of the traditional cherry favorites

Far right: Yellow cherries such as these *Stark Golds* can be less susceptible to bird damage at harvest time because they are not as easy for birds to see as red cherries.

Bing, a traditional favorite, in bloom. The flower buds are tender once they begin to swell; planting in an appropriate site can lessen the chances of the blossoms being killed by frost.

such as *Bing* have their drawbacks, especially concerning disease susceptibility.

The variety chart on pages 346–347 describes some of the most well adapted, hardy, and pest-resistant varieties for the entire East as far as the Rockies. (These varieties also do well in the far West, but more disease-susceptible and crack-susceptible varieties can be grown there because of the drier climate.)

Flavor depends as much or more on tree vigor, crop load, and stage of fruit maturity at harvest as it does on variety. Fruit cracking also varies, being worse on a tree with a light crop load than on the same variety with a heavy crop load. Fruit cracking may not occur on any varieties in a dry season, but a wet season will encourage it.

In most areas, stay clear of most commonly sold varieties. *Bing* can be grown successfully on the West Coast where winters are mild and dry air makes fruit cracking and brown rot less of a problem, but seldom does well in the East. Even where *Bing* can be grown, there are better varieties for home gardeners, such as *Starkrimson*, a self-fertile genetic dwarf with bigger, sweeter fruit.

Bing and *Napoleon* (also called *Royal Ann*) are most susceptible to winter injury. Other varieties that are highly susceptible to winter injury are *Republican*, *Black Tartarian*, *Rainier*, and *Van*. *Emperor Francis*, *Napoleon*, *Republican*, *Vista*, and

Essentials

Planning

- Tart cherries thrive in zones 4 to 6, sweet cherries in zones 5 to 7.
- Plant cherry trees in early spring.
- Tart cherries are self-fertile. Sweet cherries need a compatible variety for cross-pollination.
- Choose sweet cherry varieties that are especially adapted to your climate and resistant to the major diseases in your area.
- Standard-size trees start bearing in about their fourth year, dwarf trees in about their third year.
- One mature, standard-size tart or sweet cherry tree will produce 30 to 50 quarts of cherries each year; a dwarf tree, about 10 to 15 quarts.

Preparation

- Choose a sunny site with good air circulation and deep, well-drained soil. Avoid low areas or places surrounded by buildings or shade trees, where cold air settles.

Planting

- Plant sweet cherries on standard rootstocks 35 to 40 feet apart; dwarfs, 5 to 10 feet apart. Space tart cherries on standard rootstocks 20 to 25 feet apart; dwarfs, 8 to 10 feet apart.
- Set trees on standard rootstocks with the graft union a few inches below the soil level. Set trees on Colt dwarfing rootstock with the graft union several inches above the soil level.

Care

- Train dwarf tart cherry trees to a central leader. Train semi-dwarf or standard-size cherry trees to a modified leader.
- Prune trees every year in late winter to encourage the growth of new fruiting wood. Don't prune in the fall.
- Fertilize each spring until trees start to bear, then fertilize only after harvest each season.
- Watch out for the larvae of the plum curculio (page 401) and the cherry fruit fly (page 400) in sweet cherries and the related black cherry fruit fly in tart cherries. The apple maggot (page 400) and peach tree borer (page 401) may also cause problems. Brown rot (page 404) and cherry leaf spot (page 347) affect both tart and sweet cherries. Black knot (page 403) and powdery mildew (page 405) are other potential disease problems.
- Prevent birds from eating your harvest.

Harvesting

- The sugar content of cherries rises dramatically in the last few days of ripening, so wait until they turn fully red, black, or yellow (depending on the variety) before harvesting.
- Harvest as the cherries ripen over the course of about a week.
- Pick the cherries with the stems attached, being careful not to tear off the fruit spur that will produce fruit year after year.

Preventing Bird Damage

Birds are much more of a problem on sweet cherries than on tarts. Clear yellow-fruited varieties may escape much bird damage because birds can't pick them out easily unless the cherries develop red spots from worm infestation or injury. Yellow-red types will be attacked as soon as the red blush begins to show. Birds cause the greatest amount of damage to early-ripening varieties but are less destructive to the latest-ripening, when more food sources are available.

Distracting objects, such as white strips of cloth and aluminum pie plates hung in the trees, will scare most birds away from tart cherries, but they don't work as well for sweet cherries. You can also throw a spool of black thread through all the branches in a tart cherry tree; the birds don't like to get their feet entangled, and stay away. Nylon mesh netting can be draped over dwarf trees and secured beneath the lowest branches. Unfortunately, mature standard-size sweet cherries are too big to cover with netting.

Growing mulberries nearby can protect sweet cherries if the mulberries start ripening before the cherries and continue producing fruit throughout the cherry ripening season. Plant a seedling (female) mulberry that ripens early. Do not plant *Illinois Everbearing* mulberry (the best-tasting to humans) because it ripens too late, the fruit are too big for many birds, and it ripens over the entire summer rather than yielding a large crop just before cherry season.

If there's no room for a mulberry tree, noisemaking devices may work, though commercial growers find that the birds get used to them after a while.

Windsor bloom earlier than most, so are more likely to be damaged by frosts in areas with fluctuating winter temperatures.

Sweet cherry varieties highly prone to fruit cracking, which leads to brown rot, include *Bing, Black Tartarian, Emperor Francis, Napoleon, Starkrimson,* and *Vega.* Varieties such as *Van* and *Vista* with fruits that hang in tight clusters are very susceptible to brown rot. Varieties highly susceptible to cherry leaf spot include *Bing, Black Tartarian, Napoleon, Rainier, Republican,* and *Van.*

Clear yellow cherries such as *Gold* (also called *Saylor*) and *Stark Gold* (*Thomas*) are crack resistant and disease resistant, but are not very sweet or tasty. Yellow-fruited cherries often escape bird predation because they are not as easy for birds to see.

Don't forget that all sweet cherries except *Stella* and *Starkrimson* must be cross-pollinated by another compatible variety, so you'll need two trees unless your neighbor has a sweet cherry of a different variety.

Some varieties will not pollinate each other because they are too closely related. Groups of cross-incompatible varieties are listed on page 347. If you select one of these varieties, be sure you select another variety from a different group with compatible pollen.

Preparation

Cherries need a sunny site with good air circulation and deep, well-drained soil. Although cherry wood is as winter-hardy as some apple varieties, the flower buds are tender once they start to swell. An elevated site will minimize frost-killed blossoms. Avoid low areas or places surrounded by buildings or shade trees, where cold air settles. Poorly drained soils can cause trees to die in a wet year even though they may have lived through several years of drier weather.

Cherries are susceptible to verticillium wilt and other diseases, so don't plant

Midwestern home grower Bob Kurle protects one of his small tart cherry trees with nylon mesh netting. He drapes the tree just before the harvest, as his somewhat light-sensitive netting can deteriorate after five or six seasons.

them where verticillium has infested the soil or where tomato family crops, melons, or strawberries grew the previous two seasons. Also avoid planting where peach or cherry trees once grew.

Planting

Plant sweet cherries on standard rootstocks 35 to 40 feet apart; dwarfs, 5 to 10 feet apart. Space tart cherries on standard rootstocks 20 to 25 feet apart; dwarfs, 8 to 10 feet. (See pages 301–303 for complete instructions on planting fruit trees.)

Care

Dwarf cherry trees are most productive when trained to a central leader. The lowest branch should be about 2 feet off the ground, and the limbs should be spaced at least 8 inches apart. Train semidwarf or standard-size trees to a modified leader. (See page 315 for details on training.)

Prune the trees every year in late winter to encourage new fruiting wood to grow. After harvest, cut back overvigorous branches to control the size of the tree. Summer pruning can be done any time until early August; the later you prune, the smaller you'll keep the tree. Don't prune in the fall, as that leaves the tree more susceptible to winter injury.

Control grass or other competing vegetation around the tree for the first few years. A heavy mulch from the tree trunk to the tree's dripline helps conserve soil moisture and control weeds.

Fertilize each spring until trees start to bear. (See page 305 for fertilizer recommendations.) Once bearing, cherries need little irrigation or fertilizer in most areas. If you apply nitrogen to bearing trees, wait until after the fruit has been harvested, but apply it no later than midsummer. This will give the tree a boost toward producing plenty of sugars in its leaves to ripen next year's crop. If nitrogen is added shortly before the harvest, the fruit will be softer and more susceptible to brown rot.

Cherry Rootstocks

Ordinarily, nurseries won't offer a choice of rootstocks when you order a cherry tree. If possible, try to find out which rootstock is being used on the trees you order.

Mazzard and *Mahaleb* are the two most common cherry rootstocks. Most nurseries use *Mahaleb* for tart cherries because it tends to induce earlier and heavier bearing. It tolerates drought and sandy and alkaline soils better than *Mazzard,* and is more winter hardy. It's resistant to bacterial canker, a disease that can be serious in very humid areas such as the Pacific Northwest Coast, but is rarely troublesome elsewhere. *Mahaleb* grows more slowly than *Mazzard* and won't live as long.

Mazzard is generally used for sweet cherries. It tolerates heavier or wetter soils and is moderately resistant to pocket gophers and moles, to which *Mahaleb* is highly vulnerable. Gardeners troubled by these pests, or by heavy soils, would be wise to buy from a nursery using *Mazzard* rootstocks.

Some nurseries now offer both sweet and tart cherries on *Colt,* a semidwarfing *Mazzard*-type roostock that produces a tree two-thirds standard size. If the nursery doesn't specify *Colt* as its dwarfing rootstock and the variety isn't a genetic dwarf, then beware. Some dwarfing rootstocks such as the western sand cherry or Nanking cherry are likely to cause premature tree death.

To prepare the tree for winter, it's a good idea to paint tree trunks white or wrap them with white plastic tree guards (page 306). Pull mulch away from the trunk and be sure to harden the tree off (page 306).

Be on the lookout for problems with pests and diseases. In the southern parts of the tart cherry–growing area, the only worm to infest the fruit is the larva of the plum curculio (see page 401), which also attacks sweet cherries. Wormy cherries are easily noticed; you can see the crescent-shaped egg-laying scars and brown frass under the skin.

Two species of cherry fruit flies are serious pests in northern areas. Their eggs hatch into maggots, easily distinguished from plum curculio larvae because they have no heads — just two dark mouth hooks at the head end.

Adult flies can be controlled with properly timed sprays of approved insecticides. Use traps to determine when the adult flies emerge and spraying should begin. Fill a jar with equal amounts of water and household ammonia. Cover the jar with a screen and hang it below a yellow board covered with Tangle Trap about 4 to 6 feet high in the tree.

In humid areas, apply a fungicide with the insecticides to prevent brown rot of the fruit and cherry leaf spot. Check with your county agent for the right product recommendation.

If brown rot has been a serious problem in the past and wet weather is prevalent, make an additional application of fungi-

High-Quality, Disease-Resistant Sweet Cherries
(Recommended for Areas East of Rocky Mountains)

Variety	Winter Hardiness		Resistance to				
	Wood	Fruit Buds	Leaf Spot	Fruit Cracking	Brown Rot	X-Disease	
Angela	hardy	hardy	*?	high	none	high	
**Bada*	hardy	hardy	?	high	slight	none	
†*Compact Stella*	moderate	moderate	?	moderate	slight	none	
Hardy Giant	very hardy	very hardy	moderate	high	none	none	
***Hedelfingen*	moderate	very hardy	moderate	mod. high	none	none	
Hudson	hardy	very hardy	?	high	slight	none	
†*Starkrimson*	hardy	hardy	none	none	none	none	
Sweet Ann	very hardy	very hardy	?	high	none	high	
Valera	moderate	moderate	high	high	none	none	
Viva	hardy	hardy	high	high	slight	none	

*?—unknown resistance.
**Bada* and *Hedelfingen* are offered on the dwarfing rootstock *Colt* by Stark Bros. Nursery, and *Hedelfingen* is offered on *Colt* by Adams County Nursery.
†Self-pollinating, genetic dwarf sweet cherries.
Compiled by Brenda Olcott-Reid.

cide (not of insecticide, which might kill the pollinating bees) during bloom. Sweet cherries are more susceptible to brown rot than tart ones, so they may need more frequent fungicide applications. During humid springs, apply a fungicide at bloom and every 10 to 14 days thereafter until you reach the waiting period before harvest (read the fungicide label carefully). Do not apply any fertilizer until after harvest; nitrogen released before harvest makes fruit more prone to rot.

Cherry leaf spot, if serious and not controlled, can cause partial to complete defoliation. If it's a problem, make another fungicide application just after harvest. In late autumn, after trees are dormant, apply a high-nitrogen material such as urea to the fallen leaves so they decom-

pose faster and are not a source of cherry leaf spot infections next spring.

Harvesting

Wait until the cherries turn fully red to harvest them; the sugar content rises dramatically in the last few days of ripening. You'll need to go over the tree every other day for about a week. Pick the fruit with stems attached, but be careful not to tear off the woody fruit spur, which will continue to produce fruit year after year.

If you're using a mechanical cherry pitter, pick the cherries by leaving the stems on the trees. Use these cherries up soon after you pick them because they'll leak juice and may spoil if left out. Using a hand-cranked cherry pitter, you can pit a quart of cherries in 10 minutes.

Groups of Incompatible Cherries for Pollination

Each variety in a group will not pollinize any other variety in that group, but will pollinize any variety in any other group.

- Black Tartarian, Early Rivers
- Bing, Merton Bigarreau, Van, Windsor

- Bing, Emperor Francis, Lambert, Compact Lambert, Napoleon, Vernon

- Victor, Viva, Vogue
- Bold, Merton Heart, Viva
- Hedelfingen, Ulster, Vic

- Hardy Giant, Hudson, Schmidt
- Hudson, Rainier
- Seneca, Vega, Vista

Fruit				Comments
Color	Flavor	Size	Ripens	
black	very good	large	late June	Blooms late; often escapes spring frost damage.
yellow red	good	medium	mid-June	Yellow-red fruit; bears fruit at a young age; moderately resistant to bacterial canker.
dark red	fair–good	large	mid-June	Bears heavily and early; hardy to zone 6; fruit is very acid; cans well.
dark red	good	medium	mid-June	81% of fruit buds survived a −21°F freeze; tree slow to bear, doesn't bear as heavily as others; susceptible to bacterial canker.
black	excellent	small–med.	late June	Old variety; tends to overbear, resulting in small fruit some years; doesn't crack much because it bears so heavily; not resistant to bacterial canker.
black	good	med.–large	early July	Survived a −21°F freeze with 85% live fruit buds; fruit ripens late.
red	very good	large	mid-June	Hardy and high quality; shouldn't be planted in areas with excessive rainfall during time of cherry ripening.
yellow red	excellent	medium	mid-June	Has withstood −20°F winter temperatures; blossoms have some frost resistance; yellow fruit less bothered by birds until fully ripe and almost solid red.
dark red	good–excel.	large	early June	Ripens early; hardy to zone 6; bears fruit at a young age; flavor varies with the season.
dark red	good–excel.	med.–large	early June	Early ripening.

Citrus

Mandarin oranges such as the *Satsuma* shown at left are available in many distinctively flavored varieties. *Ponderosa* lemons (*above*) make good indoor trees; the fruits can be much larger than store-bought lemons.

Most people don't realize just how large the citrus family is. What you see in the supermarket is only a small portion of what can be grown. Pummelos, blood oranges, limequats, and myriad mandarin varieties offer exciting new taste experiences and landscape possibilities.

The commercial citrus belt extends roughly from California through Arizona, Texas, along the Gulf Coast, and into Florida; but home growers are not necessarily limited to this area. Small changes in elevation and distance from the coast can make a significant difference in minimum temperatures at a given location. Warm spots around buildings and on hillsides can provide safe growing areas in sections that would not appear suitable from a climate map. The important thing to know is a variety's tolerance to cold, especially the minimum temperature it can tolerate. There are many hardy varieties that can be grown much farther north or inland. If your citrus trees are planted in containers and moved to protected locations during cold weather, you can even grow them in Minnesota or Maine.

Planning

The traditional citrus climate extends from northern California down through southern California and into the low Arizona desert. There is a break in New Mexico, a state that has mostly high elevation with cold winters. Then the citrus belt picks up again in southern Texas and extends along the Gulf Coast and into Florida.

Not all types of citrus can be grown in all parts of the citrus belt. Climatic differences within the region markedly affect fruit characteristics and quality. What can be grown in Florida cannot always be grown in California and vice versa.

The warm, dry days and cool nights of California develop brightly colored fruit with balanced sugar and acid and thick rinds. The warm, humid days of Florida and the Gulf Coast are usually accompanied by equally warm nights; such even temperatures promote lighter colored fruit without pronounced acidity.

Humidity and day-to-night temperature fluctuations also influence which varieties are best adapted to an area. Almost all lemons in the supermarket come from western states because in Florida lemons do not develop enough acidity. On the other hand, some types of citrus naturally high in acids, such as many tangelos, are too tart when grown in California. They reach peak quality and sweetness only in Florida or along the Gulf Coast.

Citrus types have varying degrees of hardiness, so tolerance to low winter temperatures is often the most important factor in determining which varieties you can grow. The foliage of limes is usually damaged if temperatures fall below 32°F; oranges are damaged at about 26° to 28°F. Kumquats and kumquat hybrids can withstand temperatures as low as 18°F, but the ripe fruit is usually less hardy than the foliage. The duration of the cold and the position of the tree in your garden also influence how badly trees are damaged.

Each citrus type has a heat requirement that must be met before the fruit will become sweet. Grapefruits need the most heat and only reach peak quality in the California and Arizona deserts, southern Texas, and Florida. Lemons can be grown in cooler climates because they don't need to sweeten.

Citrus trees are evergreen and can have both flowers and fruit at the same time, so they are treated a bit differently than other fruit trees. They store food reserves in their leaves and must therefore be protected from stresses that will cause leaf drop. Although the cycles are not as obvious as the cycles in temperate fruit trees, citrus trees go through different stages throughout the year. When temperatures drop below 56°F, the trees stop growing and go into a semidormant state. After a period of such cool weather, they can withstand brief cold snaps much more easily than when they are actively growing. It only takes a few days of warmer temperatures to make them more vulnerable, though.

In the spring they have a flush of growth and their major bloom period. Some varieties tend to bloom lightly throughout the year; water shortages or other stresses can trigger a second bloom.

Citrus can be planted any time of year. Spring is the best time to set out container-grown trees from a nursery. Select strong and healthy trees for planting.

Preparation

Citrus trees will grow in most soils except salty ones. Add organic matter to very heavy or sandy soils to improve their structure. Water stress is the single most important source of problems, so the goal is to have moist but well-drained soil.

Choose a site in an area protected from wind and with maximum heat and sun, unless you live in desert regions where a little midday shade might be appreciated. If you live in a cooler area, try to provide extra protection for your trees. Put them against a light-colored, south-facing wall that reflects heat. Planting on a slope

Far right: **The calamondin, a kumquat hybrid, produces good fruit outdoors. It can be striking when grown indoors as an ornamental, for it can bear hundreds of small, bright orange fruit.**

where air drains away can often prevent frost damage.

Planting

Place the tree in its planting hole no deeper than it was in the nursery container. If the trunk is in constant contact with damp soil, it is more susceptible to the fungus disease gummosis.

Planting distances will depend on type and variety. For example, standard orange trees should be 20 feet apart and standard-size grapefruit 25 feet apart, while standard limes and lemons require less space and can be set 12 to 15 feet apart. Set dwarf trees 6 to 10 feet apart.

Care

Keep a good layer of mulch around the trees, but spread it several inches away from the trunk. The roots are fairly shallow and extend well beyond the dripline, so water the entire root area. The trees should receive a deep soaking about once a week; the soil should dry a bit before the next watering.

When trees are young, they occasionally produce some overvigorous branches. Prune these back so the tree remains well balanced. Limit later pruning to removing dead, broken, and diseased branches; it can be done any time of the year.

The nutrient most needed by the trees is nitrogen; mature trees need 1 to 1½ pounds per year. Apply it in four portions

Essentials

Planning

❧ *In the citrus belt, trees can be planted any time of year. Spring is the best time to plant container-grown trees from a nursery outside.*

❧ *Standard-size orange and grapefruit trees grow 18 to 22 feet tall; dwarf varieties grow 8 to 12 feet tall. Dwarf varieties are suitable for growing outdoors or in containers.*

❧ *Most citrus trees begin to bear at 3 to 6 years.*

❧ *Pollination is generally accomplished by insects and sometimes by the wind. Indoor gardeners can hand-pollinate. Most citrus varieties are self-fertile so you need only one tree.*

Preparation

❧ *Citrus will grow in most soils that are moist but well drained. Avoid salty soils.*

❧ *Choose a site protected from wind, with maximum sun exposure.*

Planting

❧ *Set standard-size trees 12 to 25 feet apart, set dwarfs 6 to 10 feet apart. (Distance will depend on type and variety.) Set standard-size oranges 20 feet apart, standard-size grapefruit 25 feet apart. Limes and lemons require less space.*

❧ *Plant the trees no deeper than they grew in the nursery container.*

Care

❧ *Water the entire root area deeply about once a week.*

❧ *Prune any time of the year. When the trees are young, prune overvigorous growth. Prune mature trees to remove dead, broken, and diseased branches.*

❧ *Give mature trees 1 to 1½ pounds of nitrogen a year. Apply in four portions throughout the year, or just once 6 to 8 weeks before bloom.*

❧ *Watch out for gophers (page 306).*

❧ *Aphids (page 400), scales (page 402), and red spider mites (page 353) may bother trees.*

❧ *Gummosis (page 404) is the most likely disease problem.*

Harvesting

❧ *Although some varieties ripen their fruit all at once, many others ripen fruit over a period of several months (fall through winter). Taste is the best indicator of ripeness.*

❧ *Clip ripe fruit off with pruning shears.*

Unusual Citrus

Home gardeners can enjoy many types of citrus fruits not found in most supermarkets. Here we suggest just a few unusual citrus types to inspire you to do more exploring. Follow the same general horticultural practices for these varieties as for the rest of the citrus family.

Blood Oranges. Once you have tasted a good blood orange, you will never forget its superb flavor, a cross between an orange and a raspberry. Their rind and flesh are a deep red color.

Blood oranges are very popular in Europe and are grown commercially in Mediterranean citrus regions. They haven't caught on in the United States primarily because their coloration is a bit unpredictable. Climate plays an important role, but the exact requirements for the development of the pigmented rind and flesh are not known. Fruits grown in hot areas of California and Arizona usually develop the best color, but even their color intensity changes from year to year. You can grow blood oranges in Florida and along the Gulf Coast, but the color is not as reliable and the flavor is often less pronounced than in fruit grown in dry summer, Mediterranean-type climates. Fruit grown in cool coastal climates seldom develops deep colors.

Regardless of color, blood oranges are worth growing for their unique flavor. Each of the three most common varieties grown, *Moro, Sanguinelli,* and *Tarocco,* has its own distinctive flavor.

Pummelos. As suggested by their botanical name, *Citrus grandis,* pummelos bear the largest fruit in the citrus family. They are usually compared to grapefruit because of their appearance; many people believe the pummelo may be one of the ancestors of the grapefruit. Supermarkets occasionally sell pummelos as Chinese grapefruit, a label that is probably confusing.

Pummelos do not need as much heat as grapefruit and they can be grown in most citrus areas. The largest, sweetest fruit is produced in hot climates; in cooler areas, fruit will be smaller and have a thicker rind, but it's still quite good.

The fruit's soft, thick rind encloses white or pink flesh. Peeling and eating one for the first time is a memorable experience.

The rind tears off and segments separate easily, but the surprise is the way the juice vesicles (the part you scoop out of a grapefruit) separate from the membrane. There is no chewy membrane or bitter rind. The flavor is delicious — mildly sweet without the bitterness common to grapefruit. The texture is firmer than most citrus and there is less juice, but they're definitely not dry. Pummelos are excellent in fruit salads or by themselves.

Two principal varieties of pummelo are grown in California and Arizona: *Chandler* has pink flesh, *Reinking* has white. Both trees are large and attractive.

Kumquat hybrids. Kumquat hybrids can be grown in all citrus regions; kumquats are among the hardiest citrus. With this in mind, the USDA crossed kumquats with other popular types of citrus to create hardy kumquat hybrids. Two of these, orangequats and limequats, are beautiful ornamental trees ideal for fruit lovers in cold areas.

The orangequat is a hybrid between the *Satsuma* mandarin and the *Meiwa* kumquat. It is eaten like a kumquat and has a mildly sweet rind and tart flesh. The fruit is larger than a kumquat, bright orange, and makes excellent marmalade. The tree is small but productive, with handsome foliage. The orangequat is an exceptional ornamental, ideal for containers. *Nippon* is the only variety.

Limequats are equally lovely trees, with light-green-to-yellow fruit borne in abundance. The fruits are juicy, with sweet rinds and tart flesh. They are an excellent lime substitute. *Eustis* is a commonly available variety.

Mandarins. As a group, the mandarins offer the greatest diversity of varieties among citrus types. Some are available in supermarkets. Home gardeners can grow many more distinctively flavored varieties.

Mandarins are usually very attractive trees, sometimes with willowy leaves. They are generally hardier than oranges, although ripe fruit can be damaged at 26° to 28°F. With wise selection of varieties, you can harvest mandarins from November to June. Three varieties with outstanding flavor are *Page, Encore,* and *Honey.*

Kumquats are among the hardiest citrus, yielding small oval fruits. *Nagami* (*top*), which has few seeds, is slightly tart and makes wonderful marmalade. The limequat (*bottom*), a cross between a lime and a kumquat, is a good lime substitute in cooler areas.

throughout the year, or apply the entire amount 6 to 8 weeks before a bloom.

Lower branches of the tree help protect the trunk from sunburn; citrus bark is very thin and can be easily damaged by too much sun. It helps to paint the lower trunk and other exposed portions with diluted white interior latex paint or to wrap the trunks of young trees with tree wrap tape.

If a tree suffers frost damage, wait until new growth starts to see just how much has been hurt, then cut out the damaged parts. Cutting too early could lead to more damage. You may have to wait 6 months to see the new growth.

Most of the major citrus pests and diseases affect commercial plantings, not home garden trees, so you do not need a preventive spray program as you do with some of the other fruits. You do need to deal with some pests, though. Gophers can destroy a tree quickly and must be kept out.

Check the leaves frequently for aphids, mealy bugs, and red spider mites. If they're present, spray the leaves frequently with a forceful stream of water or use an insecticidal soap spray. Scale can be controlled with a horticultural oil spray applied in the fall, when temperatures are moderate and trees have been well watered.

Harvesting

You usually can't tell if citrus is ripe by looking at it. When some of the fruit reach full size, taste them to see if they're ripe. Unlike most temperate fruits, many citrus varieties ripen over a period of many months and keep well on the tree even when ripe, so you're not faced with an enormous harvest all at once. Some will ripen a late summer crop from the spring bloom, others will take up to a year or more to mature, and some continue to bloom and fruit year-round. Clip ripe fruit off with pruning shears instead of pulling it to avoid damage to twigs.

Citrus Rootstocks

Rootstock choice can increase the hardiness of citrus varieties. *Trifoliate* orange is a popular dwarfing rootstock that increases hardiness and keeps most trees 8 to 12 feet tall, depending on variety. The *Cunningham* citrange rootstock is slightly less dwarfing and less hardy.

A new rootstock, *Flying Dragon*, provides even greater dwarfing. Trees will maintain a wonderfully compact height of 5 to 6 feet, perfect for containers or small spaces.

Standard orange or grapefruit rootstocks will produce a tree 18 to 22 feet tall. The *Trifoliate* and citrange rootstocks are preferred by many for backyard use — they will keep tree size at 40 to 50 percent of standard height and live for many years.

Grapes

Whether purple, green, blue, or black, let your grape crop ripen fully before harvesting; the berries do not ripen off the vine.

It's a wonder more gardeners don't plant grapevines. Just 2 years after planting, you can be sampling your own grapes; in 3 years, you can be harvesting up to 15 pounds of grapes from each vine — plenty for eating and making jellies, juice, or wine. Two healthy vines are enough for most home growers.

Many gardeners who raise everything from Brussels sprouts to plum trees have never tried grapes. Often, it isn't because they don't like them, but because they think grapes are difficult to prune properly. However, many home gardeners know that grapes are easy to grow. After the first year, you just need to give vines a simple annual pruning to keep them bearing well.

There are three major groups of grapes. American grapes (*Vitis labrusca*) are generally quite winter hardy and grow well in most parts of the United States. European grapes (*Vitis vinifera*) grow best in warm, dry areas. Crosses between European- and American-type grapes have produced hybrids that are hardier and can be grown over a greater range. Muscadine grapes (*Vitis rotundifolia*) are native grapes well adapted to growing conditions in southeastern United States.

Red Flame seedless

Thompson Seedless

Muscadine grapes

Planning

Choose grape varieties carefully. American-type grapes such as *Concord* and *Catawba* do well in the cool climate of New England, in the Midwest, and in the Northwest. The *Concord,* developed in the 1850s, is still a mainstay in many home gardens; it's vigorous, hardy, and easy to propagate from cuttings. European grapes (usually wine varieties such as *Zinfandel* or *Chardonnay*) flourish in California where bright, dry summer days and mild winter temperatures provide a favorable environment. Tougher-skinned muscadine grapes do best in the Deep South.

Some of the new hybrid crosses between European and American types, such as the *Baco Noir* and *Seibel* varieties, are hardy and have extended the range in which wine grapes can be grown. Vineyards in New York State, where winter temperatures drop well below zero, produce high-quality wines.

Over the years plant breeders have introduced earlier-ripening and more-winter-hardy grapes. *Swenson Red,* for example, produces delicious medium to large red table grapes and is winter hardy to −25°F.

Most grapes are self-fertile, but check to be sure when you place your order. A few will need pollinizing plants. Muscadines come in self-fertile and self-sterile lines. The best fruits are from the self-sterile vines; to assure pollination you have to grow a pollinizing vine, too. Whether a variety is from a self-fertile line or not should be noted in the mail-order catalog or at the nursery.

Many garden centers sell grape plants in containers (in 8-inch pots, for example). There's usually a thin, 8- to 10-inch-tall stem that will develop over the years into a sturdy trunk. Vines grown in containers are easy to plant because the roots are less stressed in transplanting. Tap the plant out of the container and set the root ball, with as much of its soil as possible, into a prepared hole.

Buying container plants locally can be more expensive than ordering from a mail-order company. If you send away, your grapevines will probably arrive bare-root with a moist packing of peat moss or other material to keep the roots from drying out. The stem is usually cut back at planting. (The planting instructions below are for bare-root vines.)

There is no advantage to buying a vine older than 1 year. Roots always have to be trimmed back at planting time, and no matter how old the vine is, it takes a certain amount of time for the roots to re-establish themselves. Older vines won't necessarily give you earlier fruiting.

Preparation

The fall before you plant, mark the location for your vines. Get rid of all weeds, especially perennial ones, as your vines can easily survive 30 years or more in the same location. Grapes don't require superior soil, but good drainage is a must.

Although you won't start training the vines until the second year, set up the trellis system before spring planting so you don't damage the roots later.

Planting

In the spring, work the soil again and plant the vines 6 to 10 feet apart. (Double this spacing for muscadines.) For each vine, dig a hole 12 inches deep and 12 inches wide to accommodate the roots. Shovel in a 4-inch layer of topsoil. Then prune the top of your grapevine back to two or three buds and trim off any broken roots or roots too long to fit into the hole without crowding. Set the vine into the hole, slightly deeper than it was grown in the nursery, and spread its roots. Cover the roots with 6 inches of topsoil, keeping the buds above the soil line. Tamp down the soil, then fill the remainder of the hole with topsoil but don't tamp it down.

Water the new plants well. Although grapevines are known to be drought tolerant, they need plenty of water right after planting so roots can get established.

Care

Grapes should be pruned yearly because fruits only form on buds that arise from the previous season's growth. There are various methods of training grapevines. Your preferences, space limitations, and the variety of grape you are growing will determine your trellis system.

Prune vines when they are dormant; in most of the country, that means very early spring, before any green shoots appear. Muscadines in the Deep South can be pruned any time after the first fall frost.

Unless your soil is very poor, grapes, which are very deeply rooted, don't require much fertilization. Where fertility is low, a soil test will determine whether you should add phosphorus or potassium.

For all soils, fertilize lightly the second year. Apply no more than ¼ pound of 10-10-10 fertilizer in a circle up to 4 feet away from each vine. In following years when the vines are established, apply about a pound up to 8 feet away from the base if growth was slow or foliage color poor the previous season. Apply it only when the buds start to swell in the spring; later fertilizing may cause extensive growth in late summer, making the plant more vulnerable to winter injury.

While grapevines can survive some neglect, they need regular attention to reach maximum yields:
• Prune carefully. Leaving too much growth causes far more problems than overpruning.
• Cultivate shallowly around the base of your plant while it's young to avoid damaging roots near the surface.
• Fertilize lightly. Unless the soil is particularly poor, grapevines need little feeding.

Grape growers encounter a few common problems. For example, if you plant a seedless variety, you may find that your grapes are smaller than those in supermarkets. Grape seeds produce a plant hormone that causes the berries to increase in size. Seedless varieties are missing this hormone and thus produce smaller grapes.

Essentials

Planning
❧ *Choose a variety that is recommended for your climate. Grapes require a long, frost-free growing season.*
❧ *Grapes start to bear 2 years after 1-year-old vines are planted. Established vines will yield up to 15 pounds of grapes per year, 30 to 40 pounds from a muscadine.*
❧ *Plant grapes in the spring.*

Preparation
❧ *Select a site with deep, well-drained, loose soil in full sun.*
❧ *Set up a trellis system before planting.*

Planting
❧ *Space vines 6 to 10 feet apart (16 feet for muscadines).*
❧ *For each vine, dig a planting hole 12 inches deep and 12 inches wide. Fill with 4 inches of topsoil. Trim off broken roots and set the vine into the hole slightly deeper than it grew in the nursery.*
❧ *Cover the roots with 6 inches of soil and tamp down. Fill with the remaining soil, but don't tamp this down.*

Care
❧ *Prune the top back to two or three buds at planting time and follow the first-year training steps (page 358).*
❧ *Prune annually when the vines are dormant according to the training system you select.*
❧ *Do not fertilize unless the soil is very poor or the plants show poor foliage color or signs of nutrient deficiencies.*
❧ *Cultivate shallowly around the base of plants to control weeds.*
❧ *Drape netting over vines to prevent birds from destroying your harvest.*
❧ *Possible insect pests include aphids (page 400) and scales (page 402).*
❧ *Watch for anthracnose (page 403), black rot (page 403), downy mildew (page 360), and powdery mildew (page 405).*

Harvesting
❧ *Grapes will only ripen on the vine. As they ripen, the sugar content rises to about 20 percent.*
❧ *Harvest table grapes when the flavor is right; harvest wine grapes when they reach the appropriate sugar content.*

Grape Training and Pruning: Three Basic Systems

Grapes must be pruned every year to keep producing because once a cane has fruited, it won't fruit again. Fruits form only on buds that arise from the previous season's growth.

Which pruning method you choose depends on the type of grape and variety you have and which seems convenient and efficient to you. For American grapes, the most widespread system is the Four-Arm Kniffen System. For the vigorous muscadine grapes grown in the South, a two-arm version of the Kniffen System prevents excessive leaf shade.

European wine grapes are generally trained to have two permanent arms and are spur-pruned. If you have only a few vines and don't want to put up a wire trellis, you can head-train European grapes instead.

Pruning is done once a year — after the coldest part of the winter. Be sure to cut back to firm, live wood; the tips are often killed back. Muscadines are usually pruned after the first severe frost in the fall.

Training the Vine

The first few years are the same for the basic systems, the goal being to produce a strong root system and trunk. Here are the steps:

1. When planting, cut the vine back to two or three buds. It's a good idea to place trellis stakes or posts by the vine at this time; the wire can be put up later.

2. Early in the first summer, pick out the strongest growing cane. Pinch out the rest and let that one grow. As it gets taller, let several side shoots develop off the main one where you intend to place horizontal supports.

3. The following winter or early spring, prune back all canes as shown. Leave three buds on each of two or four lateral spurs (depending on how many arms you want). Put up wire supports.

4. The second summer, tie the side shoots to the wires as they grow. Remove flower clusters — you don't want the vine to fruit yet. Also remove shoots from all buds except those on the spurs. By late fall the vines should look like the one shown at right.

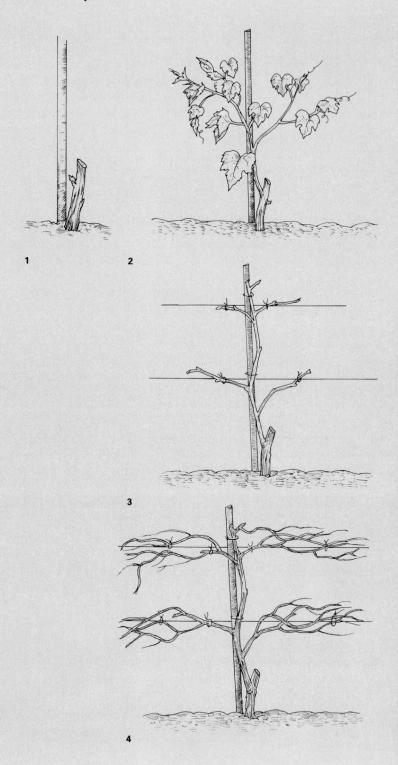

Four-Arm Kniffen System

Second winter: Choose four healthy, well-spaced arms to train on the wire for fruit production. If they are very long, trim back to ten buds. Choose four more canes for renewal spurs; cut these back to two buds. Remove all other canes. The following summer, the buds on the fruiting canes will grow into long shoots, each bearing two to three bunches of grapes. The buds on the renewal spurs will also produce shoots; if they are vigorous, let them fruit. If not, remove their fruiting clusters.

Third winter: Remove the canes that fruited and choose one replacement from each renewal spur to tie to the wires. Trim to ten buds. Cut back another four canes to form renewal spurs. Your vine should now look approximately as it did a year ago. Repeat each year.

Spur Pruning: Two-Arm

In this system you develop two permanent arms with spurs that produce fruiting wood each year.

Second winter: Remove all canes except the best two; tie these to the support wire. The next summer each bud along the arm will send out a fruiting shoot. Weave these in and out of the upper wires.

Third winter: Check the horizontal branches for the strongest vertical shoots and cut each of these back to two buds. These will be the fruiting spurs. Space them about 6 to 10 inches apart. Every bud you leave on the spurs will produce a fruiting shoot the following year. Each year, repeat the process.

Spur Pruning: Head-Trained

For this system, the vine will need only a strong, vertical, 4-foot post for support.

1. Allow the vine to grow to the top of the post and cut just above that point. Tie to the post. Remove any branches below. Next year, let four or five branches grow.

2. In the winter, cut each of the branches back to two or three buds. Remove any weak branches and any on lower parts of the trunk. Buds left on spurs will produce fruiting shoots next year. You can allow more branches to develop as the vine matures so there will be more fruiting shoots each year. A mature head-trained vine can have more than seven main branches.

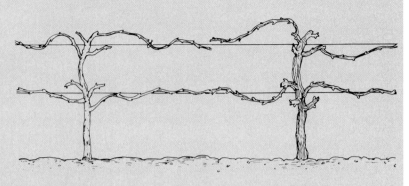

Second winter   **Third winter**

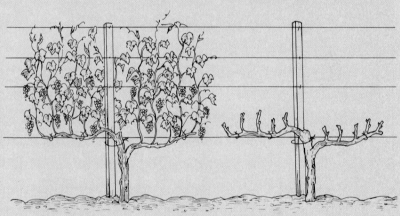

Second winter   **Third winter**

1   2

How Grapes Grow

1. Shown before growth starts in the spring: the main trunk is several years old, the shaded spur is 2 years old. The unshaded spur was produced the previous growing season; therefore, bud "a" is fruitful. Bud "b" is on 2-year-old wood and bud "c" on mature wood; because "b" and "c" are on old wood, neither is fruitful.

2. During the growing season, fruitful bud "a" grows into a shoot with fruit clusters, tendrils, leaves, and a new bud at the base of each leaf. The number of fruit clusters on each shoot varies according to the variety, but the average is three per shoot. Buds "b" and "c" also grow into shoots with tendrils, leaves, and new buds, but no fruit.

3. After harvest and leaf-fall, there is extensive wood present that was produced during the season. All the many buds on this new wood are fruitful. One of several choices is shown on where to prune to retain a single fruitful bud and thus return to the conditions in the first illustration. In practice, several canes and their fruitful buds are retained, and the cane with sufficient buds and best placement would be selected.

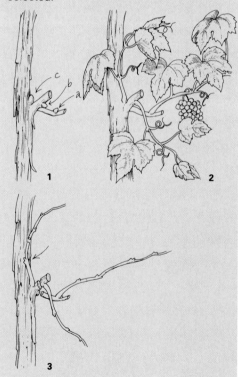

If you want larger grapes, keep more buds at pruning and thin out one cluster of every three just before spring bloom.

If your grapes are of mature size but fail to ripen on the vine in the fall, the leaves may be shading the grapes, which inhibits ripening. Try pinching foliage-bearing side shoots back to one leaf, which will bring more sunlight and warmth to the clusters.

Your first planting of grapes may escape insect or disease attacks for a while, but eventually some trouble usually arrives. In humid areas, mildew diseases can be a problem; European grapes are very susceptible to downy mildew, for example.

Black rot, caused by a fungus, develops in warm, moist climates of Eastern states. Anthracnose, another fungus disease, flourishes in wet spring weather.

Japanese beetles, aphids, and mites are common garden insects that you may find.

The grape berry moth is a pest in central and eastern regions. Larvae of the moth feed on buds, blossoms, and berries, tying berries together with silken threads as they feed. Two generations usually occur. Clean up grape leaves in the fall to reduce the number of overwintering pests. The following spring, cultivate around plants to turn up overwintered pupae.

The grape phylloxera is a pest common in California, where it attacks roots by sucking juices from them and creating galls, and in the East, where it attacks leaves as well as roots. Galls about the size of peas form on leaf undersides. American varieties are resistant, but other types are not. No chemical controls exist; if you have a severe problem, grow American types or European varieties with resistant American rootstocks.

Harvesting

Grapes do not ripen off the vine, so pick them when they are completely ripe. Use a sharp knife or small pruner to cut the bunches. Bees and wasps may occasionally light on the grapes to feast on some sweet juice, so watch for them.

Some Good Grape Varieties and Their Uses

Variety	Color	Comments	Sources
Table Grapes			
Buffalo	blue-black	Early ripening; delicious for jams and jellies.	*135, 141, 154*
Canadice	red	Early, seedless, disease resistant, winter hardy; a favorite for homes, where it's also used for red wines.	*135, 141, 154*
Concord	blue-black	The most common U.S. grape; good for wine, juice, jelly; tough skin; susceptible to powdery mildew, black rot; hardy.	*6, 17, 119, 135, 141, 154, 168*
Delaware	pink	For white wine, jelly; top commercial variety; needs good growing conditions; midseason ripening.	*119, 135, 154*
Edelweiss	white	Very hardy, high-quality, early, table or white wine grape; for northern gardens.	*11*
Fry	white	Muscadine.	*17*
Glenora	black	Dessert grape; hardiest of the seedless varieties.	*141, 154*
Golden Muscat	gold	Delicious, late season, matures only in warmer zones.	*135, 141, 154*
Himrod	white	Seedless, early, dessert grape; moderately winter hardy.	*6, 119, 135, 141, 154*
Interlaken	white	Very early, winter tender, seedless; favorite of birds.	*6, 17, 119, 135, 141, 154, 168*
Jumbo	black	Largest muscadine; needs pollinator.	*17, 119*
Reliance	pink	New seedless grape of high quality; very hardy.	*15, 21, 135, 154*
Schuyler	black	Seeded, very early; excellent for home vineyard.	*141*
Scuppernong	bronze-green	Most popular muscadine in South, perhaps over-rated; dessert, jam, or jelly; plant with *Higgins* (also sold by Burpee) for pollination.	*6, 17, 119*
Steuben	dark blue	Seeded, late grape, sweet with spicy tang; easy to grow; strong vines; can also be used for wine.	*135, 141, 154*
Swenson Red	red	Very hardy; excellent for far north gardens.	*21*
Venus	blue	Seedless, with large clusters of big grapes; slight muscat flavor.	*128, 135, 154*
Wine Grapes			
Aurore	gold	White French-American, hardy, vigorous, productive; early; can be used for table; favorite of birds.	*6, 119, 135, 154*
Baco Noir	dark red	For red wine; vigorous, disease resistant, French-American.	*6, 119, 141, 154*
Carlos	white	Medium-size muscadine with dry stem scar (some muscadines have a leaky stem scar that's messy).	*6, 17, 119*
Catawba	red	Late; top commercial wine grape also used for New York champagne. Vigorous, productive.	*6, 119, 135, 154, 168*
Foch	black	For red wine; hardy, early producer; another bird favorite.	*6, 141, 154*
Fredonia	black	Concord-type, early to midseason; makes red wine.	*17, 119, 135, 168*
Magnolia	white	May be the finest wine muscadine; sweet, medium size, tough skin, texture like Eastern bunch grape.	*17, 164*
Niagara	white	Leading white commercial grape in U.S. for juice and wine; not as cold hardy as Concord; midseason.	*6, 17, 119, 135, 141, 154, 168*
Villard Blanc	white	Resistant to Pierce's disease.	*17, 119*

Peaches

Showy peach blossoms (*above*) are a welcome sight in the spring. At left are large and sweet *Red-haven* peaches.

Few gastronomical treats come close to the season's first bite into a peach: the faint tingle of fuzz on your lips, the flesh, softer and sweeter than you remembered, and the trickle of juice down your chin, warm, sticky, and wonderful.

You may have shied away from growing peaches in the past because you've heard about all the things that could go wrong. Yet thousands of gardeners grow marvelous peaches. As with most fruit trees, the trick is to start out with the peach variety that suits your climate. Peaches will grow in zones 5 to 8; they do especially well in zones 6 and 7. Since most peach varieties are self-fertile, you can plant just one tree at a time (*J. H. Hale* and *Elberta* are among the exceptions).

Peaches ripen from mid-July through mid-September. If you are planting more than one tree, be sure to select varieties with different ripening periods to extend the harvest.

Planning

Peaches have very specific needs for dormancy, and at certain times, can be extremely susceptible to frost damage. It's important to choose the correct variety and rootstock for your area.

In order to break dormancy and begin flowering, peach trees require a certain number of chilling hours below 45°F during the winter; most need between 650 and 950. If you choose a variety that needs fewer hours of chilling than your area provides, your peach tree could start to bloom during a January or February thaw. A cold snap could then spoil your whole crop of blossoms. Or, if you pick a variety that needs more chilling hours than your area provides, dormancy will never be broken properly, blossoms might appear one month on one branch, one month on another, shoots will be bare, and your crop poor.

Some varieties are more cold tolerant than others. Most peach trees will not blossom and often cannot survive temperatures below −10°F. A few varieties such as *Reliance* tolerate temperatures as low as −20°F, but the flavor of the fruit will not be top quality.

Peach trees are also susceptible to frost damage right near the end of dormancy. A cold snap in early spring can damage the flower buds on a tree with little spring frost resistance. Trees in areas with cold winters tend to develop buds slowly and bloom late enough so they're not bothered by spring frosts. But trees in areas with mild winters develop buds rapidly and are vulnerable to early spring frost.

If you live in a good peach-growing area (zones 5 to 8, and especially zones 6 and 7), you can worry less about cold resistance and focus instead on flavor when choosing a variety. Many growers rate midseason peaches as the best in flavor. Of those, some favorites are *Red Globe, Loring, Suncrest, Madison, J. H. Hale, Jefferson,* and *Jerseyqueen.* Others claim that white peaches such as *Nectar* and *Belle of Georgia* are the gourmet's choice. Traditionalists swear by such old varieties as *Late Crawford.*

For canning, both cling and freestone have their advantages and drawbacks. Cling peaches have a firm flesh that doesn't bruise easily with handling. Freestones have softer flesh and easy-to-remove pits. You can also grow nectarines, a genetic variation of peaches that produces fuzzless fruit. Nectarines are grown the same way as peaches, but they are more susceptible to brown rot.

Preparation

Never plant peaches in low areas that can become frost pockets. To delay bloom in an area with frequent spring frosts, plant on the north side of a one- or two-story building. This will shade the tree in late winter, retarding the bloom, but allowing the tree to receive needed sun in the summer. Peaches do best in well-drained, sandy soils.

Planting

Plant in the spring so the tree will be well established by winter. Space trees 15 to 20 feet apart. (See pages 301–303 for further information on planting.)

Care

Fertilize the young tree with a nitrogen-containing fertilizer such as 1 pound of 10-10-10 or its equivalent about 6 weeks after planting. In the second year, add ¾

Far right: Standard-size peach trees can grow 25 feet tall if left unpruned. For small-growing peach trees that grow to only 6 feet, look for genetic dwarf varieties such as *Compact Elberta* and *Compact Redhaven.*

Nothing beats the home-grown flavor of a tree-ripened peach. Pictured here are *Rio Oso Gem* peaches.

pound of the fertilizer in the spring and another ¾ pound in early summer. Seeding the lawn around the tree with white clover as well as grass, or with bird's-foot trefoil or crimson clover, will provide extra nitrogen. (Clover and trefoil are nitrogen-fixing legumes.) Once the tree starts bearing, it shouldn't grow quite as vigorously and won't need as much nitrogen. From the third year on, mature trees need about 1 pound of actual nitrogen per year, applied in the spring when growth is starting.

Slowing the tree's growth is a good way to make it stronger, more winter hardy, and longer lived. Don't apply fertilizer within 2 months of the average first fall frost, and let the lawn grow up around the tree in late summer and early fall. Don't apply any more water than necessary at this time and never prune in the fall.

To prevent winter sunscald, you can paint the trunk white (see page 306). Remove any mulch from around the base of the tree to avoid attracting rodents and place a mouse guard around the trunk if

Essentials

Planning

᠊ᡧ Plant peach trees in the spring.

᠊ᡧ Plant large, vigorous 1-year-olds. Standard-size trees will bear fruits at 3 years of age, dwarfs at 1 to 2 years.

᠊ᡧ Most varieties are self-fertile, so it is not necessary to plant more than one tree.

᠊ᡧ Choose varieties that are right for your area and resistant to disease.

᠊ᡧ A standard-size peach tree will stand 15 feet at maturity if kept pruned, 25 feet if left unpruned. Dwarf trees reach 6 feet in height.

Preparation

᠊ᡧ Choose a site with well-drained, sandy soil. Avoid low-lying areas that can become frost pockets.

Planting

᠊ᡧ Plant standard-size trees 15 to 20 feet apart, dwarf trees 10 to 12 feet apart.

Care

᠊ᡧ Fertilize young trees with nitrogen in early spring and early summer. Fertilize older trees at a rate of 1 pound of actual nitrogen per year. Do not fertilize within 2 months of the average first fall frost date or when fruits are maturing.

᠊ᡧ Prune trees to an open center shape.

᠊ᡧ Thin fruits to 6 to 8 inches apart 4 to 6 weeks after bloom.

᠊ᡧ Watch for peach tree borers (page 401) and the plum curculio (page 401).

᠊ᡧ Prune trees, thin fruit, and pick fruit when ripe to increase resistance to fruit diseases such as brown rot (page 404) and powdery mildew (page 405). Peach leaf curl (page 405) may also be a problem.

Harvest

᠊ᡧ Pick peaches when fully ripe. There should be no green on the fruit, and fruit should come off the branch with a slight twist.

᠊ᡧ Store peaches in a cool place.

Control of the Peach Tree Borer

The peach tree borer is the larval stage of a moth that lays its eggs in burrows near the bases of peach trees. The eggs hatch during the summer, and the larvae enter the peach bark to feed throughout the late summer, early fall, and the following spring and early summer. Damage becomes apparent in the spring and summer as masses of gum and brown frass appear around the bases of infested trees. Young trees can be killed during the first season of infestation; older trees can take longer to die as a result of girdling by the insect.

Para-dichlorobenzene (PDB), or moth crystals, is commonly recommended for control of the peach tree borer. Unfortunately, most sources of this information neglect to give specific enough instructions for its use. The best time to apply moth crystals is in the fall when the larvae are most susceptible, damage is not yet great, and soil temperatures are warm enough to volatilize the crystals. Consult your Extension Service agent to find out the best dates for application. Soil temperature must be around 60°F 4 inches below the surface for at least 2 weeks after application.

Before applying the crystals, scrape away all the grass and a few inches of topsoil from the base of each tree. Remove gum deposits from the trunk above and below the soil line. Then spread the crystals in a ring around the tree, between 1 and 3 inches from the base of the trunk. The amount depends on the age and size of the tree. Apply ¼ pound the first year, ¼ to ½ pound the second year, ¾ pound the third to fifth year, and 1 to 1½ pounds the sixth year and after.

Cover the crystals with about a foot of soil. The soil temperature will volatilize the crystals, and the vapor will travel into the larval burrows. Keep the crystals in the ground for 1 month for trees between 1 and 5 years old. For trees 6 years and older, leave the crystals for 6 months. After removing the crystals and soil cover, be sure to maintain the original level of soil around the tree.

necessary. In late winter or early spring, after the ground has thawed, put a heavy layer of organic mulch around the trees to keep the soil cool — this will delay blooming.

Train peaches to an open center (see pages 313–315) and prune annually. Remove dead or diseased wood first, then any branches that grow straight up or droop down. Peaches and nectarines bear fruit only from lateral buds on 1-year-old branches. They need more dormant-season pruning than other fruit trees to stimulate growth of new fruiting wood each year and to keep the fruiting wood closer to the trunk. When bloom is heavy, lightly head back the longer fruiting branches to reduce the fruit load and prevent branch breakage. Summer pinching helps control tree size, encourages formation of next year's buds, and improves fruit quality.

When the tree is 5 or 6 years old, remove all the wood produced in the previous 2 years. This will keep the tree from growing too tall and will restore vigor to the older wood.

Far right: **This tree should have been thinned of excess fruit about 4 to 6 weeks after bloom. A heavy fruit load must be reduced to prevent branches from breaking. Fruits should be spaced 6 to 8 inches apart on the branch.**

A *Reliance* **peach tree is shown here with a mouse guard and a support for a heavy limb; its trunk is painted white for protection from winter sunscald.**

About 4 to 6 weeks after bloom, thin some of the excess fruit if you have an abundant crop. Remove and destroy any fruit with signs of insect puncture. Thin so the fruits are spaced 6 to 8 inches apart on the branch. The remaining fruits will be larger and sweeter than they would have been without thinning.

Harvesting

Never shortchange yourself by picking your peaches too early. The reward for your labor is the special, home-grown flavor of a tree-ripened peach; one that has to sit for a while on the kitchen windowsill just isn't reward enough.

If there's still some green on the peach, chances are it's not ready to be picked. A peach should come off the branch with one slight twist — nothing more vigorous than that. Be careful while harvesting because most varieties, especially the soft-fleshed *Reliance* and *Champion*, bruise easily when ripe.

To store peaches, keep them in a cool place to prevent further ripening.

Peach Rootstocks

If you have a choice when buying your peach trees, stick with such standard rootstocks as *Lovell* or *Halford* in most parts of the country. Both are widely adapted, widely offered seedlings, and they perform similarly. Although both are susceptible to nematodes, verticillium wilt, crown rot, and peach tree borers, properly cared for trees on these rootstocks will outlive trees on other rootstocks. Choose an especially well drained site for peaches to avoid crown rot and leaf yellowing from excess moisture.

If you live on the northern fringe of the peach's range (Michigan, Ontario, and northern New York), you can try *Siberian*, which is adapted to steady, prolonged winter cold. It cannot withstand the fluctuating winter temperatures common in most peach-growing areas, so don't buy this rootstalk in areas any further south of those named.

Nemaguard is useful in the Southwest because it resists root-knot nematodes. However, it is more susceptible than *Lovell* or *Halford* to lesion nematodes, some other damaging nematodes common in the East, and bacterial canker, and it is not as cold hardy. It's not a good idea for the very humid Northwest Coast and Southeast, where bacterial canker is a serious problem.

Do not choose dwarfing rootstocks. Those currently used are western sand cherry (*P. besseyi*), Nanking cherry (*P. tomentosa*), and *St. Julien,* a damson plum (*P. institia*). These are not closely related to peaches, so graft incompatibility problems often develop, causing the trees to be unproductive and die young. A new dwarfing rootstock developed in California, a peach-plum hybrid named *Citation,* shows promise. However, if you really want a miniature peach tree, several genetic dwarf varieties are sold, including *Compact Elberta* and *Compact Redhaven*.

Peach Sources

Belle of Georgia *119, 123, 152, 157*
Champion *119, 133, 152*
Compact Elberta *154, 155*
Compact Redhaven *154, 155*
Elberta *119, 124, 129, 152*
Glohaven *119, 122*
Halberta *154*
Jefferson *119, 124, 157*
Jerseyqueen *119, 124, 152, 157*
J. H. Hale *119, 124, 129*
Late Crawford *152*
Loring *119, 124, 157*
Madison *119, 124, 154, 157*
Nectar *121, 129*
Norman *124*
Redskin *119, 124, 152, 157*
Red Globe *119, 121, 124, 157*
Reliance *119, 124, 133, 152, 154*
Rio Oso Gem *119, 124, 129, 157*
Suncrest *119, 152*
Sunhigh *119, 124, 133, 157*
Topaz *119, 124, 133*
Velvet *142*
Washington *119, 157*
Winblo *124*

Rootstock Sources

Citation *154*
Elberta *158*
Halford seedling *135, 155, 157*
Lovell seedling *119, 141, 157*
Nanking cherry *154*
Nemaguard *124, 158, 159*
Sand cherry *135*
Siberian C seedling *119, 141, 142*
St. Julien plum *154*

Pears

Red pears such as the *Rogue Red* at left have been introduced by plant breeders to attract more pear enthusiasts. Pear trees bloom early (*above*); to avoid frost damage, it's best to select a site that allows trees to receive plenty of summer sun but little spring sun.

The extensive selection of high-quality pear varieties available that can't be found in grocery stores make pear trees well worth growing by home gardeners. Pears require less spraying than peaches, plums, or apples and are easy to train to fit small spaces in a yard.

Unfortunately, pear trees can be affected by two serious problems. The insect pest the pear psylla can be difficult to control. And the bacterial disease fire blight has made larger-scale commercial pear growing difficult in many parts of the country. Because of fire blight, most of the United States pear crop now comes from northern California, Oregon, and Washington, where the predominantly dry climate discourages the spread of this disease.

If you live outside of this region, you can still grow pears successfully by selecting blight-resistant varieties and rootstocks. With good planning and vigilance during the season, you can grow fresh, tender pears year after year with minimal use of chemical products.

Planning

Pears can usually be grown wherever apples are successful, though they are somewhat less resistant than apples to extremes of heat and cold. Pears, however, need less attention than apples in matters of pruning and insect control and are more tolerant of moist soil conditions. So if you have predominantly clay soil, pears will probably do better for you than apples on the same site.

Compared to other tree fruits, pears are slower to start producing. Many apple varieties begin bearing in 3 to 4 years; with pears, the wait for good crops is longer. Standard types will take about 4 to 8 years to begin bearing; dwarfs, 4 to 6. As a general rule, pears must be cross-pollinated to produce fruit, so plan to plant two varieties; most combinations of pear varieties will work except for *Bartlett* and *Seckel*, which don't cross-pollinate well with each other.

Out of nearly three thousand varieties, perhaps a hundred have good yields, flavor, texture, and keeping qualities. However, fewer than twenty are grown commercially. Thus, the home gardener has a wide choice of top-quality specialty pears.

There are several pear varieties that offer effective resistance to fire blight, such as *Moonglow, Magness, Maxine, Seckel,* and *Kieffer* (see page 375 for other varieties). In the South, plant resistant varieties such as *Hood, Leconte, Hawaiian,* and *Baldwin.*

Preparation

Pears need soil with moderate fertility. Frosts during the bud and blossom period can damage the flowers and reduce yields significantly. Try to locate pears on a slope for better air drainage, or on the north side of a building to retard flowering.

Planting

Space standard trees 20 to 25 feet apart, dwarf trees 12 to 15 feet apart. (See pages 301–303 for planting information.)

Bosc pears are excellent for canning as well as fresh eating. They can be kept for several months after harvest if conditions are right.

Care

Keep young trees weed-free, and water well during dry spells to help the roots get established quickly.

Fertilize lightly in early spring of the second and succeeding years about 2 weeks before bloom. In moderately fertile soils, use ammonium nitrate at ⅛ pound or its equivalent per tree, multiplied by the number of years the tree has been set. Use less if you have highly fertile soil.

If shoot growth on the tree is more than 12 inches in a season, use less fertilizer the following spring. If the leaves are pale green or yellowish in midsummer, add slightly more fertilizer the next year.

Be careful applying fertilizer around your pear trees. Too much nitrogen promotes succulent growth, which allows fire blight disease bacteria to enter the tree's tender young shoots more easily. Also, pears require several months to harden off in the fall. High nitrogen levels after midsummer delay this hardening-off process.

If your pear tree is located in a lawn area, cut back on turf fertilizer applications when you feed your lawn so as not to give your trees too much nitrogen.

Dwarf pears are often trained to a central leader (see pages 311–313). Semi-dwarf and standard-size trees also yield best when trained to a central leader, but they are usually trained to a modified leader because that form is easier to maintain with a larger tree. In an area prone to fire blight, you can prune your tree to multiple leaders. That way an infected leader can be removed while the others keep growing.

Pears are trickier to prune well than apples because all their branches grow nearly straight up. This growth habit promotes weak branches and dense foliage around the center of the tree, which encourages fire blight, fungus diseases, and pear psylla. Once you get the knack of pruning, the results will be worth the trouble. Prune regularly, though generally very lightly.

Spreaders will help direct the tree's scaffold branches to a more outward, horizontal direction, and will encourage early development of fruiting spurs. Fortunately, pears are easier to train than most trees. Start in early summer of the first year. Toothpicks or clothespins can be used when branches are small; later, use wooden slats with the ends notched in a "V" to hold them in place. Sharp ends of spreaders can poke into the trunk and branch slightly, but won't hurt the tree. (An alternative practiced by some growers in the West is to hold branches down with a string tied to a clip in the ground.)

Pears bear their fruit mainly from terminal buds on short branches or spurs. Mature trees need only light pruning during the dormant season, mostly to thin out unfruitful, diseased, or crowded branches. Avoid heading back cuts during dormant pruning since this will result in new, long, unfruitful shoots.

If you have a variety that bears at an early age, such as *Bosc* or *Bartlett*, remove fruit developing on the ends of thin fragile branches to keep the limbs from breaking.

Pollination can be a problem with pears because bees are not partial to their blossoms; pear nectar contains less than 10 percent sugar, compared to nearly 50 percent in apple nectar, and pears often flower when it's too cold (below 55°F) or wet for the bees to fly. To make matters worse, pear blossoms are fertile only for a short time.

Pollination is most likely if the weather is warm during pear blossom time. If you're fortunate enough to live near an ocean coast or large lake, the cooling influence of the water in the spring promotes later blooming of pears and facilitates pollination. Ask other pear growers if pollination in your area is erratic from year to year; if so, you may need a beehive when your trees are coming into their bearing years for consistent fruit set. Move it to within 50 feet of your pear trees when blossoming starts. Even with a

Essentials

Planning
✦ *Choose fire blight–resistant varieties and rootstocks, especially in areas outside dry western regions.*
✦ *Most varieties will start to bear significant harvests after 5 to 6 years.*
✦ *Plant at least two different varieties for cross-pollination.*

Preparation
✦ *Choose a site with full sun, moderate fertility, and good air circulation and water drainage.*
✦ *Pears will do well in a wide range of soil types.*

Planting
✦ *Space standard-size trees 20 to 25 feet apart; space dwarf trees 12 to 15 feet apart.*

Care
✦ *Pears do best with a small amount of fertilizer early in the year. Heavy doses of nitrogen will make the tree more vulnerable to fire blight.*
✦ *Use spreaders to encourage horizontal branching and earlier fruiting spurs.*
✦ *Watch for pear psylla (page 401), codling moths (page 401), apple maggots (page 400), cherry fruit flies (page 400), plum curculios (page 401), aphids (page 400), and mites (page 397).*
✦ *Be on guard for fire blight (page 404).*

Harvesting
✦ *Don't let pears ripen on the tree. Harvest them when they reach a mature size but are still hard.*
✦ *Early pears will ripen at room temperature in a few days to a week. Storage varieties will keep 1 to 2 months or more in a cool (40°F), dark place.*

beehive, you may have occasional years of near-total crop failure owing to frosts or poor flying weather for the bees.

Fire blight, unlike most fruit tree diseases, is caused by a bacteria that can be spread from tree to tree by bees, aphids, pear psylla, and other insects. The bacteria mainly attack twigs and young shoots. Affected branches wither and turn black or brownish black, as if scorched. Most branch tips, once infected, wilt rapidly, taking on a shepherd's crook shape.

The bacteria enter the tree through the blossoms or through lush, tender new growth. Once inside, they multiply rapidly and begin to work toward the roots. An orange-brown liquid will ooze from pustules on the tree, particularly on warm days. This liquid contains a great number of bacteria, which may be spread by rain or insects. The bacteria form a canker under the bark and survive there through the winter, infecting more trees the following year.

Fire blight is a very serious disease in most parts of the country; it can wipe out all susceptible trees in an orchard in one season. It can be controlled, however.

Fire blight is most damaging during bloom, when the blossoms become entry points for the bacteria. If you have a mini orchard — 20 to 30 pear trees — it would pay to use an antibiotic spray or dust during bloom and shortly after to prevent the blight bacteria from reproducing.

Fire blight spreads rapidly in periods of warm, humid weather, so check the trees carefully at such times for signs of wilting. Remove all suckers and cut off any infected branches before the bacteria attack the tree further. Using a sharp set of pruning shears, cut off the wilting branch at least 8 inches below the point of last visible wilt. After each cut, dip the shears in a solution of 1 part household bleach to 9 parts water to avoid transmitting bacteria from one branch to another. (When you are finished, wash and oil your tools to prevent damage from the bleach.)

Notched-board branch spreaders encourage horizontal limb growth. The spreaders prompt the tree to produce more fruiting spurs and result in earlier harvests.

Discourage lush growth because it is very susceptible to fire blight damage. If possible, remove other plants that may serve as hosts for the disease, including wild apples, hawthorns, mountain ash, and cotoneaster hedges. Control aphids and pear psylla to prevent them from spreading the disease.

Prune out fire blight cankers in the winter when trees are dormant. Leaves remaining on blighted branches in autumn can indicate trouble spots. If you prune before the sap starts to flow in the spring, you don't have to sterilize your tools after each cut.

The chief pest of pear trees in eastern and western (but not central) United States is the pear psylla. This reddish-brown insect rapidly develops resistance to chemical controls; it causes significant damage by spreading pear decline and fire blight and sucking out the plant sap. The insects emit a sticky substance called honeydew on which a black fungus grows. Yellow jackets may congregate around the black fungus, indicating pest activity.

Control adults with dormant oil spray in the fall when they are most susceptible. A fall spraying is better than a spring spray because it will not affect many of the beneficial insects that are present in the trees in very early spring.

If necessary use a dormant oil spray in the spring to inhibit egg-laying and to kill any active adults present. The adults begin to lay eggs when the temperature gets up to 70°F, sometimes at slightly lower temperatures on a sunny day with no wind. You will have to use a 10-power magnifying glass to see the little yellow eggs at the base of the bud scales.

As soon as you find any eggs, the first oil spray should go on. Spray again 7 days later. The insects don't seem to like laying eggs on this oily surface. Be sure to cover the tree thoroughly — until it's dripping. During the growing season use an insecticidal soap spray to keep pear psylla activity down.

Pear Rootstocks

A seedling pear tree growing on its own roots can grow 35 to 40 feet tall and live for a century or more. The standard pear is much taller, but narrower, than a standard apple tree. Standard-size pears can take up to 8 years to start bearing and require careful pruning to control growth.

Most of the standard rootstocks are seedlings of the *Bartlett* variety, producing a tree that can easily grow 25 to 35 feet tall. This rootstock adapts to a wide range of soils, tolerating a certain amount of drought as well as excess soil moisture. It's highly susceptible to fire blight, though, as well as pear root aphids and nematodes. The threat of fire blight may be reduced by choosing a blight-resistant variety grafted onto a *Bartlett* rootstock.

Bartlett seedlings are winter hardy to zone 5, as are most pear varieties. Seedlings of hardier pear varieties are sometimes used as rootstocks by northern nurseries. Cold-hardy rootstocks of the Siberian pear (*Pyrus ussuriensis*) and the Snow pear (*P. nivalis*), are also used, though the Siberian pear rootstock is very susceptible to pear decline, and the Snow pear rootstock is susceptible to fire blight. If you live in zones 2, 3, 4, or the colder sections of zone 5, be sure the pears you order from your nursery are on cold-hardy rootstocks.

In zones 4 and 5 you can try *Old Home* rootstocks as well. Cuttings of *Old Home* pear offer a rootstock hardier than *Bartlett* seedlings. *Old Home* is resistant to pear decline (a common disease in the West) and moderately resistant to fire blight. However, it is just as susceptible to pear root aphids and nematodes. *Old Home* rootstock produces a semidwarf tree, 70 percent of standard size.

Cuttings of quince (a different species of fruit) are the most commonly used dwarfing rootstocks for pear, good for zones 5, 6, 7, and 8. It is the rootstock Western commercial growers depend on. Quince rootstock produces a tree about 35 percent of standard size that will bear fruit a year or two sooner.

Quince is not reliably hardy north of the warmer sections of zone 5, and is more sensitive to high soil pH and excess soil moisture than pear. Use it only on sites with excellent air and water drainage and a near-neutral pH. Quince produces a weak root system, and the pear variety tends to overgrow the rootstock, so pears on quince roots should be staked or trellised all their lives. The trees tend to die much sooner than standard pears, sometimes breaking off at the graft union. Quince roots are resistant to pear root aphids and nematodes, and the pear variety on quince resists pear decline. Quince, however, is highly susceptible to fire blight; if it is chosen as a rootstock, choose a blight-resistant variety.

The graft union on a dwarf pear cannot be buried, or the variety roots and overcomes the rootstock's dwarfing effect. However, if *Old Home* was used as an interstem (you'll see two graft unions), the tree can be planted with the lower union 3 to 4 inches below ground level, and the *Old Home* interstem will root in 1 to 4 years. The quince root acts as a nurse root for the first few years, inducing earlier fruit production. *Old Home* becomes the dominant root system, producing a semidwarf tree that's more winter hardy, better anchored, and blight resistant. This is a good choice for zone 5.

For zones 6 and warmer areas, a better fully dwarfing rootstock for pear is OH × F 51. This was the fifty-first seedling of a cross between *Old Home* and *Farmingdale* seedlings and is propagated by cuttings. Though not quite as winter hardy as quince and susceptible to nematodes, it's better anchored and resistant to fire blight, pear decline, and pear root aphids. It will produce trees about 50 percent of standard size. Unfortunately, demand for it is great and the supply is low at the present time.

Some West Coast nurseries use the standard-size Oriental pear rootstocks *Pyrus betulaefolia* and *P. calleryana* for European pears. Both are highly resistant to fire blight and pear root aphids. However, neither is hardy north of zone 6, and trees on these rootstocks should always be planted with the graft union several inches below ground to protect the rootstock from freezing damage. *Betulaefolia* roots are highly susceptible to nematodes and induce very vigorous tree growth, so aren't recommended. *Calleryana* roots are subject to pear psylla and pear decline, but are useful in the Southeast where decline and cold damage aren't problems and fire blight is a severe problem.

A traditional, very sweet-tasting pear, *Flemish Beauty.*

The codling moth ("codling" is an old name for a tiny apple) is a key pear and apple pest. The first adults appear at the time blossom petals fall. The adult insects lay eggs on young fruit, twigs, and leaves. Adults can be killed with a spray of ryania when 75 percent of the blossom petals have fallen. Trichogramma wasp parasites will attack codling moth eggs and should be released about 10 days after the ryania application.

As the eggs start to hatch, the young caterpillars feed on the leaves for a few days. This is a good time to spray the tree with *Bacillus thuringiensis,* which kills various leaf-chewing caterpillars. The larvae don't feed heavily on the leaves so you might consider adding one or two tablespoons of skim milk powder as a feeding enhancer to your spray mixture.

After feeding on the leaves briefly, the worms enter the pears and eat for about a month. Although the fruits will be ruined that year, you should try to intercept the larvae after they leave the pear and descend the trunk to reach the soil, where they will finish their life cycle. A strip of burlap about 6 inches wide and covered with Tangle Trap (a sticky, trapping substance) can be tightly wrapped around the trunk and stapled together to form a formidable and usually lethal barrier.

Several turns of corrugated cardboard around the trunk will entice many of the surviving larvae to spin their cocoons in it, and after a while you can simply remove the cardboard from the tree and burn it. If there are two or more generations of codling moths in your area, use the burlap strip as a monitor of caterpillar activity and destroy the cardboard about a month after the first larvae are caught in the Tangle Trap. Don't apply Tangle Trap directly to the tree because it will injure the bark.

Woodpeckers, particularly the downy and the hairy, will eat up to half of the larvae that overwinter in the orchard area. Hang a block of suet in the trees to attract woodpeckers. Scrape off old, flaky bark by using chicken wire like a bath towel to deny winter cover to the larvae and make the birds' job that much easier.

Harvesting

Pears should be harvested when they are mature, but still hard, and ripened off the tree for the best eating and canning quality. If you wait until the pears get ripe on the tree they'll be mushy inside within a day or two. The early varieties will take a few days to a week to ripen after harvest; later ripening varieties often require several weeks or more to reach best quality.

Mature pears will be full size and the color of many varieties at this stage turns from green to light yellow. Generally, if you lift the fruit up it should break away easily from the stem. (The *Bartlett* pear will need a slight twist to loosen it.)

Pears grow larger and get softer all through the picking period. If you're going to keep some pears in cool storage for eating a month or two in the future, pick them when they are full size but still quite hard. Even though the skin is firm, handle them gently; they bruise easily. Pears that you will eat right away can be harvested later when the skin is a bit softer.

Many varieties can be kept for a few weeks in a cool, dark place. For longer storage, pears need refrigeration at 32° to 40°F. Bring them out to room temperature for a week or so before eating them.

Pear Varieties

New varieties are released every year and many are not only resistant to pear diseases, but quite tasty as well. Don't be afraid to try a pear variety simply because it isn't well known or readily available in the stores. On the other hand, depending on your needs, there are some varieties you'll want to avoid. (Where no mail-order source is indicated, check at a local nursery.)

Oriental Pears

Interest in Oriental pears has increased substantially in recent years. Unlike the buttery soft European pears, Oriental pears remain firm and are crisp and juicy when ripe. Most of them are round like an apple, but the flavor is entirely different. To yield good-size fruits, Oriental pears require more severe pruning than European pears. Most Oriental pears are susceptible to fire blight but less so than *Bartlett*.

Variety	Comments	Sources
Hardy Pears for Zones 2, 3, and 4		
Clapp's Favorite	A large, well-colored pear that ripens with Melba apples; very good quality, but it doesn't keep well; very sensitive to fire blight.	6, 119, 133, 152, 160
Golden Spice	Small, reddish-yellow pear with good quality and a spicy flavor; sweet and aromatic; cans well; fire blight resistant.	137, 154
Nova	Large, round, yellow pear; juicy, buttery, and sweet most years; fire blight resistant; unknown hardiness in zone 3.	153
Patten	Large, yellow pear that resembles the better-known *Bartlett*; fire blight resistant and much hardier than *Bartlett*, but of somewhat lower quality.	11, 153
Temperate Pears for Zones 5 to 8		
Anjou	A large, round, good late pear that stores and ships very well; will keep for up to 6 months with little loss of quality; not a heavy producer.	118, 119, 129, 151, 152
Bartlett (Williams)	High-quality pear for dessert and canning; accounts for three-quarters of North American commercial production; very vulnerable to fire blight, but probably worth the trouble for home gardeners.	118, 119, 121, 129, 133
Bosc	A brown pear with a very narrow neck; high quality for canning or eating out of hand; ripens about 3 weeks after *Bartlett*; will keep for several months.	118, 129, 133, 141, 149
Comice	A large russeted, rounded pear with superb flavor and texture; highest quality in the Pacific Northwest; ripens late.	119, 129, 130, 133, 149, 151
Kieffer	A medium-size pear whose main virtue is its fire blight resistance; by December they may be soft enough to can.	17, 119, 125, 158
Magness	A medium-size pear of high quality; somewhat resistant to insect damage; very resistant to fire blight; produces no pollen and needs a companion variety to set fruit, and a third variety is needed to pollinize the companion.	119, 125, 130, 157
Maxine (Starking Delicious)	Large pears of very good quality, somewhat blight resistant.	15, 118, 125, 137, 152, 159
Moonglow	A large, soft, juicy, excellently flavored pear; early ripening; fire blight resistant; can or use fresh.	17, 119, 125, 152, 154, 158
Seckel	A very small, brownish green pear of high quality, which does best on dwarfing roots; quite sweet, not a keeper.	17, 119, 121, 130, 150, 153
Southern Pears for Zones 9 and 10		
Baldwin	Medium to large oblong pear; semihard to use fresh or canned; ripens in early fall; moderately blight resistant.	17
Garber	A round pear for canning and preserving.	158, 159
Hawaiian	Fire blight resistant; for canning.	Check locally
Hood	Fire blight resistant; for canning.	Check locally
Leconte	Good-quality pear for eating out of hand, pickling, or preserving; fire blight susceptible.	125, 158, 159
Oriental Pears		
Twentieth Century (Nijisseiki)	Mottled greenish yellow, somewhat lopsided; the white flesh is mild and refreshingly tart with only a few grit cells; very good to excellent quality; hardy in zones 6 to 9.	146, 155
Chojurŏ	Best of the russet-skinned Oriental pears; greenish brown to brown; slightly astringent skin, mildly sweet flesh; less tender than the green-skinned varieties; good quality; hardy in zones 6 to 8.	146, 147

Compiled by Brenda Olcott-Reid.

Plums

Japanese plums (*left*) have juicy flesh and are excellent for fresh eating, but the trees require more pruning and fruit thinning than other types. European plums such as the versatile, widely adapted *Stanley* variety above are generally easier to grow.

Widely adapted, reliably prolific, more compact, and less demanding than most fruit trees, plums are a natural choice for the home grower. Plums are delicious cooked in jams, jellies, butters, sauces; baked in pies and coffee cakes; dried as prunes; or — best of all — eaten juicy fresh right off the tree. For the home gardener, plums offer an additional bonus: the trees add a beautiful, graceful touch to any home landscape.

Which variety of plum tree to plant depends partly on your location. Hardy European plums are the most widely planted plum across the United States. The more delicate Japanese plums thrive where peach trees thrive. Where neither European nor Japanese plums will flourish, American hybrids will survive. Combining the hardiness of the native American trees with the flavor and size of the Japanese plums, American hybrids will often survive even under the harsh wintry conditions of the northern plains and Canada.

Planning

Japanese plums actually originated in China but were brought to this country via Japan in the 1800s. They are not quite as sweet as European plums, though their flesh is much juicier. Two varieties that are excellent for fresh eating and canning are *Satsuma,* a large, dark red, sweet plum, and *Santa Rosa,* a large plum with crimson skin and purple flesh that turns yellow near the skin.

European plums will grow where it's neither too cold nor too hot. The fruits are high quality and very uniform. *Stanley* is a versatile European plum that is widely adapted and particularly well suited to the eastern regions and some of the Northwest. It's self-fertile and very productive. A medium to large freestone plum, *Stanley* is excellent for eating fresh, cooking, or canning. *Italian* plums are similar to Stanley. These large, freestone purple plums are

Top: Green Gage European plums. *Bottom: Satsuma,* one of the most highly recommended Japanese plums. European plums should be harvested when they are tree-ripe; Japanese plums should be harvested slightly early and allowed to ripen in a cool place.

very sweet, perfect for drying, eating fresh, or canning. *Seneca* is a high-quality European plum that's just now being tested and looks promising for the home gardener. It matures about one week before *Stanley.* The fruit is large, oblong, and purple, with good flavor for eating fresh.

If you live in a place where neither Japanese nor European plums will grow because of the climate or disease problems, American plums or bush plums may be your best bet, but they're hard to find.

Though very winter hardy, American bush plums will produce well as far south as Florida. Fruits are ¾ inch in diameter or larger, yellow or red, with a flat stone. There's also the hardy beach plum, or shore plum, which is found along the eastern shore from Maine to Delaware. The fruit is delicious in preserves. The plants are available commercially and can be pruned to a shrub shape or small tree. Beach plums are very hardy and enjoy poor, sandy soils.

American hybrid trees are a good choice for regional extremes. Combining the virtues of both breeds, the fruits are as tasty as the Japanese plums and as hardy as our native plum species.

Climate plays a large role in determining which plum variety to plant. European plum trees are adapted to conditions throughout most of the United States. They are generally more tolerant of the cold than Japanese varieties. On the other hand, Japanese plums are better able to tolerate summer heat. They bloom earlier than European plums, so they are more vulnerable to late frost damage. Generally, Japanese plums don't set fruit well in regions with cold, damp springs.

American hybrids look very promising in the Southeast where there are many disease problems. Also, some native hybrids do well in the northern Midwest, where you can't grow any other plums because of freeze damage. These hybrids are often able to survive on the northern plains because of the unbroken, persistent cold, although they may not fare as well in other northern regions where warm spells frequently interrupt winter conditions.

The European plum is generally easier to grow than the Japanese because Japanese plum trees need more pruning and more fruit thinning. They generally spoil faster than European plums after harvest. Europeans tend to stay on the tree longer, and they last longer after they are picked.

European plums also offer more leeway in cross-pollination planning. They are more often self-fertile; one variety, or even one tree, can be planted alone and still bear fruit. Some varieties such as *President* require cross-pollination. (European plums classified as self-fertile may produce better crops when cross-pollination is provided.) Japanese plums almost always require the presence of another Japanese, Japanese/American hybrid, or American plum variety nearby in order to set fruit. European and Japanese will not cross-pollinate, as their pollen is incompatible.

Preparation

Choose a site with loamy, well-drained soil in full sun. Avoid low-lying areas where frost settles. If possible, remove wild plums to prevent them from spreading disease to your new trees.

Planting

When you plant plums, keep the graft union an inch above the soil line. Space trees 20 to 25 feet for standard varieties, 15 to 20 for dwarfs. (Refer to pages 301–303 for information on planting fruit trees.)

Care

During their formative years, Japanese plum trees should be trained to an open center. They grow vigorously and so require relatively heavy pruning to keep fruiting wood close to the trunk. These varieties will bear fruit on 1-year-old shoots as well as on long-lived spurs. Remove 1-year-old shoots to promote bearing only on the older spurs to prevent trees from overbearing.

Essentials

Planning

❧ *Some plums are self-fertile but all plums will yield better if planted with a second variety for cross-pollination. Japanese plums need to cross-pollinate with other Japanese or American hybrid plums.*

❧ *Order bare-root, rather than potted trees, if possible.*

❧ *A well-established tree will yield up to 2 bushels of plums.*

Preparation

❧ *Select a site that offers loamy, well-drained soil in full sun.*

❧ *Avoid frost pockets.*

Planting

❧ *Set the tree in the prepared hole keeping the graft union an inch above the soil line.*

❧ *Space standard-size varieties 20 to 25 feet apart, dwarfs 15 to 20 feet apart.*

Care

❧ *Water young trees heavily every week through the first season.*

❧ *Train Japanese trees to an open center shape; train European trees to a conical shape with a central leader.*

❧ *Japanese plum trees benefit from a moderate fruit thinning; do not thin European plums unless the crop is especially heavy.*

❧ *Plums are relatively pest-free, but may be visited by the plum curculio (page 401). Other possible insect pests include the apple maggot (page 400), cherry fruit fly (page 400), and peach tree borer (page 401).*

❧ *Watch for two fairly common fungus diseases: black knot (page 403) and brown rot (page 404). Powdery mildew (page 405) may also be a problem.*

Harvesting

❧ *Harvest European plums when they are tree-ripe. They will be a little soft and should come off easily with a slight twist. Late-maturing varieties should be near-ripe with firm flesh for storing for a few weeks.*

❧ *Pick Japanese plums slightly early and allow them to ripen in a cool place.*

European varieties bear fruit only on spurs older than 1 year, so they bear less heavily and require less pruning. Don't prune out the 4- to 6-inch fruit-bearing spurs; remove young shoots instead. European plum trees should be trained to a conical shape with a central leader, much like apple trees.

Unless the crop is unusually heavy, European plum trees require little fruit thinning. The closely related *Damson* plums require none at all. Japanese plums, on the other hand, tend to overbear and should be moderately thinned.

All plum trees naturally thin themselves after the fruit has formed. During the spring drop, nearly every other plum may fall. Don't panic; it's natural. Follow up with a hand-thinning soon after to end up with fruits spaced about 3 to 4 inches apart. European plums should be spaced one fruit every 2 inches. This encourages larger, better tasting plums.

Plum trees are afflicted with pests less often than are most fruit trees. However, there are a few pests that can be truly devastating if given the chance, such as the plum curculio.

The plum curculio is a ½-inch-long beetle that is common just about everywhere east of California. It also plagues apples, peaches, cherries, pears, and apricots. Adult plum curculios overwinter in the soil and emerge in the spring. Females pierce the developing fruit and lay eggs under the surface. The larvae tunnel deep into the fruit, causing it to rot and drop.

The easiest and most effective way to control these voracious insects is to follow a low-toxicity spray schedule recommended by your local county Extension Service office.

Another method offers some control in the case of minor infestations, and can be used to monitor populations to time sprays. Starting just after bloom, check the newly formed fruit for egg-laying scars. Early in the morning, spread plastic sheets under each tree and jar the limbs to check

A mesh guard around the trunk protects the bark from rabbits and mice during the winter. White paint reduces the threat of winter bark injury due to fluctuating day and night temperatures.

for adult weevils. They'll fall from the tree and play dead, looking like bud scales or pieces of debris. Carry the insects away to their demise before they know what hit them. This procedure must be repeated daily when the bugs are most active in the spring, shortly after the fruit set, and then periodically throughout the summer. As soon as you find adults or egg-laying scars, apply the first insecticide, then spray again 2 weeks later.

Good cultural practices can also reduce plum curculio damage; they will increase the effect of insecticides, but will not provide the same degree of control if used in place of them. Collect and burn wormy fruit. Prune the trees to keep them open, since curculios do the most damage in deep shade. Lightly cultivate the soil around the trees in late spring and early summer to destroy the larvae and pupae in the soil. In late fall, remove all leaf litter and mulch from around the trees; curculios hibernate under it during the winter. Also clean up overgrown hedges and fence rows, two other favorite overwintering locations.

Black knot and brown rot are fungus diseases that can attack the trees. Remove all blighted twigs and fruit, including what falls to the ground. Remove refuse after the last harvest.

Harvesting

Wait until some fruits soften before harvesting. The plums should come off easily with a slight twist. European plums are best when they ripen on the tree. But they, as well as Japanese varieties, can be harvested just as they begin to soften, and then stored in a cool place to ripen fully. Late-maturing varieties may last for several weeks in a cool place if picked when firm but quite near the softening stage.

Though plums on early-bearing trees may ripen at different rates (allowing two or three harvests), most of the fruit on plum trees will ripen at roughly the same time.

Rootstocks for European and Japanese Plums

Peach seedlings — *Lovell, Halford,* and *Nemaguard* — are often used as standard rootstocks for plums because they provide higher yields than many plum rootstocks. *Lovell* and *Halford* are also moderately resistant to bacterial canker. However, a peach rootstock reduces the nutrient uptake of a plum. The common peach rootstocks are also very susceptible to both northern and southern root-knot nematodes (except for *Nemaguard,* which has other drawbacks; see page 367) and to crown rot. Plum rootstocks are not quite as susceptible as peach rootstocks to verticillium wilt and peach tree borers.

The most widely used plum rootstock, *Myrobalan* cherry plum (*P. cerasifera*), is closely related to European plums and adapted to many soil types. *Damas,* a hybrid plum rootstock propagated from cuttings, induces better yields than peach rootstocks and dwarfs the tree by about 20 percent. It resists bacterial canker and does well even in heavy, slightly wet, or alkaline soils.

A native American plum, *P. americana,* is sometimes used as a rootstock because it's very hardy. It produces a slightly smaller tree, but the combination is weak, so it's best planted with the graft union several inches below ground so the variety roots. It's moderately susceptible to bacterial canker.

A good semidwarfing rootstock is *St. Julien,* a damson plum (*P. institia*) that's closely related to European plums. Grown from cuttings, it's not as deep-rooted as seedling rootstocks, but has good anchorage. It's cold-hardy, resistant to bacterial canker, does well on loamy and heavy soils, and doesn't sucker readily.

Full dwarf plum trees offered today are propagated on sand cherry (*P. besseyi*) or Nanking cherry (*P. tomentosa*). Trees start bearing sooner on these rootstocks, and fruit may be larger, but trees tend to die sooner. Japanese plums seem to do better on these rootstocks than Europeans. These cherry rootstocks restrict water and nutrient uptake, so you'll need to fertilize and irrigate more. The root system is shallow so the trees should be staked. Trees on sand cherry have especially poor anchorage, while Nanking cherry is especially susceptible to bacterial canker.

Plum Sources

Beach (shore) plums
check locally
Bush plums *128, 153*
Damson *127, 142, 154*
French prune *121, 129*
Green Gage *142*
Italian *129, 142*
President *119, 121, 129*
Santa Rosa *119, 121, 129, 142*
Satsuma *119, 121, 129*
Sprite *17, 131, 146*
Stanley *119, 142, 154*
Weeping Santa Rosa *146*

Rootstock Sources

American plum *15, 154*
Halford peach *133, 155, 158*
Lovell peach *124*
Myrobalan cherry plum seedling *116*
Myrobalan seedling *142, 149, 152, 154, 157, and others*
Nemaguard *124, 159*
Sand cherry *12, 158*
St. Julien *154*

Raspberries

Summer-bearing raspberries (*left*) should begin to yield in their second year. You can trellis certain types of raspberries (*above*) to make pruning and harvesting easier.

Raspberries are so delicate and perishable they're scarce at the supermarket and fruit stands and expensive if you find them. Fortunately, they can be very easy to grow at home.

Though naturally adapted to a cool climate, varieties have been developed for virtually all parts of the country. Besides the familiar red varieties, there are also black, purple, and yellow ones. Black raspberries, or "blackcaps," have a distinctive and slightly musky aroma and taste; good eaten fresh, they make great jams and desserts. Purple raspberries are vigorous red-black hybrids with an unusual flavor richer than a blackcap. Purples process well; eating out-of-hand is often an acquired taste. Yellow raspberries are a variation on the red but can be even more tender and sweet.

Most varieties bear one crop in the summer soon after the strawberry harvest ends. Certain varieties known as everbearers or fall-bearers bear twice each year, midsummer and fall. A well-tended raspberry patch can thrive indefinitely.

Planning

The first step is to select a variety that's right for your region. Study the variety chart on page 389 and try to find out what works for neighboring growers.

You can save money by digging plants from a friend's patch, but there is always the risk of acquiring diseased plants when you get them secondhand. Infected plants usually have reduced vigor and may decline after only a year or two. There may be no obvious, visible symptoms until that occurs. A safer bet is to buy certified virus-free plants from a nursery.

Black raspberries are by far the most vulnerable to disease. To avoid problems, buy plants from nurseries that use *tissue culture* propagation. These plants are not only virus-free, but also free of all other diseases. Some of the more progressive nurseries are propagating by tissue culture;

most small fruit plants available from the New York State Fruit Testing Co-op, for example, are now being propagated by tissue culture.

While this precaution is a good idea for all types of raspberries, it's less critical for red raspberries, which are naturally more vigorous, and purple raspberries, which can be the most vigorous and disease resistant of all. But when it comes to blackcaps, tissue culture can make the difference between a bountiful crop and a trickle of berries.

Preparation

Raspberries thrive in well-worked, well-fed, slightly acid soil (pH 5.5 to 6.8). Like most fruits, they crave sunlight and plenty of moisture, but adequate drainage is critical.

Take the time to eliminate perennial weeds as much as possible, either by repeated tilling or by planting a cover crop a year in advance. Be sure to mix in some 10-10-10 fertilizer (1 to 2 pounds per 20 feet of row) or plenty of manure in early spring before you plant.

Not even virus-free or tissue culture plants are immune to infection, so destroy any neighboring wild raspberries or black-berries (within about 300 feet) that might harbor disease.

Planting

Early spring (late winter in the South) is the best time to plant raspberries. If you're importing plants from a friend's patch (or moving plants around in your own expanding patch), spring is the time to dig them. Keep bare-root raspberry roots moist by covering them with damp peat moss or soil until planting time. Soak the roots in a bucket of water for an hour before setting plants in the garden.

Set each plant in a well-watered hole that's wide enough and deep enough for the roots to spread out. Firm the soil over the roots and cover each cane an inch or two deeper than it was previously grown. Water some more.

Far right: Latham raspberries growing in a hedgerow. Red and yellow raspberries can be confined to hedgerows but not to separate plants. *Below:* Everbearing *Fall Gold* raspberries have a reputation for sweetness and flavor.

Cut each cane back to an 8-inch handle to give the roots a chance to get established. To prevent anthracnose disease in black raspberry canes, cut them right back to ground level. The handle usually dies back anyway unless conditions are perfect; it's not a problem as long as the roots are all right underneath.

Red and yellow raspberries multiply by root suckers that spread rapidly in all directions; they can be confined to a hedgerow but not to rows of individual plants. Blackcaps produce no root suckers at all and propagate only by tip-layering (see page 386); they can be limited easily to isolated hills without crowding neighbors.

Purple raspberries can be trained to a row of discrete plants, but some do produce root suckers which can fill out a hedgerow in time.

Essentials

Planning

- *Plant in late winter or early spring.*
- *Select plants that are bare-root or rooted in soil.*
- *Buy only certified virus-free plants. Black raspberries are especially vulnerable to disease, so plant resistant varieties when possible.*
- *Summer-bearers should yield some berries in their second year and then full crops each succeeding summer. Everbearers may produce some fruit the first fall.*

Preparation

- *Select a site in full sun; avoid frost pockets.*
- *Eliminate perennial weeds, preferably with a cover crop planted 1 year in advance. Mix in 1 to 2 pounds of 10-10-10 fertilizer for every 20 feet of row or plenty of manure in early spring before you plant.*
- *Destroy neighboring wild raspberries or blackberries to prevent disease from spreading to your plants.*

Planting

- *Set plants in the garden an inch or two deeper than previously grown. Space plants 3 feet apart in rows 6 to 7 feet apart. Allow red and yellow raspberries to fill in a hedgerow not more than 2 feet wide (some purples will also create a hedgerow); blackcaps and most purples will remain as separate plants.*
- *Cut black raspberry canes back to ground level; leave an 8-inch handle on others. Water well.*

Care

- *Keep the aisles between rows tilled bare or plant grass and keep it mowed.*
- *Cultivate to control weeds early the first summer, then mulch thickly. Once the plants are established, maintain a layer of mulch 4 to 8 inches deep year-round.*
- *Dig or till up suckers that spread beyond row boundaries.*
- *Erect a T-trellis if your canes don't stand up on their own.*
- *Prune during the dormant season. Remove dead and weak canes; thin out the healthiest ones. Blackcaps must also be summer-topped (see page 387).*
- *A sudden wilting of cane tops may mean that cane borers (page 402) are present; the raspberry crown borer (page 402) may also cause damage.*
- *Watch for diseases, including anthracnose (page 403), orange rust (page 404), and powdery mildew (page 405).*

Harvesting

- *Berries usually ripen over a period of 2 to 3 weeks during early summer; everbearers yield again for several weeks in early fall.*
- *When they slide easily off the small white core, berries are ripe.*
- *Pick into small containers so bottom berries are not crushed.*

Propagating Raspberries

With absolutely no encouragement, red, yellow, and some purple raspberries will produce new plants from root suckers. In the early spring, as soon as the suckers emerge, dig up whole clumps of sucker roots and soil. Separate the roots of the suckers from the mother plant. Then transplant.

Raspberry roots and crowns are perennial, but their canes are biennial. In the raspberry bed at right, the old, harvested canes have been cut away, leaving the leafy primocanes.

Blackcaps and the remaining purples require a different procedure. Give the plants a year or two to get established before prodding them to multiply. In mid-summer, the current season's new canes (or their lateral branches) will be ready for *tip-layering:* insert the tips of some healthy and actively growing young canes straight down about 4 inches deep into loose, moist soil. Several shoots should emerge in the fall. Early next spring, separate the new plant from its mother and transplant.

In either case, set the plants about 3 feet apart in a row. Those that sucker can be allowed to fill out a hedge no more than 2 feet wide; those that don't will stay in a single row of hills. Leave about 6 or 7 feet between rows to promote good air circulation for healthy plants and berries. You can till the aisles bare and mulch them heavily, or plant grass and keep it mowed.

Care

There's little to be done for your berry plants during the first year. Cultivate to keep weeds down at least through early summer to let the plants get established, then apply a layer of mulch thick enough to smother weeds — 4 to 8 inches deep. Mulches rich in nutrients produce superior-tasting fruit. Composted leaves around the plants, supplemented with manure, are a good choice.

Besides mulch, moisture is the critical ingredient throughout the life of your raspberry patch. For plenty of plump, juicy berries, trickle irrigation of some kind — perhaps a soaker hose under the

Pruning Made Easy

Pruning raspberries is relatively simple once you understand their growth pattern. The roots and crowns of raspberries are perennial; the canes are biennial, called primocanes (leafy canes) their first year and floricanes (fruiting canes) their second. Primocanes are produced every year so you'll never miss your annual crop.

Summer-bearers send up primocanes in the spring, which grow vigorously during the summer, initiate flower buds in the fall, and then go dormant for the winter. The following year, they become the floricanes, bear fruit, dry up, and die.

Everbearers produce two crops on the same canes. Besides the regular summer crop on floricanes, they first bear fruit on primocanes in the fall. The fall crop is borne near the tips; the summer berries grow farther down the cane.

How to Prune Summer-Bearers

Some growers remove dead floricanes after the harvest and then prune again during the winter, but you can save yourself some trouble by doing it all in one shot, during the dormant season, any time after the canes have stopped growing and have lost their leaves.

You can tell the difference between a dormant primocane and a dead floricane by fruiting laterals that give the dead wood a branched appearance. Cut out the dead wood and the weakest primocanes — they're not going to be fruiting anyway. Leave only the healthy, strong canes. Then for reds and purples (and yellows, too), use hedge shears to cut them off at about 5 feet, or 4 feet if they're really vigorous. Leave the healthiest canes spaced 4 to 8 inches apart in a hedgerow, or about half a dozen canes per hill.

In addition to dormant pruning, black raspberries must also be *summer-topped.* Snip 2 to 4 inches off the top of each new primocane when it's about 2 feet tall (usually around the time you're harvesting berries on the floricanes). This will promote strong laterals that will bear heavily the next year.

How to Prune Everbearers

With everbearers, you can take a real shortcut and use a lawnmower. Cut all canes to within 2 inches of the ground every year before growth starts in the spring. The primocanes will bear earlier and more heavily in the fall. If you use this method you'll lose your summer crop from last year's canes, so they won't be everbearing, but the fall harvest should be larger.

If you want both crops, you can still do all your pruning during the dormant season. As with other raspberries, cut out the dead floricanes and leave the dormant primocanes. However, it will be harder to distinguish between the canes because the primocanes will also have fruiting laterals.

Check the location of the laterals to be sure. Dormant primocanes will just have laterals only near the tip, whereas the canes that have already borne in the summer (the dead floricanes) will have laterals halfway down the cane. Also, the bark of dead canes will be gray and peeling and look dried up.

Once you know your primocanes from your floricanes, follow the same pruning instructions given for summer-bearers.

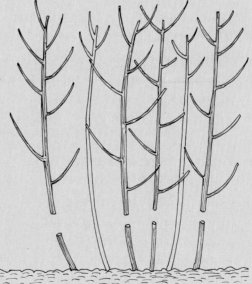

Raspberry canes are called primocanes (leafy canes) their first year and floricanes (fruiting canes) their second. When pruning, keep the primocanes to produce fruit the following season.

mulch — is ideal. Short of that luxury, at least ensure 1 inch of water per week, more during dry spells.

By the second year you will have to work at keeping the canes within the 1- or 2-foot-wide hedgerow boundaries if you planted a variety that spreads through root suckers. Periodically dig up any stray canes and transplant or destroy them, or just run a tiller alongside the rows. Beyond that, put off any substantial pruning until the third year.

A year or two after planting you will know whether or not your canes need support. All black and most purple raspberry plants can be individually staked, but this is obviously impractical for reds, yellows, and those purples with a propensity for spreading underground. For those types, a T-trellis system works nicely. Certain varieties are more upright than others; you may not need to support them at all. Just grow them, see how droopy they are, then decide if you need to put up a T-trellis afterward. You don't have to tie the canes; they'll just grow up and rest against the wires.

Besides producing a tidier berry patch, trellising makes for cleaner fruit, less breakage, and easier pruning and harvesting.

Raspberries are bothered by insects and disease less often than most other fruits. Nevertheless, the risk is there. In most cases, you can avoid sprays by practicing careful garden sanitation and removing wild plants nearby.

Two insects in particular may be attracted to your raspberry patch. The cane borer makes itself known by a sudden wilting near the tops of new canes, where the adult beetle lays its eggs. If undisturbed, the larvae will travel down the cane, kill it, and infect others. Look for a slight swelling and two rings on the cane that pinpoint the borer, cut off the cane just below the lower ring, and burn it. To stay ahead of the borers, remove affected canes as soon as you notice them.

The tarnished plant bug, which feeds on young berries and flowers, is less easily controlled. Ideally, you should situate your raspberry patch away from hay or corn fields where the bugs breed. If you're not getting fully developed fruit, you may have to resort to more direct methods of control, possibly pesticides.

Raspberries may also fall prey to several fungal diseases (anthracnose, cane and spur blights, orange rust [black raspberries only], and verticillium wilt), bacterial diseases (crown and cane gall), viruses (mosaic, leaf curl, and ringspot), mildews, and fruit rot.

Harvesting

Summer-bearers should begin to yield in their second year and bear full crops each succeeding summer. Vigorous everbearers may even produce some fruit the very first fall. Heavy picking usually lasts about 2 or 3 weeks in early summer; everbearers produce another crop for several weeks in early fall.

To enjoy top-quality fruit and prevent pest problems, pick berries as soon as they ripen; they should easily slide off the small white core that stays on the stem. At the peak of the season you may have to pick daily if the plants are dry enough — wet berries mold fast. Pick the berries directly into pint or smaller containers so they don't get crushed and keep them out of the sun. Don't wash the delicate fruit or you'll spoil its texture.

Sudden wilting of cane tops is a sign of cane borer presence. To prevent the borers from destroying your crop, remove the affected canes as soon as you notice them.

Raspberry Varieties

Varieties are summer-bearers unless otherwise noted.

Variety	Comments	Sources
Red Raspberries		
August Red	Everbearer; very hardy; bears early and for many weeks; especially good for northern extremes.	*128*
Canby	Large berries; hardy, vigorous, and productive; especially good for Pacific Northwest.	*128, 146, 160*
Dormanred	Especially good for southern regions (zones 7 to 9); bears late but heavily; good for processing.	*125, 154*
Fairview	Large berries, good flavor; productive; adapted to Northwest.	*107, 129*
Fall Red	Everbearer; hardy, bears early; excellent quality; especially good for Northeast.	*128, 141, 165*
Heritage	Everbearer; hardy and vigorous, adapted to Northeast; high quality; upright canes need no support; fruit remains in good condition on the cane even when overripe.	*128, 146, 149, 155, 160*
Latham	Relatively small fruit, average quality; very hardy; good for processing; nearly thornless.	*119, 125, 128, 151, 154*
Reveille	New variety; very large fruit, sweet and soft.	*119*
Scepter	Everbearer; hardy and vigorous; tolerates fluctuating winter temperatures, especially good for mid-Atlantic states and upper South.	*119, 165*
Sentinel	Hardy and vigorous; productive; tolerates fluctuating winter temperatures, especially good for mid-Atlantic states and upper South.	*119*
Southland	Everbearer; bears early; high-quality berries; highly disease resistant; especially good for upper and mid-South.	*12, 119, 154*
Sumner	Ripens late; very good flavor; disease resistant; well adapted to heavy soils of Pacific Northwest.	*107, 128, 149*
Willamette	Large, firm, good-quality berries; vigorous and productive; widely grown in Pacific Northwest.	*107, 128, 146, 155*
Yellow Raspberries		
Amber	Pinkish-yellow; good quality; productive.	*5*
Fall Gold	Everbearer; very hardy and widely adaptable; high-quality berries, extremely sweet and flavorful; for fresh eating.	*125, 128*
Purple Raspberries		
Brandywine	Released in 1976; large berries, good tart flavor; vigorous and productive; propagated like blackcaps by tip-layering; adapted to Northeast.	*125, 128, 142*
Clyde	Large, tart berries ripen late; hardy; some disease resistance; propagated by tip-layering and suckering; adapted to Northeast.	*125*
Royalty	Purple-red cross, released in 1982; widely adaptable; large, sweet berries, good fresh and processed; vigorous and productive; easily propagated either by tip-layering or natural suckering; insect and disease resistant.	*128, 141, 142, 154*
Black Raspberries		
Allen	Large, sweet berries; vigorous and productive; adapted to North Central states and Northeast.	*141, 142*
Black Hawk	Large, good-flavored berries; very hardy, vigorous and productive; ripens late; widely grown in eastern United States; somewhat resistant to anthracnose.	*119, 128, 154*
Bristol	Large, firm, good-flavored berries; hardy, vigorous and productive; upright canes produce heavily; popular in eastern United States.	*119, 128, 142, 154*
Cumberland	Large berries, very good flavor; hardy and productive; suited to eastern states.	*119, 128, 157*
Huron	Large, firm, good-flavored berries; hardy, vigorous, and productive; especially good in Great Lakes region; somewhat resistant to anthracnose.	*142*
Jewel	Glossy, rich-flavored berries; very hardy; some disease resistance; adapted to Northeast.	*128, 141, 142, 160*
Munger	Large, firm, good-flavored berries; especially popular in Oregon.	*107, 146*

Strawberries

Strawberries are most abundant when plants are in their second year of growth; most growing systems call for pinching out blossoms (*above*) in the first season.

Probably nothing beats the taste of a just-picked, sun-ripened strawberry. Strawberries are loaded with natural sugars, but these sugars rapidly convert to starch once the berry is picked. So it is not mere pride that makes a freshly picked home-grown strawberry taste better — it really does. The fresher the berry, the sweeter the taste.

Strawberries are high yielders. From a single, well-cared-for 2-year-old plant, you can expect to harvest 1 to 2 quarts of strawberries. That's 50 to 100 quarts of berries from a bed 15 feet long and three plants deep — about 50 plants.

You can maximize yields by continually renewing your strawberry bed with new plants. Many gardeners try to keep old plants producing year after year, but this inevitably leads to decreased yields and increased disease problems. If you follow the plan outlined in this chapter, you can start out in the spring with ten plants that will each produce five healthy daughter plants in the first year — and they'll bear an abundant crop of strawberries the second year. Keep two beds in rotation and every year you can count on 50 to 100 quarts of juicy red berries — enough for about thirty strawberry-drenched shortcakes *and* fifty pints of preserves to enjoy all winter *and* fifty helpings of Sunday brunch strawberry waffles, not to mention the sweetest possible berries for eating straight out of the garden.

Planning

Strawberries are in full production in their second year. The first year, you buy plants — usually in bunches of 25 or 50. (For large quantities or special varieties, order from a mail-order nursery.) These plants are sometimes called mother plants because 5 or 6 weeks after planting they will start sending out runners, a few or many, depending on the variety.

When a runner reaches 8 to 10 inches in length, it will bend upward and begin to form a new daughter plant; the runner will continue outward and set several more daughter plants. The daughters provide most of the crop the following year.

Right: "Mother" plants may produce three to ten or more runners, depending on the variety. When a runner is 8 to 10 inches long, it bends upward to set a new daughter plant. *Far right:* It's important to leave 18 inches between plants the first season; runners need room to extend and establish new plants.

Runner

How many plants you'll need depends on how many strawberries you want. As a rule of thumb, buy one plant for every 1 or 2 quarts of berries you'd like to harvest. Of course, this formula assumes you'll be taking good care of every plant. If you start with 10 plants the first year — and they each produce five healthy daughter plants — you'll get from 50 to 100 quarts of berries.

Selecting the right type of strawberry requires a little research. You can buy varieties that are resistant to diseases such as red stele or verticillium wilt, and different varieties are suited to different parts of the country.

Everbearing varieties yield a light crop in early summer, a few berries during the summer, and then another heavier crop in late summer or fall. ("Day-neutral" varieties bear all season, but this term is often used interchangeably with everbearers. To be really technical, day-neutrals are some-times everbearing, usually on the West Coast, but the reverse is never true.) Regular spring- or June-bearing varieties yield more than everbearers, but over a shorter season. Everbearers often fare poorly in the southern and northern extremes of the country; they are best suited to the middle regions, zones 5 to 8.

Whatever variety you choose, try to buy new plants from a commercial grower. Digging your own daughter plants from an old bed leads to diseased, weakened, unproductive plants that aren't worth the money saved. When ordering from a commercial grower, specify fall-dug plants (commercial suppliers are able to store them well over the winter). These may look scrawny and pathetic after winter storage, but they will rapidly overtake the more attractive spring-dug plants. If you do use spring-dug plants, however, they will suffer some root loss, so you should remove about half the leaves to balance the tops with the reduced root systems — and keep them moist while they await planting.

Preparation

Strawberries will do best in soil that has been thoroughly prepared. If your future strawberry bed was plowed last year, you're ahead of the game. But if you're starting with land that was in sod, allow an extra year or the soil will be tough to cultivate, and you'll really pay later when you are confronted with weeds (especially grass) and grubs.

Strawberries do best in soil with a pH of 5.5 to 6.5. Apply aged manure and a complete fertilizer such as 5-10-10 (½ pound per 25-foot row) before planting in the spring. To further improve the soil, you can plant a winter cover crop (see pages 35–37).

If you have heavy soil, raised beds will provide better drainage and encourage healthy roots.

Planting

You can usually set out your new plants in the strawberry bed when the trees in your area are just beginning to leaf out. Suppliers try to ship them at the appropriate time for your region. If you're not ready when the plants arrive, you can store them in the refrigerator for a couple of weeks. Let out any moisture from the shipping bag and wrap the roots in plastic. Do not let the roots dry out.

Space your rows 4 feet apart, and leave 18 inches between plants. Cut back the

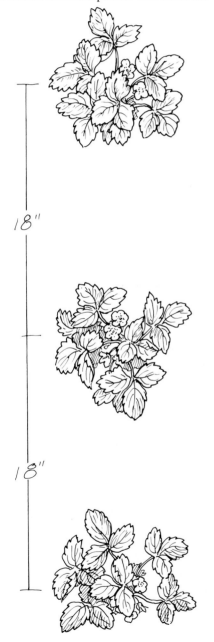

18"

18"

Essentials

Planning
❧ *Plants bear in their second season.*
❧ *Plan to set your new plants out in early spring, just as the trees in your area leaf out.*
❧ *For best yields, start a new bed of plants each year and take out beds that have fruited.*

Preparation
❧ *Select a site that offers full sun and good drainage and air circulation.*
❧ *Apply aged manure and a complete fertilizer such as 5-10-10 (1 pound per 50-foot row) before planting in the spring.*

Planting
❧ *Space your rows 4 feet apart.*
❧ *Trim the roots of the new plants to no more than 6 inches long. Soak the roots in water for about an hour before planting.*
❧ *Set the plants 18 inches apart in the rows.*
❧ *Dig holes in the ground deep enough so the roots are covered but the crown isn't buried. Pack the soil against the roots and add about ¹/₂ pint of water mixed with a diluted soluble fertilizer.*

Care
❧ *First year, spring: Keep the bed free of weeds. Pick off blossoms to prevent fruiting and encourage production of healthy daughter plants.*
❧ *Late spring: 5 to 6 weeks after planting, train daughter plants to take root in a 9-by-9-inch spaced row system.*
❧ *Late spring and summer: Side-dress with ammonium nitrate (¹/₂ pound per 100-foot row), 5-10-10 (2¹/₂ pounds per 100-foot row), or manure tea (¹/₂ to 1 pint per plant). Side-dress again 1 month later.*
❧ *Late fall: After a few freezes, mulch with 5 to 6 inches of straw or 4 to 5 inches of pine needles.*
❧ *Second year, late spring: Remove the mulch gradually in spring, but protect blossoms from late frost with covers of mulch, if needed. Provide 1 inch of water per week while the fruit is developing, through harvest.*
❧ *Cover the patch with tobacco cloth or strawberry netting to keep birds out.*
❧ *Summer: After harvest, till the plants under, plant a cover crop, and prepare the bed for new plants next spring.*

Harvesting
❧ *The berries will ripen about 1 month after the plants bloom. Expect 2 to 3 weeks of harvesting for each variety.*
❧ *Pick the plants clean every 2 or 3 days. Avoid the green-tipped berries; they're not fully ripe.*
❧ *When harvesting, don't leave berry remnants on the plants. They encourage plant rot.*

Regional Notes

Performance of a strawberry variety is influenced markedly by local soil and climate conditions. A variety that is highly successful in the East may be of little value in the West. Select varieties on the basis of performance in your area.

Below are listed varieties for several regions based on recommendations from Extension Service specialists in each region. These are general recommendations. For best results, get more local information before ordering plants.

Midwest: *Surecrop, Cyclone*

Northeast: *Sparkle, Midway, Raritan, Red Chief, Earliglow*

Mid-South: *Sunrise*

North Central: *Midway, Catskill, Surecrop, Sparkle*

Mid-Atlantic: *Earliglow, Sparkle, Guardian, Midway*

Southwest: *Arking*

Southeast: *Florida 90, Cardinal, Tioga*

Northwest: *Shuksan, Hecker, Tillikum*

Nationwide: *Sweetheart* (seeds)

You can usually set out new plants when the trees in your area have just begun to leaf out. Be sure to plant them at the proper depth so the crown remains above the soil level.

Many kinds of netting will keep birds away from the harvest.

roots of your new plants to not more than 6 inches long; put them in a bucket and soak the roots in water for about an hour just before planting.

Make absolutely sure you set them in the ground at the right depth so the roots don't dry out and the crown isn't buried. Pack the soil against the roots, and water each plant with about ½ pint of water mixed with a soluble fertilizer; don't overdose.

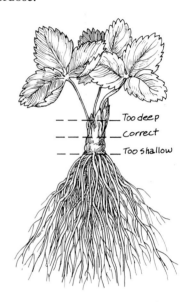

Too deep
Correct
Too shallow

Care

You won't be idle until your first harvest. You must not let the new plants set berries in their first year. They will try to fruit, but you must pick off the blossoms as they appear. This way, instead of fruiting, the mother plants will produce vigorous daughters that will yield well the following year.

Keep the bed weed-free throughout the growing season. Some people use a sheet of black plastic to smother weeds, leaving holes for the strawberry plants, but that's more work than weeding when it comes time to position the runners and the daughter plants.

After 5 or 6 weeks in the ground, your plants will begin to "run." A first daughter plant will form and root, then the runners will set more daughters. Keep only the first daughter of each runner. It will bear better than a second or third daughter on the same runner.

When most mothers have produced daughters that are ready to take root, it's time for you to establish the 9-by-9-inch spaced row system designed by John Page, an Extension Service strawberry expert. Although it's more work, it's more berries.

Let five strong daughters from each mother plant take root; clip off all others. (If you don't have five daughters on a plant, make do with what you have.) As these daughters grow, space them around the mother at 9-inch intervals, as shown at right. Weigh the runners down with soil, stones, or hairpins to hold the daughters in place; they'll root by themselves. It will take two or three passes over the course of the summer to arrange the plants correctly and get rid of unwanted runners.

While the arrangement may not look quite as tidy in your strawberry patch as it does on paper, you will have created three parallel rows with plants spaced roughly 9 inches apart in each one. Unlike other systems in which all plants are permitted to run freely, this system discourages sibling rivalry and gives each selected plant plenty of room to grow. The result is more and bigger berries.

When the first bearing season is over, you'll do best to till in all the plants and start again. Each successive year you prolong their lives will yield fewer berries — and more weeds and disease. To have strawberries every year, you should maintain two beds: one to bear fruit and one to produce next year's fruit-bearers.

After the harvest, plant a short-season vegetable where the berries were, if you like, then a winter cover crop like buckwheat or rye. Crop rotation has many advantages: the roots of the strawberry plants don't have a chance to get bound up, infestations of diseases are less likely, and rotation is an effective method of weed control. The following spring, you'll set new strawberry plants in that bed and begin the cycle again.

Many gardeners prefer to *renovate* their beds, thinning out most of the plants and leaving some strong ones to produce runners and daughter plants for the third year. If you've enjoyed a productive, disease-free season, you may decide to renovate at least part of the bed for another year or two before cleaning out the whole bed entirely:

• Just after harvest, cut off all the leaves with a scythe, sickle, or lawnmower set high enough not to hit the crowns.
• Turn under the two daughter plants on either side of each mother row (preferably with a tiller), which should leave a 6-inch-wide row.
• Add a complete fertilizer such as 5-10-10 (½ pound per 25-foot row) to the bed and get rid of all weeds. Thin the plants to stand 9 inches apart, leaving only the strongest ones.
• Allow only two runners from each plant; set each runner 9 inches from the mother plant on either side.
• Side-dress with 2½ pounds of 5-10-10 or its equivalent per 100 feet of row.
• Apply winter mulch as before. Await spring and your second — and somewhat smaller — harvest.

Harvesting

In the second year, the berries will ripen about 1 month after the plants bloom, with the bigger berries developing at the center of each cluster. To harvest, don't squeeze a ripe berry; pinch the stem behind it with your thumbnail.

Every 2 or 3 days, pick all the ripe berries. Avoid picking green-tipped berries — they're not fully ripe. They'll taste much better in a day or two. Don't leave berry remnants on the plants because they encourage plant rot.

You can expect 2 to 3 weeks of harvesting for each variety. If you find yourself deluged by berries, you can make them into jam or freeze them.

Strawberry Sources

Arking *128*
Cardinal *128, 161*
Catskill *128, 161, 166*
Cyclone *12, 128*
Earliglow *128, 162, 166*
Florida 90 *128*
Guardian *128, 162, 166*
Hecker *129, 146*
Midway *128, 162, 166*
Raritan *128, 162, 166*
Red Chief *128, 162, 166*
Shuksan *107, 150*
Sparkle *128, 162, 166*
Sunrise *128, 161, 166*
Surecrop *128, 161, 166*
Sweetheart *6, 33*
Tioga *128*
Tillikum *146, 149*

When the mother plants have produced daughters that are ready to take root, space four or five daughters around the mother at 9-inch intervals. This 9-by-9-inch spaced row system gives each plant plenty of room, resulting in bigger berries and bigger yields.

Fruit Pests and Diseases

The following section describes a selection of common fruit pests and diseases. This is by no means an exhaustive list. For more information on the pests and diseases that are prevalent in your area and how to identify and control them, consult your local county Extension Service agent. Remember that any pesticides you use must be applied according to the label instructions; see page 275 in the vegetable section for more information on using pesticides safely and effectively.

Fruit Pest Management

A great number of pests — insects, diseases, animals, and birds — can attack fruit plants. Fortunately, only a few pests usually cause serious damage in any particular location. Prevention, when possible, is always the best pest control. Before purchasing any fruit plants, contact your Extension Service agent to find out which pests commonly attack those plants in your area.

Even if you choose resistant varieties and rootstocks, you'll still need to plan controls for some pests. Many books and Extension Service publications recommend spray schedules that time pesticide applications by the trees' blossom development or by the calendar. Often, the recommended pesticide is a combination of broad-spectrum insecticides and fungicides, which controls many kinds of pests in one fell swoop. This type of pest control is easy, but has serious drawbacks. Sprays made on a fixed schedule may be a waste of time and money if pests and diseases are not a problem on the indicated spray dates, and unnecessary pesticide applications can hinder the natural control of many pests.

The vast majority of fungi, bacteria, insects, spiders, mites, birds, and other organisms on fruit plants are not harmful, and many are beneficial — they actually help control pests. Sometimes pesticide sprays hurt the "good guys" as much or more than the pests, causing outbreaks of other pests which would have been adequately controlled by beneficial organisms had sprays not been used.

Integrated pest management (IPM), also called ecological pest management, is a better approach than just using pesticides. Gardeners who control pests with IPM use several different pest control strategies — resistant varieties, biological control agents, pesticides, and cultural practices. Instead of applying pesticides on a fixed schedule, they watch weather conditions, monitor populations of pests and beneficials, and spray only when a damaging pest outbreak is predicted. Rather than applying broad-spectrum pesticides, those who practice IPM choose materials that effectively kill pests but do the least harm to beneficials.

So before applying any pesticide, consider whether the pest causes real damage to the tree or crop, or just cosmetic damage to the fruit, such as surface scarring or a small amount of interior damage that can easily be cut out. Lightly blemished fruit tastes just as good, is fine for cooking or preserving, and may be less hazardous to your health than perfect fruit that has been treated with pesticide.

Insecticides

Try to avoid using broad-spectrum insecticides (such as Sevin, malathion, methoxychlor, pyrethrum, or diatomaceous earth), which kill many beneficial insects. Don't assume that natural pesticides are less harmful than chemical pesticides; some are just as harmful to beneficial organisms as chemicals. Always evaluate the environmental impact of a pesticide before using it. Try to use insecticides that are harmful only to specific insects. Ryania is a natural insecticide effective against moth pests, sabadilla controls moth larvae and plant bugs, rotenone is short-lived but effective against fruit flies. Imidan, a synthetic insecticide, is effective against most fruit pests, including the hard-to-kill plum curculio, but easy on beneficials. A few insecticides such as *Bacillus thuringiensis* (Dipel or Thuricide) are actually forms of biological control. If properly timed, *Bacillus thuringiensis* is effective against moth larvae.

Don't use combination fruit sprays or home orchard sprays; they usually contain two insecticides and two fungicides, three of which may not be needed.

If leafrollers, mites, aphids, pear psylla, or scale insects are a problem, spray with horticultural-grade dormant oil as the buds swell. It kills many of these pests on the tree without killing many of their predators, which overwinter in the groundcover. During the growing season, insecticidal soap sprays can be used against aphids, leafhoppers, and mites, and repeated high-pressure hosings with plain water will wash off mites effectively.

If you use anything toxic to bees, such as pyrethrum, Imidan, malathion, or Sevin, spray in the evening, if possible, after bees have stopped flying. Never apply an insecticide during fruit tree bloom. Mow the groundcover under fruit trees 3 to 4 days before spraying if it has flowers that attract bees, such as clover or dandelions. Don't mow groundcover for 1 to 2 days before or after spraying because beneficial insects move to the trees after mowing.

Aiding Beneficial Insects, Spiders, and Mites

Insect and mite pests are attacked by other insects, spiders, and mites, both predators and parasites. Predators such as lady beetles, lacewings, predator mites, spiders, assassin bugs, and trash bugs are larger and more powerful than their prey. Both adults and juveniles feed on pests by devouring them or sucking their body juices. These predators require prey in quantity to grow and develop. They can quickly destroy many pests, but often require high populations of pests and/or alternate prey to support themselves.

Parasites — usually tiny braconid or ichneumonid wasps or tachinid flies — are smaller and weaker than the pests they attack. The adult parasite attacks its host by depositing an egg or larvae in or on it. The egg hatches and the parasitic larvae feeds on the juices or internal organs of the host. When the parasite reaches maturity, the host usually dies. Because each parasite kills just a single pest, parasites do not provide quick control of pests, but a large parasite population can provide continuing control of even a small pest infestation.

Neither predators nor parasites live on pests alone. Growing a diversity of plants near fruit plants provides the habitat beneficials need to be most effective. The adult stage of some parasites needs the nectar and pollen from flowers to live. Legumes and grasses planted as groundcover under trees, and other plants in the yard, aid predators by supporting other insects for them to prey on. This allows the number of predators to increase to a level where they can effectively control fruit pests.

Releasing Additional Predators and Parasites

If you provide alternate food for predators, you will probably have an adequate supply of them to help get rid of pests. Although many predators and parasites are available from commercial insectaries, gardeners find that releasing these beneficial insects often provides poor control because the beneficials die or leave the area. Parasites may do poorly if the release is not timed properly and there aren't enough pests in the proper developmental stage for parasitism, or if adult parasites didn't receive enough nourishment from nectar and pollen to live long. Predators will fly away if they run out of food after devouring a low pest population.

Monitoring and Mass Trapping Insect Pests

Using traps, you can monitor pest populations and spray only when pests are present at damaging levels, or you may be able to control pests by trapping the majority of them. Many of these traps can be made at home; others can be purchased. You can monitor moth populations with pheromone traps, which contain the scent of female moths to attract males of that species. Or you can put a mixture of 10 percent honey, 10 percent molasses, water, and a little bit of yeast in some cans and hang them in your trees. Bright yellow boards

(or red spheres for apples) coated with sticky Tangle Trap attract fruit flies. Tarnished plant bugs can be trapped with nonreflective white sticky boards.

If you use traps to time sprays or releases of parasites, you will only need one trap for each type of insect pest. Place the traps in the trees when petals fall, and check them every 2 or 3 days. For the cleanest fruit, spray after you've found two or more adults of one pest species per night. If you can tolerate some culls for preserving, wait until you find four or five adults per night. With moths and flies, spray about 10 days after you start trapping at these levels. This will allow time for eggs to begin hatching. Continue monitoring and spray again as necessary.

Some pests can be mass trapped. You can catch male peach tree borer moths with pheromone traps. To trap the egg-laying females and newly hatched larvae, wrap heavy paper around the trunk, from 2 inches below ground to at least 6 inches above, and coat it with sticky Tangle Trap. Destroy the wrap weekly, and keep replacing it until no more larvae are trapped.

Coddling moth or cherry fruitworm larvae may also be mass trapped when they leave the fruit in search of a place to pupate. Tie 6-inch strips of burlap or corrugated cardboard around the trunks in midsummer. Larvae will crawl under these traps and pupate. Remove and destroy the bands every week if they're made of cardboard, or if you've used burlap, remove the larvae and replace the traps. Such traps may be left on trees all winter when pupae are hibernating; woodpeckers will eat many of the pests in the traps. The rest can be removed and destroyed in late winter.

Some insects can simply be removed from the plants and destroyed as they are spotted. These include green fruitworms feeding on young fruits, leafrollers hidden in folded leaves of many kinds of fruit trees, cherry fruitworm cocoons, colonies of larvae such as red-humped caterpillars on apples, and webs of tent caterpillars. You can remove colonies of insects in webs by sticking a pole with several nails on its end into the web, and then winding the web onto the pole.

Cultural Controls for Insect Pests

Cultural pest controls include careful variety selection, site selection and preparation, groundcover management, pruning, and fruit thinning. Some require extra time, but many just require some planning.

Few truly insect-resistant fruit varieties have been developed, but some varieties often escape insect damage. For example, in many areas, early maturing varieties of peaches and apricots escape fruit damage from the Oriental fruit moth, even if the pest is abundant. Prevent grape phylloxera damage by choosing resistant American varieties or European varieties grafted onto resistant native rootstocks.

Consider pest problems when choosing a site. Don't plant strawberries or brambles where a lawn or corn has grown during the past 2 years. White grubs, serious pests of these fruits, build to high populations in grasses. If you plan to convert a lawn area to strawberries or brambles, treat the area with milky spore disease powder and plant it with a legume cover crop at least a year in advance.

Keep vegetables such as tomatoes, potatoes, beans, and okra as far as possible from fruit plants because they can harbor tarnished plant bugs and stinkbugs, which may seriously deform young fruit. Control weeds around the plants for the same reason, and if you plant a groundcover, use low-growing legumes such as clovers or trefoil, and keep them mowed.

For more details on cultural control methods, refer to the individual fruit chapters.

Helpful and Harmful Animals

Many birds help control fruit insect pests, especially woodpeckers, nuthatches, warblers, bluebirds, wrens, chickadees, titmice, swallows, orioles, thrushes, and purple martins. Encourage them by providing water, bushes for breeding areas and shelter, and nesting boxes. Leave some dead snags of nonfruit trees for woodpeckers, and nail boards under eaves for swallows to nest on. Hang out suet during the winter to keep woodpeckers around, and supply seeds such as sunflower, millet, and thistle for other birds.

Birds that eat ripening fruit can be kept away with nylon netting. Support the netting with metal or bamboo stakes so it doesn't get entangled in the branches. Providing alternate fruit that the birds prefer, such as mulberries or juneberries, can minimize damage to cherry crops, provided it is available during the entire time that the cherries are ripening.

Squirrels can be pests in fruit trees. Attach a 2-foot-wide band of sheet metal around the tree trunk about 6 feet from the ground; this will keep squirrels from climbing up the trunk. Prune the tree so that no branches are within 6 feet of the ground, another tree, or an adjoining building from which the squirrel could jump. Live trapping is also useful.

Prevent rabbits from feeding on bark in the winter by placing tree guards around your trees. Make sure the guards reach above the expected snow level. See pages 72–73 for more information on preventing animal damage.

Fruit Disease Management

Fruit disease management, like insect management, shouldn't be based solely on spraying. Use other disease prevention techniques — choosing disease-resistant varieties and rootstocks, finding a good site, buying certified disease-free plants, and certain cultural practices — along with or in place of pesticides. Often, for best disease control, you'll need to combine a number of different methods. Some diseases can only be controlled by practicing disease prevention techniques.

As with vegetable diseases, prevention is the best control for fruit diseases. Once symptoms are evident, damage has already been done and control is more difficult. This is why calendar-based spray schedules were developed. However, if you monitor the weather conditions that encourage certain diseases, you may be able to reduce the number of sprays needed.

Many fruit varieties resist infections from one or more diseases. The degree of resistance varies, but in general, the more resistant a variety is rated, the less you will need to spray.

Most fungicides are better at preventing an infection than in curing an established one. Sprays should be timed carefully. Try to spray a day or two *before* an infection period — before, for instance, a spell of wet weather. Don't spray within a few hours before a rain or the fungicide will be washed off and a repeat spray needed. If you don't get to spray before a rain, spray as soon as the foliage dries off. As with insecticides, fungicides and bactericides kill helpful microorganisms as well as harmful ones. Several fungicides, notably benomyl and sulfur, can cause pest mite outbreaks by killing predator mites, so avoid these if possible.

If you try to prevent stress to your trees, they will be less susceptible to disease. Choose a well-drained site with good air circulation. Fertilizing and watering properly help reduce stress, as do training and pruning, fruit thinning, and preventing cold damage. Remove and destroy all prunings, dropped and thinned fruit, fallen leaves, and disease-infected tissues to reduce the spread of diseases.

Fruit Pests

APHIDS: Different species of aphids attack most kinds of fruits throughout the United States. These small, soft-bodied, pear-shaped insects may be black, green, pink, or yellow; some species are covered with a white, waxy or woolly substance. Aphids cluster in large numbers on the tips of new growth and the undersides of leaves. They feed by sucking out the plants' juices, causing leaves to become distorted and yellow. Aphids secrete a sticky, sugary substance called honeydew which attracts ants and may cause the growth of a sooty black fungus on the leaves. In small numbers aphids do little damage, but they reproduce rapidly and can spread disease, so it is best to begin control at the first sign of infestation.

CONTROLS: Use an insecticidal soap or other approved insecticide. Spray trees with a strong stream of water. For other controls on apples, see page 326.

APPLE MAGGOT: Found in all parts of the country except the Southwest and extreme Southeast, but are a major problem primarily in colder northern areas. Also known as the railroad worm because of the brown winding tunnels that the larvae make in the apple flesh as they feed, this pest also attacks European plums, pears, and cherries. Fruit is pitted and misshapen, and the flesh is brown and pulpy, with white maggots feeding in it. Infested fruits usually drop prematurely. The adult looks like a housefly. Females lay eggs inside the fruit; after feeding, the larvae emerge to pupate in the soil over the winter. Adults begin emerging in early summer, continuing through the summer. Early maturing varieties of apples are often more heavily infested than later ones.

CONTROLS: See apple chapter, page 325.

CHERRY FRUIT FLY: These flies cause problems for cherry, and to a lesser extent, plum and pear growers throughout the United States — all except the extreme Southwest and Florida. Cherries are small and misshapen, with rotten flesh in which maggots are found feeding. Cherries may drop prematurely. After overwintering as pupae in the soil, adults resembling small houseflies with barred wings emerge in late spring or early summer. Females lay eggs inside the developing fruits. The maggots that hatch out are yellowish-white and legless with two dark mouth hooks.

CONTROLS: Once the eggs have been laid inside the fruit, controls are ineffective. Control adults as soon as they emerge, using approved insecticide sprays. Use traps to monitor emergence (see page 398). Cultivating the top 2 inches of soil under the cherry trees in the fall exposes overwintering pupae to cold and predators and may reduce numbers.

CODLING MOTH: One of the major pests on apples, the codling moth is found in all areas where apples are grown. It attacks pears, apricots, and quinces as well as apples. Small holes are found on the fruit, usually at the blossom end; inside, pinkish-white worms with brown heads feed on the flesh, leaving tunnels full of sawdustlike frass. Fruits may drop prematurely. The codling moth larvae overwinter in cocoons under loose bark on the trunk or under debris on the ground. In midspring they pupate, emerging as grayish-brown moths in late spring. The females lay eggs on leaves, twigs, and fruits. The larvae feed briefly on the leaves before tunneling into the fruits. After feeding for 3 to 5 weeks, they emerge and crawl down the trunk in search of a spot to pupate. There may be up to three generations per year.
CONTROLS: Use a combination of physical traps and approved insecticides. See pear chapter, page 374, and apple chapter, page 326.

PEACH TREE BORER: A problem in just about all areas where peaches are grown, the peach tree borer also attacks cherry, plum, and apricot trees. Holes in the trunk near the base of the tree from which frass and gum exude are signs that borers are at work. Wasplike moths lay eggs around the base of the trunk in late summer and early fall. These hatch into white caterpillars with brownish heads, about 1 inch long, that burrow into the trunk as high as a foot above ground or several inches below. The caterpillars overwinter in the trunk, pupate in their tunnels from late spring to early summer, then emerge in midsummer to lay eggs. If not controlled, borers can kill a tree. There is usually one generation per year.
CONTROLS: See peach chapter, page 366.

PEAR PSYLLA: A pest on pear trees mainly in eastern and western, rather than central, parts of the country, the pear psylla not only causes damage by feeding, but can spread fire blight. After overwintering on or near pear trees, adults emerge in spring and mate. Females begin laying eggs on twigs in early spring. The immature insects and adults feed by sucking out the plant's juices, causing leaf yellowing and a general decline in vigor. Severely infected trees may drop their leaves. The pear psylla secretes honeydew, a sticky, sugary substance that coats leaves and may cause the growth of a sooty black mold. There are usually three to four generations per year.
CONTROLS: Control with dormant oil spray in the fall. Spray again in the spring if necessary. Use an insecticidal soap during the growing season. See pear chapter, page 372.

PLUM CURCULIO: Only found east of the Rockies. These pests attack apples, peaches, cherries, apricots, and pears as well as plums. Infested fruits often drop prematurely and are misshapen, with small crescent-shaped scars on the skin. Inside, grayish-white grubs with brown heads feed on the flesh. In late summer, they eat small holes through the skin of the fruit. The adult, a brown beetle with a long curved snout, becomes active about the time that apples and peaches bloom. After the female lays eggs, the grubs hatch out and feed in the fruit for about 2 weeks, then emerge to pupate in the soil. In midsummer a new generation of adult beetles emerges, feeding on fruit until hibernating for the winter. In the South there may be more than one generation in some years.
CONTROLS: See plum chapter, page 380.

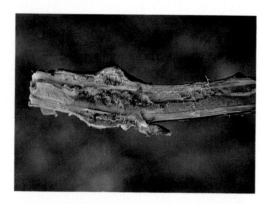

RASPBERRY CANE BORER: Found throughout the eastern United States. Sudden wilting of the tips of raspberry canes is the first sign of infestation. Closer examination of the canes shows two rows of punctures about 1 inch apart at the tip of the cane. The half-inch-long, black and yellow adult beetle lays an egg between the rows of punctures that hatches into a grub. It tunnels down through the cane for two seasons, killing the cane as it feeds. *CONTROLS: To destroy the larvae cut off the wilted tips below the lower row of punctures, and burn them as soon as you notice them.*

RASPBERRY CROWN BORER: This pest can attack all brambles in the northern part of the country. Infested canes may wilt and die in early summer, break off easily at the base, or show an overall lack of vigor. You can often find white grubs feeding in the crown or the roots. Crown borers have a 2-year life cycle. In late summer, females lay round, rust-colored eggs on the undersides of the leaves. Grubs pupate in the soil at the base of the plant over the winter. The following spring, they enter the roots and crown and feed there until late in the summer of the next year. *CONTROLS: Drench the base of the plants with an approved insecticide in early spring; this should be done annually for two seasons. Cut out and destroy infested canes below the soil line to kill larvae. Look for eggs on the leaves in late summer and destroy them.*

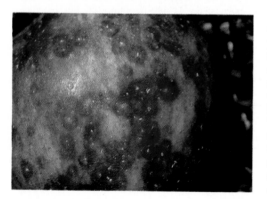

SCALES: Different species of scale insects attack various kinds of fruits in all parts of the country. Branches, twigs, and leaf undersides are covered with numerous small bumps. These may be flattened and brown, or thick, white, and covered with a waxy or woolly substance. Leaves on infested plants turn yellow and the overall vigor of the tree declines. Severely infested plants may die within several seasons. Mature females lay eggs or produce live young under the bumps. Eggs hatch into crawlers that feed by sucking out the plant's juices. They then begin to produce a scale over themselves and lose their legs. There may be several generations per year. *CONTROLS: Use a dormant oil spray in early spring before bud break. Time insecticide sprays to coincide with vulnerable stages of the life cycle when the insects are not protected by the scale; consult your county Extension Service agent for help identifying and controlling specific types of scale insects.*

Fruit Diseases

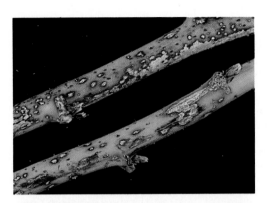

ANTHRACNOSE: Occurring throughout the United States, this fungus disease can attack all brambles, but is most severe on black and purple raspberries. Small, raised purple spots appear on canes in spring. The spots enlarge as the disease progresses, the centers turning gray and sunken. Leaves may have yellow spots with purple edges. Overgrown, crowded bushes are most susceptible, with most of the infected canes found in the center of the plant. Wet spring and early summer weather promotes the spread of the fungus, which overwinters in infected canes.
CONTROLS: *Prune out and destroy infected canes after harvest. Follow proper pruning practices. Destroy wild brambles in the vicinity that may harbor the disease. Spray plants with an approved fungicide in early spring when the leaf buds have swollen to expose about ¼ inch of new leaf.*

BLACK ROT: A problem of grapes in the eastern half of the country (including Texas), this fungus can be very destructive. The first signs of infection are light brown spots with dark edges on the fruits. These enlarge and the grapes turn black and shrivel up like raisins, but remain hanging on the vine. Reddish-brown spots may appear on the leaves, and dark sunken areas on canes, leaf stems, and tendrils. The fungus overwinters on infected plant parts. Warm, wet weather in spring and early summer encourages the spread of the disease.
CONTROLS: *Use an approved fungicide. Time sprays precisely; once fruits start to shrivel, sprays won't help. Make the first application when the shoots are 6 to 10 inches long; repeat just before and just after bloom. Continue at 10- to 14-day intervals if weather conditions favor the spread of the disease. If black rot is a big problem in your area, consider planting resistant varieties such as* Fredonia.

BLACK KNOT: This fungus disease is a problem for plum growers in the eastern half of the country, although cherries can be infected occasionally. Soft, green swellings appear on branches, eventually becoming hard, black galls that may be up to 1 foot long and 1½ inches in diameter. As the galls grow, they cut off water and nutrients to the parts of the branches beyond the galls, stunting and possibly killing them. Infection spreads by spores produced on the knots in spring. Warm, wet weather encourages the spread of the disease.
CONTROLS: *Prune out and destroy infected branches in early spring, cutting at least 4 inches back from the knot into healthy wood (see pages 309–310). Spray trees just before buds open with an approved fungicide, making two more applications at 7- to 10-day intervals. Avoid planting extremely susceptible varieties such as* Damson *and* Stanley.

BROWN ROT: Occurring in most parts of the country, this is one of the major fungus diseases on stone fruits (apricot, peach, plum, cherry). The first sign of trouble is when blossoms and leaves wilt and turn brown in the spring. Infection often spreads through the base of the flowers, causing many twigs to die. Blighted flowers hang on the tree and are covered with masses of gray spores during humid weather. These spores spread infection to branches, causing cankers that ooze a thick gum. Maturing fruits are most susceptible to the fungus. Small brown spots enlarge rapidly; infected fruits become covered with gray spores during wet weather. The fungus overwinters in infected fruits and twigs. *CONTROL: Pick and destroy all infected fruits, both on and under the tree. Spray fungicides during early bloom to prevent blossom infection; once blossoms are infected, fungicides are ineffective. Spray later in the season to protect developing fruits.*

FIRE BLIGHT: This bacterial disease is a major problem for pear growers in most parts of the country. It can also infect apples and some other members of the rose family grown primarily as ornamentals, such as mountain ash and serviceberry. In the spring, infected blossoms turn black and die, as do the new shoots, the ends of which bend over into a characteristic "shepherd's crook." The tree looks as if it has been scorched by fire; hence the name of the disease. Infected fruits shrivel, turn black, and remain on the tree. Dark, sunken areas (cankers) appear on branches, from which a sticky substance oozes during wet weather. The bacteria overwinter in the cankers, oozing out in spring to be carried by insects, wind, and rain to the blossoms. Infection spreads into the branches through the flowers. Severe infection can kill a tree; less severe, chronic infections greatly decrease fruit yield. *CONTROL: See pear chapter, page 372.*

GUMMOSIS: A problem in all citrus-growing areas, this fungus disease causes sunken cankers in the bark at the base of the tree from which a thick brownish gum oozes. Leaves turn yellow and die as the tree declines in overall vigor. Cankers form when a soil-borne fungus, *Phytophthora*, which thrives in heavy, wet soil, splashes up onto the trunk. Wounds in the bark provide a good avenue of infection, but the fungus can also penetrate the bark directly. Limes and lemons are most susceptible. *CONTROLS: Cut out small cankers in the bark as soon as you notice them, going ½ inch into healthy bark. Use Phytophthora-resistant rootstocks such as Trifoliate orange and Troyer citrange. When watering trees, don't wet the soil directly at the base of the trunk. Spray the base of the trunk with an approved fungicide.*

ORANGE RUST: This fungus disease infects blackberries all over the country, but is most severe in the Northeast and mid-Atlantic states. One of the most serious diseases affecting blackberries, it can also infect black raspberries but won't bother red or purple ones. Bright yellow pustules cover the undersides of the leaves, which are yellow and distorted. The pustules open to release masses of bright orange, powdery spores. Infected plants rarely bloom or set fruit. Once a plant is infected, it cannot be cured. *CONTROLS: Dig out and destroy infected plants. Destroy any nearby wild blackberries that may harbor the disease. Grow rust-resistant varieties.*

PEACH LEAF CURL: A fungus disease that attacks peaches and nectarines throughout their growing range, it causes leaves to curl and pucker. Leaves are tinged with red when they first appear, but later turn yellow or brown and become covered with powdery gray spores before dropping from the tree. Spring rains wash spores from the bark where they overwinter in the leaf buds, which become infected as they open. Premature loss of foliage weakens the tree and fruiting is poor. Cool, wet weather encourages the spread of the disease; depending on the weather conditions as buds are breaking, leaf curl may be severe one year and not the next.
CONTROLS: Spray trees with an approved fungicide either in the fall right after leaves have dropped, or in the spring as the buds begin to swell. Fungicides applied after buds are open are ineffective. Remove and destroy infected leaves as they appear in the spring.

POWDERY MILDEW: The leaves of plants infected with this fungus disease are covered with a gray-white powder. New growth is stunted and distorted, and dries up and dies. Infected buds may fail to open, while infected fruits may be russeted (in the case of apples) or covered with powdery white patches. A number of different fungi cause similar symptoms in a wide variety of plants. The species that infects apples will also infect peaches, plums, pears, and cherries, while other species infect strawberries and raspberries. The fungus overwinters in infected plant parts, becoming active in spring. Warm days and cool nights promote its spread. The fungus competes with the plant for nutrients, causing an overall decline in vigor and reducing fruit yield.
CONTROLS: Prune out infected twigs. Spray with an approved fungicide at 10- to 14-day intervals, starting when plants begin to bloom and continuing until after petal fall. See apple chapter for resistant varieties.

RED STELE: Strawberries become stunted, weak, and bear few fruits if they are infected by this soil-borne fungus. Leaves turn yellow and red. The core, or stele, of roots dug in the spring is reddish-brown rather than a normal pale yellow. The fungus, which can survive in the soil for many years, infects and kills roots in the spring. As new roots are produced during the summer, symptoms often go away temporarily. Heavy, poorly drained soil promotes the growth of the fungus.
CONTROLS: There are no chemical controls. Plant strawberries in well-drained soil. Check with your county Extension Service agent for red stele–tolerant varieties that do well in your area.

RESOURCES

The Cooperative Extension Service

The Cooperative Extension Service is a government organization that provides home gardeners with a wealth of information and advice, especially for specific information on local gardening needs and problems. There is an office in every county of every state. Many helpful gardening publications are available from your local Extension Service office, either free or at a very reasonable price. The agricultural agent can help you solve gardening problems and is your best source of current information on correct pesticide use in your state. All it takes is a phone call to find out what services your local office provides.

To contact your local Extension Service office, you may need to be a little creative. We've found the phone numbers of local offices listed in phone directories a variety of ways: under "Cooperative Extension," "Extension," or the name of the county (for example, "Chittenden County Extension Office").

Vegetable Seeds — General

The following is a list of companies that offer a good selection of varieties of common vegetables; many also offer the common culinary herbs.

The list is numbered; the numbers are cross-referenced to the tables and list of variety sources in each fruit and vegetable chapter. Any unusual features or specialties offered by a company are given at the end of the entry.

The Canadian companies listed in this general section do sell to U.S. gardeners.

Unless otherwise stated, the catalogs were available free of charge as of 1985. Some companies will deduct the catalog price from your order.

1. *Agway, Inc.*
   P.O. Box 487
   Elizabethtown, PA 17022
   A mail-order catalog is no longer available, but the varieties referenced are generally available in Agway stores.

2. *Alberta Nurseries & Seeds*
   Bowden, Alberta
   CANADA T0M 0K0
   (Catalog, $2)

3. *Archias' Seed Store*
   P.O. Box 109
   Sedalia, MO 65301

4. *Burell's*
   Rocky Ford, CO 81067
   Large selection of melons.

5. *Burgess Seed & Plant Co.*
   905 Four Seasons Rd.
   Bloomington, IL 61701
   A few unusuals, such as stuffing tomato; also fruit.

6. *Burpee (W. Atlee) Co.*
   Warminster, PA 18974
   Also fruit, garden tools.

7. *Comstock, Ferre & Co.*
   Box 125
   Wethersfield, CT 06109
   Established company with some unusual vegetables.

8. *Dam (William) Seeds*
   P.O. Box 8400
   Dundas, Ontario
   CANADA L9H 6M1
   Several varieties hard to find in the United States.

9. *De Giorgi Company*
   P.O. Box 413
   Council Bluffs, IA 51502
   Some old and imported varieties. (Catalog, $1)

10. *Early's Farm & Garden Center*
Box 3024
Saskatoon, Saskatchewan
CANADA S7K 3S9
(Catalog, $1)

11. *Farmer Seed & Nursery*
818 N.W. 4th St.
Faribault, MN 55021
Also fruit.

12. *Field (Henry) Seed & Nursery*
Shenandoah, IA 51602
Includes a number of unusual varieties and some rare vegetables; also fruit and nuts.

13. *Garden Magic*
P.O. Box 6570
Zephyr Cove, NV 89449

14. *Gardenimport*
P.O. Box 760
Thornhill, Ontario
CANADA L3T 4A5
Only North American supplier for Suttons, a famous English seed company. (Catalog, $1)

15. *Gurney's*
Yankton, SD 57079
Some unusual varieties; also nut and fruit trees.

16. *Harris Seeds*
Moreton Farm
Rochester, NY 14624
New hybrids often featured.

17. *Hastings*
P.O. Box 4274
Atlanta, GA 30302
Many southern varieties.

18. *Hume (Ed) Seeds*
P.O. Box 1450
Kent, WA 98032

19. *Island Seed Co.*
P.O. Box 4278, sta. A
Victoria, B.C.
CANADA V8X 3X8

20. *Johnny's Selected Seeds*
Albion, ME 04910
Fine selection of old and new varieties suited for short seasons; also grains, cover crops.

21. *Jung Seed Co.*
Randolph, WI 53957
Old family-owned company with a number of hard-to-find varieties; also fruit and nuts.

22. *Lagomarsino Seeds*
5675-A Power Inn Dr.
Sacramento, CA 95824

23. *Landreth's Seeds*
180–188 West Ostend St.
Baltimore, MD 21230
Oldest seed company in the U.S.; mostly hybrid varieties. (Catalog, $2)

24. *Ledden & Sons*
P.O. Box 7
Sewell, NJ 08080

25. *Letherman's Seeds*
1221 Tuscarawas St.
Canton, OH 44707

26. *Liberty Seed Co.*
P.O. Box 806
New Philadelphia, OH 44663

27. *Lindenberg Seeds*
803 Princess Ave.
Brandon, Manitoba
CANADA R7A 0P5

28. *Lockhart Seeds*
P.O. Box 1361
Stockton, CA 95205
Extensive selection of hybrids; also cover crops. (Catalog, $1)

29. *May (Earl) Seed & Nursery*
Shenandoah, IA 51603
Also fruit.

30. *McFayden Seed Co.*
P.O. Box 1800
Brandon, Manitoba
CANADA R7A 6N4

31. *Mellinger's*
2310 W. South Range Rd.
North Lima, OH 44452
Mostly garden products; a selection of vegetables; many biological pest controls and soil amendments.

32. *Meyer Seed Co.*
600 S. Caroline St.
Baltimore, MD 21231

33. *Olds Seed Company*
P.O. Box 7790
Madison, WI 53707
Several varieties not available elsewhere; also fruit.

34. *Ontario Seed Co.*
Box 144
Waterloo, Ontario
CANADA N2J 3Z9
(Catalog, $1; cash only)

35. *Park Seed Co.*
P.O. Box 31
Greenwood, SC 29646
Includes many varieties recommended for southern areas.

36. *Rawlinson Garden Seed*
269 College Rd.
Truro, Nova Scotia
CANADA B2N 2P6

37. *Rohrer's*
P.O. Box 25
Smoketown, PA 17576

38. *Seedway, Inc.*
Hall, NY 14463

39. *Stokes Seeds*
Box 548
Buffalo, NY 14240
Large selection of varieties for short seasons; some old varieties and uncommon hybrids.

40. *T & T Seeds, Inc.*
Box 338
Grand Forks, ND 58206

41. *T & T Seeds, Ltd.*
P.O. Box 1710
Winnipeg, Manitoba
CANADA R3C 3P6

42. *Tait & Sons*
P.O. Box 2873
Norfolk, VA 23504

43. *Twilley Seed Co.*
Trevose, PA 19047
Good selection of sweet corn.

44. *Vesey's Seeds*
York, P.E.I.
CANADA C0A 1P0

Heirloom, Foreign, and Unusual Varieties

45. *Abundant Life*
P.O. Box 772
Port Townsend, WA 98368
Heirloom varieties. (Catalog, $1)

46. *Bountiful Gardens*
5798 Ridgewood Rd.
Willits, CA 95490
Organically grown, open-pollinated varieties; also green manures, and biological pest controls. (Catalog, $1)

47. *The Cook's Garden*
P.O. Box 65054
Londonderry, VT 05148
Salad vegetables, including many European lettuce varieties.

48. *Epicure Seeds*
P.O. Box 450
Brewster, NY 10509
European gourmet varieties.

49. *Exotica Seed Co.*
8033 Sunset Blvd., Suite 125
West Hollywood, CA 90046
Tropical and subtropical vegetables and fruits. (Catalog, $2)

50. *Fisher's Garden Store*
P.O. Box 236
Belgrade, MT 59714
High-altitude, short-season varieties; some originals. (Catalogs to Montana only)

51. *Garden City Seeds*
Box 297
Victor, MT 59875
Emphasizes organically grown, open-pollinated varieties.

52. *Garden Delight*
Box 55316
Madison, WI 53705
Open-pollinated and hybrid varieties; inexpensive seed packets.

53. *Gleckler's Seedsmen*
Metamora, OH 43540
Unusual vegetables, including rare foreign varieties.

54. *Grace's Garden*
10 Bay St.
Westport, CT 06880
Unusual vegetables, especially giant and foreign varieties.

55. *Greenleaf Seeds*
P.O. Box 89
Conway, MA 01341
Unusual foreign vegetables, especially salad plants; descriptive and historical information. (Catalog, 25¢)

56. *Heirloom Garden Seeds*
P.O. Box 138C
Guerneville, CA 95446
Herbs and a few old vegetable varieties. (Catalog, $2; price list, free)

57. *Herb Gathering*
5742 Kenwood Ave.
Kansas City, MO 64110
Formerly J. A. Demonchaux Seeds. French vegetable varieties; also herbs. (Catalog, $1)

58. *High Altitude Gardens*
P.O. Box 4238
Ketchum, ID 83340
Open-pollinated varieties for short seasons and high altitudes; planting, culture, pest, and seed-saving information. (Catalog, $2)

59. *Jardin du Gourmet*
West Danville, VT 05873
Foreign varieties, especially French; inexpensive seed packets; also herbs. (Catalog, 50¢)

60. *Johnson Seed Co.*
227 Ludwig Ave.
Dousman, WI 53118
Modern and heirloom varieties; heirloom seed potatoes. (Catalog, two first-class stamps)

61. *Kerncraft*
434 W. Main St.
Kutztown, PA 19530
European vegetable varieties.

62. *Le Marché*
P.O. Box 566
Dixon, CA 95620
Hard-to-find varieties, including foreign and heirloom; extensive descriptions and some historical information. (Catalog, $2)

63. *Meredith Seeds*
13563 N.W. Cornell Rd.
Portland, OR 97321
Compact and dwarf varieties for small gardens, patios, and containers.

64. *Mountain Seed & Nursery*
P.O. Box 9107
Moscow, ID 83843
Traditional and hybrid varieties for short growing seasons. (Catalog, $1; deductible)

65. *Native Seeds/SEARCH*
3950 West New York Dr.
Tucson, AZ 85745
Native American varieties, especially those for the Southwest. (Catalog, $1)

66. *Nichols Garden Nursery*
1190 North Pacific Hwy.
Albany, OR 97321
Good selection of hybrid and open-pollinated varieties; also herbs, Oriental vegetables.

67. *Pine Tree Garden Seeds*
Rt. 100
New Gloucester, ME 04260
Mostly hybrids; some unusual heirlooms such as *Jenny Lind* melon; many short-season varieties.

68. *Plants of the Southwest*
1812 Second St.
Santa Fe, NM 87501
Includes native, heirloom, and modern vegetable varieties. (Catalog, $1)

69. *Redwood City Seed Co.*
P.O. Box 361
Redwood City, CA 94064
Foreign and old-fashioned varieties and unusual vegetables (jicama, rampion, burdock); also herbs, useful plants. (Catalog, $1)

70. *Sanctuary Seeds*
2388 West 4th St.
Vancouver, B.C.
CANADA V6K 1P1
Open-pollinated, untreated seed; some varieties little known in the U.S. (Catalog, $1)

71. *Seeds Blum*
Idaho City Stage
Boise, ID 83706
Family company emphasizing heirloom varieties; also herbs, edible flowers. (Catalog, $2; free to previous customers)

72. *Shepherd's Garden Seeds*
7389 West Zayante Rd.
Felton, CA 95018
European varieties chosen for flavor, including unusual salad plants. (Catalog, $1)

73. *Southern Exposure Seed Exchange*
P.O. Box 158
North Garden, VA 22959
Open-pollinated varieties, especially those suited for mid-Atlantic region. (Catalog, $2; free to previous customers)

74. *Thompson & Morgan*
P.O. Box 1308
Jackson, NJ 08527
U.S. branch of British company with many hard-to-find varieties.

75. *Vermont Bean Seed Co.*
Garden Lane
Bomoseen, VT 05732
Full vegetable catalog specializing in beans and peas.

76. *World Seed Service*
P.O. Box 1058
Redwood City, CA 94064
Open-pollinated varieties, including unusual and Mexican; also rare plants from around the world. (Catalog, $1)

Oriental Vegetables

77. *Dr. Yoo Farm*
P.O. Box 290
College Park, MD 20740
Chinese and Japanese vegetables.

78. *Japonica Seeds*
P.O. Box 919
Jackson Heights, NY 11372
Japanese vegetables.

79. *Kitazawa Seed Co.*
356 W. Taylor St.
San Jose, CA 95110
Mostly Japanese vegetables.

80. *Sunrise Enterprises*
P.O. Box 10058
Elmwood, CT 06110
Large selection.

81. *Tsang and Ma International*
P.O. Box 294
Belmont, CA 94002
Chinese vegetables and some Oriental cookware.

Specialty Companies

The companies listed below offer a wide choice of varieties of the following vegetables.

Corn

82. *Prairie State Commodities*
P.O. Box 6
Trilla, IL 62469
Feed seeds, including a few hard-to-find corn varieties; also cover crops.

Lettuce and Greens

The Cook's Garden, *see 47*

Greenleaf Seeds, *see 55*

Melons

Burell's, *see 4*

Weeks Seeds, *see 102*

Willhite Seed Co., *see 103*

Onions, Etc.

83. *Kalmia Farm*
P.O. Box 3881
Charlottesville, VA 22903
Unusual multiplying onions, garlic, shallots.

84. *S & H Organic Acres*
P.O. Box 757
Newberg, OR 97132
Unusual multiplying onions, garlic, etc.

Peppers

85. *Horticultural Enterprises*
P.O. Box 810082
Dallas, TX 75381
Three dozen varieties; a few other Mexican vegetables.

86. *The Pepper Gal*
10536 119th Ave. N.
Largo, FL 33543
Over 100 edible varieties.

Potatoes

87. *Moose Tubers*
Box 1010
Dixmont, ME 04932
A dozen varieties of seed potatoes.

Sweet Potatoes

88. *Fred's Plant Farm*
Rt. 1, P.O. Box 707
Dresden, TN 38225
Sweet potato plants; over a dozen varieties.

89. *Margrave Plant Co.*
Gleason, TN 38229
Ten varieties of sweet potato plants; free grower's guide with each shipment.

90. *Steele Plant Co.*
Gleason, TN 38229
Good variety selection; also onions and cole crop plants. (Catalog, two first-class stamps)

Tomatoes

91. *Tomato Growers Supply Co.*
P.O. Box 2237
Fort Myers, FL 33902
Over 100 varieties, mostly hybrids.

92. *The Tomato Seed Co.*
P.O. Box 323
Metuchen, NJ 08840
Over 250 varieties, including many old-time; gives growing habit, maturity, resistance, and if hybrid for each variety.

Inexpensive Seed

93. *Broom Seed Co.*
P.O. Box 237
Rion, SC 29132

94. *Butterbrooke Farm*
78 Barry Rd.
Oxford, CT 06483
Untreated, organically grown seed. (Price list, SASE)

95. *FEDCO Seeds*
52 Mayflower Hill Dr.
Waterville, ME 04924
Inexpensive source for large orders; minimum order $25.

Garden Delight, *see 52*

Jardin du Gourmet, *see 59*

96. *Seeds for All*
Keating Stage
Baker, OR 97883
"Home of $.25 seed packet" is the company's claim.

Regional Vegetable List

Northeast

97. *Allen, Sterling & Lothrop*
191 U.S. Rt. 1
Falmouth, ME 04105
Turn-of-century company with varieties for northern New England, including a few older ones.

Johnny's Selected Seeds, *see 20*

Pine Tree Garden Seeds, *see 67*

Mid-Atlantic Region

Southern Exposure Seed Exchange, *see 73*

South and Southwest

98. *Aurora Garden*
321 Texas Blvd.
Texarkana, TX 75501
Good selection of varieties suitable to the Southwest, including older ones such as cowhorn okra. (Price list, 50¢)

Hastings, *see 17*

99. *Kilgore Seed Co.*
P.O. Box 2158
Sanford, FL 32772
Good selection of Florida varieties. (Catalog, $1; deductible)

Park Seed Co., *see 35*

Plants of the Southwest, *see 68*

100. *Porter & Son*
P.O. Box 104
Stephenville, TX 76401
Good small company with some hard-to-find, open-pollinated varieties; large selection of melons.

101. *Roswell Seed Co.*
P.O. Box 725
Roswell, NM 88201
Mostly hybrids; also field seed.

102. *Weeks Seeds*
921 Dickinson Ave.
Greenville, NC 27834
Specializes in large melons.

103. *Willhite Seed Co.*
P.O. Box 23
Poolville, TX 76076
Varieties for Texas; large selection of melons.

104. *Wyatt-Quarles Seed Co.*
P.O. Box 379
Garner, NC 27529
Also cover crops.

Rocky Mountain Region

105. *Rocky Mountain Seed Co.*
P.O. Box 5204
Denver, CO 80217
Many cold-hardy varieties. (Catalogs to Rocky Mountain states only)

Northwest

Nichols Garden Nursery, *see 66*

106. *Territorial Seed Co.*
P.O. Box 27
Lorane, OR 97451
Untreated seed; many varieties adapted to areas west of the Cascade Mountains.

107. *Tillinghast Seed*
P.O. Box 738
La Conner, WA 98257
Oldest seed company in Northwest; also fruit.

California

108. *California Gardeners Seed Co.*
904 Silver Spur Rd., Suite 414
Rolling Hills Estates, CA 90274
Mostly open-pollinated varieties; untreated seed.

Lockhart Seeds, *see 28*

Redwood City Seed Co., *see 69*

109. *Specialty Garden Supply*
418 Sumner St.
Santa Cruz, CA 95062
Many varieties for coastal climates.

Herbs

This list of herb companies includes those selling plants, seeds, or both.

110. *Borchelt Herb Gardens*
474 Carriage Shop Rd.
East Falmouth, MA 02536
Seed; over 100 types. (Price list, SASE)

111. *Companion Plants*
Route 6, Box 88
Athens, OH 45701
Plants; over 300 listed, including 20 basils. (Catalog, $1.50; deductible)

112. *Richters Herbs*
Goodwood, Ontario
CANADA L0C 1A0
Seed; nearly 300 types, many hard-to-find; also gourmet vegetables, wildflowers. (Catalog, $2)

113. *Rutland of Kentucky*
P.O. Box 182
Washington, KY 41096
Plants and seed; over 200 types, several hard-to-find. (Catalog, $2; deductible)

114. *Sandy Mush Herb Nursery*
Rt. 1, Surrett Cove Rd.
Leicester, NC 28748
Plants and seed; over 300 selections, including 39 thymes. (Catalog, $2)

115. *Well-Sweep Herb Farm*
317 Mt. Bethel Rd.
Port Murray, NJ 07865
About 500 plants; no descriptions. (Catalog, $1)

General Fruit Nurseries

Most of the firms listed below sell trees and plants, not seed. Many carry both tree fruits and small fruits; most offer nut trees as well.

It is always better, if possible, to purchase from local nurseries where you have a chance to look over the stock before you buy.

Unless noted otherwise, catalogs are available free of charge as of 1985.

116. *Adams County Nursery*
P.O. Box 108
Aspers, PA 17304
Also apple rootstocks, dwarf apple.

117. *Barnes & Son*
P.O. Box 250L
McMinnville, TN 37110
Also nuts.

118. *Bear Creek Farms*
P.O. Box 411
Northport, WA 99157
Hardy fruits and nuts. Many old apple varieties. Also rootstocks. (Catalog, two first-class stamps)

119. *Bountiful Ridge*
P.O. Box 250
Princess Anne, MD 21853
Good selection of hard-to-find varieties in easy-to-read catalog.

120. *C&O Nursery*
P.O. Box 116
Wenatachee, WA 98801

121. *California Nursery Co.*
Niles District, Box 2278
Fremont, CA 94536

122. *Columbia Basin Nursery*
P.O. Box 458
Quincy, WA 98848
Also apple rootstocks.

123. *Converse Nursery*
73 Lawn St.
Cambridge, MA 02138
Heirloom apples.

124. *Cumberland Valley Nurseries*
P.O. Box 471
McMinnville, TN 37110
Large peach selection.

125. *Eastville Plantation*
P.O. Box 337
Bogart, GA 30622
Specializes in southern varieties.

126. *Edible Landscaping*
Rt. 2, Box 343A
Afton, VA 22920
Unusual fruits, including many varieties of figs, hardy kiwis, and persimmons.

127. *Emlong Nurseries*
Stevensville, MI 49127

Exotica Seed Co., *see* 49.
Seeds only.

128. *Foster (Dean) Nurseries*
Hartford, MI 49057
Very large strawberry selection.

129. *Fowler Nurseries*
525 Fowler Rd.
Newcastle, CA 95658
Some older varieties; also subtropicals, Asian varieties, and genetic dwarfs. (Catalog, $2; price list, free)

130. *Greenmantle Nursery*
3010 Ettersburg Rd.
Garberville, CA 95440
Family-run, interested in old varieties; extensive descriptive and historical information. (Catalog, $3; price list, SASE)

131. *Harmony Farm Supply*
P.O. Box 451
Graton, CA 95444
Emphasizes old varieties; has subtropicals, genetic dwarfs. (Catalog, two first-class stamps)

Hastings, *see* 17
Many persimmons, pecans; also genetic dwarfs.

132. *Hidden Springs Nursery*
Rt. 14 Box 159
Cookeville, TN 38501
Old apple varieties and several unusual fruits; also herbs. (Catalog, 60¢)

133. *Hilltop Orchards*
Rt. 2
Hartford, MI 49057
Also rootstocks.

134. *Johnson Nursery*
Rt. 5
Ellijay, GA 30540

135. *Kelly Bros.*
Dansville, NY 14437

136. *Lakeland Nurseries*
Unique Merchandise Mart, Bldg. 4
Hanover, PA 17331
Catalog of ornamentals; has some giant and a few hardy fruit varieties.

137. *Lawsons Nursery*
Rt. 1 Box 294
Ball Ground, GA 30107
Specializes in old-fashioned and unusual apple varieties; also some pears.

138. *Leuthardt Nurseries*
Montauk Hwy., Box 666
East Moriches, NY 11940
Specializes in dwarf and espa-
lier fruit trees; has older
varieties.

139. *Living Tree Center*
P.O. Box 797
Bolinas, CA 94924
Over three dozen old apple
varieties; historical and cul-
tural information. (Catalog,
$4.50; deductible)

140. *Mayo Nurseries*
Rt. 14 N.
Lyons, NY 14489
Dwarf apple varieties, other
tree fruits, some small fruits;
also rootstocks.

141. *Miller Nurseries*
5060 West Lake Rd.
Canandaigua, NY 14424

142. *N.Y. State Fruit Testing*
Association
Geneva, NY 14456
Trial varieties featured.

143. *Northwoods Nursery*
28696 Cramer Rd.
Molalla, OR 97038
Varieties for Northwest; specializes in edible landscaping;
holds classes.

144. *Pacific Tree Farms*
4301 Lynwood Dr.
Chula Vista, CA 92010
Tropical and subtropical
plants, including fruit and
nuts; large selection of citrus.
(Catalog, $1.50)

145. *Patrick's Nurseries*
P.O. Box 130
Ty Ty, GA 31795

146. *Peaceful Valley Farm Supply*
11173 Peaceful Valley Rd.
Nevada City, CA 95959
Fruit and nut varieties for
West Coast; some organically
grown; a few unusuals like
jujubes and carob; also genetic
dwarfs.

147. *Possum Trot Tropical Fruit*
14955 S.W. 214th St.
Miami, FL 33187
Tropical fruits and nuts.

148. *Preservation Apple Tree Co.*
P.O. 607
Mt. Gretna, PA 17064
Classic apple varieties on
dwarfing rootstocks; mini-
mum purchase, 25 trees.

149. *Raintree Nursery*
391 Butts Rd.
Moreton, WA 98356
Some old varieties; information on edible landscaping;
also rootstocks.

150. *Savage Farms Nursery*
P.O. Box 125 PL
McMinnville, TN 37110

151. *Sonoma Antique Apples*
4395 Westside Rd.
Healdsburg, CA 95448
Old apple varieties and some
pears.

152. *Southmeadow Fruit Gardens*
15310 Red Arrow Hwy.
Lakeside, MI 49116
Large selection of old varieties; 100-page catalog
includes descriptive and historical information. (Catalog,
$8; price list, free)

153. *St. Lawrence Nurseries*
R.D. 2
Potsdam, NY 13676
Extremely hardy trees, organi-
cally grown; some unusuals
such as edible mountain ash.

154. *Stark Brothers Nurseries*
Louisiana, MO 63353
Carries genetic dwarfs.

155. *Van Well Nursery*
P.O. Box 1339
Wenatchee, WA 98801
Also apple rootstocks.

156. *Vermont Fruit Tree Co.*
Box 34
New Haven, VT 05472
Modern apple varieties, espe-
cially scab-resistant ones.

157. *Waynesboro Nurseries*
P.O. Box 987
Waynesboro, VA 22980

158. *Well's Nursery*
Box 606
Lindale, TX 75771
Southwest fruit varieties.

159. *Womack's Nursery*
Rt. 1, Box 80
De Leon, TX 76444
Southwest fruit and nuts.

160. *Zilke Brothers Nursery*
Baroda, MI 49101

Berry Catalogs

161. *Ahrens Strawberry Nursery*
Rt. 1
Huntingburg, IN 47542
Mostly strawberries.

162. *Boston Mountain Nurseries*
Rt. 2
Mountainburg, AR 72946
Strawberries, brambles, grapes.

Foster (Dean) Nurseries, *see* 128

163. *Hartman's Plantation*
Rt. 1
Grand Junction, MI 49056
Blueberries — highbush and
rabbiteye. (Hartman's has a
southern plantation: Earlton,
FL 32631)

164. *Ison's Nursery & Vineyard*
Rt. 1 Box 191
Brooks, GA 30205
Specializes in grapes.

165. *Makielski Berry Farm*
7130 Platt Rd.
Ypsilanti, MI 48197
Specializes in raspberries;
some unusual Canadian
varieties.

166. *Nourse Farms*
Box 485 RFD
South Deerfield, MA 01373
Strawberries, raspberries,
blackberries.

167. *Owen's Vineyard & Nursery*
Georgia Highway 85
Gay, GA 30218
Muscadine grapes and rabbiteye blueberries for South.

168. *Rayner Brothers*
P.O. Box 1617
Salisbury, MD 21801
Mostly strawberries; also other small fruit, dwarf trees, and nuts.

Canada Only

These companies sell only to residents of Canada.

Vegetables

Becker's Seed Potatoes
RR 1
Trout Creek, Ontario P0H 2L0
Unusual potato varieties. (Catalog, SASE)

Bishop Farm Seeds
Box 338
Belleville, Ontario K8N 5A5

Charles Seeds
Box 28 Station B
Ottawa, Ontario K1P 6C3
(Catalog, 50¢)

Dominion Seed House
111 Guelph St.
Georgetown, Ontario L7G 4A2

Halifax Seed Co.
P.O. Box 8026, sta. A
Halifax, Nova Scotia B3K 5L8
(Catalog, free to Maritime provinces; $1 elsewhere)

Jenkins Seed House
359 Rideout St. N.
London, Ontario N6A 4G3
(Catalog, $1.50)

W. H. Perron Co.
515 Labelle Blvd.
Laval, Quebec H7V 2T3
(Catalog, $1)

Seed Centre, Ltd.
P.O. Box 3867, sta. D
Edmonton, Alberta T5L 4K1

Tregunno Seeds
126 Catherine St. N.
Hamilton, Ontario L8R 1J4
Untreated, heirloom seeds.

Fruits

Golden Bough Tree Farm
Marlbank, Ontario K0K 2L0
Hardy fruits and nuts, including some Canadian natives. (Catalog, $1)

Lakeshore Tree Farms
RR 3
Saskatoon, Saskatchewan S7K 3J6
Small selection of fruit, including some native Saskatchewan varieties. (Catalog, $1)

McConnell Nurseries
Port Burwell, Ontario N0J 1T0

Seed Exchanges

The organizations listed below are dedicated to locating, exchanging, and preserving edible plants. Though they may be a source for heirloom varieties, they are not seed companies. In fact, they are rather fragile organizations run by one or two committed volunteers who have jobs and families competing for their time. If these organizations are to grow, those who participate must be equally committed.

Before obtaining seeds or plants from any of these groups, make a pledge to yourself that you will keep that variety going and share it with others.

When you write to them, be sure to enclose a self-addressed, stamped envelope.

Blue Ridge Seed Savers
Box 106
Batesville, VA 29924
Seed exchange for Virginia gardeners.

Corns

c/o Carl Barnes
Rt. 1, Box 32
Turpin, OK 73950
Over 200 varieties of open-pollinated corn.

KUSA Research Foundation
P.O. Box 761
Ojai, CA 93023
Old varieties of grains.

Native Seeds/SEARCH, see 65

North American Fruit Explorers
c/o Robert Kurle
10 S. 055 Madison St.
Hinsdale, IL 60521
Publishes quarterly newsletter that carries ads for rare varieties.

Will Bonsall, Scatterseed
c/o Khadighar
Box 1167
Farmington, ME 04938
Acts as intermediary with National Germplasm Preservation system in locating extremely rare varieties.

Seed Savers Exchange
P.O. Box 70
Decorah, IA 52101
Publishes a seed yearbook, listing seed available from member gardeners, and sells a seed inventory, listing commercial sources for hundreds of old-time varieties.

Plant Finders of America
532 Beaumont
Fort Wright, KY 41044
This is not an exchange but a source for extremely rare plants. With contacts all over the world, it will try to find a source for "any plant in cultivation." Fee, $5 per plant; refunded if source can't be located.

Tool Companies

The following companies offer a wide assortment of tools and gardening aids for home and market gardeners.

Clapper's
1125 Washington St.
West Newton, MA 02165

Garden Way
102nd St. & 9th Ave.
Troy, NY 12180

Gardener's Supply Co.
113 Elm St.
Winooski, VT 05404

Green River Tools
P.O. Box 1919
Brattleboro, VT 05301

A. H. Hummert
2746 Chouteau Ave.
St. Louis, MO 63103

A. M. Leonard's
Piqua, OH 45356

Mellinger's, Inc.
2310 W. South Range Rd.
North Lima, OH 45356

Walt Nicke
Box 667G
Hudson, NY 12534

Ringer Research
6860 Flying Cloud Dr.
Eden Prairie, MN 55344

Smith & Hawken
25 Corte Madera
Mill Valley, CA 94941

Organic Gardening Supplies

The following companies specialize in natural fertilizers or natural pesticides, insect traps, insect monitors, etc. Write for a listing of products.

Growing Crazy
2460 S. Beyer Rd.
Saginaw, MI 48601

Harmony Farm Supply
8515 Sonoma Ave.
Graton, CA 95444

Necessary Trading Co.
Box 305
New Castle, VA 24127

North Country Organics
Box 107
Newbury, VT 05051

Organic Control, Inc.
5132 Venice Blvd.
Los Angeles, CA 90019

Organic Farm & Garden Supply
Rt. 2 Box 587
West Columbia, SC 29169

Progressive Agri-Systems
201 Center St.
Stockertown, PA 18083

Soil Labs

Before sending soil samples to any of the labs below, gardeners should write to the company and inquire about types of testing available, costs, and sampling instructions.

Biosystem Consultants
P.O. Box 43
Lorane, OR 97451

Brookside Farms Laboratory Association
New Knoxville, OH 45871

Peaceful Valley Farm Supply
11173 Peaceful Valley Rd.
Nevada City, CA 95959

Soil and Plant Laboratory
P.O. Box 1648
Bellevue, WA 98009

Stemilt Testing Laboratory
4173-18 Joe Miller Rd.
Malaga, WA 98828

Woods End Laboratory
Orchard Hill Rd, RFD Box 128
Temple, ME 04984

Glossary

A

Acidic. Having a pH of less than 7.0. The pH level indicates a concentration of hydrogen and aluminum ions in proportion to hydroxyl ions. Acidic soil limits the availability of all the major plant nutrients and the activity of bacteria in the soil.

Agricultural gypsum. Hydrated calcium sulfate used to reclaim sodic, alkaline soils.

Alkaline. Having a pH greater than 7.0 or a high level of exchangeable sodium, or both. Alkalinity usually interferes with plant growth.

Ammoniacal nitrogen. Synthetic nitrogen fertilizer, a potentially caustic material that should be handled with care. Ammoniacal nitrogen fertilizers include anhydrous ammonia, urea, ammonium nitrate, and ammonium sulfate.

Ammonium nitrate. Synthetic nitrogen fertilizer that contains 33 percent nitrogen.

Ammonium sulfate. Synthetic nitrogen fertilizer that contains 21 percent nitrogen.

Annual. A plant that completes its life cycle, going from seed to mature plant to seed again, in one growing season.

Anther. The pollen-bearing part of a stamen. The male flower part.

B

Bacillus thuringiensis. A biological insecticide used to control the immature stage of moths and butterflies. This material is harmless to other insects and to all warm-blooded animals. It is rendered ineffective by environmental factors such as ultraviolet rays, and repeated applications may be needed. Sold as Dipel, Thuricide, and BT.

Bacteria. Microscopic, one-celled organisms lacking chlorophyll, which multiply by fission and live either parasitically or saprophytically on nonliving organic matter.

Balanced fertilizer. A fertilizer formulation that contains nitrogen, phosphorus, and potassium (N-P-K), i.e., 10-10-10.

Balled-and-burlapped. Referring to tree roots bound in burlap cloth with soil still attached to the roots.

Bare-root. Refers to plants taken from the soil and marketed with little or no soil left attached to the roots.

Biennial. A plant that requires two growing seasons to complete its life cycle. Vegetative growth takes place the first year and flowering and fruiting the second.

Blanching. Depriving plant tissue of sunlight to create a pale coloration, often accomplished by mounding soil around the base of the plant.

Blocking. Dividing the growing medium of seedling plants into blocks for easier transplanting.

Blood meal. An organic source of nitrogen that contains approximately 10–14 percent nitrogen.

Bolting. Premature flowering and fruiting of a crop not grown for its fruit; often caused by light and climatic conditions.

Branch bark collar. The point where a branch meets the trunk of a tree.

Breaker. A hose attachment that regulates the flow of water into the garden without the gardener's needing to be present; a type of drip irrigation.

Broadcasting. Planting by spreading seeds all over the surface of the soil, as in a hay field.

Brush-hog. A piece of machinery that takes down coarse grasses and small brush and tree saplings, often operated with a power take-off system on a tractor or tiller.

Bud. Naked or scale-covered embryonic tissue that will develop into a vegetative shoot, flower, or stem.

Budding. Grafting a single bud to a stem or branch by inserting it under the bark.

Bud union. The place where the stem or canopy portion of a tree has been grafted onto the rootstock portion of the tree; identifiable from a graft scar.

C

Cadmium. A heavy metal that can accumulate in plant tissue and in animal tissue when ingested.

Cambium. A layer of cells in stems and roots that divides into primary and secondary tissue. The green inner bark of a tree that carries food from canopy to roots.

Cane. A long, woody, pliable stem, as on grapes and bramble fruits, which are also known as cane fruits. Also, the stem of roses, reeds, and grasses.

Capsaicin. The substance responsible for making hot peppers hot.

Chelation. The addition of one substance to another to prevent its loss or alteration by fixing it chemically in a stable form. The process involves multiple chemical bonds.

Chemical fertilizer. "Manmade" fertilizer; technically, fertilizer made without carbon or derived from nonliving material.

Clay soil. Soil containing more than 40 percent clay, less than 45 percent sand, and less than 40 percent silt. A clay particle is less than 0.002 mm in equivalent diameter. A clay soil is heavy in texture and has a tendency to drain slowly.

Cloche. A covering for plants that protects them from damaging climatic conditions such as frost and wind. Originally made of glass, many cloche arrangements are now made of plastic sheeting.

Clubroot fungus. A soil-borne fungus (*Plasmodiophora brassicae*) that attacks the cabbage family and can persist in the soil for many years. The fungus is spread by gardening tools that come in contact with the millions of spores that are released when the infected tissue starts to decompose. Soil on shoes and tires can also transport the fungus. Crop rotation is an essential control measure.

Cold frame. An outdoor glass- or plexiglass-covered, solar-heated place where plants can be started early in the season. It is usually a simple rectangular box with a sloped top on which a salvaged window or a newly constructed transparent cover is placed. The top can be manually propped open or opened electronically to adjust heat and moisture retention.

Cold hardiness. Tolerance of a plant to cold temperatures.

Cole crop. Any of the cultivated *Brassicas*, including cabbage, brussels sprouts, broccoli, and cauliflower.

Compost. The end product of aerobic decomposition of organic matter such as plant residues, manures, clippings, and so on.

Copper. A necessary plant micronutrient; 50 ppm is recommended in the surface soil. Also known as a trace element, copper aids in the utilization of iron and in the plant's respiration.

Copper naphthenate. A safe wood preservative that can be used on the wood supports of raised beds or wooden garden edging.

Cordon. A single-stemmed espalier design for apple trees; best suited to spur-forming varieties.

Cover crop. A crop grown to improve soil structure and nutrient-holding capacity by its addition of organic matter, or a crop grown for the purpose of holding the soil to protect against erosion.

Crotch angle. The angle at which a branch meets the branch or trunk of a tree. The angle where a branch originates.

Crown. The place where stem and root meet on seed plants. Also, the canopy of a tree.

Cucurbit. Any member of the family *Cucurbitaceae*, including cucumbers, squashes, and melons.

Cultivar. Synonymous with variety, except that it refers only to cultivated plants.

Cultivation. Disturbing the soil so as to promote the movement of water and air and discourage weed growth.

Cultural pest control. The modification of cultural practices to avoid pest attacks on crops. For example, the timing of planting can be adjusted to avoid the emergence of a particular pest, given a knowledge of the pest's life cycle.

Curing. Allowing allium crops such as onions and garlic to dry prior to storage. Curing is usually done in a dry, airy, protected place for as long as a few weeks.

Cytokinin. A plant growth hormone that increases cell division, used as a growth regulator.

D

Damping-off fungus. Any one of a number of soil-borne disease-causing fungi, including *Pythium, Rhizoctonia, Fusarium, Phytophthora,* and *Sclerotium.* The condition caused by the fungus is most serious where nitrogen levels are high and drainage is poor.

Decomposition. The breakdown of organic materials into their constituent parts due to the action of microorganisms.

Determinate. A flowering and fruiting habit that occurs at the terminus of a twig or branch, ending twig elongation.

Diatomaceous earth. A substance made from the ground bodies of marine and freshwater algae. The product is almost pure silica. Very abrasive, it is used to control soft-bodied pests such as snails and slugs and is thought to repel several other insects as well. It leaves no harmful residues and is not at all harmful to birds and mammals.

Diazinon. An insecticide that is primarily used in granular form to control soil insects.

Direct seeding. Placing seeds directly into the garden, in the place where the plants will grow for the season.

Dolomitic limestone. A classification of limestone containing a proportion of magnesium.

Dormancy. The period of inactivity in a plant's life cycle, as in seeds, bulbs, or buds.

Dormant pruning. Pruning done during the winter while the tree is in dormancy.

Double-digging. A method of garden soil preparation in which the soil is worked to two shovels' depth. The soil is dug, removed, and replaced in a systematic way at intervals of one shovel's width.

Draw. A sprouted sweet potato used to start plants outdoors.

Dried blood. See Blood meal.

Drip irrigation. A system of adding water to garden soil in a slow, gentle stream from sources such as a hose with a bubbler attachment placed along the ground. Drip irrigation prevents soil from being disturbed and cuts down on runoff.

Dwarf. A fruit tree bred for its small size. Dwarfs bear earlier than standard-size trees and are easier to maintain in terms of pruning and harvesting.

E

Espalier. A method of training trees or woody shrubs to grow with support, such as on a trellis or against a wall, in a specific geometric design.

Eye. The vegetative growing point of the potato tuber.

F

Fish emulsion. Liquid fertilizer made from fish and fish parts, sold as a water-soluble plant food that contains the three major plant nutrients: nitrogen, phosphorus, and potassium.

Flat. A box in which transplants are started.

Floricane. The fruit-producing second-year cane of bramble fruit.

Foliar fertilizing. Applying plant nutrients directly to the leaves rather than to the soil. The leaves can absorb the nutrients through their cuticles.

Frass. Sawdustlike material found around the opening made by a boring insect, such as the squash vine borer or peach tree borer.

Fruit set. The comparative density of fruit formed on a tree in a given season.

Fungus. One of the lower order of plants not containing chlorophyll that depend on organic matter in the soil for their energy. Both beneficial and detrimental fungi are present in the soil. They are characterized by their filamentous vegetative growth.

Fungicide. A chemical pesticide used to kill fungi.

Furrow. The slice a plow makes in the soil as it is dragged along.

G

Gall. A knobby growth on a plant, usually formed in response to insect, disease, or mechanical damage.

Germination. The growth of a plant embryo or spore. Also, the growth of the pollen tube, or the sprouting of a seed.

Girdling. Damage to the bark of a tree around its circumference which prevents the normal movement of water and nutrients.

Grafting. Splicing two trunks or branches together so that they will grow as one.

Graft union. The place where a graft has been made between two plant materials.

Green manure. A crop grown for the express purpose of tilling it back into the soil to add organic matter.

Ground limestone. A substance that supplies calcium and raises the pH of soil.

Growing cube. A peat cube used to start one plant. Growing cubes can be set directly into the garden.

Gynoecious. Refers to a plant having only female flowers and requiring a pollinizer plant with male flowers for pollination and fruit set.

H

Hardening off. The gradual exposure of seedlings started indoors to natural climatic conditions.

Heat mat. A mat used to provide a heat source for developing plants.

Hilling. Growing plants in groups in a small hill, a system used often for cucurbits.

Honeydew. The substance excreted by feeding aphids, made of unused sugar and sap. This substance will support black mold, and ants are attracted to it.

Humus. A stable organic constituent of soil that persists after the decomposition process is well under way, made up of lignin, protein, and polyurinides.

Hybrid. A cross between two individuals that differ in one or more genes.

I

Indeterminate. An inflorescence whose terminal flower buds open last and do not arrest the growth of the main stem axis by the opening of flowers.

Inoculant. Nitrogen-fixing bacteria that are added to soil to increase the population of these bacteria; used in association with legume crops.

Insecticidal soap. Soap containing fatty acids that has an insecticidal effect. Soaps containing potassium are the most effective. Care must be taken that the soap does not harm plant leaves.

Insecticide. An insect-killing chemical.

Intercropping. Growing two or more crops together because of their lack of competition or their mutually beneficial effect.

Interplanting. See Intercropping.

Interstem. (interstock) The stock grafted between rootstock and scion in tree construction.

Invasive. Refers to a plant with a tendency to spread beyond the bounds of its original planting.

L

Larva. The immature stage of an insect. The worm, grub, or caterpillar stage of insect development that is responsible for extensive crop loss.

Leaching. The movement of materials through the soil profile, away from the root zone.

Lead arsenate. An insecticide used in orchards in the past. Lead residues may be present in soils where lead arsenate was once commonly used.

Legume. A plant characterized botanically by fruit called a legume or a pod. Members of the family *Leguminosae* include alfalfa, clover, peas, and beans. Many plants are associated with nitrogen-fixing bacteria.

Loam. A soil type made up of a mixture of sand, silt, and clay with many subdivisions such as sandy loam, clay loam, and so on.

M

Macronutrient. A nutrient required by plants in large amounts, including calcium, nitrogen, phosphorus, potassium, and sulfur. Macronutrients are found in concentrations of up to 1 ppm in the plant tissues.

Mattock. A digging and prying tool, similar to a pick with a flat blade on one side, used to remove roots and loosen soil.

Micronutrient. A nutrient essential to plant growth and needed in relatively small amounts, including iron, manganese, zinc, boron, copper, chlorine, cobalt, and molybdenum.

Min-max thermometer. A thermometer that records minimum and maximum temperatures that can be used to determine the best time to plant a given crop.

Miticide. A mite-killing chemical.

Modified leader. The result of a pruning technique that is a cross between central leader and open center.

Monoecious. Referring to a plant with unisexual flowers and both sexes on the same plant, such as corn or pine trees.

Mulch. Any material such as straw, plastic sheets, stones, wood chips, or compost placed on the surface of the soil or around plants to conserve moisture, limit weed growth or erosion, and protect from inimical climatic conditions such as frost.

Mycoplasm. A disease-causing microorganism similar to bacteria.

N

Nematode. A soil- or water-inhabiting unsegmented worm ranging in size from microscopic up to 1 meter in length. Nematodes are responsible for many diseases of plants, animals, and humans.

Nitrate nitrogen. A source of nitrogen in nitrate form that is readily available to plants. Nitrates leach from the soil easily.

Nitrification. The biological conversion of ammonium gas to nitrate nitrogen.

Nitrogen. An essential plant macronutrient that plays a central role in the vegetative growth of plants.

Node. The place on a plant stem where leaves or buds are formed.

Nymph. The immature stage of some insects. Nymphs look like small adults.

O

Open center. The result of a tree-pruning technique in which there is no main or dominant vertical trunk, and the tree is shaped like a vase.

Organic fertilizer. Fertilizer derived from plant or animal origins. The term is also used loosely to describe all naturally occurring compounds used to increase soil fertility.

Organic matter. Technically, compounds containing carbon. Generally, materials that have once been living. Organic matter in soil has a very high nutrient exchange capacity and moisture-retentive capacity, and it influences soil flocculation, improving soil structure.

Oxidization. The process of combining with oxygen.

P

Parasite. An insect, disease organism, fungus, or plant that lives off a host plant at the host's expense. The parasite cannot survive without the host.

Parthenocarpic. Referring to plants that develop a sporophyte from a female gamete without benefit of fertilization.

Pasteurization. Exposure of a material to high temperatures in order to destroy microorganisms present in that material and to arrest fermentation.

Peat moss. Partially decomposed vegetative material harvested from wet, marshy regions, used to mulch soil or to add moisture-holding ability and porosity to soil.

Perennial. A woody or herbaceous plant that lives from year to year. The plant's life cycle does not end with flowering.

Perlite. A porous volcanic material used as a rooting medium and a means of lightening soil for potted plants and container gardening.

Petiole. A leaf stalk.

Pheromone trap. An insect trap with sticky insides used to catch insects lured by the sexual attractant (pheromone) of that particular insect species. Used to prevent and to predict an outbreak of insect pests.

Phosphorus. An essential macronutrient for plant growth. One of its major functions is promoting root formation.

Photosynthesis. The process by which plants synthesize complex organic compounds such as carbohydrates from water, carbon dioxide, and inorganic salts using energy from the sun.

Pollination. The transfer of pollen from the anther to the stigma of a flower, resulting in fertilization.

Pollinator. The agent of pollination, such as an insect, a bird, or the wind.

Pollinizer. The plant that provides the pollen for pollination.

Potash. Potassium, an essential macronutrient of plants, important for plant maturity and hardiness.

Primocane. The first year's growth of a cane, such as raspberries; nonfruiting cane.

Pruning. Cutting branches of a tree, shrub, or vine to increase yield and maintain vigor.

Pupa. The stage in the life cycle of an insect between larva and adult. The stage when the insect is not feeding or at all active.

Pyrethrum. An insecticide derived from *Chrysanthemum coccineum*, potentially very irritating to skin and mucous membranes.

R

Rake thinning. Thinning a planting of seedlings with a metal rake to establish the ideal spacing for optimum plant growth.

Remay. A durable commercial row covering used to extend the growing season of a crop by protecting it from climate extremes.

Rhizobium. A nitrogen-fixing bacterium that lives symbiotically with higher plants, especially in association with legumes.

Rhizome. A horizontal underground stem that gives rise to roots and shoots that survive from season to season.

Root crop. A crop grown for the harvestable roots it develops.

Root sucker. A leafy shoot arising directly out of a root or below the soil surface.

Rose nozzle. The nozzle on a watering can that breaks the flow of water into fine streams that do not disrupt the soil.

Rotenone. A botanical insecticide.

Rototilling. Soil preparation done with a rototiller, which is a gasoline-run machine that turns the soil, creating a fine seedbed.

Row cover. Any material used to cover growing plants to extend the growing season by protecting them from climate extremes.

Runner. A horizontal stem or branch forming roots at nodes or tips.

Ryania. A botanical insecticide, not harmful to birds or mammals, made from the roots of the Ryania shrub.

S

Sabadilla. A botanical insecticide made from the seed of a South American member of the Lily family.

Sandy loam. Loam containing a high percentage of sand. See also Loam.

Scaffold branch. A branch making up the structural framework of a fruit tree.

Scion. A grafting term for the wood above the graft union.

Scuffle hoe. A hoe that cuts weeds just below the surface of the soil.

Secondary nutrient. See Micronutrient.

Self-fertile. Referring to plants with flowers that contain both male and female parts and not requiring pollinators such as insects or wind movement.

Self-infertile. Referring to plants that need another plant to pollinate them, perhaps from another variety that flowers at the same time.

Set. The small propagative part of a plant such as a bulb, tuber, or shoot that can be put directly into the ground.

Side-dressing. The application of fertilizer to soil around growing plants during the course of the growing season.

Slip. A propagative shoot for starting sweet potato plants in the garden. Also called a draw.

Sod. A mat of growing grasses.

Sodic soil. Soil containing more than 15 percent sodium, a concentration sufficiently high to interfere with most plant growth.

Soil. A dynamic natural layer of mineral and organic materials covering the surface of the earth which supports plant life. Soil is created by the action of climate, time, and the functions of living organisms on the parent material.

Soil amendment. Any material added to the soil that changes its texture, drainage, or moisture- and nutrient-holding capacity in order to improve its ability to support plant life. Soil amendments include fertilizer, manures, compost, and so on.

Soil test. An analysis of nutrient levels, pH, and textural classification of soil.

Spore. A minute reproductive body composed of a single gametophytic cell.

Spur. A short shoot or branch on a fruit tree; fruit-bearing flower buds in apples.

Spur type. A variety of tree with a strong tendency to form spurs.

Stigma. A protuberance on the tip of the style for receiving pollen.

Style. An elongated structure that connects the stigma to the ovary in the female part of a flower.

Succession planting. Staggering plantings so that crop maturity coincides with need or the potential utilization of the harvest.

Sucker. A leafy stem arising from a root or below the surface of the soil.

Sunscald. Damage to fruit caused by overexposure to the sun.

Superphosphate. Phosphate fertilizer readily available to plants with a phosphorus content of 22 percent.

T

Taproot. The tapering main root of a plant with smaller lateral roots growing off it.

Terminal. Short for terminal shoot, the shoot at the end of a tree branch.

Thinning. Removing seedlings in a systematic fashion to provide optimum spacing for plants to grow and mature.

Tines. The teeth of a rake or pitchfork.

Tip layering. Propagation that occurs when the tip of a berry cane arches to touch the ground and sends down roots at the point of contact.

Trap crop. A crop grown for the purpose of luring pests away from the main crop.

Trellis. A structural support for various climbing plants.

Trickle irrigation. A system of delivering water to the soil gradually and from a source on the soil surface. The result is minimum runoff and very little soil disturbance.

True leaves. The first leaves to form after the seed leaves or cotyledons.

Tuber. An enlarged underground stem modified as a food storage organ and having scale leaves, buds, or "eyes," such as on the potato.

U

Urea. A synthetic nitrogen fertilizer containing up to 45 percent nitrogen which provides both ammonium and nitrate nitrogen for an immediate and long-term nitrogen supply.

V

Variegation. Color variation in leaves.

Vermiculite. An absorbent substance composed of mica minerals exposed to very high temperatures, which expands their size to create a loose, porous structure. Vermiculite is used as a mulch and a rooting medium.

Verticillium wilt. A disease affecting many garden plants caused by a soil-borne fungus (*Verticillium albo-atrum*) that can persist in the soil indefinitely. Using resistant plant varieties is the best defense against the disease.

Viroid. An organism that resembles a virus.

W

Water sprout. An upright, nonfruiting tree shoot that sprouts from older, larger branches.

Weevil. A pest, characterized by its habit of playing dead when disturbed. Immature weevils are usually legless grubs. The adults and immatures feed on a great variety of host plants.

Whip. A young, usually one-year-old tree.

Z

Zeolite-type water softener. A water softener in which sodium is used instead of calcium. Water thus treated may be too high in salts to use in the garden.

Photo Credits

2–3 Didier Delmas
5 Heather Hale Hutchins
6 Thomas E. Eltzroth
7 Kit Anderson
8 Didier Delmas
10 Sandra Wagner
12–13 John Still
76 Kit Anderson
77 Thomas E. Eltzroth
78, 80 Didier Delmas
81 George Thabault
82 Kit Anderson
83 Heather Hale Hutchins
85 (both photos) Didier Delmas
86 David Cavagnaro
87 Thomas E. Eltzroth
89 Heather Hale Hutchins
92 Didier Delmas
93 Thomas E. Eltzroth
94 Didier Delmas
97 Rosalind Creasy
98 Thomas E. Eltzroth
99 David Cavagnaro
101 George Thabault
102 (both photos) Didier Delmas
104 Didier Delmas
105 Kit Anderson
107 Didier Delmas
108 Heather Hale Hutchins
109 Kit Anderson
112 (left) National Gardening Association; (right) Heather Hale Hutchins
113 Kit Anderson
114 Didier Delmas
115 Thomas E. Eltzroth
117 (top) Rosalind Creasy; (bottom) Thomas E. Eltzroth
118 Thomas E. Eltzroth
119 Didier Delmas
120 Lynn Ocone
122 Thomas E. Eltzroth
123 Didier Delmas
124 George Thabault
125 Didier Delmas
126 (top) George Thabault; (bottom) Didier Delmas

128, 129, 131 Thomas E. Eltzroth
133 (top) Steven A. Frowine; (bottom) George Thabault
134 (top) Thomas E. Eltzroth; (bottom) Maggie R. Cavagnaro
136 Kit Anderson
137 Didier Delmas
138 Thomas E. Eltzroth
139 Lynn Ocone
141 George Thabault
142 (first and fourth) Didier Delmas; (second) Thomas E. Eltzroth; (third) Kit Anderson; (fifth) Heather Hale Hutchins
144 Thomas E. Eltzroth
145 Kit Anderson
146 Didier Delmas
148 Thomas E. Eltzroth
149 Holly H. Shimuzu
150 Thomas E. Eltzroth
151 Kit Anderson
152, 154 Thomas E. Eltzroth
155 (top) Thomas E. Eltzroth; (bottom) Heather Hale Hutchins
156, 157 Thomas E. Eltzroth
158 George Thabault
159 Didier Delmas
160 (top) National Gardening Association; (middle and bottom) Didier Delmas
162, 164 George Thabault
165 Thomas E. Eltzroth
168 Kit Anderson
169 David Hoag
170, 171 Thomas E. Eltzroth
172 Kit Anderson
173 Didier Delmas
174 Rosalind Creasy
176 Thomas E. Eltzroth
178 Rosalind Creasy
179 Ken Klotz
184 Heather Hale Hutchins
185 George Thabault
186 Didier Delmas
188 Thomas E. Eltzroth
189 Kit Anderson
190 (both photos) Winston Cooke
192 Heather Hale Hutchins
193 Read D. Brugger
195, 197 Didier Delmas

199 Heather Hale Hutchins
200, 201 Thomas E. Eltzroth
204 Didier Delmas
205 (top) Thomas E. Eltzroth; (bottom) Didier Delmas
206 Thomas E. Eltzroth
207, 208 Didier Delmas
209 Heather Hale Hutchins
213 Lynn Ocone
214 Didier Delmas
216 Thomas E. Eltzroth
217 Fred Taylor
218 Didier Delmas
220 Thomas E. Eltzroth
222 Didier Delmas
223 Lynn Ocone
224 Didier Delmas
226 Thomas E. Eltzroth
227, 229 Lynn Ocone
230, 231, 232 Didier Delmas
235 (top) Didier Delmas; (bottom) Thomas E. Eltzroth
236 Didier Delmas
237 Lynn Ocone
238, 240 Didier Delmas
241 George Thabault
242 Didier Delmas
243 Fred Taylor
244, 245 Thomas E. Eltzroth
249 Darlene Sproul
250 Thomas E. Eltzroth
251 Didier Delmas
258 Thomas E. Eltzroth
262, 263, 264, 265 Didier Delmas
266 Thomas E. Eltzroth
267 Heather Hale Hutchins
268 (top) Heather Hale Hutchins; (middle) National Gardening Association; (bottom) Thomas E. Eltzroth
270 Kit Anderson
276 (top) Ralph S. Byther; (middle and bottom) Ron West
277 (first and fourth) Ralph Adkins; (second and third) Ron West; (fifth) Dale K. Pollet
278 (first, fourth, and fifth) Ron West; (second and third) Ralph Adkins
279 (top and middle) Ron West; (bottom) Dale K. Pollet

280 (first and second) Ron West; (third and fourth) Dale K. Pollet; (fifth) George MacCollum
281 (first and second) Ron West; (third) Ralph Adkins; (fourth) Dale K. Pollet
282 (first and third) Ralph Adkins; (second and fifth) Thomas A. Zitter; (fourth) Gary W. Simone
283 (first and fifth) Gary W. Simone; (second, third, and fourth) Ralph S. Byther
284 (first) Heather Hale Hutchins; (second) Stephen A. Johnston; (third) Arden F. Sherf; (fourth and fifth) Gary W. Simone
285 (first) Ralph Adkins; (second) Ralph S. Byther; (third and fifth) Gary W. Simone; (fourth) Ron West
286 (first and second) Ralph S. Byther; (third and fourth) Gary W. Simone; (fifth) Ralph Adkins
287 (first) Ralph Adkins; (second) Ralph S. Byther; (third and fifth) Thomas A. Zitter; (fourth) Heather Hale Hutchins
288–289 John Still
318 Heather Hale Hutchins
319, 320 Kit Anderson
322 Heather Hale Hutchins
323 Jesse Pomozal
326 Kit Anderson
328 Rosalind Creasy
329, 330 Thomas E. Eltzroth
331, 333 Rosalind Creasy
334 George Thabault
335, 336 Kit Anderson
340 Brenda Olcott-Reid
341 George Thabault
342 Rosalind Creasy
343 Thomas E. Eltzroth
344 George Thabault
348 Thomas E. Eltzroth
349 Kit Anderson
351 Thomas E. Eltzroth
352 (both photos) Thomas E. Eltzroth
354 Kit Anderson
355 Heather Hale Hutchins
356 (top and middle) Thomas E. Eltzroth; (bottom) Kit Anderson
362 Heather Hale Hutchins
363, 364 Thomas E. Eltzroth

365 Rosalind Creasy
366, 367 Heather Hale Hutchins
368 Thomas E. Eltzroth
369 Kit Anderson
370 Thomas E. Eltzroth
372 George Thabault
374, 376 Heather Hale Hutchins
377 Kit Anderson
378 (top) Heather Hale Hutchins; (bottom) Thomas E. Eltzroth
380 Heather Hale Hutchins
382, 383 Didier Delmas
384, 385, 386 George Thabault
388 Heather Hale Hutchins
390 Didier Delmas
391 Heather Hale Hutchins
394 George Thabault
400 (top) Brenda Olcott-Reid; (middle and bottom) New York State Agricultural Experiment Station
401 (top and middle) Bill Reid; (bottom) New York State Agricultural Experiment Station
402 (top and bottom) Brenda Olcott-Reid; (middle) New York State Agricultural Experiment Station
403 (top) Ralph S. Byther; (middle) Alan L. Jones; (bottom) Brenda Olcott-Reid
404 (first) Alan L. Jones; (second and third) Gary W. Simone; (fourth) Ralph S. Byther
405 (top) Brenda Olcott-Reid; (middle) Alan L. Jones; (bottom) Ralph S. Byther
406–407 John Still

Index

About the National Gardening Association

The National Gardening Association is a non-profit, member-supported organization promoting gardens for all and dedicated to helping people garden successfully at home, in community groups, and in institutions. We believe gardening adds joy and health to living while improving the environment and encouraging our appreciation for the proper stewardship of the earth.

Established in 1972, this national organization of close to a quarter million members is now the premier membership organization for gardeners in the country.

Members receive monthly the color *National GARDENING* magazine, can call the NGA Gardening Answer Service, receive discounts on gardening books and tools, and have an array of other member benefits. *National GARDENING* newsmagazine provides in-depth, how-to articles for the home gardener, profiles of members and their gardens, and evaluations of garden tools and products. It also features a "Seed Swap" exchange column, a news column, and seed- and recipe-finder columns.

The National Gardening Association promotes gardening on numerous fronts. Well known as a clearinghouse for community garden programs, we offer manuals, technical assistance, research, and a national grants program to all kinds of community gardeners — for neighborhoods, landless groups, the elderly, youth, schools, churches, clubs, and institutions.

We produce an annual report, the *National Gardening Survey,* from research conducted for NGA by the Gallup organization. This is the most comprehensive and reliable source of information on trends in home gardening in America, and it is widely used by the media and by the lawn and garden industry.

The National Gardening Association has established itself as a leading gardening advocate and resource for the print and broadcast media. Information is provided monthly to more than 2,400 key media contacts.

Our organization continues to explore new ways to gather and share information, to connect gardeners with other gardeners, and to further our mission — gardens for all!

If you would like a free sample copy of the *National GARDENING* magazine and information on how to join the National Gardening Association, please write or call:

The National Gardening Association
180 Flynn Avenue
Burlington, VT 05401
(802) 863-1308

NATIONAL Gardening   Nov. '85

GARDENS FOR ALL

THE GARDENER'S NEWSMAGAZINE